PSYCHOTHERAPY AND SUBSTANCE ABUSE

THE GUILFORD SUBSTANCE ABUSE SERIES
HOWARD T. BLANE and THOMAS R. KOSTEN, Editors

PSYCHOTHERAPY AND SUBSTANCE ABUSE

A Practitioner's Handbook

Edited by

ARNOLD M. WASHTON

THE GUILFORD PRESS
New York   London

©1995 The Guilford Press
A Division of Guilford Publications, Inc.
72 Spring Street, New York, NY 10012

Printed in the United States of America

This book is printed on acid-free paper.

Last digit is print number: 9 8 7 6 5 4

Library of Congress Cataloging-in-Publication Data

Psychotherapy and substance abuse : a practitioner's handbook /
edited by Arnold M. Washton.
    p. cm.—(The Guilford substance abuse series)
    Includes bibliographical references and index
    ISBN 0-89862-838-5.—1-57230-202-X (pbk.)
    1. Substance abuse—Treatment. 2. Psychotherapy.
  I. Washton, Arnold M. II. Series.
    [DNLM: 1. Substance Abuse—therapy. 2. Psychotherapy
—methods.
WM 270 P975 1995]
RC564.P86   1995
616.86'0651—dc20
DNLM/DLC
for Library of Congress   95-183
                                          CIP

Contributors

Ann Bordwine Beeder, MD, Department of Public Health, Cornell University Medical College, New York, NY

Insoo Kim Berg, PhD, Brief Family Therapy Center, Brookfield, WI

Thomas H. Bien, PhD, Health Psychology Associates, Albuquerque, NM

F. Michler Bishop, PhD, Institute for Rational-Emotive Therapy, New York, NY

Dennis C. Daley, MSW, Center for Psychiatric and Chemical Dependency Services, University of Pittsburgh Medical Center, Pittsburgh, PA

Lisa Director, PhD, Clinical Psychologist , New York, NY

Marc Galanter, MD, Division of Alcoholism and Drug Abuse, New York University School of Medicine, New York, NY

James Garrett, CSW, CAC, Al-Care Treatment Center, Albany, NY

Reid K. Hester, PhD, Behavior Therapy Associates, University of New Mexico, Albuquerque, NM

John E. Imhof, PhD, Director of Mental Health Services, New York University School of Medicine, North Shore University Hospital, Manhasset, NY

Ronald M. Kadden, PhD, Department of Psychiatry, University of Connecticut Health Center, Farmington, CT

Edward J. Khantzian, MD, Department of Psychiatry, Harvard University Medical School, Cambridge, MA

Jerome David Levin, PhD, Director, Alcohol Counselor Training Program, New School for Social Research, New York, NY

Judith A. Lis, MSN, Alternative and Cocaine Treatment Center, University of Pittsburgh Medical Center, Pittsburgh, PA

Ruby Malik, PhD, Washton Institute, New York, NY

Robert Margolis, PhD, Director of Psychological Services, Ridgeview Institute, Smyrna, GA

Robert B. Millman, MD, Department of Public Health, Cornell University Medical College, New York, NY

Michelle Morgan, PhD, School of Psychology, University of Wales, Cardiff, Wales, UK

Susan Lyden Murphy, PhD, Department of Psychiatry, Harvard Medical School, Cambridge, MA

Christopher R. Penta, MA, CCMHC, Alcohol and Drug Abuse Treatment Center, University of Connecticut Health Center, Farmington, CT

Richard A. Rawson, PhD, Department of Psychiatry, University of California at Los Angeles, School of Medicine, Los Angeles, CA

Melissa Robbins, MSW, CAS, Division of Addictions, Harvard Medical School, Cambridge, MA

Stephen Rollnick, PhD, Department of General Practice, University of Wales College of Medicine, Cardiff, Wales, UK

Debra Rothschild, PhD, CAC, Psychologist, PsychologicA, New York, NY

Howard J. Shaffer, PhD, CAS, Division of Addictions, Harvard Medical School, Cambridge, MA

Douglas Stellato-Kabat, ACSW, CAC, Al-Care Treatment Center, Albany, NY

Joanna Stellato-Kabat, ACSW, CAC, Al-Care Treatment Center, Albany, NY

Nannette Stone-Washton, MS, CSAC, Washton Institute, New York, NY

Marsha Vannicelli, PhD, Department of Psychology, Harvard University, Cambridge, MA

Barbara C. Wallace, PhD, Department of Health and Nutrition Education, Teachers College, Columbia University, New York, NY

Arnold M. Washton, PhD, Washton Institute, New York, NY

Mark G. Winiarski, PhD, Department of Family Medicine, Montefiore Medical Center, Bronx, NY

Enid B. Young, PhD, private practice, Berkeley, CA

Sheldon Zimberg, MD, Department of Psychiatry, Columbia University College of Physicians and Surgeons

Joan Ellen Zweben, PhD, Department of Psychiatry, School of Medicine, University of California at San Francisco, San Francisco, CA

Preface

Substance abuse is one of the most prevalent and troublesome health care problems in the United States today. Never before has it been so important for health care professionals to become familiar with substance abuse and its treatment. This is especially true for mental health professionals, because substance abuse is rampant among persons seeking mental health services. Use of powerful brain-modifying chemicals such as alcohol or cocaine can severely exacerbate and complicate preexisting mental conditions; it can also induce behavioral disturbance in persons with no preexisting mental illness. This means that mental health professionals must always consider the possible involvement of substance abuse when assessing a patient's presenting complaint.

The purpose of this book is to familiarize mental health practitioners (including psychologists, psychiatrists, social workers, and other psychotherapists) with psychotherapeutic approaches to alcohol and drug abuse. It is designed to provide clinically useful information on a wide range of topics directly relevant to the treatment of alcohol and other substance abuse. The intended reader is the *nonspecialist* who works in a mental health facility, hospital, private practice, or other clinical setting that is not a specialized chemical dependency treatment program, whether inpatient or outpatient. The current volume was conceptualized along the lines of what a general psychotherapist or mental health clinician needs to know about substance abuse in order to properly identify, assess, and refer or possibly treat a patient who is using psychoactive substances, regardless of clinical setting. This is an important point since much of what is written about the treatment of substance abuse presumes that either the reader works in a specialized program or has the flexibility (or inflexibility as the case may be) to operate like one. Both assumptions are unwarranted for many, if not most, mental health professionals.

Several recent developments have contributed to the need for this volume: (1) the extraordinary prevalence of substance abuse among persons seeking mental health services of every kind, whether or not substance abuse is the presenting complaint; (2) recognition that no single approach to treating substance abuse is superior to all others; (3) increasing frustration among mental health professionals with the dogmatic "one size fits all" stance that has dominated the substance abuse treatment field for so long; (4) increasing appreciation for the role of psychotherapeutic approaches (including cognitive, behavioral, and psychodynamic), especially in difficult-to-treat patients; (5) increasing demand by nonspecialists for practical knowledge of assessment and treatment techniques; and, (6) demands by managed care and other third-party payers that all psychotherapists be able to properly identify and assess patients who may be using psychoactive substances.

The book is organized into three major sections: (I) Basic Issues and Perspectives; (II) Clinical Strategies and Techniques; and (III) Special Populations and Considerations.

Section I addresses several core issues of particular interest to psychotherapists such as attitudinal and countertransference barriers to treating substance abusers, clinical assessment techniques, the efficacy of psychotherapy with substance abusers, integrating 12-Step and psychotherapeutic approaches, and co-morbidity of psychopathology and substance abuse.

Section II focuses on specific clinical approaches and techniques such as motivational interviewing, brief therapy, solution-focused therapy, relapse prevention, group therapy, network therapy, family therapy, and structured inpatient and outpatient programs.

Section III addresses clinical considerations with a variety of special populations: adolescents, women, minorities, elderly, incest victims, and patients afflicted with HIV and AIDS.

Two additional chapters—one on gay and lesbian issues and another on the impact of managed care—were planned for inclusion in this volume, but unfortunately, due to unforeseen circumstances, the authors were unable to fulfill their commitments.

The aim of this book is to enhance knowledge with the hope that this will enhance patient care.

Contents

I. BASIC ISSUES AND PERSPECTIVES

I

BASIC ISSUES
AND PERSPECTIVES

1

Overcoming Countertransference and Other Attitudinal Barriers in the Treatment of Substance Abuse

JOHN E. IMHOF

INTRODUCTION

Since the widespread presence of negative attitudes toward substance abusers in those who treat them was reviewed a decade ago (Imhof, Hirsch, & Terenzi, 1983), what looked then like an underreported phenomenon has become a fixture in the substance abuse treatment field. Despite a growing number of studies of negative stereotyping, labeling, and stigmatizing of substance abusers (Abed & Neira-Munoz, 1990; Allen, 1993; Brooks, 1990; Carroll, 1993; Chachkes, Kaufer, Primack, & Ullah, 1991; Farrell & Lewis, 1990; Hanna, 1991; Hirsch & Imhof, 1975; Imhof, Hirsch, & Terenzi, 1983; Kaufman, 1990; Marshall & Marshall, 1993; Nurco et al., 1988; Ross & Darke, 1992; Toumbourou & Hamilton, 1993; Vannicelli, 1991) and comments on the subject (Blansfield, 1991; Cohen, 1990; Gallant, 1990; Imhof, 1979, 1986, 1989, 1991; Imhof & Hirsch, 1993; Imhof, Hirsch, & Terenzi, 1985), we continue to see pejorative terms such as *addicts, junkies,* and others applied to them in both the professional and the popular literature. Blansfield (1991), in a letter that appeared in his state medical journal, urges his fellow physicians to "discard . . . bias and archaic preconceptions . . . and fight chemical dependency as we have fought cancer and heart disease with dedication, intelligence, and compassion" (p. 361). Ironically, his letter is titled "Addictophobia," and he himself refers to chemically dependent people and users of illegal drugs as addicts. In an editorial intended to review the implications of President Clinton's health care proposals on substance abuse treatment, the *Wall Street Journal* ("Review and Outlook," 1994) prints, "An addict is an addict," and in his *Further Along the Road Less Travelled,* popular writer M. Scott Peck (1993) acknowledges that although he writes and lectures "about self-discipline . . . , I must confess that I am an addict. In particular, I am almost hopelessly addicted to nicotine." As recently as 1993, a headline in *Clinical Psychiatry News* (Newman, 1993) referred to hard-core addicts. Although some substance abuse treatment professionals may be sensitized to the use of "politically correct" language when referring to their patients and clients, overall, underlying attitudes do not seem to have shifted significantly since 1979, when Davies (1979) noted that professionals "see drug abusers as lying, manipulative, aggressive people who lack motivation" (quoted in Carroll, 1993, p. 706). Wurmser's (1972) observation that "drug abuse is the nemesis to haunt psychiatry itself" is a recurrent truth; his prescience in noting that the sheer mass of "emotional problems" substance abusers bring to treatment "dwarfs our skills" (p. 406) remains a salient clue to persistent countertransferential and attitudinal barriers that professionals continue to erect.

Even recent advances, such as board certification for physicians in addiction medicine and the increasing availability of specialized clinical training and credentialing for nurses, psychologists, social workers, and counselors, do not appear to have moved the field of psychiatry forward in terms of professional attitudes toward substance and alcohol abusers. A small sampling of recent studies illustrates that negativity continues to impede progress in treatment. Among family therapists treating substance abusers, Reichelt and Christensen (1990) have noted that therapists' expectations negatively influenced treatment outcome. Hanna (1991), in a comparison of treatment and referral patterns among first-year psychiatric resident physicians and alcoholism treatment professionals when patients identified themselves as alcoholics, found conclusively that the label "alcoholic" stimulated negative attitudes on the part of the physicians, leading to their failure to provide the kind of comprehensive evaluation that leads to appropriate treatment referrals. Farrell and Lewis (1990) found that the psychiatrists they surveyed were likely to perceive patients with a previous alcoholism dependence diagnosis as not compliant with treatment recommendations, unwilling to accept their advice, and generally poor prospects for recovery. They assessed a need for hospitalization and prescribed antidepressants for such patients less frequently, and said that they were "more annoying and less likely to arouse sympathy"

(p. 887). The "common social prejudice" identified in this study, which led the authors to conclude that alcoholism is a "stigmatizing diagnosis" (p. 888), suggests that the attitude of the psychiatrists they studied is not unique or even particularly remarkable.

Those of us in the substance abuse treatment field have known for some time that most of our patients are in fact psychiatric patients, referred to as dual-diagnosis patients, with varying degrees of psychopathology whose drug use is symptomatic of an underlying pathological state. As previously noted (Imhof et al., 1983), most may be diagnostically assessed as having narcissistic and borderline personality disorders. The experience of O'Malley, Kosten, and Renner (1990) with dual-diagnosis patients bears this out. As they have noted, when patients with these psychiatric diagnoses act out, their behavior often brings out strong negative reactions in their treaters, especially when these patients continue to abuse substances or relapse during treatment. A nearly inevitable pattern then ensues: The therapist, angry and rejecting, discharges the patient, often prematurely and often at a point in treatment when treatment is most needed.

In their study of attitudes toward injecting drug users among professionals in a drug and alcohol research unit and an AIDS (acquired immunodeficiency syndrome) treatment facility, Ross and Darke (1992) confirmed that attitudes toward intravenous drug users have (IDUs) several dimensions:

> [1] seeing injecting drug use as a matter of public concern (as opposed to private choice) and seeing it as an indication of personal inadequacy or psychopathology . . . [2] a more rigid rejection of IDUs as criminals who should be removed from society, and . . . [3] a social and affective rejection of IDUs as people one would want to have no contact with. [Hence their title:] These three dimensions may be popularly characterized as seeing IDUs as, respectively, mad, bad, and dangerous to know. (p. 74)

Perhaps the most heartening aspect of their work is their convincing argument that process variables such as attitudes *can* be measured and must be because they influence treatment provision and outcomes. The research instrument this team developed deserves widespread attention among researchers in the field.

The attitudes of treatment professionals toward substance abusers and alcoholics are at least partly a mirror of societal attitudes in general, apparently extending even to the families and children of individuals in treatment. Burk and Sher (1990) studied negative labeling and stereotyping of adolescents by two groups, one composed of their adolescent peers and the other made up of mental health professionals and paraprofessionals—counselors, aides, nurses, psychiatrists, psychologists, social workers, and general medical practitioners, almost half of whom had worked with substance abusers. In both studies, videotaped actors iden-tified as children of alcoholics (COAs) were consistently seen by par-ticipants to have greater psychopathology than those not identified as such, and most participants rated them as more likely to have emotional and interpersonal difficulties as they matured. Spouses of alcoholics have traditionally been labeled as codependent, enabling, and generally dys-functional adults and partners. Gallant (1990), concerned about the "detrimental as well as therapeutic effects" of such stereotyping and generalization, advises professionals:

> It is unwise and possibly harmful to "lump" or categorize all COAs in one group and all spouses or families in another group, labeling them with the nonscientific term of "codependents" in an attempt to throw a therapeutic net over all of them. Each alcoholic patient and family member has unique and distinct backgrounds and characteristics which deserve different therapeutic approaches. (p. 630)

Given that a fundamental change in underlying attitudes toward sub-stance and alcohol abusers does not appear to be coming from within psychiatry or substance abuse treatment, it is perhaps instructive to look further afield at what *has* changed in the last decade; the remainder of this chapter focuses on emerging trends that appear to offer a cautiously optimistic prognosis for substance abuse treatment. First, reports in the professional literature increasingly deal with the impact that negative stereotyping is having on the quality of health care delivered by those in other professional and paraprofessional disciplines. Second, the increas-ing attention paid to *attitudes* among caring professionals bodes both well and ill for the goal of achieving a substantial shift in attitudes among psy-chiatric and substance abuse treatment professionals. Finally, new solu-tions are beginning to take shape, largely because of the work carried out among members of other treatment disciplines. In addition to dis-cussing these trends, this chapter includes a case vignette to illustrate the impact of attitudes on the treatment process and potential solutions to removing the impediments to progress in treatment represented by nega-tive attitudes and stereotyping.

ATTITUDES AMONG NONSUBSTANCE ABUSE TREATMENT PROFESSIONALS

The role that negative attitudes play as genuine impediments to quality health care has been the focus recently of investigators from nursing, var-ious medical specialties, physician education, and other health-related disciplines. Interest in stigmatization in health care is a fairly recent phenomenon, stimulated by the groundswell of consumerism in mental health; research on the psychosocial aspects of AIDS, among many factors, has had an added benefit for those of us interested in the stigmatization of substance and alcohol abuse.

Typical of these recent studies is the work of Carroll (1993), who compared the attitudes of counselors, general nurses, prison nurses, psychiatric nurses, and social workers toward drug abuse and drug abusers on the bases of the professionals' role, socialization, and prior experience with substance abuse treatment. He hypothesized that attitudes among professionals would be different on these bases. Carroll also hypothesized that those who had experience working with substance abusers before, especially those patients with HIV (human immunodeficiency virus) infection, would have more positive attitudes toward their patients. The results showed that the professional specialists, those addiction counselors and psychiatric nurses who had had substance abuse training and clinical experience in treatment, and most of whom had specifically chosen to work in the addictions field, had the most positive attitudes toward drug abuse and drug abusers. Prison nurses had the least positive attitudes; Carroll speculated that their negative attitudes derived from their dual role as disciplinarians and caregivers and from their perception of substance abusers as prisoners first and as people with treatable disease second. Although Carroll was not surprised at the expression of negative attitudes by nonspecialist health care professionals, he found "the hostility to drug users . . . disturbing and unethical. The fact that even 2% of respondents agree that drug users should be sterilized indicates the prevalence of punitive attitudes." He concluded, somewhat conservatively, "These [punitive attitudes] do not have a place in a caring profession" (p. 710).

As a curious sidelight, a brief review of the professional education literature has revealed a minor trend in studies of health professionals' attitudes toward their colleagues who are impaired by substance abuse or dependence. A brief summary of three of many studies should suggest the extent of the growing concern. Smith (1992), for instance, studied the attitudes of nurse managers and assistant nurse managers toward their impaired colleagues, noting that attitudes influence institutional response to impaired nurses and that *negative* attitudes may "act as barriers to the identification, intervention, referral, rehabilitation and re-entry of the impaired nurse into the profession" (p. 295). They cite a few studies from the late 1970s and early 1980s describing nurses as "moralistic, pessimistic, stereotypical and authoritarian toward substance abusing patients" (p. 296). "Stereotypic and stigmatic attitudes toward chemical dependency contribute both directly and indirectly to the lack of response to chemical dependency in the nursing professional" (p. 296).

Baldwin, Hughes, Conard, Storr, and Sheehan (1991) included attitudes in their study of substance use among senior medical students, distinguishing among occasional use, dependence, and impairment. They found that "most medical students appeared to accept the occasional use of alcohol and marijuana among colleagues'' (p. 2076). ''The majority recommended treatment for alcohol and marijuana dependence, but suspension or expulsion for dependence on the other substances surveyed'' (p. 2077). The other substances were cocaine, tranquilizers, LSD, psychedelics other than LSD, amphetamines, barbiturates, opiates other than heroin, and heroin.

Gopalan, Santora, Stokes, Moore, and Levine (1992) reported on the results of nine annual surveys of the classes of 1989–1992 at The Johns Hopkins University School of Medicine, on measures of knowledge, attitudes, beliefs in role responsibility, and confidence in clinical skills. These reports are a fascinating glimpse in the evolution of a medical student, but the attitude information is what interests us. Gopalan et al. found a significant increase in positive attitudes (toward belief that alcoholism and other drug problems are illnesses that can be diagnosed and treated successfully) between the students' sophomore and senior years, and between the sophomores of the classes of 1989 and 1990. The attitudinal pattern of the seniors in the class of 1990 and those in the class of 1989 was less positive (p. 262).

A substantial body of investigative work on attitudes has been done with nurses as subjects, perhaps as a reflection of the number of medical cases in which substance abuse is a factor. The Carroll (1993) study, for example, included prison and general nurses, as well as ''straight'' drug abusers and drug abusers with AIDS. Cole and Slocumb (1993), aware that AIDS is socially stigmatized among nurses in a way that other terminal illnesses are not, studied the influence of mode of acquiring AIDS on nurses' attitudes toward AIDS patients and found that association of the disease with drug use was a factor increasing the negativity of their attitudes. The nurses in their study generally had more positive attitudes toward a male patient who had acquired HIV through a blood transfusion than toward a male patient who had acquired the virus through sharing needles.

In another nursing study, Boland (1990) found that negative attitudes among the nurses in the study were associated with psychosomatic health complaints and lower productivity, and were partly responsible for increased incidence of sick days, transfer requests, and choices of career moves that would take nurses away from the bedside. In a study of student nurses' attitudes toward AIDS patients (Breault & Polifroni, 1992), the investigators also found negative attitudes among their subjects toward AIDS patients who had contracted the disease through intravenous drug use.

Allen (1993) studied the attitudes of community hospital general nurses toward alcoholic patients in a general hospital population, expecting those attitudes to reflect the negative attitudes generally ascribed to society at large (as Estes & Heinemann, 1986, suggested), that is, acceptance of drinking and rejection of the person whose drinking gets out of control. However, the nurses in her sample counted emotional problems as contributors to alcoholism, perceived loss of control as a symptom, believed that a alcoholic does not necessarily drink continuously, and labeled alcohol an "addicting chemical" (pp. 927–928). Overall, their attitudes scored as more positive than negative. In contrast, nurses at a large university hospital said they had very little patience with and did not know much about substance abuse. They said they felt disgusted, angry, and used by alcoholic patients. Allen concluded that the milieu might account for the different attitudes.

A number of substance abuse treatment professionals are aware that institutional or milieu countertransference can be expressed in unwritten policies and guidelines that apply only to substance-abusing individuals. Consider the following vignette.

Evelyn Kramer, the intake social worker for Island Metro's Drug Program, was quite unprepared for the experience of meeting William, a 34-year-old white, homosexual intravenous drug user, who was diagnosed as having AIDS 3 years ago. Accompanied by his lover and two aunts, William had, at 3 A.M. that morning, flamboyantly presented to Island Metropolitan Hospital's Emergency Room insisting he was addicted to Valium (diazepam), Darvocet (propoxyphene and acetaminophen), and Seconal (secobarbital) and, in dramatic gestures, demanding immediate inpatient hospitalization in order to detoxify from the drugs. His reason for wanting admission to Island Metro was primarily related to the fact that his AIDS doctors were on the staff at Island and he reasonably expected he would receive greater coordination of care if he were admitted there. William's personality is usually brittle and provocative, and he was no less provocative the morning he sought admission. Alternately demanding his rights as a patient and accusing the doctors of not wanting to admit him because he had AIDS, William angrily confronted the psychiatric resident with a threat that, unless he were admitted "within the hours," he would "bite someone and give them AIDS."

The psychiatry resident, Dr. Andrea Martin, found herself feeling both panic and rage. Her first impulse was to call security, which she did immediately, and then contacted the medical resident. Dr. Martin felt it essential to first assess William's medical status prior to proceeding with a mental status examination as part of his inpatient evaluation. With a security guard now present in the consultation room, William was no less belligerent with the medical resident, Dr. Richard Smith, with whom William now started to flirt, and wondered aloud, so all in the emergency room could hear, whether Dr. Smith himself was homosexual. In an attempt to set limits with the patient, Dr. Smith informed William that he would refuse to proceed with the examination unless William refrained from his now obnoxious behavior. Dr. Smith suspected, as was later confirmed by toxicology, that William was indeed stoned.

While Dr. Smith was conducting his medical evaluation, Dr. Martin had also contacted the chief resident in psychiatry to inquire whether or not, because the psychiatric unit was at full census, a consideration should be made to go over census. In learning of the circumstances of the case, the chief resident decided he would not consent to admitting the patient and would instead recommend a referral to the county hospital. That recommendation was supported by the medical resident, who stated that despite William's stoned condition and his insistence on being addicted to three substances, a referral should be made to the county hospital, because "all the beds at Metro are full."

Upon hearing he would not be admitted to the hospital of his choice, William suddenly began crying and pleading for help, stating he was out of drugs and would start withdrawal soon. Dr. Martin insisted that the county hospital would attend to his medical and psychiatric needs, but that he could always pursue other treatment choices at Island Metro's Drug Treatment Center. At that point, William put on his clothes and, without another word, bolted from the emergency room.

When Evelyn arrived for work at 8 A.M., William was seated in the intake unit, having announced he was referred from the emergency room, where he was told the drug program would find him a bed in a hospital "other than the county hospital." True to his style, William continued to act in a provocative and confronting manner, at which point Evelyn immediately stated, "Listen, unless you just talk to me in a respectful manner, you can go and sit in the waiting room for another two hours." Her tone and demeanor apparently motivated William to address his presenting problem without the usual attendant drama, and Evelyn proceeded with an intake evaluation.

She determined that William did indeed require inpatient detoxification, although he again insisted on being hospitalized at Island Metro so he could be near his AIDS doctors. He expressed a willingness to be placed on a waiting list, and overall began comporting himself in a manner quite different from what was evidenced in the emergency room. Evelyn arranged for an evaluation with Dr. Judd, the program's staff psychiatrist, who supported Evelyn's findings and himself began to make a number of telephone calls to investigate why William had not originally been admitted to Island Metro earlier that morning.

The vignette illustrates the ways in which society's overall attitudes toward substance abusers are translated into an institution's attempt to deal with the problem by isolating it, in this case, in a specific treatment unit. There are also other forces at work in this vignette, those having to do with individual professionals' countertransferential responses to the acting-out behavior of some substance abusers. Table 1.1 outlines the kinds of reactions treatment professionals may experience when they encounter specific defenses associated with substance and alcohol abusers.

TABLE 1.1. A Sampling of Patient Defenses and Transference Manifestations and Various Countertransference Reactions by Treatment Staff

Patient	Therapist/counselor
1. The patient as victim—"Poor me—I'm helpless," or "Everyone is against me," or "Why does everything happen to me"	Anger at the helplessness Feeling the need to rescue and save the patient Becoming an advice giver Experiencing sadistic feelings toward the masochistic element of patient's transference
2. Overt anger and hostility by patient toward therapist and other treatment staff	Emotional withdrawal from patient's anger Becoming frightened for one's safety Meet anger with greater anger Discharge patient for inappropriate behavior Passive–aggressive behavior toward anger, that is, appearing to listen, then making changes with regard to patient's appointment time, date of session, frequency, lateness, etc.
3. The perfect patient—does everything right: on time, verbal, drug free—seeming appropriate in all aspects	Becoming complacent and bored Experiencing a sense of great therapeutic effectiveness, if not grandiosity
4. The perfect patient acts out: misses appointments, overdoses, gets arrested, etc.	Therapist becomes enraged Feelings of inadequacy, incompetence; shattering of illusion of the effective therapist Depressive reaction, as a defense against rage Impulsive acting out by the therapist, that is, discharging patient Provoke patient to leave therapy
5. The patient intellectualizes behavior and experiences; no apparent contact with emotions and feelings	Therapist resorts to interpreting Attacks the primary defense of intellectualization, telling patient he/she is using his/her head, not heart Anger at patient for not conforming to role of the "good" patient who should talk about feelings Therapist becomes complacent with intellectualizing, as it avoids necessity of addressing underlying emotions
6. Provocative and obnoxious toward therapist: belittling, devaluing, confronting	Anger at patient Emotional withdrawal; cowering under attack Seek to discharge patient as uncooperative and/or "unsuitable for outpatient therapy"
7. Patient insists on knowing personal information about therapist prior to self-revelations	Reveal personal information to soothe patient Silence Anger at feeling intruded upon *(cont.)*

TABLE 1.1. *(cont.)*

Patient	Therapist/counselor
8. Cannot maintain ground rules of session; wants to eat and drink during therapy; several telephone calls throughout week; a scattered, often chaotic patient	Therapist permits eating and drinking in session Anger at telephone calls and feeling intruded upon Warns patient about discharge if calls don't cease Changes patient's appointment time or cancels sessions
9. Insists that he/she cannot be helped; wants to constantly leave therapy unless results are seen quickly	Feels pressure and sense of being manipulated Anger at patient Feelings of helplessness and ineptitude Recommends discharge

Note. From Imhof (1991, pp. 939–940). Copyright 1991 by Marcel Dekker. Reprinted by permission.

Tucker (1990), in an article written for surgical nurses on postoperative medication of patients, including those with histories of or current substance abuse, notes that both nurses and physicians tend to undermedicate patients who admit to current or historical substance or alcohol use, because they lack of knowledge about substance abuse and because they fear it. Tucker's position is that although it is well established that abusers of narcotics require greater-than-usual doses of pain medication postoperatively, they are seldom given the larger doses they need for pain relief and that is simply poor-quality care. She quite rightly identifies lack of knowledge and "erroneous attitudes" as the reason. She makes this stern admonition: "When an addict is in pain, narcotics should not be withheld as a *punitive* or rehabilitative measure" (p. 346, emphasis added). She explains the nurse's dilemma:

> The neuroscience nurse may view substance abuse as too complicated a problem to be addressed, or may develop a negative attitude toward patients diagnosed as having a substance abuse problem. Few engender as much anger and hostility among health care professionals as alcoholics and drug abusers. The nurse experiences conflict when a patient who abuses a substance asks for more postoperative medication than a patient who does not abuse a substance. Feelings of conflict not only interfere with the provision of appropriate care but are also quickly detected by the patient resulting in a vicious cycle of mutual antagonism and hostility. (p. 345)

It is ironic that in her plea for sensitive consideration of patient with substance abuse histories, Tucker herself cannot avoid the all-too-common pitfall of labeling the substance abuser an addict. However, the "vicious cycle" Tucker refers to is none other than the countertransference experienced even by those treatment professionals who have knowledge about substance abuse, who have learned by experience that it is not to be feared, but whose own feelings are so highly aroused by therapeutic interactions with their patients.

This broadening of interest and focus on discrimination, stigmatization, and hostility toward patients who need health care in general and substance abuse treatment in particular is welcome. It has encouraged researchers to discover ways to measure the influence of attitudes on treatment outcomes. Ross and Darke (1992), in particular, in developing the AIDUS (Attitudes toward Injecting Drug Users Scale), have created a psychometric instrument that shows great promise. Broad interest in stigmatization is welcome too as part of a larger trend toward raising the consciousness of clinicians regarding the various factors that constitute each patient's *individuality.* However, increasing interest in attitudinal barriers to successful treatment outcomes on the part of caregivers in fields outside substance abuse may have problematic implications for those of us still trying to combat stigmatization within the field. One concern is that substance abuse treatment professionals, by identifying with the issues of stigmatization, labeling, and negative stereotyping as they are being articulated in a more general context, may become less sensitive to the very real therapeutic problems and issues that exist within substance abuse treatment *and nowhere else.* Creating an attitudinal link between the negative stereotyping that occurs among those who treat substance abusers and those who treat people with AIDS, for example, may only serve to strengthen the negative attitudes, as it is well known in the treatment community that substance abusers are at greater risk of infection with HIV than is the general population.

ATTITUDINAL BARRIERS UNIQUE TO SUBSTANCE ABUSE AND ALCOHOLISM TREATMENT

As noted earlier, Gallant (1990) has argued persuasively for recognition that "each . . . patient and family has unique and distinct backgrounds and characteristics which deserve different therapeutic approaches" (p. 630). His concern was stereotyping among the children and families of alcoholics. Vannicelli (1991), too, is eloquent in her plea that special care is to be taken in working with adult children of alcoholics (ACOAs), a specialty within the field of substance abuse treatment admittedly but with lessons for practitioners in other areas of substance abuse treatment. Particularly when therapists are themselves ACOAs or have had a drug or alcohol problem in their own families are they at great risk of allowing countertransference issues to cloud or even impede the treatment. She believes:

> It is particularly important that these ACOA therapists be reflective about their motives in choosing to work with this population and the feelings that get stirred up in the course of their work with ACOA clients. The extent to which the ACOA group leader resonates with the clinical material may be his or her greatest treasure in working with ACOA clients. This resonation, however, may also get the therapist into trouble if it is not adequately examined and understood. . . . It is important to consider the possibility . . . that the therapist's level of development and integration may impose a ceiling on the level of development and integration that will be reached by the group as a whole or by individual patients within it. (pp. 297–299)

Vannicelli (1991), in exploring a danger of ACOA therapists working with ACOA patients that she calls the assumption of sameness, puts her finger on a kind of stereotyping that is far from what we consider stereotyping and negative labeling behavior in those who treat mentally ill patients or people with AIDS. The very thing that can make the therapy work, she implies, can keep it from working:

> The assumption of sameness among group members (or between group members and a leader who is known to be an ACOA) may at times be used as a defense against exploring issues in greater depth and *against tolerating differences and conflict*. Thus, at times of stress in the group, members may attempt to abort further exploration with comments such as, "This is a typical ACOA issue." However, assumptions about "shared understanding" and "sameness" may create a "you know how it is" mentality in the group about "typical ACOAs," leading to tunnel vision and a reluctance to explore "the obvious." Because the assumption of sameness may prevent the group from moving from one stage of group life to the next, it is important that leaders challenge this assumption when it emerges. An ACOA label should not be accepted as an adequate summary or explanation of what is going on but rather should be understood as the patient's attempt temporarily to close the door on painful issues. (p. 299, emphasis added)

Further, when patients label their own behavior, "That's my ACOA behavior," Vannicelli urges that this labeling not be confused by the leader with explaining: "It is important that group leaders go beyond the naming [i.e., the labeling] to find out more about the real phenomenon."

Bell (1992) noted another phenomenon in the substance abuse treatment community, which he calls treatment dependence syndrome, which he feels is prevalent among those working in substance abuse. He has noted that researchers and treatment professionals "frequently exhibit behaviors which bear a striking resemblance to the alcohol dependence syndrome [as it is described in DSM-III]; [for those afflicted] treatment and research become ends in themselves, displacing concern for clients' welfare or genuine curiosity about how best to help them'' (p. 1049). He identifies the features of the syndrome as narrowing of the treatment repertoire and rigidity when patients do not fit or are resistant to the narrow range of treatments offered, the belief that all substance abusers must have treatment, the view that abusers' reluctance to seek treatment is their own denial when the treater is really seeking the gratification that comes with providing treatment, repeated withdrawal symptoms, relief of symptoms by further treating, compulsion to treat, and reinstatement after abstinence.

Bell (1992) believes that drug and alcohol treatment professionals are at great risk of becoming dependent on treatment itself because in the field, ''the obvious solutions are so elusive, the goals of treatment are difficult to define. The benefits of treatment are uncertain. The public is ambivalent in its support for treatment services, and clients are ambivalent about seeking help. There is doubt whether treatment is an appropriate societal response to the problems of alcohol and drug abuse'' (pp. 1052–1053).

BREAKING DOWN ATTITUDINAL BARRIERS IN SUBSTANCE ABUSE TREATMENT

A major benefit of general interest in and acceptance of the concept that attitudes are a primary consideration in attempts to improve quality of substance abuse treatment is that widespread attention is being paid to solutions. Those remedies previously proposed (Imhof et al., 1983) remain the solid foundation on which to base a program to improve professionals' attitudes toward their patients and thus improve their patients' prognosis. These solutions include the following.

The Therapist's Therapy

As Imhof et al. (1983) have noted, ''only through an examination of one's own emotional development can the therapist most effectively recognize, tolerate, and begin to sort out'' (p. 29) the wide variety of attitudinal factors influencing the treatment of individual patients. Vannicelli (1991), echoing this belief, points out that ''although there is always the possibility that the therapist can grow along with the [ACOA] group, it is the therapist's responsibility to take care of his or her own growth in another arena (i.e., in the therapist's own psychotherapy)'' (p. 299).

Clinical Supervision

A number of authors recognize the value of supervision and teamwork in counteracting the effects of negative attitudes on treatment decisions and the treatment process itself. O'Malley et al. (1990) even recommend creating treatment teams in order to help therapists avoid burnout by sharing the treatment responsibility. As team members, therapists are less likely to act out their negative countertransferential feelings. Bell (1992) sees teamwork as a form of intensive clinical training as well, noting that team members grow personally and professionally "by attending to group dynamics within the team, by recognition of different skills, and by fostering both a genuine curiosity and compassion" (p. 1053). He also believes that when treatment staffs have a real structure, a coherent, shared philosophy regarding treatment that is constantly being reviewed and discussed, and a research and study effort that supports their work, the potential "chaos and confusion" (p. 1053) endemic to many treatment units may be reduced.

Clinical Training and Continuing Education

Farrell and Lewis (1990) speculate that training in addiction medicine could be the reason that some physicians had more positive attitudes toward substance and alcohol abusers, and they wondered whether the training or the individuals who chose addiction work were "less judgmental" (p. 889). Cole and Slocumb (1993), noting that education consisting of information only is ineffective in changing negative attitudes toward AIDS patients and IDUs, recommend measuring nurses' attitudes toward their patients *before* establishing the content of their continuing education. Smith (1992) believes that his study of attitudes toward impaired nurses held by their colleagues strongly supports the need to increase education on impairment and chemical dependency in the nursing schools, as nurse managers and assistant nurse managers have apparently "not been effectively trained to deal with impaired nurse colleagues" (p. 299). Smith also suggests that "education about chemical dependency in nursing will need to take cultural differences into account" (p. 299), because his study showed significant deviation in attitude toward chemical dependency among subjects in the black group and the Filipino/Oriental group who, generally, believed chemical dependency to be a personality weakness rather than a treatable illness.

Baldwin et al. (1991) reported that fewer than 22% of U.S. medical schools had a formal written policy on substance abuse among their (medical) students, yet 64% of the students in their study reported that there was some teaching about substance abuse at their schools, and 45% indicated that there was some teaching about physician impairment (p. 2078).

Personnel Standards

Unlike any other area of mental health treatment, "having had the illness" is a requirement for employment in a number of therapeutic communities, methadone maintenance programs, and residential rehabilitation centers that require the treaters to have been substance or alcohol abusers at one time (Imhof, 1991, p. 941). Unfortunately, a previous drug history on the part of the treating professional may itself provoke countertransferential and attitudinal barriers to impede treatment, as Imhof et al. (1983) suggested:

> The drug patient may serve as a constant and perhaps uncomfortable reminder of the therapist's past. . . . The therapist who is a former compulsive drug abuser might inadvertently seek to utilize the identical therapeutic framework with the patient that the therapist himself experienced, and currently views as responsible for his own successful rehabilitation. In such cases, a "what worked for me will work for you" attitude may result in unreasonable therapeutic expectations, often leading to premature treatment termination." (pp. 940–941)

In addition, Vannicelli's (1991) interpretation of the dangers for ACOA therapists treating ACOA patients is a further argument for taking great care in assessing the credentials of treatment professionals.

Responsible Professional Literature

Whereas individual attempts to self-monitor one's attitudes toward substance abuse patient are appropriate and encouraged, it would appear that concurrent responsibility lies with those who publish and edit mental health and substance abuse journals to ensure that all published articles avoid inadvertently labeling the very patients we all seek to help. It is heartening to see that the *Journal of Substance Abuse Treatment* recently revised its editorial policy to read as follows:

> The *Journal* will not consider articles that utilize pejorative and stereotypical expressions when discussing individuals who abuse, or who are addicted to, drugs and alcohol.
> Individuals addicted to drugs and alcohol are often viewed as social outcasts, criminals, or social misfits. It is the view of the Editors that scientific articles should insure that discussions about substance-abusing patients do not inadvertently perpetuate negative stereotypes by the use of value-laden labels such as "addict," "junkie," etc. Inclusion of these and other similarly-related expressions will result in papers being returned to authors for correction. Following is an example to assist authors in the development of their papers:
> *Unacceptable:* "This study reviews a sample of 100 heroin addicts."
> *Acceptable:* "This study reviews a sample of 100 heroin-addicted patients (or individuals, clients, etc.)."

The review of the field of attitudinal barriers in the treatment of drug and alcohol abuse has detected faint stirrings of ideas that may change the face of treatment radically over the next few years. For example, adherents of treatment approaches that were traditionally considered at opposite poles philosophically have begun a dialogue that focuses on their common interests and positive contributions to treatment success rather than on their differences. Piercy (1991), among others, argues persuasively that family therapists treating substance abusers, particularly adolescents, need to tap the power of the family to challenge substance abuse and support recovery more often and more effectively. He even generalizes that "we in the mental health field need to be mutually supportive and respectful of our different ways of thinking and helping. In essence, we need to shed our ethnocentrism and learn to be more culturally sensitive" (p. 529).

Kaufman (1990) has argued that psychodynamic psychotherapy can be successfully integrated into substance abuse treatment, along with family therapy and 12-Step programs such as Alcoholics Anonymous (AA). He believes that this integration is possible, in part, because professionals in the substance abuse treatment field are coming to understand the role countertransference plays.

> In the field of substance abuse treatment, countertransference is often relabeled as therapist "codependency" or "enabling" and is one of the most frequent causes of "burnout." The concept of codependency can enhance our understanding of many different forms of countertransference. The concept of codependency gives the therapist a frame of reference for changing his/her antitherapeutic countertransference reactions. The overprotective, overcontrolling, or overinvolved therapist can relate these behaviors to codependency and change them through personal psychotherapy, as well as through Al-Anon, Co-Dependents Anonymous, or, where appropriate, Adult Children of Alcoholics groups. (p. 105)

Smith, Buxton, Bilal, and Seymour (1993) argue persuasively for cultural sensitivity in adaptations of treatment of addictions to specific cultural groups. In a detailed account of a specific project, to bring AA to an African American community, the authors note that "addiction takes place in and must be treated within a culturally specific milieu. The whole fabric of successful treatment needs to be woven around cultural realities. The same can be true for individuals. Individuals were not produced on an assembly line like so many interchangeable units. . . . The same is true for both treatment and recovery within a multicultural society" (p. 101). Even though AA and other 12-Step groups are perceived as exclusionary, as exclusively white, mainstream, and middle class, the authors were able to adapt AA concepts to an African American community by recognizing what was culturally operating for African Americans in relation to substance abuse: low self-esteem (based on lack of knowledge of African American history and contributions to the growth of the United States); late introduction into recovery, usually through the criminal justice system, and so regarded as punitive; historic focus on short-term abstinence rather than long-term recovery; "a unique, often dysfunctional family structure that is traditionally matrilineal; use of dialect; institutionalized racism; and internalized racism (p. 99).

The wave of consumerism, so prevalent in other areas of society, has finally reached health care in general, and psychiatry and substance abuse in particular. With patients taking a more active role in their treatment, caregiver attitudes are being scrutinized. Smith (1992), in a study of the attitudes of nurse managers and assistant nurse managers toward their chemically impaired nurse colleagues, found that the non-Caucasians among their subjects were less likely to "believe the illness concept of impairment, the treatability of impairment, nursing colleagues' ability to assist the impaired nurse and the recognizability of the impaired nurse" (p. 298). There was also a "statistically significant correlation between experience with a family member having an alcohol and/or drug problem and racial/ethnic background" (p. 298).

> The Philippine/Oriental group demonstrated a strong need to know when a colleague is impaired or receiving treatment, exhibited a lesser belief in the treatability of impairment and displayed a strong belief of impairment as a personality weakness. These findings may be indicative of the strong values held by the Philippine/Oriental culture of chemical dependency being a moral and personality weakness, instead of a disease. The Black group was also less likely to believe in the illness concept and treatability of impairment. Studies have shown that Blacks believe alcoholism and chemical dependency are personality weaknesses . . . and that alcoholics and drug addicts are morally weak. (p. 299)

From the broader perspective that includes other treatment disciplines and approaches and substance abusers themselves, the phenomenon of treatment codependency begins to look like narrowmindedness on the part of some practitioners.

TOWARD THE MILLENNIUM . . .

In 1930, Karl Menninger observed that "the public has many erroneous ideas about drug addiction. . . . Very few criminals are drug addicts and relatively few drug addicts are criminals. They are not dangerous or loathsome, but they are monstrous liars" (p. 136). As was noted in earlier studies (Imhof et al., 1983; Imhof, 1991), the current negative views toward individuals who abuse drugs stem in large part from the essentially pessimistic view of Menninger and most of the addiction treatment pioneers. As we approach the turn of the century, however, prospects are brightening. We can sense a gradual shift in attitudes as professionals outside psychiatry and substance abuse begin to study the effects of labeling and stereotyping people with drug abuse problems, effects that reach further than might have been suspected in Menninger's time. Cautiously, we may even begin to anticipate a time when labels will have lost their force, pejoratives will be powerless, and stereotypes will have become empty symbols.

ACKNOWLEDGMENT

The author wishes to express appreciation to Judith Pynchon, M.A., for the editorial assistance she provided.

REFERENCES

Abed, R. T., & Neira-Munoz, E. (1990). A survey of general practitioners' opinions and attitudes toward drug addicts and addiction. *British Journal of Addiction, 85,* 131–136.

Allen, K. (1993). Attitudes of registered nurses toward alcoholic patients in a general hospital population. *International Journal of the Addictions, 28,* 928–930.

Baldwin, D. C., Jr., Hughes, P. H., Conard, S. E., Storr, C. L., & Sheehan, D. V. (1991). Substance use among senior medical students: A survey of 23 medical schools. *Journal of the American Medical Association, 265,* 2074–2078.

Bell, J. (1992). Treatment dependence: Preliminary description of yet another syndrome. *British Journal of Addiction, 87,* 1049–1054.

Blansfield, H. N. (1991). Addictophobia [Editorial]. *Connecticut Medicine, 55,* 361.

Boland, B. K. (1990). Fear of AIDS in nursing staff. *Nursing Management, 21,* 40–44.

Breault, A. J., & Polifroni, E. C. (1992). Caring for people with AIDS: Nurses' attitudes and feelings. *Journal of Advanced Nursing, 17,* 21–27.

Brooks, M. A. (1990). *The impact of negative therapist feelings on the accuracy with which therapists predict attributes drug abusing clients have assigned to themselves.* Unpublished doctoral dissertation, Catholic University of America, Washington, DC.

Burk, J. P., & Sher, K. J. (1990). Labeling the child of an alcoholic: Negative stereotyping by mental health professionals and peers. *Journal of Studies of Alcohol, 51,* 156–163.

Carroll, J. (1993). Attitudes of professionals to drug abusers. *British Journal of Nursing, 2,* 705–711.

Chachkes, E., Kaufer, S., Primack, S., & Ullah, E. (1991). Countertransference in professionals working with chemically dependent clients with HIV. *Journal of Chemical Dependency Treatment, 4,* 159–170.

Cohen, K. D. (1990). Compliance with treatment—Transference and countertransference issues. *Carrier Letter, 148,* 1, 7.

Cole, F. L., & Slocumb, E. M. (1993). Nurses' attitudes toward patients with AIDS. *Journal of Advanced Nursing, 18,* 1112–1117.

Davies, P. (1979). Motivation, responsibility and sickness in the psychiatric treatment of alcoholism. *British Journal of Psychiatry, 134,* 449–458.

Estes, N., & Heinemann, M. (1986). Issues in identification of alcoholism. In N. J. Estes & M. E. Heinemann (Eds.), *Alcoholism: Development, consequences, and intervention* (pp. 317–333). St. Louis, MO: C. V. Mosby.

Farrell, M., & Lewis, G. (1990). Discrimination on the grounds of diagnosis. *British Journal of Addiction, 85,* 883–890.

Gallant, D. M. (1990). Problems in alcoholism treatment: Labeling and negative stereotyping [Letter]. *Alcoholism: Clinical and Experimental Research, 14,* 630–631.

Gopalan, R., Santora, P., Stokes, E. J., Moore, R. D., & Levine, D. M. (1992). Evaluation of a model curriculum on substance abuse at The Johns Hopkins University School of Medicine. *Academic Medicine, 67,* 260–266.

Hanna, E. Z. (1991). Attitudes toward problem drinkers, revisited: Patient-therapist factors contributing to the differential treatment of patients with alcohol problems. *Alcoholism: Clinical and Experimental Research, 6,* 927–931.

Hirsch, R., & Imhof, J. E. (1975). A family therapy approach to the treatment of drug abuse and addiction. *Journal of Psychedelic Drugs, 7,* 181–185.

Imhof, J. (1986). Here we go again! [Editorial]. *Journal of Substance Abuse Treatment, 3,* 241.

Imhof, J. (1989). What ever happened to patient confidentiality? [Editorial]. *Journal of Substance Abuse Treatment, 6,* 1.

Imhof, J., Hirsch, R., & Terenzi, R. E. (1983). Countertransferential and attitudinal considerations in the treatment of drug abuse and addiction. *International Journal of the Addictions, 18,* 491–510.

Imhof, J., Hirsch, R., & Terenzi, R. (1985). AIDS and the substance abuse treatment clinician [Editorial]. *Journal of Substance Abuse Treatment, 2,* 137.

Imhof, J. E. (1979). "Addicts," "addicts," everywhere: But has anyone seen a person? [Editorial]. *Contemporary Drug Problems, 8,* 289–290.

Imhof, J. E. (1991). Countertransference issues in the treatment of drug and alcohol addiction. In N. S. Miller (Ed.), *Comprehensive handbook of drug and alcohol addiction* (pp. 931–946). New York: Marcel Dekker.

Imhof, J. E., & Hirsch, R. (1993). 10th anniversary editorial [Editorial]. *Journal of Substance Abuse Treatment, 10,* 1.

Kaufman, E. (1990). Critical aspects of the psychodynamics of substance abuse and the evaluation of their application to a psychotherapeutic approach. *International Journal of the Addictions, 25,* 97–116.

Marshall, M. J., & Marshall, S. (1993). Treatment paternalism in chemical dependency counselors. *International Journal of the Addictions, 28,* 91–106.

Menninger, K. A. (1930). *The human mind.* New York: Literary Guild.

Newman, A. (1993). Hard-core addicts becoming predominant cocaine users. *Clinical Psychiatry News, 21*(4), 6.

Nurco, D. N., Hanlon, T. E., Shaffer, J. W., Kinlock, T. W., Duszynski, B. A., & Stephenson, P. (1988). Differences among treatment clinic types in attitudes toward narcotic addiction. *Journal of Nervous and Mental Disorders, 176,* 714–718.

O'Malley, S. S., Kosten, T. R., & Renner, J. A., Jr. (1990). Dual diagnoses: Substance abuse and personality disorders. *New Directions for Mental Health Services, 47,* 115–137.

Peck, M. S. (1993). *Further along the road less travelled.* New York: Simon and Schuster.

Piercy, F. P. (1991). Ethnocentrism and beyond: Letters between a family therapist and an advocate of Alcoholics Anonymous. *Contemporary Family Therapy, 13,* 521–530.

Reichelt, S., & Christensen, B. (1990). Reflections during a study on family therapy with drug addicts. *Family Process, 29,* 273–287.

Review and outlook: A therapeutic state? (1994, January 3). *Wall Street Journal,* pp, 6–7.

Ross, M. W., & Darke, S. (1992). Mad, bad, and dangerous to know: Dimensions and measurement of attitudes toward injecting drug users. *Drug and Alcohol Dependence, 30,* 71–74.

Smith, D. E., Buxton, M. E., Bilal, R., & Seymour, R. B. (1993). Cultural points of resistance to the 12-step recovery process. *Journal of Psychoactive Drugs, 25,* 97–108.

Smith, G. B. (1992). Attitudes of nurse managers and assistant nurse managers toward chemically impaired colleagues. *Image: Journal of Nursing Scholarship, 24,* 295–300.

Toumbourou, J., & Hamilton, M. (1993). Perceived client and program moderators of successful therapeutic community treatment for drug addiction. *International Journal of the Addictions, 28,* 1127–1146.

Tucker, C. (1990). Acute pain and substance abuse in surgical patients. *Journal of Neuroscience Nursing, 22,* 339–349.

Vannicelli, M. (1991). Dilemmas and countertransference considerations in group psychotherapy with adult children of alcoholics. *International Journal of Group Psychotherapy, 41,* 295-312.

Wurmser, L. (1972). Drug abuse: Nemesis of psychiatry. *American Scholar, 41,* 393–407.

2

Clinical Assessment
of Psychoactive Substance Use

ARNOLD M. WASHTON

INTRODUCTION

Because substance abuse and mental health problems are so often linked, a substance use history is an essential part of every mental health assessment no matter what the patient's presenting complaint. Given the high incidence of substance use disorders among the general population in the United States, especially among persons with mental illness (Miller, Belkin, & Gibbons, 1994; Schottenfeld, Carroll, & Rounsaville, 1993), every mental health clinician needs to learn how to conduct an accurate substance use evaluation.

In persons with no preexisting psychopathology, chronic substance use often produces behavioral symptoms that mimic nearly every kind of psychiatric disorder. For example, symptoms of depression, anxiety, and psychosis can be produced by chronic use of central nervous system (CNS) depressants or stimulants (e.g., alcohol or cocaine). For individuals who do have preexisting psychiatric illness, psychoactive substance use can severely complicate and exacerbate these problems. When not properly identified, substance-abusing patients are likely to be treated only for their presenting mental health complaint(s) while their alcohol and drug use escalates.

Patients whose substance abuse is especially likely to be overlooked or minimized by therapists lacking specific substance abuse training are that group whose use of alcohol and/or other drugs appears to be a form of "self-medication" aimed at enhancing functioning. Especially if the patient is educated, articulate, and insightful, the therapist may feel encouraged to focus on the psychological factors that drive the patient's felt need for self-medication while the drug-taking behavior itself is ignored.

Some therapists feel reluctant to raise the issue of substance use with patients who have not mentioned the issue themselves. There is concern that asking pointed questions, particularly about *illicit* drug use, might offend patients who have no history of involvement with drugs, or the therapist may be uncomfortable treading too deeply into areas that are beyond the scope of his/her clinical training. Whatever the reason, failure to identify individuals who have problems with alcohol and/or other drugs has serious consequences. Early-stage drug and alcohol problems tend to escalate into more serious problems when left unaddressed. Moreover, it is highly unlikely that a patient's presenting mental health problem will be successfully resolved in the face of continuing substance abuse.

This chapter provides the mental health practitioner with clinical techniques for conducting an accurate and thorough substance use assessment.

The purposes of the assessment are severalfold: (1) to screen for possible substance abuse problems; (2) to initiate a therapeutic interaction with the patient; (3) to provide the patient with objective feedback about his/her substance use behavior; (4) to establish a diagnosis and, where indicated, to offer treatment recommendations; and (5) to enhance the patient's motivation to change.

PSYCHOLOGICAL "TONE" OF THE INTERVIEW

In the treatment of substance abuse, as in any type of therapy, perhaps no single factor is more important to success of the interview than the psychological atmosphere created by the clinician's attitude and behavior toward the patient. The initial interview is always much more than an information-gathering activity: It is the starting point of the therapeutic relationship and offers a unique opportunity to engage and motivate the patient to accepting the need for positive change. The interview should provide realistic feedback about troublesome behavior, but the tone must be distinctly encouraging, friendly, and optimistic. Especially in the treatment of substance abuse, it is a serious mistake to assume that strong confrontational tactics are required to get at the truth. The intense shame, guilt, and self-loathing commonly associated with substance abuse place additional demands on the clinician to convey an empathetic, nonjudgmental, and accepting attitude toward these patients. Simple expressions of interest and caring can go a long way toward creating a trusting atmosphere that encourages truthful self-revelation. Strong confrontation aimed at counteracting denial, although a standard feature of traditional addiction counseling, tends only to exacerbate the patient's feelings of shame and guilt and to produce alienation rather than cooperation. Therapists who are skilled at finding ways to "start where the patient is" and know how to creatively join or sidestep resistance rather than assault it are more likely to elicit the information needed to conduct an accurate assessment. Operating from a stereotypical view of addicts as manipulators and liars is distinctly countertherapeutic. It engenders negative interactions between patient and therapist, power struggles, and destructive acting out of negative countertransference (see Imhof, Chapter 1, this volume).

It is often assumed that substance-abusing patients will minimize or lie about their alcohol and other drug use. But quite often the patient neither perceives nor experiences substance use as a "problem" requiring treatment. The patient may be focused solely on alleviating the distress being caused by the presenting problem, even if substance abuse is the prime generator of that problem. For example, a patient who sought therapy for marital problems complained of irritability, short temper, and loss of sex drive. He also complained about his wife's constant "nagging" and problems disciplining his two teenage children. He did mention that he used cocaine but did not consider it a "problem." In his eyes, it was the marital and family problems that were causing him severe pain and distress. In taking a detailed substance use history it became apparent that cocaine use was indeed a problem and that it was severely exacerbating or directly causing the patient's presenting complaints. Cocaine at first made him feel more sociable and more talkative and increased his libido, but with chronic, escalating use its effects turned predictably negative. He became irritable, short-tempered, impotent, and withdrawn. This led to arguments with his wife, who strongly resented and disapproved of his drug use. It had also led him to be impatient and intolerant with his teenage children, who responded by ignoring their schoolwork and rebelling against curfews and other basic household rules. The patient's clinical history revealed that almost all his presenting complaints had existed for some time prior to cocaine use, but escalation of these problems was clearly linked to escalation in his drug use. In this case, it would have been futile to treat him for the presenting problems without first addressing his cocaine use.

It is beyond the scope of this chapter to provide a detailed description of clinical interviewing techniques. Recent publications (Miller & Rollnick, 1991; Rollnick & Morgan, Chapter 9, this volume) provide excellent descriptions of motivational interviewing: a client-centered approach to assessing patients with addictive behaviors. In contrast to the traditional confrontation-of-denial approach, motivational interviewing (1) de-emphasizes acceptance of labels such as "alcoholic" or "addict" as pre-requisites for change, (2) emphasizes the patient's personal choice and responsibility for change, (3) views resistance as a behavior directly in-fluenced by the clinician's behavior toward the patient, (4) promotes negotiation of goals rather than unequivocal submission to treatment recommendations, and (5) sees ambivalence rather than denial as the core issue to be addressed (Miller & Rollnick, 1991). The strategies of motiva-tional interviewing represent a significant breakthrough in dealing with the most difficult aspect of addiction: the client's ambivalence about giv-ing up mood-altering substances. Interestingly, this approach sees the *ther-apist's* behavior as the most important factor influencing the outcome of the interview. This is a refreshing departure from the usual tendency to lay blame on the substance-abusing patient for any and all therapeutic failures.

REASONS FOR SEEKING TREATMENT

Among the most critical questions to be asked at the beginning of the interview are: What brings you to see me? Why now, at this particular point in time, rather than several days, weeks, or months ago? Is sub-stance use part of the presenting complaint? Does the patient consider substance use a "problem," and if so, does he/she want professional help? Is this individual being coerced by others (e.g., family member, employ-er, or criminal justice system) to seek treatment for an alcohol or a drug problem? If so, exactly what are the coercing agency's or person(s)' de-mands? What will it take to satisfy their demands? What are the conse-quences of not complying with their demands?

The patient's initial presentation is strongly affected by the circum-stances that have brought him/her to the clinician's door. This is espe-cially true with substance-abusing patients because they are most likely to appear for treatment when faced with an acute crisis or emergency that demands immediate attention. More often than not, the precipitat-ing crisis has been created by negative consequences (e.g., job jeopardy, arrest or incarceration, financial problems, or marital problems) directly linked to the patient's use of alcohol and/or other drugs. Sometimes the first session must focus on crisis intervention and a full assessment must be deferred until the immediate crisis has stabilized.

Coerced Patients

Patients who are coerced by an external force (e.g., court, employer, or family member) into appearing for the assessment pose a special challenge and dilemma for the therapist. The challenge is: How can the therapist conduct an accurate, thorough substance use assessment in someone who comes to the interview with reason to actively withhold and/or falsify information? First, it is essential that the therapist fully expect the patient to feel angry, mistrustful, resentful, controlled, infantilized, humiliated, fearful, anxious, defensive, and suspicious. Accepting this reality can help the therapist to find an effective way to "start where the patient is." Suggestions for dealing with coerced patients have been described at length by others (Berg & Miller, 1992; Berg, Chapter 12, this volume; Miller & Rollnick, 1991). These suggestions include the following: (1) be sympathetic to the patient's plight and validate his/her appropriately negative feelings in light of the unpleasant circumstances that brought him/her to your door; (2) accept without challenge the individual's likely goal for the interview—to get the coercing agent off his/her back; (3) compliment the patient for recognizing the importance of at least showing up for the interview; (4) emphasize that showing up for the interview was a matter of personal choice and a positive indication of caring about oneself as it was entirely possible to not show up and face the self-destructive consequences of that choice; (5) detach yourself from the coercing person or agency by stating clearly that your goal is *not* to coerce this individual into doing anything but rather to help him/her achieve an accurate assessment and understanding of the nature of his/her involvement with psychoactive substances. If the therapist is, in fact, required to issue an assessment report and treatment recommendations to the coercing person/agent, it is essential to say so very clearly and straightforwardly at the outset of the interview but still to emphasize that his/her primary goal is to provide the patient with realistic feedback about the patient's substance use behavior.

Intoxicated Patients

It is impossible to conduct a meaningful clinical interview with a person who is actively intoxicated. If the patient exhibits significant, observable signs of substance-induced impairment in cognitive and motor functioning (e.g., slurred speech, stumbling gait, inappropriate affect, or impaired responsiveness), the interview should be deferred until the individual is sober. In cases in which the patient reports having used alcohol and/or other drugs in the hours immediately preceding the interview but shows no significant signs of impairment, a preliminary interview can be attempted, but a second interview should be conducted when the patient is not under the influence of any psychoactive substances.

ASSESSMENT TOOLS

The substance use assessment questionnaire developed at Washton Institute is shown in Appendix 2.1. This is a self-administered instrument that the patient fills out in the waiting room immediately prior to the face-to-face interview. Unlike most other assesment tools developed primarily for research purposes, this instrument is specifically designed for use in a clinical setting. The questionnaire is divided into several sections: (1) current substance use (i.e., within the past 30 days), (2) lifetime history of use and whether involvement with any substance was ever a "problem," (3) consequences of use, (4) withdrawal symptomotology, (5) treament history, and (6) psychiatric risk profile.

Using a self-administered questionnaire such as this one has at least several advantages. It provides structure and focus to the assessment interview. It relieves the clinician of having to verbally ask and then record the patient's response to each question, thus leaving more time to interact (and make eye contact) with the patient. The clinician can devote more energy to forming a therapeutic alliance with the patient than to recording data. Moreover, the specific content of the questionnaire conveys a clear message to the patient that substance use behavior will be examined in considerable detail during the face-to-face interview.

PSYCHOACTIVE SUBSTANCE USE

The most commonly abused psychoactive substances that should be asked about in every assessment interview are listed in the questionnaire (Appendix 2.1). To obtain an accurate assessment, it is important to ask specific questions about each of these substances.

For each substance it is essential to determine the method/route of administration as well as the frequency, pattern, and quantity of consumption. Assessment should start with use during the past 30 days. For any substance the patient reports using within the past 30 days, the therapist should obtain a day-by-day detailed assessment of use during each of the 7 days immediately preceding the interview, including any use on the day of the interview itself. Lifetime history, including age of first use for each substance and any changes in pattern and intensity of use over time, should also be evaluated.

It is also important to determine whether the person frequently uses two or more substances simultaneously or in succession. For example, cocaine users may drink substantial quantities of alcohol while high on cocaine or when "crashing" in order to alleviate unpleasant cocaine side effects such as restlessness and irritability. In cases of polysubstance use it is extremely important not to overlook or downplay the clinical significance of the secondary substance use even if this use does not seem as problematic. In cocaine addicts, for example, it has often been noted that any level of alcohol consumption (including "social" drinking) during attempted cocaine abstinence markedly increases the likelihood of relapse to cocaine (Rawson, Obert, McCann, & Ling, 1993; Washton, 1989a).

Method of Use

The patient's preferred and current method of drug administration, especially with substances such as cocaine and heroin, is an important indicator of the depth and malignancy of the person's involvement with the drug. Intensive methods of drug administration, such as smoking and injecting, are almost always associated with addictive patterns of use and serious adverse consequences. For example, it is extremely difficult for individuals who are smoking crack cocaine to maintain control over their drug use and to prevent rapid escalation to compulsive patterns of use with resulting adverse effects on psychosocial functioning. Crack smoking is commonly characterized by patterns of daily use or by marathon binges lasting for days or weeks on end. It is important to point out, however, that compulsive/addictive patterns of use can occur with any method of drug administration. Prior to the cocaine epidemic of the 1980s, many people believed that snorting cocaine could not lead to addiction, but this misconception was refuted by dramatic reports of cocaine snorters whose drug use had escalated out of control (Washton, 1989a).

Cocaine hydrochloride, a white crystalline powder, can be taken intranasally (i.e., inhaled or "snorted" through the nostrils), or it can be dissolved in water and injected intravenously. It cannot be smoked because the active drug is destroyed (pyrolyzed) by temperatures achieved with a match or lighter. In order to smoke cocaine, it first must be converted into cocaine alkaloid or "freebase," now known as "crack." Heroin, on the other hand, can be snorted, smoked, or injected without any chemical conversion. Smoking (also know as pulmonary administration) has become a very popular method of drug delivery in recent years, partly as an outgrowth of fears about exposure to HIV (human immunodeficiency virus) infection from contaminated needles. Smoking is an extremely rapid and efficient method for delivering large quantities of a drug into the brain in a very short period of time. The instantaneous and extremely intense drug euphoria or "rush" experienced with intravenous use is also achieved with smoking but without the medical risks (e.g., exposure to AIDS, hepatitis, and other infections) commonly associated with intravenous use. Also, smoking carries less of the sick, dangerous, desperate connotations associated with intravenous use and thus it is appealing to people who might never allow themselves to experiment with intravenous use. Smoking and injecting drugs are reliably associated with faster progression from initial use to compulsive/addictive use and more severe drug-related dysfunction.

Amount and Frequency of Use

The dosage or amount of alcohol and other drugs consumed during each episode of use is another important variable that characterizes a person's involvement with psychoactive substances. It is essential to ask exactly how much of each substance the person consumes during a typical episode of use. Determining amount or dosage of use is fairly straightforward with legally manufactured substances such as alcohol or prescription drugs but can be confusing or obscure when it comes to illicit (street) drugs.

With alcohol, consumption is typically measured in ounces of each type of alcoholic beverage consumed (e.g., beer, wine, or distilled spirits). It is helpful to keep in mind that one 8-ounce glass of wine, one can of beer, and one shot glass of distilled spirits each contains about the same amount of ethyl alcohol. When an individual says, "I don't have a problem with alcohol, I only drink beer or wine, I never touch hard liquor," it is important to keep in mind that it is the total amount (dose) of alcohol consumed in a given period rather than the particular type of alcoholic beverage one drinks that determines its impact on the individual's functioning.

With street drugs such as cocaine, heroin, and marijuana, an accurate measure of consumption is difficult to obtain because of wide variations in street price, purity, and packaging. Often one has to rely on the patient's report of the amount of money he/she is spending on drugs as the best indicator of consumption level. Money spent on drugs may reveal less about the exact amount consumed than about the relative value of drugs to the user. It is important to know, for example, what proportion of the patient's income or savings is being spent on drugs and whether it has become necessary to borrow money in order to support the drug use. Does the patient sell drugs to offset the cost of personal use? Are there depleted bank accounts, overdue bills, large credit card debts, or other unmet financial obligations due to drug use? This information provides at least some indication of the strength of an individual's attachment to the drug and the level of priority it has achieved in his/her life. In those individuals who are capable of supporting their drug use without financial consequence, evidence of the drug's priority in their lives must be identified in other areas of functioning. A diagnosis of addiction should not depend on the patient's income.

Assessing amount and cost of an individual's illicit drug use requires familiarity with certain street terms. Heroin is typically sold in ten-dollar ("dime") bags. It is not uncommon for an intravenous heroin addict to be using anywhere from 3 to 10 bags spread over the course of a day. Crack cocaine is commonly sold on the street in plastic vials containing 1 to 3 tiny pea-size pellets or "rocks" at a price of $5 to $30 per vial depending on the number and size of the rocks. Each pellet provides a few puffs of cocaine vapor to be inhaled into one's lungs. Each puff provides an intense but short-lived euphoria lasting only a few minutes, followed by a rebound dysphoria or "crash" and cravings for more cocaine. It is not difficult to see how this drives the development of compulsive use patterns. Cocaine powder is sold by the gram, the ounce (28 grams), the "quarter" ounce (7 grams), or the "eighth" ounce (3.5 grams). Prices may vary anywhere from $40 to $75 per gram. Marijuana is typically sold in the form of individually rolled cigarettes (known as "joints" or "reefers") for a few dollars each, in dime bags that contain a quantity of loose plant material sufficient to roll two or three marijuana cigarettes, or by the ounce.

Another important aspect of drug consumption is the frequency or pattern of use. Frequency can range from occasional use to intensive marathon binges separated by days or weeks of abstinence to continuous use every single day. Binge patterns often create diagnostic dilemmas because it is frequently assumed that a person who does not use drugs every day must not be addicted, especially if the individual seems able to refrain from using for several days in a row. To the contrary, binge patterns are among the most difficult to break and result in problems as severe as if not more so than problems from daily usage at lower doses. Binge use rather than daily use is the most common pattern associated with smoking crack cocaine. During a typical crack binge lasting 2 or 3 days, the user may consume upwards of several hundred dollars worth of the drug while sitting alone in a crack house or an empty apartment lost in fantasies and reveries, and in some cases tormented by paranoid delusions. The binge comes to end when the user collapses from physical exhaustion or runs out of money, whichever happens first. Binge patterns are also quite common among alcoholics who regularly disappear on "benders" for several days on end. On the other hand, binge use is relatively uncommon among heroin users (especially intravenous users) whose physical dependence on the drug demands daily dosing to stave off withdrawal symptoms.

Setting and Circumstances of Use

A detailed accounting of the specific settings, circumstances, and immediate precursors of the individual's substance use may provide clues about its functional significance in the patient's life and helps to identify precipitants or "triggers" of the drug use. This information is potentially crucial in determining what behavioral changes will be required to achieve abstinence if and when that is defined as a goal. The patient should be asked to describe the people, places, and things most reliably associated with his/her drug use as well as any particular moods and emotional states that seem related to the drug use. For example, does the patient use drugs at work, at home, at bars/clubs, alone, with dealers, with friends, with coworkers, with sex partners (including prostitutes)? How and where are drugs procured? Does anyone else in the patient's household use drugs? Is the drug use associated with feeling stressed, depressed, lonely, or otherwise unhappy? Does it occur on the heels of arguments with the patient's mate, boss, parent, or significant other? If there have been previous periods of sustained abstinence, what factors precipitated a return to drug use?

It is crucial to acknowledge and explore the patient's perceived benefits of using psychoactive substances while neither condoning nor condemning this perception. It must be accepted that psychoactive substances do provide desirable effects that may actually enhance one's ability to cope and function. Some individuals report that substance use improves performance (e.g., sexual arousal or endurance, meeting new people in a social setting, and artistic or musical creativity) or alleviates negative mood/feeling states such as anxiety, boredom, or depression. Others state more generally that drug use helps them to relax or just plain "have a good time." Whether and to what extent drug use is currently helping or hindering the patient's functioning is best evaluated during a trial period of abstinence.

CONSEQUENCES OF USE

Doing a careful, detailed assessment of recent drug-related consequences to the patient's health and psychosocial functioning serves at least two critical functions: (1) It helps to identify problems that may require immediate attention or, at the very least, consideration in the treatment plan, and (2) it can heighten the patient's awareness of the toll that the substance use may be taking on his/her life. The Washton Institute questionnaire constains an extensive checklist inventory of substance-related consequences (Appendix 2.1).

Biomedical Consequences

Alcohol and other drug use can certainly have adverse effects on physical health. For this reason, it is essential for the nonmedical practitioner at least to inquire about possible health problems, including those most commonly associated with certain types of drugs and methods of use. For example, it is well-known that excessive alcohol use may (1) cause serious liver, gastrointestinal, and other internal organ damage; (2) exacerbate and aggravate a wide range of other medical conditions; and (3) interfere with or nullify the therapeutic action of medications being prescribed for other medical conditions. Snorting cocaine can cause sinus congestion, nose bleeds, ulcers in the nasal mucosa, and in extreme cases perforation of the nasal septum. Smoking crack cocaine can impair pulmonary functioning and suppress appetite to the point of causing malnutrition and severe weight loss. Intravenous heroin use may be associated with hepatitis, endocarditis, or AIDS and with ulcerated sores or discolored scar tissue ("tracks") at injection sites. In all cases of severe or chronic substance abuse, the patient's health status should be evaluated by a physician who can conduct a physical examination and laboratory tests, where indicated.

Psychosocial Consequences

It is essential to determine whether and to what extent the patient's substance use is associated with problems at work or at home. For example, is there a drug-related pattern of absenteeism, lateness, poor productivity, argumentativeness, and apathy at work? Are there frequent arguments with parent, mate, or significant others? Has a significant relationship broken up as a result of the patient's drug use? Is there a current threat of this happening? Is there a pattern of social isolation and withdrawal? Are there financial or legal problems due to substance use? Whether and to what extent does the patient perceive that the substance use is having any negative impact on his/her life?

Sexual Consequences

Sexual functioning can be profoundly affected by psychoactive substance use. Short-term and/or low-dose use of alcohol, cocaine, marijuana, and other drugs tends to enhance sexual performance by reducing anxiety and inhibitions. Chronic and/or high-dose use, on the other hand, tends to severely impair or in some cases totally obliterate sexual functioning. Complaints about lack of sex drive and inability to achieve erection or orgasm are often heard from substance-abusing patients. Fortunately, these problems usually remit on their own after several weeks or months of drug abstinence.

Hypersexuality is a problem uniquely associated with cocaine and other stimulants. Studies have shown that as many as 70% of cocaine-dependent men report a strong link between cocaine use and a variety of sexual acting-out behaviors (Washton, 1989b; Schneider, 1994). Cocaine-induced hypersexuality often involves compulsive masturbation and marathon encounters with prostitutes or other unknown sexual partners while high on cocaine. Some patients report that cocaine stimulates intense sexual fantasies, often involving "taboo" sexual behaviors such as cross-dressing, sadomasochism, exhibitionism, and homosexuality. Many men who use cocaine chronically or in high doses become impotent and nonorgasmic, but this does not thwart their sexual acting-out behavior. To the contrary, if anything their sexual acting-out behavior escalates in the face of increased sex drive and inability to achieve satisfaction, Preliminary observations suggest a much lower incidence of cocaine-induced hypersexuality (20–30%) among cocaine-using women (Washton, 1989b). The reasons for this discrepancy between males and females may involve both biological and social factors, but to date no studies have explored this phenomenon.

The clinical importance of identifying cocaine-related hypersexuality centers on its contribution to chronic relapse patterns. It appears that once the cocaine–sex connection has been established, it is extraordinarily difficult to break. The sexual aspect of the individual's cocaine use adds a dimension to the drug-induced euphoria with awesome power to drive compulsive drug-seeking behavior. Sexual thoughts and feelings, even in the absence of cocaine use, can stimulate intense cravings and urges for the drug. Similarly, thoughts about cocaine tend to stimulate urges to act out sexually, The treatment of patients with cocaine-related sexual compulsivity must actively address the cocaine–sex connection if it is to have any chance of succeeding.

Psychiatric Consequences

Substance abuse is typically associated with alterations in the user's mood, mental state, personality, and behavior. Thus, a complete mental status evaluation is an essential part of the assessment. In the author's clinical experience it appears that suicidal ideation is particularly rampant among patients who abuse cocaine and/or alcohol. Some report that they experience suicidal thoughts only while actively intoxicated, while others experience these thoughts only when hung over or "crashing." Obviously, it is essential in every case to assess the patient's potential for inflicting harm on self or others. The risk assessment section of the intake questionnaire can assist in this process (Appendix 2.1).

When the patient presents with serious psychiatric symptoms such as severe depression, mood swings, panic anxiety attacks, paranoid thinking, and the like, it can be difficult to discern whether the patient is suffering from a primary psychiatric disorder or a secondary substance-induced psychiatric disorder. Understanding the temporal relationship between the psychiatric symptoms and the use of psychoactive substances can help in making this determination. For example, did the onset of the psychiatric symptoms predate the substance use? If so, were they exacerbated by the substance use? Did the psychiatric symptoms persist unabated during significant periods of drug abstinence (if any)? In many cases, the psychiatric symptoms are directly linked to substance use and disappear or markedly diminish within a few days or weeks after the substance use stops. Sometimes, however, the psychiatric problems persist or worsen despite sustained periods of abstinence. In the absence of significant risk factors, it is preferable to wait until the patient is free of all psychoactive drugs for at least 4 to 6 weeks before attempting a psychiatric evaluation or starting the patient on a trial of nonaddictive psychotropic medication.

PHYSICAL DEPENDENCE
REQUIRING MEDICAL DETOXIFICATION

If there has been no alcohol or other drug use in the preceding 2 to 3 weeks, there is no generally reason to be concerned about acute withdrawal. Abrupt withdrawal from alcohol, barbiturates, benzodiazepines and other CNS depressants can be fatal. Consumption of CNS depressants in daily dosages exceeding roughly three times the therapeutic dose range may require management in a hospital. In some cases, outpatient detoxification from CNS depressants is a viable alternative if the patient is closely monitored, shows up reliably, and follows prescribed medication regimens. Alcohol withdrawal can often be safely managed in an outpatient setting provided there is no history of seizure disorders or medical complications (e.g., delirium tremens) during previous detoxification attempts and the patient is reliable and capable of complying with medical instructions. Withdrawal from heroin and other opioids is very distressing and uncomfortable, but not fatal (except in a fetus or neonate). Outpatient withdrawal can be effective in motivated patients, but most opioid addicts (especially intravenous and high-dose users) must be denied access to drugs by admission to a hospital or other inpatient facility in order to endure the drug cravings and withdrawal discomfort long enough to achieve a drug-free state. Cocaine does not produce a withdrawal syndrome requiring medical management or detoxification. Some high-dose users complain of depression, irritability, and insomnia that may last for several days or weeks after last use, but many others experience no postcocaine symptoms of clinical significance.

How can the clinician determine when medical detoxification under the auspices of a physician is required? In other words, how does one decide whether the patient is (1) physically dependent on one or more substances and in need of medical detoxification or (2) not physically dependent and at no medical risk if drug consumption is stopped abruptly? The substances of greatest concern in this regard are alcohol and other CNS depressants. With opioids one need only ask the patient whether he/she experiences withdrawal symptoms and wants medication to quell those symptoms. The most common symptoms of opioid withdrawal are stomach cramps, diarrhea, chills, restlessness, tearing eyes, runny nose, and insomnia. These symptoms are usually not health threatening, but they do cause substantial discomfort and may become too intolerable for the patient to sustain the motivation to remain abstinent. With alcohol and other CNS depressants, however, it can be more difficult to determine whether the patient is physically addicted and whether there is a strong likelihood of medical complications if consumption is reduced or stopped too quickly. There is a great deal of individual variability in susceptibility to experiencing withdrawal complications from chronic use of alcohol and other depressants. For example, whereas one person who consumes a six-pack of beer every day may experience significant withdrawal symptoms upon stopping abruptly, another person with exactly the same level of consumption may experience no withdrawal problems whatsoever. Furthermore, often the patient does not know whether he/she is addicted either because there have been no recent periods of abstinence where consumption has ceased long enough to allow withdrawal symptoms to appear or because the patient has not recognized the early signs of withdrawal as such and so has inadvertently ignored them. The clinician should ask pointed questions about any recent periods of abstinence that have extended for 2 or more consecutive days and what if any physical symptoms the patient experienced during those periods. For example, when was the last time the patient consumed no alcohol and no other depressant drugs for at least 2 days in a row? Did the patient feel sick or notice any physical changes during that time? Did the patient experience any vomiting, sweating, nausea, or insomnia? If so, did these symptoms stop when the patient subsequently drank alcohol or took depressant drugs? Has the patient ever experienced withdrawal symptoms or any other physical problems during previous attempts to remain abstinent? The final determination of whether a patient who has been consuming alcohol and/or other depressant drugs on a chronic daily basis requires medical detoxification should be made only by a physician.

FAMILY HISTORY OF SUBSTANCE ABUSE

Substance abuse problems often run in families. There is evidence suggesting that a history of chemical dependency in one or both parents is associated with an increased likelihood of chemical dependency in the offspring (Anthenelli & Schuckit, 1992). One implication of this finding is an increased level of concern about the potential consequences of even occasional or sporadic use of psychoactive substances by sons and daughters of people who have a history of serious problems with alcohol and/or other drugs. The therapist should determine whether there is any such history in the patient's family, including parents, grandparents, aunts/uncles, and siblings. If so, what if any treatment did these individuals receive? Are they currently abstinent or actively using? Did any family member die from substance-related causes such as cirrhosis of the liver or drug overdose? If there is a significant family history of substance abuse problems, this information should be considered when formulating treatment recommendations.

Perhaps even more important than the history of substance abuse in the family is the current role that family members might play in unintentionally perpetuating the patient's substance abuse. It is often said that chemical dependency is a "family disease," not only because there may be a familial biological (genetic) component to the problem but also because the behavior of family members (and significant others) toward the active substance abuser can provoke, maintain, or otherwise "enable" the patient's continuing substance abuse. It is important to assess, for example, whether any family members (1) financially support the patient's drug use, (2) assist the patient in obtaining drug supplies and/or use drugs together with the patient, (3) sabotage attempts by the patient to stop using, or (4) tolerate and compensate for the patient's dysfunctional, irresponsible behavior so as to shield the individual from experiencing negative consequences directly linked to his/her substance use.

Whether or not family members are directly involved in the patient's substance abuse, it is generally helpful to interview the patient's spouse, parent(s), or significant others, provided the patient consents to such interviews.

PRIOR TREATMENT FOR SUBSTANCE ABUSE

If the patient has received any prior treatment for substance abuse, the particulars of that treatment can be very informative (see section on treatment history of questionnaire in Appendix 2.1). In addition to asking when, where, and what type of treatment, it is important to know whether the patient completed the recommended course of treatment or dropped out prematurely; whether he/she thought the treatment was helpful; and, if so, what aspects of the treatment were most helpful and what aspects were least helpful? How long did the patient remain substance-free after treatment? What helped in maintaining abstinence? What contributed to subsequent relapse? Similar questions should be asked about any past or present involvement in self-help groups such as Alcoholics Anonymous, Narcotics Anonymous, Rational Recovery (RR[SM]), or others.

URINE TESTING

Testing body fluids (e.g., blood or urine) for the presence of psychoactive drugs is the only objective way to determine whether an individual has used any of these substances in the recent past (Verebey, 1992). A urine test may confirm the patient's verbal report of recent use or identify additional, unreported use. A urine test can determine only the presence or absence of certain drugs that a person may have used in the preceding several days and says nothing about the extent or frequency of use.

Although it may not be very practical or comfortable for the therapist (especially a nonmedical therapist) to take a urine sample from every patient who presents with a mental health complaint, urine testing should be part of every comprehensive assessment of substance use behavior and any ongoing treatment of a substance-abusing patient. This can be accomplished in a variety of ways: (1) The therapist can arrange with a local laboratory for direct pickup of urine samples at his/her office, (2) the therapist can ask the patient to go to a local laboratory to give a sample for testing and request that the results be sent directly to the therapist, or (3) the therapist can make arrangements with a physician colleague to take the urine sample from the patient and send it to a laboratory for testing. Every sample should be tested for the most commonly abused drugs, including alcohol, cocaine, amphetamines, benzodiazepines, barbiturates, opioids (e.g., heroin, methadone, or codeine), cannabinoids (e.g., marijuana), and hallucinogens (e.g., LSD, mescaline, PCP). (It is important to note that alcohol cannot be reliably detected in the urine much beyond 2 to 4 hours after the last drink, and the same limits generally apply to breathalyzer devices.) The preferred method of testing to be requested from the laboratory (for most drugs) is enzyme immunoassay (or EMIT), because this method is highly accurate and reasonably priced (usually $15 to $35 per sample depending on the specific number and types of drugs to be tested).

FORMULATING A DIAGNOSIS

The therapist is charged with the task of synthesizing the raw data obtained during the interview into a coherent diagnosis and treatment recommendations (if any). First, the clinician must appropriately place the patient's behavior on a substance use continuum that ranges from nonpathological use at the low end to abuse in the middle and dependency at the high end. Most diagnostic schemes, including the newly released fourth edition of the *Diagnostic and Statistical Manual of Mental Disorders* (DSM-IV; American Psychiatric Association, 1994), approach this task by the process of elimination. First, the clinician determines whether the patient's substance use behavior meets clinical criteria to warrant a diagnosis of dependency. If no, he/she determines whether the behavior meets criteria for a diagnosis of abuse. If no, by default, the behavior falls into the category of nonpathological use. (It should be noted that where *illegal* drug use is concerned, moral and political considerations can sometimes complicate the diagnosis, especially with regard to a diagnosis of nonpathological use. Politicians and lawmakers have often argued, for example, that any use of illicit drugs and any underage drinking of alcoholic beverages de facto constitute *abuse* because possession and use of these substances are against the law and this behavior must, therefore, be considered a "problem." For purposes of this chapter, the clinical criteria described in DSM-IV are utilized.)

Criteria for Dependence

An informal working definition of dependence utilized for many years by substance abuse treatment professionals rested on the simultaneous presence of all three of the following diagnostic features: (1) inability to control onset, cessation, amount, and frequency of use; (2) a sense of craving, obsession, and compulsion to use; and (3) continued use despite significant adverse consequences. Similarly, DSM-IV defines dependence by a cluster of three or more of the following symptoms occurring at any time in the same 12-month period:

1. Tolerance as defined by either the need for increasing amounts of a substance to achieve the desired effect or a markedly diminished effect with use of the same amount of the substance;
2. Withdrawal as manifested by a substance-specific characteristic withdrawal syndrome, or intake of a substitute drug to relieve or avoid withdrawal symptoms;
3. Using a substance in larger amounts or over a longer period of time than intended;
4. Persistent desire or unsuccessful efforts to cut down or control substance use;
5. Spending a great deal of time procuring, using, or recovering from effects of the substance;
6. Giving up or reducing important social, occupational, or recreational activities because of substance use; and
7. Continuing to use the substance despite knowledge of having recurrent or persistent physical and/or psychological problems likely to have been caused or exacerbated by the substance use.

It is important to note that in this diagnostic scheme, neither tolerance nor withdrawal must be present in order to meet criteria for dependence. In other words, a diagnosis of dependence can be assigned based on the presence of certain *behaviors* even in the absence of traditional hallmarks of physical addiction.

Criteria for Abuse

DSM-IV defines abuse as a maladaptive pattern of substance use leading to clinically significant impairment or distress, as manifested by one or more of the following, occurring within a 12-month period, provided that the patient has never before met criteria for dependence for this type of substance:

1. Recurrent substance use resulting in a failure to fulfill major role obligations at school, work, or home;

2. Recurrent substance use in situations in which it is physically hazardous (e.g., driving an automobile);
3. Recurrent substance-related legal problems; and
4. Continued use despite persistent or recurrent social or interpersonal problems caused or exacerbated by effects of the substance.

It should be noted that repeated episodes of substance intoxication are almost always prominent features of substance abuse or dependence, but one or more episodes of intoxication alone are not sufficient for either diagnosis.

Specifiers

DSM-IV also offers various types of "specifiers" in an attempt to further differentiate a diagnosis of abuse or dependence. For example, for persons who have stopped using there are four "remission" specifiers based on time elapsed since any of the criteria for abuse or dependence were present. These are:

1 *Early full remission.* For at least 1 month but less than 12 months, no criteria for abuse or dependence have been met.
2. *Early partial remission.* For at least 1 month but less than 12 months, one or more criteria of abuse or dependence have been met but the full criteria have not been met.
3. *Sustained full remission.* None of the criteria for abuse or dependence have been met at any time during a period of 12 months.
4. *Sustained partial remission.* Full criteria for dependence have not been met for 12 months or longer; however, one or more criteria for dependence or abuse have been met.

There are also specifiers to denote whether the patient is receiving substitute medication (e.g., methadone) or is residing in a controlled environment (e.g., hospital or rehab) where access to psychoactive substances is blocked.

PROVIDING FEEDBACK

Toward the end of the interview, it is useful to provide the patient with a summary that pulls together material that has been gathered thus far. It is important to decide what material to include, what to exclude, what to emphasize, and what to deemphasize. The tone of the summary statement must be objective, dispassionate, and optimistic. Any "scare tactic" or "arm twisting" must be avoided. The clinician should not try to pressure or convince the patient to accept a diagnosis or a particular course of action. An overbearing, controlling approach is likely to diminish the patient's receptiveness to feedback and stimulate defensiveness. At this point in the interview, no conclusions or treatment recommendations should be offered. Simply stated, the goal is to present information in an objective, dispassionate, straightforward manner so the patient will be able to hear it and, it is hoped, reflect on it. Success is evidenced when the feedback elicits the patient's own concerns and he/she requests the clinician's input and advice. The following is an example of a summary statement:

> Well, Jim, let me summarize what I think I've heard from you thus far and then I'd like to hear your reactions. You said that you came here because your boss threatened to fire you if you didn't take care of your "drinking problem" as he saw it. He seemed to be reacting to your most recent failure to show up for work on Monday, following your unexpected absence on several previous Mondays over the course of the past two months. You report that you drink, on average, two or three times per week, and most heavily on weekends. You don't always drink to the point of getting "drunk", but you have noticed that on weekends your drinking has led to some problems including getting into arguments in bars, getting into a car accident when you were driving under the influence, and failing to show up for work on at least several Monday mornings. You say that your wife gets angry when you come home smelling of alcohol, but so far your drinking has not led to major problems in your marriage. You have also emphasized that despite your recent absences, you are a good worker and feel that your boss considers you to be a valuable employee. You have also made clear that you are not sure that your drinking is enough of a "problem" to warrant being in treatment and that you would prefer to try to stop drinking on your own. On the other hand, you were quick to add that you have tried to stop on your own many times in the past, but were able to stay sober for no more than two or three weeks at a time before drinking again.
>
> So, what do *you* make of all this? Would you like to correct or add to anything I've just said? I'm interested in hearing *your* view of the situation.

TREATMENT RECOMMENDATIONS

When the assessment reveals a pattern of substance *abuse* or *dependence* (according to DSM-IV criteria), or the patient subjectively defines his/her use as a "problem," a clear course of action should be formulated to specifically address the substance use behavior. Often the most useful and informative course of action is to discuss with the patient the potential benefits of attempting a relatively short-term (e.g., 30-day) trial period of abstinence from all psychoactive substances. (If the patient requires medical detoxification or there is reason to think that abrupt reduction/cessation of use may be dangerous to the patient's health, as described earlier in this chapter, the therapist should refer the patient for medical evaluation before recommendating any reduction or cessation of substance use.) It is essential that this trial period not be presented in an insistent or controlling manner but as an important next step in the assessment process. The rationale for this trial period is to provide an opportunity to examine the nature of the individual's attachment to these substances and to determine their functional significance in his/her life. For example, how much does he/she depend on psychoactive substances in order to have a good time, to tolerate stress at work, to quell interpersonal anxiety, to obliterate bad moods, or to experience sexual pleasure? Helping the patient examine his/her daily thoughts, feelings, and behaviors during a period of total abstinence from all mood-altering chemicals is the most reliable way to arrive at an accurate assessment.

When the patient seems unable to sustain abstinence for more than a few days at a time, despite a sincere effort (an important qualification), referral to either a specialist practitioner or a structured outpatient program for further evaluation may be indicated. It is quite possible that the patient will require more specialized, intensive care (e.g., group counseling, peer suport, urine monitoring, or family counseling) than the therapist alone is able to provide. However, even when this is true, the therapist may still be able to help by providing adjunctive individual therapy that is carefully coordinated with the specialized care that the patient is receiving elsewhere. When the patient requires inpatient care for medical detoxification or serious coexisting psychiatric problems, the therapist may wish to continue seeing the patient upon discharge as part of a comprehensive aftercare plan.

CONCLUSION

Every mental health clinician needs to know how to accurately assess a patient's involvement with psychoactive substances in order to arrive at a working diagnosis and make appropriate treatment recommendations. The assessment relies most heavily on engendering the active participation and cooperation of the patient being assessed. Information from collaterals or laboratory tests can help to round out the clinical picture, but for the most part an accurate assessment depends on the patient's voluntary report. To what extent the patient is willing to cooperate in a detailed exploration of past and present substance use, both legal and illegal, depends on the particular circumstances that have brought this person to the clinician's office, as well as on the clinician's attitude and behavior during the interview. Taking too aggressive a stance about substance use behavior can alienate the patient and preclude a therapeutic outcome; taking too passive a stance can enable and perpetuate destructive behavior.

REFERENCES

American Psychiatric Association. (1994). *Diagnostic and statistical manual of mental disorders* (4th ed.). Washington, DC: Author.

Anthenelli, R. M., & Schuckit, M. A. (1992). Genetics. In J. H. Lowinson, P. Ruiz, R. B. Millman, & J. G. Langrod (Eds.), *Substance abuse: A comprehensive textbook* (pp. 39–50). Baltimore: Williams & Wilkins.

Berg, I. S., & Miller, S. D. (1992). *Working with the problem drinker: A solution-focused approach.* New York: Norton.

Miller, N. S., Belkin, B. M., & Gibbons, R. (1994). Clinical diagnosis of substance use disorders in private psychiatric populations. *Journal of Substance Abuse Treatment, 2*(4), 387–392.

Miller, W. R., & Rollnick, S. (1991). *Motivational interviewing: Preparing people to change addictive behavior.* New York: Guilford Press.

Rawson, R. A., Obert, J. L., McCann, M. J., & Ling, W. (1993). Neurobehavioral treatment for cocaine dependency: A preliminary evaluation. In F. K. Tims & C. G. Leukefeld (Eds.), *Cocaine treatment: Research and clinical perspectives* (Research Monograph No. 135, pp. 92–115). Rockville, MD: National Institute on Drug Abuse.

Schneider, J. P. (1994). Sex addiction: Controversy within mainstream addiction medicine, diagnosis based on the DSM-IIIR, and physician case histories. *Sexual Addiction and Compulsivity, 1*(1), 19–44.

Schottenfeld, R., Carroll, K., & Rounsaville, B. (1993). Comorbid psychiatric disorders and cocaine abuse. In F. K. Tims & C. G. Leukefeld (Eds.), *Cocaine treatment: Research and clinical perspectives* (Research Monograph No. 135, pp. 31–47). Rockville, MD: National Institute on Drug Abuse.

Verebey, K. (1992). Diagnostic laboratory screening for drug abuse. In J. H. Lowinson, P. Ruiz, R. B. Millman, & J. G. Langrod (Eds.), *Substance abuse: A comprehensive textbook* (pp. 425–436). Baltimore: Williams & Wilkins.

Washton, A. M. (1989a). *Cocaine abuse: Treatment, recovery, and relapse prevention.* New York: Norton.

Washton, A. M. (1989b). Cocaine abuse and compulsive sexuality. *Medical Aspects of Human Sexuality, 23,* 32–39.

APPENDIX 2.1

The Washton Institute Intake Questionnaire

IMPORTANT: All information you give us will be held STRICTLY CONFIDENTIAL as required by state and federal law. These laws and our obligation to protect your confidentiality are described in the Policies and Procedures form included in this packet. We cannot release any information about you to anyone unless you give us written permission to do so.

TODAY'S DATE: _____ WHO REFERRED YOU? _____ TEL #_____

Last Name _____ First _____ Middle _____

Street Address _____ City _____ State _____ Zip _____

Home Phone (   ) _____ Work Phone (   ) _____

Occupation _____ Annual Income: $_____

Employer _____

Work Address _____ City _____ State _____ Zip _____

SS# _____ Birthday _____ Age _____ [ ] Male [ ] Female

Race: [ ] Black [ ] White [ ] Oriental [ ] Native American [ ] Other: _____
Hispanic: [ ] Puerto Rican [ ] Cuban [ ] Mexican [ ] Other Hispanic origin
Marital Status: [ ] Never married [ ] Married [ ] Living as married [ ] Widowed
  [ ] Separated [ ] Divorced
Sexual Orientation: [ ] Heterosexual [ ] Homosexual [ ] Bisexual
  [ ] Choose to NOT answer this question
Do you have any children? [ ] No [ ] Yes *If so, how many? _____
  (give names and ages below)

Name: _____ Age: _____ Living with you? Y N

Name: _____ Age: _____ Living with you? Y N

Name: _____ Age: _____ Living with you? Y N

Name: _____ Age: _____ Living with you? Y N

Name: _____ Age: _____ Living with you? Y N

Name: _____ Age: _____ Living with you? Y N

Your Best Personal Contact (someone who usually knows where you are):

Name _____ Tel# (   )_____ Relationship to you _____

Highest School Grade Completed:
[ ] Dropped out of high school: Grade # completed: _____
[ ] Graduated high school
[ ] GED equivalency diploma
[ ] Some college
[ ] Associate degree in:
[ ] Bachelor's degree in:
[ ] Graduate degree in:

Have you ever served in the military? [ ] No [ ] Yes: Did you receive an Honorable
  Discharge? [ ] Yes [ ] No
Veteran's Status [ ] None [ ] Disabled Veteran [ ] Vietnam Veteran
  [ ] Other: _____

Your Current Employment Status:
[ ] Employed full-time (at least 35 hours per week)
[ ] Employed part-time (less than 35 hours per week)
[ ] Unemployed, looking for work
[ ] Not in labor force, homemaker [ ] Not in labor force, student
[ ] Not in labor force, disabled
[ ] Not in labor force, other:

EMPLOYMENT HISTORY
Please provide the information requested below, starting with your most recent job:

Employer	Type of Job	Dates	Reason for Leaving

Your Current Living Arrangement
[ ] Living alone   [ ] Living with spouse/relatives
[ ] Living with nonrelated persons   [ ] mate or lover   [ ] friend(s)   [ ] other

Have you ever been ARRESTED? [ ] No [ ] Yes, please describe below

Year: _____ Reason for Arrest: _____ Disposition _____
Year: _____ Reason for Arrest: _____ Disposition _____

Your Current Criminal Justice Status
[ ] None [ ] Parole [ ] Probationer [ ] Court—on bail or conditional discharge
[ ] Other (explain):

Please indicate for each drug listed below whether you have EVER used that drug; whether
your use of that drug was ever a PROBLEM FOR YOU; at WHAT AGE YOU FIRST USED
that drug; and, HOW LONG AGO you last used that drug.

	Ever Used?	Ever a Problem?	Age of 1st Use	Time since Last Use
Cocaine	Yes No	Yes No	_____	_____
Crack	Yes No	Yes No	_____	_____
Alcohol (beer, wine, liquor)	Yes No	Yes No	_____	_____
Heroin	Yes No	Yes No	_____	_____
Methadone	Yes No	Yes No	_____	_____
Percodan	Yes No	Yes No	_____	_____
Codeine	Yes No	Yes No	_____	_____

	Ever Used?	Ever a Problem?	Age of 1st Use	Time since Last Use
		Demerol	Yes No	Yes No
Dilaudid	Yes No	Yes No	_____	_____
Other Prescription Opiates	Yes No	Yes No	_____	_____
Marijuana or Hashish	Yes No	Yes No	_____	_____
Valium	Yes No	Yes No	_____	_____
Librium	Yes No	Yes No	_____	_____
Xanax	Yes No	Yes No	_____	_____
Halcion	Yes No	Yes No	_____	_____
Other Tranquilizers	Yes No	Yes No	_____	_____
Tuinol	Yes No	Yes No	_____	_____
Seconol	Yes No	Yes No	_____	_____
Quaalude	Yes No	Yes No	_____	_____
Other Barbiturates or Sleeping Pills	Yes No	Yes No	_____	_____
Methamphetamine	Yes No	Yes No	_____	_____
LSD	Yes No	Yes No	_____	_____
Mescaline	Yes No	Yes No	_____	_____
Other Hallucinogens	Yes No	Yes No	_____	_____
PCP	Yes No	Yes No	_____	_____
Special "K"	Yes No	Yes No	_____	_____
Nitrous Oxide	Yes No	Yes No	_____	_____
Butyl Nitrate	Yes No	Yes No	_____	_____
Amyl Nitrate ("snappers")	Yes No	Yes No	_____	_____
Other Inhalants	Yes No	Yes No	_____	_____
Ecstasy (MDMA)	Yes No	Yes No	_____	_____
Other (specify) ____	Yes No	Yes No	_____	_____

How often have you used in the PAST 30 DAYS? (x equals times)

Cocaine	[ ] None [ ] 1–3 x [ ] 1–2 x/wk [ ] 3–4 x/wk [ ] 5–6 x/wk [ ] daily
Crack	[ ] None [ ] 1–3 x [ ] 1–2 x/wk [ ] 3–4 x/wk [ ] 5–6 x/wk [ ] daily
Alcohol (beer, wine, liquor	[ ] None [ ] 1–3 x [ ] 1–2 x/wk [ ] 3–4 x/wk [ ] 5–6 x/wk [ ] daily
Heroin	[ ] None [ ] 1–3 x [ ] 1–2 x/wk [ ] 3–4 x/wk [ ] 5–6 x/wk [ ] daily
Methadone	[ ] None [ ] 1–3 x [ ] 1–2 x/wk [ ] 3–4 x/wk [ ] 5–6 x/wk [ ] daily
Percodan	[ ] None [ ] 1–3 x [ ] 1–2 x/wk [ ] 3–4 x/wk [ ] 5–6 x/wk [ ] daily
Codeine	[ ] None [ ] 1–3 x [ ] 1–2 x/wk [ ] 3–4 x/wk [ ] 5–6 x/wk [ ] daily

Demerol   [ ] None [ ] 1–3 x [ ] 1–2 x/wk [ ] 3–4 x/wk [ ] 5–6 x/wk [ ] daily
Dilaudid   [ ] None [ ] 1–3 x [ ] 1–2 x/wk [ ] 3–4 x/wk [ ] 5–6 x/wk [ ] daily
Other Prescription
  Opiates   [ ] None [ ] 1–3 x [ ] 1–2 x/wk [ ] 3–4 x/wk [ ] 5–6 x/wk [ ] daily
Marijuana or
  Hashish   [ ] None [ ] 1–3 x [ ] 1–2 x/wk [ ] 3–4 x/wk [ ] 5–6 x/wk [ ] daily
Valium   [ ] None [ ] 1–3 x [ ] 1–2 x/wk [ ] 3–4 x/wk [ ] 5–6 x/wk [ ] daily
Librium   [ ] None [ ] 1–3 x [ ] 1–2 x/wk [ ] 3–4 x/wk [ ] 5–6 x/wk [ ] daily
Xanax   [ ] None [ ] 1–3 x [ ] 1–2 x/wk [ ] 3–4 x/wk [ ] 5–6 x/wk [ ] daily
Halcion   [ ] None [ ] 1–3 x [ ] 1–2 x/wk [ ] 3–4 x/wk [ ] 5–6 x/wk [ ] daily
Other Tran-
  quilizers   [ ] None [ ] 1–3 x [ ] 1–2 x/wk [ ] 3–4 x/wk [ ] 5–6 x/wk [ ] daily
Tuinol   [ ] None [ ] 1–3 x [ ] 1–2 x/wk [ ] 3–4 x/wk [ ] 5–6 x/wk [ ] daily
Seconol   [ ] None [ ] 1–3 x [ ] 1–2 x/wk [ ] 3–4 x/wk [ ] 5–6 x/wk [ ] daily
Quaalude   [ ] None [ ] 1–3 x [ ] 1–2 x/wk [ ] 3–4 x/wk [ ] 5–6 x/wk [ ] daily
Other Sleeping
  Pills   [ ] None [ ] 1–3 x [ ] 1–2 x/wk [ ] 3–4 x/wk [ ] 5–6 x/wk [ ] daily
Methamphet-
  amine   [ ] None [ ] 1–3 x [ ] 1–2 x/wk [ ] 3–4 x/wk [ ] 5–6 x/wk [ ] daily
LSD   [ ] None [ ] 1–3 x [ ] 1–2 x/wk [ ] 3–4 x/wk [ ] 5–6 x/wk [ ] daily
Mescaine   [ ] None [ ] 1–3 x [ ] 1–2 x/wk [ ] 3–4 x/wk [ ] 5–6 x/wk [ ] daily
Other Hallu-
  cinogens   [ ] None [ ] 1–3 x [ ] 1–2 x/wk [ ] 3–4 x/wk [ ] 5–6 x/wk [ ] daily
PCP   [ ] None [ ] 1–3 x [ ] 1–2 x/wk [ ] 3–4 x/wk [ ] 5–6 x/wk [ ] daily
Special "K"   [ ] None [ ] 1–3 x [ ] 1–2 x/wk [ ] 3–4 x/wk [ ] 5–6 x/wk [ ] daily
Nitrous Oxide
  gas   [ ] None [ ] 1–3 x [ ] 1–2 x/wk [ ] 3–4 x/wk [ ] 5–6 x/wk [ ] daily
Butyl Nitrate
  gas   [ ] None [ ] 1–3 x [ ] 1–2 x/wk [ ] 3–4 x/wk [ ] 5–6 x/wk [ ] daily
Amyl Nitrate
  ("snappers")   [ ] None [ ] 1–3 x [ ] 1–2 x/wk [ ] 3–4 x/wk [ ] 5–6 x/wk [ ] daily
Other
  Inhalants   [ ] None [ ] 1–3 x [ ] 1–2 x/wk [ ] 3–4 x/wk [ ] 5–6 x/wk [ ] daily
Ecstasy
  (MDMA)   [ ] None [ ] 1–3 x [ ] 1–2 x/wk [ ] 3–4 x/wk [ ] 5–6 x/wk [ ] daily
Other (specify)
  _____   [ ] None [ ] 1–3 x [ ] 1–2 x/wk [ ] 3–4 x/wk [ ] 5–6 x/wk [ ] daily

In the spaces below, list the specific drugs and amounts you have used (including alcohol) during each and every one of the past SEVEN days (if none, write "NONE"; do NOT leave any space blank).

Today: _____

Yesterday: _____

2 days ago: _____

3 days ago: _____

4 days ago: _____

5 days ago: _____

6 days ago: _____

On the average, how much money have you been spending on drugs?
per week $_____ per month $_____

What is the *one* drug that causes you the *most* problems? (check only one)
[ ] Cocaine   [ ] Crack   [ ] Alcohol   [ ] Heroin   [ ] Marijuana
[ ] Other: (specify) _____

By what METHOD do you use this drug? [ ] Smoke [ ] Snort [ ] Inject [ ] Oral

At what age did you first try this drug? _____

When you drink alcohol, what do you usually drink? [ ] Beer [ ] Wine [ ] Vodka [ ] Gin
[ ] Sherry [ ] Blended Whiskey [ ] Scotch [ ] Rye [ ] Other (specify): _____

How many drinks do you usually have?   per week _____   per day _____

Do you experience any physical symptoms when you try to stop drinking? [ ] No [ ] Yes
If so, which ones?   [ ] Shakes/tremors   [ ] Sweating/perspiration   [ ] Seizures
[ ] Continuous Vomiting   [ ] Sleeplessness   [ ] Disorientation   [ ] Hallucinations

Are you currently taking any PRESCRIPTION MEDICATIONS? [ ] No   [ ] Yes

Name of drug(s) _____ Reason for use _____
Prescribing physician _____

Name of drug(s) _____ Reason for use _____
Prescribing physician _____

Is your drug or alcohol use associated with SEX? [ ] No   [ ] Yes
Does it involve: [ ] Seeing prostitutes   [ ] Having sex with unknown partners
  [ ] Sadomasochistic sex   [ ] Cross-dressing   [ ] Having unwanted sex
  [ ] Compulsive masturbation   [ ] Pornography or "peep shows"
  [ ] Other:

Do you feel that your sexual behavior is out-of-control or excessive? [ ] No   [ ] Yes

Is your alcohol or drug use associated with gambling? [ ] No   [ ] Yes
Is your gambling out-of-control or excessive? [ ] No   [ ] Yes

Have you ever had a problem with Bulimia, Anorexia, or Obesity? [ ] No   [ ] Yes
If yes, please describe:

CONSEQUENCES RELATED TO ALCOHOL OR DRUG USE

1. Check below any PHYSICAL problems caused or worsened by your use of alcohol or drugs:

[ ] Convulsions with loss of consciousness [ ] Coughing up black phlegm
[ ] Nasal sores, bleeding [ ] Severe weight loss (without dieting)
[ ] Chest congestion, wheezing [ ] Sinus problems
[ ] Hepatitis or other liver problems [ ] Ulcers or other stomach problems
[ ] Severe or frequent headaches [ ] Heart palpitations
[ ] Drug overdose requiring treatment in an Emergency Room or hospital
OTHER (specify):

2. Check below any PSYCHOLOGICAL problems caused or worsened by your use of alcohol or drugs:

[ ] Irritability, short temper [ ] Severe depression [ ] Paranoia, suspiciousness
[ ] Panic attacks [ ] Memory problems [ ] Suicidal thoughts
[ ] Violent thoughts
OTHER (specify):

3. Check below any SEXUAL problems caused or worsened by your use of alcohol or drugs:

[ ] Loss of sex drive [ ] Sexual obsession or preoccupation
[ ] Sex with strangers [ ] AIDS-risky sexual behavior
[ ] Sexually out of control
OTHER (specify):

4. Check below any RELATIONSHIP OR SOCIAL problems caused or worsened by your use of alcohol or drugs:

[ ] Arguments with spouse or mate [ ] Arguments with parents, brothers, or sisters
[ ] Thrown out of household [ ] Spouse or mate has threatened to leave or
[ ] Loss of friends has already left
OTHER (specify): [ ] Social isolation

5. Check below any JOB OR FINANCIAL problems caused or worsened by your use of alcohol or drugs:

[ ] In jeopardy of losing my job [ ] Already lost at least one job
[ ] Late to work [ ] Missed days of work
[ ] Less productive at work [ ] Missed opportunity for promotion or raise
[ ] In debt [ ] Behind in paying bills
OTHER (specify):

6. Check below any LEGAL problems caused or worsened by your use of alcohol or drugs:

[ ] Arrested for possession of illicit [ ] Arrested for sale of illicit substances
  substances [ ] Arrested for DWI or DUI
[ ] Arrested for forging prescriptions [ ] Arrested for violent or disorderly
[ ] Auto accident while under the influence conduct
[ ] Arrested for assaulting someone [ ] Arrested for theft or robbery
[ ] Arrested for embezzlement or check forgery

OTHER (specify):

Are you currently using HEROIN?
[ ] No—SKIP TO NEXT PAGE
[ ] Yes—answer questions below and then go to next page

Method of heroin use: [ ] Injecting   [ ] Snorting   [ ] Smoking

How many times per day do you take a dose of heroin? _____

How long after your last dose, do you start to feel withdrawal symptoms? _____

When you try to detox, what symptoms do you experience? [ ] Insomnia   [ ] Stomach cramps   [ ] Chills   [ ] Muscle and bone pain   [ ] Low energy   [ ] Runny nose [ ] Tearing eyes   [ ] Restlessness   [ ] Craving for heroin   [ ] Other:

Do you ever take methadone to prevent opiate withdrawal? [ ] No
[ ] Yes: When was the last time you took methadone? _____

Have you ever taken clonidine (Catapres) to reduce opiate withdrawal symptoms?
[ ] No   [ ] Yes: Did you find it helpful? _____

When was the last time you successfully detoxed and stayed off heroin and all other opiates for at least one week (NOT in a residential treatment program or hospital)?

During previous attempts to detox, what helped you to get through the withdrawal?

What do you think will help you now?

YOUR TREATMENT HISTORY

1. Have you ever been treated in an INPATIENT DRUG-ALCOHOL REHAB?
   [ ] No [ ] Yes

Facility Name: _____ City: _____ State: _____ Dates: _____
How long were you there? _____ Did you complete the program? [ ] Yes [ ] No
How long did you stay alcohol and drug free after leaving the program? _____

Facility Name: _____ City: _____ State: _____ Dates: _____
How long were you there? _____ Did you complete the program? [ ] Yes [ ] No
How long did you stay alcohol and drug free after leaving the program? _____

2. Have you ever been treated in an OUTPATIENT DRUG-ALCOHOL PROGRAM?
   [ ] Yes [ ] No

Facility Name: _____ City: _____ State: _____ Dates: _____
How long were you there? _____ Did you complete the program? [ ] Yes [ ] No
How long did you stay alcohol and drug free after leaving the program? _____

Facility Name: _____ City: _____ State: _____ Dates: _____
How long were you there? _____ Did you complete the program? [ ] Yes [ ] No
How long did you stay alcohol and drug free after leaving the program? _____

3. Have you ever been treated in an INPATIENT PSYCHIATRIC HOSPITAL?
   [ ] Yes [ ] No

Facility Name: _____ City: _____ State: _____ Dates: _____
How long were you there? _____ Did you complete the program? [ ] Yes [ ] No
How long did you stay alcohol and drug free after leaving the program? _____

Facility Name: _____ City: _____ State: _____ Dates: _____
How long were you there? _____ Did you complete the program? [ ] Yes [ ] No
How long did you stay alcohol and drug free after leaving the program? _____

4. HAVE YOU EVER SEEN A PSYCHOLOGIST, PSYCHIATRIST, OR OTHER MEN-
   TAL HEALTH PROFESSIONAL ON A REGULAR BASIS? [ ] Yes [ ] No

Name of therapist: _____ Dates of treatment: _____
Reason for seeking help: _____

Name of therapist: _____ Dates of treatment: _____
Reason for seeking help: _____

5. HAVE YOU EVER ATTENDED AA, CA, OR NA MEETINGS? [ ] No [ ] Yes

  For how long? _____

  Did you get a sponsor? [ ] No [ ] Yes

  Did you attend step meetings? [ ] No [ ] Yes

FAMILY HISTORY

1. Which members of your family ever had an alcohol or drug problem? (check all that apply):
   [ ] None [ ] Mother [ ] Father [ ] Brother(s) [ ] Sister(s)

2. How many children including you were in your family of origin? _____ brothers
   _____ sisters

3. Did anyone in your immediate family ever have serious psychiatric problems?
   [ ] No [ ]Yes

4. Did anyone in your immediate family ever attempt or commit suicide? [ ] No [ ] Yes

5. Does anyone in your current household use drugs? [ ] No [ ] Yes
   If yes, please explain:

Please answer ALL questions below. Do not leave any blank.
If you answer "Yes" to any questions, please explain your answers at the bottom of this page.

1. Have you ever been hospitalized or treated in an emergency room for a drug overdose?   [ ] No [ ] Yes

2. Have you ever been treated with medication for serious depression?   [ ] No [ ] Yes

3. Have you ever been treated with medication for any other psychiatric condition?   [ ] No [ ] Yes

4. Have you ever "heard voices" or had hallucinations when you were NOT intoxicated?   [ ] No [ ] Yes

5. Have you ever been treated with medication to get rid of hallucinations or delusions?   [ ] No [ ] Yes

6. Have you ever felt suicidal or had repeated thoughts about harming yourself?   [ ] No [ ] Yes

7. Have you ever felt suicidal while drunk, high or crashing?   [ ] No [ ] Yes

8. Have you ever felt suicidal while NOT under the influence of alcohol or other drugs?   [ ] No [ ] Yes

9. Have you ever planned out or chosen a specific method for killing yourself?   [ ] No [ ] Yes

10. Have you ever attempted to kill or seriously harm yourself?   [ ] No [ ] Yes

11. Have you ever been hospitalized because of a suicide attempt or suicidal thoughts?   [ ] No   [ ] Yes

12. Has any member of your immediate family ever attempted suicide?   [ ] No   [ ] Yes

13. Do you fear that you might try to kill or harm yourself at any time in the near future?   [ ] No   [ ] Yes

14. Do you have a history of being violent toward other people?   [ ] No   [ ] Yes

15. Have you ever had persistent thoughts or fantasies about harming other people?   [ ] No   [ ] Yes

16. Have you ever been sexually abused by a family member or anyone else?   [ ] No   [ ] Yes

17. Have you ever been physically abused by a family member or anyone else?   [ ] No   [ ] Yes

DURING THE PAST 90 DAYS, HAVE YOU EXPERIENCED ANY OF THE FOLLOWING PROBLEMS ON A PERSISTENT BASIS FOR TWO WEEKS OR LONGER?

[ ] Severe depression   [ ] Persistent feelings of hopelessness   [ ] Difficulty in falling asleep
[ ] Difficulty in staying asleep   [ ] Unable to get out of bed in the morning
[ ] Persistent thoughts about harming or killing yourself
[ ] Persistent thoughts about harming or killing someone else
[ ] Dramatic reduction in your food intake   [ ] Dramatic increase in your food intake
[ ] Loss of interest in sex

Please explain any "Yes" answers below:

3

Is Psychotherapy Effective for Substance Abusers?

RICHARD A. RAWSON

INTRODUCTION

The use of psychotherapy with substance abusers has generated and continues to generate controversy and debate. Clinicians who have worked with substance abusers point to numerous examples of substance abusers who have benefited from psychotherapy. Conversely, many substance abuse patients can recount long, frustrating experiences in psychotherapy while their lives deteriorated as a result of unaddressed substance abuse problems. Both scenarios are accurate. The question in the title cannot be meaningfully addressed without considering which types of psychotherapy are effective for which types of substance abuse patients in which treatment contexts.

This chapter is intended to provide clinicians with an overview of some empirical evidence concerning psychotherapeutic techniques with substance abuse patients. It is not designed to be a technical review of psychotherapy research or a comprehensive listing of all outcome studies. Rather, this chapter highlights some of the most influential research on psychotherapy treatments for substance abusers. In addition, the chapter attempts to describe briefly some of the most promising psychotherapeutic approaches currently being developed for the treatment of substance abuse disorders.

How Is Psychotherapy Defined in This Chapter?

This book includes a compendium of topics on the use of psychological, psychosocial, and other "talk therapies" for the treatment of substance abuse disorders. Using the broadest definition of psychotherapy, all these techniques can be considered forms of psychotherapy, yet they include methods as diverse as intensive psychodynamic therapies (Murphy & Khantzian, Chapter 8) to psychoeducational approaches (Director, Chapter 21, and Washton, Chapter 15) to brief therapies (Hester & Bien, Chapter 11). For purposes of this chapter, psychotherapy will incorporate the definition used by Woody, Luborsky, McLellan, and O'Brien (1989) as "psychological treatment that aims to modify intrapsychic and interpersonal conflicts" (p. 1417). In addition to this definition of traditional psychotherapy, the chapter includes those specific psychological, behavioral, and cognitive-behavioral strategies that have been developed for the treatment of substance abuse disorders. Hence, for purposes of this review, a broad definition of psychotherapy is applied. However, the definition excludes drug abuse counseling, a set of techniques defined by Woody et al. (1989) "as the regular management of drug dependent patients through monitoring of behavior (urinalysis, employment), the enforcement of program rules (no loitering, attendance regulations) and the provision of concrete services such as referral for job counseling, medical services or legal aid" (p. 1417).

What Types of Substance Abuse Disorders Are Included in This Discussion?

The clinical population addressed in this chapter includes patient groups that meet criteria for substance abuse or dependency disorders according to the fourth edition of the *Diagnostic and Statistical Manual of Mental Disorders* (DSM-IV). Most of the literature in this area presents information on patient groups according to substance of abuse. There is a significant psychotherapy literature with alcoholics, cocaine abusers, and opiate addicts. Although other categories of substance abusers (e.g., benzodiazepine users and marijuana users) have received treatment with psychotherapeutic methods, there is little empirical evidence on the effectiveness of psychotherapy with these groups. Although some of the treatment strategies used with the major categories of substance abusers may be applicable for these groups, there is not a sufficient body of literature to meaningfully assess therapeutic efficacy with these less frequently encountered patient populations. In addition, the chapter does not address the value of psychotherapeutic techniques with substance-using adolescents or the use of psychotherapy as a drug-prevention strategy.

How Is Effectiveness Defined?

For purposes of this chapter, effectiveness is defined as the degree to which a therapeutic technique decreases the amount or frequency of drug or alcohol use, promotes prosocial behavior changes compatible with a drug-free life-style, and/or increases the engagement or retention of patients in a treatment process. Measurement of drug/alcohol use by self-report is a frequently used indicator; however, in more recent research efforts, confirmation of these self-reports by biological measures (e.g., urinalysis, breathalyzer, and liver function tests) or collateral reports (e.g., spouse or employer) have become standards for experimental rigor. The best multidimensional instrument for measuring behavior change is the Addiction Severity Index (McLellan, Luborsky, Woody, & O'Brien, 1980). This instrument measures change in seven behavioral domains to provide a valid and reliable method for assessing meaningful change. Finally, numerous studies on outcome in the substance abuse field suggest a positive relationship between time in treatment and favorable outcome. Hence, duration of time in treatment has become an accepted measure of a treatment's effectiveness.

PSYCHOTHERAPY AND SUBSTANCE ABUSE TREATMENT: A BRIEF HISTORICAL CONTEXT

During the first half of this century, psychotherapy was the primary method used for treating patients with substance abuse disorders. Psychotherapy was the primary approach, not because of its efficacy but rather because there were few available alternatives. Much of the psychoanalytically based psychotherapy conceptualized substance abuse behavior merely as symptomatic of underlying psychopathology. During this period, it was a generally accepted principle that the primary role of psychotherapy for substance abusers was to address the underlying psychological distress that led patients to take drugs or alcohol. Successful resolution of these underlying psychological dynamics was presumed to result in a resolution of the substance abuse problem.

During the 1940s and 1950s, two self-help movements emerged as alternative forms of support for alcoholics and addicts. The Alcoholics Anonymous (AA) fellowship, established in the 1930s, grew into a significant network of support during this period as a program of assistance for alcoholics. Borrowing from the principles and methods of AA, a number of residential self-help programs, including Synanon and Daytop, were established in the late 1950s for the treatment of drug addictions. These therapeutic community (TC) programs became cornerstones of the existing substance abuse treatment system. Although officially neither the

AA nor the TC advocates opposed psychotherapeutic techniques for substance abuse treatment, many of the members of these self-help movements had previous unsuccessful treatment experiences in psychotherapy. As a result of these experiences, many of the members of these self-help programs discouraged the use of professional psychological and psychiatric treatments as contradictory to recovery activities.

The frustration surrounding the inadequacy of psychotherapy for substance abusers was experienced by treating professionals as well as by patients. One of the pioneering clinicians and researchers in the area of opiate addiction treatment was Dr. Marie Nyswander, a psychiatrist. Together with her husband, Dr. Vincent Dole, they initiated a methadone research program that led to methadone maintenance as a widely used treatment modality for opiate addiction (Dole, Nyswander, & Warner, 1976). Nyswander's work with methadone followed her discouraging experiences treating opiate addicts with psychotherapeutic techniques at the Lexington Narcotics Treatment Center and in her private practice in New York City. She observed that "a careful search of the literature failed to disclose a single report in which the withdrawal of drug and psychotherapy has enabled a significant fraction of the patients to return to the community and to live as normal individuals" (Nyswander, 1956, p. 42).

There are similar conclusions concerning the usefulness of psychotherapy with alcoholics. Miller and Hester (1980) concluded that controlled treatment outcome studies prior to 1980 failed to yield persuasive evidence for the effectiveness of psychodynamic psychotherapy with alcoholics. In addition to the poor evidence of efficacy, there has been a powerful antipathy concerning psychotherapy for alcoholism. Some of the sources of the antagonism between proponents of the AA fellowship and the field of psychotherapy have been noted by Brown (1985):

> Many therapists expect their alcoholic patients to stop drinking and forfeit their main defenses to demonstrate their motivation and capacity to form a traditional treatment alliance. Because many alcoholics are not able to meet such conditions at the time they seek treatment, a climate of animosity and mistrust has developed between both helpers and those needing help. More recently, Zimberg (1982) suggested that there exists a therapeutic nihilism regarding alcoholism. There is strong prejudice against alcoholics and a belief that alcoholism can't be treated.
>
> Animosity also has developed between professional helpers and sober alcoholics. The latter recall negative, unhelpful experiences with therapists when they were drinking (Brown, 1977) and are reluctant to trust the therapist or the therapy process now that they are sober (Zinberg & Bean, 1981). Many of these individuals state specifically their fear that therapy will interfere with Alcoholics Anonymous (AA), their newfound base for abstinence and security.
>
> Thus, drinking and nondrinking alcoholics fear psychotherapy: For

the drinking alcoholic, therapy might come too soon between the patient and the bottle; for the sober alcoholic, therapy was a potential
wedge between the patient and AA. Understandably, therapists respond
to these feelings with defensiveness. (p. 3)

In a survey research project with active AA participants, Brown
reported that 77% of alcoholics had been in psychotherapy while drinking and 30% felt that the therapy had not been helpful. However, 45%
of these AA participants also reported they had been in psychotherapy
once abstinent and only 3% felt the therapy had not been helpful. These
results suggest that alcoholics in AA believe that psychotherapy can be
of help once drinking has stopped, but they are mistrustful of the efforts
of psychotherapists with actively drinking alcoholics.

> AA research participants saw psychotherapists as being relatively un-
> aware of and incompetent to handle alcohol issues. They criticized ther-
> apists for their failure to identify and label alcohol as the major problem.
> Murphy (1980); Zimberg (1982); and Bissell (1982) found that failure
> to diagnose and mismanagement by the therapist were the primary
> sources of hostility. One respondent described a collusion of denial be-
> tween herself and her psychiatrist:
>   "Therapy allowed me the illusion of doing something about my-
> self while continuing to drink. I had expressed concern about my drink-
> ing to several therapists, who as I, chose not recognize it as a problem."
> (Brown, 1985, p. 4)

During the 1970s, a major dichotomy emerged concerning the use
of psychotherapy with substance abusers. In general mental health settings, psychotherapy was the treatment of choice for substance abusers.
For the most part, professional mental health practitioners viewed substance abuse problems as symptoms of underlying psychopathology and
focused their psychotherapeutic effects on the presumed underlying
mechanisms of the substance abuse. Very little substance abuse-specific
information was incorporated into these treatment efforts. Many therapists viewed the 12-Step program as a quasi-religious cult and most
professionals were uninformed about the nature of formal substance abuse
treatment options.

Within the substance abuse treatment system, there was a clear movement in the opposite direction. Within the alcoholism treatment network,
hospital-based programs using AA-based models (e.g., the Minnesota
model) became the de facto standard for alcoholism treatment. In the
drug abuse treatment arena, methadone maintenance and therapeutic
communities were treatment standards and innovative pharmacotherapies
and behavioral strategies were in research development for the treatment
of drug dependence. Specialized strategies for substance abusers were developed and evaluated and insight-oriented psychotherapy as a modality for substance abuse treatment was discouraged or disparaged.

During the 1980s, psychotherapeutic efforts for the treatment of substance abuse disorders expanded and became increasingly sophisticated. Specific techniques were developed for specific elements of substance abuse disorders such as cue exposure for craving reduction (Childress et al., 1993). Systematic research efforts have created an empirical base for cognitive-behavioral strategies used with a variety of substance abuse disorders. One of the most impressive of these efforts is the work in the area of relapse prevention developed by Marlatt and Gordon (1985) and applied to a variety of substance abuse problems including alcoholism (Annis, 1990) and cocaine abuse (Carroll, Rounsaville, & Gawin, 1991). Other clinical researchers have combined a number of psychotherapeutic elements into integrated outpatient treatment experiences (McAuliffe, 1990; Washton, 1989; Rawson, Obert, McCann, Smith, & Scheffey, 1989). These integrated outpatient models have become accepted treatment options within the mainstream substance abuse treatment system.

In the 1990s, psychotherapeutic efforts with substance abuse disorders have continued to increase. Both federal substance abuse institutes—the National Institue on Drug Abuse (NIDA) and the National Institute on Alcohol Abuse and Alcoholism (NIAAA)—have major psychotherapy and/or behavior therapy research initiatives. With a federal commitment to the development and evaluation of new techniques there will certainly be a greater emphasis on the use of psychotherapeutic strategies in the substance abuse treatment field.

PSYCHOTHERAPY FOR OPIATE ADDICTION

Psychotherapeutic techniques have been widely used for the treatment of opiate addiction. As Nyswander (1956) said, psychotherapy as a singular treatment method with actively addicted or detoxifying opiate addicts has produced very little success. Although there is a large amount of literature on the underlying psychodynamics and psychoanalytical dimensions of opiate addiction (Brehm & Khantzian, 1992), there is no evidence to suggest that insight-oriented psychotherapy alone is an adequate treatment for the actively addicted opiate addict or for the recently abstinent opiate addict. Even the most eloquent supporters of psychotherapy for substance abuse treatment view insight-oriented psychotherapy for opiate addiction as useful only in combination with other formal addiction treatment efforts (Khantzian, 1985). Psychotherapy as a singular approach for the currently addicted or recently detoxified opiate addict cannot be clinically justified.

These conclusions do not suggest that psychotherapy with opiate addicts at later stages of recovery or in combination with other techniques is ineffective. In fact, there is evidence to support the use of psychotherapy as one component to a multicomponent opiate addiction treatment approach. McAuliffe (1990) described a treatment model for opiate users which he calls recovery training and self-help (RTSH). This model combines a cognitive behaviorally based relapse prevention approach with recreational activities and self-help involvement as an outpatient aftercare program for opiate addicts who have achieved some degree of abstinence. In his report, there is evidence that this combination of techniques increases the duration of opiate abstinence and promotes prosocial behavior change. Although it is unclear what the "active ingredients" of RTSH are, the overall combination of techniques appears to provide opiate addicts with a viable outpatient treatment experience.

Psychotherapy Combined with Opiate Pharmacotherapies

An even more well-researched role for psychotherapy with opiate addicts has been established regarding psychotherapy in combination with both methadone and naltrexone.

Psychotherapy and Methadone Treatment

Woody, Luborsky, McLellan, and O'Brien (1983) conducted a study evaluating the differential benefits of drug counseling, supportive expressive therapy, and cognitive-behavioral therapy in conjunction with methadone maintenance treatment. In this study, 110 newly admitted methadone maintenance patients were randomly assigned to one of three therapy conditions. One group of subjects received drug counseling alone, one group received drug counseling plus supportive expressive psychotherapy delivered by a professional therapist, and one group received drug counseling plus cognitive-behavioral treatment delivered by a professional therapist. All subjects received weekly drug counseling sessions and the subjects in the two therapy groups received weekly therapy sessions. All subjects were treated for a period of 6 months.

The study supported the value of psychotherapy as an adjunct to drug counseling for patients in methadone maintenance treatment. Both groups of patients receiving psychotherapy showed a superior treatment response to patients receiving drug counseling only. With this patient population, there did not appear to be a significant difference between the two modalities of psychotherapy. Although all subjects showed treatment gains during treatment, only the patients receiving psychotherapy sustained the gains they made during treatment to a 12-month follow-up interview. The drug-counseling-only group demonstrated some erosion of treatment gains by the 12-month point.

An equally important finding in the Woody et al. (1983) study was the differential effect of psychotherapy on patients with different levels and types of psychopathology. Patients with relatively low levels of psy-

chopathology showed approximately as much progress in the drug counseling condition as they did in the psychotherapy conditions. Patients
with moderate levels of psychopathology showed gains in all three treatment conditions but more gains in the two psychotherapy conditions.
Finally, those with severe psychopathology showed little progress with
drug counseling only but substantial gains in the two psychotherapy
groups. One specific diagnostic group, those with antisocial personality
disorders, did not show treatment gains in any of the treatment conditions.

A study conducted at Yale also evaluated the value of psychotherapy with methadone maintenance patients. In this study (Rounsaville, Glazer, Wilber, Weissman, & Kleber, 1983), methadone patients were
randomly assigned either to a condition in which they received weekly
interpersonal psychotherapy or to a low-contact condition that consisted of a 20-minutes session once a month. Treatment involvement was
designed for a duration of 6 months. The outcome of this study indicated few differences between subjects in the two conditions. However, as
pointed out by two of the authors, the interpretation of these study data
must consider the circumstances of the study implementation (Rounsaville
& Kleber, 1985). Subjects in this project were difficult to recruit and retain in either treatment condition. One contributing factor was that the
psychotherapy program was in a separate location from the methadone
program. The geographic separation of these two treatment settings led
to a much poorer integration of the psychotherapy condition with the
methadone treatment. As a result, the overall study involvement of subjects was obstructed to such a degree that the high dropout rate may have
obscured any psychotherapeutic effect.

These two studies of psychotherapy with methadone maintenance
patients illustrate a number of points important in establishing an empirical base to the use of psychotherapy for substance abusers. First, the nature of the psychotherapies being studied must be carefully and
systematically designed and issues regarding study implementation must
be carefully considered in order to ensure an adequate test of psychotherapeutic methods. In the Rounsaville et al. (1983) study, the physical location of the two treatment settings may have been a more important
factor than the effectiveness of the therapies. The Woody et al. (1983)
study demonstrated that research on psychotherapies with substance
abuse populations has to carefully consider the patient groups being
studied. Psychotherapy studies must determine the nature and extent of
concurrent psychopathology. The Rounsaville et al. (1983) study also
demonstrated the methodological problems in psychotherapy studies with
substance abusers created by problems of high subject attrition. Attrition
from psychotherapy studies has often been reported with substance
abusers and makes the interpretation of outcome results difficult. The
design of experimental evaluations of psychotherapy with substance

abusers must have a sufficient sample size and adequate safeguards against attrition and other compliance problems to ensure a valid set of study findings.

Psychotherapy and Naltrexone Treatment

During the 1970s, there was a tremendous interest and enthusiasm in the development of the narcotic antagonist naltrexone. Naltrexone, which is a nonaddicting opiate blocker, was thought to be a medication that would be widely used in the treatment of opiate addiction. However, following the introduction of naltrexone into the field in 1985, there has been little clinical use of this medication. One of the primary problems concerning the use of naltrexone has been premature treatment attrition. Because patients do not receive the opiate agonist effects from naltrexone and because they are not dependent on the naltrexone, there is little pharmacological incentive for them to remain in treatment. Patients started on a treatment regimen with naltrexone frequently discontinue treatment after a few weeks, before achieving significant clinical benefits. Hence, naltrexone has gained the reputation of being a highly effective pharmacological blocker that has a limited clinical role.

One of the strategies that has been suggested for improving the use of naltrexone has been to combine the pharmacological agent with an appropriate program of psychotherapeutic support. The rationale is that if the proper set of psychotherapeutic strategies can be combined with naltrexone, attrition will be reduced and greater treatment gains will be achieved. In a controlled evaluation of psychotherapy as an adjunct to naltrexone treatment, Resnick, Washton, and Stone-Washton, (1981) randomly assigned subjects to naltrexone treatment with either a weekly psychotherapy session or a minimal case management session. Of the subjects who were started on naltrexone, a significantly higher percentage of the subjects receiving therapy completed the fourth month of treatment (77%) than did subjects in the case management group (33%). Similar to the Woody et al. (1983) study, it was reported that the value of the psychotherapy was different with different groups of addicts. In this study, the psychotherapy produced a significant benefit to heroin addicts off the street but did not produce a similar benefit with subjects who transferred from methadone maintenance.

A summary of the use of psychotherapeutic strategies with opiate addicts suggests that with acutely addicted or recently detoxified addicts, there is little evidence that general psychotherapy is of value as a singular treatment procedure. However, psychotherapeutic techniques are valuable as elements in multi-component treatment models and as adjuncts to pharmacotherapy treatments. When used in these contexts, proper diagnosis and assessment are important as there is differential effectiveness of psychotherapies with different subsets of opiate users.

PSYCHOTHERAPY FOR COCAINE ABUSE
AND DEPENDENCE

Prior to 1980, there was very little literature on the use of psychotherapy for cocaine abuse. In fact, there was very little literature on the treatment of cocaine abusers with any form of treatment. During the decade of the 1980s, almost every approach imaginable was attempted with cocaine abusers. Hospital treatments, therapeutic community approaches, pharmacotherapies, behavioral techniques, acupuncture, and a wide variety of experimental and "new age" techniques were applied to the problems of cocaine abusers. However, psychotherapy was a component in many of the modalities. In addition, specific psychotherapeutic approaches have been developed for the treatment of cocaine abusers. Since there are no effective pharmacotherapies for cocaine abuse treatment, psychotherapies have been the major modality employed with cocaine abusers. Presently, psychotherapies alone and in combination with other elements of multicomponent outpatient models are the predominant form of cocaine abuse treatment. The question for this chapter is: How effective are these psychotherapeutic techniques with cocaine abusers?

Carroll et al. (1991) have compared a cognitive behaviorally based relapse prevention (RP) model with an interpersonal therapy (IPT) model. In this study, 42 cocaine abusers were randomly assigned to either a weekly RP session using cognitive-behavioral materials, or a weekly IPT session using a short-term psychodynamic model. Treatment duration was 12 weeks for both groups. The format was 1-hour individual sessions. Treatment retention data suggested a superior outcome for the RP procedure, as 67% of the RP group subjects completed the 12-week trial, whereas only 38% of the IPT group completed. In other measures of outcome there were no significant differences between groups. However, there were some interesting findings if subjects were grouped by pretreatment level of addiction severity. With subjects who had lower levels of pretreatment severity, there was comparable improvement in both groups. However, in subjects with severe cocaine abuse problems on admission, there was a significant difference between groups. With the severely addicted subset, 58% of the RP group met a 3-week criteria for cocaine abstinence whereas only 14% of the IPT group achieved such criteria. Hence, the abstinence results as well as the retention rate differences suggested that RP strategies resulted in a more desirable outcome with cocaine abusers.

In another evaluation of an individual therapy approach, 122 cocaine abusers were randomly assigned to one of three forms of cocaine outpatient therapy (Kang et al., 1991). These three modalities were individual supportive expressive psychotherapy, family therapy, or group counseling led by a paraprofessional counselor. The project was designed to deliver the weekly sessions over a 12-month period. Outcome was evaluated according to the self-report of cocaine use and change scores using the Addiction Severity Index. The results of the Kang et al. (1991) study highlight the issue of subject attrition in substance abuse psychotherapy studies. Due to high dropout rates, it was not possible to evaluate treatment differences between conditions. Over 40% of all subjects dropped out before the first session following the data collection sessions. Between the first and the fifth session, 33% of all subjects dropped out. Only 26% of the subjects attended six or more sessions.

The authors concluded from this study that the high attrition rates from all conditions indicated that weekly therapy sessions are inadequate as a primary treatment modality for cocaine abusers. Furthermore, they found no association between the number of weekly treatment sessions and improved treatment outcome. The results of this evaluation suggested that if psychotherapy is to be useful for cocaine abusers, it must be conducted within a more intensive treatment framework that is delivered more frequently than once a week and includes information specifically directed toward the achievement of cocaine abstinence.

Higgins et al. (1991) and Higgins et al. (1993) adapted a behavioral treatment package from the alcoholism literature—the community reinforcement approach (CRA) (Hunt & Azrin, 1973) for cocaine abuse treatment. In both studies, Higgins's group combined a positive reinforcement voucher system with the CRA collection of behavioral counseling techniques into a multicomponent outpatient treatment approach. The approach includes the following elements: reciprocal relationship counseling with patients and significant others, information about cocaine antecedents and cocaine cues that may illicit craving, employment counseling, and a program to assist in the developments of new recreational activities. Over a 12-month period, cocaine abusers attend twice-weekly sessions in which the above four topic areas are addressed. The authors have added a positive reinforcement voucher system to enhance this combination of techniques. With this reinforcement system, patients earn credit toward vouchers by giving urine samples free from cocaine. The schedule for delivery of the vouchers is progressive in that larger payoffs occur as the patient achieves larger numbers of consecutive cocaine-free weeks. The vouchers are redeemed for a preagreed-on set of reinforcers compatible with drug-free prosocial activities.

The results with this approach have been impressive. Higgins et al. (1991) have demonstrated in a series of well-controlled studies that this combined set of behavioral interventions produced substantial suppression of cocaine use when compared to a traditional 12-Step-based counseling procedure. Furthermore, the reduction in cocaine use was maintained over a 24-week period (Higgins et al., 1993). In a more recent study (Higgins et al., 1994), the value of the behavioral counseling strategies with and without the voucher system was evaluated. The recent study demonstrated that the CRA counseling alone produced a superior treatment response than was seen with the initial study control group. Furthermore, the treatment response from the therapeutic interventions was significantly enhanced by the addition of the voucher reinforcement system.

The demonstration of the robust treatment effect of the CRA is an extremely important development. This series of studies clearly establishes the value of the CRA model with cocaine users. Although, the subjects treated in this study were from an exclusively Caucasian, non-crack-using population, which may somewhat limit the generalizability of the findings, these reports establish this approach as a promising clinical procedure. The concept of combining psychotherapeutic/behavioral strategies with an explicit contingency system provides an innovative strategy for cocaine abuse treatment. This approach will certainly receive much more research and will require the innovation of clinicians to move this technique into mainstream clinical practice.

Several other groups developed treatment models that employ psychotherapeutic components for the treatment of cocaine abuse. Washton (Chapter 2) and Wallace (Chapter 26) describe treatment materials they developed for cocaine abuse treatment elsewhere in this book. Rawson et al. (1989) created a manual for cocaine abuse treatment, which has received extensive use with a variety of stimulant-using populations. This approach, the Matrix neurobehavioral model, contains individual sessions, group RP sessions, family therapy techniques, psychoeducation, and 12-Step involvement into a structured 1-year outpatient treatment approach. In a series of evaluation studies, the authors reported that this outpatient model (1) produces outcome results comparable to outcome from a much more expensive inpatient treatment approach (Rawson, Obert, McCann, & Mann, 1986); (2) demonstrates statistically significant reduction in cocaine use in a dose-related manner (i.e., more sessions attended, more reduction in cocaine use) (Rawson, Obert, McCann, & Ling, 1993); (3) produces a significant improvement in prosocial behavior (Addiction Severity Index scores) and a reduction in HIV-related risk behavior (Shoptaw, Rawson, McCann, & Obert, 1995). In addition, this model has been employed in the treatment of cocaine-using methadone maintenance patients with considerable promise (Magura et al., in press).

The psychotherapeutic treatment efforts with cocaine abusers have produced a sense of optimism and promise. There is a clear caution from the Kang et al. (1991) study that once-a-week psychotherapy is not an adequate treatment experience for cocaine abusers. Further information on optimal methods and parameters of successful treatment with cocaine abusers is likely to be forthcoming in future clinical research efforts.

PSYCHOTHERAPY FOR ALCOHOLISM AND ALCOHOL ABUSE

Although psychotherapy for alcoholism has been widely criticized (Vaillant, 1981), there are proponents of psychodynamic psychotherapy for the treatment of alcohol issues (e.g., Levy, 1987; Forrest, 1985). However, these proponents of psychodynamic models of therapy advocate for specific therapeutic modifications when working with alcoholics. One specific theme repeatedly encountered in the literature on psychotherapy with alcoholics is that therapy cannot be a passive, reflective process. Regardless of the psychotherapeutic orientation, there is a consensus that psychotherapy with alcoholics must include an explicit focus on alcohol use and that the therapist must be an active, directive agent who promotes specific behavioral change.

According to Levy (1987), psychodynamic techniques with alcoholics require a clear awareness of the central nature of the alcohol use on all aspects of the therapy process. The therapist must be alert to the degree of physiological dependence that the alcoholic presents on treatment initiation. It is impossible to begin any meaningful program of therapy until needed medical attention is provided to address issues of withdrawal. Extended exploration of the original reasons for drinking is, in most cases, unnecessary. Awareness of the alcoholic's propensity to use defense mechanisms including denial and projection is important. Particularly noteworthy are the defense mechanisms in which the consequences of the alcohol use (e.g., marital discord and work-related problems), become viewed by the alcoholic as reasons for the alcohol use (Vaillant, 1978). Levy also points out that giving advice, which may not be a frequently used tool for some therapists, is essential when working with alcoholics. Giving specific strategies for achieving abstinence and reducing exposure to alcohol-related situations and new strategies for coping with alcohol-related problems is an important component of therapy with alcoholics. Teaching patients about the alcohol craving process and providing strategies for handling craving without drinking are useful, as are contingency contracting procedures to help alcoholics commit to specific periods of alcohol abstinence. Therapists need to be ready for relapse and able to help alcoholics construct new abstinence plans following instances of relapse. Because alcohol use influences all aspects of the therapeutic relationship and therapy process, any efforts to conduct psychotherapy with alcoholics without a central focus on this issue will result in an unproductive therapy experience.

Psychotherapy Research Evidence with Alcoholics

Although there are a wealth of outcome studies with alcoholics (see Emrick, 1974, 1975; Miller & Hester, 1986), there are few well-controlled studies that explicitly evaluate psychodynamic psychotherapy for problem drinking. The majority of outcome studies evaluated multicomponent models of alcoholism treatment that combine psychotherapy, group milieu therapies, AA, and alcoholism education. The literature does contain several studies that do specifically focus on the impact of psychotherapy for alcoholism treatment. These studies, including Olson, Devine, and Dorsey (1981), Pomerleau, Pertschuk, Adkins, and D'Aquili (1978), and Zimburg (1974), report negative findings about the value of insight-oriented psychotherapy for alcoholism treatment. The varieties of insight-oriented psychotherapies evaluated did not include the modifications described above by Levy (1987). However, even with the modifications suggested by Levy and others, there are no data to support even modified insight-oriented therapy as a primary treatment for problem drinking disorders.

These negative findings concerning insight-oriented techniques do not suggest that there are not promising psychologically and behaviorally based treatment models for alcoholism treatment. Much of the clinical research effort sponsored by the NIAAA over the past 15 years has centered on the development of specific psychotherapeutic and behavioral strategies for the treatment of alcoholism. Among those strategies that have the most promise for the future treatment of alcoholism are social skills training, stress management techniques, and community reinforcement models. A brief discussion of these strategies provides an overview of the models that are currently undergoing evaluation and are likely to increasingly influence psychotherapy models of alcoholism treatment. In addition, other techniques described in this book, including motivational interviewing (Rollnick & Morgan, Chapter 9), brief interventions (Hester & Bien, Chapter 11) and network therapy (Galanter, Chapter 19) have strong potential to be widely integrated into future alcoholism treatment efforts.

Social Skills Training

The rationale for the social skills training (SST) for alcoholism treatment is that for alcoholics, alcohol use is a nonadaptive manner of coping with a range of problem areas. Alcohol use serves a variety of functions in providing a social peer group, a recreational activity, a structure for free time, and a method to control negative affective states. As alcohol use increases, other, more adaptive responses decrease in frequency. Frequently, alcohol use becomes the only response to almost all situations and circumstances.

SST provides a set of alternative behaviors that give the alcoholic a new range of options for problem solving. SST is frequently conducted in a group setting, but the techniques and methods can be used in an individual setting. SST initially involves the assessment of those situations in which a problem drinker frequently uses alcohol. A number of assessment scales have been developed to aid in obtaining this information in a structured manner (Chaney, 1989). Using this background information, it is possible to create role-play situations that give patients new options for dealing with these problem settings. In these role-play exercises, the therapist can suggest and demonstrate adaptive nondrinking ways to cope with problem situations. Frequently, homework assignments are used to promote generalization of skills into real-world settings. The context of SST is a positive teaching environment with the therapist providing positive reinforcement for behavior change.

A number of outcome studies (Chaney, O'Leary, & Marlatt, 1978; Ferrell & Galassi, 1981; Oei & Jackson, 1982) provided empirical support for SST. These studies indicated that SST can be effective in reducing alcohol use, slowing relapse to alcohol use following inpatient treatment, and improving alcohol use status at follow-up. As reviewed in several recent articles (Holder, Longabaugh, Miller, & Rubonis, 1991; Miller, 1992), SST is one technique that has strong empirical support of effectiveness.

Stress Management

One of the commonly reported roles of alcohol use for alcoholics is to relieve stress. Stress can be defined as any interaction between the individual and the outside world that produces a negative affective state. Stressors can involve relationships, career issues, financial issues, health problems, etc. Alcohol use is perceived by drinkers to be a response to relieve the negative affective state. Stress management introduces the use of a variety of specific recommendations for problem drinkers which give them alternative methods for relieving stress. These methods include relaxation techniques, physical exercise, and biofeedback. The therapist's role in using stress management strategies is to give the patient a range of new response alternatives, to monitor the use of these new strategies, and to provide positive reinforcement for use of these techniques. It is hoped that the use of these techniques increases the patient's behavioral repertoire for coping with stress situations, thereby reducing relapse vulnerability. A number of studies have demonstrated the efficacy of these techniques in assisting with the achievement and maintenance of alcohol abstinence (Stockwell & Town, 1989).

Community Reinforcement Approach

The CRA was described earlier as a promising approach for the problem of cocaine abuse (Higgins et al., 1991, 1993). Hunt and Azrin (1973), in studies with problem drinkers, described the original work with this program. This combination of techniques created a model with an established methodology and base of empirical support. CRA techniques were demonstrated to substantially reduce the number of drinking days for patients compared to those treated in a traditional hospital program. In addition, patients showed gains in employment as well as other positive behavioral changes (Hunt & Azrin, 1973). In a later study, the addition of disulfiram to the CRA program was demonstrated to add to the reduction in the number of drinking days produced by CRA (Azrin, Sisson, Meyers, & Godley, 1982).

Project Match

The NIAAA has funded a multisite collaborative study at 19 sites throughout the United States (Project Match Research Group, 1993). The study is a carefully controlled evaluation of a cognitive-behavioral program, a 12-Step facilitated program, and a motivational interviewing protocol. The project is a landmark study on the efficacy of these three psychological approaches for the treatment of alcohol-related problems. The methodology developed in this study will set the standard for alcoholism treatment research for many years to come. The results of Project Match are likely to substantially influence alcoholism treatment and research developments into the next century.

IS PSYCHOTHERAPY EFFECTIVE WITH SUBSTANCE ABUSERS?

This chapter has used a broad definition of psychotherapy to include a wide range of behavioral, cognitive-behavioral, and psychodynamic techniques. Using this broad definition of psychotherapy, it is accurate to conclude that psychotherapeutic strategies have demonstrated robust positive treatment effects with all major categories of substance abuse disorders. Not surprisingly, however, it is important to qualify this affirmative assessment by clarifying some of the specific areas of strength and weakness that have been reported in the psychotherapy research.

There is a consensus among clinicians and clinical researchers that traditional weekly, insight-oriented psychotherapy sessions are not appropriate treatment for substance abusers who are actively using or recently detoxified from alcohol/drugs. Insight-oriented psychotherapeutic approaches require substantial modification or integration with other techniques to benefit substance abusers in early recovery. Clinicians can modify their psychotherapeutic approaches as described by Levy (1987) or Forrest (1985) or they can combine them with other treatment elements. Zweben (Chapter 6, this volume) describes how 12-Step involvement can be successfully combined with insight-oriented psychotherapeutic techniques. Studies by Woody et al. (1983) and Resnick et al. (1981) document how psychotherapeutic methods can benefit substance abuse patients in pharmacotherapy treatment.

A variety of treatment models employing psychotherapeutic techniques have been created for the treatment of substance abuse disorders. The fields of behavioral and cognitive-behavioral therapies have created some methods that have produced impressive results. The CRA has clearly demonstrated efficacy with both alcohol and cocaine users. The transfer of this package of psychological and behavioral techniques into clinical settings will provide a new option for clinicians. Relapse prevention techniques, drawn from the cognitive-behavioral literature, have demonstrated efficacy and have already been incorporated into numerous treatment models. Specific behavioral strategies, including SST and stress management procedures, give clinicians a set of treatment tools that can be applied in a variety of clinical settings. New approaches including motivational interviewing, brief therapies, and network therapy all add important new resources for clinicians.

The integration of substance abuse strategies into general clinical settings is likely to increase. As mental health professionals struggled to meet the challenge of the influx of cocaine users in the 1980s, it was apparent to many that general psychotherapeutic strategies were dramatically unsuccessful. Hence, therapists have been much quicker to adopt substance abuse treatment strategies into their clinical practice. This need for greater skills in substance abuse treatment strategies has been acknowledged and supported by the organized mental health establishment. Professional organizations including the American Psychiatric Association, the American Psychological Association, the American Society of Clinical Social Workers, and the American Association of Marriage and Family Therapists have all initiated training efforts in the area of substance abuse treatment. Similarly, substance abuse training is a mandatory topic area for professional licensing and certification requirements. Hence, information about psychotherapeutic methods and treatment issues with substance abusers has become much more widely disseminated among mental health clinicians.

Another development that has emphasized the importance of psychotherapy in the treatment of substance abusers is the increasing attention to the needs of dual-diagnosis patients. Standard substance abuse treatment programs are inadequate to successfully engage and retain these patients. The use of psychotherapy can greatly augment the treatment of substance abusers with concurrent acute Axis I disorders and the entire range of Axis II disorders which are commonly encountered in substance abuse populations. The study by Woody et al. (1983) provided clear support for the value of psychotherapy in the treatment of patients with concurrent psychopathology.

Finally, the emergence of the managed mental health movement has created a major shift in the reimbursement practices for substance abuse care. Reimbursement for treatment in 28-day inpatient programs has been severely restricted. Treatment of substance abuse patients has been shifted to outpatient settings in which structured outpatient models have combined psychotherapeutic strategies into multicomponent treatment models. More recently, many of the managed care organizations have further shifted their referral practices by sending substance abusers into general clinical settings rather than specific substance abuse programs. This latest trend will increase the need for clinicians to become aware of and competent with substance abuse treatment strategies that can be adapted for individual practice settings (e.g., network therapy) (Galanter, 1986).

As therapeutic methods are developed and evaluated for substance abuse populations, the success of treatment efforts will continue to improve. The professional mental health community has recognized the need to gain competence with this population and has actively promoted the adaptation of substance abuse treatment techniques to mainstream mental health training. Many of the criticisms about the unresponsiveness of psychotherapists to the needs of addicts and alcoholics are no longer accurate. As the fields of substance abuse treatment and mental health treatment are brought closer together, there is the promise that substance abuse treatment will benefit by a mutual sharing of information from both disciplines.

REFERENCES

Annis, H. M. (1990). Relapse to substance abuse: Empirical findings within a cognitive-social learning approach. *Journal of Psychoactive Drugs, 22,* 117–124.

Azrin, N. H., Sisson, R. W., Meyers, R., & Godley, M. (1982). Alcoholism treatment by disulfiram and community reinforcement therapy. *Journal of Behavior Therapy and Experimental Psychiatry, 13,* 105–112.

Brehm, N. M., & Khantzian, E. J. (1992). A psychodynamic perspective. In J. H. Lowinson, P. Ruiz, R. B. Millman, & J. G. Langrod (Eds.), *Substance abuse: A comprehensive textbook* (pp. 106–117). New York: Williams & Wilkins.

Brown, S. (1985). *Treating the alcoholic: A developmental model of recovery.* New York: Wiley.

Carroll, K. M., Rounsaville, B. J., & Gawin, F. H. (1991). A comparative trial of psychotherapies for ambulatory cocaine abusers: Relapse prevention and interpersonal psychotherapy. *American Journal of Drug and Alcohol Abuse, 17,* 229–247.

Chaney , E. F. (1989). Social skills training. In R. K. Hester & W. R. Miller, (Eds.), *Handbook of alcoholism treatment approaches* (pp. 206–221). Boston: Allyn & Bacon.

Chaney, E .F., O'Leary, M. R., & Marlatt, G. A. (1978). Skill training with alcoholics. *Journal of Consulting and Clinical Psychology, 46,* 1092–1104.

Childress, A. R., Hole, A. V., Ehrman, R. N., Robbins, S. J., McLellan, A. T., &

O'Brien, C. P. (1993). Cue reactivity and cue reactivity interventions in drug dependence. In L. S. Onken, J. D. Blaine, & J. J. Boren (Eds.), *Behavioral treatment for drug abuse and dependence* (NIDA Research Monograph, No. 137, pp. 92–115; NIH Publ. No. 93-3639). Rockville, MD: National Institute on Drug Abuse.

Dole, V. P., Nyswander, M. E., & Warner, A. (1976). Methadone maintenance treatment: A ten-year perspective. *Journal of the American Medical Association, 235,* 2117–2119.

Emrick, C. D. (1974). A review of psychologically oriented treatment of alcoholism. Part I: The use and interrelationships of outcome criteria and drinking behaviors following treatment. *Quarterly Journal of Studies on Alcohol, 35,* 523–549.

Emrick, C. D. (1975). A review of psychologically oriented treatment of alcoholism. Part II: The relative effectiveness of different treatment approaches and the effectiveness of treatment versus no treatment. *Quarterly Journal of Studies on Alcohol, 36,* 88–108.

Ferrell, W. L., & Galassi, J. P. (1981). Assertion training and human relations training in the treatment of chronic alcoholics. *International Journal of the Addictions, 16,* 959–968.

Forrest, G. G. (1985). Psychodynamically oriented treatment of alcoholics and substance abusers. In T. E. Bratter & G. G. Forrest (Eds.), *Alcoholism and substance abuse: Strategies for clinical intervention* (pp. 307–336). New York: Macmillan.

Galanter, M. (1986). Social network therapy for cocaine dependence. *Advances in Alcohol and Substance Abuse, 12,* 159–175.

Higgins, S. T., Budney, A. J., Bickel, W. K., Foerg, F., Donham, R., & Badger, G. (1994). Incentives improve outcome in outpatient behavioral treatment of cocaine dependence. *Archives of General Psychiatry, 51,* 536–541.

Higgins, S. T., Budney, A. J., Bickel, W. K., Hughes, J. R., Foerg, F., & Badger, G. (1993). Achieving cocaine abstinence with a behavioral approach. *American Journal of Psychiatry, 150,* 763–769.

Higgins, S. T., Delaney, D. D., Budney, A. J., Bickel, W. K., Hughes, J. R., Foerg, F., & Fenwick, J. W. (1991). A behavioral approach to achieving initial cocaine abstinence. *American Journal of Psychiatry, 148,* 1218–1224.

Holder, H. D., Longabaugh, R., Miller, W. R., & Rubonis, A. V. (1991). The cost effectiveness of treatment for alcoholism: A first approximation. *Journal of Studies on Alcohol, 52,* 517–540.

Hunt, G. M., & Azrin, N. H. (1973). A community reinforcement approach to alcoholism. *Behaviour Research and Therapy, 11,* 91–104.

Institute of Medicine Report. (1990). *Broadening the base of treatment for alcohol problems.* Washington, DC: National Academy Press.

Kang, S-Y, Kleinman, P. H., Woody, G. E., Millman, R. B., Todd, T. C., Kemp, J., & Lipton, D. S. (1991). Outcomes for cocaine abusers after once-a-week psychosocial therapy. *American Journal of Psychiatry, 148,* 630–635.

Khantzian, E. J. (1985). Psychotherapeutic intervention with substance abusers: The clinical context. *Journal of Substance Abuse Treatment, 2,* 83–88.

Levy, M. (1987). A change in orientation: Therapeutic strategies for the treatment of alcoholism. *Psychotherapy, 24,* 786–793.

Magura, S., Rosenblum, A., Lovejoy, M., Handelsman, L., Foote, J., & Stimmell,

B. (in press). Neurobehavioral treatment for cocaine-using methadone patients. A preliminary report. *Journal of Addictive Diseases.*

Marlatt, G. A., & Gordon, J. R. (Eds.). (1985). *Relapse prevention: Maintenance strategies in the treatment of addictive behaviors.* New York: Guilford Press.

McAuliffe, W. F. (1990). A randomized controlled trial of recovery training and self-help for opioid addicts in New England and Hong Kong. *Journal of Psychoactive Drugs, 22,* 197–210.

McLellan, A. T., Luborsky, L., Woody, G. E., & O'Brien, C. P. (1980). An improved diagnostic evaluation instrument for substance abuse patients: The Addiction Severity Index. *Journal of Nervous and Mental Diseases, 168,* 26–33.

Miller, W. R. (1992). The effectiveness of treatment for substance abuse: Reasons for optimism. *Journal of Substance Abuse Treatment, 9,* 93–102.

Miller, W. R., & Hester, R. K. (1980). Treating the problem drinker: Modern approaches. In W. R. Miller (Ed.), *The addictive behaviors* (pp. 102–126). Elmsford, NY: Pergamon Press.

Miller, W. R., & Hester, R. K. (1986). The effectiveness of alcoholism treatment: What research reveals. In W. R. Miller & N. Heather (Eds.), *Treating the addictive behaviors: Processes of change* (pp. 121–174). New York: Plenum Press.

Nyswander, M. E. (1956). *The drug addict as a patient.* New York: Grune & Stratton.

Oei, T. P. S., & Jackson, P. R. (1982). Social skills and cognitive behavioral approaches to the treatment of problem drinking. *Journal of Studies on Alcohol, 43,* 532–547.

Olson, R. P., Ganley, R., Devine, V. T., & Dorsey, G. C., Jr. (1981). Long-term effects of behavioral versus insight-oriented therapy with inpatient alcoholics. *Journal of Consulting and Clinical Psychology, 49,* 866–877.

Pomerleau, O., Pertschuk, M., Adkins, D., & D'Aquili, E. (1978). Treatment for middle income problem drinkers. In P. E. Nathan, G. A. Marlatt, & T. Loberg (Eds.), *Alcoholism: New directions in behavioral research and treatment* (pp. 143–160). New York: Plenum Press.

Project Match Research Group. (1993). Project Match: Rationale and methods for a multisite clinical trial matching patients to alcoholism treatment. *Alcoholism: Clinical and Experimental Research, 17,* 1130–1145.

Rawson, R. A., Obert, J. L., McCann, M. J., & Ling, W. (1993). Neurobehavioral treatment for cocaine dependency: A preliminary evaluation. In F. M. Tims & C. G. Leukenfeld (Eds.), *Cocaine treatment: Research and clinical perspectives* (NIDA Research Monograph No. 135, pp. 92–115; NIH Pub. No. 93-3639). Rockville, MD: National Institute on Drug Abuse.

Rawson, R. A., Obert, J. L., McCann, M. J., & Mann, A. J. (1986). Cocaine treatment outcome: Cocaine use following inpatient, outpatient and no treatment. In L. S. Harris (Ed.), *Problems of drug dependence* (NIDA Research Monograph No. 67, pp. 271–277). Rockville, MD: National Institute on Drug Abuse.

Rawson, R. A., Obert, J. L., McCann, M. J., Smith, D. P., & Scheffey, E. (1989). *The neurobehavioral treatment manual: A therapist manual for outpatient cocaine addiction treatment.* Beverly Hills, CA: Matrix Center.

Resnick, R. B., Washton, A. M., & Stone-Washton, N. (1981). Psychotherapy and naltrexone on opioid dependence. In L. S. Harris (Ed.), *Problems of drug dependence, 1980* (NIDA Research Monograph No. 34, pp. 109–115). Rockville, MD: National Institute on Drug Abuse.

Rounsaville, B. J., Glazer, W., Wilber, C. H., Weissman, M. M., & Kleber, H. D. (1983). Short-term interpersonal psychotherapy in methadone-maintained opiate addicts. *Archives of General Psychiatry, 40,* 629–636.

Rounsaville, B. J., & Kleber, H. D. (1985). Psychotherapy/counseling for opiate addicts: Strategies for use in different treatment settings. *International Journal of the Addictions, 20,* 869–896.

Shoptaw, S., Rawson, R. A., McCann, M. J., & Obert, J. L. (1994). The Matrix model of outpatient stimulant abuse treatment: Evidence of efficacy. *Journal of Addictive Diseases, 13*(4), 25–34.

Stockwell, T., & Town, C. (1989). Anxiety and stress management. In R. K. Hester & W. R. Miller (Eds.), *Handbook of alcoholism treatment approaches* (pp. 222–230). Boston: Allyn & Bacon.

Vaillant, G. (1978). Alcoholism and drug dependence. In A. M. Nicholi (Ed.), *The Harvard guide to modern psychiatry* (pp. 78–94). Cambridge, MA: Belknap Press of Harvard University Press.

Vaillant, G. (1981). Dangers of psychotherapy in the treatment of alcoholism. In M. Bean & N. Zinberg (Eds.), *Dynamic approaches to the understanding and treatment of alcoholism* (pp. 55–96). New York: Free Press.

Washton, A. M. (1989). *Cocaine addiction: Treatment, recovery and relapse prevention.* New York: W. W. Norton.

Woody, G. E., Luborsky, L., McLellan, A. T., & O'Brien, C. P. (1983). Psychotherapy for opiate addicts: Does it help? *Archives of General Psychiatry, 40,* 639–645.

Woody, G. E., Luborsky, L., McLellan, A. T., & O'Brien, C. B. (1989). Individual therapy for substance abuse. In W. H. Reid (Ed.), *Treatment of psychiatric disorders* (pp. 1417–1430). Washington, DC: American Psychiatric Association Press.

Zimberg, S. (1974). Evaluation of alcoholism treatment in Harlem. *Quarterly Journal of Studies on Alcohol, 35,* 550–557.

4

Treatment Strategies
for Comorbid Disorders:
Psychopathology and
Substance Abuse

ANN BORDWINE BEEDER
ROBERT B. MILLMAN

INTRODUCTION

Drug taking may be at once a cause and a result of psychopathology. In recent years, it has become apparent that sizable psychiatric populations have comorbid drug use. Substance abuse populations also demonstrate significant psychopathology. The terms *dual diagnosis* and *MICA* (mentally ill chemical abuser) were developed in programs devoted primarily to the treatment of substance abusers to identify the patients with psychopathology.

The etiology of dual-diagnosis conditions has been described by four hypotheses: primary mental illness with subsequent substance abuse, primary substance abuse with psychopathologic sequelae, dual primary diagnosis, and situations in which there is a common etiology, (i.e., one common factor causing both diseases) (Lehman, Myers, & Corty, 1989).

It is the task of the clinician to provide a comprehensive evaluation of each patient to assess the pattern of drug abuse, to characterize current and past psychopathology and behavioral patterns, and to attempt to define the relationship of the drug-taking patterns to the psychopathology. Following evaluation, patients should be provided with appropriate treatment and referrals. Effecting treatment and referrals depends on an appreciation of the varying determinants of the drug-taking patterns as well as their consequences (Zweben, 1987). It is necessary to assess the meaning of the drug taking at the particular stage of the patient's comorbid psychiatric illness. This meaning will vary over the course of the patient's disease (Millman, 1986).

PREVALENCE

Dual-diagnosis patients represent approximately half of all patients seen in psychiatric emergency rooms and present with severe symptoms that are difficult to assess because of the complex and changing relationship of the drugs used and the psychopathology, which both fluctuate over time (Osher & Kofoed, 1989).

The prevalence of this comorbidity varies remarkably depending on the bias of the assessment team, the clinical situation in which the evaluation takes place, the severity of the disorders, and the patient's perspective.

According to a psychiatric perspective, the prevalence of coexisting substance abuse, dependency, and psychopathology is remarkably high. Data from the latest of the Epidemiologic Catchment Area (ECA) study, a survey of 20,000 people from five sites using the National Institute of Mental Health (NIMH) Diagnostic Interview Schedule, suggests that more than half the people who abuse drugs other than alcohol have at least one comorbid mental illness, with cocaine abusers demonstrating an additional psychiatric illness in 76% of cases (Helzer & Pryzbeck, 1988). The prevalence of comorbid substance abuse disorders and psychiatric illnesses was 81% (Regier, Farmer, & Rae, 1990).

A large number of clinicians view the coexistence of chemical dependence and psychopathology quite differently. In their view, the incidence of psychopathology in their substance-abusing populations in treatment is no higher, or perhaps no more than slightly higher, than that of the general populations. According to this perspective, embraced by the majority of inpatient rehabilitation programs, the psychopathology noted is most often a result of the drug taking and the symptoms will decrease markedly or disappear with time and abstinence. These programs generally are informed by a chemical dependency model; the drug or alcohol use is perceived as a disease characterized by a profound inability to control drug use (Nace, Davis, & Gaspari, 1991).

GENERAL TREATMENT STRATEGIES

Evaluation and Early Recovery

Evaluation of the patient should continue throughout the initial stages of treatment whether the setting is inpatient or outpatient. A complete evaluation must consider five areas:

1. *A psychiatric evaluation* should contain a history of past treatment including hospitalizations, therapies, and medications; a thorough review of prior symptomatology including any history of suicidal ideation or acts or violence to others; an understanding of the current symptom picture with emphasis on the possible presence of psychosis, depressions, panic attacks, suicidality, homicidality, and cognitive impairment; and a complete mental status examination. Permission should be obtained from the patient for the evaluator to contact family, friends, and past treatment providers as soon as possible. Medical records, when available, should be reviewed.

2. *A complete drug history* should include five elements:

- The events leading to treatment;
- The age of onset of drug use for each drug used;
- The duration and pattern of use of each drug: the most intense period of use, periods of abstinence, the last time the drug was used, routes of use, etc.;
- The subjective and objective effects each drug had on the individual and his/her symptomatology; and
- An exploration of the meaning the chosen drug has for an individual patient at the current moment.

A drug history should also include an understanding of the changing pattern of the patient's drug use, withdrawal symptomatology, and medical sequelae. Characterization of the extent of loss or social deterioration associated with drug use is essential to understand the interpersonal, legal, education, medical, and employment consequences the patient faces. The determination of premorbid psychopathology is enhanced by assessing the choice of drugs, pattern of use, and positive and negative effects the drugs have had on the patient. For example, a borderline person may take drugs in a disorganized chaotic pattern, whereas an obsessive–compulsive physician may take fentanyl or alcohol at carefully prescribed intervals. Patients are often poor historians due to denial, deliberate obfuscation, or memory problems subsequent to the drug use. Outside sources such as family, friends, employers, and probation officers are critical.

3. *A physical examination* including a detailed neurological exam-

ination is imperative. Given the increasing impact of AIDS (acquired immunodeficiency syndrome), consideration of this diagnosis should be made.

Treatment of withdrawal symptoms should be provided concurrently with treatment of severe psychiatric symptoms which might interfere with early treatment compliance. In the short term, severe psychiatric symptoms such as psychosis, depression, and anxiety must be identified and treated aggressively in order to maximize the patient's ability to participate in treatment. In most cases, psychiatric symptoms will decrease in importance when withdrawal symptoms are adequately treated in a supportive and safe environment. The effects of the drugs vary in each patient depending on the personality, expectation, and milieu of the user. As well, the severity and characteristics of the withdrawal symptoms will vary in patients.

4. *Regular urine drug testing* for the major drugs of abuse should be a routine element in the treatment process. As part of the initial evaluation procedures with a reluctant patient, it is generally useful to obtain an observed urine for toxicological analysis. This obviates the need to rely on self-report data. It may be difficult for many therapists to accomplish this because of logistics or because of an unwillingness to be so intrusive. They may believe that testing will hinder the development of a therapeutic alliance. Most experienced therapists have come to the conclusion that it significantly facilitates the evaluation process.

Certainly, toxicology tests should be performed on patients when there is evidence suggesting drug use. During the treatment process, it is often useful to obtain drug screens at intervals.

5. *Structured and unstructured interviews,* such as rating scales, neuropsychological screening tools, and other psychometric scales, may contribute significant data to the evaluation during early phases of treatment (Mirin, Weiss, & Michael, 1988).

Long-Term Treatment

During this phase, treatment contacts may be reduced to weekly group sessions to maintain the commitment to abstinence, to enhance interpersonal skills to combat renewed denial, and to work toward goals. Continued participation in self-help groups should be advised. In programs based on 12-Step principles, people are encouraged to continue to think of themselves as recovering addicts. This has proven useful for drug-dependent adults. With respect to adolescent abusers, it may be unnecessary to maintain this identification. After one year or more of abstinence and appropriate social adjustment, young people might be encouraged to think of themselves as similar to their peers, though with the recognition that they continue to be at increased risk.

Treatment of psychopathology should be continued as needed. During this phase, continuation of evaluative procedures can more precisely characterize the psychopathology that may have antedated the drug use or may be a result of it.

The concept of rationalization must be understood and dealt with in the treatment process. Many patients prefer to see themselves as drug addicts rather than mentally ill. This frequently occurs in young people, who often involve themselves heavily in the drug culture to avoid facing the demoralization experienced when grappling with psychiatric disorders. The society involved in the drug culture is more tolerant of the strange ways and eccentricities often seen with these individuals. For example, a young schizophrenic male may become a pot dealer, only rarely partaking in its use because he knows that it will amplify his voices.

Collusion among patients, families and even treatment providers to minimize the psychopathology and use the evidence of drug use to explain all the problems can undermine appropriate treatment of psychiatric conditions and increase vulnerability to relapse.

TREATMENT FACILITIES AND PROCEDURES

Inpatient Treatment

Institutionalization is indicated by the following criteria:

1. Psychiatric or medical conditions that require close observation or treatment, such as psychotic states, severe depressive symptoms, suicidal or homicidal ideation, severe debilitation, and severe withdrawal phenomena.
2. The inability to cease drug use despite appropriate outpatient maneuvers.
3. The absence of adequate psychosocial supports that might be mobilized to facilitate the cessation of drug use.
4. The necessity to interrupt a living situation that reinforces continued drug use.
5. The need to enhance motivation or break through denial. (Millman, 1988, 1989)

Dual-diagnosis patients are difficult to place in programs. Their drug taking makes them less attractive to psychiatric facilities, and their psychopathology may disqualify them for admission to such drug treatment programs as rehabilitation facilities, therapeutic communities, halfway houses, and methadone maintenance.

Programs vary considerably, but some generalizations can be made. If a patient's psychiatric condition is sufficiently severe to require skilled care, a psychiatric hospital is necessary. These facilities often lack struc-

tured drug treatment and may be insensitive to the needs of dually diagnosed patients. Therapeutic communities and rehabilitation programs
often lack psychiatric backup and are too confrontational for disturbed
patients (Bell & Khantzian, 1991).

There are few data on which programs are most effective for which
patients, and referrals are often made on tenuous grounds. Yet, sophisticated inpatient facilities that combine perspectives from the various
models of treatment are now becoming available. Examples include a psychiatric hospital with a unit that also integrates the traditional disease
model of chemical dependency, with structured days that include groups,
12-Step meetings, peer support, and family work. Some rehabilitation programs have included psychiatric backup in their programs. There are therapeutic communities that now treat patients on methadone maintenance.
Once a patient is stabilized and committed to abstinence, referral to outpatient treatment is indicated to prevent relapse and recurrence of psychiatric symptoms.

Outpatient Treatment

Again, existing outpatient programs that can accommodate dually diagnosed patients are currently not able to meet the demand. Outpatient programs based on the chemical dependency treatment models that provide
integrated psychiatric care are being developed, although only a few exist. Future programs should be able to provide comprehensive treatment
including drug treatment in all phases (outpatient detoxification, early
recovery, relapse prevention), psychiatric services (evaluation, medication, psychotherapy), family treatment, and primary medical care.

Group Therapy

Chemical dependency treatment strategies depend to a large extent on
peer support and process. Equally, the treatment of psychopathology
often requires individualized attention, which can distract both patients
and clinicians from the group process. The group setting often inhibits
patients from discussing psychiatric symptomatology because of fears of
stigmatization or feelings of shame, particularly in regard to psychotic
symptoms, sexual deviance, and antisocial behaviors. A balanced curriculum that includes psychoeducation about the mode of action of
drugs, the nature of psychopathology, issues related to stigmatization,
the ethos of drug taking, and medical and psychiatric effects of drug use
is essential. Flexibility with respect to individualizing treatment should
include fitting group placement to patients' needs, providing individual
counseling at frequent intervals, medication administration, and monitoring.

Family Therapy

There is a high prevalence of both substance abuse and psychiatric disorders in family members in these patients (Rounsaville, Weissman, & Kleber, 1982). Family members and, when appropriate, friends should be included in the treatment process. Involving the people most important to the patient has proven effective. This paradigm, "network therapy," mandates family and friends to participate in the treatment process and addresses problems that reinforce drug abuse behaviors, attempts to decrease the likelihood of relapse by intense communication facilitated by group meeting, and installs protocols for network members to use when relapses occur in order to insulate the slip (Galanter, 1993).

The 12-Step Programs

Twelve-Step programs may be an essential element for dually diagnosed patients' treatment. Yet, many patients refuse to participate because of their psychopathology, sense of isolation, or past unpleasant experiences. Sophisticated treatment now attempts to prepare these patients by teaching them how the group works, what they must do to participate, and how to handle various situations. Special 12-Step programs for patients with psychopathology ("double trouble" groups) have emerged. Well-prepared patients can begin to attend, slowly integrating the preparatory information with significant support, and gain benefit from their membership in the fellowship (Woody, McLellan, O'Brien, & Luborsky, 1990).

Behavioral Treatment

Although there are no good studies demonstrating efficacy, many of the techniques currently utilized by drug treatment programs are informed by behavioral perspectives. Clinical experience and some controlled studies do suggest that certain methods are effective. With patients dependent on narcotics and cocaine, there is evidence that cognitive-behavioral, supportive-expressive, and interpersonal psychotherapeutic techniques may be effective (Marlatt, 1985). Other methods include skill-building techniques (e.g., relaxation exercises and assertiveness training) and positive reinforcement for attaining and maintaining of sobriety or other positive behaviors. Contingency contracting has proven useful with abusers of various drugs, particularly in the treatment of marijuana abuse and dependence with adolescents.

DRUG TREATMENT STRATEGIES
FOR PSYCHIATRIC DISORDERS

Schizophrenia and Psychotic Illnesses

Prevalence

The prevalence of drug use and dependence in association with psychotic states is significant, although the relationship between these disorders is complex. For example, ECA data found schizophrenia to be four times more prevalent in alcoholics than in nonalcoholics (Helzer & Pryzbeck, 1988). Ross, Glaser, and Germanson (1988) studied a large sample of alcoholics and found 8% to be schizophrenic.

Diagnosis

It is both difficult and necessary to attempt to determine whether the psychotic symptomatology was caused or precipitated by the drug use or whether the drugs were being used to self-medicate a preexisting psychopathological state. In predisposed individuals, acute and chronic psychotic disorders may be activated by the use of amphetamines, cocaine, marijuana, hallucinogens, and severe withdrawal states from opiates, alcohol, benzodiazepines, and barbiturates.

Treatment

The treatment of psychotic states requires the careful integration of chemical dependency and psychiatric models. Patients suffering from acute or chronic psychosis may be paranoid or have poor attention and concentration and an inability to relate to others.

Initial treatment must be supportive, providing the patient with a warm, safe environment with frequent reassurance that the feelings and thoughts experienced are a function of the drug use and will pass ("talking down"). Anxiolytic drugs should be administered as necessary to allay anxiety. Diazepam 10–30 mg orally and lorazepam 1–3 mg intramuscularly are effective due to their rapid onset. Neuroleptics may exacerbate psychotic symptoms or cause delirium through their anticholinergic side effects and should be reserved for later stages of treatment when any drug effects have subsided.

Clinical experience suggests that individuals are variably vulnerable to psychotic episodes from any combination of drugs at different dose and frequency intervals. A psychotic episode predisposes individuals to subsequent ones. It has been postulated the psychotic disorders frequently seen in young adult chronic patients who are often homeless and living in the inner city may be a function of chronic psychotomimetic drug use.

Long-term treatment should focus on minimizing symptoms, improving patients' function, and relapse prevention. Unlike traditional chemical dependency treatment models, the group treatment, 12-Step meetings, and counseling must be highly supportive, with minimal intensity and confrontation. The characteristics and severity of the symptoms require careful attention so that employment of highly supportive treatment can be integrated with conventional treatment strategies when appropriate.

If psychotic symptoms persist after several days of abstinence, the symptoms should be treated as a functional psychotic disorder. Pharmacotherapy with neuroleptics is generally indicated. As with all patients on neuroleptics, the smallest possible dose with the fewest side effects should be used. Treatment may require the addition of anticholinergic medicines such as Cogentin (benztropine mesylate) or Artane (trihexyphenidyl), or antihistaminic medications such as diphenhydramine. Akathisia may require dose adjustment or adjunct propranolol. Clinicians must be well informed about both transient and permanent side effects caused by these drugs, knowing that patients respond idiosyncratically to different classes of neuroleptics.

Frequent contacts are necessary with these patients and their unwillingness to take these medications makes it useful to incorporate administration of the neuroleptic into the routine of each visit. Use of longer-lasting depot medicines should be considered. Obtaining routine urine drug screens with the visit is indicated. Integration of these procedures enhances compliance and reduces relapse liability.

Relapse occurs frequently in this population. Relapse may be secondary to medication noncompliance that ensues as the side effects of the neuroleptics become less tolerable. Some patients say that the medications make them feel "dead inside." For example, relapse may begin with patients abusing their use of anticholinergic medications in order to achieve a sense of more feeling. Often this progresses to the common drugs of abuse and escalates into a full-blown relapse.

Schizophrenic patients who use illicit drugs are often attempting to reduce the intensity of psychotic symptoms or to alleviate the dysphoria associated with the medications or social pressures integral to the disorder. Heroin and other opiates have been shown to be powerful antipsychotic agents, and alcohol and sedative depressants are known to initially reduce the magnitude of psychotic symptoms (Millman, 1982). Interestingly, many psychotic patients also use psychotomimetic agents such as cannabis and cocaine, knowing that amplification of already uncomfortable symptoms will result (Castaneda, Galanter, Lifshutz, & France, 1991; Vardy & Kay, 1983). Dynamically, the use of pychotomimetic agents may represent the patient's attempt to direct delusional and hallucinatory symptoms by using substances that cause or exacerbate them and give a sensation of control. Even though the outcome is negative, the patient has determined it. As previously noted, a patient's drug use may represent an attempt to rationalize the psychopathology.

Affective Disorders

Prevalence

Affective disorders have been linked with drug use and dependence for some time. For example, the ECA data suggest that major depression and dysthymia occur one and a half to two times more commonly in alcoholics (Helzer & Pryzbeck, 1988). Hesselbrock, Meyer, and Keener (1985) found that female alcoholics had a tenfold increased incidence of mania and male alcoholics had a threefold greater incidence of mania.

Diagnosis

In patients with major depression, dysthymia, bipolar disorder, and related disorders, it is difficult to determine whether the mood states are the cause or the sequelae of protracted drug use. Affective symptoms can represent a distinct illness, a result of the agonist effects of the drugs such as opiates or depressants, part of an abstinence syndrome as from cocaine and opiates, or any combination of these factors. A careful history must include assessment of mood pathology that antedated the drug use and determination of whether the drugs were used as self-medication for the observed symptoms. Patients often describe drug use as an attempt to alleviate depression or anxiety or to enhance a desirable mood state such as hypomania. Information from family and friends should be obtained to clarify these issues.

Treatment

Initial treatment should include use of appropriate medications for withdrawing patients from their drugs of abuse. Whenever possible, careful observation over extended periods of time with no medication can clarify diagnostic issues. In most patients, severe drug-related affective symptomatology abates within 1 to 4 weeks. Educating the patient both individually and in groups with respect to how cocaine and alcohol, for example, exacerbate depressive symptoms that may or may not have preceded drug use is often useful.

In recent years, following the initial work of Martin and Jasinki (1969), there has been an increasing appreciation of the existence of the protracted abstinence syndrome. Variable symptoms associated with protracted abstinence appear to include physical complaints, waxing and waning dysphoria, anxiety, drug craving, persistent insomnia, poor concentration, and diminished creativity. Early discussions forecasting these often persistent symptoms can allay anxiety in patients whose expectations frequently include rapid return to normal function. This should be coupled with repeated reassurance that protracted abstinence symptoms will lessen progressively over time and end. If patients can learn to identify depressed feelings and learn coping techniques that are nonpharmacological (exercise, acupuncture, meditation, etc.), relapse may be prevented.

Long-term treatment includes monitoring patients for ongoing symptomatology, continued efforts to help patients learn to identify and cope with their feelings (psychotherapy, groups, 12-Step programs, etc.), and relapse prevention techniques. After several weeks to months of observation and treatment with no reduction or worsening of symptoms, pharmacotherapy is indicated. In addition, when the depressive symptomatology is sufficiently severe that sobriety is threatened, or when repeated relapses have occurred, it is reasonable to institute a trial of antidepressant medication. The choice of the medication will depend on the individual patient, but several generalizations can be made. Certainly, medications subject to misuse or abuse should be avoided where possible. For example, amitriptyline with its profound sedating properties should be avoided in depressant abusers. Initially, a tricyclic antidepressant (TCA) with less sedation such as nortriptyline or desipramine should be used. Because the TCAs have been related to decreased cocaine craving, administration of this class of medications may provide dual benefit (Millman, 1988). Serotonergic reuptake inhibitors can be useful in patients who have severe psychomotor retardation, poor motivation, or significant side effects from TCAs. Monoamine oxidase inhibitors have limited usefulness in this population due to the severe hypertensive crisis that may occur in patients who might ingest certain wines that contain tyramine, such as Chianti, or analeptic drugs including cocaine or amphetamines (Greenberg, 1989).

Anxiety Disorders

Prevalence

People diagnosed with anxiety disorders, including generalized anxiety disorder, panic attacks, and obsessive–compulsive disorder, have a lifetime prevalence rate of alcohol dependence of 13.3% (Regier, Boyd, & Burke, 1988). In another study, approximately 25% of those with an anxiety disorder were diagnosed as having a substance abuse disorder. A lifetime prevalence of 8–16% for panic disorder patients and 3–55% for lifetime prevalence of phobia patients has been diagnosed (Hesselbrock et al., 1985; Schuckit, 1985).

Diagnosis

Anxiety symptoms may be due to a premorbid generalized anxiety disorder or to panic attacks or secondary to drug or alcohol abuse. Controversy persists relative to the relationship of anxiety symptoms and drug use. For example, Vaillant (1983) postulated that in alcoholics, most psychopathology occurs secondary to the alcohol use itself. The relationship in most individuals is probably more complex, often marked by a vacillating interaction of multiple variables including the drugs and anxiety in different settings over time (Kranzler & Liebowitz, 1988). Importantly, Kushner, Sher, and Beitman (1990) showed that anxiety and panic attacks were most likely to follow the compulsive consumption of alcohol. Worsening of symptoms may be a result of acute or protracted abstinence syndromes, particularly from alcohol, sedative depressant drugs, and opiates. Long-term cocaine use has been implicated in producing both chronic anxiety states and panic attacks.

Szuster, Pontius, and Campos (1988) examined the pattern of marijuana use in patients known to have panic attacks and found that these patients experienced significantly more anxiety with marijuana use than did matched controls. Notably, this study found that users with panic attacks typically discontinued marijuana use.

Obtaining a careful history can clarify the relationship a patient's drug use has to anxiety symptoms. Individuals may use a variety of drugs to allay anxiety, including alcohol, benzodiazepines, tranquilizers, and narcotics. Initially, those who start out with high anxiety states obtain relief by using drugs (Johannessen, Cowley, Walker, Jensen, & Parker, 1989). Over time, the anxiety symptoms may not be perceived as such but instead become a conditioned stimulus for drug craving that reinforced patients' continued drug use (Linnoila, 1989).

Treatment

Initial treatment must include careful evaluation of the determinants of these symptoms and treat patients in a timely fashion because the condition can be so debilitating. Clearly, acute withdrawal symptoms may represent psychophysiological stress that can precipitate a variety of psychiatric symptoms in predisposed, individuals including psychosis, affective, and anxiety disorders. Yet, protracted abstinence symptoms may also occur in individuals who do not present with psychiatric sequelae in the acute phase of drug abstinence.

After detoxification, a period of observation combined with supportive counseling or psychotherapy and peer support is optimal. Behavioral treatments such as biofeedback, hypnosis, or cognitive psychotherapy benefit most patients. Cognitive labeling can also be an effective treatment strategy used to break the cycle of anxiety leading to drug use and the converse.

Long-term treatment of chemically dependent patients who experience anxiety, whatever the etiology, should focus on the anxiety symptoms inextricably intertwined with the experience of withdrawal and/or drug craving. Patients should be encouraged to identify symptoms of anxiety separate from drug withdrawal and craving during periods of abstinence. If anxiety symptoms persist or threaten sobriety, TCAs can be useful in controlled dose regimens. Benzodiazepines are rarely indicated because of their reinforcing properties and abuse liability (Roth, 1989). In unusual circumstances, minor tranquilizers with low reinforcing properties such as chlordiazepoxide may allay symptoms in patients recalcitrant to other treatment. Low-dose carbamazepine (200–600 mg per day) has been a useful adjunct to patients experiencing difficult detoxification and/or severe anxiety symptoms. Because of the associated rare but serious side effect of aplastic anemia, monitoring of patients' blood count is indicated. Acupuncture and electroacupuncture appear to offer a treatment for both acute and chronic anxiety disorders, particularly those associated with withdrawal states

Personality Disorders

Prevalence

There are significant problems inherent in many of the studies reporting the prevalence of comorbid substance abuse and dependence with personality disorders. Many patients are diagnosed while under the influence of the drugs or soon after, and follow-up studies after significant periods of abstinence generally have not been done. For example, Khantzian and Treece (1985) working with a diverse sample of narcotic addicts found that 65% met criteria for an Axis II personality disorder.

Diagnosis

Personality disorders are frequently diagnosed in chronic drug users, although these conditions are fraught with confusing criteria when comorbid with drug use. The criteria necessary to make the diagnoses are often not clear, depend on the perspective of the therapist, and change over time and varying settings. For example, in programs informed by a psychiatric perspective, the diagnosis of borderline, antisocial, and narcissistic personality disorder is made in drug users with alarming frequency. Programs working from a traditional chemical dependency model rarely diagnose patients with personality disorders, perceiving this as a hindrance to therapeutic zeal.

Antisocial personality disorder is often overdiagnosed due to the construct of events that lead to treatment, such as legal problems, interpersonal violence, and dissembling. This sort of labeling can create hopelessness in both the patient and the treatment team, which can inhibit effective treatment. For example, Gerstley, Alterman, McLellan, and Woody (1990) noted the overdiagnosis of antisocial personality disorders in drug-taking, crime-committing populations. They suggested that the reliance on behavioral criteria and the failure to require that antisocial behaviors occur independently of substance abuse tend to unduly increase the number of substance abusers labeled as antisocial personality disorders. It should be stressed that diagnosis of antisocial personality disorder is often based on the substance abuse and dependence and the related behaviors rather than lifelong personality patterns (Grande, Wolf, Schubert, Patterson, & Brocco, 1984). Diagnosis of antisocial personality disorder should be reserved for patients whose behaviors clearly precede the drug use and/or seem to be independent of it.

Chronic drug use may cause personality changes incident to the pharmacological actions of the drugs and the associated denial, particularly in the context of societal norms that tend to reject drug use and users and consider it to be abnormal and shameful (Zinberg, 1975). In attempts to conform to societal expectations, drug users may develop character dysfunction, including compulsive lying, poor ability to relate to others, a sense of unreality associated with the drug effects, and feelings of isolation (Bean-Bayog, 1986). Chronic users often become impulsive and manipulative over time in attempts to control both feelings of inadequacy and the feelings associated with the drug experience.

A diagnosis of personality disorders with drug users must be made with respect to the complicated interaction occurring in individuals negotiating both the effects of the drug and the response from others which appears to alter personality factors over time. Patients with premorbid personality disorders often demonstrate amplification of dysfunction with drug use.

Treatment

Initial treatment strategies must focus on interruption of drug taking and containment of dysfunctional behaviors, particularly self-destructive acts. Symptoms equivalent to those seen in patients with personality disorders will quickly subside with abstinence and remain absent in many patients who sustain a drug-free state. When behaviors are extreme or dangerous, brief hospitalization is indicated. If behaviors consistent with any of the personality disorders persist or worsen after several weeks of abstinence, treatment providers should consider both a diagnosis and long-term treatment.

Long-term treatment in patients with narcissistic, borderline, and antisocial personality disorders is typically difficult as the symptomatology is unyielding. Individual psychotherapy is frequently employed to address the dysfunctional behavior; yet, results are often poor with these patients. The disease model of chemical dependency treatment, which is based on tight structure, peer support, and confrontation that addresses the significant denial of these patients, appears to be more useful. Group process and structure may improve the ability of these patients to learn appropriate behaviors and new perceptions that will enhance their ability to relate to others. Group process also serves to diffuse inevitable transference issues that can undermine treatment in an individualized setting.

Patients with histrionic, passive–aggressive, and self-defeating personality disorders present with other concerns. Often healthier than the previously described group, these patients tend to sabotage their treatment in subtle ways that often lead to relapse. Therapeutic strategies using both individual and group treatment should target identification of these behaviors as the treatment progresses. The psychopathology of these patients is significant but more subtle than that of other impaired patients and minimization of their behaviors by treatment providers can occur, resulting in poor outcomes. Diagnosis should be considered in any patient who begins to lose ground in later stages of treatment.

No definitive pharmacological treatment has been identified for personality disorder patients. Medication can be beneficial for patients in various settings, particularly when symptoms appear to be threatening sobriety. For example, a borderline patient with severe mood lability may benefit from low-dose lithium. The use of non-dependency-producing anxiolytics such as buspirone or even low-dose neuroleptics such as perphenazine for anxiety or impulse-related symptoms is a reasonable consideration. Generally, use of minor tranquilizers is unwarranted due to their abuse potential; yet, in the setting of repeated relapses this class of medication may be beneficial when closely monitored and used over time limited periods.

Minimal Brain Dysfunction

Prevalence

Minimal brain dysfunction (MBD) and attention deficit disorders (ADD) are generally diagnosed in children with obvious symptoms. Only recently has the appreciation for the presence of subtle and ongoing symptoms been noted in adult populations. It is these adult individuals who tend to self-medicate with illicit drugs and alcohol to allay their symptoms. Accurate estimates of the prevalence of these disorders in adults are unclear because diagnostic criteria are vague for describing a wide spectrum of patients.

Diagnosis

This population presents with varying and often subtle symptomatology, including inability to concentrate, decreased attention span, disorganization, and impulsiveness. Symptoms often are not sufficiently well defined. Generally, children are diagnosed when school performance declines or behavior is consistently disruptive. Adults diagnosed as children often do not pursue follow-up both because symptoms lessen and they learn adaptive behaviors to compensate. Adults and children with subtle symptoms often do not present for treatment unless stressors such as drug use exacerbate difficulties. Careful evaluation, thorough history, and psychologic testing enhances the assessment for the presence of these disorders.

Mirin and Weiss (1991) found patients with MBD preferred to use stimulants such as cocaine and amphetamines. They noted that patients described improved organization and concentration when using these drugs. This parallels pharmacoactions of the agents employed in the treatment of children with ADD: methylphenidate hydrochloride and amphetamines. Less well recognized is the widespread use of alcohol, sedative-hypnotics, and tranquilizers in adult patients with MBD; they report lessening of impulsivity and, surprisingly, improved concentration.

Treatment

Initial treatment should attempt nonpharmacologial interventions such as conventional, well-structured chemical dependency procedures. Because many of these patients experience feeling "out of control," treatment should be geared toward helping them gain a sense of control. Cognitive-behavioral therapy, insight-oriented psychotherapy, relapse prevention techniques, and peer supports provide useful treatment strategies for MBD patients.

Long-term treatment relies on continuation of structured therapy that can become less intense over time as patients improve. Use of TCAs, particularly desipramine, which has a tolerable side effect profile, can be beneficial for patients who do not respond to nonpharmacological treatment or for those who have severe difficulty due to impaired concentration and impulsivity. Fluoxetine (Prozac) and Zoloft have not been studied in this population; the analeptic and antidepressant properties of this class of medications make their use intriguing. For patients with severe disorganization, concentration, and impulsivity problems who do not respond to other treatments, low-dose neuroleptic medication may be effective.

Triple Diagnosis

Prevalence

Estimates vary widely, but it is approximated that in the United States there are 1.5 million HIV-positive individuals and 200,000 individuals with AIDS. As the spread of HIV (human immunodeficiency virus) increases in the drug-abusing population, the psychopathology noted may be premorbid, drug related, or a result of AIDS, particularly as it affects the central nervous system.

Diagnosis

In our experience, diagnosing of HIV or AIDS early has helped many patients mobilize their resources to become abstinent and more responsible. It creates a situation for these patients to recognize the need to take control of their lives and remain drug-free in order to live. Increased monitoring with respect to the complications and progression of the disease with appropriate treatment implemented early is life sustaining for many patients. In rare cases, the diagnosis may accelerate the patient's self-destructive behavior, including drug use, needle sharing, and unsafe sex. This both diminishes the patient's chance of survival and puts others at risk (Rothenberg et al., 1987). Widespread testing should be strongly encouraged in high-risk populations. Opponents of widespread testing note these adverse reactions and castigate the currently inadequate treatment systems and the bias often directed toward patients when they are identified.

Triple diagnosis is the term used to describe the concurrent presence of a psychiatric illness, substance abuse and/or dependence, and HIV or AIDS. These patients can present with significant physical signs and symptoms and severe psychiatric symptoms. Depression, cognitive impairment, short-term memory loss, and emotional lability may be early signs of central nervous system involvement. End-stage patients present with a wide variation of symptoms.

Treatment

Treatment strategies for these triple-diagnosis patients have been described by Batki (1990), who concluded that patients whose management was organized through intensified interdisciplinary communication and treatment procedures resulted in improved outcomes. Medical treatment for the complications of HIV, abstinence-based drug treatment, evaluation, and access to treatment of both psychiatric and neuropsychiatric conditions best describes this model. An essential element is case management that promotes frequent communication among programs and clinicians to effectively integrate the interdisciplinary treatment model necessary to care for this population. Patients tend to experience less anxiety with the consistency inherent to this model and will often demonstrate improved compliance (Smith, 1989). Perry and Jacobson (1986) found that close observation and extensive evaluative procedures were necessary to diagnose cognitive impairment. Further, they found that the use of psychostimulants was beneficial to many patients experiencing apathy and dysphoria.

MANAGEMENT OF INTOXICATION, WITHDRAWAL, DRUG CRAVING, AND PSYCHOPATHOLOGY

Alcohol and Psychopathology

In some dual-diagnosis patients, *alcohol intoxication* and *withdrawal syndromes* can produce profound behavioral and cognitive difficulties as well as life-threatening medical complications (Schuckit, 1989). Intoxication may cause depression, mood lability, agitation, and impaired judgment. Withdrawal syndromes include uncomplicated alcohol withdrawal, alcohol withdrawal delirium, alcohol hallucinosis, alcohol amnestic disorder, and dementia.

Withdrawal symptoms begin between 4 to 6 hours after the last drink or as a result of decreased intake in chronic drinkers. Symptoms peak between 48 and 72 hours and can persist for days. Tremulousness, agitation, labile pulse and blood pressure, sweating, and insomnia are typical. Generalized seizures can occur both during withdrawal or during a drinking episode. Seizures usually occur 7 to 48 hours after the last drink. Reliable predictors for seizures include a past history of seizures and photophobia. Hypomagnesemia, hypoglycemia, and respiratory alkalosis have also been associated with alcohol seizures.

Symptoms can subside without treatment or progress to delirium tremens, even with appropriate detoxification procedure. The severity of the withdrawal is related both to the history of use and the patient's state of health. Delirium tremens is associated with significant mortality marked by autonomic lability, hyperreflexia, waxing and waning consciousness, disorientation, and both visual and auditory hallucinations.

Uncommonly, *alcohol hallucinosis* occurs. This syndrome is defined by the presence of a clear sensorium and hallucinations. Visual, tactile, and/or auditory hallucinations may last 1 to 2 weeks after withdrawal. In rare cases, symptoms persist for long periods.

The *alcohol amnestic syndrome,* once called Wernicke's encephalopathy and Korsakoff's psychosis, can occur with remarkable variability in the chronic alcoholic. Etiology remains unclear, although nutritional deficiency caused by long-term alcohol use is recognized as a significant correlate. Paralysis of lateral gaze and/or nystagmus, ataxia, and confusion are the triad of symptoms. Treatment includes intravenous thiamine, magnesium stabilization, and closely monitored supportive care. Symptoms often reverse within 1 to 6 hours of treatment. Severe deficits in short-term memory with concurrent confabulation and other cognitive impairment may persist indefinitely, even with appropriate treatment (Nace & Isbell, 1991).

Alcohol, sedative-hypnotic, and barbiturate withdrawal require systematic treatment, which generally includes (1) use of a long-acting benzodiazepine such as chlordiazepoxide; (2) vitamin replacement including intravenous or intramuscular thiamine, folic acid, and multivitamins; (3) rest; (4) and proper nutrition.

Disulfiram is highly beneficial in alcohol-dependent patients with psychopathology. Relapse often results from impulsive behavior due to negative experiences, worsening psychotic symptoms, depression, and/or anxiety. Disulfiram 250 mg orally per day can reduce the frequency of relapse by placing the patient in a situation in which, although impulsive feelings are prompting alcohol consumption, the medication makes the option unavailable, allowing the moment to pass. Disulfiram should be administered routinely in treatment for optimal compliance as many patients cease taking the medication when left to their own devices. This often occurs after a period of sobriety when patients feel that they can remain abstinent without it or when they consciously decide to relapse. Caution should be used with severely disturbed patients who cannot make the connection between taking the disulfiram and having a severe reaction if alcohol is consumed.

Opiates and Psychopathology

Self-medication with opiates commonly occurs in a variety of psychiatric conditions. Most patients experience dysphoria, depression, anxiety, and an alteration in personality style with chronic use of these drugs. Perhaps the euphoric release and unreality induced by the opiates reinforces narcissistic or antisocial personality traits.

A small population of psychotic and borderline patients probably abuse these drugs for their well-known antipsychotic properties. Methadone has been used in a well-controlled clinical trial with refractory schizophrenics based on this feature. Acutely, psychotic symptoms were markedly reduced, only to return as tolerance occurred. Future work in this area is warranted (Brizer, Hartman, Sweeney, & Millman, 1985).

The withdrawal syndrome typically described with respect to narcotics is "flu-like" and, distinct from sedative depressant withdrawal, is not life-threatening. The physical symptoms most often described in the literature surely occur and include diarrhea, nausea, vomiting, dilated pupils, itching, and bone pain. Yet, it is generally misunderstood that the central features of narcotic withdrawal are profound depression and anxiety. It is the intolerable feeling state that is largely responsible for frequent relapse. Withdrawal may precipitate psychosis in predisposed individuals. Detoxification with methadone usually relieves the symptoms. Where methadone or other narcotics are unavailable, clonidine at doses from 0.1–0.6 over 24 hours may be useful. Syncope can result and patients' vital signs should be routinely monitored. In patients with severe psychopathology, clonidine alone is generally not useful in effecting the significant psychiatric symptomatology amplified by a withdrawal state.

Whereas acute withdrawal is a time-limited experience, relapse to opiates is extremely frequent. Dole (1988) and others have postulated that chronic use of exogenous opiates may result in suppression or alteration of the endogenous opioid neurotransmitter system that results in a profound neurochemical deficit that drives chronic drug craving. Protracted abstinence symptoms could be related to this proposed mechanism and account for the remarkably high relapse rate after opiate detoxification. Methadone maintenance is widely used to treat opiate addicts because it effectively allays drug craving and blocks or lessens the effects of other opiates. It may also represent an effective treatment for debilitating symptoms postulated to occur due to a neurochemical deficit. Significant controversy exists in the treatment community with respect to methadone maintenance. Yet, in the light of the increasing transmission of HIV, newly available inexpensive and potent heroin, and the other well-known risks associated with heroin dependence, methadone maintenance provides a powerful treatment strategy for patients who might otherwise die.

Cocaine and Psychopathology

A largely unappreciated natural history of cocaine use is worthy of discussion. It includes initial use producing hyperalertness, energy, and euphoria. These early positive experiences often lead to frequent, higher-dose use.

Chronic use typically is associated with the onset of anxiety, agitation, and paranoia. Increased use of cocaine in high doses generally leads to intense anxiety, paranoia, and even psychotic symptoms in some individuals. Psychotomimetic effects are probably related to premorbid psychopathology and the personality of the user. It appears that psychotic symptoms are inevitable in any user at high enough doses and frequency. Chronic users report the onset of negative symptoms at lower doses than were once necessary. With increasing anxiety and paranoia at decreasing doses, the use of depressant and sedative drugs such as alcohol or opiates become inextricably linked to the cocaine use to counter adverse reactions.

Although cocaine use may cease, patients often escalate use of the other drugs. Post and Kopanda (1976) posited the theory of kindling and sensitization that may account for the effect of increasing adverse symptoms on decreasing dose. As well, it has been hypothesized that chronic cocaine users may develop anxiety disorders and panic attacks and even psychotic symptoms that persist after cessation of cocaine use. Rounsaville et al. (1991) studied a large sample of cocaine users and found that affective disorder usually preceded cocaine use, whereas anxiety disorders, attention deficit disorders, and antisocial personality disorders usually followed. The possibility that these reactions can be produced by cocaine in individuals who appear to have no premorbid psychopathology must be further studied.

Although controversy persists with respect to the existence of a withdrawal syndrome following the cessation of cocaine use, symptoms of an acute "crash" marked by somnolence, apathy, and depression commonly occur. In addition, agitation and paranoia can be severe and require treatment (Gawin & Kleber, 1986). Short-term use of benzodiazepines in conjunction with supportive care reduce acute symptoms. Persistent or unmanageable symptoms may require neuroleptics that should be used with caution.

Depression and ahedonia with or without anxiety often occur with prolonged cessation of cocaine use. Our experience suggests that symptoms vary considerably and depend on multiple factors such as the set and setting (Zinberg, 1975).

Medications have not proven to be particularly effective in the treatment of reducing symptoms of cocaine withdrawal or craving. Research devoted to the use of dopamine agonists such as tricyclic antidepressants, bromocriptine, amantadine, and the anticonvulsant carbamazepine have yielded minimal results. Although these agents can be effective in some patients, it has been found that dopiminergic agents can exacerbate paranoia and anxiety in others.

Amphetamines and Psychopathology

The effects of amphetamines are similar to those of cocaine. Amphetamines have been associated with more prolonged adverse effects due to both higher potency and longer duration of action. Agitation, paranoia, and anxiety should be treated with benzodiazepines, and persistent psychotic reactions may require neuroleptic medication such as haloperidol. Chronic amphetamine users often report severe depression, hypersomulence, hyperphagia, decreased energy, and motivation occurring both with tolerance effects associated with drug use and with abstinence. Treatment of these symptoms with supportive psychotherapy and groups usually is sufficient, although severe depressive symptoms may warrant a trial of antidepressant medication.

Cannabis and Psychopathology

Acute adverse effects of marijuana use typically include anxiety, panic attacks, and, on rare occasions, psychotic episodes. Usually these symptoms occur in naive users who are using the drug in an unfamiliar setting. In the vast majority of individuals, prolonged psychotic episodes occurring in tandem with cannabis use cannot be distinguished from functional psychotic disorders and probably relate to premorbid vulnerability. Treatment should include provision of a supportive environment with reassurance. Benzodiazepines can be used for severe symptoms. When psychotic symptoms persist for prolonged periods, treatment should follow the standards of those used for functional psychotic episodes including neuroleptics.

An amotivational syndrome has been described in chronic high-dose users of marijuana in various parts of the world, marked by apathy, diminished goal-directed activity, and an inability to master new problems. Personal habits deteriorate, and users are described as withdrawn, passive, and easily distracted with poor judgment (Stefanis, Boulougouris, & Liakos, 1976). Subsequently, other reports of chronic users and controlled laboratory studies failed to demonstrate the existence of this syndrome (Carter, 1980; Rubin & Comitas, 1975; Brady, Fotin, Fischman, & Capriotti, 1986).

The pharmacological actions of cannabis include sedation, disruption of concentration, and impairment of short-term memory, and do seem to stifle ambition and drive and impair school performance in certain people. In other young people, chronic heavy cannabis use has been associated with profound changes in perspective, dress, and behavior, and they often demonstrate laudable energy and ambition in the pursuit of varied obscure goals such as intense involvement with computer bulletin boards or popular music. An example is reflected by the long-term existence of the distinct community of followers of The Grateful Dead. "Dead Heads" may organize their lives around touring with the band and participating in predictable group practices including drug use, ritualized dancing at concerts, and styles of dress and carriage unique to this society (Millman & Beeder, 1994). The term *aberrant motivational syndrome* has been suggested as a more precise description of this phenomenon (Millman & Sbriglio, 1986).

Recent anecdotal experience has revealed a new pattern of cannabis abuse emerging where certain individuals employ a combination of marijuana and high-dose zoloft (150–600 mg). These users note significantly enhanced creative abilities and markedly improved productivity not experienced using either agent alone. It appears that hypomanic symptoms may follow, requiring discontinuation of both agents with close follow-up.

Hallucinogens and Psychopathology

The terms *hallucinogen* and *psychedelic* are used to describe about 12 naturally occurring and approximately 100 synthetic compounds that induce alterations in perception, emotion, and cognition. These are primarily derivatives of indoles or phenylalklamines such as LSD, peyote, psilocybin, phencyclidine, and ketamine (Weiss & Millman, 1991). Perceptual distortions are induced with this class of drugs; yet, frank hallucinations are rare. Adverse sequelae are similar to those seen with cannabis use, including anxiety, panic, paranoia, and occasional psychosis. Treatment strategies are equivalent to those previously described with cannabis.

Some patients have persistent low-level perceptual distortions such as halos or "trails" (lines of light following moving objects), depersonalization, and derealization. These symptoms usually fade with time though when prolonged a trial of short-term benzodiazepines followed by a TCA trial. Low-dose neuroleptics may be employed when symptoms are recalcitrant and not responsive to other treatment. Despite pharmacological treatment, rarely patients report unremitting symptoms that can be bothersome. Adaptation to the symptoms is usually possible for these patients.

CONCLUSION

Treatment Outcome

Few studies have attempted to systematically relate treatment strategies to outcome of drug abusers with psychopathology. Clearly, research devoted to this question is imperative. This is particularly relevant as existing literature suggests that factors traditionally associated with poor prognosis such as severity of psychopathology and intensity of symptoms do not necessarily affect outcome (Case, 1991).

Treatment strategies for dually diagnosed patients are primarily based on clinical experience. Factors that do appear to positively affect outcome include family support, likability, ability to relate to others, and a higher level of education.

Future Goals in the Study of Dual Diagnosis

Innovative treatment models informed by both clinical experience and research must be developed and evaluated to address the needs of this growing population. The complex relationship between drug use and psychopathology makes questions about what elements of treatment are most effective for particular groups of patients key factors in determining the specific goals in improved treatment strategies. Finally, increased understanding of the relationship of drug use to psychiatric symptoms enhances the studies of both addiction and psychopathology.

REFERENCES

Batki, S. L. (1990). Drug abuse, psychiatric disorders and AIDS, dual and triple diagnosis. *Western Journal of Medicine, 152,* 547–552.

Bean-Bayog, M. (1986). Psychopathology produced by alcoholism. In R. E. Meyer (Ed.), *Psychopathology and addictive disorders* (pp. 334–345). New York: Guilford Press.

Beeder, A. B., & Millman, R. B. (1992). Treatment of patients with psychopathology and substance abuse. In J. Lowinson, P. Ruiz, R. B. Millman, & J. G. Langrod (Eds.), *Substance abuse: A comprehensive textbook* (2nd ed., pp. 675–690). Baltimore: Williams & Wilkins.

Bell, C. M., & Khantzian, E. J. (1991). Contemporary psychodynamic perspectives and the disease concept of addiction: Complementary or competing models? *Psychiatric Annals, 21,* 273–281.

Brady, J. V., Fotin, R. W., Fischman, M. W., & Capriotti, R. M. (1986). Behavioral interactions and the effects of marijuana. *Alcohol, Drugs and Driving, 2*(1), 93–103.

Brizer, D. A., Hartman, N., Sweeney, J., & Millman, R. B. (1985). Effects of methadone plus neuroleptics in treatment-resistant chronic paranoid schizophrenia. *American Journal of Psychiatry, 142*(9), 1106–1107.

Carter, W. E. (1980). Cannabis in Costa Rica. In *A study of chronic marijuana use.* Philadelphia: Institute for the Study of Human Issues.

Case, N. (1991). The dual diagnosis patient in a psychiatric day treatment program: A treatment failure. *Journal of Substance Abuse Treatment, 8,* 69–73.

Castaneda, R., Galanter, M., Lifshutz, H., & France, H. (1991). Effect of drugs of abuse on psychiatric symptoms among hospitalized schizophrenics. *American Journal of Alcohol Abuse, 17,* 178–185.

Dole, V. P. (1988). Implications of methadone maintenance for theories of narcotic addiction. *Journal of the American Medical Association, 260,* 3025–3029.

Galanter, M. (1993). Network Therapy for addiction: A model for office practice. *American Journal of Psychiatry, 150*(1), 28–36.

Gawin, F. H., & Kleber, H. D. (1986). Abstinence symptomatology and psychiatric diagnosis in cocaine abusers. *Archives of General Psychiatry, 43,* 533–545.

Gerstley, L. J., Alterman, A. I., McLellan, A. T., & Woody, G. E. (1990). Antisocial personality disorders in patients with substance abuse disorders: A problematic diagnosis. *American Journal of Psychiatry, 147,* 173–178.

Grande, T. P., Wolf, A. W., Schubert, D. S., Patterson, M. B., & Brocco, K. (1984). Associations among alcoholism, drug abuse and antisocial personality: A review of literature. *Psychological Reports, 55,* 455–474.

Greenberg, R. (1989). The patient with cardiovascular disease. In L. Jarvik (Ed.), *Treatments of psychiatric disorders* (pp. 913–914). Washington, DC: American Psychiatric Association.

Helzer, J. E., & Pryzbeck, T. R. (1988). The co-occurrence of alcoholism with other psychiatric disorders in the general population and its impact in treatment. *Journal of Studies on Alcohol, 49,* 219–224.

Hesselbrock, M. N., Meyer, R. E., & Keener, J. J. (1985). Psychopathology in hospitalized alcoholics. *Archives of General Psychiatry, 42,* 1050–1055.

Johannessen, D. J., Cowley, D. S., Walker, R. D., Jensen, C. F., & Parker, L. P.

(1989). Prevalence, onset and clinical recognition of panic states in hospitalized male alcoholics. *American Journal of Psychiatry, 146,* 1201–1203.

Khantzian, E. J., & Treece, C. (1985). DSM-III psychiatric diagnosis of narcotic addicts. *Archives of General Psychiatry, 42,* 1067–1070.

Kranzler, H. R., & Liebowitz, N. R. (1988). Anxiety and depression in substance abuse: Clinical implications. *Medical Clinics of North America, 72,* 867–885.

Kushner, M. G., Sher, K. J., & Beitman, B. D. (1990). The relationship between alcohol disorders and the anxiety disorders. *American Journal of Psychiatry, 147,* 685–694.

Lehman, A. F., Myers, C. P., & Corty, E. C. (1989). Assessment and classification of patients with psychiatric and substance abuse syndromes. *Hospital and Community Psychiatry, 40,* 1019–1030.

Linnoila, M. I. (1989). Anxiety and alcoholism. *Journal of Clinical Psychiatry, 50* (suppl. 11), 26–29.

Marlatt, G. A. (1985). Lifestyles modifications. In G. A. Marlatt & J. R. Gordon (Eds.), *Relapse prevention: Maintenance strategies in the treatment of addictive behaviors* (pp. 201–279). New York: Guilford Press.

Martin, W. R., & Jansinki, D. R. (1969). Psychologic parameters of morphine dependence in man-tolerance, early abstinence, protracted abstinence. *Journal of Psychiatric Research, 7,* 9–17.

Millman, R. B. (1982). The provision of opioid therapy to the mentally ill; conceptual and practical considerations. In K. Verebey (Ed.), *Opioids in mental illness: Theories, clinical observations and treatment possibilities* (pp. 178–185). New York: New York Academy of Sciences.

Millman, R. B. (1986). Considerations on the psychotherapy of the substance abuser. *Journal of Substance Abuse Treatment, 3,* 103–109.

Millman, R. B. (1988). Evaluation and clinical management of cocaine abusers. *Journal of Clinical Psychiatry, 49* (suppl. 2), 27–33.

Millman, R. B. (1989). Cannabis abuse and dependence. In *American Psychiatric Association Task Force on Treatments of Psychiatric Disorders* (Vol. 2, pp. 1241–1260). Washington, DC: American Psychiatric Association.

Millman, R. B., & Beeder, A. B. (1994). The new psychedelic culture: LSD, "Rave" parties and The Grateful Dead. *Psychiatric Annals, 24*(3), 148–150.

Millman, R. B., & Sbriglio, R. (1986). Patterns of use and psychopathology in chronic marijuana users. *Psychiatric Clinics of North America, 9,* 533–545.

Mirin, S. M., & Weiss, R. D. (1991). Substance abuse and mental illness. In R. J. Frances & S. I. Miller (Eds.), *Clinical textbook of addictive disorders* (pp. 271–298). New York: Guilford Press.

Mirin, S. M., Weiss, R. D., & Michael, J. (1990). Psychopathology in substance abusers: Diagnosis and treatment. *American Journal of Drug and Alcohol Abuse, 14,* 139–157.

Nace, E. P., Davis, C. W., & Gaspari, J. P. (1991). Axis II comorbidity in substance abusers. *American Journal of Psychiatry 148,* 118–120.

Nace, E. P., & Isbell, P. G. (1991). Alcohol. In R. J. Frances & S. I. Miller (Eds.), *Clinical textbook of addictive disorders* (pp. 43–68). New York: Guilford Press.

Osher, F. L., & Kofoed, L. (1989). Treatment of patients with psychiatric and psychoactive substance abuse disorders. *Hospital and Community Psychiatry, 40,* 1025–1030.

Perry, S., & Jacobson, P. (1986). Neuropsychiatric manifestations of AIDS-spectrum disorders. *Hospital and Community Psychiatry, 37,* 135–142.

Post, R. M., & Kopanda, R. T. (1976). Cocaine, kindling and psychosis. *American Journal of Psychiatry, 133,* 627–634.

Regier, D. A., Boyd, J. H., & Burke, J. D., Jr. (1988). One month prevalence of mental disorders in the United States. *Archives of General Psychiatry, 45,* 977–985.

Regier, D. A., Farmer, M., & Rae, D. (1990). Comorbidity of mental disorders with alcohol and other drug abuse: Results from the epidemiologic catchment area study. *Journal of the American Medical Association, 264,* 2511–2518.

Ross, H. E., Glaser, F. B., & Germanson, T. (1988). The prevalence of psychiatric disorders in patients with alcohol and other drug problems. *Archives of General Psychiatry, 45,* 1023–1031.

Roth, M. (1989). Anxiety disorders and the use and abuse of drugs. *Journal of Clinical Psychiatry, 50* (suppl. 11), 30–42.

Rothenberg, R., Woefel, M., Stoneburner, R., Milberg, J., Parker, R., & Truman, B. (1987). Survival with the acquired immunodeficiency syndrome. *New England Journal of Medicine, 317,* 1297–1302.

Rounsaville, B., Anton, S. F., Carroll, K., Budde, D., Prusoff, B. A., & Gawin, F. (1991). Psychiatric diagnoses of treatment-seeking cocaine abusers. *Archives of General Psychiatry, 48,* 43–51.

Rounsaville, B., Weissman, M., & Kleber, H. (1982). Heterogeneity of psychiatric diagnosis in treated opiate addicts. *Archives in General Psychiatry, 39,* 161–166.

Rubin, V., & Comitas, L. (1975). *Ganja in Jamaica.* The Hague: Mouton.

Schuckit, M. A. (1985). The clinical implications of alcoholism and affective disorder. *Archives of General Psychiatry, 42,* 1081–1086.

Schuckit, M. A. (1989). Goals in treatment. In *Treatments of psychiatric disorders, section 12* (pp. 1072–1075). Washington, DC: American Psychiatric Association.

Smith, D. (1989). The role of substance abuse professionals in the AIDS epidemic. *Advances in Alcohol and Substance Abuse, 7,* 175–195.

Stefanis, C., Boulougouris, I., & Liakos, A. (1976). Clinical and psychophysiological effects of cannabis in long-term users. In M. C. Brause & S. Szara (Eds.), *Pharmacology of Marijuana.* New York: Raven Press.

Szuster, R. R., Pontius, E. B., & Campos, P.E. (1988). Marijuana, sensitivity and panic anxiety. *Journal of Clinical Psychiatry, 49,* 427–429.

Vaillant, G. (1983). *The natural history of alcoholism.* Cambridge, MA: Harvard University Press.

Vardy, M. M., & Kay, S. R. (1983). LSD psychosis or LSD-induced schizophrenia? A multimethod inquiry. *Archives of General Psychiatry, 40,* 877–883.

Weiss, C. J., & Millman, R. B. (1991). Hallucinogens, phencyclidine, marijuana, and inhalants. In R. J. Frances & S. I. Miller (Eds.), *Clinical textbook of addictive disorders* (pp. 146–170), New York: Guilford Press.

Woody, G. E., McLellan, A. T., O'Brien, C. P., & Luborsky, L. (1990). Addressing psychiatric comorbidity. In R. W. Pickens, C. G. Leukefeld, & C. R. Shuster, (Eds.), (NIDA Research Monograph No. 106). Rockville, MD: National Institute on Drug Abuse.

Zinberg, N. E. (1975). Addiction and ego function. In R. S. Eissler, A. Freud, M. Kris, & A. J. Solnit (Eds.), *The psychoanalytic study of the child*. New Haven: Yale University Press.

Zweben, J. E. (1987). Recovery-oriented psychotherapy: Facilitating the use of 12-step programs. *Journal of Psychoactive Drugs, 19,* 243–251.

5

Psychotherapy for Addictive Behavior: A Stage-Change Approach to Meaning Making

HOWARD J. SHAFFER
MELISSA ROBBINS

> Whilst part of what we perceive comes through our
> senses from the object before us, another part (and it
> may be the larger part) always comes out of our head.
> —WILLIAM JAMES (1890).

INTRODUCTION

Purpose

This chapter develops three interactive themes that can be applied to facilitate the conduct of psychotherapy for persons with addiction: (1) how conceptual approaches to addiction are manufactured and the diverse implications of this perspective for the conduct of psychotherapy; (2) a rationale for integrating a time-limited stage-change treatment approach through psychotherapy; and (3) consideration of various conceptual, strategic, and tactical approaches to treatment that can be informed by a developmental stage-change model to avoid or resolve common therapeutic impasses. In this chapter, we examine the utility and limitations of using various models of addiction with a range of clients at different points or stages during the treatment process. This discussion features how clinicians can get stuck within one treatment paradigm and the therapeutic tactics derived from these world views (i.e., explanations of addiction). Under these conditions, psychotherapists can lose their ability to promote therapeutic change because of what they perceive as limited clinical alternatives (i.e., the "blinding" function of paradigms) (Shaffer & Gambino, 1979; Shaffer, 1986a). Before we examine how clinicians manufacture conceptual meaning in the addictions, a brief digression is necessary to review some background to this approach.

Conceptual Background

The concept of psychotherapy has a long and complex history (e.g., Urban & Ford, 1971). In the discussion that follows, we consider only the technique of *talk* psychotherapy and not the full range of possible therapeutic activities. Furthermore, we are approaching psychotherapy from the most generic perspective; consequently, in this chapter, all references to psychotherapy refer interchangeably to counseling. This universal posture yields a discussion that, in this instance, will focus on the general interactive aspects of talk psychotherapy and not on specific benchmark events that occur within the conduct of any psychotherapy (e.g., assessment and termination). Whether individual, couples, family, or group oriented, talk psychotherapy provides the opportunity for participants to examine how they feel, think, and behave as well as the interaction among these experiences. Psychotherapy is an opportunity to understand self-deception and its motivation (N. E. Zinberg, personal communication, 1978), which provides an opportunity to reduce unsatisfying or self-defeating motifs of experience.

The material throughout this chapter derives from the perspective that all theoretical models of addiction and its treatment are cultural products or social constructions (e.g., Kleinman, 1987, 1988; Pfifferling, 1980; Shaffer, 1987; Sontag, 1979). These illness constructions, conventional wisdoms, and ideological frames reflect and interact dynamically with society's prevailing values and norms. Consequently, we describe multidimensional images of both the concept of "addiction" and its treatment. For example, even our contemporary view of AIDS (acquired immunodeficiency syndrome) as a disease (Sontag, 1989) is biased by cultural influences: "The way a society responds to problems of disease reveals its deepest cultural, social, and moral values. These core values—patterns of judgment about what is good or bad—shape and guide human perception and action. This . . . has most certainly been the case with AIDS; the epidemic has been shaped not only by powerful biological forces but by behavioral, social, and cultural factors as well" (Brandt, 1986, p. 231). Similarly, Watzlawick (1990) recognized that "like any other discipline, psychiatry relies on the epistemology considered valid at any given time" (p. 49). Time and clinical epistemology share a vital relationship within the context of psychotherapy. Therefore, this chapter also examines the notion of *time-limited* constructions of addiction (Shaffer & Robbins, 1991). Specifically, the discussion considers how these ideas can be used within a transactional process over the course of addiction treatment by applying a natural history of addiction and recovery stage-change treatment matching to the process of psychotherapy.

Metaphors, Models, Manufacturing, and Reality

Previously, we described the utility of considering different theories of addiction as helpful metaphors employed during psychotherapy to facilitate the evolution of a meaningful dialogue with patients (Shaffer & Robbins, 1991). Rather than engaging in ideological debate as to the "true" etiology and "right" treatment for addiction (cf. Havens, 1973, for an enlightening discussion of various approaches to the mind), we consider models and theories of addiction as symbolic constructs that clinicians and clients both employ to manufacture meaning (Szasz, 1970; Shaffer & Robbins, 1991; Watzlawick, 1984). Social constructions of addiction have included, but not been restricted to, models of excessive behavior as a moral weakness, a symptom of character pathology, the result of efforts to self-medicate an affective disorder, a metabolic deficiency, and a primary progressive disease. Each of these perspectives conveys a disparate view of the etiology of addiction and suggests a different course of treatment. Rather than assume—as is conventional—that theories of addiction reflect a tangible underlying reality, we suggest that all theories of addiction—as do scientific theories in general (Casti, 1989; Cohen, 1985)—manufacture or construct a "reality" that is temporary (e.g., Burke, 1985). This temporary world view remains active until essential new information is assimilated. This integrative process is iterative and recursive (Bateson, 1972), constantly but gradually revising reality; however, protracted periods of relative stability can be observed during this cyclical process. As with the evolution of scientific perspectives on the universe (Cohen, 1985; Kuhn, 1962), these recensions can be abrupt and revolutionary or more gentle and relatively imperceptible.

PERSPECTIVES ON ADDICTION

Manufacturing Clinical Meaning: Formulations as Visions and Views

The three descriptions of Ms. S. that follow reveal different visions of her problem based on the belief system(s) employed by the psychotherapist. The first case summary describes a psychological view of Ms. S.; the second features an understanding of Ms. S. from a biological perspective; and the third summary explains Ms. S. primarily in behavioral terms.

Psychological Formulation

Ms. S. is a 21-year-old woman with a 4-year history of drug abuse and self-destructive behavior. Her background of physical and sexual abuse and emotional deprivation has left her with low self-esteem, poor object relations, and an inability to tolerate intense affect. The patient's use of cocaine began at age 17 and continues to be her method of managing the demands of adult life for which she feels ill equipped.

Biological Formulation

Ms. S. is a 21-year-old woman with a 4-year history of depression and cocaine dependence. Prior to her use of cocaine, the patient experienced a major depression with severely impaired functioning. The patient has a positive family history for affective illness. Ms. S.'s mother has been hospitalized twice following depressive episodes, her maternal aunt is diagnosed with bipolar illness, and her father's alcoholism may mask an underlying depression.

Behavioral Formulation

Ms. S. is a 21-year-old woman who has been using cocaine excessively for the past 4-years. Her exclusive route of cocaine administration is intranasal. She uses between 0.50 and 0.75 gram of cocaine two to three times daily. Ms. S. reports that cocaine acts as a positive reinforcer by relieving her feelings of malaise and discomfort. Because she has few alternative activities that produce positive reinforcement, her repertoire of behaviors has become narrow. Consequently, she has withdrawn from her primary social support systems.

The Social Design of Formulations

As in all narratives (e.g., formulations), each clinical account of Ms. S. tells the reader as much about the author/clinician as it does about the protagonist/patient. Referring to how we understand disease, Blum (1985) said that "it is best to think of any affliction—a disease, a disability . . . as a text and of 'society' as its author" (p. 221). In addition to the broad social and cultural influences that bias how we perceive and explain addictive disorders, each individual's (e.g., psychotherapist, researcher, and social policymaker) understanding of explanations of addiction involves the prejudice of his/her own unique frame of reference. Consequently, in the language of psychotherapy, formulations (Perry, Cooper, & Michels, 1987; Shaffer, 1986b; Weiner, 1975) such as those above reflect how various clinicians use different conceptual models to understand a case and identify a treatment plan (Lazare, 1973). Clinicians create, construct, or "tell" different stories with and about their patients by manufacturing formulations that depend on a complex transaction between personal, cultural, and professional ideologies. Mechanic (1968) illustrated that this dynamic confluence of factors can, on occasion, yield unusual formulations of pathology. Mechanic described that dyschromic spirochetosis, a disease characterized by spots of various colors on the skin, was so common among a tribe of South American Indians that those who were absent the condition were considered abnormal and excluded from marriage because of this abnormality. Health and disease are indeed determined by the culture and context within which these occur (Mechanic, 1968).

Therapeutic Meaning Making: Prescriptively Revising Formulations as Reframes

Clinicians regularly manufacture meaning during the conduct of psychotherapy. For example, rather than construing "a problem" of addiction as the painful consequences of a poor adaptation to reality, or a disease process that travels relentlessly forward once set in motion, one theorist describes it as "the painful present consequences of a specific as-if fiction . . . [that] must be replaced by the effect of a different as-if fiction which creates a more tolerable reality" (Watzlawick, 1990, p. 143). In other words, as effective agents of change, psychotherapists learn to understand and appreciate how individuals make meaning or "as-if fictions," and offer reframes that permit effective problem resolution and relief from personal distress. Consider a reframing response for a patient who, while struggling with bulimia nervosa, presents her bingeing problem as out of control. A therapist might wonder with her whether the problem is also a solution to a more intolerable kind of distress. By so doing, clinician and client are beginning to reframe, rewrite, or formulate new meaning for this experience: Now the client is a person coping rather than someone helplessly out of control. Reframes can cast the proverbial glass half full or half empty depending on which view maximizes change. The terms remain the same, but the emphasis changes; meaning is revised; figure and ground are shifted.[1]

If psychotherapists are willing to accept *every* model of addiction as tentative rather than "real" and "true," they gain the opportunity to choose from a treatment array that resonates with each patient's unique way of creating meaning. Clinicians can select an approach to effect change by matching a patient's construction (i.e., world view) with a syntonic treatment approach. This therapeutic transaction permits psychotherapists to meet patients where they are and then take them where they have found it difficult to go. This view of addiction and addiction treatment features and advances each patient's perception of his/her dilemma as the foreground of psychotherapy and theoretical models as the landscape against which these personal perspectives ebb and flow, constantly changing hue and texture. This treatment style is a variation on what Budd and Zimmerman (1986) called the potentiating therapist:

> The potentiating clinician cares for people by restoring them to their own remarkable humanity. His or her compassion takes the form of empowering people to "listen" to the linguistic distinctions in which they exist with dignity. His or her attentiveness involves listening to the linguistic distinctions that patients are, so that those patients can create new distinctions and, hence, new possibilities. (p. 50)

Many substance abuse therapists already work this way. In fact, when clinicians utilize *any* theoretical model in their work with clients, they are using a new (i.e., new for the client) and sometimes very specific frame to reorganize or rewrite the client's as-if fiction. Understanding psychotherapy as a manufacturing process allows therapists the freedom and flexibility to be pragmatic when choosing which model or elements of a treatment model to employ. Addiction treatment specialists, for example, are now beginning to ask, "which method of care for which patient should be applied at which specific time during the process of recovery" (Shaffer & Gambino, 1990, pp. 365–366).

Psychotherapy:
Therapeutic Reframes as Time-Limited Realities

A motion picture is the presentation of a rapid sequence of single photographic frames. When stopped, each frame of the movie depicts a static moment, frozen in time. Although each frame is only a cross-section of the movie experience, the meaning of this image evolves within the context of the film sequence as each frame "constructs" or slightly revises the film narrative. Similarly, during psychotherapy each reframe shifts a client's perspective so that experience is revised. As experience changes, so does reality. Each revision or set of revisions teaches clients and clinicians alike that experience is plastic and socially constructed. These evolving time-limited constructions serve as the architecture of time.

When psychotherapists conceptualize therapy in this way—as a developmental process—it becomes possible to think about how clinicians and clients can use a series of reframes, rather than a single treatment approach, to encourage change (e.g., Marlatt & Fromme, 1987). Clinicians may find that the various languages of the disease, family systems, psychodynamic, and behavioral models all provide useful reframes at different points during the psychotherapy process. Until recently, however, there has not been a coherent conceptual approach that recognizes addiction as a developmental process requiring different interventions or treatment frames at different points during recovery. Recently, a diverse group of clinicians and researchers (e.g., Brown, 1985, 1988; Marlatt, Baer, Donovan, & Kivlahan, 1988; Maisto & Connors, 1988; McAuliffe & Albert,1992; Shaffer & Jones, 1989) described in various ways the emergence of a significant theoretical movement that is capable of integrating a multitheoretical treatment appraoch: the evolution of the concept of "stage change"[2] to understand and explain the entire addiction process.

Vaillant's (1983) natural history approach to addictive disorders provided the supportive conditions for stage-change theory to emerge. Prochaska and DiClemente (1985) stimulated and nourished the movement by giving theoretical substance and empirical sustenance to the idea of developmental stages of addiction. As a result, any consideration of contemporary approaches to the psychotherapeutic treatment of addiction would be incomplete without an illustration of a current developmental stage-change model of addiction. Within the last decade, for example, Prochaska and DiClemente (1985) began to articulate a transtheoretical model that encompassed the full course of change as a dynamic transactional process. They organized this process into four identifiable stages of change that people go through during episodes of transformation; these stages were defined as precontemplation, contemplation, action, and maintenance. Although a full discussion of stage change theory is beyond the scope of this chapter, we are interested in examining how a stage-change model can be employed to clarify and guide the use of treatment frames across the life span of addictive process.

THE NATURAL HISTORY OF ADDICTION: STAGE CHANGE AS A NARRATIVE FOR UNDERSTANDING THE REVISIONARY PROCESS

Shaffer (1992, 1994) recently offered a developmental model that extends the stage-change theory to (1) an account of the "natural recovery" process reported by "cocaine quitters" (Shaffer & Jones, 1989) and intoxicant abuse in general (Shaffer & Gambino, 1990) and (2) a guide to psychotherapy for persons with addiction (Shaffer, 1994). By listening to addicts' stories, their way of making sense of their addiction and recovery experience, Shaffer has elaborated a new addiction narrative that suggests fresh ways of utilizing different treatment frames over time. This approach suggests six stages of change that can describe both the emergence of addiction and the evolution of recovery.

The Emergence of Addiction: Initiation

The genesis of addiction begins with an individual's initiation into drug use or other potentially addictive activity (e.g., gambling). Of course, most individuals who experiment with substances or potentially addictive behaviors do not become addicts. But for some, these initial episodes provide the portal into the addictive process.

Positive Consequences

During this early phase, an individual participates in a potentially addictive activity (e.g., alcohol use, drug use, gambling, overeating, and high-risk sexual activity) and experiences a positive consequence. Positive effects can be a direct result of the pharmacological properties of the drug or other neurochemical changes resulting from the activity, or the psychological reinforcement (e.g., relief of depression or reduced sexual inhibition) obtained by participating in the activity. The consequences also can be positive in an indirect manner. For example, some drug users experience social rewards, are held in higher esteem, and have more to do when they are using the psychoactive substances or gambling to excess. Without some positive consequences, an activity or drug use would not be continued to the point that addiction would emerge. This experience of positive consequences is essential to understanding the development of ambivalence during the next stage and the often repetitive cycle of addictive behaviors.

Adverse Consequences Emerge

For most individuals who experience a potentially addictive behavior, their recognition of negative consequences will restrict and help modify their activity by encouraging moderation or abstinence. For example, at a party an individual may act in a way that he/she later regrets (e.g., waking up the next morning feeling ill equipped to go to work). This experience will alter future behavior by encouraging more temperance. For a person developing an addiction, however, this instructive information or "feedback" remains unusable. Although adverse consequences of the activity (e.g., drug use or gambling) emerge, the cause of these problems remains out of the addict's awareness. Prochaska and DiClemente (1985) describe this absence of awareness as the precontemplation stage. This is a period when one is in the throes of addiction.

Shaffer (1992, 1994) noted that the essence of addiction is that it continues to provide some of the previous positive consequences while simultaneously producing adverse consequences that begin to weigh more heavily. Addictive behaviors serve while they destroy. The reason these behavioral patterns can be so extremely destructive rests on the notion that addicts are not fully aware that the adverse effects of their addictive behavior are, in fact, the result of that same behavior. During this phase, addicts believe their behavior has little to do with their suffering. They perceive others as the source of their problems. The urging of friends and family to reduce or stop the addictive behavior is of little consequence; in fact, their pleading can become the fuel that energizes the addictive behavior so that the pattern intensifies further. At this level, addicts are capable of making sense of their world, with one exception: They cannot make any causal association between their addictive behavior and the life problems that they have had to endure. To minimize the discomfort associated with these problems, people with addiction persist in engaging in those behaviors that previously produced positive consequences. The result is the maintenance of repetitive, excessive behavioral patterns—addictive behaviors—that repeat without the *apparent* presence of a regulatory mechanism capable of restoring control by breaking this cycle.

The Evolution of Quitting: The Turning Point(s)

For addicts who successfully recover, the adverse consequences of their addictive behavior eventually enter awareness. This "turning point" into awareness, or insight, has often been considered the end of denial. This is the beginning of an epistemological shift. People with addiction are confronted by their emerging recognition of a causal connection between their addictive behavioral pattern and the adverse consequences of these activities (e.g., poor health, financial difficulty, and/or family disintegration). During the transition from the previous stage to a turning point, people with addiction struggle with ambivalent conflicts as they begin to recognize the importance of relinquishing the sought after positive consequences of their behavior while concurrently gaining access to the negative outcomes that the addictive behavioral pattern stimulated. Often experienced as a life crisis, people struggling with addiction recognize that their life-style must now change if they are to regain personal control, direction, and purpose in their lives. Prochaska and DiClemente (1985) framed this phase of addiction and recovery as the contemplation stage. However, this is much more than simply a thoughtful time in the history of addictive experience. For the recovering person with addiction, a turning point ushers in a period of increased awareness of ambivalent moods and shifting emotions.

Ambivalence

Ambivalence is a feeling of conflict. It is a simultaneous sense that we both want and do not want to change. Ambivalence creates a mixed feeling that we both like and do not like what we have, want, or experience. In spite of the obvious destructive power of addiction, addicts cling to the part of addiction that they like, the part that was adaptive originally and produced *positive consequences* during the second phase of addiction development. As people with addiction become increasingly aware and tolerant of their ambivalence, denial diminishes and they begin to express a *wish* that they would want to quit—but they do not yet actually want to stop. Heightening levels of self-observation develop and people with addiction now begin to realize that the costs of excessive behavioral patterns surpass the benefits. Gradually, addiction becomes explicitly identified as the major destructive agent in their life. It is at this point that quitters often enlist friends and significant others to help them stop. Before a turning point, the burden of self-control had been delegated more to others than to oneself; the acceptance of personal responsibility represents the actual turning point.

Active Quitting

Once a turning point is experienced, the process and tasks associated with active quitting can begin. Prochaska and DiClemente (1985) identify this as the action stage of change. Shaffer and Jones (1989) identified two basic approaches to cocaine quitting: "tapered quitting" and "cold-turkey quitting." It is possible for a successful quitter to mix these approaches to find a method that works. The majority of quitters, however, fall predominantly or entirely into one style or the other. Few successful quitters actually mix their stopping strategies during a quitting episode.

The notion of *active* quitting is critical. Successful quitters make observable changes during the stopping phase of addiction. Methods for quitting drugs include energetic attempts to avoid the drug, shift social activities, gain social support for personal change, and engage in some form of self-development. Thus, active quitting is characterized neither by contemplative thoughtfulness nor ambivalence. It is identified by important and marked behavioral change and life-style reorganization. New activities are elevated to a position of prominence; these events innervate intra- and interpersonal value. Old behaviors become devalued and less meaningful.

Relapse Prevention or Change Maintenance

Few individuals who stop their addictive activity remain totally abstinent from that moment. Marlatt and Gordon (1985) examined how slips (i.e., single episodes of drug use) can lead to full-blown relapse. Biological, psychological, and sociological factors interact to influence the risk of relapse for any individual. Prochaska and DiClemente identify this phase of the recovery process as the maintenance stage of change. Change maintenance involves the use of new skills and life-style patterns that promote positive, independent patterns of behavior. The integration of these behaviors into regular day-to-day activities is the essence of relapse prevention (e.g., Brownell, Marlatt, Lichtenstein, & Wilson, 1986). These new behaviors will be integrated most successfully if they approximate or satisfy the needs that were met by the addictive behavior. As we discuss later in this chapter, to identify these requirements, psychotherapists must be willing to investigate the positive aspects of addictive behavior as well as the adverse consequences (Shaffer, 1994). This strategy of stimulating and exploring painful ambivalence permits both clinicians and patients to fully appreciate the unique meaning, power, and function of addiction.

Speaking Psychotherapeutic Language: Facilitating Stage Change

Prochaska, DiClemente, and Norcross (1992) persuasively demonstrate that the most robust and reliable predictor of treament outcome, regardless of treatment strategy, is an index of patient readiness to change. Consequently, psychotherapists should attend to (1) the overall readiness of a patient to change and (2) a patient's specific stage of change. By identifying a patient's specific level of development within the natural history of addiction, treatment can be directed to facilitate movement to the next stage of development and not impede this natural process.

To help patients progress through the stages of quitting, clinicians must begin to speak a language that promotes and encourages this natural progression instead of inadvertently complicating the tasks of recovery with irrelevant or restricting ideas. To accomplish this goal, therapists must first learn to match the tasks of clinical work to the stage of change that clients are experiencing (e.g., Marlatt, 1988; Shaffer, 1994). For example, it is not useful to explore ambivalence in detail when a patient has resolved their ambivalence and is ready to actively quit. Similarly, it is equally useless to help patients develop quitting strategies when they have not become resolute about their readiness to change because painful ambivalence is fueling denial. Helping individuals move from one stage of experience to the next requires clinicians to recognize and interact with their clients' particular frame of reference. In other words, clinicians must become fluent in the language of each stage of addiction and recovery for each patient. Clinicians must be adept listeners and observers as they inhabit the role of students learning to navigate their clients' subjective realities. Put simply, if clinicians fail to become "fluent" in their clients' particular "language," there is little hope that a genuine, empathic, meaningful dialogue, capable of facilitating change, will develop.

Clinical Fluency: A Case Example

The following case illustrates some of the challenges facing clinicians who enter into psychotherapeutic relationships with persons struggling with addictive disorders. "Jill" and the problems she brings with her for psychotherapeutic attention represent a common set of dilemmas facing contemporary addiction treatment specialists.

Jill is a 34-year-old married woman with two children under the age of 6. She works in public relations and lives in an affluent suburb with her husband John, who is a lawyer in a successful downtown law firm. Jill arrives 15 minutes late to her first therapy appointment and presents her therapist with the following complaint: "I'm here because my marriage is falling apart." Jill describes her marriage as explosive with frequent blowouts and subsequent periods of silent withdrawal. She describes the cause of these fights as her husband's obsession with her alcohol use. In fact, Jill admits that part of why she originally made this therapy appointment was to appease her husband during their most recent fight.

Jill comes from an Irish Catholic family of "drinkers." Her memories of childhood—which she characterizes as "nearly perfect"—are interspersed with her father's drunken rages and her mother's silent passivity. Jill argues, "My whole family drinks more than I do, and no one hassles them about it. In fact," Jill adds, "my friends are also a hard partying bunch. Some of them make me look like a teetotaler." In Jill's social and familial world, she insists, her alcohol use is not unusual; she has between three and four glasses of wine a day.

As Jill's story unfolds, she confesses that she had been bulimic between ages 19 and 30. She gave up bingeing and purging only after her husband discovered this secret behavior. He threatened divorce; as a result, they briefly entered into couples therapy, which she describes as "excruciating." It is no surprise that she refuses a couples meeting or referral to a couples therapist this time around.

Jill is bright and articulate. She is able to describe in detail how her husband "makes" her drink more. All her life, she explains, she has felt overly controlled by her father, her brothers, and now her husband. She admits to feeling a certain measure of shame at their constant criticism as well as a sometimes overwhelming dose of rage. In response to their control and to coping with her feelings, she describes herself as becoming a "rebel." As a teenager, she disobeyed orders, was impertinent, and generally "raised hell." Even her bingeing and purging was her assertive solution to the strict dieting, deprivation, and the pursuit of thinness as required by her college sorority culture. When Jill's husband searches for empty liquor bottles, scrutinizes her, questions her, and generally attempts to control her liquor consumption, Jill feels both shame and anger. The more he attempts to control her, she argues, the more she will drink. "If he would just back off, things would be OK."

Like all clinicians, Jill's therapist hears her story through a set of clinical and personal assumptions and biases. For example, the clinician can view Jill as an active alcoholic in denial. Jill has a probable family history of alcoholism, selected a peer group that enables her to comfortably sustain her level of drinking, and has marital problems directly linked to alcohol.

Alternately, Jill's therapist could see her as engaged in a difficult marriage within which intimacy issues are manifested in a set of distance regulating maneuvers that include Jill's involvement with substances. From this perspective, the fight about Jill's alcohol use may be one step in a homeostatic dance that maintains a tolerable level of closeness for both partners.

Jill's therapist also could choose to understand her patient as having self-deficits. From this perspective, Jill's childhood experience of her unpredictable raging father and her emotionally withdrawn mother have left her without certain self-regulating capacities; she has managed to regulate her life with both her bulimia and her alcohol use. Similarly, Jill's psychotherapist must also consider additional formulations: whether Jill's addictive behaviors mask a neurochemical depression, how Jill's young children are being affected, and so forth.

Jill's therapist is facing a complex and difficult choice point: how to establish a therapeutic frame with Jill that will maximize the possibility of forming a fruitful working alliance, which, in turn, will facilitate positive changes. Jill's therapist is also facing a gordian set of clinical risks. To treat Jill without directly confronting her alcohol abuse would be collusion, whereas beginning treatment with her alcohol use adds one more person who is attempting to control Jill's behavior, increasing the risk of premature termination. On the other hand, if Jill's psychotherapist attempts to establish an alliance by avoiding the issue of alcohol and, instead, explores her patient's difficult marriage, she risks communicating to Jill an unwillingness or inability to face an issue that secretly may be causing Jill considerable anxiety. This strategy can create a therapeutic alliance that may not be clinically productive.

If Jill's therapist takes as her task establishing a meaningful and productive dialogue, she must consider Jill's particular frame of reference. This understanding includes Jill's cultural view, her past experience with personal change, the particular meaning that alcohol use may hold for Jill, and where she is in the addiction and recovery process. In other words, for her psychotherapist to engage Jill in a fertile therapeutic conversation, she must avoid taking a dichotomous stand either for or against Jill's alcohol use. One of the goals of this therapy is to help Jill understand that she is a competent adult in charge of her own decisions, as well as someone who is responsible for the consequences of her actions. Therefore, the therapeutic task is to involve Jill in a discussion that gently challenges her mind-set and encourages her to revise personal perspectives and sense of identity—all without overwhelming her.

Clinicians also can view Jill as in the midst of a painful ambivalent conflict that is energizing her denial. If Jill's psychotherapist considers the initial treatment task as one that will help Jill recognize and become tolerant of these painful, conflicted ambivalent feelings (regarding Jill's use of intoxicants and her relationship with her husband), therapy can utilize aspects of a range of formulations without having to assume one particular perspective as an accurate representation of reality. For example, Jill's therapist might inquire about Jill's bulimic experience, exploring with her the adaptive and problematic aspects of this behavioral pattern. She might also wonder what Jill's marriage would be like if Jill and her husband did not have her alcohol to fight about. Alternately, the therapist might wonder with Jill how Jill would regard her own alcohol use if her husband backed out of the issue. Jill's childhood memories of her father's alcohol-induced rages might also be a useful avenue of discussion.

When working this way, an implicit aspect of any psychotherapeutic discussion is the task of enhancing a patient's sense of self as a responsible individual who is coping actively and adapting to a range of very difficult situations. For example, Jill's alcohol use might be framed as an attempt to save her marriage. By keeping her husband focused on her problems, Jill protects them both from confronting the less familiar and perhaps overwhelming task of tolerating and building marital intimacy. Jill's therapist might wonder whether there are ways that both her alcohol use and bulimia have functioned to calm her down or numb out other painful emotions. These sorts of questions are designed to build a safe context for Jill to think about the present cost of her solutions to some difficult problems and to enhance her sense of herself as an empowered agent of change. By so doing, Jill's psychotherapist establishes a meaningful, productive dialogue within which Jill safely can claim responsibility for her choices. This experience permits Jill to understand and learn to tolerate her ambivalence about both drinking and not drinking in addition to the vast array of emotional issues associated with change. This tolerance naturally diminishes the need for denial and will permit Jill to resolve this life impasse and move on with her development.

THERAPEUTIC IMPASSES: RESISTANT CLIENTS OR INTRACTABLE CLINICIANS?

Addicts have "a reputation" in the therapeutic community. They are often described as difficult clients who resist change and need the stern medicine of confrontation and disciplinary measures in order to shape up and comply with "recovery.". Unfortunately, clinicians often are as vulnerable as their clients to becoming locked into one story. When this story no longer works, they tend to blame their clients for misbehaving. In fact, in what could be described as a parallel process to addiction, therapeutic impasses become clinical projections: the client's problem rather than the therapist's responsibility.

Impasses in the Treatment of Substance Dependence and Abuse

In spite of the best intentions, psychotherapy can—and often does—reach an impasse. An impasse occurs when a treatment strategy or tactic fails to keep pace with a patient's shifting experience. In other words, the treatment no longer matches clinical need. An impasse is often experienced as a clinical dead-end where treatment progress comes to a full stop. This is a serious clinical predicament; that is, a potentially dangerous situation because lack of treatment progress often stimulates palpable countertransference among therapists and provocative transference among patients (Maltsberger & Buie, 1974; Shaffer, 1994). Therapists often experience frustration with patients who challenge their authority actively with anger or passively with lack of progress. This feeling of frustration can lead to unbearable malicious impulses that are expressed as patient blaming and ultimately as a dangerous need to terminate treatment (Maltsberger & Buie, 1974).

The Detoxification Impasse

Impasses result most commonly from seemingly benign therapeutic motives that can only be understood as countertransference. For example, imagine a methadone patient who announces that he intends to detoxify. This pronouncement is met with an instinctive congratulatory response from the psychotherapist. However, evidence suggests that as many as 90% of patients who become abstinent will slip and use psychoactive substances again during the course of their recovery (Marlatt & Gordon, 1985; Marlatt et al., 1988); thus, this patient will find it difficult to continue to confide in his therapist who has inadvertently revealed praise of abstention and disdain for using. Praise of use and disdain for abstention, although atypical among almost all addiction treatment specialists, are equally destructive to a therapeutic relationship and must be interpreted as countertransference even if the strategy is construed as a tactic to engage a resistant and chonic substance abuser in treatment. Under either of these countertransference-laden conditions, patients reveal less and begin to withdraw from the therapeutic alliance. Psychotherapists often have difficulty understanding the source of this impasse. A predicament of this type could have been avoided by responding to the original proclimation of detoxification by asking any of a variety of questions: When did you decide? Will you mind? How will that be for you? Questions of this variety require patients to become aware and consider the full range of alternative choices. Awareness and contemplation of alternative choices are the sine qua non of psychotherapeutic treatment for addiction in general and impulse disorders in particular.

Resolving Impasses:
The Art of Psychotherapy

To resolve impasses, clinicians must examine their motives for patient change. Patients resist change in response to the therapeutic context. What clinicans present to patients determines in large measure how patients respond (Miller & Rollnick, 1991). This view represents a significant shift from the common "patient must be motivated to change" view of psychotherapy. The task of therapists is simply to help patients (gradually) shift their experience so they can move to the next stage of a natural process. For example, when patients present for treatment experiencing adverse effects from their behavior and unaware that they are indeed causing these painful events (i.e., stage three of the stage-change model presented earlier), the goal of treatment is not active quitting (i.e., stage five). The task of psychotherapy is for patients to experience and begin to tolerate their ambivalence so that denial is no longer necessary; consequently, patients naturally experience a turning point (stage four, when they begin to accept responsibility for their behavior). Similarly, when patients who have reached the relapse prevention stage of treatment do relapse, in addition to identifying the specific relapse "triggers" so that patients can learn the most from their experience, clinicians also must attend to any ambivalence that has resurfaced. Miller and Rollnick (1991) offer a variety of useful clinical suggestions that minimize countertransference and, as a consequence, therapeutic impasses. To begin, therapists must express empathy; this notion is similar to becoming fluent in a patient's representation and experience of the world. Instead of being argumentative, clinicians should develop discrepancies—between patients' behavior and their stated goals—to help them see the self-deception in either their goals or their behavior. This discrepancy is an expression of ambivalent conflict and must be exercised if it is to dissipate denial. Therapists need to roll with patient resistance; clinicians must remember that they stimulate defensiveness by their probing, confronting, and clarifying comments. Psychotherapists need to actively support patient self-efficacy. Thus, clinicians should implement strategies that will increase a patient's sense of hope, range of alternatives, and ultimately the possibility of change. This can be accomplished through a variety of tactics. For example, during the course of therapy, a caregiver can ask a patient how uncomfortable the patient is at that moment along any emotional dimension (e.g., anxiety). Later, in the very same session, usually as the patient leaves the treatment office, the therapist can ask how the patient feels now along the same dimension. Inevitably, patients will respond with a somewhat different value to their feelings. Even if they are more uncomfortable, the therapist can note that "things are already beginning to change." (Sometime things do indeed get worse before getting better.)

The Treatment of Painful Ambivalence: The Essence of Psychotherapy for Addiction

Similar tactics can be used to explore and exercise painful feelings associated with ambivalent conflicts. As we described earlier in this chapter, it is essential to the psychotherapy of substance abuse that clinicians explore with patients *what addiction does for them* and not simply how it may hurt them. Denial is the result of painful ambivalence: the feeling that one both wants and does not want an object, feeling, or behavior. Denial is a defense mechanism that removes one side of the painful conflict by erasing it from consciousness. Overcoming denial within the context of psychotherapy requires clinicians to stimulate and exercise ambivalent feelings. Not only will this approach to treatment increase a patient's ability to tolerate painful ambivalence and, therefore, diminish the underlying need for denial, but this tactic adds considerable credibility to any therapist's position. Patients who abuse intoxicants know full well that these drugs reliably do something for them— even though they also may experience significant adverse effects. Once patients know that the therapist is aware of this fact and can tolerate a candid discussion of this matter, there is much less to be defensive about.

During psychotherapy sessions, ask open-ended questions, listen reflectively, and be affirmative—support the client's efforts to participate in change (e.g., Miller & Rollnick, 1991). This can be done by occasionally summarizing what has transpired during treatment. For example, "So far you have said that . . . and we have come to think. . . ." Finally, elicit self-motivational statements by asking evocative questions. Help patients to recognize their responsibility by challenging their motivation to change (Miller & Rollnick, 1991). This requires patients to defend change; do not impose change so patients defend the status quo (e.g., patients struggling with addiction often say they are in treatment because their parent or spouse wanted them to come); "do you always do what they ask you to? If not, what brings you here now?" Guide patients to look both backward (before problem) and forward (after problem) so they can develop a mental image of their life before and after substance abuse. Finally, contact patients (i.e., by telephone or letter) after their first office visit. This tactic will minimize the dropout rate after evaluation and encourage the development of a treatment adherence (typically 30–60% of patients do not follow treatment prescriptions) (Miller & Rollnick, 1991).

CONCLUSION

This chapter presented an overview of how conceptual thinking in the addictions is manufactured and how these explanatory ideas can be applied to the process of psychotherapy. Specifically, we suggest that, in spite of personal preferences, clinicians acquire a willingness to employ the entire range of theoretical explanations for addictive behavior to help them match a theoretical frame with each patient's world view. Similarly, using language that patients understand and resonate with strengthens the treatment alliance.

Shifting language and theoretical explanations for addiction and recovery can be applied incrementally as time-limited realities. Psychotherapists should apply these shifts in explanation by first matching a particular patient's subjective experience and then reframing his/her difficulties so that hope, change, and efficacy become possible: Manufacture new meaning from the available evidence. Next, gradually titrate alternative explanations as patients adapt to, and evolve through, the operative but time-limited explanation of their changing behavior as well as their shifting world view. The task of treatment, language, and theory matching is facilitated by understanding and including in the psychotherapeutic formula the specific stage of change, or moment in the natural history of development, that a patient is experiencing.

Impasses during psychotherapy with patients struggling against their impulses and addictive disorders are very common. Usually these problems result when clinicians fail to include patient perspectives about the meaning of their addiction and impose their own instead. For example, clinicians often fail to attend to the full range of benefits that patients experience from their relationship with the object of addiction; during the early stages of an emerging excessive disorder there are always some positive consequences that appear—otherwise the behavioral pattern would stop naturally from lack of interest or benefit. Similarly, by attending exclusively to denial, instead of ambivalence as its primary root cause, clinicians cause psychotherapy to become an inordinately painful and combative process. This uncomfortable state of affairs also can result in a therapeutic impasse. Alternatively, clinicians must learn to attend and tolerate patients' feelings of ambivalence. By recognizing patients' wishes to "use" and the losses that they will incur by stopping, therapists can help to identify or manufacture meaningful substitutes that provide healthy alternatives to the objects of addiction.

NOTES

1. Barker (1985) and Marlatt and Fromme (1987) provide and analyze a selection of metaphorical reframes for use during psychotherapy in general and the addictions in particular.

2. Prochaska and DiClemente (1985), Marlatt and Gordon (1985), Marlatt et al. (1988), and Vaillant (1983) provide the intellectual framework that stimulated much of the developmental stage change thinking that led to a modern reformation of addiction explanations. These workers are true pioneers. We are indebted to them for providing the conceptual and intellectual platform on which many of the stage-change ideas in this chapter rest.

REFERENCES

Barker, P. (1985). *Using metaphors in psychotherapy*. New York: Brunner/Mazel.

Bateson, G. (1972). *Steps to an ecology of mind*. New York: Ballantine Books.

Blum, A. (1985). The collective representation of affliction: Some reflections on disability and disease as social facts. *Theoretical Medicine, 6*, 221–232.

Brandt, A. M. (1986). AIDS: From social history to social policy. *Law, Medicine and Health Care, 14*, 231–242.

Brown, S. (1985). *Treating the alcoholic: A developmental model of recovery*. New York: Wiley.

Brown, S. (1988). *Treating adult children of alcoholics: A developmental perspective*. New York: Wiley.

Brownell, K. D., Marlatt, G. A., Lichtenstein, E., & Wilson, G. T. (1986). Understanding and preventing relapse. *American Psychologist, 41*, 765–782.

Budd, M. A., & Zimmerman, M. E. (1986). The potentiating clinician: Combining scientific and linguistic competence. *Advances, 3*, 40–55.

Burke, J. (1985). *The day the universe changed*. Boston: Little, Brown.

Casti, J. L. (1989). *Paradigms lost: Images of man in the mirror of science*. New York: William Morrow.

Cohen, I. B. (1985). *Revolution in science*. Cambridge, MA: Harvard University Press.

Havens, L. (1973). *Approaches to the mind*. Boston: Little, Brown.

Kleinman, A. (1987). Culture and clinical reality: Commentary on culture-bound syndromes and international disease classifications. *Culture, Medicine and Psychiatry, 11*, 49–52.

Kleinman, A. (1988). *The illness narratives: Suffering, healing and the human condition*. New York: Basic Books.

Kuhn, T. S. (1962). *The structure of scientific revolutions*. Chicago: University of Chicago Press.

Lazare, A. (1973). Hidden conceptual models in clinical psychiatry. *New England Journal of Medicine, 288*, 345–351

Maisto, S. A., & Connors, G. J. (1988). Assessment of treatment outcome. In D. M. Donovan & G. A. Marlatt (Eds.), *Assessment of addictive behaviors* (pp. 421–453). New York: Guilford Press.

Maltsberger, J. T., & Buie, D. H. (1974). Countertransference hate in the treatment of suicidal patients. *Archives of General Psychiatry, 30*, 625–633.

Marlatt, G. A. (1988). Matching clients to treatment: Treatment models and stages of change. In D. M. Donovan & G. A. Marlatt (Eds.), *Assessment of addictive behaviors*, (pp. 474–484). New York: Guilford Press.

Marlatt, G. A., Baer, J. S., Donovan, D. M., & Kivlahan, D. R. (1988). Addictive behaviors: Etiology and treatment. *Annual Review of Psychology, 39,* 223–252.

Marlatt, G. A., & Fromme, K. (1987). Metaphors for addiction. *Journal of Drug Issues, 17,* 9–28.

Marlatt, G. A., & Gordon, J. R. (Eds.). (1985). *Relapse prevention: Maintenance strategies in the treatment of addictive behaviors.* New York: Guilford Press.

McAuliffe, W. E., & Albert, J. (1992). *Clean start: An outpatient program for initiating cocaine recovery.* New York: Guilford Press.

Mechanic, D. (1968). *Medical sociology: A selective view.* New York: Free Press.

Miller, W. R., & Rollnick, S. (1991). *Motivational interviewing: Preparing people to change addictive behavior.* New York: Guilford Press.

Perry, S., Cooper, A. M., & Michels, R. (1987). The psychodynamic formulation: Its purpose, structure, and clinical application. *American Journal of Psychiatry, 144,* 543–550.

Pfifferling, J. H. (1980). A cultural prescription for medicocentrism. In L. Eisenberg & A. Kleinman (Eds.), *The relevance of social science for medicine* (pp. 197–222). Boston: D. Reidel.

Prochaska, J. O., & DiClemente, C. C. (1985). Common processes of self change in smoking, weight control, and psychological distress. In S. Shiffman & T. A. Wills (Eds.), *Coping and substance abuse* (pp. 345–363). New York: Academic Press.

Prochaska, J. O., DiClemente, C. C., & Norcross, J. C. (1992). In search of how people change: Applications to addictive behaviors. *American Psychologist, 47,* 1102-1114.

Shaffer, H. J. (1986a). Conceptual crises and the addictions: A philosophy of science perspective. *Journal of Substance Abuse Treatment, 3,* 285–296.

Shaffer, H. J. (1986b). Assessment of addictive disorders: The use of clinical reflection and hypothesis testing. *Psychiatric Clinics of North America, 9*(3), 385–398.

Shaffer, H. J. (1987). The epistemology of "addictive disease": The Lincoln-Douglas debate. *Journal of Substance Abuse Treatment, 4,* 103–113.

Shaffer, H. J. (1992). The psychology of stage change: The transition from addiction to recovery. In J. H. Lowinson, P. Ruiz, & R. B. Millman (Eds.), *Comprehensive textbook of substance abuse* (2nd ed., pp. 100–105). Baltimore: Williams & Wilkins.

Shaffer, H. J. (1994). Denial, ambivalence and countertransference hate. In J. D. Levin & R. Weiss (Eds.), *Alcoholism: Dynamics and treatment* (pp. 421–437). Northdale, NJ: Jason Aronson.

Shaffer, H. J., & Gambino, B. (1979). Addiction paradigms II: Theory, research, and practice. *Journal of Psychedelic Drugs, 11,* 299–304.

Shaffer, H. J., & Gambino, B. (1990). Epilogue: Integrating treatment choices. In H. B. Milkman & L. Sederer (Eds.), *Treatment choices for alcoholism and substance abuse* (pp. 351–375). Lexington, MA: Lexington Books.

Shaffer, H. J., & Jones, S. B. (1989). *Quitting cocaine: The struggle against impulse.* Lexington, MA: Lexington Books.

Shaffer, H. J., & Robbins, M. (1991). Manufacturing multiple meanings of addiction: Time-limited realities. *Contemporary Family Therapy: An International Journal, 13*(5), 387–404.

Sontag, S. (1979). *Illness as metaphor.* New York: Vintage Books.

Sontag, S. (1989). *AIDS and its metaphors.* New York: Farrar, Straus and Giroux.

Szasz, T. (1970). *The manufacture of madness: A comparative study of the inquisition and the mental health movement.* New York: Dell Publishing.

Urban, H. B., & Ford, D. H. (1971). Some historical and conceptual perspectives on psychotherapy and behavior change. In A. E. Bergin & S. L. Garfield (Eds.), *Handbook of psychotherapy and behavior change: An empirical analysis* (pp. 3–36). New York: Wiley.

Vaillant, G. (1983). *The natural history of alcoholism.* Cambridge, MA: Harvard University Press.

Watzlawick, P. (1984). *The invented reality: How do we know what we believe we know?* New York: W. W. Norton.

Watzlawick, P. (1990). *Munchhausen's pigtail, or psychotherapy and "reality": Essays and lectures.* New York: W. W. Norton.

Weiner, I. B. (1975). *Principles of psychotherapy.* New York: Wiley.

6

Integrating Psychotherapy and 12-Step Approaches

JOAN ELLEN ZWEBEN

INTRODUCTION

Successful recovery from addiction requires life-style changes in which the patient disengages from patterns and circumstances that promote alcohol and drug use and replaces them with those that support abstinence. For some, this requires alterations of a major magnitude. The work of the psychotherapist can be enhanced and accelerated in many different ways by maintaining awareness of the profound changes needed to support recovery (Brown 1985; Zweben, 1986). A productive integration with 12-Step programs offers the psychotherapist a major advantage in addressing addiction at all stages of the recovery process. This chapter describes the characteristics of 12-Step programs, and discusses strategies for fostering effective utilization. This will be approached in part in the framework of the recovery-oriented psychotherapy model (Zweben, 1986, 1987, 1989, 1993), which describes how the therapist's tasks shift according the the patient's stage in recovery. Twelve-Step program participation has advantages and challenges at all stages.

"Twelve-Step programs" is the generic name for the many descendants of Alcoholics Anonymous (AA), which was founded in 1935 and accelerated its growth rapidly during the 1940s. According to the most recent (1989) survey of membership, there were almost 1 million members in the United States and Canada (Alcoholics Anonymous World Survey, 1990). Recent data suggest that of the U.S. adult population, 9% have been to an AA meeting at some time, 3.6% in the prior year. Of these, only about one third attended for problems of their own, the remaining likely prompted by curiosity and concern about someone else's drinking (Room & Greenfeld, 1993). Room and Greenfeld (1993) describe the heart of the AA movement, based on current attendance, as middle-aged women and younger men. The coalcoholism movement is centered on middle-aged women, the group also most likely to be involved in psychotherapy as well as self-help. Systematic data on other self-help groups are considerably more scant, but literature from the alternative groups are available from the groups themselves and often in local bookstores. Table 6.1 contains a listing of those in the San Francisco Bay area, including those with national telephone numbers (*Recovering,* 1993).

These alternative groups provide at least two essential elements that are available with minimal or no financial barriers. They offer a social support system for recovery and a process for personal development that encourages looking inward and addressing issues obscured by alcohol and drug use. Inasmuch as recovery is more than the absence of alcohol and drug use, 12-Step programs provide both a catalyst and guidance for moving through the issues (Carnes, 1989). Certainly both functions overlap with psychotherapy. It is important to understand the areas of similarity and differences to better facilitate use of both modalities.

One essential difference between 12-Step programs and psychotherapeutic activities pertains to accountability and the nature of the group process. Although sometimes referred to as a treatment, these programs are self-help groups, which by nature do not have a leadership hierarchy or any other objective means of holding the patient accountable. Thus, treatment programs, probation officers, or others can mandate attendance and ask the secretary of the meeting for signatures, but this practice gives a false sense of accountability that is in many ways worse than none at all. Many a fine meeting has been destroyed by an influx from the local chemical dependency program, or others mandated to attend, who sign each other's slips at the back of the room and disrupt the meeting with negative attitudes and behaviors. Twelve-Step programs are fundamentally "programs of attraction," and the therapist must achieve a fine balance between getting someone over the initial obstacles to attendance and engagement and exerting a level of coercion that inspires rebellion. Once the patient becomes involved, the therapist will see it through increasing discussion of experiences in meetings (positive and negative), stimulation of insights, and increasing application of the concepts not only to the addictive patterns but to other life issues as well. For example, H.A.L.T. is one such guideline; it is the recognition that one is vulnerable when *h*ungry, *a*ngry, *l*onely or *t*ired and it is wise to avoid difficult situations at that time.

TABLE 6.1. The *Recovering* Directory

National telephone numbers included where available.

Adult Children of Alcoholics
Adult Survivors of Child Abuse
Al-Anon/Alateen: (800) 344–2666
Alcoholics Anonymous
Arts Anonymous
Cocaine Anonymous
Chronic Fatigue Immune Disease Syndrome Anonymous
Chemically Dependent Anonymous
Codependents Anonymous: (602) 277–7991
Emotions Anonymous (612) 647–9712
Emphysema Anonymous: (813) 391–9977
Debtors Anonymous
Gamblers Anonymous: (213) 386–8789
Incest Survivors Anonymous: (213) 428–5599
Marijuana Anonymous: (800) 766–6779
Nar-Anon Family Group: (213) 547–5800
Narcotics Anonymous
Nicotine Anonymous
Overeaters Anonymous
Partners of Survivors of Incest Anonymous
Phobics Anonymous: (619) 322–COPE
Prostitutes Anonymous: (818) 905–2188
Racism and Bigotry Anonymous
Recovering Couples Anonymous: (314) 830–2600
Self-Help Group Information: (800) 222–5465
Self-Mutilators Anonymous
Sexual Addiction Hotline: (800) 321–2066
Sex and Love Addicts Anonymous
Sexaholics Anonymous
Shame Anonymous
Shoplifters Anonymous: (800) 848–9595
Smokers Anonymous
Survivors Reaching Out: (916) 967–0424
Survivors of Incest Anonymous
Workaholics Anonymous

The second important difference pertains to the nature of the group process. Twelve-Step programs have a particular group process, which has its own strengths and limits. The policy of "no cross-talk" emphasizes that helping occurs through learning from the experience of others. Participants are not to confront, inquire, or otherwise interfere with another's "share." This reduces the perils of aggressive interrogation by untrained persons and creates an atmosphere of acceptance and some protection against other kinds of invasiveness. However, it may also mean that someone in great distress receives no immediate response or support, although he/she may once the meeting is over. Many of the benefits of interaction and feedback do not occur within the framework of the meeting, and lack of confrontation may make it difficult to control unacceptable behavior on the part of participants who may be disruptive though sober.

The lack of intrusiveness can be a crucial element in allowing someone to settle in and feel secure as a participant.

Tammy enlivened her traditional therapy group with her poetically stated insights derived from her many years of active participation in AA. She reported that when she first started going to meetings, she was terrified and spent the first year observing. She took care to sit in the back and left immediately as the meeting ended to avoid attention. She felt that had it not been possible to do that, she would have been unable to sustain participation. Since then, she has been a highly articulate, active member.

It is useful for the therapist to maintain simultaneous focus on encouraging the patient to begin attending meetings, and using attitudes and feelings about meetings as a mirror of feelings about addiction and recovery. Through inquiry about resistance to meeting attendance, the therapist can often get a clearer picture of the nature of resistances at each recovery stage.

Peter was a highly paid professional who had entered treatment for amphetamine use, which he relied on to energize him to cope with long periods of intense work demands. After entering treatment for the first time, he attended meetings for 4 to 5 months before discontinuing, insisting that because he was doing well (i.e., completely abstinent), he did not need to go any more. After a year of abstinence, he had a major relapse, signaled by a return to "social drinking," soon followed by a resumption of amphetamine use. At that time, he shared that his previous refusal to continue 12-Step meetings was based on a strong dislike of the opening declaration, "I am Peter, I am an addict." This was also a key factor in his resistance to abstaining from alcohol; he preferred to compartmentalize his problem as one of stimulant use alone, yet "social drinking" was a recurrent indicator of an impending relapse.

Although it is highly desirable for patients to begin 12-Step program participation as soon as possible, many currently enthusiastic participants took a long time to settle in. Brown (1985) reports on her research study of self-declared AA members in a Stanford Alcohol Clinic sample studied in the mid-1970s and found that an average of 20 months elapsed between initial contact and acknowledged membership in AA, and another 8 months passed before the average respondent achieved abstinence. Thus, almost 2 years passed between the time an individual recognized enough of a drinking problem to check out AA and the time he/she embraced AA membership, with its corresponding declaration of a desire to stop drinking. It took an average of another 8 months after that before participants actually stopped drinking. Although appropriate treatment can certainly accelerate progress, it is important to maintain the perspective that these achievements can take a long time. The therapist needs to have a realistic time frame while insisting that the issue remain on the table for discussion.

HELPING PATIENTS USE 12-STEP PROGRAMS

Prochaska, DiClemente, and Norcross (1992) offer a framework for therapists to assess the stage of the patient's readiness for change and tailor interventions accordingly. Because the initial obstacles to meeting attendance are often motivational, it is useful to determine where the patient can be located along this continuum. These stages include precontemplation (resistance to recognizing or modifying a problem), contemplation (seriously considering the problem and possible approaches), preparation (making some unsuccessful behavioral changes and intending to take further action in the forseeable future), action (highly visible behavioral changes to overcome the problem), and maintenance (working to consolidate the gains attained and prevent relapse). The therapist addresses 12-Step program participation in different ways depending on the stage of change. For example, patients in the contemplation phase can be reminded that AA is for anyone *concerned* about drinking, not just for those who declare themselves alcoholic. They can be asked to take a "field trip" to three different meetings to see what they are like. They can be prepared with the information that although many of the rituals are quite compelling, AA is actually tolerant of a wide range of behaviors and they can pass at any time, or describe themselves in any way they want:

> Jane was highly conflicted both about labeling her drinking and about going to AA, particularly since therapist inquiry had resulted in her concluding that both parents were in fact alcoholic. At her first meeting, she preferred to announce: "I am Jane, and I am a basket case."

The therapist needs to find a balance between encouraging the patient to take some action and exploring the issues that serve as obstacles. It is useful to ask patients to describe their picture of what goes on in meetings and what they would find difficult. This usually reveals stereotypes about alcoholics and addicts that can be addressed by the therapist, partly by supplying information (e.g., the skid row bum is only a small percentage of alcoholics) and partly by exploring the issues. Gentle encouragement toward some kind of action (getting information about meetings, asking a friend who is familiar with meetings to go, actually attending a meeting) is important, and negative feelings need not be a deterrent to some form of action. "Bring the body, the mind will follow," "It's OK to do the right thing for the wrong reason," and "Take what you need and leave the rest" are useful AA maxims to present to patients who believe thay have to resolve their ambivalence before they can benefit. Those who do share their reservations about involvement often find that regular participants readily understand their issues and offer support.

Patients often wonder whether they should go to AA, Narcotics Anonymous (NA), Cocaine Anonymous (CA), or some other variant of a 12-Step meeting. It is usually more important to pick a place to start and begin with meetings of a similar socioeconomic group in the neighborhood of home or work. However, for many, there may be distinct advantages in starting with a group organized around drug of choice (e.g., CA for cocaine users). Engaging the patient in the treatment and recovery tasks is the main goal in the beginning, and patients often report being able to identify more readily with other stimulant users because they are more likely to hear "their story." It is also quite common for patient preference to evolve quickly. For example, many find the CA meetings "too wired" and feel more stability and a calmer atmosphere in the AA meetings. Although alcohol is the theme of AA meetings, it is difficult to find pure alcoholics under the age of 50 because polydrug use patterns are so widespread, and in many locales, most participants identify themselves as addicts and alcoholics. Inasmuch as AA is the oldest of the groups, it is usual to find a greater percentage of people with long-term sobriety to serve as role models. NA and CA meetings in some settings can be magnets for drug dealers, and patients in early recovery should be encouraged to find other meetings if this appears to be the case, and it is practical to do so. In general, patients should be encouraged to follow their attractions in selecting an AA or other kind of 12-Step meeting. They should "shop" until selecting a "home" meeting, one in which to become regularly involved. This can include speaking frequently, in small "shares" of extended personal or step presentations and taking responsibilities such as setting up refreshments, bringing cake, making coffee, cleaning up, acting as treasurer, and so on. It also includes using the meeting as a springboard for developing relationships outside the meetings, increasing support and understanding of recovery tasks, and building a social support system that facilitates a satisfying abstinent life-style. Confining participation solely to attending meetings may indicate a tendency to compartmentalize the addiction problem and resist the far-reaching developments that occur once abstinence is achieved.

COMMON RESISTANCES AND PROBLEMS

Resistance to stating, "I am an alcoholic/addict," as described in the case of Peter, is a common obstacle to going to meetings. The therapist should avoid the pitfall of trying to persuade the patient to accept this term as a justification for recommending total abstinence or as a basis for attending meetings. These labels are highly stigmatized, and many are only able to integrate them over a long period. An "experiment with abstinence" can be undertaken on pragmatic grounds, to allow the patient to explore the role of intoxicants in his/her life (Zweben, 1989). The patient can also be encouraged to attend meetings as part of the process of finding out about addiction and be asked to listen particularly carefully to accounts of the beginning stages of recognition that alcohol or drugs were a problem. Another useful strategy is to ask whether the patient is willing to do something seemingly unrelated to the presenting problem in order to get better. This provides a place to begin without pressure to settle the question of the severity of the alcohol and drug problem.

Attitudes and feelings toward groups are a prominent facet of early resistance. The term *fellowship,* which so aptly describes the spirit of cohesion and vitality pervading many meetings, can be a source of discomfort to newcomers, particularly if the issue of being an outsider is especially loaded. Many deliberately select their first meeting site partly to assure they will not be recognized by anyone they know, and this can heighten the stranger anxiety that fuels resistance. Therapist encouragement that discomfort passes with each exposure can be crucial in getting beyond these feelings, which are often surprisingly easy to pass beyond. Many meetings offer a warm welcome to strangers, although occasionally an abrasive experience may occur. It is useful for the patient to arrange to attend a meeting with someone else, as this reduces anxiety about a room full of strangers. Some addiction specialists have a pool of people (including current and former patients) willing to take newcomers to meetings, and they feel that the benefits of this intervention outweigh the risks.

Fear of being engulfed by the group is another issue that arouses resistance, and often takes the form of protesting, "I don't want to lose my identity." This may reflect the addict/alcoholic's desire to be exempt from the rules that govern others or insistence that he/she is different (less badly off, less crazy, etc.) from those who speak in meetings. As someone in later stages of recovery described it, "When I first went to AA, I was a star. Over time, I learned to join the chorus." Reassurance that AA is fundamentally accepting of people's needs to choose their relationship to it, despite the peer pressure generated by the enthusiasm of many members, can be important at this time. "Take what you need and leave the rest" is another AA tenet that supports patients' finding a way to relate to 12-Step programs that fits for a particular point in time.

Providing a place for patients to talk regularly about what they are experiencing in meetings is another way for the therapist to facilitate participation. Although many speakers describe their initial ambivalence about 12-Step programs, it is less common to hear those who are currently ambivalent speak up in meetings. The therapist can provide an outlet for ambivalence, as many react to the enthusiastic endorsement of the old timers and feel guilty about their own mixed feelings. Some conclude that 12-Step programs cannot work for them because of their negative feelings, so the therapist's permission to explore ambivalence and reassurance that participation can nonetheless yield benefits can be important in fostering engagement.

For patients for whom prescribing the resistance may be effective, Gorski (1991) offers the following guaranteed method for having a terrible experience:

> If your first meeting is bad, you have a perfect excuse never to go back. Here are the steps you take:
>
> First, find a meeting that is many miles from your home. Why? If you go to a meeting close to home, someone may know you and you don't want any friends or neighbors to know you're an alcoholic.
>
> Second, leave late for the meeting. Figure out how long it will take to get there and substract four minutes. Rationalize by saying that if you arrive too early, you are going to be hanging around for five or ten minutes with nothing to do. This forces you to drive fast and become anxious.
>
> Third, don't find out the exact location of the meeing; just know it's in the church between 152nd and 153rd streets. When you get there, you'll figure out which of the three churches on the block has the meeting. Don't find out the exact room, either. Discover that there are seven meetings going on at the same time. Open each door and ask, "Is this the Twelve Step meeting?" Above all, don't call the central office of the Twelve Step group you want to attend. If you do, someone might offer to take you to the meeting so you won't get lost or be embarrassed.
>
> Fourth, when you finally find the right meeting, be sure to try to sneak in quietly. If the door hinges squeak loudly as you open the door, smile warmly as everyone turns around and looks at you. Now you have a perfect excuse to sit in the corner feeling embarrassed.
>
> Fifth, as you listen to the people talk, don't just listen—judge. That's very important. Judge others. When you arrive, look over each person in the room and try to guess what psychiatric problem of social deviancy brought him or here here. Pick out the schizophrenics, the child molesters, the criminals and the rapists. Then "compare out." Say to yourself, Hey, I'm not like any of these people. I don't belong here, I don't fit in. Become very critical. If you agree with something, ignore it. If you disagree with it, remember it so you can tell your therapist about it.

Sixth, isolate yourself. You already arrived late and sat in the corner. During the break, don't talk to anybody, don't introduce yourself to anyone. Don't comment at the meeting and then leave about two minutes before the meeting is over. Then, on your way home, sit in the car and tell yourself, What an unfriendly bunch of people they were! Convince yourself you didn't really care. (pp. 26–27)

Gorski's comments often elicit sheepish smiles by those who have "tried meetings and didn't like them."

Gitlow (1985) offers straightforward, practical recommendations for fostering engagement:

1. Attend at least a meeting each day until one or, better, two groups seem to offer more to you than do the others.
2. Thereafter, never fail to attend these particular meetings.
3. Always arrive before everyone else (and with such consistency that your absence would be noteworthy).
4. Always sit in the first row.
5. Introduce yourself to the people seated about you should there be any with whom you are not acquainted.
6. Always raise your hand to enter a discussion, no matter how minor your comment.
7. Ask the chairperson to assign a task to you, whether passing the basket, picking up the chairs, or pouring the coffee. Volunteer to qualify as soon as you pass 90 days.
8. Never leave a meeting without sharing a beverage and some discussion with another attendee.
9. Be the last to leave the meeting and always request someone's company (for a "bite to eat," coffee, and one-on-one dialogue).
10. Whether or not you designate someone as your formal sponsor, choose a successfully abstinent member of the group who attends regularly and meet that person "socially" between meetings.

Gitlow's recommendations stress the need for active participation (except in cases where this is too threatening) and using the meetings to expand the social network supporting recovery. Clinicians have noted that finding another newcomer buddy is often a predictor of successful engagement. Patients should be encouraged to keep checking out meetings until they identify a "home" meeting, one in which they feel they can fit in and benefit from regular attendance. Even if they reduce 12-Step meeting attendance in later stages of recovery, it is important that patients maintain enough of a connection with their home meeting that it can readily serve as a support and reinforcer of coping strategies that work. This connection also helps patients weather upheavals such as loss of job or intimate relationship, major illness, death, or great success.

A key element in successful engagement and fruitful participation is the sponsor (Alcoholics Anonymous, 1983). A sponsor is an experienced, recovering member who acts as an adviser, guide, or teacher on how to work a program of recovery. AA encourages participants to find a sponsor quickly and to choose a person with whom they can feel comfortable and talk freely. Although there are no formal or written rules for sponsorship, newcomers are encouraged to select someone who has a year or more of sobriety and who appears to be *enjoying* sobriety. It should also be someone who is not an object of sexual or other interest that might distract from the primary purpose. Sponsors can be temporary or enduring; members are encouraged to change or add sponsors if they identify someone else whom they believe will be helpful. There is also a wide range of ways in which the role is carried out, from making suggestions to actual instructions on decisions. Because the emotional attachment may be intense, and the triadic relationship inherently difficult, sponsors sometimes provide a difficult clinical challenge to therapists. Brown (1985) notes that it is important for therapists to appreciate the patient's need to maintain a behavioral focus in early recovery; resistance to insight-oriented work may be highly adaptive at that point. Statements and attitudes that appear to run counter to therapeutic norms may engender conflict between 12-Step participation and treatment, and these may manifest as a division between the sponsor and the therapist. It is crucial that the therapist have a good understanding of stages of recovery and also of the range of healthy sponsor relationships in order to assess how best to further the patient's well-being. Many times, a sponsor's sound suggestions about how to achieve a good sobriety seem contrary to the therapist's values. There are also sponsor relationships that are pathological by any standards, and the patient needs assistance in extricating from them.

Professionals often express concerns about low long and how frequently patients need to attend meetings, and some wonder at what point meetings themselves become an "addiction." The guiding principle is the presence of adverse consequences. For many, the social elements of meetings are very important, and meetings serve as a catalyst for rewarding experiences. The therapist needs to help the patient explore the balance of benefits and detrimental factors, keeping in mind that premature disengagement is more common. For example, for those in the first year of recovery, diminished attendance at meetings may reflect a desire to regard the substance abuse as "the problem I used to have" or may signal an impending relapse. It is often useful to examine how the patient decided to disengage: Was the decision planned, impulsive, or not even conscious? Patients can then be asked how they expect to replace the recovery resources available in 12-Step programs. Once freed of addictive pursuits, a patient may become involved in various sports or recreational activities that are incompatible with drug use and hence may rely less on meetings as a recovery support. In such cases, it is important that some vehicle for psychological development also be maintained. Thus, the issue is not to struggle over meeting attendance but to define the patient's current recovery tasks and how they will be met. For many 12-Step program members, the relationships they develop become like an extended family, an integral core of their new support system.

Patients in later stages of recovery often disconnect completely from meetings, having absorbed an "all-or-none" attitude toward meeting participation. This is fostered by the presence of many members who attend frequently and regularly. Patients may conclude they have to adopt this pattern in order to benefit, whereas minimal attendance designed to maintain connection and familiarity may stand the person in good stead when a life crisis occurs. The therapist can again encourage the "take what you need and leave the rest" posture, which advocates maintaining affiliation at a level that is comfortable instead of completely dropping out.

RESISTANCE TO THE SPIRITUAL DIMENSION

Discomfort with the spiritual emphasis is a common objection to becoming involved in 12-Step programs. It is often useful to begin with understanding how the patient understands the spiritual focus. Many do not appreciate that it is not necessary to accept the Christian framework; although the movement originated in part with Christian fundamentalist groups and many meetings take place in churches, the founders and AA literature are quite explicit that the program is nondenominational and participants need to identify their own Higher Power, however they understand it. In addition, many communities offer humanist and atheist meetings and locate meetings in synagogues, hospitals, mental health facilities, community centers, and a wide range of other places. Treatment programs can compile lists of meetings that are congenial to persons concerned about this issue. Once misconceptions are addressed, the therapist can move on to other areas of exploration.

Attitudes toward spirituality can reflect many other issues, and exploration can proceed as with any other clinical themes. One area to investigate is the nature of the patient's negative experiences with institutionalized religion, particularly those occurring in childhood, and how to distinguish these from the inner experience of a spiritual connection. It is also common for patients to project harsh superego forces and authority conflicts onto their concept of God or Higher Power:

Jan, who grew up with a father who was verbally and physically abusive, was struggling with the prospect of attending Overeaters Anonymous, complaining bitterly about "all that God stuff." She dismissed repeated suggestions from group members that she set aside such considerations for later ("take what you need and leave the rest") or that she take advantage of the many alternatives available in her community. One day she declared exuberantly: "I did it! I finally figured it out. God is *not* my father. God is God and my father is my father." From then on, she began to attend OA and use the process in a productive manner.

Further exploration may also reveal a level of resistance based on self-esteem issues. "I don't deserve it" or "it's too good for me" frequently emerges as a source of resistance to an inner or outer spiritual force. These patients may also have problems accepting affection and positive regard for others or taking pleasure in their accomplishments. Gestalt techniques visualizations, or meditation can also be used to develop a compassionate internal witness and to transform harsh internal judges into more positive inner voices (Krystal & Zweben, 1988). Thus, exploring issues around spirituality can provide a catalyst for developing beneficent internal forces.

SPECIAL ISSUES FOR DUAL DIAGNOSIS PATIENTS

Special preparation may be needed for patients who have coexisting disorders, particularly if they are on medication. Despite a long-standing and clear-cut AA position that medication is quite compatible with recovery (Alcoholics Anonymous, 1984), it is still quite common to encounter negative attitudes about medications on the part of other meeting participants. This is particularly difficult for patients who are currently feeling quite vulnerable. It may be useful to describe to the patient the context in which these attitudes developed. Professionals generated mistrust by previous failures to respond appropriately to a wide range of addiction issues, and in the case of physicians, to select medication without considering the special needs of those in a high-risk group, that is, a personal or family history of addiction. Many 12-Step program participants describe experiences that clearly reflect misguided professional interventions. However, many others speak enthusiastically about their experiences with psychotherapy and some speak openly about benefiting from medication. In addition, individual meetings establish their own "culture," with some being more comfortable for those with coexisting disorders. Thus, the patient can be encouraged or assisted in finding meetings more hospitable to patients on medication. Highly disturbed patients can be taken to meetings or directed to meetings more tolerant of eccentric behavior. Hospital-based meetings are generally more accepting of patients on medication; this can be verified by contacting the hospital in which the meeting is located. Professionals who work extensively with the dual-diagnosis population need to be able to make informed referrals to specific meetings. It should not be left to the patient to do this research alone.

Simulated 12-Step meetings on the treatment site can familiarize the patient with group norms for behavior as well as 12-Step program philosophy and content; exposure to the rationale for the rituals and traditions can facilitate greater utilization of these programs. In these simulated meetings, a facilitator provides explanations and offers opportunity for discussion. Zweben (1991) describes one such successful endeavor with methadone patients. Such an activity may be useful for mental health facilities or hospital-based psychiatric programs as a way of introducing the patient to the concepts. More disturbed patients can be given explicit instructions about how to behave or not behave (Evans & Sullivan, 1990a), as they may have more difficulty recognizing and adapting to social norms. There are also workbooks available offering modified stepwork for dual-diagnosis patients (Evans & Sullivan, 1990b).

It is important to provide continuing support to patients whose deviance is especially uncomfortable, as they are often able to benefit greatly from the contact and the structure available in meetings. Therapists should remain attentive to the possibility that those with severe disorders may become discouraged by seeing others improve more rapidly than they do and may need to be reminded of the dangers of such comparisons.

SPECIAL NEEDS
OF DISEMPOWERED GROUPS

Many people object to 12-Step programs because they feel the philosophy ignores important parts of their culture and personal experiences, especially when those revolve around a painful history of being powerless and anonymous. They often object that more of such experiences are unlikely to bring healing and struggle with the emphasis on surrender in the early steps. The therapist can reframe the issue, emphasizing how the patient *gains* control over his/her life by abandoning efforts to engage in controlled drug use (i.e., admitting powerlessness over drugs.) Eating disorders are an example of how controlling behaviors over food mask an intense, desperate sense of helplessness, and hence an emphasis on giving up control may exacerbate resistance. Sensitivity to this issue suggests that the therapist does better to focus on the empowering consequences of giving up alcohol and drugs rather than on admitting powerlessness, as the patient in early recovery may be unable to appreciate the merits of the paradox.

RECENT VARIATIONS AND OTHER SELF-HELP GROUPS

Cultural adaptations of 12-Step programs are likely to become increasingly common, as various communities add their own variations. In San Francisco, Rev. Cecil Williams, of Glide Memorial Methodist Church, has adapted the strengths of 12-Step programs in a manner that regularly draws crowds from a multitude of different groups. He looked at the roots of recovery and developed an approach in keeping with African American cultural values. He saw recovery as both a "miracle of healing" and a "movement for social change for our people." He saw African Americans as a communal people, needing recognition, a voice, an acknowledged heritage, and to take responsibility within a spiritually extended family dedicated to recognition, self-definition, and rebirth in recovery and community (Williams, 1992; Smith, Buxton, Bilal, & Seymour, 1993).

Acting on these insights, Reverend Williams offered "Terms of Resistance," repeated at recovery meetings:

Terms of Resistance
1. I will gain control over my life.
2. I will stop lying.
3. I will be honest with myself.
4. I will accept who I am.
5. I will feel my real feelings.
6. I will feel my pain.
7. I will forgive myself and forgive others.
8. I will rebirth a new life.
9. I will live my spirituality.
10. I will support my brothers and sisters.

The magnetic power of Glide meetings to attract diverse groups suggests that they are responding in a meaningful way to a deeply felt cultural need. Indeed, self-help programs appear to be filling a need for community that was once met by other social institutions, such as the church and extended family. In a highly mobile society, the possibility of attending meetings in another city, state, or country and still finding some familiar rituals is comforting and stabilizing.

Many other adaptations are becoming evident, as various individuals and groups express their own distinctiveness through this medium. Olitzky and Copans (1991) demonstrate how the 12 Steps are not only compatible with Jewish tradition but can all be found within the Torah and Talmud. Philip Z. (1990), a compulsive overeater and confirmed skeptic, describes his own coming to terms with addiction and spirituality. Rational Recovery and Secular Organization for Sobriety offer a secular model based on cognitive-behavioral principles. The latter attracts persons who desire alternatives to the spiritual emphasis of 12-Step programs.

PREPARING THERAPISTS TO MAKE EFFECTIVE
12-STEP PROGRAM REFERRALS

Therapists become far more effective in facilitating the use of 12-Step programs when they are familar with meetings in their community. Program literature is available at low cost from the various offices (usually listed in the telephone book), and many other books and workbooks can be found in local bookstores. In addition, "field trips" are invaluable as a way of developing an understanding of what actually goes on in meetings. I offer the following assignment to students and new staff members:

Understanding 12-Step Programs

A good understanding of 12-Step programs (the generic term for all the descendants of Alcoholics Anonymous) is crucial for anyone working in the addiction field. These programs offer a wealth of resources at every stage of the recovery process, with no financial barriers. One of the most important jobs of the therapist or counselor is to help the client make a good connection with these programs, and learn to use them effectively. This is a complex task.

To increase your effectiveness, it is important that you have some familiarity with the meetings in your community. Please look up the telephone number of the central office in your telephone book (you can start with Alcoholics Anonymous) and select a meeting in your area. It can be an AA meeting, or Al-Anon, Narcotics Anonymous, Cocaine Anonymous or anything else you prefer. Be sure it is an open meeting (i.e., people who do not consider themselves addicts or alcoholics can attend). You can also ask for a nonsmoking meeting. If you are not recovering, you can introduce yourself by first name only, or you can give your name and identify yourself as a guest, therapist, or counselor.

Within 24 hours of your visit, please make some notes (journal style) on the following issues:

1. What you felt in anticipation of going; avoidances, resistances, etc.
2. What you felt on arriving, throughout the meeting, and afterwards.
3. Your observations on the group process (both the standard rituals, like introductions and the informal aspects), its advantages and limitations.

Please distinguish between your feelings, observations, and analyses and include all three.

The number of meetings assigned is determined by the length of the course. For staff, with a more open time frame, it is recommended that they go to 6 to 12 meetings of different types. Those in recovery or who have attended some meetings are encouraged to broaden their perspective by going to meetings outside their previous focus. It is important to provide a forum for discussion, as attendance at meetings generates many feelings and often clarifies attitudes about addiction.

CONCLUSION

In summary, 12-Step programs offer a valuable resource, widely available (often 24 hours a day), with minimal financial barriers. Participation often greatly enhances the patient's ability to address shifting needs throughout the recovery process. The issue is itself a remarkable mirror and powerful catalyst to revealing and exploring resistance, and so therapists are encouraged to maintain a focus on both the patient's feelings and behavior. As these programs usually are a natural resource with no financial barriers, therapists are encouraged to acquire firsthand experiences of what occurs in them.

ACKNOWLEDGMENT

Thanks to Pat Shields, L.C.S.W., for her feedback on this chapter and her many insights over time which are incorporated into the text.

REFERENCES

Alcoholics Anonymous. (1983). *Questions and answers on sponsorship.* New York: Alcoholics Anonymous World Services.

Alcoholics Anonymous. (1984). *The AA member—Medications and other drugs. Report from a group of physicians in AA.* New York: Alcoholics Anonymous World Services.

Alcoholics Anonymous World Survey. (1990). *Analysis of the 1989 survey of the membership of AA.* New York: Author.

Brown, S. (1985). *Treating the alcoholic: A developmental model of recovery.* New York: Wiley,

Carnes, P. (1989). *A gentle path through the Twelve Steps.* Minnesota: CompCare.

Evans, K., & Sullivan, J. M. (1990a). *Dual diagnosis: Counseling the mentally ill substance abuser.* New York: Guilford Press.

Evans, K., & Sullivan, J. M. (1990b). *Step study counseling with the dual disordered client.* Center City, MN: Hazelden.

Gitlow, S. (1985). Considerations on the evaluation and treatment of substance dependency. *Journal of Substance Abuse Treatment, 2,* 175–179.

Gorski, T. (1991). *Understanding the Twelve Steps.* New York: Prentice Hall.

Krystal, S., & Zweben, J. E. (1988). The use of visualization as a means of integrating the spiritual dimension into treatment. *Journal of Substance Abuse Treatment, 5*(4), 201–206.

Olitzky, K. M., & Copans, S. A. (1991). *Twelve Jewish steps to recovery.* Woodstock, VT: Jewish Lights.

Prochascka, J. O., DiClemente, C. C., & Norcross, J. C. (1992). In search of how people change: Applications to addictive behaviors. *American Psychologist, 47*(9), 1102–1114.

Recovering. (1993, October). *58,* 14.

Room, R., & Greenfield, T. (1993). Alcoholics anonymous, other 12-step movements and psychotherapy in the US population, 1990. *Addiction, 88,* 555–562.

Smith, D. E., Buxton, M. E., Bilal, R., & Seymour, R. A. (1993). Cultural points of resistance to the 12-Step recovery process. *Journal of Psychoactive Drugs, 25*(1), 97–108.

Williams, C. (1992). *No hiding place: Empowerment and recovery for our troubled communities.* San Francisco: HarperCollins.

Phillip, Z. (1990). *A skeptic's guide to the 12 steps.* Center City, MN: Hazelden.

Zweben, J. E., (1986). Recovery oriented psychotherapy. *Journal of Substance Abuse Treatment, 3*(4), 255–262.

Zweben, J. E. (1987). Recovery oriented psychotherapy: Facilitating the use of 12 step programs. *Journal of Psychoactive Drugs, 19*(3), 243–251.

Zweben, J. E. (1989). Recovery oriented psychotherapy: Patient resistances and therapist dilemmas. *Journal of Substance Abuse Treatment, 6*(2), 123–132.

Zweben, J. E. (1991). Counseling issues in methadone maintenance treatment. *Journal of Psychoactive Drugs, 23*(2), 177–190.

Zweben, J. E. (1993). Recovery oriented psychotherapy: A model for addiction treatment. *Psychotherapy, 30*(2), 259–268.

7

Rational-Emotive Behavior Therapy and Two Self-Help Alternatives to the 12-Step Model

F. MICHLER BISHOP

INTRODUCTION

For the past 60 years, Alcoholics Anonymous (AA) and its spinoffs Narcotics Anonymous (NA) and Cocaine Anonymous (CA) have played a valuable role in helping people control their problems with alcohol and other mood-altering chemicals. As a self-help organization, AA is available in a way psychiatrists, psychologists, and other helping professionals are not. Although AA may not be quite as successful as some people believe (Emrick, 1994), it is not difficult to find members who assert that AA kept them from destroying their lives. However, many other recovering people find aspects of the AA program difficult, if not impossible, to accept. People who have never attended an AA meeting or who are not familiar with the program are often unaware of the degree to which a particular conceptualization of the relationship between God and humans is an integral part of the 12 steps (Alcoholics Anonymous, 1980). The third step, for example, states: "We made a decision to turn our will and our lives over to the care of God as we understand him," and the sixth step asserts: "We were entirely ready to have God remove all these defects of character."

AA urges participants to interpret the word *God* in any way that is helpful to them; for example, one may think of god as standing for "good orderly direction." But this approach sidesteps two significant problems. Many nonreligious people feel that suggesting that god "can mean anything you want it to" is just a device, albeit well-intentioned, to get them into the program. But, in addition, avowedly religious and spiritual people may also experience difficulties with the particular form of religious belief suggested by the AA credo. They may believe in God but not in giving over their will to God. Rather, it is for them to solve their addiction problems; God may help, but they must use their own resources.

The point of this chapter is not to attack AA, which has without question been a lifesaver for many thousands of people. Nor, in my opinion, is there any value in pitting one organization against another, especially as research clearly indicates that outcomes are better when alternative treatment modes are available (Miller, 1989). Many people are looking for help, and each organization offers a significantly different philosophical approach to recovery that is correct for some but not for others.

Originally, as a clinical psychologist in New York, I had no alternative but to urge my addicted clients to become active in 12-Step programs all having the same philosophical and spiritual bases as AA (e.g., NA, Overeaters Anonymous, Debtors Anonymous, Gamblers Anonymous, Sexual Compulsives Anonymous, etc.). However, there are a number of alternatives available now including Rational Recovery (RR^{SM}), SMART Recovery (Self-Management and Recovery Training), SOS (Secular Organization for Sobriety), and Women for Sobriety (cf. Gelman, 1991). This chapter focuses on RR and SMART Recovery and the therapeutic modality from which they were largely derived, rational-emotive behavior therapy (REBT).

Rational Recovery^{SM} was started in 1986 by Jack Trimpey, a clinical social worker in California who asserted that he had overcome his problems with alcohol by using the techniques of REBT developed over the past 35 years by Albert Ellis (1962).

In 1985, Trimpey authored *The Small Book,* an obvious play on the title of the famous AA (1980) source book, *The Big Book.* Although some of the chapters are devoted to what has been characterized as polemical AA bashing, there are many others that forcefully and convincingly challenge some of the basic AA tenets.

Because each RR group was to have a professional adviser, preferably trained in REBT, Trimpey asked professional mental health workers to become involved. A lay coordinator was to run the meetings, but the professional adviser was to attend meetings on occassion and to be available if problems arose. As RR was in the beginning years based on REBT, a cognitive-behavioral approach, a large number of psychologists became involved and started to help set up meetings in their communities.

In 1990, Trimpey set up Rational Recovery Systems, Inc. (RRS), a privately owned corporation to license professionals and hospitals to offer RR training and services. For many people involved in RR at the time, RRS presented a problem as they were uncomfortable about organizing a network of lay-led, self-help groups that was closely linked with a for-profit organization. As a result, in September 1993, RRSN (Rational Recovery Self-Help Network) was set up as a separate nonprofit entity with its own bylaws. Officers were elected, mainly psychologists from diverse regions of the United States.

During 1993 and 1994, Trimpey developed his Addictive Voice Recognition Training (AVRT^SM) and began to move away from REBT as his theoretical base, presenting his "structural model" of addictions, which argues that addictions are the result of urges emanating from the mid-brain. Most recently (1994a, 1994b), he not only split with REBT as the choice of treatment, but also asserts that "treatment is dead" and "in AVRT^SM, there are no steps, sponsors, Higher Powers, psychological theories, enablers, triggers, warning signs of relapse, or religious teachings" (1994b, p. 2). According to Trimpey (1994a, 1994b), the "sole cause of addiction is the Addictive Voice," which he describes as "a subcortically-driven mentality that enlists all neocortical resources in its quest for endless intoxication" (1994b, p. 3). He also now believes that only a previously addicted person can effectively treat an addicted person.

Consequently, many of the psychologists who had been active in developing RR groups created a new organization, SMART Recovery, based primarily on REBT and other cognitive-behavioral therapeutic (CBT) techniques. And because many RR members remain enthusiastic about REBT, some meetings have changed while others have continued to operate using a mixture of AVRT and REBT/CBT techniques; in addition, some have been licensed by Trimpey to provide AVRT.

Defining Characteristics

As noted, SMART Recovery, as well as some RR groups, utilize principles and techniques drawn from REBT. Ideally consisting of 12 people, groups meet once or twice a week to help participants overcome addictive behaviors by gaining better control over their thinking, behaviors, and emotions and by developing more effective relapse preventive social skills.

Despite variations from one group to the next, meetings reflect a number of basic tenets:

1. People are largely responsible for their behaviors, including addictive behaviors.
2. A person can recover; that is, a person can gain control over his/her addictive behaviors.
3. Lifetime membership is not required; many people can recover in a year or two.
4. Labeling of all kinds is discouraged; a person does not have to call him/herself an alcoholic to begin to recover.

5. Alcoholism may or may not be a disease; however, a person has to find a way to cope and take responsibility for his/her life in any case.
6. The value of a person is not linked to his/her behavior, addictive or otherwise. A person will not be a better person if he/she gives up alcohol or some other addictive behavior; he/she may be a happier person, a person who has better relationships and can keep a job, but behavioral change does not affect the "goodness" of the self.
7. A person is not necessarily, ipso facto, "in denial" if he/she does not accept the basic AA tenets.
8. A person is not doomed to a life of alcoholism if he/she does not accept help from AA, a rehabilitation clinic, a hospital, and so on. People can recover on their own with or without the help of professionals and/or self-help groups.

As is evident, many of these principles take issue with basic AA teachings. AA members who believe that the organization has saved them and who see other people destroying their lives by continuously denying their dependency often regard SMART's and RR's messages as dangerously harmful to addicted people. Thus, on occasion they vehemently oppose this new development in self-help groups.

But to many addicted people who have had difficulty with the AA program, these ideas are like a breath of fresh air. Several of my private clients, having read *The Small Book* (Trimpey, 1992), have told me: "I've finally found someone who is telling me that I'm not crazy. I don't have to think their [AA's] way." They are relieved to find a different approach available to them, one explicitly arguing for the development of greater *self*-control rather than dependency on an external God for help.

This alternative message has proven to be a compelling force. More than 500 groups have been set up by recovering people in the United States and in Australia over the past few years. This development was no doubt aided by widespread media attention following a front-page *New York Times* article about RR (Hall, 1990).

In addition, there is growing research evidence indicating that cognitive-behavioral techniques can work with addictive behaviors (cf. Heather, Miller, & Greeley, 1991; Miller, 1989; Miller, Benefield & Tonigan, 1993; Monti, 1990; Oei, Lim, & Young, 1991). Thus, an increasing number of psychiatrists, psychologists, and social workers are integrating cognitive-behavioral techniques into their practice.

Nevertheless, it is clear from attendance figures that these new groups are not for everyone. Of every 100 people who inquire, about 50 attend if an organizational meeting is held. Of these, 20 may return, but often fewer. And during the initial period, many people attend but do not remain. For example, some may come to a meeting out of curiosity but do not return because they prefer AA's approach. Or they may find RR or SMART as unsatisfactory to them as AA. Undoubtedly, some attend hoping to find a way to continue drinking, despite the fact that both organizations are abstinence programs. Such dropping in and out is often discouraging to coordinators and professionals attempting to facilitate the formation of a new group in their community. It also makes building a close-knit, effective group difficult. However, the dropout rate at this point may be high because the organizations are still developing, and there are few coordinators with significant experience and few "old hands" to inspire and motivate newcomers. Eventually, however, a core of approximately 8 to 12 interested, motivated people usually develops and the group begins to function effectively.

Most groups are established by a recovering person who acts as the coordinator, although in some localities, professionals have organized meetings. The coordinator is primarily responsible for practical matters, for example, opening and closing the room and collecting the money if rent has to be paid. Many coordinators also run the meetings, but this is not always the case; sometimes the role of facilitator or leader for the meeting is shared among the members. Each SMART Recovery group also has a professional adviser, preferably one trained in cognitive-behavioral techniques. The adviser may attend meetings occasionally to help the participants learn new REBT or related cognitive-behavioral therapy methods. He/she is also available for expert advice regarding hospitalization or other professional referrals and may be called by the coordinator in the event that a group member appears to be in crisis.

To date, most meetings do not currently follow a set pattern, but many groups have elected to spend approximately 10 minutes per member. "Drunkalogs" are discouraged as groups encourage members to focus on current problems or on the specific thinking, feelings, and behaviors that precede lapses. No doubt the testimonials typical of many AA meetings can be effective in increasing hope and resolve, but many members often report finding them repetitive and, more importantly, ineffective. Stories of other people's struggles, while inspiring, often fail to provide usable suggestions.

In contrast to most AA meetings, "cross-talk" is encouraged. That is, members are expected to help each other identify the irrational beliefs and distorted cognitions that members use to convince themselves to engage in addictive behaviors and/or to recognize the role of the addictive voice. In SMART Recovery, role playing and other typical group therapeutic techniques to enhance social skills development may also be employed.

Believing that people may become dysfunctionally dependent on 12-Step groups, Trimpey (1992) stresses that RR promotes self-*help*, not self-*support*. In fact, in *The Small Book,* he asserts that after 1 year or so in an RR group, one can safely move on to join other social, nonrecovery groups without fear of relapse (Trimpey, 1992). Of course, this short-term feature of RR is a powerful attraction for some and dramatically distinguishes it from AA.

As it turns out, however, many people need more than 1 year to integrate REBT principles into their lives and to practice new, relapse-preventive social skills. Hence, although they may have joined a new self-help group partly because they liked the thought of only having to work for 1 year to resolve their problem, many remain longer in recognition that they need more time. This is not surprising, because many people stay in group therapy for several years even when their original hope was for short-term treatment. And although none of the new groups establish formal sponsor–member relationships, participants frequently take each other's telephone numbers, call when someone misses a meeting, and support each other during difficult times.

As lay-run, self-help organizations, the new groups invite replication by recovering people who seek an alternative to AA and feel that a new approach can help them and others in their community. However, the need for training and support is evident. Following the model of Recovery, Inc., a self-help organization founded in 1937 by Abraham Low (1978) to provide no-fee, self-help meetings primarily for patients after a stay in a mental hospital, advisers in some cities hold once-a-month leadership meetings for current and prospective coordinators. Half-day workshops at relatively low cost are also provided by REBT-trained professionals for lay, recovering people who want to learn more about relevant self-help cognitive-behavioral techniques. In addition, longer 2- and 3-day workshops for both laypeople and interested professionals have been conducted in various locations nationwide.

A recent study by Galanter, Egelko, and Edwards (1993) provides an initial look at the impact of RR when it was based primarily on REBT and AVRT. Among members who had been attending for 3 months or more, 73% were abstinent; of those who had been attending for 6 months or more, 58% reported at least 6 months of abstinence. Similar data were found for those who had been heavy users of cocaine. Although 80% felt strongly that they should "maintain abstinence from alcohol permanently," a minority (23%) of the "engaged" members—those attending for more than 3 months—continued to drink. However, among the "recruits," defined as those attending for less than 1 month, 57% were still drinking, suggesting that continued attendance increases the proportion who opt for abstinence.

The Role of Rational-Emotive Behavior Therapy

The meeting procedures and techniques of both new groups have not been fully standardized or even agreed on. As a result, meeting content differs from place to place. In addition, coordinators reflect a wide range of personality and leadership styles. Consequently, some groups are more supportive, some more didactic, and yet others more confrontational, although the last approach seems to be the least effective. Nonetheless, as noted earlier, most Smart Recovery groups draw most of their techniques from REBT. Thus, Ellis's ABCDE model (Ellis, 1962; Ellis & Dryden, 1987; Ellis, McInerney, DiGiuseppe, & Yeager, 1988) either explicitly or implicitly becomes the backbone of many meetings. According to this paradigm:

"A" represents an "Activating Event" or "potential trigger" for addictive behavior (e.g., drinking). As Marlatt (1985), Annis (1982), and others have noted, this may be either an external activating event, often interpersonal (e.g., getting a gift of a bottle of Scotch from a business associate or being yelled at by one's boss), or an internal, intrapersonal event (e.g., feeling lonely and depressed in the evening or becoming exhilarated after a successful day at the office and wanting to enhance that feeling).

"B" stands for "Beliefs," which constitute a lens through which one interprets and evaluates all life events. Some of these may be helpful and are frequently referred to as rational beliefs or "RBs" by REBT therapists and clients; others are unhelpful and referred to as irrational beliefs or "IBs." Beliefs can be categorized as helpful or unhelpful by examining them in terms of one's goals and values. Abstinence is the focal goal of SMART Recovery and RR groups; in individual therapy, other goals, such as moderation, can be negotiated.

"C" represents the "Consequences" of what a person does, feels, and thinks as a result of the activating event. These thoughts, feelings, and behaviors often become new "A"s or potential triggers, initiating a subsequent ABC cycle.

"D" indicates "Disputing/Intervening." The point of REBT is to learn how to intervene, how to change the way one usually reacts to a trigger situation. This may involve disputing irrational beliefs and questioning cognitive distortions, but it often also involves behavioral interventions as well (e.g., relaxation training and social skills training).

"E" stands for "Effects," that is, the results of the intervening/disputing. The overall process goal of REBT is to promote new, and, it is hoped, more helpful, less self-defeating cognitions, behaviors, and emotions to produce the desired outcomes—in the case of SMART Recovery and RR, abstinence and effective relapse prevention.

Ellis (1991) suggested that people become addicted in two ways. For some, the addiction results primarily from pleasure seeking and low frustration tolerance. That is, initially people may begin to drink or use drugs to enjoy themselves with their peers, but then, when they try to moderate or quit, their low tolerance for discomfort and frustration is the primary contributing factor to their inability to do so.

The second group, however, drinks or uses drugs primarily to deal with general emotional disturbances, for example, unpleasant emotions such as depression and anxiety. Initially this solution may help, but when problems begin to surface and the person tries to quit, he/she experiences what Ellis (Ellis et al., 1988) has termed *discomfort anxiety,* that uncomfortable feeling that many people get when they deny themselves or are unable to do something they like. This discomfort anxiety then becomes a new "A," activating event/potential trigger.

Sooner or later, low frustration tolerance or discomfort anxiety is likely to become coupled with irrational beliefs which, in turn lead people to use the chemical again. Typical of self-talk arising from mediating IBs in such cases would be: "I can't stand it anymore." "It shouldn't be this hard." "One more time won't make a difference." "I can start tomorrow." "Other people party, so why can't I (as I must)."

For many, the ABC model is a powerful tool for analyzing and understanding what is occurring. It is not uncommon, for example, for group members to report that at the outset, they feel that the urge to drink or to walk into the delicatessen to buy some beer is automatic, almost robotic—and they have no way to explain from where that drive comes. However, through repeated use of the ABC model to examine more closely what has occurred or is occurring, this perceptual veil tends to lift.

Although there is considerable evidence that cognitions, emotions, and behaviors all interact, it is often helpful from a therapeutic standpoint to use a linear model which the ABC framework provides. No doubt, some professionals will find this paradigm simplistic. However, it offers many people an understandable tool to explore both the causes and dynamics of their own complex problems. Moreover, the ABC perspective also appears to increase a sense of self-efficacy because it provides an uncomplicated way to get a handle on otherwise hard to discern situations. What group members are doing or what they feel is happening to them may be the result of some intensive complex interaction of genetic, familial, environmental, biological, sociological, economic, political, and perhaps even spiritual factors. But they can often gain better control of their behaviors by simplifying the situation via the ABC model.

SMART Recovery meetings, in particular, may include specific guidance and mutual assistance in identifying the "A's" (i.e., to describe as succinctly as possible what was happening before a relapse), the "B's" (i.e., related irrational beliefs and cognitive distortions), and the "C's" (i.e., what they did and felt as a result of their interpretation of the events). Although the ABCs may not be explicitly referred to, the model gives direction to the questioning and also often helps people, once they have learned REBT, to conceptualize problematic situations for themselves.

For those who find the ABCs difficult at first, we use other exercise sheets which focus on the same issues but in a slightly more user-friendly

TABLE 7.1. REBT Relapse Review Form

1. What was the problem situation?
2. How were you *feeling* just before you decided to drink or drug?
3. What were you *thinking* to yourself just before drinking or drugging? (Look for hidden thoughts and beliefs.)
4. What did you *do*?
5. What *could* you have said to yourself that would have been more helpful?
6. What *could* you have done differently
7. What *could* you have pushed yourself to feel?
8. How do you feel now about what happened?
9. What are you telling yourself *now*?

___

manner. As shown in Table 7.1, if a person answers the questions, he/she will have in essence accomplished an ABC analysis. People may take a copy of this form home, fill it out, and bring it back to the next session. This helps the the group leader and members see what the person understands and what he/she does not.

In some RR and SMART Recovery groups, members refer to the BEAST, a combination of acronym and metaphor serving as a mnemonic:

B = *B*oozing opportunity, when you *think* of drinking.
E = *E*nemy recognition, when you *hear* the mental voice.
A = *A*ccuse the *thought* of drinking of being the *real* enemy.
S = *S*elf-control and self-worth are now yours for the taking.
T = *T*reasure your sobriety; a lot is at stake.

For group members who like the BEAST metaphor, it serves as a forceful but simple reminder that the urge to drink must be seen as a dangerous "enemy" which must be immediately and vigorously stopped. Considerable time may also be spent on Trimpey's AVRT. Members are encouraged to recognize that people are always ambivalent about what they want and do not want to do. Moreover, they are always thinking and talking to themselves about their various options and reasons for choosing one over the other. It is critical that members recognize that much of their thinking and inner self-talk constitutes an "addictive voice," and that while expressing the addictive side of their ambivalence, they unrelentingly, creatively and cleverly attempt to convince themselves to relapse. Members are encouraged to acknowledge that relapse does not just "happen" to them, and that they are not helpless before choosing to drink or use drugs.

RATIONAL-EMOTIVE BEHAVIOR THERAPY
AND THE STAGES OF SELF-CHANGE

Many groups and REBT therapists are finding it useful to use REBT within the context of Prochaska, DiClemente and Norcross's (1992) "stages of self-change" model. AA's 12 steps suggest by the word *steps* that there is a path that if followed will lead to recovery. The Prochaska et al. (1992) model suggests that there are six stages through which all self-changers pass:

> Stage One: Precontemplation. As the name suggests, you are not contemplating change in stage one. You either do not realize you have a problem (although others around you may claim you do) or you are too demoralized to admit it or to think about trying to change again.
>
> Stage Two: Contemplation. Stage two is primarily characterized by ambivalence. You are not sure whether you want to change or not, but you begin to contemplate changing.
>
> Stage Three: Preparation. Here you begin to prepare to change. You may read a book or inquire about a program to help you.
>
> Stage Four: Action. In stage four, you take some actions in a real attempt to change. Lapses and relapses often occur at this stage.
>
> Stage Five: Maintenance. Actions are not enough; you have to work at maintaining the change. Relapse prevention is the focus of stage five.
>
> Stage Six: Termination. The change has become an almost permanent part of your behavioral repertoire. You do not have to spend much attention or energy any longer to maintain the change.

Three aspects of this model are worth noting. First, most people recycle through various stages several times before achieving the level of change they desire. Second, this is a model of self-change, not specifically a model focused on changing addictive behaviors. And third, although members assert that (some) people can move on to stage six, others may think it wiser and safer to always consider themselves in stage five, the maintenance stage.

The model provides group members with a way of orienting themselves and a way of conceptualizing what they might expect ahead. At the same time, it gives therapists and coordinators a way of thinking about people and their problems. In addition, we are now working to explore whether there may not be specific irrational beliefs and/or cognitive distortions that impede people from moving forward from one stage to the next. For example, people in stage two, contemplation, may be telling themselves: "If I tried and failed, I'd feel even worse. I'd be a real jerk and I'd probably start to drink even more.'' Or people in the action stage may contribute to a relapse by thinking to themselves: ''It shouldn't be this hard. This is *too* hard.''

Prochaska et al. (1992) have suggested that cognitive-behavioral approaches may be most appropriate or forceful during the action stage. However, REBT may be effective at each stage because of the large number and variety of techniques most good therapists employ. Despite the fact that many people with only a brief exposure to REBT think that disputing *is* REBT, good REBT therapists incorporate many more techniques into their sessions beside disputing. And formulating their approach in terms of the hypothesized stage the client or group member is in may help group leaders and individual therapists decide which techniques to use.

Many of the people attending group meetings appear to be in the action or maintenance stage, although some of the hundreds of people who show up for one or two meetings and then drop out may be in the contemplation or preparation stage. To date, no one has done any research on this question. Increasingly, people are being court ordered to meetings, and these participants are frequently in the precontemplative stage. Nevertheless, because REBT places such emphasis on accepting oneself even with one's problem and failures, these people may move toward self-change as opposed to change resulting from coercion by the justice system.

REVIEW AND REHEARSAL

As noted above, most of the people attending meetings of most self-help groups are probably in the action or maintenance stage of change. Hence, most groups focus on relapse prevention, with the emphasis on review and rehearsal. This approach clearly focuses attention on the immediate past week or so. In fact, in some groups, members are encouraged to consider only the past 2 weeks and the 2 weeks to come. Participants are told that serious problems in their distant past (such as abuse as a child) probably have to be taken up with a professional as the groups themselves are not prepared to deal with such issues.

REBT therapists and group coordinators ask people who have successfully dealt with a potential trigger situation to explain how they managed to remain sober. In this way, they not only review how they managed to intervene to be successful but also demonstrate to others in the group what is possible and how to do it; although less structured than AA's ''qualifying,'' it has the effect of a testimonial and may be very encouraging to new members.

Clients or group members who have lapsed are encouraged to carefully reflect on what happened. Using a five-step model frequently helps to clarify what happened and when; it also provides a way to explore what interventions and/or disputes might have prevented the slip and where they might best have been utilized.

> *Step 1: Potential trigger or activating event.* An activating event may be the result of an intra- or interpersonal event.
>
> *Step 2: Imagining/fantasizing what if. . . .* A person begins to imagine or fantasize, perhaps only for fleeting moments, what would happen *if* they had a drink or used a drug or engaged in some other kind of addictive behavior. They can sense the change that would occur and may go on to step 3.
>
> *Step 3: "Stinking thinking."* At this step, people engage in irrational thinking and/or cognitive distortions to convince themselves to move on to steps 4 and 5; for example, "I can't stand not having a cigarette." "It should not be this hard." "It won't really matter." "I can get away with it."
>
> *Step 4: Planning.* Planning is involved in almost every addictive episode, although for legal substances such as alcohol, cigarettes and food, it is not as involved as for heroin or crack.
>
> *Step 5: Action.* At this step, a person engages in the addictive behavior.

Especially after a relapse, clients are encouraged to "slow down the mental videotape" of these five steps and to "look at what happened, second by second" to (1) help them analyze and understand how they progressively slipped down the path to another addictive episode and (2) encourage them to take responsibility—without self-downing, guilt, or shame—for the role their cognitions, emotions, and behaviors played in the process at each step.

Then they are helped to see what they might have done at each step to stop their "slip," the purpose being to learn to intervene. They are encouraged to come up with alternative ways they could have thought about the situation and could have behaved. In a group setting, everyone in the group is encouraged to share his/her ideas. In addition, a member may volunteer to role-play the situation so as to give another member an opportunity to rehearse what he/she could say and do when confronted with the situation again in the future.

During one group session, a member, a jazz musician, reported that he had relapsed. He was new to the group and he reported that he was really surprised. He thought he had discovered the answer to his problem. But then, suddenly, late at night after a gig, he "just found himself" going into a delicatessen and buying two 40-ounce bottles of beer. The group leader and the group members began to probe, exploring what occurred from both the five-step framework and the ABC model. At first, the musician insisted that he had no idea what had happened; he was completely confused. But eventually one member got him to laugh and admit that, in fact, as he had been walking to the club, he had thought, "Damn, I think I've found the answer to my problem." But then, almost immediately, he had also thought, "Jeez, that means I can't ever get a buzz on again." And then, under more questioning, he acknowledged that while he was playing, for only a moment, he first thought about drinking and then, a little later, he imagined himself going into the deli near his apartment for some beer.

Because REBT has such a confrontational reputation, it is important to note that the questioning arose from curiosity on the part of the members and leader: How *did* it happen? It was not motivated by a demand to know or to confront. But it motivated the musician to reflect and to gain a better understanding of the dynamics that had occurred. In some circles, REBT has gained the reputation of being excessively confrontational. This view may result from Ellis's style in lectures and demonstrations. However, in groups and individual sessions (as evidenced, for example, in a recent video of Ellis working with a substance abuser), Ellis and most REBT therapists exhibit a gentler, supportive, accepting/nonjudgmental style while still being active and directive. Moreover, REBT often involves Socratic questioning to create constructive cognitive dissonance between, on the one hand, the client's stated goals and, on the other, his/her dysfunctional actions.

To prepare for the future, clients and group members are also asked whether they know of any potential dangerous situations coming up, such as a wedding or office Christmas party. If they do, they are helped to rehearse what they might say, do, and feel as they are in the situation. They are queried about possible irrational/unhelpful beliefs and helped to see how those beliefs might best be disputed. Other possible interventions, cognitive, emotive, and behavioral, are explored. To aid such prophylactic rehearsal, they may be given a form such as the one in Table 7.2 to work on outside the session.

REBT therapists and group leaders also spend considerable time reviewing what a person might do if he/she lapses in order to limit the episode's length and severity. Here again, IBs typical to relapse situations and possible disputes are reviewed, as well as other interventions.

RATIONAL-EMOTIVE BEHAVIOR THERAPY
AND THE ROLE OF EMOTIONS

Critics of cognitive therapy sometimes question the focus on thinking (i.e., on cognitive distortions and IB's) given that emotions play such an important role in addictions. It is interesting to note that REBT contains an E, something missing from CBT (cognitive-behavioral therapy) and BT (behavioral therapy). This is not an accident. Initially, rational-emotive

TABLE 7.2. REBT Recovery Rehearsal Form

Potential event: . . . .

1. What do you think you *might* tell yourself that *would not* be helpful? (Or, if you are far along in recovery, what do you think you *might have* told yourself in the past?)

2. If others are involved, what do you think you *might* tell them that would *not* be helpful? (Or, in the past, what do you think you might have told them that would not have been helpful?)

3. How do you think you *might* feel *at first* which would *not* be helpful? (Or, how do you think you might have felt in the past?)

4. What do you think you *might* do that would *not* be helpful? (Or, in the past, what do you think you might have done?)

5. What *could* you *tell yourself instead* that would be *more* helpful?

6. What *could* you *tell someone else* that would be *more* helpful?

7. What *could* you try to *feel* instead that would be more helpful?

8. What *could* you *do* instead that would be *more* helpful?

9. What are you telling yourself now?

---

therapy was named rational therapy by Ellis, but he quickly recognized that an emotive element was always involved in the way he worked. Hence he changed the name (Ellis, 1962). He recently added the word *behavior,* making it rational emotive behavior therapy, in what he called a long overdue acknowledgment that RET always had a very strong behavioral component (e.g. homework assignments and social skills training) (Ellis, 1993).

A key element of REBT is learning to take responsibility for one's emotional life. To many clients and self-help group members, this is a revolutionary concept. They all along felt that their mood swings and the emotional ups and downs were largely uncontrollable, even though they often tried hard to cope with them with and without the help of chemicals. They tend to believe that whatever they feel, they *have to* feel because certain things have happened. Their boss yelled at them, so they automatically have to feel angry. Their uncle abused them, so they must naturally feel ashamed, helpless, hopeless, depressed, and rageful whenever they think about it. Or they just find themselves feeling anxious, bored, angry or depressed and know very few ways to cope successfully with such feelings.

As noted earlier, according to REBT, people drink either to enhance their pleasure or to cope with some kind of emotional disturbance; the latter may be a disturbance about a disturbance. For example, one may drink because he is depressed about being depressed, or another may drink to rid herself of the discomfort anxiety she experiences whenever she tries not to drink. But in all cases, they drink or use drugs to change their emotions, either enhancing pleasant ones or attempting to alleviate or eliminate unpleasant ones.

Many people discover that drinking something, eating something, smoking something, etc., often helps change their feelings much more rapidly and easily and with greater certainty than anything else. They may try to stop ruminating about a boss's critical remark by using thought substitution, but the thought keeps returning, and they may not realize that they have to persist. Or they may use disputing to convince themselves that although they would *prefer* that their boss not speak like that, there is no law in the universe that he absolutely must not. But again, many clients find that these techniques require too much time and effort. Drinking or drugging helps them affect a change with much faster and better results, at least in the short run. This may be due, in fact, as much to changes in their cognitions as to the chemicals, but to them the chemical route still seems a lot easier and surefire.

Hence, it helps to clarify that REBT and other change techniques are generally more difficult to apply, take time to learn, require practice, and do not work nearly as quickly as the substance-based pleasure or coping "methods." And it is important to help learners understand that their goal of eliminating or changing emotions may be at the root of their problem. As long as they continue to believe, "I can't stand it" or "I must change it," they remain vulnerable to relapse.

The philosophical idea that one can take responsibility for one's emotional life inevitably presents the problem of emotional goals. What is it that one would prefer to feel? Substance abusers often say they want to feel "calm"; others say "happy"; some say "normal." We need to explore with them what they mean by each term and also what is realistic. It also helps to expand their vocabulary of possible choices. In a therapy session, I sometimes ask: "Do you think I'm happy right now?" When I say that I am not, many are surprised. But I usually feel alert, focused, engaged, challenged, determined to try to be of some help. I always point out that I have not used words they may associate with feelings because I have difficulty finding such words in the English language. Happy, content, calm, all seem inappropriate, especially while I am working with a client. Perhaps I may feel those emotions later, at the end of the day, although I may also feel discontented, unhappy, irritated, concerned, or sad depending on what has occurred and what I am thinking about at the moment.

It is a mistake to focus on eliminating the negative emotion because, at least at the outset, people are likely to experience those feelings—just as they have for years and years. To get out of this bind, a three-pronged approach has proven its worth. The first step is to make a case for self-acceptance even if and when one engages in self-defeating, self-destructive behavior. People who relapse frequently feel shame, which, in turn, often fuels more drinking or drugging. But the vicious circle can be avoided. Other emotions may be more appropriate and helpful, such as strong irritation and annoyance at the behavior combined with a determination to continue to work to change. Constantly rating one oneself tends to be self-defeating, whereas rating one's behavior may help. The second prong is to teach people how to reduce the frequency, severity, and duration of unhelpful, self-defeating, unhealthy emotions using a variety of cognitive, emotive, and behavioral techniques. Third, some negative emotions such as sadness and boredom are not necessarily unhelpful or self-defeating, and sometimes it is healthier and more appropriate to live with these unpleasant (but tolerable) feelings for a while. And it may be in people's best interests to accept that they cannot change these feelings immediately.

EMOTIVE-RATIONAL THERAPY?
RATIONAL THERAPY?
BEHAVIORAL THERAPY?
RATIONAL-EMOTIVE BEHAVIOR THERAPY?

Some clients appear to go to REBT therapists or groups because, without realizing it, they want to do "rational therapy" (RT). They do not like to feel and they want to learn how to "feel" even less often. Or they are poor at identifying their feelings and do not think learning would help. They sometimes seem to want to emulate Mr. Spock in the *Star Trek* series without the benefit of his redeeming qualities. They are already using RT in their life, often to the consternation of people living around them, but they want to learn how to do it even better and REBT therapists seem to be the people who can teach them.

Some professionals may be attracted to REBT for similar reasons. Working with them in workshops, they clearly have difficulty getting in touch with their feelings. One can imagine their likely discomfort when confronted by a client who expresses deep emotions. As a result, they may respond with a "good" cognitive therapy or REBT question, "What are you telling yourself to make yourself so angry (so anxious? so depressed?)?" effectively shutting down the display of feelings.

REBT practitioners who unwittingly prefer to be RT therapists reinforce the irrational beliefs of substance abusers by failing to dispute beliefs that "I can't stand many of the emotions that I experience and I have to learn ways to eliminate them as quickly as possible." If we think in terms of emotive-rational therapy, focusing on the emotions and emotive techniques first may be wise. Such an approach may be particularly appropriate for women who have been socialized to deny their angry feelings. It may also be especially appropriate when we are working with someone who has never discussed a particularly traumatic event with a therapist before. One can think of such clients as being in the precontemplation stage of the Prochaska et al. (1992) model. They cannot and will not feel their anger or grief; they will deny that they are angry or depressed. As noted earlier, this may be particularly true for women, but it is also so common among the men in professions such as engineering, computer sciences, and law, as to have become the stuff of social stereotypes. In fact, many of these men may have decided early in life that emoting was inappropriate behavior for a man and therefore they make every effort not to feel. If they were to emote, they are afraid they might easily get out of control—which might be true considering that they have so little history of either experiencing or expressing emotions. As they may have practiced denying and repressing their emotional responses for many years, so the therapist may have to be quite creative to help them come in contact with their emotions and to express them.

Similarly, with women who have been or are still in abusive relationships or are struggling to juggle a career and a family, or are coping with oppressive working conditions, little progress may be made before they can acknowledge and begin to express their anger. Therapists can use a variety of evocative emotive techniques, some borrowed from gestalt therapy, to help such clients become aware of how they feel (e.g., "emotional thermometers," shame attacks, and the empty chair exercise). At the same time, they can show clients how they can use rational/cognitive approaches (e.g., disputing, reframing, and thought substitution) or behavior therapy approaches (e.g., relaxation techniques and assertiveness training) to control and moderate their emotions when and if they choose to.

On the other hand, there are clients who come to REBT therapists after working for years with other therapists. These people may be quite well trained in emoting. In fact, they may have difficulty functioning because they feel so angry or so depressed throughout the day. In such cases, emotive-rational therapy might only encourage them to continue along this path. It might be more useful to take a more rational/cognitive or behavior therapy approach. The practicioner might explore with them the advantages and disadvantages of continually thinking about, discussing, and emoting over events that occurred in the past. And traditional REBT disputing might be more appropriate, in conjunction with other approaches such as thought stopping.

RATIONAL-EMOTIVE BEHAVIOR THERAPY AND ALCOHOLICS ANONYMOUS

As McGrady (1990) has pointed out, "The alcoholism field delights in periodic fits of internecine warfare" (p. 477). The most recent example is the recent break between Jack Trimpey's RR and SMART Recovery.

Although many people disagree on various elements of REBT, SMART Recovery, RR and AA, there are far more therapists and even group members who have no difficulty effectively utilizing and integrating REBT with spirituality, religion, and even AA. Ellis and Trimpey are avowed atheists, but most of the people involved with RRSN were not (Willis, 1992) and REBT has been shown to work effectively with even very religious people (Young, 1989; Robb, 1993).

The basic issue remains, how can therapists best help clients cope with the conditions that precipitate substance abuse and relapse? The questions an REBT therapist or self-help group leader or member might ask, although in some ways unique, will not often conflict with a person's spiritual and/or religious beliefs. For example, on the emotive level: How do you feel about that? What other feelings do you think a person might have in a similar situation? On the cognitive level: How are you upsetting yourself? depressing yourself? angering yourself? shaming yourself? or What are you telling yourself that may contribute to how you are feeling? or What does what has happened (or what is happening) *mean* to you? And on the behavioral level: What did you do? What else could you have done under the circumstances? What do you think someone else might have done? If calling your sponsor or praying helps, no REBT therapist and few self-help group members would object; some might wonder whether that would be sufficient over the long run, but none would object. Even Ellis (Ellis & Schoenfeld, 1990) agrees that "acceptance of AA's Step 1 is vital if an individual is to overcome an addiction" (p. 461).

The issue for many therapists and counselors who subscribe to the concepts and techniques of REBT is to stay out of trouble with their superiors who are avid AA and 12-Step proponents and who associate anything sounding like REBT with denial. This is truly unfortunate considering that much of AA is cognitive behaviorally oriented and REBT techniques can be integrated so easily. It is zealousness on both parties part that creates most of the difficulties. But as long as some people remain convinced that there is only one answer to addictions, mistrust and acrimony will probably prevail.

REFERENCES

Alcoholics Anonymous. (1980). *The big book.* New York: Alcoholics Anonymous World Services.

Annis, H. M. (1982). *Inventory of drinking situations (IDS-100).* Toronto, Canada: Addiction Research Foundation of Ontario.

Ellis, A. (1962) *Reason and emotion in psychotherapy.* New York: Lyle Stuart.

Ellis, A. (1991). *REBT and the treatment of addiction.* Paper presented at the Institute for Rational-Emotive Therapy, New York, NY.

Ellis, A. (1994). Changing rational-emotive therapy (RET) to rational emotive behavior therapy (REBT). *The Behavior Therapist, 16*(10), 257–258.

Ellis, A., & Dryden, W. (1987). *The practice of rational-emotive therapy.* New York: Springer-Verlag.

Ellis, A., McInerney, J. F., DiGiuseppe, R., & Yeager, R. J. (1988). *Rational-emotive therapy with alcoholics and substance abusers.* New York: Pergamon Press.

Ellis, A., & Schoenfeld, E. (1990). Divine intervention and the treatment of chemical dependency. *Journal of Substance Abuse, 2*(4), 459–468.

Emrick, C. D. (1994). Alcoholics Anonymous and other 12-Step groups: Establishing an empirically based approach for the health care provider. In M. Galanter & Kleber, H. (Eds.), *Textbook of substance abuse treatment* (pp. 351–358). Washington, DC: American Psychiatric Press.

Galanter, M., Egelko, S., & Edwards, H. (1993). Rational recovery: Alternative to AA for addictions. *American Journal of Drug and Alcohol Abuse, 19*(4), 499–510.

Gelman, D., Leonard, E. A., & Fisher, B. (1991, July 8). Clean and sober and agnostic. *Newsweek,* pp. 62-63.

Hall, T. (1990, December 24). New way to treat alcoholism shuns spiritualism. *The New York Times,* p. 1.

Heather, N., Miller, W. R., & Greeley, J. (Eds.). (1991). *Self-control and the addictive behaviors.* New York: Macmillan.

Low, A. A. (1978). *Mental health through will-training: A system of self-help in psychotherapy as practiced by Recovery, Inc.* Winnetka, IL: Willett.

Marlatt, G. A. (1985). Situational determinants of relapse and skill-training interventions. In G. A. Marlatt & J. R. Gordon (Eds.), *Relapse prevention: Maintenance strategies in the treatment of addictive behaviors* (pp. 71–127). New York: Guilford Press.

McGrady, B. (1990). The divine, the saturnine and the internecine: Comments on Ellis and Schoenfeld. *Journal of Substance Abuse, 2*(4), 477–480.

Miller, W. R. (1989). Matching individuals with interventions. In R. K. Hester & W. R. Miller, *Handbook of alcoholism treatment approaches* (pp. 261–272). New York: Pergamon Press.

Miller, W. R, Benefield, R. G., & Tonigan, J. S. (1993). Enhancing motivation for change in problem drinkers: A controlled comparison of two therapist styles. *Journal of Consulting and Clinical Psychology, 61*(3), 435–461.

Monti, P. M. (1990). Communication skills training, communication skills training with family and cognitive behavioral mood management training for alcoholics. *Journal of Studies on Alcohol, 51*(3), 263–270.

Oei, T. P. S., Lim, B., & Young, R. M. (1991). Cognitive processes and cognitive behavior therapy in the treatment of problem drinking. *Journal of Addictive Diseases, 10*(3), 63–80.

Prochaska, J. O., DiClemente, C. C., & Norcross, J. C. (1992). In search of how people change: Applications to addictive behaviors. *American Psychologist, 47,* 1102–1114.

Robb, H. B., III (1993). Using RET to reduce psychological dysfunction associated with supernatural belief systems. *Journal of Cognitive Psychotherapy, 7*(4), 281–289.

Trimpey, J. (1992). *The small book.* New York: Delacorte.

Trimpey, J. (1994a). The shortcomings of RET in addictions. *Journal of Rational Recovery, 6*(6), 7–12.

Trimpey, J. (1994b). "Treatment" is dead. *Journal of Rational Recovery, 6*(6), 1–2.

Willis, C. S. (1992). *A preliminary look at Rational Recovery as an alternative to Alcoholics Anonymous.* Paper presented at AABT annual convention, Boston, MA.

Young, H. (1989). Practicing RET with Bible-belt Christians. In W. Dryden (Ed.), *Howard Young: Rational therapist* (pp. 77–96). Loughton, Essex, England: Gale Centre.

8

Addiction as a "Self-Medication" Disorder: Application of Ego Psychology to the Treatment of Substance Abuse

SUSAN LYDEN MURPHY
EDWARD J. KHANTZIAN

INTRODUCTION

Substance abuse and dependence are tied intimately to an individual's attempt to cope with his/her internal and external environments. Viewed from a contemporary psychoanalytical perspective, substance dependence can best be understood by examining how such a person's ego organization and sense of self serve or fail the individual's attempts to cope, and how the specific effects of various substances facilitate or impede such attempts (Khantzian, Mack, & Schatzberg, 1974; Wurmser, 1974; Blatt, Rounsaville, Eyre, & Wilber, 1984; Treece & Khantzian, 1986).

The psychodynamic study and treatment of substance-abusing individuals has yielded findings that indicate that a range of self-regulation vulnerabilities and disturbances are involved in addictive disorders. These vulnerabilities and disturbances are accessible, understandable, and modifiable through psychodynamic treatment methods (Khantzian, Halliday, & McAuliffe, 1990). Findings based on psychodynamic approaches are supported in the main by empirical diagnostic findings that document coexisting psychiatric disorders, including a range of personality disorders (Khantzian & Treece, 1985; Rounsaville, 1990).

Clinical findings suggest that addiction results when individuals discover that the drugs they experiment with can relieve or control the painful affects and suffering that derive from deficits in ego capacities, the sense of self, and object relations. In other words, it is the vulnerable and disregulated self which is the central problem in addiction.

The psychodynamic perspective is valuable because it provides a basis to explain some of the subjective and experiential aspects of the meaning and function of substances in a person's life. It also explains some of the qualities and functions that characterize substance abusers and provides a basis for understanding that individuals, through their substance abuse, are trying to work out and solve human problems in coping.

A psychodynamic perspective does not and should not compete with findings that derive from biology, social science, and systems theory. These latter perspectives complement those derived from a psychodynamic one. Ultimately, the challenge remains to understand and think about addictive disorders in integrative terms. It may be helpful at this point to present some of the alternative theories that account for substance abuse. Each of the perspectives of genetics, social science, psychodiagnostics, and family and systems theory has an advantage in describing certain features and etiologial determinants of substance abuse.

For ease of presentation, this review of competing theories will use Lettieri, Sayers, and Wallerstein's (1980) framework, which identifies four areas of theoretical focus: whether the theory focuses on one's relationship to nature, to others, to society, or to the self.

Theories that focus on one's relationship to nature include those that propose a genetic marker or predisposition to alcoholism or other substance abuse in certain individuals and those that posit a primary role for chemical receptors in the brain.

Although these theories, including those of Schuckit (1985), note the importance of environmental factors in the initiation of substance use, the point here is that biology truly is destiny. Substance abuse, in these theories, does not denote psychological problems but simply the existence of a biological system programmed to respond in a certain way to chemical agents. Indeed, these researchers suggest that the psychopathology associated with substance abuse is a consequence, not a cause, of chronic substance use, and that much of this psychopathology disappears with successful treatment.

Theories that focus on one's relationship to others are most often seen within the context of family and systems theory. The substance abuser is seen as the "symptom bearer" for a disturbed system that is able to maintain a precarious state of equilibrium only by assigning the responsibility for all family problems to a designated member. Here the addictive behavior of the patient serves a function for the family, which has an investment in maintaining the system.

These theories, which are often used to explain concepts such as codependence, assume the existence of concordant psychological disorders within the family system, including the member whose role is that of identified patient.

Theories that focus on society include those that attempt to explain the addictive process in terms of drug subcultures. Here, substance abuse and addiction secure a role for those individuals who are otherwise alienated from or disenfranchised by society.

This phenomenon is often referred to as substance abuse as a career. The drug provides more than a means of getting high; it provides a reason to get up in the morning and to embark on those activities that will provide the money needed to maintain a habit and a way of filling time in a productive fashion that would otherwise be denied to those individuals who cannot get or keep a normal job. In this context, substance use is also seen as providing the user with a community of like-minded individuals who acknowledge and accept the user's place in the substance-using culture.

Societal theories also help to explain the use of alcohol and the place of the neighborhood bar in our culture. Individuals who might otherwise have difficulty forming and maintaining affectional bonds have a ready-made environment in which they can find both comfort and status.

The question of preexisting psychological disorders that might predispose people to substance abuse is an important philosophical question for the societal theorists. If people cannot find and keep a satisfying position in their culture, is it the individual who is disordered or the society? In general, however, the incomplete socialization assumed in these examples is seen as signifying characterological impairment or deficit.

There are also competing theories of self, or psychodynamic theories, which have been put forward to explain substance abuse. Early psychodynamic formulations were based on drive theory, which placed an emphasis on pleasurable and aggressive drives and the unconscious meanings of substance use, as well as models that emphasize the "sensation-seeking" nature of those individuals who are predisposed to abuse substances. In these models, the instinctive and pleasurable aspects of substance use explain the compelling nature of addiction (Carrol & Zuckerman, 1977; Zuckerman & Neeb, 1979).

Other models stress the self-destructive aspects of substance use, or what Menninger referred to as "chronic suicide." These psychodynamic models presuppose the existence of unconscious death wishes and self-destructive trends and see substance abuse as a neurotic compromise formation between conflicting drives and needs, a compromise that allows the person to stay alive while acting on the need to harm the self.

More recent psychoanalytical formulations have placed greater emphasis on problems in adaptation, ego and self disturbances, and related psychopathology as etiological factors in substance dependence (Krystal & Raskin, 1970; Murphy, Rounsaville, Eyre, & Kleber, 1983; Bell & Khantzian, 1991).

A variety of substance use patterns and degrees of dependence may be identified in which everyday problems of living are involved. However, we believe that becoming and remaining addicted to substances is in most instances associated with a range of psychological vulnerabilities and related characterological disturbances. Taken from the psychoanalytical perspective, the meaning, causes, and consequences of substance use can be understood best by considering how the personality organization, particularly ego psychological and self structures, of an individual interact with subjective states of distress, environmental influences, and substance effects. Such an approach can explain both more benign, self-limited degrees of substance involvement and the more malignant patterns of misuse and dependence.

THE SELF-MEDICATION HYPOTHESIS

Khantzian's self-medication hypothesis holds that substance-dependent individuals are predisposed to use and to become dependent on substances primarily as a result of ego impairments and disturbances in their sense of self, involving difficulties with drive and affect defense, self-care, dependency, and need satisfaction. The theoretical work that follows focuses on these impairments and disturbances in the ego and the sense of self.

The use of substances as an adaptive device was explored in Khantzian's early work (Khantzian et al., 1974; Khantzian, 1974, 1975), which focused on the relationship of heroin use to a range of human problems, including pain, stress, and dysphoria. In attempting to adapt to one's emotions and one's environment, the action of the substance and immersion in the drug subculture could be used to mute, extinguish, and avoid a range of feelings and emotions. Rather than settling for more ordinary defensive, neurotic, characterological, or other adaptive mechanisms as a way of dealing with distress, substance users adopt an extraordinary solution by using a powerful drug (Khantzian et al., 1974). Dysphoric feelings, when experienced by individuals whose ego stability is already subject to dysfunction and impairment as a result of developmental arrest or regression, are a disorganizing influence on these individuals' ego functions. Thus, it appeared that the use of substances by such individuals was in the service of drive and affect defense.

In recent years, considerable attention has been focused on self psychology. In contrast to ego psychology, in which the emphasis is on disturbance in structure and function in coping with drives and emotions, self (or narcissistic) psychology relates more to troubled attitudes and experiences about the self and others. Kohut (1971) and Kernberg (1975) explored how disruptions and disturbances in a person's early development, particularly around nurturance and dependency needs, lead to self-pathology in adult life. Both investigators consider substance abuse and dependence manifestations of such disorders, although neither Kernberg nor Kohut has systematically explored this relationship. A number of investigators have attempted to relate this recent understanding of narcissistic processes and disturbances to substance dependence. Reports by Weider and Kaplan (1969), Krystal and Raskin (1970), and Wurmser (1974) stressed narcissistic vulnerabilities and decompensation as predisposing factors. Wurmser, in particular, noted that substances are used to counteract the distress and dysphoria associated with decompensated narcissistic states, and he emphasized the importance of painful affects involving hurt, rage, shame, and loneliness. More recently, Dodes (1990) pointed out the role of helplessness and reactive narcissistic rage as important factors that precipitate relapse to the use of substances.

Both the ego psychological and self structures of an individual contribute to the individual's personality organization, and as part of the personality, these structures interact with painful affects, environmental influences, and substance effects.

ADDICTION AS A SELF-REGULATION DISORDER

Clinical work with substance abusers suggests that four areas of self-regulation problems, namely, affect life, self-esteem, relationships, and self-care, predisposed these individuals to become dependent on and to relapse to substances of abuse.

Self–Other Deficits and Satisfaction of Needs

A feeling of self-worth derives from the comforting, valuing, and valued aspects of early parenting relationships. When these relationships have been optimal, individuals can comfort and soothe themselves or reach out and depend on others for comfort and validation. When developmental deficits and impairments occur in relation to such needs, we see extreme and contradictory patterns around needs and wants, qualities not uncommon in substance abusers (Khantzian, 1990).

These narcissistic disturbances lead to problems in accepting dependency needs and in actively pursuing goals and satisfactions. Such problems often attach themselves to and painfully play themselves out in family life, personal relationships, and career issues. They also manifest themselves in certain attitudes incorporated into one's personality organization, such as excessive self-sufficiency, disavowal of needs, bravado, and counterdependence, all of which make human contact more difficult and substance abuse more likely. These defenses and the related character traits are employed in containing a range of longings and aspirations, but particularly those related to nurturance and dependency needs. It is because of the massive repression of these needs that such individuals feel cut off, hollow, and empty. It is the inability of these individuals to acknowledge and pursue actively their needs to be admired, and to love and be loved, that leaves them vulnerable to substance use (Khantzian, 1990).

Self-Care

Self-care as an ego function is complex. It is probably the result of a number of component functions and defenses such as signal anxiety, reality testing, judgment, control, and synthesis. When this function is impaired, defenses such as denial, justification, and projection are used. We are all subject to our instincts, drives, and impulses, and if they are expressed indiscriminately, we are subject to hazard and danger. Most of us check ourselves and automatically exercise caution, or we are appropriately worried and fearful of the prospects of danger or hazardous involvements. Such checking or cautionary responses are an integral part of our ego mechanisms of defense. However, it is exactly in this regard that substance abusers are deficient in their ego capacities for self-care (Khantzian, 1991).

Problems with self-care develop out of a failure to adequately internalize self-protective survival functions which are established in early phases of development. Self-care problems such as accidents and preventable medical, legal, and financial difficulties are evident in histories predating substance abuse, where we see a persistent inability to worry about, anticipate, or consider the consequences of action or inaction (Weiss, Mirin, Michael, & Schugub, 1986; Khantzian, 1991).

These self-care deficits are also evident in the disregard for danger seen in the substance use itself. Characterological features of this vulnerability are evident in the substance abuser's counterphobia, hyperactivity, impulsivity, aggressiveness, and denial of danger (Brehm & Khantzian, 1992). In our opinion, it is the combination of deficits in self-care and affect defense that malignantly combine to make substance use and dependence likely and persistent.

Affect Regulation and Affect Defense

Problems with affect defense are at the heart of substance dependence problems. We see in these patients significant developmental failures in which substances have been adopted to protect against overwhelming, confusing, or painful affect as a consequence of structural impairments.

In other words, substances are used to ward off or calm intense affects or to relieve dysphoric states (Milkman & Frosch, 1973).

Individuals differentially medicate themselves with various classes of substances to compensate for and to counter intense and threatening affects associated with the defects and distortions in affect defense. The choice of substances used generally correlates with the affect defended against: Opiates are most often deployed against rage and aggression, whereas stimulants are used either to counter states of depletion, anergia, and depressive affect, which often is atypical or subclinical in nature, or to augment hypomanic states. Depressants, including alcohol, are used to ameliorate states of emptiness and isolation due to rigid, overdrawn, and counterdependent defenses. Khantzian (1975) referred to this process as self-selection, in which a person discovers that the short-term effect of a certain substance results in improved functioning or a sense of well-being by augmenting shaky or impaired defenses or by producing a release of feelings from rigid and constraining defenses.

However, the literature on infant research and affect development suggests that much of the substance abuser's experience of affects is painful, not only because feelings are intense and overwhelming but because feelings are often absent, confusing, and without words.

This quality has been referred to by such terms as *alexithymia, disaffected, affect deficit, hypophoria,* and *nonfeeling responses* and appears to be a key reason why such patients often appear superficially to be free of distress (Wurmser, 1974; Krystal, 1982; McDougall, 1984).

The use of substances as an affect defense thus also points to what Krystal describes as affect regression: a global and undifferentiated experience of emotions that can only be poorly verbalized and are therefore partly converted to somatic sensations.

The Control of Addictive Suffering

Although substance abusers attempt to relieve their suffering through the use of drugs and alcohol, it appears that their main goal is the control, rather than the eradication, of their feelings.

These individuals suffer with their feelings because they often do not recognize, understand, or control them, but when they take substances, they can produce a condition which, over time, they are able to recognize, understand, and control.

Even when the effects and aftereffects are unpleasant and painful, these people have managed to substitute a dysphoria that they have invented and controlled in place of a dysphoria that is elusive and that they do not control. This is a use of the defense of turning the passive into the active, a resort to external action in order to deny inner helplessness. Having failed to develop adequate internal mechanisms for coping with internal drives and emotions, the addiction-prone individual is constantly involved with a range of behaviors and activities, including substance use, in the external world to serve the needs for a sense of well-being, security, and pleasure. Shaky or rigid defenses and low self-esteem cause the addiction-prone individual to turn more exclusively to the external environment for the satisfaction of needs and wants. Wurmser has referred to this predisposition as an addictive search and has expanded eloquently on how such predispositions are part of the necessary and sufficient causes that lead to addiction. It is the constant search and hunger for satisfactions from one's environment, interacting with the more incidental and adventitious influences such as exposure to drugs, drug availability, and peer-group pressure, that determine the initiation and continuation of substance use.

Physical and Psychological Dependence and Progression

Addiction-prone individuals' ego and self disturbances predispose them to dependence on substances, given the general and specific appeal of these substances. There is a natural tendency in such individuals to use heavier and heavier amounts, resulting in physiological dependence. However, it appears that there is also a psychological basis to depend increasingly on substances. Substance use and dependence predispose individuals to progression in their usage patterns, with a tendency to preclude the development of more ordinary human solutions to life's problems. In repeatedly resorting to a substance to obtain a desired effect, the individual becomes less and less apt to come upon other responses and solutions in coping with internal life and the external world. It is in this respect that an addiction takes on a life of its own. There is an ever-increasing tendency for regression and withdrawal, which is compounded by society's inclination to consider such behavior as deviant and unacceptable. Regressed and withdrawn individuals discover that, in the absence of other adaptive mechanisms, the distressing aspects of their condition can be relieved only by either increasing the use of this preferred substance or switching to other substances to overcome the painful and disabling side effects of the original drug of dependence.

The addict's relationship with and dependence on a substance are the result of failure to find more ordinary solutions to the human problems of coping with emotional distress and seeking satisfaction for one's needs and wants. Substances have been substituted as an extraordinary solution for a range of problems, but particularly as a means to cope with major ego and self disturbances. However, these solutions are at best short term and tenuous, and the long-term dependence on substances has serious, maladaptive aspects and consequences. As a result, substance abusers may be very ambivalent about their substances. Often, consequences such as legal, medical, and interpersonal crises that result from long-term substance use break down the rationalizations and denial that have supported their continuing substance use and dependence. At these times, alternative solutions and satisfactions become possible and realizable and may—for the first time with some people, and once again for some others—make possible the replacement of substance use with human involvements such as relationships, benign compulsive activities, religious immersion, and becoming the treater rather than the treated. This may occur with or without treatment interventions or relationships.

CLINICAL VIGNETTES

In this chapter, we have reviewed some of the psychological vulnerabilities that govern a reliance on and relapse to the use of substances of dependence. We have focused primarily on painful and dysphoric affect states and related vulnerabilities in self-regulation involving self-other relationships and self-care that predispose to substance use and that make reliance on substances likely and compelling. In this section, we present some brief clinical vignettes to highlight how certain individuals use the psychoactive properties of addictive drugs to modulate painful affects; to manage with a deficient, restricted; or inadequate sense of self; and to overcome interpersonal difficulties.

Vignette 1: Alcohol and the Bipolar Self

The two women described here, Marge and Ann, shared a tendency to be quite verbal and articulate. Although different in other respects, both women discovered that alcohol served them well, temporarily, to overcome subtle and painful problems with relating to people and expressing their emotions.

Marge was a hypomanic 48-year-old woman who despite her verbal facility was surprisingly restricted in expressing her emotions. During an interview in which she was struggling to describe her problems with expressing herself and where her use of alcohol fit in to this, she said, "I get on the phone and I want to drink and drink and drink. I want to be able to feel sad—and to get happy." In the following psychotherapy hour, she related how she had a wonderful joke to tell and that she drank three glasses of wine in order to be able "to call people and share it." In contrast, during her interviews with her therapist she spoke rapidly and circumstantially in a manner that was defensive, irritable, and distancing.

Ann, a 42-year-old professor of art history who was active and effusive, described how she used alcohol to overcome her characteristic ways of responding to hurt and disappointment, especially in important relationships. She described how in her relationship with her boyfriend she responded to distress with a "deep, icy calm." She spontaneously related how she had discovered that at these times, and in similar instances when she felt cold and cut off, alcohol "always warmed" her.

Technical and lay accounts of alcohol effects often stress its appeal as an antidepressant. In fact, alcohol is a poor antidepressant. The two cases here, however, do bring out its short-term "beneficial" action. In Marge's case, alcohol augmented both her experience and expression of sadness and happiness. In Ann's case, the alcohol helped to soften the characteristic and rigid defenses of isolation and withdrawal, which left her feeling cold, empty and cut off.

Vignette 2: Cocaine and the Restricted, Depressive Self

Jeff was an appealing and articulate 47-year-old college dean of students with a long history of alcoholic drinking which progressed to a heavy dependence on cocaine.

Jeff described how, since his high school years, "alcohol had allowed me to get outside myself and put aside my reserved character." Without alcohol, he said he was "retiring and quiet—[but when] drinking, I was more expressive and better company."

In his mid-30s Jeff discovered cocaine. He said, "It allowed me to be a lot of things I had been in the past. My energy returned, I had a sense of humor and felt like a worthy companion again." Jeff had been feeling anergic and had been avoiding social situations before this discovery. As is often the case, Jeff's increasing use of cocaine prompted an escalating use of alcohol, culminating in an admission to a detoxification and rehabilitation program which allowed him to remain abstinent for 5 years. About 1 year before being seen by one of us (EJK), the patient sought out psychiatric treatment in the context of marital difficulties in which he was again becoming increasingly isolated and uncommunicative. Not insignificantly, treatment with Prozac (fluoxetine hydrochloride) had dramatically reversed his symptoms to the point where, as he said, "words now come out, unfiltered—I look forward to going home to my wife—and I can laugh again."

In this case, alcohol had originally served Jeff as a disinhibiting agent. Later, he discovered that cocaine acted as a powerful antidote to his depressive anergia, low self-esteem, and tendency to avoid meaningful or enjoyable social contact. His description of the more recent therapeutic and corrective action of Prozac provides compelling testimony of how individuals such as Jeff both knowingly and unknowingly attempt to self-medicate a painful sense of restriction through the use of addictive drugs.

Vignette 3: Opiates, Anger, and Self-Hatred

Lorraine was a 39-year-old psychiatrist who sought consultation for dependence on Darvon (propoxyphene napsylate), a synthetic opioid-type analgesic. She had become dependent on the drug in the context of a stormy, painful psychotherapy. The drug was originally prescribed for a painful colitis condition, but her use of the drug escalated when she discovered that it could also attenuate the intense emotions being stirred up in psychotherapy.

She reported in the consultation that "the opiates calm me down— they make me feel peaceful. The drug quiets down my self-hatred and anger that I have from time to time. I become more optimistic—I use it to cope."

Lorraine's description of the antirage, antianger, and ultimately calming influence of opiates is consistent with our experience in interviewing over 250 opioid-dependent individuals from many different backgrounds, including professionals, street addicts, and patients like Lorraine, who have become iatrogenically dependent on narcotics. In our experience, the drug's major action, and thus its appeal, is that it has a powerful antiaggression and antirage action which ameliorates the disorganizing subjective distress associated with such intense affect, as well as the fear of counteraggression engendered by these emotions.

SPECIFIC GUIDELINES FOR CLINICAL APPLICATION

We are hopeful that the vignettes given here conveyed some of the specific painful feeling states that make various classes of drugs appealing and addictive. We also hope that these vignettes made evident our belief that it is suffering, not pleasure seeking or self-destruction, that is at the root of addictive disorders. Individuals who suffer with addictions do so because they are unable to regulate their emotions, their behaviors, and their self–other relationships. Treatments that are successful are those that effectively help individuals identify, understand, and modify their self-regulation vulnerabilities ●nd deficits.

Effective evaluation and treatment of substance abusers must take place within the context of a gradually evolving treatment alliance. Such a gradual approach allows individuals first to perform the necessary shoring up of their self-regulation vulnerabilities, including difficulties in establishing conditions of safety, trust, and mutuality, before attempting to uncover and examine the self-defeating personality characteristics that obscure and belie their suffering.

The outcome of such treatment is that many of those patients who were unable to sustain abstinence from substance abuse because of underlying psychological factors escape the suffering that originally caused them to attempt self-medication and become able to maintain abstinence and sobriety.

EVIDENCE OF EFFECTIVENESS
AND COST CONSIDERATIONS

Studies testing the efficacy and cost-effectiveness of treatments based on a psychodynamic understanding of substance abusers are few in number. Some of the most important empirical work has been done through the University of Pennsylvania/Veterans Administration Medical Center with patients enrolled in their methadone maintenance programs. Woody, McLellan, Luborsky, and O'Brien (1986) were able to demonstrate that patients with moderate to severe depression treated with supportive–expressive psychotherapy responded more favorably and improved more in terms of symptom reduction and overall functioning than did patients treated with methadone and drug counseling alone. In our own work at Cambridge Hospital and the Harvard Cocaine Recovery Project, we have preliminary evidence that a modified dynamic group approach that targets deficits in affect management, self-esteem, relationships, and self-care helps to retain membership in groups and to achieve the benefits of symptom reduction and improved functioning for a majority of the patients who were in the project (Khantzian et al., 1990). More recently, a report by Walsh et al. (1991), in which the benefit and cost of inpatient treatment for alcoholics was compared both to 12-Step programs and to a choice of programs, provided evidence that more intensive, inpatient psychosocial treatments were cost-effective and beneficial when measured in terms of postdischarge criteria such as number of days of alcohol use and time lost from work as a result of drinking. A more extensive review of the literature would, unfortunately, go beyond the scope of this chapter.

CONCLUSION

Neither pleasure seeking nor self-destructive motives explain the compelling nature of addictive disorders, which represent an extraordinary solution to human suffering. Instead, it is vulnerability in or damage to the psychological structures controlling affect defense, self-care, dependency, and need satisfaction that lead people to use and to become dependent on substances to regulate themselves.

Although suffering is an inevitable and unavoidable aspect of life, it appears that substance abusers have disabling problems with affect recognition, affect tolerance, and qualities of self–other relations that produce a special relationship with suffering which these patients seek to relieve while perpetuating it.

These individuals have discovered that the psychoactive properties of addictive substances can temporarily regulate, by relieving or controlling, painful and confusing feelings, including emotions that they feel about themselves and others. Thus, these substances may be used to relieve painful emotional states such as depression, rage, or anxiety; or drug effects may be employed to counter states of emptiness, anhedonia, or the inability to access or give words to their feelings.

What Wurmser (1974) describes as deficits in affect defense, and Krystal and Raskin (1970) refer to as the defective stimulus barrier of addicts, are vulnerabilities described in psychoanalytical terms that implicate early trauma and developmental disturbances. The accompanying problem of being unable to regulate their self-care blinds addicts to the costly, precarious, and even lethal hazards entailed in their attempts to correct their self-regulation difficulties. What originally was discovered to be a self-corrective measure more often turns out, if unbridled and untreated, to be self-destructive (Khantzian, 1975).

Before his suicide, the poet John Berryman suffered himself with substance abuse. Describing his emotional turmoil and his attempts to escape from it, Berryman wrote: "Now there is further a difficulty with the light / I am obliged to perform in complete darkness / operations of great delicacy / on my self."

This is, in essence, what the perspective of ego and self psychological approaches to substance abuse holds: that those who suffer with unbearable structural deficits are attempting to operate, in the dark, on their damaged selves.

REFERENCES

Bell, C., & Khantzian, E. J. (1991). Drug use and addiction as self medication. In M. S. Gold & A. E. Slavy (Eds.), *Dual diagnosis in substance abuse*. New York: Marcel Dekker.

Berryman, J. (1970). I don't operate often. *77 dream songs*. New York: Farrar, Straus, & Giroux.

Blatt, S. J., Rounsaville, B., Eyre, S. L., & Wilber, C. (1984). The psychodynamics of opiate addiction. *Journal of Nervous and Mental Diseases, 172,* 342–351.

Brehm, N., & Khantzian, E. J. (1992). The psychology of substance abuse: A psychodynamic perspective. In J. H. Lowinson, P. Ruiz, & R. B. Millman (Eds.), *Substance abuse: A comprehensive textbook* (2nd ed., pp. 107–117). New York: Williams & Wilkins.

Carrol, E. N., & Zuckerman, M. (1977). Psychopathology and sensation seeking. In Downers, speeders, and trippers: A study of the relationship between personality and drug choice. *International Journal of Addictions, 12,* 591–601.

Dodes, L. M. (1990). Addiction, helplessness, and narcissistic rage. *Psychoanalytic Quarterly, 59,* 398–419.

Kernberg, O. (1975). *Borderline conditions and pathological narcissism.* New York: Jason Aronson.

Khantzian, E. J. (1974). Opiate addiction: A critique of theory and some implications for treatment. *American Journal of Psychotherapy, 28,* 59–70.

Khantzian, E. J. (1975). Self selection and progression in drug dependence. *Psychiatry Digest, 10,* 19–22.

Khantzian, E. J. (1990). Self-regulation and self-medication factors in alcoholism and the addictions: Similarities and differences. In M. Galanter (Ed.), *Recent developments in alcoholism* (Vol. 8, pp. 255–271). New York: Plenum Press.

Khantzian, E. J. (1991). Self-regulation factors in cocaine dependence: A clinical perspective. In S. Schover & E. Schade (Eds.), *The epidemiology of cocaine use and abuse* (NIDA Research Monograph No. 110, pp. 211–216). Rockville, MD: National Institute on Drug Abuse.

Khantzian, E. J., Halliday, K. S., & McAuliffe, W. E. (1990). *Addiction and the vulnerable self: Modified dynamic group therapy for substance abusers.* New York: Guilford Press.

Khantzian, E. J., Mack, J. E., & Schatzberg, A. F. (1974). Heroin use as an attempt to cope: Clinical observations. *American Journal of Psychiatry, 131,* 160–164.

Khantzian, E. J., & Treece, C. (1985). DSM-III psychiatric diagnosis of narcotic addicts: Recent findings. *Archives of General Psychiatry, 42,* 1067–1071.

Kohut, H. (1971). *The analysis of the self.* New York: International Universities Press.

Krystal, H. (1982). Alexithymia and the effectiveness of psychoanalytic treatment. *International Journal of Psychoanalytic Psychotherapy, 9,* 353–388.

Krystal, H., & Raskin, H. A. (1970). *Drug dependence: Aspects of ego functions.* Detroit: Wayne State University Press.

Lettieri, D. J., Sayers, M., & Wallerstein, H. W. (Eds.). (1980). *Theories of addiction* (NIDA Monograph No. 30). Rockville, MD: National Institute on Drug Abuse.

McDougall, J. (1984). The "dis-affected" patient: Reflection on affect pathology. *Psychoanalytic Quarterly, 53,* 386–409.

Menninger, K. (1938). *Man against himself.* New York: Harcourt, Brace, & World, Inc.

Milkman, H., & Frosch, W. A. (1973). On the preferential abuse of heroin and amphetamine. *Journal of Nervous and Mental Diseases, 156,* 242–248.

Murphy, S. L., Rounsaville, B. J., Eyre, S. L., & Kleber, H. D. (1983). Suicide attempts in treated opiate addicts. *Comprehensive Psychiatry, 24*(1), 79–89.

Rounsaville, B. J. (1990). Psychiatric comorbidity in alcoholics. *Substance Abuse, 11*(4), 186–191.

Schuckit, M. A. (1985). The clinical implications of primary diagnostic groups among alcoholics. *Archives of General Psychiatry, 42,* 1043–1049.

Treece, C., & Khantzian, E. J. (1986). Psychodynamic factors in the development of drug dependence. *Psychiatric Clinics of North America, 9*(3), 399–412.

Walsh, D. C., Hingson, R. W., Merrigan, D. M., Levenson, S. M., Cupples, L. A., Heeren, T., Coffman, G. A., Becker, C. A., Barker, T. A., Hamilton, S. K., McGuire, T. G., & Kelly, C. A. (1991). A randomized trial of treatment options for alcohol-abusing women. *New England Journal of Medicine, 325,* 775–782.

Weider, H., & Kaplan, E. H. (1969). Drug use in adolescents: Psychodynamic meaning and pharmacogenic effect. *Psychoanalytic Study of the Child, 24,* 399–431.

Weiss, R. D., Mirin, S. M., Michael, J. L., & Schugub, A. C. (1986). Psychopathology in chronic cocaine abusers. *American Journal of Drug and Alcohol Abuse, 12,* 17–29.

Woody, G. E., McLellan, A. T., Luborsky, L., & O'Brien, C. P. (1986). Psychotherapy for substance abusers. *Psychiatric Clinics of North America, 9,* 547–562.

Wurmser, L. (1974). Psychoanalytic considerations of the etiology of compulsive drug use. *Journal of the American Psychoanalytic Association, 22,* 820–843.

Zuckerman, M., & Neeb, M. (1979). Sensation seeking and psychopathology. *Psychiatry Research, 1,* 255–264.

II

CLINICAL STRATEGIES
AND TECHNIQUES

9

Motivational Interviewing: Increasing Readiness for Change

STEPHEN ROLLNICK
MICHELLE MORGAN

INTRODUCTION

Uncertainty about change is such an apparently simple notion that it might seem strange to devote a whole chapter to it. However, from both the literature on addiction (e.g., Orford, 1985) and clinical encounters, it would appear that ambivalence about change is close to the heart of any addictive problem. How can a counselor provide a client with the opportunity to resolve this ambivalence? This question, which is the focus of motivational interviewing, is the subject of this chapter.

OVERVIEW AND BACKGROUND

A New Look at Motivation

Fluctuating motivation to change has bedeviled many an encounter with clients with addictive problems. Until fairly recently, responsibility for this problem was laid squarely on the shoulders of the client. Motivational interviewing emerged when one clinician, William R. Miller, began to question why counselors in the addictions field argued so often with their clients (Miller, 1983). The traditional answer to this question was a straightforward one. Lack of motivation was part of the problem. Resistance, in keeping with principles derived from Freudian psychoanalysis, arose within the patient. Therefore, people with addictive problems had an inherent tendency to deny the severity of the problem. Verbal battles in interviews were to be expected from this client group.

Miller's starting point was that he might also be responsible for the emergence of these problems. Put simply, a confrontational counseling style involving the use of direct persuasion could evoke resistance and denial. The development of motivational interviewing was an attempt to construct alternative strategies for enhancing motivation to change (see Miller & Rollnick, 1991).[1] In the process, the understanding of motivation itself was enhanced. This was defined not as a tendency or personality trait but as a fluctuating state of readiness to consider behavioral change.

Two Useful Concepts

Readiness to Change

The stage change model (see Shaffer & Robbins, Chapter 5, this volume) emerged in parallel with motivational interviewing and provided an immediately useful framework for describing different motivational states and corresponding therapeutic tasks (Prochaska & DiClemente, 1986; Davidson, Rollnick, & MacEwan, 1991). It was also used as the basis for distinguishing between the two phases of motivational interviewing: building motivation and strengthening commitment to change.

One simple way of plotting the varying degrees of readiness to change among clients is presented in Figure 9.1, where the stages of precontemplation, contemplation, and preparation have been placed on a continuum. A client moving sucessfully along this line will eventually make a decision to move through a "decision gate" into the ready phase (preparation stage), followed some time later by a change in actual behavior (the vertical line in Figure 9.1). Besides challenging the clinician to respond sensitively to a client's position on this continuum, a number of other observations can be made about it: First, individuals move to and fro along it; confrontational interventions from the interviewer can lead to backward movement. Second, most substance abusers are probably around the "unsure" position on the continuum; ambivalence is likey to be most common at this point and will increase as someone approaches the decision gate. Third, resistance can be seen as a measure of the extent to which the clinician has jumped ahead of the client's position on the line. Put simply, if you talk to clients as if they *should* be ready to change, when in fact they are unsure about it, resistance will be the outcome; seen in this light, resistance is a signal for the counselor to go back along the continuum and align him/herself with the position of the client.

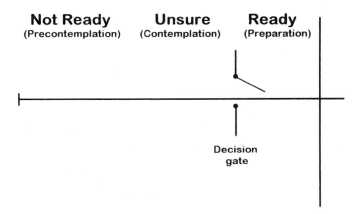

FIGURE 9.1. Readiness to change.

The assessment of readiness to change can be done formally, using any of a range of questionnaires. Less formally, it can be done simply by drawing a line and asking clients to tell you where they would place themselves. Such explicit assessment is not always necessary in the conduct of an interview. Essential however, is the counselor's willingness to understand readiness to change on an ongoing basis.

Is there any evidence that taking readiness to change into account makes any difference to the conduct and outcome of counseling? This issue is dealt with in the section on patient–treatment matching.

Ambivalence

Clients entering treatment may feel intense ambivalence. They may feel motivated to move toward a treatment goal while simultaneously feeling a desire to avoid it. It is common to find people shifting between moods of defensiveness and commitment. It is this sensitivity that makes substance abusers so vulnerable to the approach used by the counselor. This ambivalence conflict, which has been described in more detail by Miller and Rollnick (1991) and Orford (1985),[2] involves a choice between continuing with substance use and changing, between indulgence and restraint. As illustrated in Figure 9.2, each option has benefits and costs associated with it.

Common sense might suggest that the most obvious way to help someone to consider change is to use some form of direct persuasion. Thus, a clinician might argue either against the costs of continued use or for the benefits of change. This approach, it has been suggested, underlies much advice giving about behavioral change (Rollnick, Kinnersley, & Stott, 1993). The problem here is that the typical response of the client is to say, "Yes, but . . . ," and to point out either the benefits of

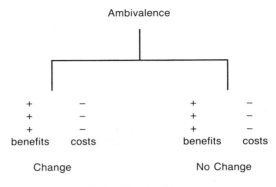

FIGURE 9.2. Ambivalence.

substance use or the costs of changing. This is precisely the opposite of what we would want such a person to say. This realization was one of the starting points of motivational interviewing, to find an alternative to falling into a "confrontation–denial trap." In essence, it should be the client, rather than the counselor, who examines this ambivalence conflict and, if appropriate, presents the reasons to be concerned about substance use and the arguments for change.

Definition and Principles of Motivational Interviewing

Underlying motivational interviewing, or any consultation about behavioral change, is a certain tension between the counselor's desire to encourage change and the expectations and aspirations of the client. Therefore, motivational interviewing has a clear directive component but is also client centered; empathizing with the client's experience of conflict is most important. Sometimes the counselor will take the lead, and sometimes he/she will follow the client. The direction pursued by the counselor is the understanding of ambivalence. A working definition of motivational interviewing is as follows: a directive, client-centered counseling style for helping clients explore and resolve ambivalence about behavioral change.

Five principles underlying motivational interviewing were identified by Miller and Rollnick (1991).

1. *Express empathy.* This is an active process in which reflective listening is used to understand the meaning conveyed by the client. The underlying attitude is one of acceptance, where the client's feelings are understood without criticism or blame. This does not necessarily imply agreement or approval but rather reflects an appreciation that the client's perspective is understandable.

2. *Develop discrepancy.* The client is actively encouraged to explore the gap between future goals (such as personal health or success) and current behavior. One goal of motivational interviewing is to develop this discrepency until it overcomes the desire to maintain the present behavior. The discomfort that sometimes arises from this process needs to be handled with respect and sensitivity. The aim of motivational interviewing is to tap the client's internal motivators as opposed to the pressure from external sources; this involves penetrating the client's value system and deeper aspirations. Crucially, however, an attempt is made to contrast these aspirations with the present problem behavior.

3. *Avoid argumentation.* Arguing with clients will only evoke further reactance (i.e., they will assert their freedom by becoming even more defensive or contrary). A topic often vulnerable to argument is diagnostic labeling; there is little to be gained from trying to persuade someone to accept a label if they appear to resist it.

4. *Roll with resistance.* Instead of using argument, the counselor should deflect or reframe client statements so that the resistance is lessened. In this way, something presented by the client as a barrier to change (e.g., reports that a spouse is constantly complaining too much about the behavior) can be reframed as a potential catalyst for change (e.g., the spouse is expressing concern). One of the most artful skills of motivational interviewing is respectfully to invite the client to consider new perspectives.

5. *Support self-efficacy.* Self-efficacy refers to the clients' beliefs in their ability to effect change in specific situations. High self-efficacy is a predictor of good outcome. The counselor needs to discuss and nurture high self-efficacy, particularly when the client moves into the preparation stage.

THE PRACTICE OF MOTIVATIONAL INTERVIEWING

The practice of motivational interviewing is described in detail in Miller and Rollnick (1991). What follows is a brief summary of the key components of motivational interviewing. Practitioners attempting to use these guidelines for the first time should be mindful of the need to keep to the spirit of the counseling style and not to become too immersed in matters of technique. Clients have within themselves the motivation to change their behavior. The task of the counselor is simply to elicit these motives in a respectful atmosphere.

Client-Centered Counseling Skills

The foundation of motivational interviewing consists of nondirective counseling skills in which it is presumed that the practice of accurate empathy is crucial. Reflective listening is obviously a key skill. So, too, open questions, summarizing, and affirmation are essential.

Eliciting Self-Motivating Statements

The directive component of motivational interviewing comes from the counselor's wish to examine the ambivalence conflict, and to encourage the client, if appropriate, to give voice to his/her concerns about the behavior and any arguments for change. When this happens, the client is making "self-motivating statements." These are statements that reflect a recognition of a problem, concern about it, intention to change, or optimism about change. Some examples are: "I have noticed that the drug doesn't just calm me down like it used to; it knocks me down." "I am concerned because if I carry on, my marriage will not last." "If I don't do something about it I don't know where I will end up."

When clients make this kind of statement, the counselor's task is surprisingly simple: to follow the client, slowly and carefully, with the singular aim of understanding in as much detail as possible. Reflective listening is particularly useful here. A common mistake made by counselors faced with self-motivating statements is to interfere with this process of exploration either by moving on too quickly, often onto the subject of change, or by introducing some new idea or hypothesis of their own.

Eliciting self-motivating statements involves listening carefully to clients, assessing their degree of readiness to change, and then choosing the right moment to explore motivation. Simple, open questions, or evocative questions, can be used to do this, as can any of a range of strategies described in Miller and Rollnick (1991). Some examples of evocative questions are: "What have you noticed about your use of alcohol that concerns you?" "What concerns do you have about your use of cocaine?" "What arguments do you see for changing?" One of the most obviously useful approaches is a simple decisional balance strategy in which the client is asked to articulate what he or she likes and dislikes about using the substance. Alternatively, it can be useful to explore the advantages and disadvantages of change, particularly as someone approaches the decision gate illustrated in Figure 9.1. It is worth noting that the exploration of ambivalence can be experienced by the client on an emotional or a cognitive level. Not enough is known about these processes to understand the advantages and limitations properly. It appears that clients, if given the freedom, will determine for themselves at what level they wish to operate.

It appears that motivation to change can increase when the client is given the opportunity to express these self-motivating statements. The principle of deploying discrepancy takes this process one step further.

The counselor attempts to contrast these statements with what the client has said about his/her personal goals or aspirations. Put simply, there is an uncomfortable contrast between, for example, "I would like to get on better with my spouse" (a personal aspiration) and "When I drink I become completely self-centered" (a self-motivating statement). Eliciting these contrasts from the client and summarizing them clearly and respectfully appear to provide a powerful impetus for change.

The Two Phases of Motivational Interviewing

Motivational interviewing has been divided into two phases on either side of the decision gate identified in Figure 9.1; in phase 1 (precontemplation and contemplation stages), the counselor's task is to build motivation; this is done by exploring ambivalence and eliciting self-motivating statements. Once the person has decided to change, the preparation stage (phase 2), the task is to strengthen commitment to change by eliciting from the client viable goals and strategies for achieving them; at this stage, because the client appears ready for change, it is tempting to come forward with solutions oneself. However, such an approach often results in the clients' asserting their freedom by telling the counselor why the solution will not work. How to avoid falling into this trap yet still remain helpful is one of the main goals in phase 2.

Dealing with Resistance

Motivational interviewing involves a set of strategies for dealing with resistance. This is viewed not as the client's problem but as a disturbance in rapport which requires a change in strategy from the counselor. Often, but not always, it arises because the counselor has overestimated the client's degree of readiness to change. Responses to resistance range from brief interventions with a range of reflective listening statements to the use of broader strategies such as shifting focus and emphasizing personal choice and control.

Exchanging Information

The simple act of sharing information or assessment results with clients can enhance motivation to change. Evidence for this has emerged from the work of Miller and colleagues (see Miller & Sovereign, 1989; Bien, Miller, & Boroughs, 1993; Brown & Miller, 1993). This activity, which can occur at any stage of counseling, is not simply a matter of giving information to clients. Adherence to a few simple guidelines can help to build motivation to change: First, discuss how much the client knows about a given topic and how much he/she would like to know. Second, give information or assessment results in a neutral and non judgmental manner: A distinction is made between the facts and the personal interpretation of them; the counselor's task is to present the facts. Finally, and most important, the client is encouraged to arrive at a personal interpretation of the information. These principles have been built into both formal assessment procedures (Miller & Sovereign, 1989) and brief motivational interviewing in medical settings (Rollnick, Heather, & Bell, 1992).

The Spirit of Motivational Interviewing

The practice of motivational interviewing involves doing a delicate dance between leading and being led, between shifting strategy and quietly listening. Thus, it is a matter of adhering to the "spirit" of the counseling style, not merely a question of applying techniques to clients. Responding to the client's degree of readiness to change is paramount. A session that is going well will take the form of occasional direction from the counselor followed by periods of more gently paced active listening. When the client is expressing concerns about the addictive behavior or arguments for change (self-motivating statements), the counselor's task is simply to listen and understand; he/she should not rush ahead or introduce too much new material; motivation to change comes from the client, not from the technical expertise of the counselor.

SPECIAL ADVANTAGES AND LIMITATIONS

The most obvious general advantage of motivational interviewing is its flexibility. Not only can it be used for any substance abuse interview, but it appears to be relevant to any encounter in which a counselor is talking to a client about behavioral change (e.g., in everyday medical consultations) (see Rollnick et al., 1993). Thus, for example, work is under way on using motivational interviewing with sex offenders, diabetics, and schizophrenics who are ambivalent about taking medication. Some clinicians have developed a set of specific techniques and deemphasized the view of motivational interviewing as a counseling style (Saunders, Wilkinson, & Allsop, 1991).

Within the addictions field, motivational interviewing need not be viewed as a discrete form of therapy but as a counseling style. It can be integrated into most other treatment approaches. For example, it is quite possible that efforts will be made in the coming years to integrate motivational interviewing with cognitive-behavioral approaches such as relapse prevention. This would involve not merely the use of client-centered counseling alongside relapse prevention strategies but the strengthening of client commitment in the manner characteristic of motivational interviewing in phase 2.

One obvious limitation of motivational interviewing is that it is not compatible with a more authoritarian approach to treatment. Some counselors will find the relatively quiet and slow pace of motivational interviewing not to their liking. It can be tiring, moving in and around a client's ambivalence conflict, where contradiction is more commonly encountered than consistency. However, we would argue that the alternative confrontational approach is not only less effective but can plunge a counselor into a tiring sequence of arguments with a client.

It appears that motivational interviewing can be used for a relatively brief period. Evidence is emerging that one or two sessions can have a powerful effect on clients. Indeed, in the wider field of medicine and primary health care, it has been possible to develop a single-session form of brief motivational interviewing (Rollnick et al., 1992) based on the use of a menu of discrete strategies that are teachable to untrained health care workers. On an anecdotal level, we recently observed an emergency medicine physician deliver a 5-minute intervention in which the patient, a drinker with oesophegal varices and liver cirrhosis, was encouraged to weigh the pros and cons of drinking. This led to a spontaneous decision to seek referral for further treatment. Brief intervention has become a discrete field of study. One argument is that it works because recipients are given a "motivational nudge" sufficiently powerful to precipitate a change in behavior (see Bien, Miller, & Tonigan, 1993).

A concern sometimes expressed about motivational interviewing is that its practice can be unethical: Clients are unwittingly manipulated into examining ambivalence and committing themselves to change. Practiced badly, we believe, ethical problems do arise. One of them is not unique to motivational interviewing; counselors in this field usually do have a clear agenda to persuade clients to change their behavior. Under these circumstances, erosion of client autonomy can occur. A number of safeguards can minimize the likelihood that motivational interviewing will descend into covert manipulation. Counselors, at various points in the session, can state openly what it is they would like to achieve with clients. Deploying discrepancy can leave clients feeling vulnerable. Ethical difficulty can be minimized if the counselor is focused on the client's core values when following this principle (Miller, 1994). Careful observation of the client will indicate if and when he/she is willing to consider the contrast between core values and the addictive behavior. As noted above, resistance from the client is a signal to change strategy. So, too, the use of reflective listening and the practice of accurate empathy are important safeguards for the counselor. This is one of the main arguments for viewing motivational nterviewing as a counseling style and not as a set of techniques to be practiced on people.

PATIENT–TREATMENT MATCHING CONSIDERATIONS

The stage-change model provides a clinically useful criterion for matching substance abusers to different forms of intervention (see Shaffer & Robbins, Chapter 5, this volume; Davidson et al., 1991). Motivational interviewing would appear most suited to those in the precontemplation and contemplation stages of change. Indeed, one of the aims of the Project MATCH study is to examine this possibility (Project MATCH Research Group, 1993).

One of the dangers in using the stage-change model in this way is that patients in the preparation, action, and maintenance stages are viewed as unsuited to motivational interviewing. In truth, people in these stages also experience crises of confidence in which their commitment to change wanes and the old specter of indulging in substance use looms once again (Saunders & Allsop, 1989). Ambivalence about change can arise at any stage of change. So, too, confrontational interviewing, or the use of direct persuasion, might be unproductive across all stages. There is an argument for viewing matching in more subtle terms, not involving the use of different treatments but different emphases depending on the stage of change of the client. Motivational interviewing could provide one of the foundations for a broad framework that includes cognitive–behavioral techniques such as relapse prevention.

COST CONSIDERATIONS

It is tempting to view motivational interviewing as a cheap treatment option, particularly since it can be condensed into a relatively brief form. Evidence for its effectiveness has begun to emerge. The argument is strengthened by the observation that most people with addictive problems change without any formal help anyway. A brief "motivational nudge" might be all that is needed for most substance abusers (see Bien, Miller, & Tonigan, 1993).

Formal evaluations of cost-effectiveness should be carried out by comparing motivational interviewing with other approaches known to be effective. Economists and planners should be warned, however, to avoid falling into the trap of viewing substance abusers as a homogeneous goup. There are some, particularly those with severe personal and social difficulties, who will need other kinds of help. One does not have to look far back into the history of substance abuse treatment to find evidence for single-minded adherence to a preferred form of treatment. It is to be hoped that sensitive clinical and economic analyses will prevent this from happening to motivational interviewing.

EVIDENCE OF EFFECTIVENESS

There is little point in spending time and resources facilitating readiness to change if this does not lead to improved treatment outcomes. The first studies of motivational interviewing have emerged only recently. Three controlled trials are described here. First, Bien, Miller, and Boroughs (1993) examined the impact of motivational interviewing as a preliminary step in outpatient treatment for severe problem drinkers. Thirty-two clients were assigned at random either to receive or not to receive motivational interviewing. This consisted of a 2-hour assessment session followed by an interview in which the results were reviewed in keeping with the principles of motivational interviewing (Miller & Rollnick, 1991). Control subjects completed the same assessment battery but received an attention placebo interview in place of the motivational interview. Superior outcome was evident in the experimental group at 3-month follow-up; by 6 months, these differences were no longer significant.

Second, Brown and Miller (1993) used a similar design to examine the impact of motivational interviewing on participation and outcome of residential treatment among 28 problem drinkers; however, in this study, control subjects continued with routine treatment after the intake assessment and did not receive an attention placebo interview. Clients who recieved the initial motivational interview participated more fully in treatment (as rated by therapists) and showed superior drinking outcome at 3 months after discharge, despite receiving the same 13-day residential program as control subjects.

Finally, Rollnick et al. (1992) gave brief motivational interviewing or skills-based counseling to 174 non–help-seeking excessive drinkers in a general hospital setting. Preliminary analyses indicate that among the 70% classified as less ready to change (precontemplation, contemplation, and preparation stages), those who received brief motivational interviewing had a superior outcome at 6-month follow-up to those who received skills-based counselling. These findings suggest that the readiness-to-change construct could form a useful basis for matching clients to treatment.

None of the above three studies were methodologically flawless. They represent provisional findings in what is a growing field of study. They also illustrate the way in which motivational interviewing can be adapted to a variety of settings; in the first two studies it took the form of an interview following detailed assessment; in the third, the whole procedure was condensed into a single session used at a patient's bedside. Put simply, these studies imply that outcome is improved when clients, rather than counselors, are encouraged to articulate the implications of assessment and their ambivalence about behavioral change.

CONCLUSION

Motivational interviewing appears to have a useful function in the addictions field as an alternative to the confrontational approaches so widely practiced for many decades. Beyond this function, what place will there be for it in the future? We have tried to show in this chapter that it represents more than simply using a nonconfrontational interviewing style with clients. Its main focus is the examinaton and resolution of ambivalence. The method involves the combined use of directive and client-centered counseling styles. Evidence for its effectiveness has begun to emerge. Whether such activity carries the name of motivational interviewing is less important than that clients are given the opportunity to get to the heart of the ambivalence conflict in a constructive atmosphere. This activity will, in turn, further enhance our understanding of motivation.

NOTES

1. Miller and Rollnick (1991) provide a more detailed account of motivational interviewing and its application in different settings. For readers interested in the wider application of motivational interviewing in medical settings, the article by Rollnick et al. (1993) provides a conceptual framework; a specific example of how the method can be condensed into a brief procedure can be found in Rollnick et al. (1992).

2. Orford (1975) provides a fascinating account of the ambivalence conflict, underlying what he has termed *excessive appetites*. This is useful background reading.

ACKNOWLEDGMENT

We would like to acknowledge the contribution of Bod Hunter, of AADAC, Alberta, Canada, who encouraged us to view the problem of resistance as one of damaged rapport which should be repaired by the counselor.

REFERENCES

Bien, T., Miller, W., & Boroughs, J. (1993). Motivational interviewing with alcohol outpatients. *Behavioural Psychotherapy, 21,* 347–356.

Bien, T., Miller, W., & Tonigan, J. (1993). Brief interventions for alcohol problems: A review. *Addiction, 88,* 315–336.

Brown, J., & Miller, W. R. (1993). Impact of motivational interviewing on participation and outcome in residential alcoholism treatment. *Psychology of Addictive Behaviours, 7,* 211–218.

Davidson, R., Rollnick, S., & MacEwan, I. (Eds.). (1991). *Counselling the problem drinker.* London: Routledge.

Miller, W. R. (1983). Motivational interviewing with problem drinkers. *Behavioural Psychotherapy, 11,* 147–172.

Miller, W. R. (1994). Motivational interviewing: III. On the ethics of motivational intervention. *Behavioral and Cognitive Psychotherapy, 22,* 111–123.

Miller, W. R., & Rollnick, S. (1991). *Motivational interviewing: Preparing people to change addictive behavior.* New York: Guilford Press.

Miller, W. R., & Sovereign, R. G. (1989). *The check-up: A model for early intervention in addictive behaviors.* In T. Lober, W. R. MIller, P. E. Nathan, & G. A. Marlatt (Eds.), *Addictive Behaviors: Prevention and early intervention* (pp. 219–231). Amsterdam: Swets & Zeitlinger.

Orford, J. (1985). *Excessive appetites: A psychological view of addiction.* New York: Wiley.

Prochaska, J., & DiClemente, C. (1986). Toward a comprehensive model of change. In W. R. Miller & N. Heather (Eds.), *Treating the addictive behaviors: Processes of change* (pp. 3–27). New York: Plenum Press.

Project Match Research Group. (1993). Project MATCH: Rationale and methods for a multi-centre clinical trial matching alcoholism patients to treatment. *Alcoholism: Clinical and Experimental Research, 17,* 1130–1145.

Rollnick, S., Heather, N., & Bell, A. (1992). Negotiating behaviour change in medical settings: The development of brief motivational interviewing. *Journal of Mental Health, 1,* 25–37.

Rollnick, S., Kinnersley, P., & Stott, N. (1993). Methods of helping patients with behaviour change. *British Medical Journal, 307,* 188–190.

Saunders, W., & Allsop, S. (1989). Relapse: A critique. In M. Gossop (Ed.), *Relapse and addictive behaviour* (pp. 249–277). London: Routledge.

Saunders, W., Wilkinson., C. & Allsop, S. (1991). Motivational intervention with heroin users attending a methadone clinic. In W. R. Miller & S. Rollnick, *Motivational interviewing: Preparing people to change addictive behavior* (pp. 279–292). New York: Guilford Press.

10

Working with Addicts
in Private Practice:
Overcoming Initial Resistance

DEBRA ROTHSCHILD

INTRODUCTION

Drug-addicted patients have a particular reputation for being "resistant." This could have a multitude of meanings yet is frequently stated with little thought as to the specific implications or reasons, and often, unfortunately, with an implicit judgment attached. It is one of the primary explanations offered for the difficulty or even impossibility of treating addicts in any but the most structured, specialized programs, and a rationalization for confrontation, prescription, or sometimes even argumentative opposition on the part of a therapist. In this chapter, I define and discuss areas of resistance and techniques for working with (not against) those resistances, thereby demonstrating why the above approaches do not and cannot possibly work and how it is possible to work with drug-dependent patients even in a private practice setting.

RESISTANCE VERSUS DENIAL

When speaking about drug addicts, the term *resistance* is often used interchangeably with *denial*. They are related but different. Denial, as we know, is a defense. All defenses serve a purpose and can be more or less adaptive depending on circumstances and the success of their use. For example, initial denial in the face of trauma or tragedy is usual and not pathological. Denial can also be extreme and psychotic. Denial has been defined as "the automatic refusal to acknowledge painful or disturbing aspects of inner or outer reality" (Bond, 1986, p. 138). In a proposal for the revised third edition of the *Diagnostic and Statistical Manual of Mental Disorders* (American Psychiatric Association, 1987) (DSM III-R), denial was described as follows: "The individual deals with internal conflicts, or internal or external stressors, by refusing to acknowledge some aspect of external reality that would be apparent to others" This definition serves our purposes well. Addicts do frequently deny the extent of their drug use and the consequences thereof. And drug use and its consequences are stressful and create great internal conflict. Denial is a rather primitive way of dealing with conflict but also perhaps an indication that it exists. It is the conflict that leads to resistance, which is a phenomenon that is frequently missed with addicts, perhaps because the interpersonal configuration developed by many clinicians is the addict who wants to get high versus the authority therapist who wants drug use to stop. So often, the chemically dependent are simply labeled resistant, as if that is all there is to it and all we have to do is convince them to "see the light."

In this context, resistance can mean resistance to admitting the addiction and acknowledging powerlessness over it, which implies an acceptance of, or even asking for, help, or it can mean resistance to any aspect of treatment. Resistance can be overt refusal to comply with recommendations, or it can manifest as passive agreement but a failure to act. Therapists who experience such resistance often become angry and frustrated. Frequently, however, these same clinicians have experienced similar resistance from many other psychotherapy patients and although they may have become frustrated, they understood it in terms of transference or conflict or some phenomenon worthy of being analyzed and worked through.

One of the most common and most dangerous misconceptions about drug addicts is that they are all sociopaths or all like spoiled, hedonistic children who simply cannot delay gratification and just want to have fun. In fact, a common and significant cause of failure to engage these patients in treatment is this misunderstanding and its consequences. One important consequence is that the therapist develops a judgmental attitude toward the patient, which the patient can quickly detect. Another is the frequent tendency on the part of clinicians to ignore the adaptive values of the drug taking. Focusing solely on the maladaptive, harmful, or apparently hedonistic aspects of the substance abuse misses the point and generally loses the patient or, if not the patient, certainly the patient's trust or feeling of being understood.

For most addicts, drug use is a way to feel not only better but "normal" or OK. When asked to describe their first experience with their drug of choice, most will describe years of multidrug experimentation, then coming upon one drug and knowing immediately that they were hooked. They knew this because suddenly they felt like they could fit in; they could be "normal," like others (Weider & Kaplan, 1969). So, an important question at the beginning of the work is, "What did your drug do for you?" Letting the patient know that the therapist knows that drug use feels essential today will go a long way toward helping the therapist to engage that person. Explore what it was like before drug use, and, especially, "What do you imagine life will be like without it?" The rationale behind this approach dates back to 1932, when Glover (1932/1956) revolutionized psychological thinking about substance abuse by labeling it progressive rather than regressive and talked about the attempt at adaptation that drug taking can signify.

CHARACTERISTICS OF ADDICTS

What follows is a review of some of the characteristics that experts have found typical of people who are addicted and how they relate to drug use. It is important to understand these characteristics not necessarily as causes of addiction but as conditions that may sustain it. In other words, whether or not these characteristics preceded the addiction, they are likely to be present when the patient presents for treatment. Understanding this will help the therapist engage the person in several ways: by empathizing, by not passing judgment, by knowing what to expect and asking the right questions, and by not expecting too much. One word of caution, however—not all addicts are alike. Ask questions.

Five ego functions have been consistently identified as impaired in most addicts (Treece, 1984). Rather than impaired or deficient, I prefer to use Khantzian, Halliday, and McAuliffe's (1990) concept of vulnerabilities, which implies danger rather than failure and a greater potential for repair. All five areas can be seen as emerging from common underlying characteristics or dynamics. They are affect management, self-care, judgment, defensive functioning, and object relations.

Affect management includes the ability to label or identify affective experience as well as the capacity to tolerate emotions. Addicts tend to have difficulty with both and are often described as living under the continual threat of being overwhelmed by affect due to its all-or-nothing quality and their inability to modulate it. Poor judgment and self-care may well derive from a need to seek thrills and increase external stimulation or an inability to use anxiety as a signal to avoid danger (related to the inability to recognize any emotion, including anxiety), or it may be related to issues of low self-esteem, masochism, or narcissistic conflicts. Similarly, difficulties with object relations would be an inevitable result of the inability to tolerate affect, a narcissistic constellation, and the use of primitive defenses such as denial, projection, and splitting.

The above reference to narcissistic conflicts or a narcissistic constellation is not meant to imply that all addicted individuals manifest narcissistic personality disorders. Rather, as Wurmser (1974) indicates, most addicted patients demonstrate some evidence of narcissistic disturbance that manifests in characteristics such as grandiosity, arrogance, entitlement, poor differentiation of self and objects, and a tenuous sense of self. Levin (1987) describes a similar observation, making it clear that these narcissistic phenomena are not necessarily due to the character of the patient but will be evident when a substance abuser enters into treatment. For some, Levin says, this is a fixation, but for others it is a regression consequent to the chronic reliance on drugs.

Clinical Implications

I am not suggesting that these characteristics be addressed early in treatment but simply that therapists recognize that most drug addicts are strikingly lacking in their ability to soothe or calm themselves, that they are overly sensitive to any stimulation they cannot control, and that they frequently live in terror of being overwhelmed by sensations or feelings for which they have no category or name and no ability to modulate. Drugs can take feelings away, increase them, decrease them, change them, and give a person the sense that he/she knows why they are there and approximately how long they will last. This may give us an idea of how frightening, or even how dangerous, it can be to give up the drugs and how much we must offer in exchange. Wurmser (1974) warns that to suppress the patient's attempt at self-treatment (i.e., the drug use) without massive support to the ego can often result in more serious forms of decompensation.

Earlier, I mentioned the importance of empathy and nonjudgmental acceptance, which would probably not even be mentioned if the diagnostic category was other than addiction. It would be assumed. Yet, with chemically dependent patients, therapists are frequently told not to be understanding but to break through denial, teach them what is right, and tell them what to do to get sober. This is a frightening and sometimes confusing concept to many clinicians, who then feel uncomfortable accepting addicted patients into treatment. The only way they know how to work is with empathy and support, and this prescription implies an oppositional stance. In fact, we can be empathic without agreeing that drug use is a good thing. We can accept nonjudgmentally without condoning behavior. We do not have to criticize the drug taking either. Most of these patients already feel bad enough about themselves and their addiction.

Conflict

Although some patients arrive in the therapist's office defending their right to drink/drug, or denying the addiction or need for help, if they really, fully believed that, they would probably brag about how much they drank rather than cover it up. We tend to hide things we are ashamed of. In general, it is safe to assume that there is a conflict. The conflict goes something like this: "It feels like I need it, yet I also know it is destroying my life." Of course, not everyone lies or denies. Many people enter treatment so tired of drugging, or in deep enough trouble, that they are begging for help. Regardless, whether someone walks in and says clearly, "I am in trouble, please help me," or, the other extreme, is mandated to treatment and indicates no desire to be there, that individual will probably be in conflict as well. For all these reasons, they want to keep using their drug. For all the reasons that are so obvious to us, they want to stop.

Conflict generally implies ambivalence. Something we know about the experience of ambivalence is that it is very hard to hold both sides of it at the same time. We generally vacillate; first to one side, then to the other. We also know that being in conflict is an uncomfortable state of affairs. One way to handle it is through projection and/or splitting. For example, addicts frequently project the wanting-to-stop side of the conflict onto the therapist, while the wanting-to-use remains unopposed for the moment, within. When the therapist allows that to happen by accepting that role, the patient can feel clearer about wanting to use.

Even without projection, but simply in discussion, this can occur. If the therapist comes across as strongly advocating sobriety and ignoring the reasons to keep using, the patient can more easily take the opposite position. The patient ends up on the side of "I want to keep using," or "I'm not an addict," and the therapist is battering away, trying to prove that the patient is addicted, or that drug use is bad and causing harm.

Managing the Resistance

As described above, the harder a therapist pushes against the drugs, the more the therapist risks solidifying the resistant client's position. Yet, of course, therapists are advocates for sobriety, and everyone including our patients, knows that. In fact, that is why our patients came to us. Following are five methods with which to handle this situation:

1. Remember that the drugging felt useful, necessary, or good in some way. Talk about that. Engage in a discussion that addresses both sides of the ambivalence. Make it personal to that addict. It might result in a statement like the following, made to a high-powered, overconfident-appearing, multimillionaire businessman who asked, challengingly, at the end of his first interview, "What can you do for me?" The therapist

replied, "I can help you live without alcohol *and* without fear." As P. Bromberg (personal communication, March 4, 1993) said, "A lot of what has been called resistance is the result of a person feeling not understood."

2. Avoid arguing. Just do not get into it. For example, try the following: "I am not an alcoholic." "Maybe you're not; let's talk about what brought you here. . . . " Remember, even in the Alcoholics Anonymous *Big Book* (1939) it says, "We do not like to pronounce any individual alcoholic, but you can quickly diagnose yourself" (p. 31).

3. Join the resistance. Joining what patients claim as their side leaves the patient available to take the opposing side. It frequently surprises the patient and creates a shift. The therapist has to be careful not to sound sarcastic, manipulative, or artificial. For example, about 3 years into treatment, an opiate addict who had also abused marijuana, benzodiazepines, and occasional alcohol was going on vacation to Club Med. He said, "Maybe I'll drink on vacation." The therapist began by talking about it as a slip, a first step toward major relapse, etc. He continued on the side of drinking. Then the therapist said, "Well, maybe it's not such a bad idea. You could drink there and come home and no one would ever know. It would be like it happened in a different world, like it never really happened at all." He paused and said, "No, I'd have to count it as a slip." The therapist sounded surprised and said, "Oh, you would? So then what?" "And then . . . " he went on and suddenly he was saying, "I think I want iced tea. That beer doesn't look so good to me anymore."

4. Make the conflict explicit and conscious. This is similar to what Miller and Rollnick (1991) call "creating cognitive dissonance" (p. 56). Miller described it as building an awareness of how the drugging is interfering with goals and desires. The goal of this method is to get the client to voice the concerns. For example, talking about goals and wishes for the future and how they might be accomplished and exploring what interfered with successes in the past can help patients articulate the ways in which alcohol or drugs create problems in living that they have previously wished to deny. It is the patient who will verbalize these concerns if the exploration is guided by a therapist sensitive to the issues and to the power of denial.

5. Accept where the patient is at. This relates to not arguing and not diagnosing. If the client comes to the office to talk about loneliness, talk about loneliness. Client and therapist will get to the drug use also, but it is best to begin with what feels important and work from there. The therapist may know that drugging is the most important issue and that nothing else will get better until the person gets sober, but the client is not necessarily concerned about that right now. The therapist will have to help the client recognize this and get there. However, building a relationship must be primary. Without it, the therapist will have no chance of helping. If this first-time patient leaves and never wants to return because he/she felt totally misunderstood or not listened to, the therapist

has probably lost the patient. It is awful to be lonely, to be having trouble at work, and so on and, of course, improving that condition is a goal. The therapist can accept that goal and begin by suggesting that they look at what is going on that led to this state of affairs and may be perpetuating it.

Addressing the issue the patient brings in is probably what most therapists do, except, for some reason, when the patient is addicted. We are scared of addiction. It feels like an emergency. It is life-threatening behavior. We want it to stop and we have been taught that if we do not confront it and intervene immediately we are doing a bad thing. I believe this has more to do with society's negative attitude toward addicts, our perception that they must be punished and controlled, and our fear of the addiction than with any clinical phenomenon.

BEGINNING TREATMENT

At this point, let us assume that the patient has acknowledged that perhaps he/she needs help. It is time to suggest what the patient should do. A discussion of treatment planning is beyond the scope of this chapter. Let me just say that it is fairly well agreed that groups are extremely useful, individual therapy is good, family work is usually important, and 12-Step involvement is considered virtually essential. How can we suggest a plan that will minimize resistance and maximize the probability of success?

Again, the same principles apply. The therapist is the expert, of course. But there is danger in coming across as an authoritarian dictator, as though the patient's feelings or desires do not count at all. Some patients are ready and willing to take on a total program of abstinence and treatment at once. Others are not. Talk about it. Sometimes I set goals for future involvement but begin with, for example, individual counseling only. If the patient is not ready for groups, we make an agreement that we will work individually and talk about his/her discomfort with being in a group. As much as we may not want to believe it, there are therapists and programs that discharge people from treatment if they do not cooperate with the whole program immediately. Many addicted patients, of course, expect just this kind of punitive treatment, and they may even invite it due to their own negative self-concepts and belief in their innate badness and need to be punished. They have always been identified as the "bad kid," or "naughty child" who cuts school, gets in trouble, and does not cooperate. Abandonment, rejection, and censure are the usual result and discharge from treatment merely confirms those self-concepts and expectations. Working with the patient, identifying his/her fears, and helping the patient to participate constructively can create a new, mutative, and healing experience for that individual.

Miller (1991) talks about the need for therapists to find the right balance between overprescribing the therapy yet not being totally non-directional. Certainly, we are experts and we have ideas about what works. We make suggestions, discuss them, and come up with a plan. This sounds so obvious, but when clinicians treat the chemically dependent it does not always happen this way, and, unfortunately, a lot of potential patients are lost to treatment because they are not properly prepared or their limitations are not respected.

Miller also warns against insisting on total abstinence immediately. I have long argued for an approach that allows an individual to find his/her way to sobriety (within reasonable limits and without risking health or safety, of course). Therapists can negotiate a trial period of abstinence, tapering, attempting moderation, and so on. For example, if someone is convinced that he/she can drink moderately, the therapist should suggest they find out whether it is true. If we get into an argument, we will probably lose the patient we just worked so hard to motivate. I usually say something like the following:

> Well, it's unusual for someone who's been drinking as much as you have to be able to control his drinking, and you may be setting yourself up for an extremely hard task, but try it. It would be great if you could. So, why not give it two weeks. Decide before you go out if you'll have one or two drinks that night, and stick to it. Let's pick some nights not to have any at all. If you find it's too difficult, we'll come up with a different plan. If you can do it, we'll keep watching and talk about what all this excess might have been about for you.

This is different from advocating controlled drinking. It is a way to help the patient become convinced, ready, and motivated. Drinking or drugging is not ignored during this period. It is explicitly monitored and talked about, with a special focus on what it feels like not to use and the consequences of using.

I believe that the notion that we must insist on total abstinence immediately is one reason that clinicians feel they cannot treat addicted individuals in private practice. They do not feel prepared or comfortable to do this, yet they believe they have no option if they are to be responsible about treating addiction.

Another issue that must be addressed is the person who agrees to whatever you suggest but simply does not show up. It can be helpful in such a situation to specifically articulate the ambivalence and talk about it in advance. Khantzian et al. (1990) say, in their book on group therapy with addicts, "The leader should specifically articulate that, given a past tendency to substitute action and activity for feeling, at some level each member will not want to come to group. This is a reaction to be expected, but not enacted" (p. 76). Predicting the feeling, getting the patient to talk about it, and making it expectable and acceptable to feel will help the patient to not act it out.

Another part of the process which contributes to denial and resistance is grief over loss. That loss is not only a loss of the drug itself, or even of its effects, but also of "friends," activities, and an identity, as in "I am a person who takes drugs (or drinks)," "I am the screw-up," and so on. The loss has to be acknowledged and grieved, and anticipating it and talking about it can help increase readiness and motivation for treatment. Not too long ago, in an early sobriety group, one female member said to another who was having trouble getting sober, "It's like when you break up with a boyfriend. You have to grieve the end of the relationship. You have to admit this relationship no longer works. It's a bad relationship and we all tend to hang out in them for too long. Then we finally break up and we have to grieve." Remember, the first phase of grief is denial, and denial is a primary defense of most addicts. It requires a delicate balance to help a patient with the denial that is part of any grieving experience yet simultaneously to work through the denial of drug use and its consequences. Bargaining, anger, and sadness follow denial in grieving before we come to acceptance.

Bromberg (1993) talks about resistance in psychoanalysis in a way that relates closely to the issues addressed here. He says:

> A person may feel himself so psychologically incapacitated and at risk in the world of people, that it is indeed similar to living alone in a burning building from which he needs to be rescued. But *that* particular burning building is the only one that exists as a self, and one's individual selfhood, no matter how painful or unadaptive, must be protected at all cost as part of any rescue operation. . . . Resistance from this perspective is an enacted communication that an analyst's effort to interpret meaning is being experienced at that moment as requiring the patient to trade off some domain of his own self-experience for something that is being offered that is "not me" and that the analyst's offering is being opposed in one way or another, because it is not felt as sufficiently negotiable at that moment. "This is not who I am!", is part of the dialectic between loyalty to old patterns of self-meaning and increased ability to state "*This* is who I am!" (pp. 2–3)

Frequently, patients addicted to drugs neglect or disown almost all other parts of their lives. One of the most frightening aspects of giving up an addiction is the thought, "If I am no longer an addict, what am I?" or more precisely, "Who am I?" The superficial bluster and defensive grandiosity that many addicts manifest can make it easy to forget the tremendous fear that characterizes the inner life of most addicted individuals. Many who have felt like failures throughout most of their lives, and/or who suffer a narcissistic sense of nothingness or emptiness inside and a vulnerable sense of self, have established a sense of identity around the addiction. Therefore, there is tremendous resistance to changing or expanding that identity.

SOME SPECIFIC SITUATIONS

At this point, I will briefly touch on some specific situations related to resistance, such as when the addict absolutely refuses to come in to the office or when he/she fails to arrive for a follow-up appointment. If the therapist cannot get the addict in at all, the therapist may feel there is not much he/she can do. However, as we know, any change in a system affects all parts of that system. So, working with any family members (or friends, coworkers, etc.) can often be helpful. As long as the therapist engages some individuals who are involved with the addict and is working on identifying and changing enabling behaviors, or just helping them come to terms with the other's addiction, the therapist has a chance of engaging the addict. Of course, there is always the option of planning an intervention. It is important to keep in mind that interventions must be carefully planned and professionally guided or else they can be dangerous. When properly and professionally done, however, interventions can be extremely powerful and successful.

Patients with addictions frequently miss appointments, especially at the beginning of treatment. With some other kinds of patients, we often consider carefully the meaning of the miss and at times decide to let it go, assuming the patient is acting out something that can be discussed at the next session, which we assume the patient will attend. With addicts, it is important to follow any missed session immediately with a telephone call and an expression of concern. Therapists who do this have a much higher return rate. In fact, Miller (1991) even suggests a routine follow-up call between the first and second sessions. He claims that the highest dropout rate for the chemically dependent is after the first session, and cites research in which 100 addicted patients were randomly divided into two groups after their initial contact at a clinic. Half of them received a single telephone call after their initial consultation and half did not. Of the two groups, 52% versus 8% returned for treatment. That is, a single further contact increased the return rate six times. Those groups were from a clinic. In private practice, this method may be a bit impractical. However, any sessions missed early in treatment should be followed up with more than one telephone call if necessary, and at the end of an initial session patients should be encouraged to call if any questions or concerns arise before the next appointment.

Another issue is relapse. The emphasis here is in terms of resistance and the readiness of the patient. (See Daley & Lis, Chapter 13, this volume, for a discussion of relapse prevention.) For some addicts, but not all, relapses are part of the recovery process and can be used as valuable learning experiences. Again, the most important principle to keep in mind is nonjudgmental acceptance. Moreover, nonjudgmental acceptance does not mean approval or even permission. (Approval is a judgment.) The idea is simply to create an atmosphere in which patients feel safe enough to tell the therapist about a relapse so that they can work on it together and it does not become a secret kept from the "punitive authority" who will drop the patient from treatment or get angry. Also, if the patient feels that the therapist is the authority keeping him/her in line, a relapse is more likely to occur as some kind of rebellion or transference acting out. If it is clear that therapist and patient are both on the same side, a relapse is deprived of this power. Drug use becomes the common adversary to avoid, not a weapon to use against the adversary therapist.

This is not to say that contingencies cannot or should not be planned for, or that continued drug use should be tolerated without limit. A mutual plan can be developed; for example, if the addict cannot stop using by a designated time, he/she will go into an inpatient rehabilitation program, or a more structured outpatient program, and then return to the therapist for continuing care.

I do not believe in discharging a patient from treatment for continuing to use drugs. Many therapists do. They believe that a patient must be fully motivated and willing to cooperate before treatment can begin. Or, a more common belief is that the therapist becomes an enabler if he/she does not insist on complete abstinence from the beginning of treatment. To me, this is tantamount to punishing the patient for asking for help with a symptom that is hard to get under control. If it were so easy to stop, perhaps that person would not be seeking assistance to begin with. Who ever dropped a depressed patient for not sleeping or still crying or feeling hopeless for too long? However, if the patient absolutely refuses all suggestions and will not cooperate with any of the treatment, it is probably in everyone's best interest to discontinue until the patient is more ready to try, at least by keeping appointments. Usually, however, a genuine sense of acceptance, a nonpunitive, nonjudgmental attitude, and explicitly addressing the ambivalence and fear are enough to allow an addict to feel safe enough to consider engaging in treatment and if not to stop drug use immediately, at least to set it up as a goal to be worked toward together.

CONCLUSION

Discussion about the ambivalence over whether to stop using substances is frequently an initial stage of addiction treatment and should be recognized as such. Too often clinicians label themselves or their clients failures if drug use continues beyond the first few sessions. As long as the focus remains on the use and the conflicts around it, therapy is occurring. Working with the resistance to engagement and to sobriety is a legitimate and valuable part of treatment. Issues that need to be addressed include fear of relinquishing the substance(s), the grief over its loss, loss of identity, finding new ways of coping, and establishing realistic goals for the future.

REFERENCES

Alcoholics Anonymous. (1939). *The big book.* New York: Author.

American Psychiatric Association. (1987). *Diagnostic and statistical manual of mental disorders* (3rd ed., rev.). Washington, DC: Author.

Bond, M. (1986). An empirical study of defense styles. In G. Vaillant (Ed.), *Empirical studies of ego mechanisms of defense* (pp. 2–29). Washington, DC: American Psychiatric Press.

Bromberg, P. (1993, November). Resistance: Obstacle or stepping stone. In *Psychoanalytic innovation and the interpersonal heritage.* Fiftieth Anniversary Clinical Symposium of the William Alanson White Institute, New York.

Glover, E. (1956). On the etiology of drug addiction. In *On the early development of mind* (pp. 187–215). New York: International Universities Press. (Original work published 1932)

Khantzian, E. J., Halliday, K. S., & McAuliffe, W. E. (1990). *Addiction and the vulnerable self: Modified dynamic group therapy for substance abusers.* New York: Guilford Press.

Levin, J. D. (1987). *Treatment of alcoholism and other addictions: A self psychology approach..* New York: Jason Aronson.

Miller, W. R., & Rollnick, S. (1991). *Motivational interviewing: Preparing people to change addictive behavior.* New York: Guilford Press.

Treece, C. (1984). Assessment of ego functioning in studies of narcotic addiction. In L. Bellak & L. A. Goldsmith (Eds.), *The broad scope of ego function assessment* (pp. 268–289). New York: Wiley.

Weider, H., & Kaplan, E. H. (1969). Drug use in adolescents: Psychodynamic theory and pharmacogenic effect. *Psychoanalytic Study of the Child, 24,* 399–431.

Wurmser, L. (1974). Psychoanalytic considerations of the etiology of compulsive drug use. *Journal of the American Psychoanalytic Association, 22,* 820–843.

11

Brief Treatment

REID K. HESTER
THOMAS H. BIEN

INTRODUCTION

Brief interventions form a class of treatments with some surprising consistencies. For one thing, such interventions often begin with thorough assessment and involve some form of feedback to the individual. There is also generally a certain style of interaction between therapist and client which focuses on enhancing client motivation for change.

"Brief" of course means different things in different contexts. In psychoanalytical therapy, a treatment of 6 months or even 1 year's duration might be considered brief. The studies in a recent review (Bien, Miller, & Tonigan, 1993), however, were generally between one and three sessions in length—remarkably brief by any standard. In most of this research, the clinical techniques employed were also quite straightforward, specifiable, and teachable. Given a minimum of specialized training, these techniques are within reach of many individuals who do not work in the mental health field (e.g., physicians and clergy) and certainly within the grasp of counselors and therapists who do not specialize in addiction. Because the need for specialized treatment of addictive behaviors consistently outstrips the availability of specialist providers, this is welcome news indeed.

In this chapter, we have limited our discussion of the literature concerning the efficacy of these treatments as our purpose is primarily practical and clinical. We begin by reviewing concepts of change relevant to brief interventions. Then we review the basic elements of these interventions and the components of an adequate assessment. Next we attempt to give the reader a concrete sense of how these interventions proceed. Finally, we make a few comments about the relevant literature supporting the efficacy of these approaches.

USEFUL CONCEPTS IN BRIEF INTERVENTIONS

We can improve our chances of being effective with brief interventions if we have an understanding of the stage-change model and motivational interviewing (MI) (Miller & Rollnick, 1991). Discussing them in detail is beyond the scope and space limitation of this chapter but fortunately they are presented in this volume by Shaffer and Robbins (Chapter 5) and Rollnick and Morgan (Chapter 9). These concepts dovetail nicely with brief interventions. For instance, being aware of where a client is in the stages of change helps clarify tasks and develop realistic expectations of what can be accomplished in a brief intervention. Knowing about MI improves chances of interacting with clients in such a way as to help move them along in the process of change. We recommend a review of these chapters before starting to conduct brief interventions.

ELEMENTS OF BRIEF INTERVENTIONS

Given that brief intervention research has been conducted by independent scientists in 14 different nations, there is surprising consistency in approach (Bien et al., 1993). To describe that consistency, Miller and Sanchez (1994) coined the acronym FRAMES (*f*eedback, *r*esponsiblity, *a*dvice, *m*enu, *e*mpathy, and *s*elf-efficacy). We comment briefly on each of these elements in turn.

Feedback

It is arguable that all therapy seeks to create a sense of discrepancy between how an individual's life is currently and how that individual would like it to be in future. In fact, it is hard to understand why someone would undertake the difficulties of behavioral change without such a discrepancy. Feedback serves to develop this sense. Because most individuals with alcohol and drug problems already receive abundant feedback from their environments that there is some sort of problem, it may not be clear why more feedback is needed. However, normal feedback may be either (1) insufficiently salient or (2) given in a manner that actually encourages continuation of the problem behavior. For instance, the more immediate, and hence more influential, consequences of drinking are positive and reinforcing. Negative consequences tend to be somewhat more remote in time. Within a drinking episode, for example, the earliest effects of consumption are usually experienced as pleasurable. Later effects, such as nausea and vomiting, are usually not experienced until the individual has reached sufficient intoxication that distortions in cognition have developed as well. These are experienced with less vividness and remembered less clearly because of increasing intoxication. This may explain why normal environmental feedback is often insufficient. The second problem with feedback, that it may actually encourage continuation of the behavior, generally has to do with the interpersonal context in which feedback is delivered. Concerned spouses or partners often give abundant negative feedback about drinking and using, but such feedback is often ineffective. The key principle involved is reactance. Reactance may be understood to mean that when the freedom of any given behavior is threatened, both the attractiveness and the probability of that behavior increase. To put this concretely, the moment we are told not to think about pink elephants, the odds are we will find ourselves both desiring to do so and doing so. Effective feedback must therefore become salient, on the one hand and avoid the problem of reactance on the other. Most forms of psychological therapy attempt in some fashion to verbally increase the salience of environmental feedback. Alcoholics Anonymous, for example, may be thought of as doing this through recitation of old "war stories." To avoid reactance, however, feedback needs to be delivered in a neutral, empathic, nonjudgmental fashion. This is discussed more extensively later.

Responsibility

Most effective brief interventions convey the message in ways both explicit and implicit that change is entirely up to the individual. In practice, we often tell clients quite specifically, "What you choose to do with this feedback is entirely up to you. If you wish to change, you and only you can do it." To avoid the reactance problem, it may be desirable to give the message, "No one can make you stop drinking or using if you do not want to." Not only does this avoid the reactance problem and help circumvent power struggles with a client (which the therapist will lose), but it is fundamentally true.

Advice

There is indeed a role for advice. The effectiveness of advice on its own is somewhat limited (Miller, 1985). Trials of advice alone have typically examined the impact of a physician's recommendation that a patient quit smoking, with positive results in 5% or 6% of cases. Such a result is not trivial when we compute 5% of the number of smokers nationally. However, advice is not sufficient for most individuals when used alone. In the context of MI, advice is generally withheld until requested and is even then given with a tinge of reluctance. When someone does request advice, we typically say something such as, "I'm not sure what will work for you." Then we ask about what the client has tried before, offering additional suggestions. We believe that such an approach to advice giving offers two advantages. Once again, it avoids the problem of reactance. Even when people seek advice, they may still resent it as a loss of freedom. Second, it takes advantage of the principle that individuals are more likely to engage in behaviors that are already within their repertoire than to engage in completely new behaviors.

Menu of Options

Research on motivation has found that offering more choices regarding approaches to behavioral change is associated with a more successful outcome (Miller, 1985). We therefore typically provide an array of possible approaches to change in this area. Because there is no one treatment that is superior to all others (Miller et al., 1995), we can offer options without fear of depriving someone of "the most effective treatment." In keeping with this approach, we also refrain from *prescribing* a specific drinking goal to clients but assist them in developing their own goal, be it lifelong abstinence, 3 months of sobriety, or moderation. It is important to remember that clients choose their own goals regardless of what the therapist says or advises. If a client is considering moderation, we provide the client with current research data about the probability of success given the level of alcohol-related problems he/she has experienced. If the client chooses moderation, we encourage the client to set limits on his/her drinking and consider pursuing moderate drinking in a systematic manner (e.g., via self-help manual or therapy). Should the client be unsuccessful in achieving or maintaining moderation, we can use the client's lack of success to help him/her consider abstinence.

Empathy

None of the reports of brief interventions has used the sort of directive, coercive style of treatment that has sometimes been used in U.S. alcohol treatment programs (Bien et al., 1993). In fact, Miller and Taylor (1980) found that higher levels of therapist empathy produce lower levels of consumption, and vice versa. What we mean by empathy is the accurate empathy described by Carl Rogers involving specific reflective listening skills. It is not a matter of, "Oh, I know just what you mean. I've been there." In fact, in this context such a statement is generally nonempathic.

Self-Efficacy

Both explicitly and in terms of general, underlying attitude, we tell clients that they can change. A good no-lose question in this context is: "Have you ever known anyone who has successfully quit drinking?" If the client says no, the therapist can respond with: "Well, no wonder you may find it difficult to imagine doing it yourself. But let me tell you each day many individuals have successfully changed this part of their behavior. They are not extraordinary individuals, but just normal people. I have personally known and worked with quite a few, and while it may not be easy, it is quite do-able." If the client has known someone, the therapist can respond with: "So you already know this can be done."

DOMAINS TO ASSESS

A comprehensive assessment of a client's history, drinking behaviors, and problems is an important aspect of brief interventions. There are several reasons for this. First, there is a surprising nonconvergence of measures. For instance, a client may be having significant problems with the law but not with his/her work performance. This nonconvergence of problems is particularly true for clients at the less severe end of the spectrum. Second, assessing a wide variety of domains increases the client's level of awareness of problems both during the assessment and during the feedback session. If we only assess two or three areas, we might miss an important aspect of the client's problem which could be a strong motivation for change. For example, whereas some of our clients do not show evidence of neuropsychological impairment from drinking, it seems to be a powerful motivator when we find leading indicators of cognitive dysfunction. Third, if the client decides to seek additional treatment following the brief intervention, having a comprehensive assessment can help guide us in our recommendations. Fourth, with a multidimensional assessment we can develop an understanding of how effective we are with different clients and different aspects of client problems. Finally, doing a comprehensive assessment is a component of a good quality assurance program. Here are the domains we recommend for assessment in brief interventions:

- Alcohol use;
- Other drug use;
- Life problems related to alcohol;
- Medical effects of overdrinking;
- Neuropsychological effects of overdrinking;
- Alcohol dependence;
- Motivation for change;
- Other psychological problems;

- Personal family history; and
- Functional importance of drinking.

Alcohol Use

There is a common misconception that clients with alcohol problems deny or minimize how much they drink. Fortunately, the research on validity of self-report indicates that drinkers can be relatively accurate in their self-report. The accuracy and validity of self-report, however, are heavily influenced by a number of factors. First, the client must be sober during the interview process. We routinely verify this with a portable breathalyzer before beginning assessment sessions. Second, the client must have assurance of confidentiality. If clients suspect or believe that their self-report of drinking will become part of a court record or their personnel file, there will be strong motivation to lie and minimize. Third, we need to develop rapport with the client and an atmosphere of a collaborative relationship rather than a superior–inferior relationship. Finally, how we phrase the questions is important. Asking a client, "Do you drink in the morning?" is likely to evoke a "no." An alternative way to ask this question might be, "How much do you drink from the time you get up until lunch?" There are several structured approaches to determining a client's quantity and frequency of drinking. The one we use in our research laboratory and in our clinical practices is the Brief Drinker Profile (BDP) (Marlatt & Miller, 1987a). It uses a grid to break down a typical week's drinking into days of the week and times of the day (morning, afternoon, evening). It has an additional section for measuring periodic or binge drinking. The BDP also assesses other drug use, life problems, personal family history, the functional importance of drinking, and some aspects of motivation. There are parallel instruments for interviewing the client's spouse or significant other and for follow-up assessments. They are the Collateral Interview Form (CIF) (Marlatt & Miller, 1987b) and the Follow-up Drinker Profile (FDP) (Marlatt & Miller, 1987c), respectively. An alternative to the BDP set of instruments is the Form 90 (Miller, 1991). The Form 90 is also a family of instruments designed to gather drinking and drug use data. Different versions are used at the initial assessment, at follow-up, and when interviewing significant others. The advantage of the Form 90 is that it gives a day-by-day picture of the client's drinking. The disadvantage is that it takes longer to administer than the quantity/frequency section of the BDP. An alternative to the structured interview approach is self-monitoring for a week or two. This involves the client in writing down each drink, how much alcohol there is in it, the time, and the day before beginning to consume it. The client returns the self-monitoring cards to the therapist for review before the feedback session (see Hester, 1995, for more specific information on how to train clients in this procedure).

Other Drug Use

If a client uses other drugs, either illegal and/or prescription, it is helpful to understand both how much and how often he/she uses drugs. The therapist will also want to know the interaction between using drugs and alcohol. For instance, a client might smoke marijuana but only when he/she drinks at a certain bar or with certain friends. In particular, it is often useful to determine the relationship between tobacco smoking and alcohol use, because they often are used together (Bien & Burge, 1991). There are several quantity/frequency measures of other drug use. Both the BDP and the Form 90 have sections on quantity/frequency of illegal and prescription drugs.

Life Problems Related to Alcohol

There are a number of good checklists of alcohol-related problems. The Michigan Alcoholism Screening Test (MAST), although of limited diagnostic utility, is a fairly good checklist. Another inventory is the Drinking Inventory of Consequences (Miller, 1991). The BDP takes an interesting approach to assessing life problems, called a card sort. First, the therapist hands the client a stack of cards, each of which has a single problem printed on it. The therapist then asks the client to sort the cards into two stacks, indicating whether or not the client currently has the problem. When the client has sorted the cards, the therapist next asks the client to rank-order the set of cards listing the problems he/she has. This allows the client to acknowledge difficulties in sensitive areas such as sex without coming right out and saying it out loud, at least initially. Finally, the therapist asks the client to indicate which problems are, in the client's opinion, at least partly related to drinking.

Medical Effects of Overdrinking

There are a large number of health problems associated with overdrinking and the severity of these problems lies on continua. Clients may have varying degrees of leading indicators for significant health problems. This is especially true for clients at the less severe end of the alcohol problems spectrum. Ideally, a client should have a comprehensive physical examination with an eye to these kinds of health problems. Realistically, however, this is not always possible. When an examination is not feasible, we recommend, as a minimum, a blood screening that includes the following enzymes: SGOT, GGTP, SGPT, and bilirubin. Mean cellular volume, high-density lipoproteins, and uric acid are also useful markers. A finding of one or more abnormal values indicates the possibility of health problems associated with drinking.

Neuropsychological Effects

As we discussed earlier, many of our clients have subtle impairments in their brain functions. Although these impairments are usually not severe enough to be noticeable to the client, they can be detected with a neuropsychological screening. There are a number of sensitive instruments to choose from. Most measures of frontal lobe functioning (e.g., Wisconsin Card Sort, the Categories test of the Halstead–Reitan battery), and many visual perceptual tasks are sensitive to the effects of overdrinking. We use the following for a brief screening: the Block Design and Digit Symbol subtests of the Wechsler Adult Intelligence Scale; the Tactile Performance Test of the Halstead–Reitan battery (using time, memory, and location scores); and the Trail Making Test, Parts A and B, which are also a part of the Halstead–Reitan battery.

The therapist does not need to be a neuropsychologist to administer this screening. However, we do highly recommend that the therapist be trained by a neuropsychologist at least until he/she reaches a level of competency and has some continuing supervision over his/her work. The implications of impairment of neuropsychological functioning are far reaching. Findings of impairment in screening often increases the client's perceived risks from drinking. When present, it is usually disturbing. Providing this information in a supportive and empathic manner makes it easier for the client to confront this issue. The good news is that if a client with mild brain dysfunction stops drinking or moderates his/her consumption, these impairments usually reverse themselves.

Alcohol Dependence

There are two good measures of alcohol dependence, both of which are self-administered paper-and-pencil tests and take 5 to 10 minutes. They are the Alchol Dependence Scale (Horn, Skinner, Wanberg, & Foster, 1984) and the Severity of Alcohol Dependence Questionnaire (Stockwell, Hodgson, & Murphy, 1983). Both measure severity of withdrawal symptoms and other psychophysiological consequences of heavy drinking.

Motivation for Change

Motivation for change and the stage of change are two important concepts to understand in a client. It is beyond the scope of this chapter to discuss these issues in detail. Fortunately, Shaffer and Robbins (Chapter 5, this volume) and Rollnick and Morgan (Chapter 9, this volume) cover these important issues well. There are several instruments available that assess stage of change and motivation. Two of them are the Stages of Change Readiness and Treatment Eagerness Scale (SOCRATES) (Miller, 1989) and the University of Rhode Island Change Assessment (URICA) (DiClemente & Hughes, 1990),

Other Psychological Problems

There are a number of psychological problems that often coexist with alcohol problems. They include, but are not limited to, depression, anxiety disorders, insomnia, sexual dysfunction, and family distress. In the brief intervention assessment, the therapist will probably only have time to screen for the presence of these difficulties. Additional evaluation may be indicated if screening is positive. Naturally, if there is evidence of depression the therapist would want to assess suicide potential and possibly the need for hospitalization. The good news here is that many psychological problems spontaneously remit once a client stops drinking or moderates consumption significantly. If a client has a current affective disorder, we recommend that the therapist at least monitor it and treat it aggressively if it persists in the abstinent or moderated drinking client.

Personal Family History

Asking about a family history of alcohol problems or alcoholism can help determine whether the client might have any genetic predisposition to alcoholism. Current data suggest that males with a strong family history of alcoholism on the male side of the family may be at greater risk. Also, it is helpful to inquire whether the client has a history of attention deficit disorder because such clients may also be at greater risk for alcohol problems.

Functional Importance of Drinking

Finally, most clients *perceive* positive benefits from drinking. Assessing these perceived benefits addresses the part of a client's ambivalence about changing that encourages the client not to change. It can also provide the therapist with valuable information about what motivates clients to continue drinking. This information can be reflected back to clients and used to pick treatment interventions if they decide to change their drinking via that route. We use the Alcohol Use Inventory—Revised Edition (AUI-R) (Horn, Wanberg, & Foster, 1987) to help us gather useful information about many aspects of the client's drinking. We strongly recommend the AUI-R for the wealth of information it provides. The AUI-R is a self-administered paper-and-pencil test which takes about 25 minutes to complete. It provides valuable information about the client's style of drinking, perceived benefits, and consequences. The normative reference group is composed primarily of individuals seeking treatment for alcohol problems. Another option is the Alcohol Expectancy Questionnaire (Brown, Christiansen, & Goldman, 1987). This paper-and-pencil test assesses positive and negative expectations about drinking. It can be used for assessment as well as follow-up.

EXAMPLE OF A BRIEF INTERVENTION

Before we present an example of a brief intervention, we want to make a few comments. The type of intervention we are presenting represents a full-scale version of a brief intervention. Some brief interventions have been described in the literature that use only screening information as the basis for a feedback and counseling session (e.g., Kristenson, Ohlin, Hulten-Nosslin, Trell, & Hood, 1983). Most, however, have used a detailed assessment as the basis for providing feedback. In other trials, the advice session lasted a total of 5 minutes (Babor & Grant, 1992). Although we cannot yet specify the minimum time for a feedback session, our recommendation is to allow for 30–60 minutes. As the therapist conducts more brief interventions, he/she will develop a sense about whether more or less time should be devoted to the feedback session.

In the example that follows, we attempt to give readers a feeling for what can take place in an MI brief intervention for alcohol or drug problems. Clearly, space does not permit a full-length transcript, so we alternate between discussion and verbatim language. The case described here is a composite based on our clinical experience and does not refer to any particular person.

First Session

The first session typically begins with a structuring comment, and may proceed, with endless variations, somewhat as follows.

DR. SMITH: Hi, Mr. Jones. I'm Dr. Smith. From our brief discussion on the phone yesterday, it seems you wanted to talk to someone about your drinking. Our goal for today is simply to get acquainted with one another, and begin to understand what it is that brings you in, as you see it. Does this fit with your understanding?

MR. JONES: (*Nods.*)

DR. SMITH: So tell me what brings you in today.

[*Comment:* Notice that Dr. Smith is using an open-ended question (a question that cannot be answered yes or no). Using closed-ended questions tends to get the therapist into the question–answer trap, encouraging passivity on the part of the client and putting the therapist into the role of the all-knowing expert. Also notice that Dr. Smith has not presumed to use such labels as disease, alcoholism, or even problem. Many individuals are still in the process of deciding whether they see their drinking or using as a problem or not. If the therapist takes one pole of the ambivalence, for example, the side of acknowledging the problem and the need for change, the client may be tempted to argue for the side of no problem and no change.]

MR. JONES: Well, to tell you the truth, it's my wife. She seems to think I drink too much. She didn't exactly say so, but lately I've begun to get the feeling that if I don't at least consult with someone about this, she might even leave me.

DR. SMITH: That must be a scary thing to consider.

MR. JONES: It sure is. We've been married fifteen years. I can hardly imagine being without her. We have three kids, too. I don't even want to imagine what a divorce would do to them.

DR. SMITH: So one concern you have about your drinking, then, is that it has begun to affect your marriage. You are really concerned about maintaining your marriage and about the effects divorce could have on your children.

MR. JONES: That's right. Why does she have to get on my case all the time about drinking? She's just constantly on me about it. I don't think I drink that much.

DR. SMITH: In your view, her concern for you is misplaced.

[*Comment:* Several things are going on here. The therapist has avoided the trap of siding with the wife, which would only encourage a stance on the part of the client in favor of the status quo or no change. Dr. Smith has also framed the wife's behavior as a problematic consequence of Mr. Jones's drinking. If Mr. Jones is concerned about nothing else regarding his drinking, he has at least gone along with seeing that its effect on his marriage is in itself something to worry about. Dr. Smith is thus already beginning to heighten a sense of discrepancy between how Mr. Jones's life is and how he might like it to be and to connect this difference specifically to drinking. He has also framed the wife's behavior as caring, even though he has not challenged the client's view that her judgment is incorrect.]

MR. JONES: I guess it's misplaced. I mean, I don't think I'm an alcoholic or anything. To tell you the truth, I've sometimes thought myself that I drink a little too much. I do spend quite a bit of money on beer, and frankly, there's a lot of other things I'd like to be doing with the money. And sometimes I don't feel quite at my best the next morning, especially if I've had a little more than usual. But Marcy's just dead wrong to call me an alcoholic. I mean, I have a good job, a nice home and family. I'm no alcoholic.

DR. SMITH: The reason you reject what Marcy tells you is that you don't see yourself as an alcoholic, on the one hand. But on the other hand, there are several concerns you have yourself. You do get concerned about the money you've been spending for beer, and it does bother you that you feel poorly the next morning at times.

MR. JONES: Besides that, to tell you the truth I've been feeling a little glum lately, too. I've started to wonder whether my drinking isn't part of that, too, but I don't know. Still, I don't think I have a problem. Most of my friends drink more than I do.

DR. SMITH: So besides the other things you've mentioned, you're worried you're drinking may be affecting your mood as well. But since your friends drink as much or more than you, it's hard to believe there's anything wrong.

MR. JONES: Right.

DR. SMITH: It may interest you to know that people tend to socialize with others who drink roughly the same as they do. That is, tee-totalers hang out with tee-totalers, heavy drinkers with heavy drinkers, and so on. Because of this, most people, whether they drink heavily or not at all, will tend to think their own level of drinking as normal. So, I could see why, looking at your friend's drinking as a comparison, you could be kind of confused about whether you drink a lot or a little.

[*Comment:* Traditional chemical dependency counselors may have been tempted to challenge Mr. Jones's assertion that he is not alcoholic as a form of denial and insist that he recognize his problem and accept the label. However, this is another of the many ways to fall into the problem of reactance. Therapist can find themselves, instead of assisting this person to acknowledge his concerns and begin to change, arguing about a label. By avoiding this, and by instead following the client's thoughts and feelings (and subtly placing weight on the side of change), the client is free to acknowledge and explore his concerns. This may never have happened if the therapist had tried to force this directly by insisting that the client accept the label. Often such an approach can result in a change of verbal behavior without affecting consumption. Notice also that the therapist has slipped in some education regarding the sociology of drinking but has done so in a way that still seems to side with the client and the client's point of view.]

DR. SMITH: What else concerns you about your drinking?

[*Comment:* The key question, not yet stated but always present in the interview, is "What concerns you about your drinking?" Through the interview so far, the therapist has attempted to follow this particular Ariadne's thread. Now he asks: what else? This implies an assumption that there will be more concerns and encourages further exploration. To ask "Is that all?" implies that the therapist expects that is all and discourages further exploration. Another helpful question at times is: "What do you like about your drinking?" We find it quite helpful to allow clients to explore this side of the equation with us. For one thing, it builds rapport when we listen to the positive aspects of drinking or using and reflect this without judgment. But furthermore, clients in the contemplation stage of change discussed earlier will be weighing the pros and cons of change in any event. By letting this happen, the therapist has a better chance of influencing that process.]

The interview above is, of course, idealized and compressed for heuristic purposes. But whereas, in an actual interview, therapist responses may not be as smooth, and whereas the whole process of therapeutic movement may occur somewhat more slowly, this is not otherwise unrealistic. The reader will notice that even the compressed example is not particularly dramatic, even though the processes of change are being quite effectively tapped. Therapists may be tempted to resort to more dramatic measures such as confrontational approaches because they feel more satisfying to the therapist, but it is these rather undramatic approaches that may have the most impact. Dramatic approaches run the risk of reactance.

At the end of the first interview, and periodically throughout the interview, MI therapists will make summaries of what has occurred so far, emphasizing the aspects of the interview that favor change though not denying the others. At the end of the first interview, such a summary may occur again, as well as a closing statement about how to proceed from that point. We skip now to this part of the interview.

DR. SMITH: Well let me try to sort of summarize what we've been discussing so far. At this point, you're not sure whether there's anything here you want to change. On the one hand, your wife's concern about you seems overblown because you don't see yourself as an alcoholic and because your friends drink the same as you or even more. This may not be the best indicator either way, as we discussed, but from your point of view, it hasn't give you the feeling there's anything to be concerned about. On the other hand, however, you are concerned that your drinking is affecting your marriage. You're worried you may end up divorced if you don't change, which could have profound effects not only on you and Marcy but also on your kids. The amount of money you spend on beer worries you, and you're concerned about feeling poorly on mornings after you drink a lot. You also wonder at times whether you're being a good role model for your kids regarding drinking, and you think it may be affecting your moods. Does that more or less cover it?

MR. JONES: I guess so. . . . Boy, it sure sounds like a lot of stuff. . . . I never thought of it all at once like that. Where do we go from here then?

DR. SMITH: Well, if it feels OK to you, let me suggest that you and I meet again in a few days. I'll ask you to spend some time here in the office filling out some questionnaires, and I'll spend another hour with you talking very specifically about your drinking. In addition, let me recommend a blood test to check the health of your liver, just to see whether your drinking is beginning to affect you physically. Then I'll collect all that information, and we can have a third meeting in which you and I discuss what it all says. You can decide at that point what you want to do about it, if anything. This information will be kept confidential, and what you do with it will be completely up to you. Does that seem reasonable?

[*Comment:* Notice the atmosphere of collaboration, confidentiality, and individual responsibility.]

Assessment Session

Because the therapist has already started to develop a collaborative relationship with the client, moving into the assessment session is relatively easy. This is the session where therapists expand on the concerns the client has already told them about. The difference here is that the therapist will be collecting information with more structured interview techniques. One question a therapist might have after reading about all the domains we have discussed is how he/she is going to get all this information in several hours. Although it might seem like a lot (and it is), therapists can gather information in all these areas in the space of several hours. Readers might also have noted some bias toward instruments developed in our clinical research laboratory at the University of New Mexico. This is in part because they are efficient instruments and we are familiar with them. Given that, allow us to describe our brief intervention assessment package instruments. They include: the BDP; the neuropsychological screening, described above; a blood screening; the AUI-R; and the CIF if significant others are available to interview.

We begin with the BDP, follow with the neuropsychological screening, and finish with the AUI-R. We ask clients to take the AUI-R at the end of the assessment session. There are three reasons for this. First, it asks many direct questions about the client's drinking which the client might be less inclined to reveal at the beginning of the assessment session. Second, it gives us time to review the data we have collected while the client is still around to provide any clarification. Third, having the client take the AUI-R at the end makes efficient use of his/her time while the therapist is interviewing the significant other (it is hoped) with the CIF. When the client has completed the AUI-R and we have interviewed the significant other, we schedule the feedback appointment for about 1 week later. Finally, we send the client to the laboratory for a blood test the next morning. The client will need to fast for 12 hours prior to having blood drawn. Waiting about 1 week between the assessment and feedback sessions gives the therapist time to score the instruments. More important, however, it gives the client several days to get to the laboratory to have blood drawn.

Interviewing the Significant Other

Selecting the most appropriate person to interview about a client's drinking can be an important decision. In our clinical practices we typically ask to speak with the client's spouse or significant other and this usually works well. At our university-based, publicly funded alcohol treatment program, however, our colleagues prefer to interview the client's drinking buddies rather than a spouse. It is their impression that they get more accurate information the former rather than the latter. Unfortunately, we do not yet have data to determine who provides more accurate information. We suspect, however, that it will probably vary according to the treatment population. Practically speaking, we may not often have a choice about whom we interview so it may be a moot point. We begin the interview of the significant other (SO) by thanking the SO for coming and for his/her willingness to discuss the client's drinking. Next we explain that we are asking for the SO's perspective so that we can develop as accurate a picture as possible of the client's drinking behaviors and difficulties with alcohol and/or drugs. To develop some rapport and enlist the SO as a collaborator, we ask about the SO's concerns about the client's drinking using open-ended questions and reflective statements. When it seems appropriate, we ease into the CIF and gradually make the interview more structured to gather the needed information as efficiently as possible. At the end of the interview, we ask the SO whether there is anything he/she wishes to tell us about the client that we might have missed. Once finished, we again thank the SO for his/her time and see the SO out. The client will usually have finished the AUI-R before the interview with the SO is completed and may be in the waiting room. If so, we remind clients of their next appointment and that they need to have their blood drawn in the next 2 or 3 days.

Feedback Session

The therapist's goals in the feedback session are (1) to present and interpret the assessment results in a neutral, nonjudgmental way; (2) to avoid resistance or denial by rolling with it rather than fighting it or arguing; (3) to elicit and empathically reflect any concerns the client articulates about this information; and (4) to begin to set the groundwork for a specific plan of change should the client appear ready to do so.

Present Feedback

The temptation is to point the finger and say, "Mr. Jones. Look here. Your liver is shot. Your drinking is above the 99th percentile for U.S. norms. You've got to cut it out, or you'll be dead." In our experience, such heavy-handed approaches, even if true, elicit reactance and denial from the client. Instead, the idea here is to present the information calmly and neutrally. For example, "You remember I asked you about your typical weekly drinking. Well I took that information and converted it into what we call standard drinks, and have compared it to norms for drinking in the United States. The drinking you reported places you at the 98th percentile for U.S. drinking, meaning that you drink more than 98% of the people in the United States. How do you feel about that?" The emphasis, you will note, is on the client's reactions and conclusions, not the therapist's.

Roll with Resistance

It is not uncommon for clients to attempt to resist the feedback process. For example, clients confronted with the percentile information above will often say, "Oh, that can't be right." If the therapist succumbs to the temptation to defend the correctness of these figures, all can be lost. Instead, we roll with the resistance. This can be done, for example, by finding some aspect of the client's reaction to agree with. "It doesn't seem right to you. And of course, you're completely correct that any one number or measure here could be wrong in some way. That's why we recommend people consider the whole pattern of results rather than just one aspect or number."

Elicit and Reflect Concerns

The therapist's continual focus is on finding what concerns the client has about his/her drinking or using, and then helping the client to hear him/herself with reflection. "It really scares you to think your drinking has started to affect your health."

Form a Plan

Unless the motivational impetus generated by the above procedures are tied to a specific plan of change that the client feels he/she can actually carry out (the principle of self-efficacy), the client is most likely to slip back into contemplation and deny the existence of the problem. Good action plans include reasonable goals, are challenging but not overwhelming, incorporate skills a client already has whenever possible, teach new skills when necessary, and often include built-in self-rewards (e.g., calculating the money spent on drugs and putting it aside until the client can purchase that car stereo he has always wanted).

Follow-Up

Even in research contexts, where the interest in follow-up procedures is primarily obtaining good data, we have observed that clients perceive follow-up as a form of caring. Scheduling follow-up meetings brings a sense of ongoing social contingencies to bear upon the client's successes and failures. Even if the therapist is nonjudgmental and empathic, clients will much prefer to be able to report success. The nonjudgmental therapist will presumably be in better position, though, to hear about failures as well. The most typical result at follow-up will be a mixture of success and failure. Often the clinical goal will be to help the client see these results as a partial success rather than a total failure, countering the tendency to see recovery in black-and-white, all-or-none terms. Slips are framed as learning opportunities rather than signs of the impossibility of change. By reviewing slips with a client in a supportive manner, and by encouraging problem-solving efforts rather than guilt or defeat, clients can become empowered to meet similar situations with needed skills in the future. Ideally, clients come to function as their own therapist in this regard, learning to reflect on slips from this perspective instead of lapsing into despair and giving up.

EFFICACY OF BRIEF INTERVENTIONS

Recently Bien et al. (1993) reviewed over 44 controlled studies investigating the effects of brief intervention on alcohol abuse. Most of these studies showed brief interventions to be superior to no-treatment-control conditions and generally about as effective as longer-term, intensive treatment on a variety of outcome measures. This surprising, counterintuitive conclusion deserves serious consideration in these days of managed care and federal health care reform proposals.

Some of the earliest studies in this area began with the modest goal of employing a brief contact with a therapist simply to facilitate referral. Chafetz (1961; Chafetz et al., 1962) found successful completion of referrals in 65% of a group randomized to receive a brief intervention in an emergency medical setting compared to only 5% of randomized controls. In a replication (Chafetz, 1968), this was increased to 78% versus 6% of controls. In another classic study with medical populations, Kristenson et al. (1983) intervened in Sweden with a general medical population screened for alcohol problems and found evidence of reduced liver damage, fewer sick days, and lower mortality compared to no treatment controls. Other studies have shown success on a variety of outcome variables with self-referred drinkers responding to an advertisement for a free and confidential "drinker's checkup" (e.g., Miller, Sovereign, & Krege, 1988) and with self-referred populations requesting addiction treatment who were doing as well as a comparison group receiving more extensive treatment (e.g., Edwards et al., 1977; Orford & Edwards, 1977; Edwards, Duckitt, Oppenheimer, Sheehan, & Taylor, 1983).

REFERENCES

Babor, T. F., & Grant, M. (1992). *Project on identification and management of alcohol-related problems. Report on phase II: A randomized clinical trial of brief interventions in primary health care.* Geneva, Switzerland: World Health Organization.

Bien, T. H., & Burge, R. (1991). Smoking and drinking: A review of the literature. *International Journal of the Addictions, 25*(12), 1429–1454.

Bien, T. H., Miller, W. R., & Tonigan, J. S. (1993). Brief interventions for alcohol problems: A review. *Addiction, 88,* 315–336.

Brown, S. A., Christiansen, E. A., & Goldman, M. F. (1987). Alcohol Expectancy Questionnaire: An instrument for the assessment of adolescent and adult alcohol expectancies. *Journal of Studies on Alcohol, 48*(5), 483–491.

Chafetz, M. E. (1961). A procedure for establishing therapeutic contact with the alcoholic. *Quarterly Journal of Studies on Alcohol, 22,* 325–328.

Chafetz, M. E., Blane, H. T., Abrams, H. S., Golner, J., Lacy, E., McCourt, W. F., Clark, E., & Meyers, W. (1962). Establishing treatment relations with alcoholics. *Journal of Nervous and Mental Diseases, 134,* 395–409.

Chafetz, M. E. (1968). Research in the alcohol clinic: An around-the-clock psychiatric service of the Massachusetts General Hospital. *American Journal of Psychiatry, 124,* 1674–1679.

DiClemente, C. C., & Hughes, S. O. (1990). Stages of change profiles in outpatient alcoholism treatment. *Journal of Substance Abuse, 2,* 217–235.

Edwards, G., Duckitt, A., Oppenheimer, E., Sheehan, M., & Taylor, C. (1983). What happens to alcoholics? *Lancet, 2,* 269–271.

Edwards, G., Orford, J., Egert, S., Guthrie, S., Hawker, A., Hensman, C., Mitcheson, M., Oppenheimer, E., & Taylor, C. (1977). Alcoholism: A controlled trial of "treatment" and "advice." *Journal of Studies on Alcohol, 38,* 1004–1031.

Hester, R. K. (1995). Self-control training. In R. K. Hester & W. R. Miller (Eds.), *Handbook of alcoholism treatment approaches: Effective alternatives* (2nd ed., pp.148–159). Needham Heights, MA: Allyn & Bacon.

Horn, J. L., Skinner, H. A., Wanberg, K., & Foster, F. M. (1984). *Alcohol Dependence Scale.* Toronto, Ontario: Addiction Research Foundation.

Horn, J. L., Wanberg, K. W., & Foster, F. M. (1987). *Alcohol Use Inventory.* Minneapolis, MN: National Computer Systems.

Kristenson, H., Ohlin, H., Hulten-Nosslin, M. B., Trell, E., & Hood, B. (1983). Identification and intervention of heavy drinking in middle-aged men: Results and follow-up of 24–60 months of long-term study with randomized controls. *Alcoholism: Clinical and Experimental Research, 7,* 203–209.

Marlatt, G. A., & Miller, W. R. (1987a). *The Brief Drinker Profile.* Odessa, FL: Psychological Assessment Resources.

Marlatt, G. A., & Miller, W. R. (1987b). *The Follow-up Drinker Profile.* Odessa, FL: Psychological Assessment Resources.

Marlatt, G. A., & Miller, W. R. (1987c). *The Collateral Interview Form.* Odessa, FL: Psychological Assessment Resources.

Miller, W. R. (1985). Addictive behavior and the theory of psychological reversals. *Addictive Behaviors, 10,* 177–180.

Miller, W. R. (1989). *SOCRATES: The Stages of Change Readiness and Treatment Eagerness Scale.* Albuquerque, NM: University of New Mexico: Author.

Miller, W. R. (1991). *The Drinker Inventory of Consequences.* Albuquerque, NM: University of New Mexico: Author.

Miller, W. R., Brown, J. M., Simpson, T. L. , Handmaker, N. S., Bien, T. H., Luckie, L. F., Montgomery, H. A., Hester, R. K., & Tonigan, J. S. (1995). What works? A methodological analysis of the alcohol treatment outcome literature. In R. K. Hester & W. R. Miller (Eds.), *Handbook of alcoholism treatment approaches: Effective alternatives* (2nd ed., pp. 12–44). Needham Heights, MA: Allyn & Bacon.

Miller, W. R., & Rollnick, S. (1991). *Motivational interviewing: Preparing people to change addictive behavior.* New York: Guilford Press.

Miller, W. R., & Sanchez, V. C. (1994). Motivating young adults for treatment and lifestyle change. In G. Howard (Ed.), *Issues in alcohol use and misuse by young adults* (pp. 55–81). Notre Dame, IN: University of Notre Dame Press.

Miller, W. R., Sovereign, R. G., & Krege, B. (1988). Motivational interviewing with problem drinkers: II. The drinker's check-up as a preventive intervention. *Behavioural Psychotherapy, 16,* 251–268.

Miller, W. R., & Taylor, C. A. (1980). Relative effectiveness of bibliotherapy, individual and group self-control training in the treatment of problem drinkers. *Addictive Behaviors, 5,* 13–24.

Orford, J., & Edwards, G. (1977). *Alcoholism: A comparison of treatment and advice, with a study of the influence of marriage* (Maudsley Monographs No. 26). Oxford: Oxford University Press.

Stockwell, T. R., Hodgson, R. J., & Murphy, R. (1983). The Severity of Alcohol Dependence Questionnaire: Its use, reliability and validity. *British Journal of Addiction, 78,* 145–155.

12

Solution-Focused Brief Therapy
with Substance Abusers

INSOO KIM BERG

INTRODUCTION

This chapter is designed to introduce the reader to the clinical application and adaptation of solution-focused brief therapy (SFBT) for the treatment of substance abusers. It is commonly believed that such a serious and difficult problem as substance abuse, which exacts tremendous social, familial, and personal costs, requires long-term, intense, and often intrusive treatment. Not only is this notion disputed by the vast amount of research data that have been available for the last 20 years (Sobell & Sobell, 1993), but clinical experience also shows that a solution can be developed rather quickly (Edwards et al., 1977).

This chapter describes step-by-step procedures that come from the tradition of the poststructural and social constructivistic approach to building solutions to this serious and difficult clinical problem. The view presented here requires a paradigm shift from the problem-solving approach to solution building (de Shazer, 1991, 1994; Berg & Miller, 1992; Berg, 1994). The result is brief treatment that can be either single contact or a series of brief and intermittent contacts through the recovery process.

Any presenting problem, including substance abuse, has exceptions. That is, most presenting problems occur sporadically, and there are periods when the presenting problem does not occur. It is the premise of SFBT that paying attention to these exceptions provides both the client and the therapist with clues and ideas for building a solution to the client's problem. (de Shazer, 1985, 1988, 1991; Berg & Miller, 1992; Berg, 1994).

This phenomenon of exception to problematic behavior is particularly characteristic of substance abusers, as most clients have periods when they do not engage in problematic activities. In fact, many clients have rather long periods of abstinence, months and even years. For some, as little as days and weeks of nonuse can be viewed as a resource and the beginning of a solution. In other words, the client already possesses the beginning step of a solution to his/her problem. For example, instead of ignoring or dismissing the client's report of 3 days of nonuse, the therapist uses this information. That is, when the therapist believes that this period of abstinence contains the initial information on which to build future solutions, he/she shifts the focus from problem to solution. Detailed information about the client's successful mastery of nonuse will offer the client and therapist clues to what the client needs to "do more." This information includes what the client does (where, when, and with whom); how successful the client was in staying healthy, productive, happy, and eating right; and the ways in which the client related to his/her family that made the client feel good about him/herself.

As previously mentioned, this treatment model is informed by postmodern, poststructural thinking and social constructivistic tradition. It is adapted from the brief therapy framework of the Mental Research Institute of Palo Alto, whose original ideas are rooted in cybernetic and communication theories. This constructivistic view postulates that the problems of living must be viewed within the context of social convention and that one's reality is created through social interaction and validation. What follows is a model of clinical application to substance abuse and its treatment implications based on the tradition described above.

DELIBERATE AND RANDOM EXCEPTIONS

Exceptions to problems seem to fall into two different types: deliberate and random. Deliberate exceptions are those situations when the client is able to describe in step-by-step fashion how, for example, he was able to stay away from drug use for 5 days or to drink only on weekends through a conscious effort to refrain from doing so otherwise.

In one case, the longest period Janice was able to stay away from her almost daily use of cocaine during the last 2 years was 9 days when she was so angry at her boyfriend for hitting her. Even though she initially forgot about this episode, the therapist's question about any periods of nonuse, however small, triggered her memory of this episode, which had occurred about a year earlier. When asked for details about the 9 days of nonuse, she remembered that she used no drugs when she was with her friends and family members who are not aware of her drug abuse. She also pointed out that when she spent time with her non-drug-using friends, got involved in her church work, kept busy with her two daughters and her first grandchild, felt good about helping others, or kept the welfare of her children "at the front of my mind," she was able to "stay clean." This is called a deliberate exception and it can become the basis for further strategies of nonuse. When the therapist asked Janice about a plan to stay drug free during the coming week, Janice thought that while her drug-using boyfriend was out of town, she could stay involved with various activities and, thus, not use drugs. Because she was able to describe the details of her non–drug-related activities, this information was used to further increase her non–drug-using days.

The next therapeutic strategy was to map out Janice's detailed plans to repeat those successful steps for "staying clean." Clearly, the more deliberately the client manages an exception, the better the client is able to repeat those successful steps because they are already within his/her repertoire. It can be said that all substance abuse treatment is designed to create deliberate exceptions in such a way that the client feels in control of his/her nonuse.

The second type of exception to problems, random exception, are those situations when clients are able to abstain or reduce their use but are unable to explain the steps they have taken to do so. Some clients feel that events or forces outside themselves are responsible for the periods of exceptions. Common descriptions are, "I just felt good and didn't feel the need to drink," or "I woke up feeling good and just did all those things," or "My wife and I were on vacation for two weeks and we were very relaxed, played lots of golf, no stress and away from jobs and all that hassles. I really had no need to drink. Even when I did, I just enjoyed a drink with meals and didn't feel the need to gulp down like I usually do. But as soon as we got back from the vacation, we were at each other's throat again. And of course I started drinking again."

Even though there clearly are periods of exceptions, the client believes they are out of his/her control; therefore, the client is unable to retrace his/her steps in a conscious way. Or, in some instances clients feel those exceptions are extremely rare and related to events outside themselves. Relying on others' behaviors or events outside of their control means that clients are not confident of their ability to replicate their exceptions to drinking. Thus, such situations require initial steps by the therapist to generate deliberate exceptions. In such situations, it is better to help clients predict their exceptions. This means bringing the exception to the client's conscious awareness by having the client predict, for example, whether he/she will stay sober on certain days of the week or how many days during the coming week he/she will stay sober. The task of predicting random exceptions forces clients to become more clear about their own behavioral control.

SOLUTION BUILDING, NOT PROBLEM SOLVING

With this approach, therefore, the therapeutic task becomes a process of helping clients develop solution-building activities by utilizing their existing resources. This approach builds on the client's vision of solution rather than having the expert therapist diagnose the problem and prescribe treatment. The following segment of this chapter briefly describes some of the key concepts of the solution-building activities that occur in either individual or group therapy.

ASSESSMENT OF CLIENT–THERAPIST RELATIONSHIPS

Building a positive client–therapist relationship starts with the therapist cooperating with the client and asking questions related to the client's reason for seeking treatment at this time. Client–therapist relationships fall into three broad categories: visitor type, complainant type, and customer type.

Visitor-Type Relationship

Visitor-type relationships occur when clients view their involvement in treatment as involuntary and feel that therapeutic tasks, goals, and solutions are being imposed on them against their wishes. Clients in this type of relationship often behave as if they are "unmotivated" or "resistant," and are often mislabled as such. Instead, clients in this situation define their "real problem" as "having to come" to treatment when their real concerns lie elsewhere. Therefore, the client who feels forced to accept treatment should be complimented for showing up for the appointment even though it is not his/her own idea, and the client should be encouraged to return for further negotiation on how to solve the dilemma of having to comply with others' demands. When the therapist cooperates with the client in this way, it makes the client feel understood and feel that the therapist is reasonable enough that the client can start to trust and negotiate the treatment goal.

Complainant-Type Relationship

The complainant-type relationship occurs when clients have goals for others, not for themselves. The most common clinical example is when the parent, spouse, or employers present another person's substance use as problematic to the complainant. This type of client is often mistaken-ly labeled codependent and asked to look into his/her need to assume the caretaker role, which is considered "unhealthy." However, when such a client is complimented for tireless efforts in seeking help for the abusing family member and his/her willingness to go the extra mile to help the person who needs treatment, this client is more likely to feel validated, supported, and, thus, able to look into his/her part in the abu-sive relationship. In other words, the client becomes more cooperative. Because the client considers him/herself the victim of another's substance abuse and is not ready to see him/herself as having to take steps to change his part in the pattern, the client is likely to feel understood by the ther-apist. Because the client has devoted a great deal of energy to analyzing the abuser's problems and has become a keen observer of the problemat-ic person's behaviors, the therapist needs to consider this tendency and to think of this investment as a resource for treatment rather than a hin-drance. The most useful approach to working with such a person may be to encourage this client to continue to think and observe but differ-ently than in the past. Because the client's continued effort has not produced the satisfactory results he/she seeks, the client is more willing to follow the therapist's suggestion at this point because he/she feels sup-ported by the therapist for the effort.

Our clinical experience is that most complainant-type clients still ex-pend a great deal of energy trying to change the problematic user, which is usually a no-win situation for both the user and the concerned family member. Certainly, sending the client to an Alcoholics Anonymous (AA) group if he/she is receptive is an option that is available to most clini-cians. However, if the therapist's clinical intuition indicates that the client in the complainant type of relationship is not receptive to examining his/her part in the dynamics of the so-called codependent relationship, the following approach is useful:

THERAPIST: Suppose, let's just suppose, that your wife stopped drinking one day somehow. If I were to ask her what she will notice is most different about you, what do you suppose she would say?

CLIENT: I suppose she would say I would be more attentive to her, like I used to be. Everytime she is drunk, it comes out that she resents the way I ignore her and don't need her like I used to. Her biggest gripe is that I and kids don't need her, but I've had to do everything since she started drinking, especially the last couple of years when it's been worse. So, I suppose she will say I will be more attentive and supportive of her.

THERAPIST: Suppose somehow she thought you were supportive again. How would she be different with you?

CLIENT: She might become more interested in the family again. She will have to care about herself first, then the kids, become a wife again. Notice what's going on with me and the kids. Be calmer, take care of herself, and spend quality time with the kids. I am really worried about the kids.

THERAPIST: Suppose she did that. What would she say about how you are different with her?

CLIENT: Well, that I'm not ignoring her. I get so angry and irritated at what she has become. If she changes, then there is no reason to nag her and criticize her about what a lush she has become. I will be more affectionate with her. After all, I still love the woman.

THERAPIST: What would she say you will be like when you are attentive to her, more openly loving and affectionate with her? What do you think has to come first, your being attentive and affectionate with her or her stopping drinking? What would she say has to come first?

CLIENT: I think she should stop drinking first. After all, I was very loving to her when we first got married, and I have never changed. She will probably say that I will have to be attentive and affectionate to her in front of the kids. She says my nagging and criticizing her drinking in front of the kids make them not listen to her. I guess she just gives up.

THERAPIST: So, what would it take for you to take the first step toward making things better for your family?

CLIENT: I guess I will have to stop nagging her about her drinking. It hasn't worked anyway. I can do that. Actually, she is right about the kids not listening to her.

As this dialogue progresses, it becomes clear that the therapist initially accepts the client's initial posture of being a complainant and gradually begins to challenge his view that there is nothing he can do.

Customer-Type Relationship

The customer-type relationship is one where clients express a treatment goal that is related to themselves and indicate in many ways that they are ready to change their behaviors. Naturally, this is the ideal type of client for most therapists, and many treatment models assume that all clients should appear in the therapist's office as a customer-type. When they do not, therapists tend to be surprised and disappointed. However, even for therapists in private practice, the proportion of substance-abusing clients who have "hit bottom" and are ready to seriously begin treatment as a customer is rather small. Becoming a customer-type is a gradual process, and the way a therapist deals with the client is critical to the successful completion of treatment. Only when clients indicate in many ways that they are serious about taking behavioral measures to solve their problems are they offered behavioral tasks that will lead toward their desired solutions. This reduces therapist frustration and anger at the client for not following through.

All Clients as Hidden Customers

It is safe to assume that most clients are "hidden customers." Even the most reluctant clients seek some sort of change, although this may be different from the expert's view of what is good for them. At times, clients are unable to articulate their goals, or the therapist has difficulty understanding what the client really wants. It is, however, helpful for the therapist to take a stance that every client is a hidden and, thus a potential, customer. That is, the client hopes that coming to the therapist will accomplish something positive in his/her life. Such a stance allows the therapist to take a positive view of the client, start where the client is, and collaborate with the client on establishing workable goals.

NEGOTIATION OF TREATMENT GOALS

Some matching theory proponents such as Miller and Hester (1985) and Prochaska and DiClemente (1992) have articulated the importance of client participation in the formulation of treatment goals. They assert that the therapist needs to match and pace the client's readiness to make necessary changes. The SFBT approach also contends that such collaboration is critical to a successful treatment outcome. Therapists tell war stories about how "difficult and resistant" their clients are and how they confronted their clients only to have them drop out of treatment entirely. Close examination of these "difficult" cases indicates that they result from the therapist's inability or unwillingness to collaborate with what the client is seeking from treatment.

Those clients who come to treatment with the referring person's agenda for treatment pose a particularly challenging task for therapists because we, as experts, have a clear sense of how much havoc, pain, suffering, and damage their substance abuse causes not only for themselves but for those who care deeply about them. We are also aware of how high a price society pays for that abuse. Our desire to ease the suffering and reduce the damage can turn into a contest of wills, often resulting in frustration and a sense of failure. However, paying attention to what the client really wants, to regain a driver's license, to keep the marriage, and so on, offers a better chance of enhancing client cooperation. Along with behaviorally measurable, concrete, and specific indicators of successful movement toward what the client seeks from therapy, the therapist must pay attention to how important this treatment goal is for the client, not what the therapist believes should be important to the client.

For example, John's referral to treatment was a condition for extending his probation on his job. Periodic confrontations with his supervisor only hardened his "devil-may-care" attitude, which neither helped nor motivated him to reduce absenteeism. It was clear that there were many other people in John's life who cared enough to repeat the same admonition to stop drinking, also without success. The following dialogue is typical of how the goal negotiation may proceed.

THERAPIST: John, what would you like to see happen different in your life as a result of your coming here?

JOHN: Actually, I don't belong here. It's not my idea to be here, you know. I don't have drinking problem as they say. If my boss thinks I have a drinking problem, he is crazy. He never liked me from the get-go because I don't take his bullshit like other guys. I don't care if he likes me or not, I don't like being told how to run my life.

THERAPIST: If your boss was here and if I were to talk to him what do you suppose he will say he needs to see you do for him to think that you don't need to come here anymore?

JOHN: Hmm . . . He will say I don't miss work without excuses and will show up for work on time on Monday mornings.

THERAPIST: Suppose you were to do that, show up for work on time on Monday mornings, and come to work regularly. What do you suppose your boss will do differently?

JOHN: He will pick on me about something else because he still thinks that I have a drinking problem, which I don't.

THERAPIST: Suppose somehow you convinced him that the drinking problem he thinks you have is solved. How would he be different then?

JOHN: I don't know I am telling you he is out to get me. But I will tell you what, if he really is convinced that I am taking care of my drinking problem, he might leave me alone and not bug me all the time.

THERAPIST: Sounds like a good idea to me. Of course nobody wants to be bugged by a boss. So, what would he say it would take for him to leave you alone to do your job?

JOHN: He will say I will have to show up for work on time on Monday mornings.

THERAPIST: So, tell me about the last time you showed up for work on time on a Monday morning.

JOHN: Let me think. Well, this past Monday I came to work on time.

THERAPIST: You did? How did you do that?

JOHN: Well, I got so tired of him hassling me I decided I would prove him wrong. It's not that hard to do when I make up my mind. I do this quite often you know, but the boss thinks I am late every Monday morning. I would have gotten fired a long time ago because he gave me warnings. But when I get mad at him I have this "don't give a damn" attitude.

THERAPIST: So, tell me what you are like when you don't have this "attitude"?

JOHN: What am I like? I'm a hard worker. I put up with lots of crap and don't mind being sent to fix other people's mistakes. I'm damned good at my job!

THERAPIST: I am curious, John. How do you manage to get to work on time on Monday mornings?

Acknowledging his desire to be a good enough employee so that he can keep his job turns out to be much more effective than trying to convince John of the need to admit his alcohol abuse. The latter is not likely to produce the desired results; instead, it will only replicate John's relationship with his boss and others who have tried to be helpful to him. In addition, when clients are given a chance to talk about successes for which they feel proud, they are more willing to look at the unsuccessful part of their life.

MIRACLE QUESTION

The clinical observation that an exception to the problem may become the key pathway to solutions led de Shazer et al., 1986; de Shazer, 1989, 1992) to realize that there is great advantage in focusing on the picture or images of solutions rather than understanding how the problem got to be a problem (Berg & Miller, 1992). The therapist focuses on what the client will do; how his life will be different; and how his family, co-workers, friends, and others will respond differently to him/her when the problem is solved. The details of this solution are achieved by asking the miracle question:

> I have a strange question to ask you. Suppose one night while you are sleeping a miracle happens and the problem that brought you to see me today is solved. But because you are sleeping you don't know that this has happened. When you wake up the following morning, what will be different that will let you know that a miracle happened and the problem is solved?

Notice that the miracle is a means to an end of the client's life being "different." Because the solution picture is generated by the client according to the client's life-style, is natural to the client's way of being and doing, and is not imposed by the expert, it is easier to implement and the client is more likely to be invested in succeeding. The therapist helps negotiate the details of this solution picture by amplifying the details, as the following dialogue with another client shows.

CLIENT: I suppose I will wake up without a hangover. That will be different.

THERAPIST: Suppose you wake up without a hangover. What will you do different that you didn't do this morning, for example?

CLIENT: Oh, I suppose I will feel like getting up and getting going instead of staying in bed all day.

THERAPIST: OK, suppose you did that. What would your wife do different that she didn't do this morning?

CLIENT: She will be friendly and not so angry. She is angry all the time. I mean, who feels like going to work when your wife is angry all the time? You can cut the tension with a knife.

THERAPIST: Suppose I were to talk to her. What will she say she will notice different about you that will let her know that a miracle happened and your problem is solved?

CLIENT: She will say I will be nice to her, friendly to her.

THERAPIST: What will she say you will do when you are friendly and nice to her that you didn't do this morning, for example?

CLIENT: She will say I will give her a smile, talk to her, give her a hug, stuff like that.

THERAPIST: Suppose you do that. Just suppose you smile at her, give her a hug, talk to her nicely, get up on time and go to work, and so on. What would she do differently that she didn't do this morning?

CLIENT: She will probably be nicer to live with. We used to do that. Gosh, it seems like it was a long time ago.

THERAPIST: What do you suppose she would say what you were like in those days when you both did these nice things for each other?

The more he describes the details of the solution state, the more it seems to generate further ideas of what he can do first to create the desired solution to his dilemma. It is important to include the significant others in this solution picture since the client's supportive social context is crucial to his/her recovery. Not only are clients affected by those around them, but they also affect those around them. This interactional, systemic point of view (Watzlawick & Weakland, 1977) makes it possible to bring in more resources even when the other family members may not be present in sessions. In this process of describing his solution picture, the client begins to remember steps he used when his life was better and steps he can reinstate easily. Remembering his past successes also raises the hope that his life can return to a more stable period.

The next step is to help the client assess how willing he is implement those solutions in order to achieve what is in his best interest.

SCALING QUESTIONS

Scaling questions are used not to measure a normative standard but to help clients assess their own situations in a more objective manner so that they can better make decisions (de Shazer, 1993). The numbers on the scale of 1 to 10, or 1 to 100, are used to assess host of issues, such as the client's motivation to solve his/her problem, how hopeful the client and others are that the client can do so, ways to contrast the client's views with those of others around him/her, the severity of the client's problem, progress the client is making in therapy, and a number of other clinically important issues. For example, how much John wants to keep his job could be assessed in the following manner.

THERAPIST: John, suppose that ten stands for you being willing to do whatever it takes to keep your job, I mean everything humanly possible, and one stands for the opposite. That is, all you are willing to do is just sit and wait for something to happen. Where between one and ten would you say you are at today?

JOHN: I would say I'm at about eight. I won't say I will do anything but just about anything to keep this job.

THERAPIST: That's very high. Suppose I were to ask your boss where he thinks you are at. What would he say?

JOHN: I think he would say I'm, at three or four. He really doesn't know how important this job is to me. He thinks I'm just blowing it off but, I want to keep this job real bad.

THERAPIST: That's very high. What would he say it would take him to believe that you have moved up just one point, to say four or five?

JOHN: He will say I have to suck up to him. But I won't do it. It's not me.

THERAPIST: Suppose I were to ask your wife. Where would she say she thinks you are at, between one and ten?

JOHN: She would say about the same, as much as my boss. She thinks I just like to make trouble but she really don't realize how much I care about her. If it wasn't for her and the kids, I wouldn't put up with all that crap. I'm only staying on the job so that I can keep my family together. That's very important to me.

This conversation indicates that John is more motivated in keeping the family together and that he sees the job as a means to his real goal of improving his relationship with his wife. As this information about his real goal becomes clear, the therapist shifts the focus away from the job issue to the marriage and his family.

THERAPIST: So, what do you suppose your wife would say she will see you do different when she believes you have moved up one point higher, to four or five?

JOHN: She would say I will go to work everyday with a good attitude. That's what she always tells me.

THERAPIST: Suppose, just suppose, you did that, go to work with a good attitude. What would she say about how she will be different with you?

JOHN: She would say she will be more friendly with me. Less nagging, less angry, yeah, more friendly in general. Gee, we used to get along and be real good to each other.

THERAPIST: Suppose you two were nicer and good to each other. What would the children say about how they will be different with you and your wife?

JOHN: I suppose they would get along with each other. They would be more relaxed and easygoing. Not so tense around the house. When my wife is irritated, it seems to affect the whole family.

This conversation gives more information on how invested John is in preserving the welfare of his family and that perhaps he sees keeping the job as a means of achieving his goal. The next sequence in the interview further assesses John's willingness to work hard to obtain what is important to him: keeping his family together.

THERAPIST: Suppose, John, that ten stands for you being willing to do whatever it takes, I mean humanly possible, to keep the family together, to be more friendly and be nicer to each other and one stands for the opposite. All you are willing to do is to just sit and wait for something to happen, where would you say you are at between one and ten right now?

JOHN: Hell, it seems like that's all I've been doing, but nothing wonderful happened. So, I guess I will have to do something if we are going to make it. I'll say about eight or nine.

THERAPIST: Wow, that's very high. I guess you really want to keep your family together badly. I wonder if your wife realizes how important your family is to you?

JOHN: I don't think so. She thinks all I care about is the bottle. Well, I don't blame her. I don't do nothing with the family anymore.

When the therapist validates what is important to the client, his motivation to pursue what is in his best interest seems to increase. This questioning method offers the client an opportunity to assess his own situation, examine his priorities, and make decisions accordingly. By cooperating with his beliefs and view of the world rather than forcing him to change his stance, the therapist collaborates with the client, thus increasing the chances of success.

The next step is to ask about exceptions to his problem and past successes. These would indicate his capacity to replicate successful strategies that he may have forgotten. This recovery of successful strategies encourages him, and increases his hopefulness, thus furthering his willingness to repeat what he already knows how to do. The following dialogue is typical of what takes place at this stage.

THERAPIST: Tell me, John, you mentioned that in recent weeks you managed to get to work on time. How did you do it?

JOHN: Gosh, people think I'm a falling-down drunk. Actually, that's not the case. If I did that all the time, I would have been fired a long time ago. Except when I get pissed at my boss or at my wife, or when I don't give a damn about anything, I usually come to work on time and I do my job.

THERAPIST: Tell me, John, how do you manage to get to work on time as often as you do?

JOHN: Actually it's not as difficult as it sounds, you know. I'm a pretty bullheaded sort of guy, but when I put my mind to it, I can do anything I want, including not drinking. It's when I don't give a damn that I end up doing things that are not good for me.

THERAPIST: So, what would it take you to be sure that you show up for work on time on Monday morning?

JOHN: I will just have to not drink on Sunday, and I've done that many times. As I said, when I make up my mind, I can do anything I want.

THERAPIST: So, what would it take you not to drink on Sunday?

JOHN: Keep busy and not get glued on the idiot box on Sunday afternoons. I have lots of projects that I never finish. Actually, once I get into a project around the house, puttering around and fixing things, I really don't need to drink because I like the feeling of getting things done. I like that but it is easier to just sit in front of TV all day and just being mindless.

THERAPIST: So, how confident are you, on a scale of one to ten where ten stands for the most confidence anybody can reasonably have that you will be able to get started on a project this Sunday and one stands for the opposite, where would you put yourself?

JOHN: I'm pretty confident. I'v done it many times. I would say about eight or nine.

THERAPIST: So, what would be the first small step you need to take to get started on the project?

This conversation shows how the therapist and the client together weave a detailed description of steps he will take to solve his current difficulties by repeating past successes.

SECOND AND SUBSEQUENT CONTACTS

When clients return in later sessions, they usually offer three possible responses when the therapist begins the session with: "What's better?" Note that the question is not *if* anything is better, but *what*. Such positive language assumes that something is likely to be better. Obviously, such expectation is conveyed in many subtle and not so subtle ways throughout the contacts in order to highlight the client's successful mastery of the problematic use of substance. There are usually three types of responses: better, same, or worse.

Better: When the client reports positive movement toward his/her goal, however small, the therapist asks details of how the client produced the change, what impact such changes has on other aspects of the client's life such as marriage, family, personal, and job-related areas. Any positive changes are supported and reinforced, both directly and indirectly. Direct reinforcement can be an outright supportive comment such as, "That's great!" which will sufficiently convey the therapist's support for what the client has initiated. Indirect reinforcement can be given when the therapist gives an admiring look and leans forward with soft, "Wow." Or the therapist can give an incredulous look and ask questions like, "Wasn't it hard to start to start eating healthy again?" or "Say that again?" or "How did you manage to get out of bed so early in the morning and go for a walk?" Frequently clients report on their own the discovery that such positive changes in life-style are reward enough and that they want to continue. The following sequence of questions is directed toward what course of action the client needs to repeat to build on these small but significant changes. The therapist can further enlarge on these small changes by asking what other people in the client's life have noticed about the client's positive changes and how they responded.

Same: When the client reports that nothing has changed the previous session, it is easy for the therapist to begin wondering whether the client is motivated or whether this approach does not work with this client's type of substance abuse problem. Our clinical experience is that such a report is a manifestation of therapist oversight and not the failure of the client or inadequacy of the treatment model: Both were looking for unrealistically big or magical changes to occur without much effort on the client's part.

Instead of giving up on the client or the treatment model, when the therapist persists in detailed inquiry, clients often discover that they took small but significant beginning steps. When the small changes are noted, the therapist needs to direct the discussion to a detailed strategy of how the client will stay focused on maintaining the small changes and increase the frequency and scope of his exceptions.

Worse: When the client reports that his/her life is getting worse instead of better, there are two possibilities. The first and most commonly reported is the occurrance an upsetting event that is not related to the therapy just prior to the session. Such events color the client's perception so that the client's life seems much worse than it actually is. The client forgets that he/she has successfully navigated the first 5 days since the last meeting Again, when clients report that their life is getting worse than it was the previous week, a detailed study of each day since the previous meeting would show these clients that they are actually doing better than they initially thought.

There are situations, however, when it is important for the therapist to pay close attention to the client's report that his/her life is getting worse. Listening for details of how things are worse from the client's point of view may provide added information about the client that was not available before, thus making it possible to revise the initial assessment of what needs to change.

TERMINATION

Termination, much as the entire treatment process, is collaborative. That is, both the client and the therapist decide when to terminate. Here scaling questions are quite useful for assessing movement toward the treatment goal during each session, as the following dialogue shows.

THERAPIST: Let's say ten stands for how you want your life to be. It's not perfect, but you are reasonably content with how your life is going overall and one stands for how serious your problem was when you first came to see me. Right now, where would you say you are between one and ten?

JOHN: I would say I'm at about eight.

THERAPIST: Wow, I would say that's a long way from one. If I were to ask your wife, where would she say she thinks you are now?

JOHN: She would probably be lot more cautious than I am, say, maybe five or six.

THERAPIST: I guess she's right to be cautious, considering what she has gone through with your drinking all these years. What would she say she needs to see you do for her to get the idea that you have moved up just one point higher on the same scale, say, to six or seven?

JOHN: Yeah, I guess she needs more time. Essentially she will say she needs more time and to see me keep at what I've been doing since I started the program here: going to meetings, changing my friends, managing my stress better, and staying away from the bottle, and being more open with her, and things like that.

THERAPIST: On a scale of one to ten where ten stands for as much confidence as anybody can have of maintaining the progress you have made so far, and one is the opposite, where would you say you are at today?

JOHN: I want to say nine or ten, but realistically I know I have just started a sober life and I've been at this point before. So I will say I'm at about seven and staying at this level. I'm determined this time, and I think I'm a lot more serious about it. I have to make it this time.

THERAPIST: If I were to talk to your wife, what would she say about where she thinks you are at, on the same scale?

JOHN: As I said, she is afraid of being disappointed again. I don't blame her, because I let her down many times before. But she knows I'm trying and we are talking more than ever before, which is different. If she was really honest about it, my guess is that she will say about seven or eight.

THERAPIST: That high? She is a little higher than you. Does that mean she has more confidence than you that you will maintain the changes you are making?

JOHN: Yeah, well, she knows how serious I am this time. Either we make it or we don't. She is that serious and me, too.

THERAPIST: Let me ask you a little different question this time. How confident are you that you can maintain at this level for the next month or so?

JOHN: I'm very confident, eight or nine. My wife would say the same.

THERAPIST: What do you suppose your boss would say about how confident he is that he doesn't have to be on your back?

JOHN: He won't say openly to my face because he is not that kind of guy, but he has been pretty decent to me lately, leaving me alone and not bugging me, that kind of stuff. I guess he knows I'm trying, too. It helps to know that my wife is supportive and encouraging me.

Because the client is realistic about his ability to stay sober over the long and short run, combined with a high degree of motivation to keep the marriage and his job, the prognosis seems more hopeful than initial ly thought. This is a good time to meet less frequently in order to give John the opportunity to experiment with success on his own in "the real world." He will be advised to repeat his successful strategies, such as attending AA, spending more time with his children, talking more with his wife, further developing a healthier life-style, and so on. The future focus will be on what other ways John is increasing his repertoire of healthy life-styles and what else he is doing to maintain his goals of keeping his family together.

APPLICATION TO GROUP TREATMENT

SFBT has been successfully adapted to the time-limited format of group treatment with various clinical populations, including sexual abuse survivors (Dolan, 1991; Linz, personal communication, 1993), parenting groups (Selekman, 1993), domestic abuse perpetrators (Uken, personal communication, 1992), and, of course, substance abusers (Gallagher, personal communication, 1993). Berg and Gallagher (in press) have adapted the popular 1-year, 2-year, or 3-year token sobriety concept into the time-limited group therapy format, expanding the miracle question into a longer time span of 1, 2, or 3 years. The token sobriety concept works as follows. Instead of reunion groups that meet years after a certain period has lapsed, the group leader can set aside a designated group meeting period during the 12-week group therapy session as the time they all return to report their progress to each other. All members report to the group as if they returned for the reunion meeting 1 year later and retrace how they have successfully accomplished the changes. The group leader's task is to focus on their successful mastery of 1 year of sobriety as if they have actually overcome many obstacles, always focusing on how each wants his/her life to change and how their significant others are reacting to these changes.

The basic principles remain the same for the group treatment. These are client goal setting by using miracle questions, using scaling questions to monitor progress, and behaviorally tracking successful strategies that work for each client. The group culture and dynamic that are fostered are to encourage and support each other's successes while holding to a minimum "drunk stories," past mistakes, blaming, or grievances against others. Instead, members are challenged about what they will do in order to make the desired changes.

THE ECONOMIC REALITY OF BRIEF THERAPY

It is no secret that the health care delivery system in this country will witness increasing demands for efficiency and accountability during the next few years. The field of substance abuse treatment is no exception. Already many health maintenance organizations (HMOs) and community mental health services offer limited detoxification and hospital stays. SFBT is ideal for those organizations that have limited economic resources along with increased demands for efficiency. In most settings, clinicians more than ever before are expected to provide more services with fewer sessions to those with more serious problems. I cannot think of a more efficient treatment model than holding clients responsible for their own treatment and utilizing their existing successful strategies as a basis.

Unlike other brief treatment models, there is no screening of clients at our center, and whoever walks through the door is seen. The majority are economically disadvantaged, inner-city people; many are court-ordered to seek treatment. Our follow-up study, based on client self-report, shows that across the board, the average number of sessions per case was 4.2, with 81% of clients stating they met their goals 6 months after termination (Kiser, 1988). Talmon's (1991) sing-session therapy excluded substance abusers. However, his study indicates that even in the HMO setting (Kaiser Permanente), where the client is entitled to 20 outpatient visits per calendar year, the overwhelming majority of "dropout" clients who did not keep a second scheduled appointment with the therapist reported satisfaction with the service. Zweben, Perlman, and Li (1993) have found with some clients at a chronic stage of alcohol abuse that a single session of advice was as effective as eight sessions of conjoint marital therapy. His more recent study of drinkers' checkup shows that many clients sustain long-term improvement with brief intervention (Zweben & Barrett, 1993). Clearly more is not always better. In fact, sometimes less is more effective.

CONCLUSION

This chapter was designed to be a brief introduction to SFBT for those with no previous exposure to this model. As is always the case, condensing the complex and complicated processes of what occurs in therapy makes it difficult to address other clinical issues such as relapses, detoxification, involvement of the family in treatment, and so on. I have described only the cursory highlights of the treatment model with the hope that the reader can be persuaded to undertake further in-depth study of this simple and innovative approach. I have been accused of being "naive," simplistic, and even "dangerous" by those who believe in the traditional disease model of treatment. I must confess that, yes, I am rather naive and rather simple-minded. Many professionals are surprised at the simplicity of the model but how difficult it is to practice because people often confuse simplicity with simple-mindedness or stupidity. No wonder. The model is based on an entirely different paradigm from the conventional deficit model.

The key component of this radically different and nonmedical model is to use the exceptions to problems that clients already have. Miracle questions work to disconnect solutions from problems, and the vision of how clients want their lives to be different becomes a goal to strive for. Along the way we have discovered that regardless of what the problems are, the solutions to them seem to be so similar and yet so mundane: to do what will be good for clients and their families, such as talking to each other, being open and honest with each other, doing kind deeds, working hard, developing healthy habits, and looking for ways to change tomorrow by creating a vision of what they want. I was surprised to find in my work with homeless substance abusers that even the most chronic abusers have periods when they "cool it" in order to maximize the high from the limited amount of substance available to them (Berg & Hopwood, 1991). It occurred to me that if the homeless abusers can do it, certainly those with more intact support systems would do better. And this seems to be true.

REFERENCES

Berg, I. K. (1994). *Family based services: A solution-focused approach.* New York: W. W. Norton.

Berg, I. K., & Hopwood, L. (1991). Doing with very little: Treatment of homeless substance abusers. *Journal of Independent Social Work, 5*(3/4), 109–119.

Berg, I. K. & Miller, S. D. (1992). *Working with the problem drinker.* New York: W. W. Norton.

de Shazer, S. D. (1985). *Keys to solution in brief therapy.* New York: W. W. Norton.

de Shazer, S. D. (1988). *Clues: Investigating solutions in brief therapy.* New York: W. W. Norton.

de Shazer, S. D. (1989). Resistance revisited. *Contemporary Family Therapy, 11*(4), 227–233.

de Shazer, S. D. (1991). *Putting difference to work.* New York: W. W. Norton.

de Shazer, S. D. (1994). *Originally words were magic.* New York: W. W. Norton.

de Shazer, S. D., & Berg, I. K. (1992). Doing therapy: Post-structural re-vision. *Journal of Marital and Family Therapy, 8*(1), 71–81.

de Shazer, S. D., & Berg, I. K. (1993) Making numbers talk: Language in therapy. In S. Friedman (Ed.), *The new language of change: Constructive collaboration in psychotherapy* (pp. 5–24). New York: Guilford Press.

de Shazer, S. D., Berg, I. K., Lipchick, E., Nunnally, E., Molnar, A., Gingerich, W. C., & Weiner-Davis, M. (1986). Brief therapy: Focused solution development. *Family Process, 25,* 207–221.

Dolan, Y. M. (1991). *Resolving sexual abuse.* New York: W. W. Norton.

Edwards, G., Orford, J., Egert, S., Guthrie, S., Hawker, A., Hensman, C., Mitcheson, N., Oppenheimer, E., & Taylor, C. (1977). Alcoholism: A controlled trial of "treatment" and "advice." *Journal of Studies on Alcohol, 38,* 1004–1031.

Kiser, D. (1988). *A follow-up study conducted at the Brief Family Therapy Center.* Unpublished manuscript.

Miller, W. R. (1985). Motivation for treatment: A review with special emphasis on alcoholism. *Psychological Bulletin, 89*(1), 84–107.

Prochaska, J. O., & DiClemente, C. C. (1986). Toward a comprehensive model of change. In W. R. Miller & N. Heather (Eds.), *Treating addictive behaviors: Processes of change* (pp. 3–27). New York: Plenum Press.

Prochaska, J., DiClemente, C. C., & Norcross, J. (1992). In search of how people change: Application to addictive behavior. *American Psychologist, 47*(9), 1102–1114.

Selekman, M. D. (1993). *Pathways to change: Brief therapy solutions with difficult adolescents.* New York: Guilford Press.

Sobell, M. B., & Sobell, L. C. (1993). *Problem drinkers: Guided self-change treatment.* New York: Guilford Press.

Talmon, M. (1991). *Single session therapy.* San Francisco: Jossey-Bass.

Watzlawick, P. & Weakland, J. (Eds.). (1977). *The interactional view.* New York: W. W. Norton.

Zweben, A., & Barrett, D. (1993). Brief couples treatment for alcohol problems. In T. J. O'Farrell (Ed.), *Treating alcohol problems: Marital and family interventions* (pp. 353–380). New York: Guilford Press.

Zweben, A., Perlman, S., & Li, S. (1988). A comparison of brief advice and conjoint therapy in the treatment of alcohol abuse: The results of the marital systems study. *British Journal of Addiction, 89,* 899–916.

13

Relapse Prevention: Intervention Strategies for Mental Health Clients with Comorbid Addictive Disorders

DENNIS C. DALEY
JUDITH A. LIS

INTRODUCTION

There is significant evidence that many mental health clients have comorbid substance use disorders (Daley, Moss, & Campbell, 1993; Robins & Regier, 1993; Ross, Glaser, & Germanson, 1988; National Institute on Drug Abuse, 1991). As a result, the focus on strategies to assess and treat alcohol and drug problems among mental health clients has increased.

There has been a significant decrease in the length of inpatient stay at many addiction residential programs as a result of pressure from managed care. These nationwide changes in health care policy have led to not only shortened stays in these traditional 28-day ''rehabs'' but also many closings. These recent developments have caused some clients alternately to seek treatment in the mental health system.

In response to these widespread changes, mental health clinicians must be able to work with clients not only with psychiatric disorders but also with a variety of substance use diagnoses. This is especially critical because untreated addiction or relapse to addiction has major implications for recovery from psychiatric illness.

There are several key issues in the treatment of substance use disorders for clients with comorbid psychiatric disorders; they are treatment entry, retention, compliance, and relapse prevention. Treatment entry, which is also referred to as engagement and motivation, is critical as many clients with substance use disorders do not enter treatment voluntarily and often receive treatment as a result of pressure or encouragement from the legal system, families, employers, and health care or social service professionals. Typically, clients entering the treatment system under these circumstances deny or minimize their substance use disorder, attributing their use of substances to their psychiatric illness and erroneously believing that successful mental health treatment will enable them to continue using substances in a controlled fashion. The first major treatment issue for clinicians is to help the client accept the reality of the substance use disorder and become motivated to engage in treatment. Mental health clinicians should become familiar with motivational counseling strategies to facilitate treatment entry and/or break through denial of the substance use disorder (Miller, 1989).

Clients with substance use problems often drop out of treatment early and thus do not benefit from the effects of treatment. There is significant evidence that length of time in treatment is correlated with positive outcome for substance abusers (Tims, Fletcher, & Hubbard, 1991). Length of treatment is correlated with reduction and cessation of drug usage as well as the improvement of general health and functioning. High rates of dropout do occur, unfortunately, especially in particular diagnostic groups, such as severe personality disorders. Therefore, a second challenge for mental health clinicians is helping the substance abuse client remain in treatment. Outreach efforts to dropouts may help some clients reengage in treatment and experience its obvious benefits.

A third major treatment issue is failure to comply with the treatment plan in relation to specific issues negotiated between clinician and client. Examples include noncompliance with total abstinence from alcohol and other drugs, poor or total lack of attendance at support groups, and failure to complete individualized recovery tasks assigned by the therapist as a way of facilitating change in the client.

Finally, a fourth issue in the treatment of substance use disorders is that of relapse. Numerous studies indicate that relapse rates are very high among individuals with substance use disorders, particularly those with comorbid psychiatric illnesses (McLellan, Luborsky, Woody, O'Brien, & Druley, 1983; Rounsaville, Dolinsky, Babor, & Meyer, 1987). Therefore, relapse prevention (RP) strategies to maintain gains realized from the treatment experience are an important part of long-term recovery.

This chapter provides a brief background of the issue of relapse among psychiatric clients who have comorbid drug and alcohol use disorders. Definitions are provided and outcome studies, precipitants of relapse, and models of treatment are reviewed. Some of the advantages and limitations of RP interventions and client treatment matching issues are pointed out. The major focus of this chapter is delineating guidelines in providing RP interventions for clients. Ten practical areas of clinical RP interventions are presented along with evidence of efficacy. Case examples are used to highlight some of the clinical issues discussed.

BACKGROUND OF RELAPSE PREVENTION

Relapse prevention refers to a number of clinical techniques and programs designed to maximize maintenance of sobriety from alcohol or other drugs. Researchers and clinicians alike have been developing new approaches to RP for over a decade in response to growing concern about the high rates of alcohol and drug abuse relapse. Outcome studies generally show 40% to 80% rates of relapse, with some studies showing even higher rates of relapse among treated alcoholics or drug addicts. There is evidence in the empirical literature that psychiatric impairment is strongly associated with relapse to substance use (Catalano, Howard, Hawkins, & Wells, 1988; Marlatt & Gordon, 1985; McLellan, Luborsky, et al., 1983). Clinicians generally agree that clients with psychiatric illness and addiction are more vulnerable to relapse to substance use and psychiatric recurrence than are clients who have a single disorder. Studies by McLellan, Luborsky, et. al. (1983) and McLellan, Woody, Luborsky, O'Brien, and Druley (1983) found that addicted clients with the highest global ratings of psychiatric severity are the most likely to relapse following treatment. In a study comparing psychiatric inpatients with and without comorbid substance use disorders, dual-diagnosis clients had significantly higher readmission rates to a psychiatric hospital than did clients without the additional substance abuse diagnosis (Salloum & Daley, 1993).

In the psychiatric field, the terms *relapse* and *recurrence* are typically used to describe two different processes (Thase, 1990). However, the term *relapse* is sometimes used to describe either one of these processes. To clarify, the term *relapse* implies a return of psychiatric symptoms during the index episode of illness. This may occur during the acute or continuation phase of treatment. The term *recurrence* refers to a separate, discrete recurrent episode of illness after a period of remission. *Webster's New Collegiate Dictionary* (1986) defines relapse as a recurrence of symptoms of a disease after a period of improvement or the act or instance of backsliding, worsening, or subsiding. This definition is applicable to both psychiatric illness or addiction.

In the addiction field, relapse is defined as a "breakdown or setback in a person's attempt to change or modify any target behavior (Marlatt & Gordon, 1985, p. 32)." The target behavior in this case is alcohol and/or drug use. This definition implies that there has been a period of improvement or remission before a person goes back to using drugs or alcohol. The other term commonly used in substance use treatment is *lapse.* A lapse refers to the initial episode of alcohol or drug use following a period of recovery. A lapse may or may not end up in a actual full-blown relapse. Some clients, for example, use substances on a limited basis during their recovery and then return to working a recovery program. Clinicians should be cognizant that there are many different patterns of lapses and relapses—not all are alike and not all require the same clinical intervention.

Although outcome studies indicate high rates of relapse in alcoholism and drug abuse treatment, drug and alcohol use is only one of several outcome variables. Other treatment outcome variables include psychological, psychiatric, occupational, medical, family, social, and interpersonal functioning as well as legal and financial status. One of the possible effects of treatment is the reduction of harmful substance use and/or a concomitant reduction in impairment in one or more of these areas. Therefore, it is helpful not to see recovery as an all-or-none phenomenon. Both the literature and clinical experience indicate that the majority of substance abusers will benefit from participation in treatment despite the actual rates of substance use following treatment.

Although relapse can occur at any point in recovery, approximately two thirds occur in the initial 3 months of abstinence. A number of different factors contribute to relapse. In most cases, it is multifactorial rather than any one precipitant that causes the actual lapse or relapse to alcohol or drug abuse. Categories of relapse precipitants include the following (Marlatt & Gordon, 1985; Daley, 1988):

1. *Affective variables or mood states.* Negative mood states such as anger, anxiety, boredom, depression, emptiness, guilt, loneliness, and anhedonia are associated with relapse. These affective states are sometimes symptomatic of the comorbid psychiatric disorder, for example, major depressive illness, bipolar disorder, and anxiety disorder. Positive emotional states are also associated with a small number of relapses.
2. *Behavioral variables.* Lack of coping skills and personal competencies are a key variable in relapse. Clients with poor problem-solving abilities, difficulties managing leisure time, and deficits in social skills are more vulnerable to relapse.
3. *Cognitive variables.* Relapse is often related to client attitudes, beliefs, and expectations regarding substance use, recovery, and relapse. Clients with higher levels of self-efficacy regarding their ability to cope with high-risk relapse situations are more likely to maintain their sobriety. Chronic alcoholics with severe deficits in cognitive functioning are less likely to maintain their recovery.

4. *Environmental and relationship factors.* Easy availability of substances, direct and indirect social pressures to use drugs or alcohol, negative social networks, a lack of a positive support system, lack of productive roles, major life changes, interpersonal conflict, social skill deficits, and other environmental problems such as homelessness contribute to relapse. Any of these factors can influence a client's decision to use alcohol or other drugs.
5. *Physiological variables.* Severity of addiction, physical illness, or symptoms such as premenstrual syndrome, physical pain, and strong physical cravings or urges to use substances can have an impact on relapse. This is particularly true for clients experiencing acute or protracted withdrawal symptoms.
6. *Psychological and psychiatric variables.* Conscious and unconscious motivations, learned behaviors, personality style or traits, psychiatric illness or severe psychological problems, other addictions or compulsive disorders, and other interpersonal issues such as tremendous emotional pain associated with being a survivor of abuse or incest may contribute to relapse.
7. *Spiritual variables.* Excessive shame and guilt, lack of meaning or purpose in life, joylessness or emptiness, and a lack of connectedness to other people have an impact on relapse.

RP techniques can be integrated into various models of counseling or professional psychotherapy for the treatment of addicted persons, mental health clients, or those with dual disorders. Clinical models of treatment include individual drug counseling (IDC), group drug counseling (GDC), cognitive behavioral treatment (CBT), supportive expressive psychotherapy (SEP), or interpersonal psychotherapy (IPT). For example, the IDC or GDC clinician educates the client about relapse warning signs and the need to avoid and/or cope with high-risk people, places, and situations associated with substance use. The CBT clinician explores the client's beliefs about relapse and helps the client alter cognitive distortions that could contribute to a lapse or relapse to substance use. Mental health clinicians can similarly help clients with psychiatric disorders learn to identify and prepare to handle high-risk factors and monitor early warning signs of recurrence of psychiatric symptoms.

RP can also be provided as a distinct clinical model of treatment in a designated skills training or RP group program. A variety of specific skills-training and RP models have been developed over the past several years that are applicable to specific types of substance use disorders and other addictions, mental health disorders, and other problems of impulse control such as sexual deviance (Annis & Davis, 1987; Chiauzzi, 1991; Daley, 1988; Daley, 1989; Gorski & Miller, 1988; Laws, 1989; Liberman, DeRisi, & Mueser, 1989; Marlatt & Gordon, 1985; Monti, Adams, Kadden, & Cooney, 1989; National Institute on Drug Abuse, 1993; Wilson,

1992). Although there are some differences in the theoretical bases and the clinical application of these various models of treatment, there is a great deal of overlap. For example, all aim to help clients identify and cope with high-risk relapse factors, identify early warning signs of relapse, and make life-style changes. These models also address issues pertinent to setbacks or actual lapses and relapses to the addictive or problematic behavior.

Above and beyond the specific clinical interventions, one of the key elements in working with substance use clients is the attitude of the clinician. A realistic attitude regarding sobriety of the substance-abusing client is absolutely necessary for treatment to succeed. Given the chronic nature of many forms of chemical dependency, clinicians must be realistic regarding how they view progress and how they work with clients who actually lapse or relapse. Unrealistic and judgmental attitudes as well as negative reactions on the part of the clinician will impede the therapeutic alliance. Therefore, clinicians must be cognizant of their personal beliefs regarding relapse and recovery and reactions to clients who relapse. Therapeutic alliance is a critical factor in treatment outcome. A positive alliance involves "connecting" with where the client is in the recovery process. The clinician needs to show concern, empathy, and regard for the client's problems and well-being. A genuine belief that the client can benefit from the treatment provided must be communicated. Without an effective alliance, techniques described in a later section of this chapter will have decreased impact.

CLINICAL INTERVENTIONS

Education, confrontation, and skill development are important clinical interventions for substance-abusing clients. Teaching specific cognitive, behavioral, and problem-solving skills and enhancing the client's self-awareness can facilitate recovery and have a positive impact on RP. A variety of action techniques such as role-plays, therapeutic assignments, workbook exercises, self-reflection journals, and monodramas can be used to teach these recovery skills. These action techniques can help clients identify, clarify, explore, or work through specific problems or recovery issues that have implications for RP. For example, role-plays or behavioral rehearsals can be used to prepare clients to deal with the pressures to use alcohol or drugs, ask for help or support from another person, negotiate interpersonal conflict, or express angry feelings toward another person. Journal assignments can be used to help clients review and reflect on previous relapses in order to identify warning signs that were ignored, as well as the context in which their relapses occurred. Coping strategies that can be used in future situations can then be discussed.

Following is a review of practical RP interventions that can be easily adapted to mental health clients who have comorbid substance use disorders. These interventions can be used in inpatient, other residential, partial hospital, and outpatient settings.

Provide Education

Provide clients with education on relapse regardless of their motivation level and where they are in the recovery process. Even if they have not accepted the severity of their addiction, education on addiction and relapse may help them further down the road in their recovery. When possible, information provided on addiction relapse should be connected with the client's psychiatric disorder. For example, many clients evidence a pattern in which substance use relapse leads to a decrease in the efficacy or a cessation of psychiatric medications or failure to attend psychotherapy sessions. As a result, psychiatric symptoms often return or worsen, leading the client to substance use in an attempt to self-medicate.

Specific areas in which to provide education include causes of relapse, typical warnings signs, ways to cope with thoughts of using, cues that trigger off cravings to use, social pressures to use drugs or alcohol, social networks, life-style balancing, and strategies to deal with setbacks such as lapses or relapses. Educational interventions are nonthreatening ways that may help break through the denial of addiction and motivate clients to change. Educational interventions can be provided systematically or spontaneously in individual treatment sessions as specific issues emerge, as part of structured psychoeducational groups or skills training groups, and through the use of readings and bibliotherapeutic assignments.

Monitor Cravings, Close Calls, or Episodes of Substance Use

Routinely ask clients about any actual episodes of substance use since the previous session and discuss close calls as well as any strong cravings or desires they have had since the previous session. If a client identifies close calls or cravings, discuss the context in which these occurred in order to help the client determine what intrapersonal or interpersonal factors contributed to an increased desire to use alcohol or drugs. It is also helpful to monitor attendance at Alcoholics Anonymous (AA), Narcotics Anonymous (NA), Cocaine Anonymous (CA), or dual-recovery anonymous (DRA) support groups as well as interactions with sponsors. Decreased or noninvolvement in support groups often precedes relapse. Regular monitoring of these activities provides clinicians with an opportunity to intervene early in this possible relapse process. Clinicians can also use objective measures to monitor alcohol and drug use or abstinence such as breathalyzers and urinalysis. Use of these measures is often a function of treatment philosophy, availability, and accessibility of staff to obtain urines or take breathalyzers, as well as mechanisms for payment.

Identify High-Risk Factors and Coping Strategies

Help clients identify their individual potential relapse risk factors. Typically, these risk factors are situations in which they abused alcohol or drugs prior to treatment or situations in which clients feel vulnerable to using. Once the client has identified specific high-risk factors, a plan can be devised to strengthen coping skills for the management of these relapse risk factors. The most common relapse risk factors include negative affect, interpersonal problems and conflicts, social pressures to use alcohol or other drugs, and cravings or desires for alcohol or drugs. Some clients report a "general" high-risk profile and exhibit a number of risk factors across a variety of areas. No one or two categories will seem a greater risk for these clients than others. Other clients evidence more "specific" relapse risk profiles. In the latter case, interventions can be devised based on the specificity of these relapse risk factors. For example, if the client identifies boredom as typically leading to alcohol or drug use, one clinical intervention is to help the client develop structure during the day to reduce the chances of feeling bored. This structure may include participation in enjoyable leisure activities as a way of enhancing satisfaction.

Identify Relapse Warning Signs
and Management Strategies

Relapse is generally viewed as a process in which discrete attitudinal, emotional, or behavioral signs show prior to the client's actually ingesting alcohol or other drugs. These warning signs often show days, weeks, or months before substances are used. However, some clients may report that warning signs develop very quickly and they use substances rather impulsively. This intervention involves teaching clients about common relapse warning signs associated with addiction as well as identifying idiosyncratic warning signs unique to each client. If the client is in treatment for the first time, he/she can benefit and relate to common relapse warning signs identified by other recovering clients in treatment and recovery.

For clients who have relapsed following a period of recovery, learning from this experience can be accomplished by conducting a "microanalysis" of the relapse. This process involves identifying specific relapse warning signs, where and when these signs occurred, who else was present when the client used, how much time elapsed between emergence of warning signs and actual substance use, the effects of relapse on the client and other people, and strategies to deal with these warning signs should they show in the future. Early warning signs are often easily identified by the client. The clinician is most helpful to the client in devising strategies to cope with warning signs because failure to cope leads to a subsequent relapse. The relapse process can be conceptualized as a series of decisions and/or events that progress and eventuate in actual substance use. By conducting a retrospective microanalysis of lapse or relapse experiences, the client is taught that relapse does not come out of the blue, that there is a context in which it occurs, and that the more the client can accept that actual warning signs preceded alcohol or drug usage, the more prepared he/she will be in the future. In essence, this microanalysis makes a "failure" a powerful "learning" experience used to facilitate recovery.

It is common for clients to report an impulsive relapse. However, upon detailed exploration of relapse experiences, the event could be predicted by specific behaviors occurring over a period of days, weeks, or even longer. Clients identify this microanalysis as one of the most helpful RP interventions. In a survey, conducted with 511 clients participating in RP groups, the specific session on understanding the relapse process was identified as the most informative and helpful (Daley, 1989).

Identify Substance Use Triggers and Coping Strategies

External cues that typically trigger alcohol or drug cravings include the sight or smell of liquor or other substances; drug paraphernalia such as pipes, mirrors, and needles; or exposure to people, places, and things associated with getting, preparing, or using substances. Helpful recovery strategies include teaching clients to avoid people, places, and things that are likely to trigger a desire to use; getting rid of paraphernalia and chemicals in their home; and exposing them to some of the situations or stimuli so that the strength of the craving is reduced. Internal triggers to cravings include negative affective states as well as obsessions or strong thoughts of using alcohol or other drugs. It helps to teach clients to identify their internal and external triggers and to be aware of the physiological and psychological manifestations of cravings. In addition, clients benefit from learning how to rate the intensity of their cravings so that they can choose the most appropriate coping strategy. For example, low-level cravings can often be dealt with simply by accepting them, letting them pass, and telling oneself that they will go away. However, stronger cravings require other techniques such as talking to a support person, talking oneself through the craving, or distracting oneself with active involvement in an activity. Another helpful coping strategy is for clients to carry a 3″ × 5″ index card that lists several craving coping strategies. This card can be easily taken from a wallet or purse and reviewed when the client has a strong craving to use. It can serve as a reminder that techniques are available to help the client successfully manage the craving.

Identify Strategies to Cope with Pressures to Use or to Stop Taking Psychiatric Medications

The second most common relapse precipitants among substance abusers are direct and indirect pressures to use alcohol or other drugs. Identifying specific relationships and social situations in which there is pressure to use substances, as well as specific strategies to cope with these specific issues, is helpful to the client. In some instances, relationships may have to be ended, particularly if they are based primarily on getting high. Perhaps the most difficult recovery issue to deal with is an intimate relationship with another active alcoholic or drug addict such as a spouse, roommate, or partner. Various options should be explored with the client so that a clear message is communicated that alternative life-styles are available. Unfortunately, some clients resist the notion of limiting contact or ending relationships with a significant other who is actively using alcohol or other drugs. As a result, relapse often occurs.

Many clients have inadequate social skills to resist offers to use alcohol or other drugs. Clinicians can help such clients first evaluate the effects of different social pressures on their thoughts, feelings, and behaviors. For instance, tremendous ambivalence may surface when a client is confronted with the possibility of using drugs, even if the client is working a solid program of recovery. One practical technique is the use of role-plays. Clients can simulate situations in which they practice different ways to refuse alcohol or drugs. Not only does the practice help them to develop coping skills, it also raises their awareness of internal thoughts and feelings that often accompany social pressure situations.

To assist in the development of life-style changes, clinicians can encourage the client to plan and participate in activities and social events that can be enjoyed without the threat of using alcohol or drugs. For some clients this is very difficult, as most social activities previously revolved around alcohol or drug use. Leisure counseling is especially important in the early stages of recovery, when the client is adjusting to living drug-free and is prone to boredom.

A strategy for clients who take psychiatric medication is preparing them for the possibility of pressure from other people to stop taking these medications. Other alcoholics and addicts in recovery may pressure a client to stop taking psychiatric medications for a variety of reasons. Some people in recovery evidence an all-or-none mentality toward this issue by advocating the cessation of all drugs even if they are medically or psychiatrically indicated. However, clients who stop taking neuroleptic, antimanic, or antidepressant medications have a greater chance of experiencing an exacerbation of psychiatric symptoms. This in turn can contribute to a substance abuse relapse. Anticipation of this possibility and behavioral rehearsal can help make dual-diagnosis clients feel comfortable in dealing with this situation should it occur. A related strategy is the reinforcement of the importance of understanding and accepting the difference between drugs used to get high and medications needed to treat a psychiatric illness.

Develop the Client's Recovery Support Network

Current support networks should be analyzed with clients so that they can identify existing gaps in their support network and new potential sources of support in recovery. Strong family and social support is associated with better recovery across a wide range of mental health and addictive disorders. Therefore, when feasible, practitioners should involve the client's family or significant others in the treatment and recovery processes. This provides the client and family with an opportunity to deal with some of the family problems caused or worsened by the addiction.

Prior to engaging the family or significant others in sessions, it is helpful to get the client to examine how the addiction affected the family and to consider ways of making amends for problems caused by the addiction. Failure to understand the impact of addiction on the family often puts clients in a position of asking for help from the very people who are angry and upset. These people may in one way or another sabotage the recovery unless an opportunity is provided for them to work through these feelings.

Asking for help and support from other people is a crucial aspect of developing a support network. Yet, many clients have tremendous difficulty making requests and asking for help from others. As a result, it is very common for clients to keep their problems and struggles to themselves. Without the involvement of a clear-cut support network in problem-solving efforts, chances of clients working through some of their difficulties without going back to alcohol or other drugs is reduced. Again, behavioral rehearsal can be a useful technique to help clients become more comfortable in asking for help and support from other people, as well as to share difficulties experienced in recovery.

Self-help groups such as AA, NA, CA, DRA, and mental health support groups should be part of the client's social network in recovery. The use of a sponsor and involvement in recovery clubs is beneficial as well. Involvement with self-help groups provides the experience of universality of understanding and a shared experience. To enhance this process, clients often need help in developing or expanding social skills such as listening, self-disclosing to others, expressing feelings and desires, and negotiating conflict.

Prepare for Setbacks and Relapses

All clients should be prepared for the possibility of coping with such set-backs as lapses or relapses. This is especially critical because return to substance abuse has implications for recurrence of psychiatric illness or exacerbation of persistent symptoms of psychiatric illness. A specific plan should be devised with clients should they go back to using alcohol or drugs. This plan could include a list of specific people that can be called on for help and support, and a plan for more serious emergencies such as severe relapses in which physical readdiction occurs or other major damage results from alcohol or other drug use. Specific intervention strategies will be contingent upon the severity of the lapse or relapse, the coping abilities of the client as well as prior relapse history, and the nature of the concurrent mental health disorder. Family involvement is often critical as family members are often able to pressure and encourage clients to get help in the early stages of a lapse or relapse. Once clients are stable from the lapse or relapse and any exacerbation of psychiatric symptoms, it is imperative to focus clinical efforts on examining, in detail, warnings signs and risk factors leading to resumption of substance use. These setbacks can be framed in a positive manner as an opportunity for learning and growth. Many clients deny the significance of these experiences. Despite this initial discomfort, it is beneficial for clients to analyze their lapses or relapse. For clients with a history of multiple relapses, such analysis may help detect clear and predictable patterns to their relapses.

Promote Life-Style Balancing

A healthy life-style ideally focuses on the need for balance in the major domains of life such as work, relationships, play, recovery, and spirituality. Identification and involvement in positive activities can bring a sense of fun, excitement, and involvement in life. Clients who are able to participate in enjoyable or fulfilling activities or hobbies are less likely to feel the need to use alcohol or drugs to fill a void or in order to experience excitement. Examination of daily patterns of living and sources of stress can help clients identify a reasonable balance between obligations and wants or desires. Structure and routine in daily life help to reduce feelings of boredom, depression, and uselessness, which are common risks for relapse. Pleasant activities should be integrated into their lives on a regular basis. These activities should be based on the needs and interests of the client and ideally should include a number of activities that can be pursued alone as well as ones that involve other people.

Encourage the Use of a Daily Inventory and Symptom Review

A simple yet powerful clinical intervention is the use of a daily inventory. At the end of each day, clients can ask themselves a few questions such as the following: (1) are there any high-risk situations that need attention, (2) are there any relapse warning signs that need to be managed; or (3) are there any problems that need to be addressed? For clients who have persistent forms of psychiatric illness, a daily rating of persistent symptoms of their psychiatric illness can track changes over time and allow them to take action when symptoms significantly worsen.

CASE EXAMPLES

Example 1: High-Risk Situations

Stan is a 32-year-old with diagnoses of recurrent major depression, antisocial personality disorder, crack/cocaine dependence, and polysubstance abuse. He has a 15 + -year history of addiction, including a 2-year history of crack addiction. Stan has been in a variety of psychiatric and addiction treatment programs during the past 10 years. His longest clean time has been 14 months. He has been attending a dual-diagnosis outpatient clinic for the past 9 months and going to NA meetings off and on for several years. Stan has been clean from all substances for 7 months. Following is a list of high-risk relapse factors and coping strategies identified by Stan and his outpatient therapist:

High-Risk Factor 1

Stan is tired and bored "with just working, staying at home and watching TV, or going to NA meetings." Recently, he has been thinking about how much he "misses the action of the good old days" of hanging with old friends and does not think he has enough things to do that are interesting.

Possible coping strategies for Stan include the following: (1) remind himself of problems caused by hanging out with other addicts and using drugs by writing out a specific list of problems associated with addiction; (2) challenge the notion of the "good old days" by looking closely at the "bad" aspects of these days; (3) remind himself of how far he has come in his recent recovery, especially being able to get and keep a job, maintain a relationship with one woman, and stay out of trouble with the law; (4) discuss current feelings and struggles with NA sponsor and NA friends to find out how they handled similar feelings and thoughts;

and (5) make a list of activities that will not threaten recovery and can provide a sense of fun and excitement, and plan to start active involvement in one of these activities.

High-Risk Factor 2

Stan is getting bored with his relationship with his girlfriend. He feels she is too much of a "home body" and wants more excitement in his relationship with her. He is also having increased thoughts of having sex with other women.

Possible coping strategies for Stan include the following: (1) explore in therapy sessions why he is really feeling bored with his girlfriend because he has a long-standing pattern of dumping girlfriends after just a few months; (2) challenge his belief that the problem is mainly his girlfriend so that he sees how his attitudes and beliefs play a role in this problem; (3) talk directly with his girlfriend in a nonblaming fashion about his desire to work together to find ways to instill more excitement in the relationship; (4) remind himself of potential dangers of casual sex with a woman he does not know very well, and remind himself that he cannot reach his goal of maintaining a meaningful, mutual relationship if he gets involved sexually with another woman. His past history is concrete proof that such involvement always leads to sabotaging his primary relationship.

High-Risk Factor 3

Stan wants to stop taking antidepressant medications. His mood has been good for several months and he does not see the need to continue medications.

Possible coping strategies include the following: (1) discuss his concern about medications with his therapist and psychiatrist before making a final decision; (2) review with treatment team the reasons for being on antidepressant medications; (3) remind himself that because he has had several episodes of depression, even during times when he has been drug-free for a long period, medications can help "prevent" the likelihood of a future episode of depression.

Example 2: Relapse Prevention Group

Following is a brief overview of a suggested 10-week RP program for dual-diagnosis outpatients. The group sessions last 1 ½ hours each. Sessions can involve brief lectures, discussions, role-plays, and completion of written recovery activities related to the topic of the group. Topics can be adapted to any diagnostic group of psychiatric disorders.

Session 1

Aid recovery and relapse prevention by reviewing key issues in recovery from dual disorders, precipitants of relapse, possible relationships between psychiatric illness and addiction, and the importance of using RP strategies on an ongoing basis.

Session 2

Identify and manage relapse warning signs by reviewing common attitudinal, emotional or behavioral changes preceding relapse (relapse warning signs) and relapse setups; using a relapse calendar; identifying the importance of understanding both intrapersonal (thoughts and feelings) and interpersonal (social context) components of the relapse process; and using cognitive and behavioral coping strategies to manage relapse warning signs.

Session 3

Identify high-risk relapse factors by reviewing common high-risk relapse factors associated with addiction and develop coping strategies to manage these risk factors.

Session 4

Learn to cope with thoughts and cravings to use chemicals by reviewing internal and external factors that trigger cravings for alcohol or other drugs, learning to be aware of ways in which cravings show and to rate their intensity, and developing coping strategies to manage cravings.

Session 5

Begin to cope with social pressures to get high or stop taking psychiatric medications by identifying social pressures (people, places, events) to use substances, thoughts and feelings experienced in social pressure situations, strategies to cope with pressures to use alcohol and other drugs, and ways to cope with pressures by others in recovery to stop taking psychiatric medications.

Sessions 6 and 7

Cope with upsetting feelings by identifying negative feelings most commonly associated with relapse and strategies to manage feelings, particularly anger, boredom and depression, without using.

Sessions 8 and 9

Develop a positive support network by reviewing its importance to recovery, through the use of 12-Step programs, dual-recovery programs, and mental health support groups, and ways to ask for help and support from others.

Session 10

Cope with setbacks and ongoing monitoring of recovery by reviewing strategies for handling different levels of substance use relapse or psychiatric recurrence and ways to monitor specific symptoms of illness (hallucinations, depression, anxiety, mania) or recovery issues (cravings to use, angry impulses) on a daily basis.

EFFICACY

There is evidence that RP and skills training approaches can have a positive impact on recovery in terms of reduction of substance use and improvement in functioning. A study of opiate addicts participating in a 6-month recovery training and RP program found that significantly more experimental group members than controls achieved abstinence or rare use of opiates during the year-long follow-up (32% vs. 18%). Clients who were unemployed when initially participating in this program also showed higher rates of employment by year-end (National Institute on Drug Abuse, 1993, p. 4). A controlled evaluation of an RP program for alcoholics derived from self-efficacy theory conducted by Annis and colleagues of the Addiction Research Foundation in Toronto showed that clients with a "differentiated profile" of drinking risk situations had a substantially lower typical daily quantity compared to clients receiving traditional counseling (Annis & Davis, 1989). After reviewing controlled studies of social skills training with alcoholics, Chaney (1989) reports that despite some methodological problems in controlled investigations of a skills-training program for alcoholics, "there continues to be a slow stream of reports supporting the effectiveness of skills training" (p. 217). A study of skills training for drug abusers conducted by Hawkins, Catalano, and Wells (1986) reports that treatment improved clients' coping skills in several areas.

PROGRAM DEVELOPMENT

RP programs can be easily integrated into existing clinical practices. Programs can be offered on a one-time basis in the form of a psychoeducational workshop or over a period of time with the inclusion of several sessions or more. Both short-term (less than 12 sessions) and longer-term RP models (up to 6 months) have been used in a variety of inpatient and outpatient treatment contexts. Many of the existing models of RP for addiction lend themselves to adaptation for dual-diagnosis populations.

The principles and practice of RP are now being applied to specific psychiatric disorders as well as to substance use disorders (Wilson, 1992; Kavanagh, 1992; Daley & Roth, 1992). Given the rate of recurrence of psychiatric illness and the high rates of relapse among alcoholics and drug addicts, clinicians are encouraged to incorporate RP interventions into their everyday clinical practice.

Following is a brief review of a process that can facilitate the development and implementation of an RP group program. This process can be used to develop an RP program in any type of inpatient, partial hospital or outpatient treatment facility.

1. Conduct a needs assessment, which involves identifying what clients need and want in the area of RP education and counseling. Interviews with clients, surveys of hospital or agency clients, and review of clinical records can help the clinician identify relapse issues that can be partially addressed in a special RP program.
2. Seek input from other clinicians and administrators, which involves collaborating with colleagues to get their ideas regarding what issues should be addressed in the RP program and in recruiting clients to participate in the program. We recommend that group programs have co-leaders if at all possible.
3. Develop a written RP program proposal, which involves delineating the specific aspects of the RP program. The proposal should specify the target population, how to recruit and screen prospective members, goals and objectives of the overall RP program, length and frequency of group sessions, format of each group session, and methods to evaluate the individual group sessions and/or the entire program.
4. Use a variety of techniques in the RP sessions, including brief educational "mini-lectures" on specific themes or topics, sharing of personal experiences of clients related to RP topics, role-plays to practice coping with RP issues (e.g., how to refuse an offer to get high or how to ask for help and support from another person), review of workbook or other bibliotherapeutic tasks, and review and discussion of educational videotapes on RP.
5. Protect the group process. Because an RP program is a specialized psychoeducation or skills group, avoid the tendency for the group to become a process therapy group, problem-solving group, crisis intervention group, or open recovery rap session in which

clients talk about whatever is on their mind. Encourage clients to take individual issues that are pressing to their individual therapists. Or, these clients can be seen briefly after the group session. One helpful strategy to keep the group on the designated topic is to take a few minutes at the start of each session and have a member read aloud group rules and norms, which should include a statement about the purpose and format of the RP group.

6. Ensure that discussions are balanced in terms of focus on problems and solutions. Make sure that group members pay sufficient attention to discussing and/or practicing coping strategies to handle the relapse issues discussed in the session. Pacing of the session is important. Our experience is that group sessions are most productive when they have a limited focus and a few well-defined objectives and involve specific activities designed to engage the clients in a discussion of ways to cope with the relapse issue that is the focus of the session. For example, if the RP group topic is "developing a support network,," help the participants identify specific strategies to enhance their support networks. Or, if the group topic is "identifying and managing relapse warning signs," help group members generate specific cognitive and behavioral coping strategies that can be used to prevent early warning signs from leading to a relapse.

CONCLUSION

Because a significant percentage of mental health clients have coexisting substance use disorders, it is helpful to focus on RP strategies, particularly as a resumption of substance use is likely to interfere with recovery from the psychiatric disorder. Numerous RP treatment models already exist that can be modified to take into account the specific nature of the psychiatric disorder. RP strategies and specific RP models can be easily integrated in individual, family, or group treatment sessions in mental health systems. Because clinical practice in today's mental health environment is becoming more and more driven by managed care and economics, clinicians are faced with the reality that they have less time to treat clients, including those with more chronic forms of psychiatric illness. RP appears to be a promising treatment approach of great value to clients suffering from mental health and addictive disorders.

REFERENCES

Annis, H., & Davis, C. (1987). Self-efficacy and the prevention of alcoholic relapse: Initial findings from a treatment trial. In T. Baker & D. Cannon (Eds.), *Addiction disorders: Psychological research on assessment and treatment* (pp. 88–112). New York: Praeger.

Catalano, R., Howard, M., Hawkins, J., & Wells, E. (1988). Relapse in the addictions: Rates, determinants, and promising prevention strategies. In *1988 Surgeon General's report on health consequences of smoking* (pp. 157–181). Washington, DC: U.S. Government Printing Office.

Chaney, E. (1989). Social skills training. In R. Hester & W. R. Miller (Eds.), *Handbook of alcoholism treatment approaches* (pp. 206–221). New York: Pergamon Press.

Chiauzzi, E. (1991). *Preventing relapse in the addictions: A biopsychosocial approach.* New York: Pergamon Press.

Daley, D. (1988). *Relapse prevention: Treatment alternatives and counseling aids.* Bradenton, FL: Human Services Institute.

Daley, D. (1989). A psychoeducational approach to relapse prevention. *Journal of Chemical Dependency Treatment, 2*(2), 105–124.

Daley, D., Moss, H., & Campbell, F. (1993). *Dual disorders: Counseling clients with chemical dependency and mental illness* (2nd ed.). Center City, MN: Hazelden.

Daley, D., & Roth, L. (1992). *When symptoms return: A guide to relapse in psychiatric illness.* Holmes Beach, FL: Learning Publications.

Gorski, T., & Miller, M. (1988). *Staying sober workbook.* Independence, MO: Independence Press.

Hawkins, J. D., Catalano, R., & Wells, E. (1986). Measuring effects of a skills training intervention for drug abusers. *Journal of Consulting and Clinical Psychology, 54*(5), 661–664.

Kavanagh, D. J. (1992). Schizophrenia. In P. H. Wilson (Ed.), *Principles and practice of relapse prevention* (pp. 157–190). New York: Guilford Press.

Laws, R. D. (Ed.). (1989). *Relapse prevention with sex offenders.* New York: Guilford Press.

Liberman, R., DeRisi, W., & Mueser, K. (1989). *Social skills training for psychiatric patients.* Elmsford, NY: Pergamon Press.

Marlatt, G. A., & Gordon, J. R. (Eds.). (1985). *Relapse prevention: Maintenance strategies in the treatment of addictive behaviors.* New York: Guilford Press.

McLellan, A., Luborsky, L., Woody, G., O'Brien, C., & Druley, K. (1983). Predicting response to alcohol and drug abuse treatments: Role of psychiatric severity. *Archives of General Psychiatry, 40,* 620–625.

McLellan, A., Woody, G., Luborsky, L., O'Brien, C., & Druley, K. (1983). Increased effectiveness of substance abuse treatment: A prospective study of patient-treatment matching. *Journal of Nervous and Mental Disease, 171,* 597–605.

Miller, W. R. (1989). Increasing motivation for change. In R. K. Hester, & W. R. Miller (Eds.), *Handbook of alcoholism treatment approaches* (pp. 67–80). New York: Pergamon Press.

Monti, P. M., Adams, D. B., Kadden, R. M., & Cooney, N. L. (1989). *Treating alcohol dependence: A coping skils training guide.* New York: Guilford Press.

National Institute on Drug Abuse. (1991). *Drug abuse and drug abuse research, third report to congress.* Rockville, MD: Author.

National Institute on Drug Abuse. (1993). *Recovery training and self-help: Relapse prevention and aftercare for drug addicts.* Rockville, MD: Author.

Robins, L., & Regier, D. (Eds.). (1991). *Psychiatric disorders in America.* New York: Free Press.

Ross, H., Glaser, F., & Germanson, T. (1988). The prevalence of psychiatric disorders in patients with alcohol and other drug problems. *Archives of General Psychiatry, 45,* 1023–1081.

Rounsaville, B., Dolinsky, Z., Babor, T., & Meyer, R. (1987). Psychopathology as a predictor of treatment outcome in alcoholics. *Archives of General Psychiatry, 44,* 505–513.

Salloum, I., & Daley, D. (1993). Unpublished data.

Thase, M. E. (1990). Relapse and recurrence in unipolar major depression: Short-term and long-term approaches. *Journal of Clinical Psychiatry, 51*(6), 51–57.

Tims, F., Fletcher, B., & Hubbard, R. (1991). Treatment outcomes for drug abuse clients. In R. Pickings, C. Leukefeld, & C. Shuster (Eds.), *Improving drug abuse treatment* (DHHS Pub. No. ADM 91-1754, pp. 93–113). Rockville, MD: National Institute on Drug Abuse.

Webster's new collegiate dictionary. (1986). Springfield, MA: Merriam-Webster.

Wilson, P. H. (Ed.). (1992). *Principles and practice of relapse prevention.* New York: Guilford Press.

SUGGESTED READINGS

Daley, D. (Ed.). (1989). *Relapse: Conceptual, research and clinical perspectives.* New York: Haworth Press.

Eriksen, L., Bjornstad, S., & Gotestam, K. G. (1986). Social skills training in groups for alcoholics: One-year treatment outcome for groups and individuals. *Addictive Behaviors, 11,* 309–329.

Frank, E., Kupfer, D. J., Perel, J. M., Cornes, C., Jarrett, D. B., Mallinger, A. G., Thase, M. E., McEachran, A. B., & Grochocinski, V. J. (1990). Three-year outcomes for maintenance therapies in recurrent depression. *Archives of General Psychiatry, 47,* 1093–1099.

Hester, R., & Miller, W. (Eds.). (1989). *Handbook of alcoholism treatment approaches.* New York: Pergamon Press.

Hollon, S. D., Evans, M. D., & DeRubeis, R. J. (1990). Cognitive mediation of relapse prevention following treatment for depression: Implications for differential risk. In R. E. Ingram (Ed.), *Contemporary approaches to depression* (pp. 117–136). New York: Plenum Press.

Jackson, H., & Edwards, J. (1992). Social networks and social support in schizophrenia: Correlates and assessment. In D. J. Kavanagh (Ed.), *Schizophrenia: An overview and practical handbook* (pp. 275–292). London: Chapman & Hall.

Lavori, P. W., Keller, M. B., & Klerman, G. L. (1984). Relapse in affective disorders: A reanalysis of the literature using life table methods. *Journal of Psychiatric Research, 18,* 13–25.

Leverich, G. S., Post, R. M., & Rosoff, A. S. (1990). Factors associated with relapse during maintenance treatment of affective disorders. *International Clinical Psychopharmacology, 5,* 135–156.

Miller, W. (1989). Matching individuals with interventions. In R. K. Hester & W. R. Miller (Eds.), *Handbook of alcoholism treatment approaches* (pp. 261–272). New York: Pergamon Press.

Rajkumar, S., & Thara, R. (1989). Factors affecting relapse in schizophrenia. *Schizophrenia Research, 2,* 403–409.

Tims, F., & Leukefeld, C. (Eds.). (1987). *Relapse and recovery in drug abuse.* (NIDA Research Monograph No. 72). Rockville, MD: National Institute on Drug Abuse.

Wanigaratne, S. (1990). *Relapse prevention for addictive behaviors.* London: Blackwell Scientific Publications.

Zackon, F., McAuliffe, W., & Ch'ien, J. (1985). *Addict aftercare: Recovery training and self-help.* (DHHS Pub. No. ADM 85-1341). Rockville, MD: National Institute on Drug Abuse.

CLIENT EDUCATIONAL MATERIALS

Following are several practical client education manuals useful in RP.

Brownell, K., & Rodin, J. (1990). *The weight maintenance survival guide.* Dallas, TX: The LEARN Education Center.

Daley, D. (1993). *Preventing relapse.* Center City, MN: Hazelden.

Daley, D., & Sproule, C. (1991). *Adolescent relapse prevention workbook.* Holmes Beach, FL: Learning Publications.

Liberman, R. (1988). *Social and independent living skills: Symptom management module.* Los Angeles: UCLA Department of Psychiatry.

Washton, A. (1990). *Staying off cocaine.* Center City, MN: Hazelden.

14

Psychotherapy in Later-Stage Recovery

JEROME DAVID LEVIN

INTRODUCTION

Although there is a long-standing controversy over whether or not antecedent psychopathology is etiological in the development of an addiction, there is universal agreement among both clinicians and researchers that by the time substance abusers are seen in treatment, there is significant and serious psychopathology concomitant with that addiction. Later-stage psychotherapy aims at the remediation of that psychopathology. The clinically addictive, as distinguished from the preaddictive personality if there is such, is characterized by depression, abysmally low self-esteem, reactive grandiosity, lack of affect tolerance, impulsivity, high levels of anxiety, self-centeredness and self-absorption seemingly paradoxically combined with self-destructiveness, difficulties maintaining goal-directed behavior, confusions about boundaries and identity, disturbances in interpersonal relations, and feelings of inner emptiness.

This chapter contends that the clinical addictive personality syndrome is usefully understood as a regression/fixation to pathological narcissism. Although the 12-Step programs, Alcoholics Anonymous (AA), Narcotics Anonymous (NA), and Cocaine Anonymous (CA), do not espouse theoretical explanations or scientific descriptions of the addictive personality, such a description is implicit in their literature, and is highly congruent with the point of view espoused here. In the words of Bill Wilson, the founder of AA, alcoholism addiction is "self will run riot." Such 12-Step slogans as "let go and let God," or "get out of the driver's seat" are cognitive-behavioral interventions aimed at aiding substance abusers in relinquishing their pathological narcissism. The issue they address is the need for omnipotent control. In general, the 12-Step programs work on reducing grandiosity and illusions of control by attempting to induce what they call ego deflation, a radical deflating of the grandiose ego in which denial is relinquished and a more realistic perception of self and world becomes possible. Later-stage psychotherapy shares these aims but goes about achieving them quite differently.

Kohut (1971, 1977), has elucidated a theory of pathological narcissism which is extremely helpful in understanding the emotional and psychological problems of recovering addicts. Psychotherapy in the later stages of recovery has as its goal what Kohut calls "the remediation of structural defects in the self"; that is, those vulnerabilities consequent upon developmental arrest and regression during the addictive process which leave the recovering substance abuser vulnerable to emotional pain and to "slips." Thus, psychotherapy in the later stages of recovery has two goals: to enable such growth as to make a sober life rewarding and worthwhile while giving the recovering person the ego strength necessary to prevent relapse. Although relapse is a possibility at any stage of recovery, it is generally the case that the more "clean and dry" time the recovering person has accrued, the better his/her chances of maintaining that state and the less the therapist needs to focus on relapse prevention and can work in a broader psychodynamic manner.

The first task of the therapist in later-stage psychotherapy is to evaluate the patient, focusing on the danger of relapse. If it is determined that the patient is highly vulnerable to relapse, the focus of therapy, regardless of the length of clean and dry experience, is of necessity on relapse prevention; that is, on the elucidation of drug signals (triggers) and of cognitive and didactic interventions intended to teach ways in which those triggers can be not only recognized but effectively neutralized so that they need not be acted on. Because relapse prevention is the subject of other chapters in this book, it will not be dwelled on here. Rather, the focus of this chapter is on the remediation of structural defects in the self.

For some substance abusers, psychological deficit and conflict are primarily the consequence of their addictive careers. These patients do extremely well once they stop using drugs. The experience of the therapist working with such patients is very different from the experience of working with the more severely damaged patients who are frequently encountered in this population. Those who became involved with drugs and suffer psychological and emotional consequences yet did not start their drug experience with major psychopathology look very different in recovery. They rarely remain long in treatment or self-help groups. Our main task with these patients is to prevent premature termination. The clinician needs to be alert to what the 12-Step programs call "the pink cloud," a manic reaction common in early sobriety which may give the recovering person a false sense of optimism and set him/her up for a slip and which may persist for several years. Our task with pink cloud patients is to engage them and keep them in treatment until life, being what it is, penetrates the pink cloud and the reality of their life situation, including all the damage they have done to themselves and others during the course of their addiction, slowly comes into consciousness. It is difficult to distinguish between pink cloud cases and "normals" who have had an episodic experience with drugs. For that reason, I urge all recovering people to stay in treatment for at least 1 year, even though they may be feeling very good in the early stages of recovery.

Addiction is a serious and potentially fatal illness. Psychodynamic therapists (Chein, Gerard, Lee, & Rosenfeld, 1964; Khantzian, 1978; Wurmser, 1978; Levin, 1987) have long stressed the severity of the emotional derangement that is concomitant with addiction, whether such derangement is a cause or a consequence of the drug abuse. Addicts are not, for the most part, neurotic individuals who happen to drug; rather, they are people suffering profound psychological disablement. Those who have become physically and psychologically dependent on drugs usually suffer grave damage in more than one of the life spheres of physical health, emotional well-being, interpersonal relations, and social and vocational functioning. Often the damage extends to all these areas. For these patients, the achievement and maintenance of sobriety are first and always the primary treatment goals. This chapter is directed toward improving the quality of recovering patients' lives against a backdrop of continued and continuous abstinence.

Although addicts with stable sobriety seek professional help for every sort of problem, two syndromes most commonly bring the stably sober to treatment. The first is that of the recovering person with considerable ego strength and growth potential who finds that NA participation has resulted in stable sobriety but feels stifled in an important area of life. The other syndrome is that of the addict who has the ego strength to achieve stable sobriety but continues to be afflicted with severe emotional conflict and psychological pain. Those who suffer from the latter syndrome require long-term treatment.

Stably sober patients may be the same patients we helped to reach sobriety, or they may be people who turn to therapy after they become sober. Although the treatment of these patients has many parallels with standard psychotherapeutic procedures, a unique dimension always remains in work with recovering people. For example, transference reactions are often acted out in psychotherapy. This acting out is later interpreted and the understanding resulting from the interpretation is utilized to facilitate growth. With the recovering patient, however, the acting out of a transference reaction may very well mean a relapse—hardly a desired step in a growth process. The therapist must *always* keep this possibility of a return to active addiction in mind when treating the stably sober. As NA says, "Addicts have a built-in forgetter." Because sobriety is the sine qua non of recovery, let us begin by discussing the process by which sobriety is internalized.

INTERNALIZATION OF SOBRIETY

Virtually no chronic drug user wants to get sober. The pain is too great. The regressive pull is too strong. That is why external events, such as the loss of a job or a mate, are so often the precipitants of the emotional crisis that results in recovery. These external events furnish the apparent motives for sobriety. At this point, the user is "doing it for them." Such motivation is often not sufficient, and external controls such as those provided by a rehabilitation facility are necessary to achieve sobriety of any duration. After leaving the rehabilitation facility, the user may remain sober out of fear of losing something valued, but it is still being done for "them." In successful recovery, a gradual process ensues in which remaining sober comes to be something that the substance abuser wants and values.

If this process is successful, the controls that were originally external become internal. Now, no asylum walls are necessary. It is not known exactly how control becomes internalized. Identification helps; in fact, it may be the key. This is one reason that 12-Step programs and peer counseling can be so effective in establishing stable sobriety. The user is provided with figures with whom to identify. They too are addicts, but they are no longer active; they are recovering. It is not with Bob or Jane or John or Sally that the addict must identify but with Bob's or Jane's or John's or Sally's sobriety. The addict may also identify with his/her nonaddicted therapist's sobriety, although here the identification is less direct. At first the identification is with the sobriety of the other, but slowly that sobriety is drawn within. It is as if the sobriety of the other is mentally ingested, digested, metabolized, and assimilated until it becomes part of the mental world of the newly recovering person. Although this is only a simile, it comes as close as we can get to an understanding of the process of internalization.

With time, sobriety becomes more rewarding. The pain of early sobriety recedes, the residual pain is endurable, and the addict wants to remain clean. Sobriety becomes part of the recovering person's ego ideal. Living up to one's ego ideal increases self-esteem and that feels good; hence, it is a behavior one tries to maintain. Remaining sober becomes less of a struggle; it is an increasingly comfortable decision.

Finally, sobriety becomes a way of life to which the recovering addict need give no thought. At this stage, there is no conscious conflict over using, although unconscious conflict remains. NA believes that this is as good as things get—that the unconscious conflict, which NA understands as the disease of addiction, always remains and that this unconscious conflict can erupt at any time, threatening sobriety. NA, therefore, teaches as part of its folk wisdom that "Nobody graduates," that addiction is "the disease that tells you that you don't have it." NA's belief is that the drug response to stress is a groove cut so deeply into the addict's brain that group support and active education in NA is a lifelong requirement for the maintenance of sobriety. Although it does not speak in these terms, NA has its doubts about both the security of internalization and the transfer of learning when it comes to sobriety. My own belief (Levin, 1987) is that sobriety depends on the building of psychic structure, so that the addict can perform the psychic tasks formerly performed by drugs.

SETTING GOALS

The treatment of choice for the still disturbed, stably sober patient is self-psychological psychodynamic therapy, a treatment that aims at expansion of self-awareness and repair of structural deficits in the self. Treatment goals are codetermined by the patient and the therapist. The patient's conscious wishes and desires must be integrated with the therapist's professional judgment. Treatment goals should be realistic, taking into account the patient's values, potential, ego strength, character structure, and life situation. Treatment goals are provisional; they are subject to change throughout the course of treatment.

The treatment of the stably sober addict proceeds, as does all psychodynamic therapy, with the establishment of the therapeutic alliance, the building of trust, the unfolding of transference reactions, the interpretation of defenses and unconscious conflicts, and the slow accretion of psychic structure through "optimal frustration." Catharsis and insight are the poles around which growth accretes. Treatment involves the weaving of a tapestry in which the woof of the release of hitherto repressed emotions is bound with the warp of understanding. The figure in the tapestry is the new self of the patient.

REMEDIATION OF STRUCTURAL DEFICITS IN THE SELF

Psychotherapy seeks both amelioration of developmental arrests *and* resolution of conflict. If Kohut is right in believing that the addictions are futile attempts to overcome deficits in the self, then the psychotherapeutic rehabilitation must remediate these deficits. The question is, how is this to be done? I have found that psychoanalytical psychotherapy that incorporates the insights of self psychology is the treatment of choice for stably sober patients.

Self psychology concerns itself with the development, pathology, and treatment of the self. The self is defined as "a unit, cohesive in space and enduring in time, which is a center of initiative and a recipient of impressions" (Kohut, 1971, p. vii). This self is both an endopsychic structure and an experience. That is, we have a self, of which we are only partially aware, which allows us to be ongoing enterprises with cohesion in space and continuity in time. This self has both conscious and unconscious contents; our self-awareness reveals only a small part of this self. At times, Kohut speaks of the self as a content of the mental apparatuses of id, ego, and superego. The self in this sense is a self-representation which may reside in any of the components of Freud's (1923/1961) tripartite model of the mind. Alternatively, Kohut regards this self as a "superordinate" concept which becomes the overarching conceptual representation of the personality. The self as a superordinate principle serves as an explanatory hypothesis that makes sense of human experience. To understand the practical applications of self psychology to the treatment of addiction, we need to know more about the development and morphology of the self.

The self has a history, a regular sequence of development in which a primary chaos is slowly organized into a coherent whole. The self is a complex achievement dependent on the successful transversing of a treacherous developmental course. Kohut (1971, 1977) believes that selves, in the sense of islands of awareness, exist from the beginning, but that building an "archaic nuclear cohesive self" is a developmental achievement. Kohut calls the first stage the fragmented self. Fragmentation is overcome by being related to as a whole self, a person rather than a collection of body parts, by empathic adults. Thus, the cohesion of the self comes about through the internalization of the experience of being treated by others as a whole, in such experiences as being securely held. Children also gain feelings of coherence through maturation and the discovery that their fingers, toes, mouth, anus, and genitals are all their own. It is this experience of the formerly isolated body parts and functions as *my* parts and functions that is alluded to in the story of the man who goes to the doctor and says, "Doctor, my head aches, my muscles are stiff, my bowels are upset, and to tell the truth, I myself don't feel so well either." It is this "I myself" that is the developmental achievement called the cohesive self.

At this stage, there is not yet a secure distinction between the self and its objects, so that the child experiences the human environment as a world of *self-objects*. The emphasis may be on *self*-objects—the world and other people as an extension of me—or the emphasis may be on self-*objects*—me as merged with the world and with other people. If this development from a fragmented to an archaic, cohesive self is successful, it results in a self secure from the danger of irreversible fragmentation, but that still experiences itself as a *self*-object and others as self-*objects.*

The archaic nuclear self has two constituents: the grandiose self and the idealized self-object; it is "bipolar." The grandiose self requires "mirroring"—that is, perfectly empathic confirming responses from the environment. Optimally, the parents will be able to enjoy the child's grandiosity and exhibitionism. What is needed is the "gleam in the mother's eye" at the child's emerging delight in self. If the parents react to the child with pride, the groundwork for secure self-esteem will be laid. However, the stage of the grandiose self has its dark side—in which the child expects to perfectly control objects who are still experienced as a part of the self. When these objects refuse to be controlled, the response is *narcissistic rage.* This rage can be murderous and unquenchable. Often it is turned against the self, leading to self-destruction. The grandiose self corresponds to Freud's (1914/1957) "His Majesty, the Baby" (p. 91). When it is thwarted, the response is the cold fury of narcissistic rage: Off with their heads! The concept of narcissistic rage makes sense out of much of the irrationality of addiction.

The other pole of the archaic nuclear self is the "idealized self-object," brought into being by the child's merger with idealized, omnipotent parents. If these stages of grandiose exhibitionism and the need to partake of the felt omnipotence of the self-objects is responded to empathically, these archaic structures will be assimilated into the mature self and will provide that mature self with a sublimated form of their primitive energy and with a feeling of fullness and inner richness. If, during the course of development, the inevitable frustration is not too great and is phase-appropriate, the archaic grandiosity becomes realistic ambition and the omnipotent self-objects are internalized as ego ideals. There is a process of gradual and nontraumatic disillusionment with ideal self-objects and their replacement by "real" objects. During this process, the functions of the self-objects as stimulus barriers, tension regulators, soothers, anxiety modulators, and self-esteem maintainers are internalized and become part of the "psychic structure of the self."

In addiction, there is a regression/fixation to the stage of the archaic self. Kohut (1977/1994) writes:

> The addict . . . craves the drug because the drug seems to him capable of curing the central defect in his self. It becomes for him the substitute for a self-object which failed him traumatically at the time when he should still have had the feeling of omnipotently controlling its

responses in accordance with his needs as if it were part of himself. By ingesting the drug he symbolically compels the mirroring self-object to soothe him, to accept him. Or he symbolically compels the idealized self-object to submit to his merging into it and thus to his partaking of its magical power. In either case the ingestion of the drug provides him with the self-esteem which he does not possess. Through the incorporation of the drug he supplies for himself the feeling of being accepted and thus of being self-confident; or he creates the experience of being merged with a source of power that gives him the feeling of being stronger and worthwhile. And all these effects of the drug tend to increase his feeling of being alive, tend to increase his certainty that he exists in the world.

It is the tragedy of . . . these attempts at self-cure that . . . they cannot succeed . . . no psychic structure is build, the defect in the self remains. (p. vii)

NARCISSISTIC TRANSFERENCES

Readers will recall that *transference* refers to the reenactment in the therapeutic relationship of early object relations. Although the transference can be regarded as resistance, as an acting instead of a remembering, it is therapeutically invaluable because it provides both the patient and the therapist with a here-and-now replication of the patient's conflicts with first objects. *Classical transference* is about relationships with objects experienced as separate from the self. *Narcissistic transferences* are about relationships with objects experienced as part of the self. In the narcissistic transferences, the therapist is experienced either as an extension of the patient's self or as an omnipotent self-object into which the patient merges.

There are two principal narcissistic transferences: the mirror transference and the idealizing transference. Both are manifestations of the archaic, nuclear self. *Mirror transferences* develop when the *grandiose self* becomes activated. *Idealizing transferences* develop when the *idealized self-object* (archaic parental imago) is activated. To speak of the activation of the grandiose self or idealized self-object is to reify and concretize a *process* in which the patient relives the developmental stage of the archaic cohesive self in the relationship to the therapist. According to Kohut (1971), the therapist need only let the transference unfold With patients who suffer from narcissistic behavior disorders, the transference that spontaneously develops will not be a repetition of early conflictual relationships with significant others experienced as separate people but rather a relationship in which either the therapist is experienced as part of the patient or the patient merges with the therapist.

TRANSMUTING INTERNALIZATION

Kohut (1971, 1977) states that once a narcissistic transference has been established, each nontraumatic failure of empathy (imperfect mirroring) or nontraumatic failure to protect (lack of omnipotence in the self-*object*) leads to the internalization of a grain of psychic structure. A small measure of that which had been done by the therapist for the patient—tension regulation, for example—now becomes part of the patient's psychological equipment. The working through of a narcissistic transference consists of hundreds or thousands of such small failures, the emotional reactions to them, and the piecemeal taking on by the patient of the function that the therapist has failed to perform adequately. Thus, psychic structure, the ability to do for oneself what was once done by others, is slowly accrued. The outcome of successful therapy is that the patient feels "full"; the empty depression dissipates; the reality ego is strengthened; and the patient is far better able to maintain a reasonably stable level of self-esteem, to modulate anxiety, to regulate tension, and to self-soothe. Transmuting internalization is a depersonified, selective identification with the functions, rather than the personality, of the therapist (parent). This selective identification builds structure. It is the process by which the structural deficits in the self are remediated.

The remediation of structural deficits in the self is a two-stage process: (1) the development of one of the narcissistic transferences and (2) the gradual internalization of psychic function through the working through of nontraumatic failures of empathy by the therapist. The patient's transference to a substance is replaced by transference to a person (the therapist) and that transference, unlike the one to the drug, is used to promote growth.

RESOLVING INTRAPSYCHIC CONFLICT

Although addicts suffer profoundly from deficits in the self, they also suffer from unconscious conflict between desire and conscience. There is conflict between the id's instinctual drives and the superego's prohibitions. When conflict is conscious, one can make a choice, however painfully, but when conflict is unconscious, no resolution is possible. Either the conflict is acted out, usually by substance abuse, or symptoms develop. It is the therapist's business to make the conflict conscious. This is done through interpretation—of genetic material, of the transference, and of the patient's behavior. Self-knowledge comes from derepression through free association, revival of early conflicts in the transference, and interpretations of the meaning of current behavior.

Case Illustration

Sally manifested most of the substance abuse–pathological narcissism syndrome. Stably clean and dry, she came for the treatment of a posttraumatic stress reaction. She was in an automobile accident and was badly shaken. Her face was scarred and she was deeply depressed. Plastic surgery later restored her face, leaving little evidence of the accident, but she did not know that was going to happen. Sally was young and very appealing. She was referred by her attorney, who had not mentioned addiction, so I was surprised when she told me that she was an addict. She said that she had been addicted since the age of 12 and had "hit bottom" 4 years ago. I asked her how old she was. She said, "Twenty-five." I asked, "How did you get clean?" She replied, "The part about getting sober wouldn't make sense unless I told you about my drugging too: should I do that?" I said, "Sure."

> Well, I don't know where to start. I come from an alcoholic family. Both my parents died of alcoholism. Well, I think my father died of alcoholism; he deserted us when I was four. I remember the last time I saw him. We were eating in a diner and I spilled my food. He screamed at me and said I was disgusting. I always felt that he left because I was so disgusting. I feel like a pig; I'm a compulsive overeater, too. I know in my head that he didn't leave because of the way I ate, but I don't know it in my heart. I still believe it. Things got worse then. My mother drank more and more and we had very little money. Sometimes there was no toilet paper in the house, but there was always beer. Later we moved to my grandfather's. He was rich, but he grabbed my pussy sometimes and I didn't know what to do. I think he was senile, but he drank too so maybe that was it. After I grew up, my mother told me she knew what he did to me, but she was afraid to do anything about it because he might have thrown us out. She was drunk when she told me that. Why did she have to tell me? I hate her for letting it happen, and I hate her for telling me that she let it happen. How could a mother do that? I have a daughter. I'd cut off his balls, if a man did that to my daughter. How could she? My grandfather got more senile and I don't know exactly what happened after that. My mother was like two people. When she was sober she was wonderful—beautiful and interested in me. But very snobby and uptight. Then I didn't think she was a snob, I thought that she was a great lady—perfectly dressed and so elegant. I loved her so much. Then there was Mother when she was drunk. Sloppy and falling down, she'd sit with her legs spread with no panties and you could see everything. She'd curse and then try to play the great lady, "Oh, my dear," and all that shit. I hated her then.
>   I was around ten when I started having sex play with my cousins and some of the neighborhood kids. Mostly with the boys, but

sometimes with the girls too. Do you think I'm a lesbian? I loved sex—it felt so good and it made me feel good about myself. Somebody wanted me. Maybe I felt guilty underneath. Later I hated myself and maybe all that sex play had something to do with it. I was raised a strict Catholic—sort of. Once I was naked—I had just gotten out of the tub and I did an imitation of the Virgin Mary—I was about six—and my mother really whaled my ass with a ruler. When I was about ten my mother met my stepfather. Eddy was a complete asshole. He drank all the time, too. Can you imagine marrying a fucking drunk like him? Then Mother really dropped me. She was more interested in drinking with Eddy. I started getting in trouble in school—at eleven I got fucked for the first time. And I mean got fucked, not made love to, by some twenty-year-old pervert. Can you imagine an eleven-year-old getting fucked? I loved it or thought that I did. I hung out with all the older boys. They had cars and liquor and pot. I can't tell you how many cocks I had in me. Big ones, small ones, white ones, black ones. And you know I was never sober once. Every one of those guys had something to get high on—beer, pot, hard stuff. I loved pot from the first time I smoked it. It was even better than sex. And I drank a lot. Any boy or man who gave me something to get high on could have me. Sometimes I really liked it, but I liked fooling around with other girls even more. I think I was really turned on by myself—when I played with the other girls. My mother and stepfather raised hell when they weren't too drunk to care, and finally my mother had me put away. Can you imagine that? What kind of fucking mother would put a kid in the places she put me? For God's sake, one place had bars and I was locked in. I hate her for doing that. Mental hospitals, homes for delinquent girls, the House of the Good Shepherd, the whole ball of wax. Finally I got out—I wasn't actually in any of those places for very long, it's just the idea—how could you do that to a kid?—and I met Calvin.

What a bastard he was. Oh, I forgot to tell you that when I was fifteen I was team banged by a gang who pulled me into an alley and fucked me until my thing was raw and bloody. They beat me real hard too, but not as hard as Calvin did later. I must have been crazy but I loved him. He took me away from my hometown and my mother didn't bother me anymore. He sort of made a prisoner out of me—if I even went to the grocery store without his permission he beat me. He had a big one, the biggest I ever saw and I had seen plenty, so I thought he was a great lover. He always had beer and weed and other stuff and I stayed high most of the time. He's the father of my child. When I went into labor he was stoned. He slapped me and called me a rotten whore. He wouldn't go to the hospital with me. Do you know what it's like for a sixteen-year-old kid to have a baby alone? Forget it.

I never cheated on Calvin but he never stopped accusing me of being with other men and hitting me. Sometimes he hit me with a wooden plank. I thought I deserved it—that I needed to be punished for all the things I had done. I needed Calvin to beat me. As long as he supplied drugs and alcohol and beat me, I would have stayed. It was the way he acted around the baby that made me leave. One day when he wasn't home and the baby was about two, I ran away. I couldn't stand his insane jealousy anymore; he was even jealous of the baby. A guy crazy enough to be jealous of his own kid, that's sick. He was real sick; sick in his head. I couldn't stand any more so I ran away and went to a town in the mountains where my older sisters and brother lived. Something in me said *enough,* you've been punished enough. Of course I kept on getting high. There wasn't any more sex, not then, just falling down stoned every day. I went on welfare and sometimes I worked off the books. I was sort of dead— no, not *sort of,* just plain *dead.* That went on for a few years and I hated myself more and more. I tried to be a good mother through it all and I don't think I did too badly, but God, was I depressed!

My stepfather was dead by then and my mother was far gone. I think I saw it in her before I saw it in me. My brother was in the Program—NA, that is. I thought he was a jerk, a real ass, an uptight loser. Who else would join those holy rollers? What I couldn't figure out was how such a raving asshole could be happy, and the damn jerk *was* happy. Even I could see that. He did something really smart; he didn't lecture me. In fact, he never even mentioned my drinking and drugging. Damn good thing he didn't, because the way I rebelled against everything and everybody I would never have listened. What he did do was tell me what had happened to him—ran his story as they say in NA. I didn't want to hear that shit and I told him so, but I did hear it in spite of myself. I was getting worse; I was more and more terrified that Calvin would come back and kill me—I guess I thought that he should because of the way I was living, but I didn't know that then, I was just scared. I was getting sicker and sicker from all the drugs and I never had any money; it got to the point where I couldn't stand any more. If it wasn't for my daughter, I would have killed myself. I don't know why, but one day I asked my brother to take me to an NA meeting. I think it was the guilt—once I didn't have Calvin to beat me I couldn't stand the guilt—I *knew*—I mean I really knew what it's like to have stoned parents. I loved my daughter—she has such a sick fuck for a father, so I wanted her to have at least one parent with her head screwed on straight. So I went to that fucking meeting. I loved it—I mean, I *loved* it—like I never loved anything. For Christ's sake, I even identified with the coffee cups. When I do something I *do* it—I went all the way—the whole nine yards. I was sick—sick, sick, sick from my crotch to my toes, not to mention my head. I was so scared; I hadn't had a sober day in years, but I've made it a day at a time. I haven't made it any too swiftly. I still can't stand the guilt and the rage; you wouldn't believe how angry I get, and the crying. I cry all the fucking time, but I don't drink, I don't drug, and I don't care if my ass falls off, I'm not going to. At least not today.

I didn't want to be like my mother. I *won't* be like her. She's dead now. I couldn't stand it when she died; she died from her drinking—she had an accident while drunk; it was kind of a suicide. I knew she was dead, but I didn't know it. I couldn't let her go—not the awful way it was—if she was sober and I was sober, I could have let her die, but she wasn't, so I knew but I didn't know she was dead. I never accepted it; she couldn't forgive me dead, nor I her. Then one day I went to the cemetery. I looked at her grave for a long time. I couldn't believe she was dead. I started screaming, "Move the fucking grass, move the fucking grass, Mother." I screamed and screamed but she didn't move the fucking grass and I finally knew she was gone. I went to my home group meeting hysterical. All I said was she couldn't move the fucking grass, and I cried the rest of the meeting. Nobody said a word, they just let me be me; they didn't try to take away my pain, and I didn't want or need anybody to take it away. What I needed was somebody to be with me in that pain, and they were.

I love the fucking program and all the crazy screwed-up people there. They're like me; I'm crazy too, but I'm sober. For God's sake, can you imagine what it would have been like if I was high when she died? Thank God I wasn't. I hate her—I love her—I still can't let go of her although I know she's dead. I hate drugs. I hate drinking; look what it did to her, to my father, to me. How did I get sober?—I don't really know—I sort of had two bottoms—a beaten bottom and a drug bottom. In that first bottom, I sort of saw myself and saw I couldn't go on exposing my daughter to that stuff; the second was luck or something. No, not exactly luck or not only luck. I had something to do with willingness—I became willing to go to that meeting. Maybe I had just had enough; I didn't want any more pain for me or for the baby; she's not a baby anymore. They say, "Why me?" in the program. When you're using, you have the "poor me's," so you're always asking, "Why me?" If you recover, you say it differently. I don't know why me. The way I lived, I should be dead, but I'm not. I don't know if I deserve it or not, but I'll take it.

Sally is a clear example of an attempted self-cure of narcissistic deficit and narcissistic injury by substance abuse. All such attempts at self-cure are futile, eventually leading to further narcissistic injury. Although alcohol and drugs turned out to be the wrong medicine, Sally found another way to heal herself or start to heal herself before she came for therapy, and I largely stayed out of her way and was nonimpinging as she continued to heal herself. My relative "inactivity" allowed identification and transmuting internalization to take place. This led to structure building, firmer self-cohesion, and greater ego strength. Most alcoholics and substance abusers do not have Sally's powerful drive for health and they require more active interventions on the part of the therapist. Self psychology has a number of powerful interventions to suggest for use in working with these patients. In their respective ways, they address what theory understands as narcissistic deficit and narcissistic injury and their attempted self-cure through the substance abuse, the attempt to fill inner emptiness due to failures in transmuting internalization, the acting out of and turning against the self of narcissistic rage, idealizing and mirror transferences to drugs, attempts at omnipotent control through substance use and abuse, attempts to boost abysmally low self-esteem through the use of drugs, and shame experiences both antecedent to and consequent with drug abuse. The following suggested ways to translate theory into concrete interventions need to be modified so a particular patient can hear them.

Elicit Admission of Powerlessness over Substances

This intervention addresses the narcissistic wound inflicted by not being able to drink or drug "like other people." The admission that one is powerless over substances, as NA puts it, or that one cannot use without the possibility of losing control, as I would put it, is extremely painful. It is experienced as a defect in the self, which is intolerable for those who are as perfectionistic as addicts usually are. The self must not be so damaged and deficient. Additionally, to be able to "drink or drug like a man" or "like a lady" may be a central component of the addict's self-concept—his/her identity. This is particularly so for *macho* men but is by no means restricted to them. The therapist must recognize and articulate the conflict between the patient's wish to stay stopped and the patient's feeling that to do so entails admitting that he or she is flawed in a fundamental way. The therapist does this by saying, "You don't so much want to use as not want not to be able to use." This makes the patient conscious of the conflict in an empathic way and allows the patient to struggle with this issue. This often opens the way for the patient to achieve a more comfortable stable sobriety. It is an intervention that can increase the patient's understanding of his/her addiction long after stable sobriety has been achieved.

Empathize with Substance Abuser's Suffering

Addictions are one long experience of narcissistic injury. Failure usually stalks the user like a shadow. As one of my patients put it, "When I use, everything turns to shit." It sure does. Career setbacks, job losses, rejection by loved ones, humiliations of various sorts, ill health, economic decline, accidental injury, and enduring "bad luck" are the all-too-frequent concomitants of addiction. Each is a narcissistic insult. Cumulatively they constitute a massive narcissistic wound. Even if outward blows have not yet come, the inner blows—self-hatred and low self-regard—are always there. The substance abuser has all too frequently heard, "It's all your fault," in one guise or another. The therapist must empathize with the abuser's suffering. "Your disease has cost you so much," "You have lost so much," and "Your self-respect is gone" are some ways the therapist can make contact with the substance abuser's pain and facilitate his experiencing this pain instead of denying, acting, out, and/or anesthetizing it.

Address Feelings of Emptiness

Substance abusers feel empty. Either they have never had much good stuff inside or they have long since flushed the good stuff out with drugs. "You drugged so much because you felt empty" makes the connection as well as brings into awareness the horrible experience of an inner void. After sobriety has been achieved, the genetic (i.e., childhood) determinants of the paucity of psychic structure experienced as emptiness can also be interpreted.

Build a Firm Identity

Substance abusers lack a firm sense of identity. How can we know who we are if our experience of self is tenuous and its inner representation lacks consistent cohesion? The therapist can comment on this and point out that being an addict is at least something definite—having an identity of sorts. When an NA member says, "My name is _____ and I am an addict," the member is affirming that he/she exists and has at least one attribute. With sobriety many more attributes will accrue—the self will enrich and cohere. Saying, "You are confused and not quite sure who you are. That is partly because of your drugging. Acknowledging your addiction will lessen your confusion as to who you are and give you a base on which to build a firm and positive identity" is a way of conveying this to the patient. The process of forming a sober identity may take a long time.

Develop the "Capacity to Be Alone"

Many people use drugs because they cannot stand to be alone. They drug to enjoy someone's companionship. They have not developed what Winnicott (1958/1965) calls the capacity to be alone. Winnicott thinks that this comes from the experience of being alone in the presence of another—from having been a small child in the presence of an empathic, nonimpinging other who has become internalized so that one is not really alone when one is by oneself. Being alone in this sense is very different from defensive isolation driven by fear. Presumably, those who use drugs for companionship never acquired the capacity to be alone. This, too, should be interpreted. "You used so much because you couldn't bear to be alone and drugs gave you the illusion of having company, of being with a friend. Now that you have stopped, it is important for us to discover why it is so painful for you to be alone."

Explore Idealizing Transference to Drug

Substance abusers form self-object (narcissistic) transferences to their drug of choice. They form idealizing and mirror transferences to drugs. The imago of the archaic idealized parent is projected onto the drug and it is regarded as an all-powerful, all-good object with which users merge in order to participate in this omnipotence. "Drugs will deliver the goods and give me love, power, and whatever else I desire" is the user's unconscious fantasy. The therapist should interpret this thus: "Your drug has felt like a good, wise, and powerful parent who protected you and made you feel wonderful, and that is why you have loved it so much. In reality, it is only a poisonous chemical, not all the things you thought it was." The therapist should go on to say, "Now that drugging isn't working for you anymore, you are disillusioned, furious, and afraid. Let's talk about those feelings."

One of the reasons that addicts are so devoted to the consumption of drugs is that it confirms their grandiosity. Another way to say this is that they form a mirror transference to the drug. I once had an addicted patient who told me that he felt thrilled when he read that a sixth Nobel prize was to be added to the original five. He read this while waiting for his connection. His not-so-unconscious fantasy was winning all six. The therapist should make the mirror transference conscious by interpreting it. "When you used, you felt that you could do anything, be anything, achieve anything and that felt wonderful. You must really miss that."

Build Genuine Self-Esteem

Substance abusers, without exception, have abysmally low self-esteem no matter how well covered over by bluster and bravado it may be. Self psychology understands this as an impoverishment of the reality ego consequent with failure to integrate archaic grandiosity, which is instead split off by what Kohut (1977) calls the "vertical split" and which manifests itself as unrealistic reactive grandiosity. This persists well into sobriety. At some point the therapist needs to say, "You feel like shit, and that you are shit, and all your claims to greatness are ways to avoid knowing that you feel that way. You don't know it, but way down somewhere inside you feel genuinely special. We need to put you in touch with the real stuff so you don't need drugs or illusions to help you believe that the phony stuff is real." The particular reasons, antecedent to and consequent upon the drug abuse, that the patient values himself or herself so little, need to be elucidated and worked through.

Sometimes the patient's crazy grandiosity is simultaneously a defense against and an acting out of the narcissistic cathexis of the patient by a parent. That is, the patient is attempting to fulfill the parent's dreams in fantasy while making sure not to fulfill them in reality. This is especially likely to be the case if the patient is an adult child of an alcoholic (e.g., Sally). Heavy drug use makes such a defense/acting out easy. If the recovering patient's grandiosity does seem to be a response to being treated as an extension of themselves by either parent, the therapist can say, "One reason you feel so rotten about yourself is that you're always doing it for Mom or Dad and not for yourself. You resent this and spite them by undermining yourself, formerly by getting high and now psychologically."

Interpret Need to Control

Substance abusers have a pathological need for omnipotent control. The drug is simultaneously experienced as an object they believe they can totally control and coerce into doing their will and an object they believe gives them total control of their subjective states and of the environment. This can be seen as a manifestation of their mirror/idealizing transferences to substances. Recovering persons frequently treat people, including the therapist, as extensions of themselves. The NA slogans, "get out of the driver's seat" and "let God and let go," are cognitive-behavioral ways of loosening the need to control. Therapists should interpret this need to control in the patient's relationship to drugs, in the patient's relationship with other people, and in the patient's relationship with the therapist. For example, "You thought and perhaps still think that when you got high, you could feel any way you wished," "You went into a rage and got stoned whenever your wife didn't do as you wished," or "You thought of using because you were upset with me when I didn't respond as you thought I should."

Identify Feelings of Shame

Substance abusers, alcoholics, and their children suffer greatly from shame experiences. Such patients are ashamed of having been shamed and often use to obliterate feelings of shame. Therapists need to help recovering patients experience rather than repress, now that they no longer anesthetize their feelings of shame. One way to do this is to identify feelings of shame that are not recognized as such. For example, "You felt so much shame when you realized that you were addicted that you kept on abusing so you wouldn't feel your shame."

Label Affects

Recovering persons, even those with considerable sobriety, often do not know what they are feeling. Krystal and Raskin (1970) speak of affect regression to a developmental stage in which affects are experienced as massive, primitive, overwhelming, and undifferentiated. Hence, *label-*

ing the affects is a crucial aspect of therapy. It provides cognitive structure; starts the process of affect redifferentiation; and reduces the terror of the experientially primitive, unfamiliar, and chaotic emerging feelings. Affect labeling is a way station on the road from feelings experienced as mysterious happenings, as lightning bolts from above, to feelings experienced as consciously owned aspects of the addict's self. Initially, affect labeling must be done by the therapist: "You are angry," or "You are sad," and so on. Although these are interpretations, the feelings are usually near the surface and are transparent to the therapist. It is the feelings that are closest to consciousness that are interpreted. Sobriety-threatening feelings, such as rage, must be interpreted.

Sally exemplifies the relationship between narcissistic deficit, narcissistic injury, and the futile attempt to remediate the former and heal the latter through the addictive use of substances—pot, coke, alcohol, and food—and compulsive actions—sex and excitement. Sally suffered massive failures of internalization, leaving her with gaping structural deficits. She also felt dead, doubting both her aliveness and her existence, and sought out stimulation of any kind, even beatings, to feel alive. Lacking idealizable parents she found Calvin; having had little phase-appropriate mirroring of her archaic grandiosity, she found drugs. In addition to mirroring her, drugs gave Sally the illusion of cohesiveness. The amazing strength she did display may have been possible because her mother very early on was "good enough." Sally's capacity for splitting also helped her preserve a good mother from whom she could draw some sustenance in face of all the "badness" of her later, and by then overtly alcoholic, mother. Sally had not integrated the two mothers. Her "bad" mother became Sally's split-off grandiosity and denial. So split off from any kind of reality testing was this side of Sally that her unassimilated grandiosity, manifested in the belief that she was invulnerable, came very close to killing her. Her mother was not so lucky. Her grandiosity proved fatal.

Sally's reality ego was impoverished, depressed, empty, fragile, and never far from fragmentation. The phase-appropriate grandiosity of the stage of the archaic nuclear self had never been integrated into her reality ego—it could not be because it had never been adequately mirrored. In Winnicott's (1960/1965) terms, her true self was buried for safekeeping from a dangerous, treacherous environment. Whether we understand this in Kohutian or in Winnicottian terms, it is clear that her defensive system made survival possible, *and* that it was now an encumbrance, and that a major aim of treatment had to be its modification.

The child of an alcoholic carries a special kind of narcissistic injury. Humiliation and shame are recurrent and the wounds go deep. Sally's narcissistic injuries were denied, repressed, and/or acted out as was the narcissistic rage as a natural reaction to these injuries. Sally's delinquency was an attempt at self-cure. As Winnicott says, when there is an antisocial tendency, there is hope. Sally found some kind of solace, responsiveness, and, in however distorted a form, mirroring in her acting out. It also allowed her to externalize her rage. However, what saved Sally was her ability to love and to seek love. She never gave up her search for good objects that she could idealize and internalize. Drugs were one such object—one that traumatically failed her, but she did not give up. Abandonment depression and abandonment rage were central to Sally's psychopathology, but they could be worked through in the transference because she transferred, because she was still searching for relationship. Her love for her baby, probably an identification with the early good mother, got her away from Calvin, and her identification with her brother resulted in her joining NA. NA then became an idealized object. She formed the same kind of transference with me, and the working through of her predominantly idealizing transference, which also had mirror aspects, enabled her to build psychic structure.

The scene in the cemetery was crucial to Sally's recovery. As long as she could not let go of the bad mother or of just plain *Mother,* there was no way that she could internalize a good object. Bad Mother was a pathological introject. Only by letting her die and then mourning her could Sally reclaim the energy to cathect a new object (i.e., to love again) and to acquire the psychic structure she lacked. Mourning is not possible during active addiction. I have found in case after case that facilitating mourning must take priority in the therapy of the stably recovering patient. Only then can the work proceed as one hopes it will.

CONCLUSION

Self-psychological psychoanalysis is not the treatment of choice for most recovering persons. Rather, what is indicated is once- or twice-weekly intensive, insight-oriented psychodynamic psychotherapy that is informed by Kohut's insights into the vicissitudes of narcissism. These patients have an intense need for mirroring, or approving confirmation, as well as a need to idealize the therapist. They are also particularly narcissistically vulnerable. The treatment should therefore focus on blows to the substance abuser's low self-esteem (addiction inflicts such terrible narcissistic wounds), failures of the childhood environment to supply sufficient phase-appropriate mirroring and opportunities for idealization, and the abuser's experience of much of the world as an extension of self. Anxiety is predominantly understood and interpreted as panic fear of regression to fragmentation experienced as psychic death, rather than as a manifestation of intrapsychic conflict, and rage is predominantly understood and interpreted as narcissistic rage, fury at the failure of the selfobject to perfectly mirror or protect, rather than as a manifestation of mature aggression.

Much seemingly irrational behavior can be understood in terms both of the abuser's need for omnipotent control and the rage that follows failure to so control. The grandiosity and primitive idealization of the archaic nuclear self also explain the perfectionism of substance abusers and the unrealistic standards that they set for themselves. Most recovering substance abusers have not developed realistic ambitions or livable ideals—these are characteristics of the mature self. The abuser's depression can be understood in terms of the paucity of psychic structure, which was never built up through the normal process of transmuting internalization. This empty depression also reflects the repression, rather than the integration, of the archaic nuclear self and the failure to integrate archaic grandiosity. This emptiness does not abate with sobriety. Further, the narcissistic rage to which the abuser is so prone can be turned against the self, resulting in intensely angry depression, sometimes of suicidal proportions. Failure to internalize the stimulus barrier and poor resources for self-soothing render the abuser especially vulnerable to psychic injury. Therefore, the ordinary events in daily life long continue to threaten the recovering person's tenuous self-esteem.

Thus, the insights of self psychology into the dynamics of pathological narcissism are indeed relevant and helpful in working with the stably sober. Kohut's approach is used in a modified form in which the narcissistic transferences are allowed to unfold, the patient's need to control and to participate in greatness is understood, and a slow working through integrates components of the archaic nuclear self into the reality ego, resulting in self-cohesion, stable self-esteem, and a vital, comfortable recovery.

REFERENCES

Chein, I., Gerard, D. L., Lee, R. S., & Rosenfeld, E. (1964). *The road to H.* New York: Basic Books.

Freud, S. (1957). On narcissism: An introduction. In J. Strachey (Ed. and Trans.), *The standard edition of the complete psychological works of Sigmund Freud* (Vol. 14, pp. 117–140). London: Hogarth Press. (Original work published 1914)

Freud, S. (1961). The ego and the id. In J. Strachey (Ed. and Trans.), *The standard edition of the complete psychological works of Sigmund Freud* (Vol. 19, pp. 1–66). London: Hogarth Press. (Original work published 1923)

Khantzian, E. (1978). The ego, the self and opiate addiction: Theoretical and treatment considerations. *International Review of Psycho-Analysis, 5,* 189–199.

Kohut, H. (1971). *Analysis of the self: A systematic approach to the psychoanalytic treatment of narcissistic personality disorders.* New York: International Universities Press.

Kohut, H. (1977). *The restoration of the self.* New York: International Universities Press.

Kohut, H. (1993). Preface. In J. D. Blaine & D. A. Julius (Eds.), *Psychodynamics of drug dependence* (pp. vii–ix). Northvale, NJ: Jason Aronson. (Original work published 1977)

Krystal, H., & Raskin, H. (1970). *Drug dependence: Aspects of ego function.* Detroit: Wayne State University Press.

Levin, J. (1987). *Treatment of alcoholism and other addictions: A self-psychology approach.* Northvale, NJ: Jason Aronson.

Winnicott, D. W. (1965). The capacity to be alone. In *The maturational processes and the facilitating environment* (pp. 29–36). New York: International Universities Press. (Original work published 1958)

Winnicott, D. W. (1965). Ego distortion in terms of true and false self. In *The maturational processes and the facilitating environment* (pp. 140–152). New York: International Universities Press. (Original work published 1960)

Wurmser, L. (1978). *The hidden dimension: Psychodynamics of compulsive drug use.* New York: Jason Aronson.

15

Structured Outpatient Treatment

RUBY MALIK
ARNOLD M. WASHTON
NANNETTE STONE-WASHTON

Driven in part by health care reform with increasing demands for cost containment and alternatives to hospitalization, structured outpatient treatment has rapidly emerged as the treatment of first choice for many if not most substance-abusing patients. Such programs typically offer a combination of specialized clinical services, including group, individual, and family counseling, as well as psychoeducation, urine and breathalyzer testing, and exposure to self-help. The historical separation of treatment programs for alcoholism from those for substance abuse has been dissolving in recent years, largely due to the increasing prevalance of cross-addiction and multiple substance use among people seeking treatment services. Today most programs offer treatment for all types of chemical dependencies, including alcohol, cocaine (crack), heroin, and other drugs.

The purpose of this chapter is to familiarize the reader with the philosophy, approach, and content of a specialized and structured outpatient treatment program for alcohol and other chemical dependencies. We describe the program offered at Washton Institute, an outpatient treatment center located in New York City (Midtown Manhattan).

PROGRAM PHILOSOPHY

A structured outpatient treatment program is a framework for configuring and delivering treatment in a planned and definable way. The goals are to enhance clients' motivation for positive change, to teach them how to break the addictive cycle, and to establish abstinence from all mood-altering substances. The program also seeks to teach the adaptive coping and problem-solving skills required to maintain abstinence over the long term and to support and guide patients through trouble spots and setbacks that might otherwise lead to relapse.

Our treatment approach views psychoactive substance dependence as a multidetermined addictive behavior and maladaptive ("self-medication") coping style with biological, psychological, and social components. Accordingly, treatment must provide (1) the structure, support, and feedback required to break the behavioral cycle of compulsive psychoactive substance use; and (2) opportunities to learn adaptive (nonchemical) problem-solving skills in order to prevent relapse.

This approach contains many original elements (Washton, 1989) and incorporates features of other approaches, including motivational counseling techniques described by Miller and Rollnick (1991), relapse prevention strategies described by Marlatt and Gordon (1985), and psychodynamic techniques described by Brehm and Khantzian (1992). The hallmarks of this approach are clinical flexibility and careful attention to individual differences. As such, it contrasts sharply with aggressive confrontational approaches commonly found in traditional treatment programs. Participation in Alcoholics Anonymous (AA) or other self-help programs is actively encouraged and is seen as helpful and highly desirable but not mandatory.

Treatment involves a combination of group therapy two to four times a week supplemented by individual counseling once a week. A supervised urine sample is taken from every patient at least twice a week and breathalyzer tests are administered on a random basis throughout the program. Although group therapy is the core treatment modality for most patients, some are not able to tolerate group as a result of psychiatric and/or interpersonal impairments. Treatment for these patients may consist of individual therapy two to three times a week, including urine and breathalyzer testing.

The program is divided into three phases: (1) early abstinence, (2) relapse prevention, and (3) continuing care. The early abstinence phase teaches cognitive and behavioral skills for breaking the cycle of compulsive substance use and works on enhancing the patient's acceptance of the problem and motivation for change. The relapse prevention phase focuses on acquiring the necessary coping skills to reduce the likelihood of returning to alcohol/drug use. The continuing-care phase focuses on solidifying and maintaining therapeutic gains.

Our approach was developed within an outpatient treatment setting and as such recognizes that the patient is continuously faced with the pressures/stressors of daily life as well as easy access to a wide variety of psychoactive substances. It also recognizes that in the outpatient setting, the client is always free to drop out of treatment and accordingly we strongly emphasize therapeutic engagement and retention strategies, particularly at the beginning of treatment when outpatient dropout rates are highest.

A distinguishing feature of the program is its variable-length format. The length of a patient's participation in the program from admission through completion ranges from 12 to 24 weeks as determined by objective measures of clinical progress such as clean urines; reliable attendance at scheduled sessions; development of a sober support network; including involvement in self-help; and exercising adaptive (nondrug) problem-solving skills. A prespecified set of behavioral contingencies adjusts the length of treatment according to individual need.

Operating from a basic philosophy of utilizing whatever seems to work best, this approach is compatible with a wide variety of other treatments. The program has no antimedication bias as long as the medications being offered are clinically appropriate and noneuphorigenic. Naltrexone and disulfiram are utilized to foster relapse prevention, when appropriate. Patients with coexisting psychiatric disorders are treated in a specialized dual-diagnosis program and often require psychotropic medication (e.g., antidepressants and antipsychotics) as part of their ongoing treatment. The program does not dispense methadone or other dependence-producing drugs.

The program actively encourages but does not mandate the client's participation in AA, Cocaine Anonymous, Narcotics Anonymous, or other self-help groups. We try to gently persuade patients to attend self-help meetings by pointing out the lasting benefits of involvement in a self-help program and by reducing barriers to giving self-help a try. For example, all patients are given a basic orientation to self-help and what it has to offer that professional treatment does not. They are also given a list of meetings in their community and provided with a ''buddy'' (fellow group member) if they feel hesitant or uncomfortable about attending self-help meetings alone. Patients are not threatened with termination from treatment for failure to attend self-help, nor is their reluctance/refusal to attend self-help meetings seen as intractable resistance or denial. The overwhelming majority of patients in the program do, in fact, attend self-help meetings.

PATIENT ELIGIBILITY

This treatment is best suited for patients who meet criteria for substance dependence according to the fourth edition of the *Diagnostic and Statistical Manual of Mental Disorders* (American Psychiatric Association, 1994) and are able to show up reliably for scheduled sessions at an outpatient clinic. The program admits patients who are actively using alcohol and other drugs as well as those who have already achieved abstinence as inpatients or outpatients. The program treats all types of chemical dependencies and cross-addictions irrespective of the patient's drug of choice (e.g., alcohol, cocaine, or heroin) and has been utilized successfully with both adult and adolescent populations (treated separately). Chronically unemployed, dysfunctional patients are treated in separate groups from patients with substantially higher levels of psychosocial functioning. The program is coed, but a special womens' group is available for those who prefer to be treated in an all-female environment. A dual-focus group (separate from the mainstream program) accommodates the special needs of patients with concurrent psychiatric illness.

Poor candidates for this approach include patients whose psychosocial functioning is so impaired that they are unable to show up reliably for treatment sessions and those who are actively suicidal, psychotic, or otherwise psychiatrically unstable and in need of more structured, intensive care such as an inpatient or partial hospitalization program.

COUNSELOR ATTITUDE AND STANCE

Counselors are expected to be warm, empathetic, engaging, tolerant, nonjudgmental, and flexible (nonrigid) in their interaction with patients. In recruiting staff, we look for therapists who have a well-developed observing ego and an ability to both receive and utilize constructive feedback, particularly with regard to the types of countertransference and control problems likely to arise with highly ambivalent (resistant) patients. They must have solid verbal communication skills and be capable of defining and implementing appropriate behavioral limits with patients in a consistently therapeutic (nonpunitive) manner. The counselor must work to motivate, engage, guide, educate, and retain patients during all phases of the program.

Utilizing a broad array of motivational, client-centered, and problem-solving techniques, counselors are expected to (1) emphasize patients' strengths rather than weaknesses, (2) join rather than assault (confront) resistance, (3) avoid aggressive confrontation and power struggles, (4) negotiate rather than pontificate treatment goals, and (5) emphasize patients' personal responsibility for change. Counselors are cautioned against being dogmatic and controlling, especially in response to reluctant and resistant clients. It is easy for counselors to lose sight of the fact that the first and foremost goal of treatment is to engage the patient in a friendly, cooperative, positive interaction that increases the patient's willingness to examine and change his/her substance-using behavior.

Counselors are taught how to avoid the most common therapeutic blunders and negative countertransferential responses with substance-abusing patients. These include (1) predicting abject failure and misery if the patient does not follow the counselor's advice, (2) telling the patient that what he/she really needs is more drug-related negative consequences in order to acquire the motivation for change, (3) ignoring discrepancies between the program's goals and the patient's goals, (4) feeling frustrated and angry at patients who do not fully comply with the program, and (5) wanting to impose "negative consequences" on noncompliant patients (e.g., depriving them of further help by "throwing" them out of treatment) rather than negotiating a change in treatment plan based on clarification of the patient's ambivalence about change.

The counselor serves a multidimensional role as collaborator, teacher, adviser, and change facilitator. In general, the patient talks more. However, the counselor does not hesitate to offer education, advice, and guidance when appropriate. The counselor takes an active role, offering specific advice and direction particularly during the early phases of treatment when immediate behavioral changes are required to establish and maintain abstinence. One of the most important aspects of this approach is the development of a cooperative relationship between patient and counselor. Building a positive therapeutic alliance requires the counselor to "start where the patient is"; that is, to accept and work within the patient's frame of reference. This is in marked contrast to traditional approaches which demand that the patient submit to the counselor's (program's) frame of reference as the starting point of treatment. For example, if the patient at first minimizes the seriousness of his/her substance use problem or rejects the idea that it is a "problem" at all, the counselor refrains from accusing the patient of being "in denial" (a tactic likely to heighten rather than reduce the patient's defensiveness) and instead asks the patient to cooperate in a time-limited "experiment" (usually involving a "trial period" of abstinence) in order to assess the nature and extent of his/her involvement with psychoactive substances.

Coerced or mandated patients pose the greatest challenge to getting a therapeutic alliance started. Typically they appear for treatment angry, suspicious, mistrustful, and ready to do battle. Relationship building under these trying circumstances requires a great deal of clinical finesse on the part of the counselor. Counselors make every effort to (1) empathize with the patient's plight and the fact that no one likes to be told what to do, (2) accept without challenge the patient's primary motivation for coming to treatment—to get the coercing agent (court, employer, etc.) "off my back," (3) compliment the patient for facing the realities of the situation by showing up for the session, and (4) detach themselves as much as possible from the coercing agent and offer to help the patient solve the problem(s) that led to the current (unfortunate) situation.

ASSESSMENT

The pretreatment evaluation process begins by asking the patient to fill out an extensive self-administered assessment questionnaire (see Washton, Chapter 2, this volume) immediately prior to a 1-hour face-to-face clinical interview with the intake counselor. The assessment questionnaire covers the domains of substance use, motivation and readiness for change, psychiatric history and status, family history, vocational history, criminal history, and treatment history. During the subsequent clinical interview, the counselor seeks to clarify and expand the information already provided by the patient on the assessment form. Perhaps more important, the counselor makes an active attempt to motivate and engage the patient in a therapeutic interaction. Where indicated, the pretreatment evaluation process may require one or more additional sessions and may also include a formal psychiatric assessment. An extremely important aspect of the pretreatment evaluation is to assess the patient's motivation and readiness for change. This involves identifying with the patient both the internal and external factors currently driving him/her to at least explore the possibility of change. It also involves helping the patient to identify his/her ambivalence about stopping psychoactive substance use by objectively exploring both the positive and negative effects of the use and defining the patient's treatment goals and to what extent these are consistent with the program's goals.

With regard to treatment goals, some patients want to reduce rather than completely stop using their drug of choice, whereas others want to give up only the one substance causing them the most obvious problems (e.g., cocaine) but not the substances they view as relatively innocuous and nonproblematic (e.g., alcohol and marijuana). In order to enter an early abstinence group, patients must agree to completely stop using all psychoactive substances for at least a trial period of total abstinence. Patients who do not meet this requirement are offered the option of time-limited individual counseling (up to 6 weeks) to help move them toward accepting trial abstinence as a short-term treatment goal.

Clinical progress is measured throughout each patient's participation in the program. A computerized office management system stores, analyzes, and reports clinical data on all patients during the course of their participation in the program. These data include (1) urine test results, (2) attendance at scheduled sessions, (3) counselor ratings of the patient's progress toward achieving specified treatment goals, and (4) patient's self-ratings of progress toward achieving treatment goals. The data are reviewed monthly (or weekly, if needed) in order to continuously adjust the treatment to individual patient needs, provide supervisory feedback to counselors, and improve overall treatment effectiveness.

SESSION FORMAT AND CONTENT

A typical group session in the early abstinence phase of the program begins with each patient stating the length of his/her "clean and sober" time (i.e., how long ago since he/she used any psychoactive substances whatsoever) and what issue he/she wishes to discuss in that session. Every patient is expected to identify at least one issue for discussion at each session. The therapist (group leader) may pull together the issues of two or more group members into a theme for that session or, alternatively, may begin the session with a specific topic as part of a revolving psychoeducational sequence. In general, two group sessions a week are devoted to day-to-day concerns and struggles raised by the patients themselves (with appropriate guidance and framing of the discussion supplied by the group leader) and one session is devoted to a specific psychoeducational or skills-training topic in which the therapist presents a brief lecture and guides a focused discussion.

TYPICAL SESSION TOPICS OR THEMES

The following is a partial list of topics and themes in the psychoeducational sequence (see Washton, 1989, 1991):

Tips for quitting
Finding your motivation to quit
How serious is your problem—taking a closer look
Identifying your high-risk situations
Coping with your high-risk situations
Dealing with cravings and urges
Why total abstinence—is it really necessary to give up *everything*?
Warning signs of relapse
Rating your relapse potential—a realistic assessment
Tips for handling slips
Managing anger and frustration
Finding balance in your life
How to have fun without getting high
Defining your personal goals
Managing problems in your relationships
Building your self-esteem
Nutrition and personal health
AIDS and other sexually transmitted diseases—how to avoid them
Overview of treatment and recovery
How your family can help without hurting—a look at codependency

The purpose of each session is to enhance the patient's motivation for change and improve his/her ability to cope adaptively with the problems of everyday life without reverting to psychoactive substance use. To successfully accomplish this purpose, sessions are neither highly structured nor totally unstructured. The psychoeducational sessions serve more to stimulate discussion rather than present material in didactic fashion. The group leader takes an active role in helping each group member to relate the lecture topic to his/her own personal situation. The goal is to foster emotional and behavioral change rather than merely supply factual information.

STRATEGIES FOR DEALING
WITH COMMON CLINICAL PROBLEMS

Lateness and absenteeism are addressed therapeutically as behavioral manifestations of a patient's ambivalence about change. The importance of patients arriving at sessions on time and attending reliably is emphasized throughout the program, starting with the initial intake interview. Patients are instructed not to come to the clinic within 12 hours of any alcohol or other drug use. If a patient arrives showing clear-cut behavioral signs of intoxication (e.g., slurred speech, uncoordinated movements, and breath smelling of alcohol), he/she is asked to leave the premises and return the next day. If the patient is severely intoxicated, a counselor will try to contact a family member to escort the patient home. According to the program's variable-length treatment protocol, each unexcused absence extends by 2 to 4 weeks the time required for program completion. On the occasion of a third unexcused absence or fifth unexcused lateness, the patient is transferred from the early abstinence group to a stabilization group that focuses more intensively on overcoming early obstacles to change.

STRATEGIES FOR DEALING WITH DENIAL,
RESISTANCE, AND POOR MOTIVATION

Enhancing patients' motivation for change is an essential part of the counselor's role in this approach. Labeling a patient "in denial," "resistant to change," or "poorly motivated" is seen as distinctly unhelpful. Problems in complying with the treatment program are framed in terms of the patient's ambivalence, reluctance, and fears about change. The counselor works collaboratively and cooperatively with the patient to overcome these obstacles. In the face of noncompliance, the counselor actively seeks to join the patient's resistance and find creative ways around it. This approach recognizes that, especially in the outpatient setting, aggressive confrontation is likely to precipitate dropout from treatment and nullify efforts to engage and retain patients. It is important to mention that although this approach avoids the use of confrontational tactics, it does not promote a "laissez faire," "anything goes" attitude toward patient noncompliance. Limit setting and constructive feedback are essential features of the approach, but there are utilized in the spirit of enhancing a patient's motivation for change rather than insisting that he/she admit to being an "addict in serious denial."

COUNSELOR'S RESPONSE TO SLIPS AND RELAPSES

Slips are treated as avoidable mistakes and manifestations of ambivalence. The thoughts, feelings, circumstances, and chain of "setup" behaviors leading up to the slip are carefully reviewed. The first goal of this debriefing is to help the patient recognize and accept the role of personal choice and responsibility in determining drug-using behavior. In order to decrease the likelihood of further use, an abstinence plan is formulated that incorporates specific decision-making, problem-solving, and behavioral avoidance strategies. The variable-length treatment protocol stipulates that each slip increases a patient's length of stay in the program by 2 to 4 weeks. On the occasion of a third slip (or sooner if the counselor deems it necessary), the patient is transferred to a stabilization group. This group focuses intensively on developing day-by-day (hour-by-hour) behavioral action plans for achieving abstinence. Upon achieving 2 consecutive weeks of total abstinence and perfect attendance in the stabilization group, the patient is eligible to return to his/her early abstinence group. In the event of a second slip while in the stabilization group, the patient is suspended from group treatment for at least 2 weeks and may be referred for inpatient care. During the suspension, the patient may also be given the option of attending the clinic for twice-weekly urine testing and once-a-week individual counseling for a maximum of 4 weeks. If the patient achieves 2 consecutive weeks of abstinence during the suspension period, he/she can return to the early abstinence group.

ROLE OF SIGNIFICANT OTHERS IN TREATMENT

Active efforts are made to involve significant others in the treatment. All newly admitted patients are encouraged to attend a family program with their significant others (mate, family members, best friend, etc.). The program consists of a conjoint multiple family group that meets once a week for 12 consecutive weeks. The group provides support, education, and counseling geared toward enhancing family members' ability to cope adaptively with their loved one's addiction and teaching them how to break the vicious cycle of enabling and provoking behaviors that perpetuate the problem. Participants learn and practice specific problem-solving and communication skills through exercises in guided role play. Couple and/or family therapy is also utilized to deal with problems that require more individualized attention.

REFERENCES

American Psychiatric Association. (1994). *Diagnostic and statistical manual of mental disorders* (4th ed.). Washington, DC: Author.

Brehm, N. M., & Khantzian, E. J. (1992). A psychodynamic perspective. In J. H. Lowinson, P. Ruiz, R. B. Millman, & J. Langrod (Eds.). *Substance abuse: A comprehensive textbook.* (2nd ed., pp. 106–117). Baltimore: Williams & Wilkins.

Marlatt, G. A., & Gordon, J. R. (Eds.). (1985). *Relapse prevention: Maintenance strategies in the treatment of addictive behaviors.* New York: Guilford Press.

Miller, W. R., & Rollnick, S. (1991). *Motivational interviewing: Preparing people to change addictive behavior.* New York: Guilford Press.

Washton, A. M. (1989). *Cocaine addiction: Treatment, recovery, and relapse prevention.* New York: W. W. Norton.

Washton, A. M. (1991). *Cocaine recovery workbooks.* Center City, MN: Hazelden Educational Materials.

16

Structured Inpatient Treatment: A Coping-Skills Training Approach

RONALD M. KADDEN
CHRISTOPHER R. PENTA

INTRODUCTION

When a patient presents with a substance abuse problem, many professionals and laymen alike think it is time to get the patient "into rehab." This evokes the image of a residential treatment facility, far removed from the pressures of everyday life, where patients reside for a fixed length of time in order to "get the program." This image is reinforced both in the popular press and in the more mundane yet authoritative language of many commercial insurance policies, which, until recently, were often weighted to steer patients toward inpatient treatment.

This chapter focuses on the considerations for inpatient treatment and the implementation of a coping-skills training approach in such a setting. A broader view of an inpatient program, including more details on the scope of services, roles of a multidisciplinary treatment team, and involvement of the self-help fellowships in the program, is provided elsewhere (Kadden & Kranzler, 1992).

An inpatient program provides opportunities for skills development and practice in a closely supervised setting without some of the stresses or inappropriate feedback that may occur in the home environment and which could be detrimental during the early stages of skills acquisition. Although the inpatient setting is an artificial one and does not provide the same opportunities for skill rehearsal in realistic situations that are an important aspect of ambulatory treatment, it does provide a safe, structured, and supportive milieu for those who are particularly skill-deficient or who live in an unsupportive environment. Staff can encourage patients to practice new skills on the unit and provide appropriate support for their efforts.

Inpatient programs usually refer to those in a hospital setting. They often are identified as a specialized unit within the context of either a general hospital or a specialized facility such as a psychiatric or rehabilitation hospital. Programs in a hospital setting are likely to attract patients with comorbid medical and/or psychiatric problems because of the easy access to resources for evaluation and treatment. Although such a setting may introduce distractions and complications to a substance abuse treatment program, it allows for assessment and treatment of factors that otherwise might interfere with the recovery process. Staffing in such settings is typically multidisciplinary, including nursing and counseling at a minimum. An internist is usually on staff, at least on a part-time basis, and the services of psychiatrists and psychologists are available either part-time or on-call. Other disciplines represented on the staff often include occupational therapy, recreational therapy, and social work. Of course, within the context of a hospital a number of other specialties are available on relatively short notice.

There are also a considerable number of residential facilities that do not operate within the context of a hospital. They tend to be stand-alone proprietary facilities, with staffing weighted in the direction of paraprofessional counselors who are recovering from substance dependence themselves (Geller, 1992). The hospital-based programs, on the other hand, tend to employ a wider range of professionals, most of whom have bachelor's degrees or master's-level training. In this chapter, we use the term *inpatient* loosely to refer to either type of facility.

Whether inpatient or residential, these treatment programs have much greater control over their patients' lives than do ambulatory programs. As such, they are particularly useful for breaking well-established, destructive behavior patterns and for training alternative, more appropriate behaviors. The skills-training approach focuses on remedying coping-skills deficits, which are a major risk factor for relapse (Monti, Abrams, Kadden, & Cooney, 1989), through the development or enhancement of behaviors that will support a sober life-style. This approach is increasingly recommended as the treatment of choice for at least the initial stages of recovery. Inpatient settings provide a milieu that is well suited for intensive skills training and a structure that encourages patients to practice new skills as well as permitting timely feedback on their performance.

SPECIAL ADVANTAGES VERSUS LIMITATIONS

Professionals considering a referral for substance abuse treatment must weigh a number of factors, including current clinical status; history of the patient's compliance with recommendations; life-style disruption, including interruption of any current therapy; and the financial resources available. Inpatient treatment at first may seem a bitter pill. It is by far the most expensive form of treatment available, particularly if provided in a hospital setting. It is disruptive to the life-style of the patient, bringing work, social, and family life to a screeching halt for a time. Many individuals resist taking the plunge for this reason. Therapists may fear that they will lose the patient to the substance abuse treatment system. Recovery programs have often perpetuated this fear by failing to include the referring therapist in treatment planning. In addition, there is no guarantee that inpatient treatment will necessarily be effective. Without adequate attention to life-style issues, inpatient treatment may only be training patients to function in the artificial environment of the treatment center.

In the face of these difficulties, what are the specific instances in which inpatient treatment would prove its special value? These include acute medical or psychiatric decompensation, the worsening of chronic disease as a result of neglected treatment, the inability to begin outpatient treatment because of continued drinking/drug use, and prior failure of outpatient treatment (Dackis & Gold, 1992; Nace, 1987). Pregnant addicts who have not established abstinence in outpatient treatment should be hospitalized as soon as possible; Gold (1992) reports that, in some parts of the country, there is cocaine involvement in 15%–20% of births. Walsh et al. (1991) even demonstrate benefits of inpatient treatment among relatively high functioning, employed alcoholics, but in the current climate of third-party reimbursement policies, this option for these patients is increasingly foreclosed.

In treating other chronic severe illnesses such as schizophrenia, professionals have long been aware that treatment takes place along a continuum of care, with the particular treatment that is provided at any point being dictated by the current severity of the condition, available options, and the patient's willingness to accept recommendations. Similarly, inpatient substance abuse treatment is no more than one point along a continuum of care. Inpatient treatment may be the only viable option for patients who have become physically or psychiatrically unstable as a result of their substance abuse. Bartels et al. (1993) found that among a group of schizophrenic patients, those who were current substance abusers were significantly more involved with hospitalization, emergency services, and jail. For such individuals who have received only fragmented care, a stay in a treatment center provides opportunities for evaluation and medication adjustment in a controlled setting. Alcohol and drug programs may improve their effectiveness by offering flexible combinations of inpatient and outpatient treatment, that allow entry at various stages based on clients' needs (Cole, Lehman, Cole, & Jones, 1981).

Hospitalization is advantageous when an individual in outpatient treatment has clearly failed to achieve abstinence. It removes the patient from the cues for craving in his/her daily environment. While recognizing that he/she will be returning to that environment, it is hoped that massed practice of coping skills, while an inpatient, will significantly alter the patient's adjustment to it. Inpatient treatment offers a measure of safety both for the patient and for others who are subjected to the patient's behavior while he/she is actively using. It forestalls, if only for the moment, the physical, psychological, and financial damage to the patient and family.

In deciding to enter the inpatient setting, the patient must commit to spending time working exclusively on recovery. The intensity of therapeutic interactions is dramatically increased. As patients work through situations that have resulted in substance abuse in their outside environment, they are taught and expected to practice new coping skills. As patients take the next step to follow-up treatment or back to the referring therapist, they must then begin to apply their new skills in the more challenging situations of real life.

In addition to the rehearsal of specific skills that have been explicitly trained, the inpatient milieu also provides opportunities for behavioral management that may be especially useful with patients who tend to act impulsively, who require a highly structured environment, or who may be poorly motivated. Contingency management can be effectively utilized in a controlled inpatient milieu to reinforce active participation in treatment activities, the practicing of behavioral skills, and engaging in discharge planning (Kadden & Mauriello, 1991). A program of this sort is most effectively managed in an inpatient environment, where appropriate consequences for behavior can be provided fairly reliably, and where inappropriate consequences, which are particularly destructive during the early phases of skills acquisition, are much less likely to occur.

PATIENT–TREATMENT
MATCHING CONSIDERATIONS

There is only a very small literature on matching patients to treatment settings. Kissin, Platz, and Su (1970) found that hospital inpatient care was advantageous only for those who were less socially stable. Welte, Hynes, Sokolow, and Lyons (1981) determined that the length of inpatient treatment made no difference for patients with high social stability, but for those with low social stability increasing lengths of stay resulted in improved outcomes. McLellan, Luborsky, Woody, O'Brien, and Druley

(1983) and McLellan, Woody, Luborsky, O'Brien, and Druley (1983) found that patients who were either low or high in psychiatric severity were not affected by the setting in which treatment was offered (low-severity patients benefited from either an inpatient or outpatient setting and high-severity patients from neither). However, those who were in the mid-range of psychiatric severity and had work-related or family-related problems did better if they received inpatient treatment. Reviews of these matching studies have concluded that although inpatient treatment may be cost-effective for only a small segment of the treatment-seeking population, it is most appropriate for those who are homeless or have poor social stability, those with severe medical or psychiatric complications, and those who have become dangerous to themselves or others (Lindstrom, 1992; Miller & Hester, 1986).

The nascent patient–treatment matching literature also contains a few studies identifying patient characteristics that indicate who may benefit from a coping-skills training approach. Although these studies have been conducted primarily in outpatient settings, they do provide some indication of variables to bear in mind when considering patients for this type of treatment. In a series of studies, Kadden and colleagues (Kadden, Cooney, Getter, & Litt, 1989; Kadden, Litt, Cooney, & Busher, 1992; Cooney, Kadden, Litt, & Getter, 1991; Litt, Babor, DelBoca, Kadden, & Cooney, 1992) found that patients who had more sociopathic characteristics, more evidence of psychopathology, and a greater urge to drink (in a role-play situation) were more likely to be abstinent and less likely to suffer alcohol-related problems if they were given coping-skills group treatment. Patients who had fewer of these characteristics at treatment intake fared better if they were assigned to interactional group therapy. Longabaugh, Rubin, Malloy, Beattie, Clifford, and Noel (1994) also found that patients with antisocial characteristics had better treatment outcomes following coping-skills treatment.

COST CONSIDERATIONS

According to a review by Holder, Longabaugh, Miller, and Rubonis (1991), inpatient treatment programs are the most expensive. Nevertheless, among them, residential facilities with minimal medical involvement are the least expensive, and in some cases are price-competitive with ambulatory treatment programs. Holder et al. (1991) were unable to evaluate the cost-effectiveness of inpatient/residential programs relative to other types of treatment because there were an inadequate number of studies assessing their treatment effectiveness.

With the rise in cost-consciousness and ever-increasing utilization of managed care, inpatient treatment is often reserved for those who have had repeated failures in ambulatory treatment. For those patients, the inpatient experience may become cost-effective (Walsh et al., 1991), offering a safe haven from high-risk situations, a controlled environment, and a greater opportunity to focus on acquiring skills to cope with the situations that led to relapse in the past. Patient–treatment matching research may in the future provide an empirical basis for assigning patients to this form of treatment without first requiring them to go through the costly process of failing at ambulatory treatment.

SPECIFIC GUIDELINES FOR CLINICAL APPLICATION

Coping-Skills Training

A coping-skills training approach is based on several assumptions about the maintenance of addictive behaviors. Among them are that (1) an addictive behavior pattern is composed of a series of maladaptive behaviors which can be modified, (2) addicted individuals are either deficient in the skills needed to effectively resist substance use or are for some reason inhibited from utilizing appropriate skills that they already possess, and (3) there are a number of factors in patients' lives, at both the interpersonal and intrapersonal levels, that may increase the likelihood of substance use unless adequately addressed. The focus of treatment, therefore, is to teach or enhance basic skills for achieving and maintaining abstinence, as well as skills to cope effectively with the problems in daily living that could set the stage for a resumption of substance use.

Many substance abuse patients have skills deficits in common, despite differences in the categories of substances they abuse. Thus, most patients will benefit from drink/drug refusal training, learning to cope with cravings, and development or enhancement of more general life skills through assertiveness training, stress management, development of appropriate leisure activities, and vocational counseling, regardless of the particular substances on which they have become dependent. They may therefore be treated together in a single program (LaPorte, McLellan, & MacGahan, 1980) as long as some of the specific issues peculiar to the use of each substance are addressed, such as the nature of the cravings they are most likely to experience, potential triggers for relapse, and typical social influences.

There are also certain to be individual differences between patients in the specific factors that trigger or maintain their substance use. This requires detailed exploration of the unique antecedents and consequences that have triggered or maintained each patient's addictive behavior, and that may be risk factors for future relapse. An essential part of the individual counseling process should be the assessment of triggers, existing coping skills, and consequences of substance use and the identification of maladaptive behaviors that are being utilized in difficult situations.

Structured assessment tools such as the Addiction Severity Index (McLellan, Luborsky, Woody, & O'Brien, 1980) and the Comprehensive Drinker Profile (Miller & Marlatt, 1984) can aid in the identification of high-risk behaviors and situations. The process of assessing risk factors not only provides the clinician with specific problems at which to aim therapeutic intervention efforts but also helps make the client more aware of the problems/deficits that are uncovered and in doing so begins the process of building the motivation needed to achieve and maintain sobriety (Miller & Rollnick, 1991).

The actual training of behavioral skills is often provided in a group setting. This allows patients to share their experiences with respect to the skills being taught and the concerns they may have regarding their ability to actually utilize them. It also provides a natural medium for role-play rehearsing of new behaviors and generating feedback regarding the adequacy of their performance. Individual counseling sessions may also be used, with the therapist providing skills training, modeling new behaviors, serving as the role-play partner, and providing feedback regarding the patient's performance (Kadden, Carroll et al., 1992).

The more experiential the process of skills training the better; recently detoxified patients are likely still to be suffering from substance-related cognitive impairment, which reduces their ability to absorb and retain didactically presented material (Becker & Jaffe, 1984). This may be countered, in part, by frequent reviews of previously taught skills to help consolidate memory and by homework assignments that require additional skills practice in the residential environment with peers, staff, and visitors.

Effective use of homework assignments in a residential milieu requires good communications among the staff, through patient charts and clinical team meetings, to most effectively integrate the skills training aspect of treatment with the total care plan.

Specific coping-skills training procedures are described in considerable detail in treatment manuals that have become available to clinicians in recent years (e.g., Monti et al., 1989). Some of the skills relate directly to alcohol/drug use, such as drink/drug refusal skills, managing thoughts about alcohol/drugs, coping with criticisms about one's addictive behavior, and handling emergency situations in which the urge to drink or use drugs is particularly strong. Other elements teach basic interpersonal skills on the grounds that social isolation and feelings of social inadequacy often provide the basis for future relapses. These include skills such as the ability to start conversations and make small talk, the effective use of body language, and assertiveness training. More complex interpersonal skills include appropriate ways for giving and receiving criticism, refusing requests that one does not want to fulfill, responding to the emotional content in the communication of others, handling intimate relationships, and developing and/or enhancing a sober social support network. Various intrapersonal skills are also taught, including problem solving, decision making, relaxation to cope with stress and anxiety, coping with anger and negative thinking, and developing enjoyable leisure activities that are incompatible with relapse. Session-by-session instructions for clinicians on the use of these interventions are provided in Monti et al. (1989).

Dual-Diagnosis Issues

Meyer (1986) summarized the variety of possible relationships between substance abuse and coexisting psychopathology. Psychopathology may be a risk factor for substance abuse, modify the course of the addictive disorder, or develop as a result of the addiction and persist into periods of abstinence. Some mental disorders strike addicts and nonaddicts alike and no meaningful connection can be found. The modern substance abuse inpatient unit is increasingly called on to provide services to patients traditionally considered unsuitable for recovery programs. In fact, the economic survival of many treatment centers is rapidly becoming dependent on their ability to service patients with disparate treatment needs using the same physical environment and staff members. With this difficult reality in mind, an overview of key treatment considerations for various patient subgroups is presented, including discussion of how to achieve therapeutic goals using the resources at hand. For the purpose of brevity, we divide special needs patients into two admittedly imperfect subcategories: (1) those with significant Axis I psychopathology (including schizophrenia, affective disorders, and organicity) and (2) those with significant Axis II conditions, with emphasis on cluster B disorders and those with involvement in the criminal justice system.

The Psychiatrically Involved Patient

This is the patient group usually associated with the term *dual-diagnosis*. It includes those with severe Axis I conditions including the schizophrenias. Because substance abuse both interacts with and imitates many forms of psychiatric illness, the incidence and clinical diagnosis of psychiatric illness are often difficult to determine. Careful evaluation is therefore essential to the successful treatment of the dually diagnosed. Family and outside treaters should be consulted as these patients are often poor historians. If possible, a medication-free period is useful in determining which symptoms are attributable to active addiction and which to psychopathology. Depression and anxiety often clear after a period of sobriety (Schuckit & Monteiro, 1988). Drug-induced psychosis, particularly from PCP, may last for several days after the cessation of active use. The diagnosis of psychiatric disorders should be delayed to prevent confusion with the effects of detoxification. Dackis and Gold (1992) recommend universal suicide, elopement, and assault precautions in addition to standard medical procedures, as well as a thorough search for contraband.

Patients with psychiatric disorders should be assessed prior to hospitalization to determine whether an addiction service is the appropriate destination after they leave the streets. Those patients with active psychosis, severe depression, or inability to tolerate discussing their behavior would best be stabilized on a general psychiatry service. They can attempt a substance abuse program after stabilization. This helps preserve the substance abuse treatment days available through the patient's insurance policy.

The dually diagnosed frequently have difficulty tolerating the demands and rules of the substance abuse unit and may flee to the general psychiatry service. Adjustments must therefore be made both in the context of treatment (ward milieu) and its content (therapeutic stratagems). Extra care must be taken to orient the patient to the milieu, repeating the orientation routine at several points throughout the program. Ward rules and restrictions should be clear but not rigid. Emphasis should be placed on working with the patient to complete the program successfully rather than on confronting "misbehavior." Schizophrenic patients have been shown to have poorer outcomes in environments where there is a high level of expressed emotion. A unit containing a high number of energetic, provocative patients is particularly challenging. Reducing the level of stimulation by excusing the patient from less well tolerated groups is helpful, as well as allowing frequent breaks from the treatment routine. Spending time alone, sometimes a sign of disengagement from therapy in other patients, can be a necessary stress reliever for the dually diagnosed. The 50-minute therapy hour is best replaced with frequent shorter contacts with the counseling staff, perhaps two to four "check-ins" per day. Ward staff may become concerned that the dually diagnosed will be perceived as "beating the system" or receiving "special treatment." The best way to handle this is to incorporate the issue into the group process. The staff should freely share that the program tries to give those with additional vulnerabilities an equivalent chance to recover. The patient community may rally around a dually diagnosed member if individual needs are clearly identified and respected.

In working with the dually diagnosed, the focus of treatment must be supportive with a relatively low degree of confrontation. This is incompatible with treatment approaches that are organized to break down massive denial and rationalization through confrontation and peer pressure. It is more helpful to establish agreement with the patient on specific difficulties he/she finds troubling and explore the role substance abuse plays in them. An example may be to explore the role of cocaine in increasing the intensity of frightening thoughts (paranoia). Many patients with psychotic disorders must learn to regard their thoughts and perceptions with a degree of "healthy skepticism." For example, the therapist might discuss the patient's assessment of the reliability of the advice the voices provide. A variety of relevant coping skills can be taught individually or in groups, such as training patients to discuss unusual ideas with a confidant, or to hum as a way of deemphasizing auditory hallucinations (see Director, Chapter 20, this volume).

We have found it useful to provide groups for a variety of disorders (especially schizophrenia, anxiety disorders, and depression/bipolar illness, as well as borderline and antisocial personality disorders). We utilize commercially available videotapes and a variety of materials written specifically for dual-diagnosis patients. There is an educational group on the topic of psychiatric medications. The overall goal is to emphasize to each patient the need for ongoing treatment and support for all their disorders. A great deal of time is spent discussing the nonaddictive nature of most psychiatric medications and the sometimes nonsupportive attitude found in 12-Step programs toward those on medications. Patients are given the opportunity to discuss their own experiences and are encouraged to discuss issues of stigma connected with dual disorders. Specific techniques for teaching skills to deal with negative moods, anxiety, negative thinking, etc., have been discussed in detail elsewhere (e.g., Monti et al., 1989).

Close contact should be maintained with the referring therapist. Visits and conjoint sessions with the outside therapist help the patient tolerate the stress of hospitalization and ease the transition to outpatient care. Discharge planning is crucial, and frequent discussions of the details of the plan should be available to the patient.

The Character-Disordered/Legally Involved Patient

Alcoholics Anonymous (AA) and other self-help groups have long acknowledged the importance of "hitting bottom" as a prerequisite to accepting help. This frequently takes the form of running afoul of the law. From those facing their first charge of driving while intoxicatd to those with extensive histories of drug-related crime, all these patients are involved in the treatment system principally as a result of external pressure. For some proportion of this group, the principal aim is the reduction of that pressure rather than the enactment of behavior change on their part. Some treatment providers may equate this "external motivation" with untreatability and have misgivings about attempting to serve this challenging population. However, any reluctance that may exist on the part of the treatment community has not impeded welfare departments, the courts, and child protective agencies from referring these patients for treatment in large numbers. Many patients with personality disorders, especially antisocial and borderline personality disorders, are among this group.

Preadmission assessment is an important part of treating these patients successfully. There should be clear criteria for admission that identify the types of patients the staff are not able to treat adequately. The limits of confidentiality and duty to warn should be clearly spelled out to avoid any appearance of trapping the patient. The referral source should be incorporated in the treatment effort, with releases of information allowing two-way information exchange. Failure on the part of the patient to grant the clinician access to his/her network, especially legal involvements, will result in significant "warping" of the therapeutic frame and is best dealt with before the patient is formally accepted into the treatment program. However, the patient's legal involvement should not become a source of stigma. The following reframe is often helpful: The fact is that *no* addict (legally involved or not) ever abstains until the negative consequences of the addiction become so painful that they outweigh the discomfort involved in giving up the substance. In other words, "it had to hurt more to use than to quit, before you began to think of quitting." Legally involved patients should be helped to identify additional negative consequences of their substance use beyond the obvious legal pressure, to enhance the likelihood of meaningful participation in the treatment program. Family involvement is invaluable in uncovering this information.

Time-limited abstinence contracts are often a useful tool in dealing with this population. If the patient can engage in a concerted effort to abstain from substance use for a specific period of time (sometimes as short as 30 days), the daunting issue of lifetime change is avoided in favor of work on specific coping skills. The successes and difficulties the patient experiences during such a period will inform his/her choice about future behavior.

A clearly written list of rules and ward routines should be given upon admission, spelling out consequences for both infractions and successful completion of program goals. Limits are best set in an empathic manner (e.g., " I see how frustrating it is for you to hear this. I'd feel the same if I were in your shoes"). This modeling of empathic behavior is helpful, as many character-disordered patients lack the ability to empathize with others and feel chronically misunderstood themselves. We have found it useful to use "warnings," with an accumulation of warnings leading to a loss of ward privileges (Kadden & Mauriello, 1991).

Privileges/rewards should be available to reinforce the development of appropriate behaviors. These can be selected from among events ordinarily available in the inpatient environment and thus implemented at minimum cost. They might include increased freedom to travel about the institution unescorted, cafeteria privileges, on-grounds and off-grounds passes, telephone privileges, increased access to stereo or television, free recovery literature, and a certificate of achievement (Kadden & Mauriello, 1991).

These patients often see themselves as victims of circumstance, always reacting to the turmoil around them, surviving by the speed of their reflexes. The patient is encouraged to "slow down the action" through coping-skills exercises that focus on delaying the expression of impulses and by encouraging them to think clearly about behavioral alternatives. Structured exercises that control treatment content are more effective than a nondirective, exploratory approach, which is easily subverted by these patients. Use of a cotherapist is often helpful in diluting the challenges offered by groups of these difficult patients (Walker, 1992).

There is evidence that a coping-skills training approach can be particularly effective for those with antisocial personality disorder (Kadden et al., 1989; Cooney et al., 1991), and patients with borderline personality disorder are also likely to benefit from the highly structured aspect of this approach. Patients with character disorders may present particular problems with respect to their motivation and may require special intervention (e.g., Miller & Rollnick, 1991) to maintain them in treatment and to limit behavior that may undermine treatment efforts.

Including Significant Others

In families in which chemical dependency has dominated the home, many basic life skills have typically broken down, if they ever were acquired at all. These skills include communication, problem solving, and fighting fair. Family members may have precious little knowledge about substance abuse, may be carrying a great deal of misinformation about their loved one's condition, and may develop troublesome behavior patterns of their own. Treatment is often offered to the patient by a family member as part of an ultimatum to "get help or get out," and it is the family member who may end up dealing with the patient's resistance and the hospital's gatekeepers. Having been disheartened by attempts to get the patient to change during the period of active addiction, family members are often skeptical of programmatic efforts to help.

Efforts must be made to include significant others in the treatment process. Family members, roommates, and friends often unwittingly become "enablers" of the patient's addictive behaviors and must be included as an important aspect of the treatment process. They may arrive at the hospital emotionally and physically exhausted. Family sessions typically provide an opportunity to vent long-standing problems and to review the treatment program's methods and goals. The overall focus of conjoint sessions should be on the identification and articulation of areas of concern that all too often went unrecognized, were not discussed, or were the basis for unproductive communications. Information is provided about assertiveness skills, the importance of praising one another for positive changes, breaking the cycle of criticism and recriminations, and discovering shared leisure activities. Patients and their significant others are urged to practice these during visits, in telephone calls, and on passes to home.

Most comprehensive substance abuse treatment programs incorporate some attempt to involve the family in the patient's recovery. There are a number of approaches:

1. Al-Anon or Nar-Anon attendance to expose the family to a supportive, spiritual self-help program.
2. Educational programs to familiarize the family with the illness of chemical dependency and the recovery process.
3. Family therapy sessions conducted by trained therapists to assess the family and, if appropriate, to induce behavior change. Difficult issues may have been avoided while the patient was in the home because of the danger of suicidal or other acting-out behavior. These may include the desire to break off a relationship, confronting issues of physical abuse, and dealing with newly diagnosed HIV (human immunodeficiency virus) infection. Inpatient settings provide opportunities to deal with such tricky issues with emergency supports readily available.
4. Multifamily groups allow the therapist(s) to work with a number of different families at the same time. This has the effect of exposing participants to situations other than their own and increasing available support from others sharing common hardships.
5. Coping-skills training approaches have been developed for use with family members, particularly spouses. These often include the facilitation of communication and teaching of problem-solving skills. Detailed descriptions of these are available for the interested professional (e.g., McCrady, 1982; O'Farrell & Cowles, 1989).

Efforts are made to involve families in the details of the discharge planning process, eliciting whatever misgivings the family members might have about the plan. A specific fallback plan should also be discussed in case the patient reengages in active substance use.

Discharge Planning and Continuity-of-Care Issues

The need for aggressive case management for the substance abuse patient has been recognized for at least 10 years (Graham & Timney, 1990). Therefore, working with inpatients on discharge planning should begin at the earliest possible opportunity, perhaps even prior to admission. Aftercare is necessary to continue the skills development that was begun during the inpatient program, so consideration should be given to continuing-care agencies or settings that would be best suited to help each patient overcome his/her particular deficits. Factors to be weighed in making discharge recommendations include length of addiction, comorbid psychopathology, available social supports, home environment, response to previous treatment, stress tolerance, and motivation.

Discharge planning for the dually diagnosed must address both illnesses. Whenever possible, the opportunity to introduce the patient to a more appropriate level of psychiatric care should be taken. For example, a patient whose symptoms had been inadequately controlled by haloperidol was, after 2 weeks on the inpatient substance abuse unit, comfortable enough to accept a transfer to the psychiatry service where he began treatment with clozapine. He was then able to enter outpatient dual-diagnosis treatment with fewer debilitating symptoms.

We have found it helpful to make agreements with patients who will only accept a lower level of aftercare than recommended, on conditions for future rehospitalization if that should become necessary. Such patients may be told that any future hospitalization will be contingent upon a prearranged commitment to obtain the recommended care. For example, a patient with 7 years of intravenous heroin abuse had only three sober friends, whom she saw only on holidays, and was estranged from her family. She insisted on individual counseling for continuing care in lieu of the recommended halfway house. She relapsed and applied for readmission the following year. The patient was reminded of the precondition in her case and consented to "try it your way." She arranged for a halfway house bed and was discharged *directly* to the follow-up program. Adoption of readmission policies such as this helps to reduce the volume of "revolving door" admissions.

In today's managed care environment, frequent and effective communication between treatment providers and funding sources is essential. Many health maintenance organizations have contracts that direct patients to particular clinics and levels of care. All too often an adversarial relationship develops between the clinician and the managed care provider. The only sure loser if this happens is the patient. The managed care representative should be brought "into the loop" and kept informed of the logic of clinical decision making, including backup plans. In some instances managed care representatives can exhibit a high degree of flexibility and be a helpful resource in securing appropriate care for their customers.

EVIDENCE OF EFFECTIVENESS

A number of research studies have been conducted to compare the relative effectiveness of treatment provided in different settings. The majority of these studies report no differences in treatment outcome between inpatient settings and outpatient or partial hospital settings (National Institute on Alcohol Abuse and Alcoholism [NIAAA], 1987; Miller & Hester, 1986). This finding has often been interpreted to mean that the two settings are largely equivalent, and that ambulatory treatment is therefore preferable in most cases on grounds of cost-effectiveness. However, as most of the comparative studies did not involve random assignment to treatment settings, the finding of no difference may simply mean that those substance abusers who are relatively less impaired do about as well in outpatient treatment, to which they are usually assigned, as those who are more impaired do in inpatient treatment (Collins, 1993). In fact, a nonrandomized study of inpatient and outpatient treatment for cocaine abuse (Budde, Rounsaville, & Bryant, 1992) demonstrated that those clients who were assigned to inpatient treatment did indeed have greater problem severity initially and showed greater improvement over a 1-year follow-up period than those assigned to outpatient treatment. However, in a study employing random assignment to treatments, O'Brien, Alterman, Childress, and McLellan (1992) generally confirmed the finding of little difference between the outcomes of inpatient and outpatient treatment. Although those patients with a cocaine problem were more likely to complete treatment if they were assigned to an inpatient program, the extent of substance-related problems reported at two follow-up points was equivalent across treatment settings. Walsh et al. (1991) also conducted a random assignment study, involving clients in an employee assistance program. Those assigned to inpatient rehabilitation fared better than those assigned to attend AA meetings. Reports specifically addressing the effectiveness of Minnesota model programs have been generally positive (Cook, 1988; Keso & Salaspuro, 1990), although, like many other treatment outcome studies, they have been subject to criticism on methodological grounds.

In a study that focused on treatment process as well as outcome in both inpatient and outpatient settings, McLellan et al. (1993) concluded that the nature and quantity of treatment services actually provided to patients were the major factors related to program effectiveness, regardless of the setting in which they were provided. Regarding the length of inpatient treatment, some studies show no differences in outcome regardless of length of stay (Miller & Hester, 1986), whereas others show some advantage for longer stays (NIAAA, 1987). When clients are subdivided according to special needs categories (e.g., psychiatric, social functioning), the benefits of lengthier inpatient stays become apparent (NIAAA, 1987).

Thus, there is some evidence to support the continued use of inpatient treatment with varying lengths of stay. However, further work is needed to identify those who will benefit most from it and which services, and in what quantities, will be most effective.

With respect to the effectiveness of coping-skills training, several controlled clinical trials found improved outcomes when skills training is added to inpatient treatment programs for alcoholics (e.g., Chaney, O'Leary, & Marlatt, 1978; Oei & Jackson, 1980). However, Jones, Kanfer, and Lanyon (1982) failed to replicate Chaney et al. (1978) with clients having a higher socioeconomic status, perhaps indicating that better-functioning alcoholics require a less concrete intervention program, a possibility that is consistent with some of the patient–treatment matching findings noted above. In a review of the literature, Chaney (1989) notes that the strongest evidence for the efficacy of skills training for alcoholics comes from studies of inpatient programs and that there has been sufficient validation to warrant recommending inclusion of skills training as a standard feature in rehabilitation programs.

CONCLUSION

We have outlined strategies for implementing coping-skills training in inpatient settings with a diverse clinical population. Such training has tentatively demonstrated effectiveness with a population that is characterized by relatively high levels of psychopathology and poor social functioning. The managed care system has increasingly allowed only such individuals access to inpatient treatment. Clinical experience has shown that targeted skills training combined with access to appropriate clinical supports after completion of inpatient treatment can make a significant difference in the durability of recovery and quality of life.

REFERENCES

Bartels, S. J., Teague, G. B., Drake, R. E., Clark, R. E., Bush, P. W., & Noordsy, D. L. (1993). Substance abuse in schizophrenia: Service utilization and costs. *Journal of Nervous and Mental Disease, 181*(4), 227–232.

Becker, J. T., & Jaffe, J. H. (1984). Impaired memory for treatment-relevant information in inpatient men alcoholics. *Journal of Studies on Alcohol, 45,* 339–343.

Budde, D., Rounsaville, B., & Bryant, K. (1992). Inpatient and outpatient cocaine abusers: Clinical comparisons at intake and one-year follow-up. *Journal of Substance Abuse Treatment, 9,* 337–342.

Chaney, E. F. (1989). Social skills training. In R. K. Hester & W. R. Miller (Eds.), *Handbook of alcoholism treatment approaches* (pp. 206–221). New York: Pergamon Press.

Chaney, E. F., O'Leary, M. R., & Marlatt, G. A. (1978). Skill training with alcoholics. *Journal of Consulting and Clinical Psychology, 46,* 1092–1104.

Cole, S. G., Lehman, W. E., Cole, E. A., & Jones, A. (1981). Inpatient vs. outpatient treatment of alcohol and drug abusers. *American Journal of Drug and Alcohol Abuse, 8*(3), 329–345.

Collins, G. B. (1993). Contemporary issues in the treatment of alcohol dependence. *Psychiatric Clinics of North America, 16*(1), 33–48.

Cook, C. C. H. (1988). The Minnesota model in the management of drug and alcohol dependency: Miracle, method or myth? Part II. Evidence and conclusions. *British Journal of Addiction, 83,* 735–748.

Cooney, N. L., Kadden, R. M., Litt, M. D., & Getter, H. (1991). Matching alcoholics to coping skills or interactional therapies: Two-year follow-up results. *Journal of Consulting and Clinical Psychology, 59,* 598–601.

Dackis, C. A., & Gold, M. S. (1992). Psychiatric hospitals for treatment of dual diagnosis. In J. H. Lowinson, P. Ruiz, & R. B. Millman (Eds.), *Substance abuse: A comprehensive textbook* (2nd ed., pp. 467–485). Baltimore: Williams & Wilkins.

Geller, A. (1992). Rehabilitation programs and halfway houses. In J. H. Lowinson, P. Ruiz, & R. B. Millman (Eds.), *Substance abuse: A comprehensive textbook* (2nd ed., pp. 458–466). Baltimore: Williams & Wilkins.

Gold, M. S. (1992). Cocaine (and crack): Clinical aspects. In J. H. Lowinson, P. Ruiz, & R. B. Millman (Eds.), *Substance abuse: A comprehensive textbook* (2nd ed., pp. 205–221). Baltimore: Williams & Wilkins.

Graham, K., & Timney, C. B. (1990). Case management in addictions treatment. *Journal of Substance Abuse Treatment, 7*(3), 181–188.

Holder, H., Longabaugh, R., Miller, W. R., & Rubonis, A. V. (1991). The cost effectiveness of treatment for alcoholism: A first approximation. *Journal of Studies on Alcohol, 52*(6), 517–540.

Jones, S. L., Kanfer, R., & Lanyon, R. I. (1982). Skill training with alcoholics: A clinical extension. *Addictive Behaviors, 7,* 285–290.

Kadden, R. M., Carroll, K., Donovan, D., Cooney, N., Monti, P., Abrams, D., Litt, M., & Hester, R. (1992). *Cognitive-behavioral coping skills therapy manual: A clinical research guide for therapists treating individuals with alcohol abuse and dependence.* Rockville, MD: National Institute on Alcohol Abuse and Alcoholism.

Kadden, R. M., Cooney, N. L., Getter, H., & Litt, M. D. (1989). Matching alcoholics to coping skills or interactional therapies: Posttreatment results. *Journal of Consulting and Clinical Psychology, 57,* 698–704.

Kadden, R. M., & Kranzler, H. (1992). Alcohol and drug abuse treatment at the University of Connecticut Health Center. *British Journal of Addiction, 87,* 521–526.

Kadden, R. M., Litt, M. D., Cooney, N. L., & Busher, D. A. (1992). Relationship between role-play measures of coping skills and alcoholism treatment outcome. *Addictive Behaviors, 17,* 425–437.

Kadden, R. M., & Mauriello, I. J. (1991). Enhancing participation in substance abuse treatment using an incentive system. *Journal of Substance Abuse Treatment, 8,* 113–124.

Keso, L., & Salaspuro, M. (1990). Inpatient treatment of employed alcoholics: A randomized clinical trial on Hazelden-type and traditional treatment. *Alcoholism: Clinical and Experimental Research, 14,* 584–589.

Kissin, B., Platz, A., & Su, W. H. (1970). Social and psychological factors in the treatment of chronic alcoholism. *Journal of Psychiatric Research, 8,* 13–27.

LaPorte, D. J., McLellan, A. T., & MacGahan, J. A. (1980). Evaluation of combined treatment for alcohol and drug abusers: Importance of patient compatibility. In J. S. Madden, R. Walker, & W. H. Kenyon (Eds.), *Aspects of alcohol and drug dependence* (pp. 290–304). Bath, Great Britain: Pitman Medical.

Lindstrom, L. (1992). *Managing alcoholism: Matching clients to treatments.* New York: Oxford University Press.

Litt, M. D., Babor, T. F., DelBoca, F. K., Kadden, R. M., & Cooney, N. L. (1992). Types of alcoholics, II: Application of an empirically derived typology to treatment matching. *Archives of General Psychiatry, 49,* 609–614.

Longabaugh, R., Rubin, A., Malloy, P., Beattie, M., Clifford, P. R., & Noel, N. (1994). Drinking outcomes of alcohol abusers diagnosed as antisocial personality disorder. *Alcoholism: Clinical and Experimental Research, 18,* 778–785.

McCrady, B. S. (1982). Conjoint behavioral treatment of an alcoholic and his spouse: The case of Mr. and Mrs. D. In W. M. Hay & P. E. Nathan (Eds.), *Clinical case studies in the behavioral treatment of alcoholism* (pp. 127–156). New York: Plenum Press.

McLellan, A. T., Grissom, G. R., Brill, P., Durell, J., Metzger, D. S., & O'Brien, C. P. (1993). Private substance abuse treatments: Are some programs more effective than others? *Journal of Substance Abuse Treatment, 10,* 243–254.

McLellan, A. T., Luborsky, L., Woody, G. E., & O'Brien, C. P. (1980). An improved diagnostic evaluation instrument for substance abuse patients: The Addiction Severity Index. *Journal of Nervous and Mental Disease, 168,* 26–33.

McLellan, A. T., Luborsky, L., Woody, G. E., O'Brien, C. P., & Druley, K. A. (1983). Predicting response to alcohol and drug abuse treatments: The role of psychiatric severity. *Archives of General Psychiatry, 40,* 620–625.

McLellan, A. T., Woody, G. E., Luborsky, L., O'Brien, C. P., & Druley, K. A. (1983). Increased effectiveness of substance abuse treatment: A prospective study of patient-treatment "matching." *Journal of Nervous and Mental Disease, 171,* 597–605.

Meyer, R. E. (1986). How to understand the relationship between psychopathology and addictive disorders: Another example of the chicken and the egg. In R. E. Meyer (Ed.), *Psychopathology and addictive disorders* (pp. 3–16). New York: Guilford Press.

Miller, W. R., & Hester, R. K. (1986). Inpatient alcoholism treatment. *American Psychologist, 41*(7), 794–805.

Miller, W. R., & Marlatt, G. A. (1984). *Manual for the Comprehensive Drinker Profile.* Odessa, FL: Psychological Assessment Resources.

Miller, W. R., & Rollnick, S. (1991). *Motivational interviewing: Preparing people to change addictive behavior.* New York: Guilford Press.

Monti, P. M., Abrams, D. B., Kadden, R. M., & Cooney, N. L. (1989). *Treating alcohol dependence: A coping skills training guide.* New York: Guilford Press.

Nace, E. P. (1987). *The treatment of alcoholism.* New York: Bruner/Mazel.

National Institute on Alcohol Abuse and Alcoholism (1987). *Sixth special report to the U.S. Congress on alcohol and health.* Rockville, MD: Author.

O'Brien, C. P., Alterman, A., Childress, A. R., & McLellan, A. T. (1992). Developing and evaluating new treatments for alcoholism and cocaine dependence. In M. Galanter (Ed.), *Recent developments in alcoholism. Vol. 10. alcohol and cocaine: Similarities and differences* (pp. 303–325). New York: Plenum Press.

Oei, T. P. S., & Jackson, P. (1980). Long-term effects of group and individual social skills training with alcoholics. *Addictive Behaviors, 5,* 129–136.

O'Farrell, T. J., & Cowles, K. S. (1989). Marital and family therapy. In R. K. Hester & W. R. Miller (Eds.), *Handbook of alcoholism treatment approaches* (pp. 183–205). New York: Pergamon Press.

Schuckit, M. A., & Monteiro, M. G. (1988). Alcoholism, anxiety and depression. *British Journal of Addiction, 83,* 1373–1380.

Walker, R. (1992). Substance abuse and cluster B disorders: II. Treatment recommendations. *Journal of Psychoactive Drugs, 24*(3), 233–241.

Walsh, D. C., Hingson, R. W., Merrigan, D. M., Levenson, S. M., Cupples, A., Heeren, T., Coffman, G. A., Becker, C. A., Barker, T. A., Hamilton, S. K., McGuire, T. G., & Kelly, C. A. (1991). A randomized trial of treatment options for alcohol-abusing workers. *New England Journal of Medicine, 325*(11), 775–782.

Welte, J. W., Hynes, G., Sokolow, L., & Lyons, J. P. (1981). Effect of length of stay in inpatient alcoholism treatment on outcome. *Journal of Studies on Alcohol, 42,* 483–491.

SUGGESTED READINGS

Geller, A. (1992). Rehabilitation programs and halfway houses. In J. H. Lowinson, P. Ruiz, & R. B. Millman (Eds.), *Substance abuse: A comprehensive textbook* (2nd ed., pp. 458–466). Baltimore: Williams & Wilkins.

Kadden, R. M., & Mauriello, I. J. (1991). Enhancing participation in substance abuse treatment using an incentive system. *Journal of Substance Abuse Treatment, 8,* 113–124.

Monti, P. M., Abrams, D. B., Kadden, R. M., & Cooney, N. L. (1989). *Treating alcohol dependence: A coping skills training guide.* New York: Guilford Press.

Walker, R. (1992). Substance abuse and cluster B disorders: II. Treatment recommendations. *Journal of Psychoactive Drugs, 24*(3), 233–241.

17

Treating Chemical-Dependent
Couples and Families

DOUGLAS STELLATO-KABAT
JOANNA STELLATO-KABAT
JAMES GARRETT

INTRODUCTION

This chapter teaches mental health clinicians to use a combined strategic
and structural marital and family therapy approach in treating chemical
dependence. We provide a description of basic principles of marital, family, and social system chemical-dependence dynamics; offer case illus-
trations; delineate practice guidelines; and give suggestions for evaluation
and referral.

Chemical dependence is a disease, like many other illnesses, that
flourishes within a social context. Multiple generations of chemical dependence result in the development of a set of family and social system
adaptations that are the primary focus of the disease and the primary focus of treatment and recovery. The disease is expressed through the complex interrelationship of the individual, family, and social network:
Chemical dependence is a biopsychosocial disorder whose occurrence,
longevity, severity, and response to treatment are largely influenced by
familial and social factors. Biology determines such aspects of the illness

as tolerance, withdrawal patterns, intensity of craving, and so forth, but the familial and social aspects largely determine its course and response to treatment.

In the absence of awareness of disease, families have always adapted to illnesses, as best they could, integrating sickness into everyday life (Rothman, 1994). In the case of chemical dependence, this adaptation is reflected in the integration into family life of routine abusive drinking and drugging and the family's accompanying patterns of denial, minimization, and rationalization. The popular term *codependence* reflects the family's adaptive strategy for maintaining optimal functioning.

A brief example illustrates these points: Sam, the adult child of an alcoholic, loans his son, Peter, the money to pay Peter's $20,000 cocaine debt. With little discussion, Sam and Peter agree that "to protect mom," the payment, and Peter's cocaine use, will be kept secret. Peter repays the loan, and as part of the father–son agreement, he stops his cocaine use. Peter has learned a number of lessons: that he can stop cocaine "whenever I want to," that husbands "protect" wives (who, after all, expect such protection) from knowing about serious family problems (this family theme has most likely been present for a number of generations), and that he should keep his complicated feelings to himself, as his father does. Five years later, when the Peter and his wife Judy have difficulties in their marriage, Peter resumes cocaine use and has difficulty using adult problem-solving skills: Chemical dependence has taken root in the marriage.

Peter's chemical-dependence problem may be effectively resolved by including his family of origin (and probably Judy's as well) in the treatment program. Peter, like most chemical dependents, is remarkably faithful to his family and its values: to develop a healthy, "clean and sober" marriage he has to change his secretive, unduly protective attitude toward Judy, as well as his belief that emotional sharing is a sign of male weakness. To truly recover, Peter must become a "family pioneer," a family member who develops new behaviors and attitudes, not only in recovery from his chemical dependence but also in the level of intimacy and style of marriage that support his recovery.

If Peter is treated individually, he may do well for a time but then will most likely relapse. Medication will probably prove of little long-term value. He will not seem to "get it" when he goes to self-help meetings. He may be labeled resistant, particularly if he relapses more than once. Peter's motivation may be missed because his loyalty makes him look ambivalent about recovery. If, on the other hand, his family is involved in treatment, and Peter's profound sense of loyalty is honored, he is likely to do well in recovery.

Using the family approach results in brief, more effective treatment outcomes that are better for clients and less expensive for payers.

THEORY AND PRACTICE RECOMMENDATIONS

The Family Is the Unit of Treatment

Our first principle is that *the family, broadly defined, is the unit of treatment, and that loyalty and love are the key systemic motivators for recovery. Therefore, we seek strategically to mobilize the recovery process within the social system, including the multigenerational family, as well as friends, and other involved professionals.* In brief, family and friends are more powerful than the therapist and the treatment system (Stanton, 1994).

There is an ongoing and constant interplay of all aspects of a chemical dependent's family and social life that reinforces or deters chemical use (Steinglass, Bennett, Wolin, & Reiss, 1987). The behavior of each important person in the chemical dependent's social sphere has an impact on chemical use: Parents, friends, spouses, lovers, and other significant persons communicate attitudes regarding the use of mood-altering chemicals. The chemical dependent assigns significance to these attitudes according to the importance he/she attaches, consciously and unconsciously, to the person. The therapist must be aware of these interpersonal pressures and be prepared to address them in an effective, therapeutic manner.

It is difficult (although not impossible) for people to change behaviors, such as drinking or drug use, that they, and their family and friends, view as adaptive, perhaps even essential, to living life well. This is true not only for the chemical dependent, who in recovery can become socially and familiarly isolated, but for spouses or significant others as well: Codependence recovery involves the same systemic dilemmas.

Loyalty, the unspoken system of debts and credits within the family and social system, is the driving force in creating recovery dilemmas. Loyalty conflicts often involve intergenerational differences between the family of origin and the family of creation. These conflicts may be expressed in difficulties maintaining abstinence, and are often a reflection of enmeshed parent–adult child relationships (Stanton, Todd, & Associates, 1982). To resolve loyalty dilemmas, it is essential to attend to the role of key hierarchical figures. These figures, typically parents or grandparents, are usually absent from the treatment room but play a significant role in the recovery process. For example, Joe, an alcohol-dependent man, will tend to have a serious loyalty conflict in accepting his alcoholism and in remaining consistently abstinent if his father is also alcohol dependent and continues to drink. Understandable and normal pressure to remain abstinent from Joe's spouse, Sandra, will compound this dilemma:

- If it is necessary for Joe to label himself as alcoholic and if "alcoholism" is perceived by his family of origin in negative terms, how is Joe to accept his alcoholism while remaining respectful to his father?

- If Joe remains loyal to his father, how is he also to remain loyal to Sandra by meeting her demand for abstinence and recovery?
- If Sandra comes from an alcoholic family, how are the loyalty conflicts for both of them to be resolved?
- How do Joe and Sandra's children deal with their grandparents' alcoholism?

The clinician must deal with the loyalty dilemmas presented by this common situation: The question for Joe, the good son, is how to respect his father while pursing a different, even superficially contradictory, life path. To address this problem, we find that a wide range of therapy interventions are essential: Individual therapy helps develop awareness and respect for one's own values (Vaillant, 1981) whereas couples work promotes fidelity to the current relationship, enhances communication, increases intimacy, and allows for conflict resolution and integration of life cycle tasks (Minuchin, Montalvo, Guerney, Russman, & Schumer, 1967; Haley, 1990; Kaufman & Kaufman, 1979; O'Farrell & Cowles, 1989; Moos & Moos, 1984). Extended family treatment supports the development of allegiance to the healthiest of family values, and social network treatment, which relies on working with all the significant persons in the family's life, encourages systemic constancy to the goal of recovery (Stanton et al., 1982; Stanton, 1994; Galanter, 1993). By consistently addressing loyalty themes, systemic dilemmas at each level of treatment are addressed and momentum toward recovery increases.

Practice Guidelines

1. Loyalty conflicts must be recognized and honored as acts of love. The clinician will quickly become aware of loyalty issues and dilemmas regarding chemical use when asking members of the system to cooperate in developing a "clean and sober" home environment. This essential first step in treatment often brings out family objections: A family with a recovering alcoholic member, which insists on keeping alcohol in the home, usually has other active chemical dependents in addition to the identified alcoholic. Expressions of uncertainty regarding developing an alcohol- and drug-free home also usually reflect family chemical abuse patterns. Similarly, discussion of the disease concept will often elicit objections from loyal family members who feel the label of chemical dependence is an accusation. In such situations, it is essential for the clinician to respectfully note the family's desire to address the issue and the difficulty of resolving a problem (i.e., chemical abuse) they may have previously perceived as a normal aspect of living. The family must be encouraged to discuss the full complexity of their situation.

2. Ambivalence, commonly labeled resistance, should be treated as a normal and healthy part of the early stage of recovery, and as a reflection of social systemic loyalties and tensions (Prochaska & DiClemente, 1983, 1986). The therapist should discuss the potential negative impact of abstinence on a wide range of social and familial relationships. It is essential to search for, find, and accept ambivalence: An unambivalent chemical-dependent client is a superficial, compliant client. Honor ambivalence as an expression of honesty. Broaden ambivalence to include the conflicted feelings of everybody in the chemical dependent social system.

3. In working with addicted families, the genogram or family tree will provide a map showing the therapist and family the pathways along which loyalties are expressed. The genogram demonstrates potential assets and liabilities in the client system and the likely direction of the most important interventions (McGoldrick, 1985). A transitional map, developed from the genogram, is useful in determining *why* treatment is occurring *now* and how previous loyalty conflicts have been resolved (J. Landau-Stanton, personal communication, September 7, 1990; Stanton, 1992). To develop a transitional map, add to the basic genogram other significant members of the client's social circle, including friends and neighbors, employers, fellow workers, religious/spiritual figures, and so forth. Adding a time line, a listing of relevant dates in the family's history, completes the transitional map and allows the clinician and family to understand how problems have been resolved and loyalties expressed at crucial times in the past (Landau-Stanton, 1988; Stanton, 1992). A transitional map not only shows relationships but also expresses a family's beliefs about men, women, children, marriage, chemical use, working, sex, and other key issues: It provides a powerful "family album" of three or four generations and allows exploration of central issues of recovery. Confused hierarchical relationships stand out and repeated marital and relationship patterns become obvious.

4. The statement of therapeutic reframe, developed by the clinician and the family, supports family recovery, resolves loyalty conflicts, and allows the family to label themselves as in a positive manner. The therapeutic reframe is an essential therapy tool, which answers the question, *Why* is the family *now* ready for recovery?" (Stanton, 1992). The case of "Susan" and "Richard" illustrates the use of reframes.

Susan, a 33-year-old historian, described seven generations of documented family alcoholism. She reported that her father and all five of her siblings drank alcoholically. Every major family event, decision, or problem-solving opportunity appeared to be associated with drinking.

Susan and her husband Richard, a 34-year-old biologist, who also grew up in an alcoholic family, reported that their relationship pattern was strongly associated with drinking. They were most open and direct with each other "when we've had a few drinks." After getting to know the therapist, they also mentioned a strong association between drinking and sexual activity; however, both expressed confidence that "we can have fun in bed even if we're not drunk." They did, however, express ambivalence regarding recovery: Richard claimed the problem "isn't that bad . . . at least it's not like my grandfather's drinking" and Susan asserted "my drinking has been a problem, but it's not that big a deal." As they began the recovery process, an initial period of pleasure in their ability to remain abstinent for an extended period was gradually replaced by a sense of emptiness and loss that surprised them.

Throughout their 4-year marriage, Susan and Richard reported feeling regularly caught in painful, difficult to resolve conflict, only alleviated by heavy drinking or intense professional work. Their families however, took delight in Richard and Susan's obvious personal and professional success.

Susan and Richard at first felt profoundly disloyal in calling themselves alcoholics: They preferred to say their drinking had "gotten out of hand" and described their treatment as "education." After a relapse, which the therapist had predicted 2 weeks previously, they expressed willingness to "do something different." At their therapist's urging, they each approached various family members whom they believed had stopped drinking. When two of Richard's brothers and Susan's maternal aunt told of their recovery, the couple found they were able, for the first time, to talk directly of their conflicts regarding the term *alcoholism* and its application to their families. Richard and Susan identify this as the point when "recovery really began."

This case illustrates that loyalty to the family of origin is often intense, that the resulting ambivalence about abstinence is expressed in the form of denial and minimization, and that recovery can only fully begin when a pathway to resolving loyalty conflicts becomes apparent. In this case, the pathway to recovery is expressed in the therapeutic reframe gradually developed by the therapist and Susan and Richard:

> Our recovery is a reflection of our commitment to becoming loving, intimate partners. Our sobriety, and our marital and professional success is an act of loyalty to the best aspects of our mutual family heritage. For us drinking isn't the issue, living our lives well is what we're interested in.

Systemic Adaptation and the Use–Abstinence Cycle

Susan and Richard's situation also illustrates our second principle: *Systemic adaptation includes a use–abstinence cycle (a broad adaptation of Steinglass's wet–dry alcoholism cycle) which may last days, weeks, months or years, and is often part of a multigenerational pattern* (Steinglass et al., 1987). Within the cycle, each intimate family member has a well defined and predictable role.

Susan and Richard's use–abstinence cycle is particularly clear: When they began treatment, they reported, as is common in early recovery, a preoccupation with basic abstinence (rather than focusing on living a healthy, chemical-free couple life, of which, abstinence was simply a necessary first condition). The couple's preoccupation with avoiding alcohol was ultimately unsatisfactory, however, as in Susan's words "it felt like we were always a little distant and superficial with each other." The pattern changed to increasing distance and work preoccupation as the couple subtly felt themselves building up to drinking ("budding" in 12-Step parlance). When they relapsed, they had intimate discussions followed by "great sex."

Susan and Richard changed again, however, as they continued to drink. There was a gradual but progressive deterioration in individual and couple functioning: Worn out and dispirited, they came back for counseling, claiming they wanted only to learn how to stay "dry" and stable. Only when Richard's brothers pointed out how happy and "sexy" they had seemed when they started drinking did they begin to seriously look at their use–abstinence cycle.

Once treatment has begun, the alert clinician will have a good likelihood of seeing all phases of the use–abstinence cycle. In this sense, relapse (i.e., resumption of old behaviors, whether chemical use or "enabling") not only communicates a more complete picture of the illness but also offers a window into the disease process. A chemical dependent or codependent who repeatedly relapses may be asking the clinician to understand the dynamics of his–her cycle, so as to allow a recovery process that includes opportunities for problem resolution that are otherwise only available during periods of use (McDowell & York, 1992).

Practice Guidelines

1. Discuss the use–abstinence cycle in detail. The clinician should get permission to ask intimate, probing questions: Honor ambivalence by asking families to "say if you want to keep certain things private and not discuss them." If the clinician finds determined resistance to discussing the role of alcohol or drugs in the family, he/she should ask the family how they want to proceed. Although the clinician may go around a few times with this discussion, "resistance" regarding family alcohol and drug use patterns can be talked through. This process helps clients to determine what has brought them into treatment and allows the clinician to develop a frame for recovery.

For many couples, loyalty conflicts and shame regarding use–abstinence cycle issues can be successfully addressed by labeling "the disease" as the causal factor and helping the couple to understand the commonality of difficulties among most recovering couples. Blaming is a common theme for couples, especially at the beginning of treatment, and may also be labeled a part of the disease, one that can play a particularly significant role in the use–abstinence cycle. Developing a frame for recovery and redefining the use–abstinence cycle promotes a feeling of safety within the family session: The therapist "rebalances" the system, lifting the burden of unnecessary guilt from the chemical dependent, removing the mantle of "innocent" suffering from the codependent spouse, promoting flexibility of marital functioning, and allowing sober discussion of treatment issues. Therapy sets the tone for "becoming a family in recovery."

2. Evaluating how ingrained the use–abstinence cycle is in family and couple functioning will help determine whether the marriage and family therapist refers a chemical-dependent family to a substance abuse clinic. The use–abstinence cycle may involve numerous key functions related to family identity, rituals, problem solving, time structuring, parenting, sexuality, loss/grief, openness with feelings, power/authority, flexibility, and life-cycle tasks. Understanding the significance and predictability of the cycle in the family's routine functioning helps the clinician to anticipate for the future what has happened repeatedly in the past, and to use this to motivate change.

3. Understanding the use–abstinence cycle will also give the clinician insight into potential mental health problems. If the client has repeated episodes of relapse or extraordinary moodiness while abstinent, it is well to evaluate for a coexistent depressive or anxiety disorder. Clients who are dysthymic often have periods of abstinence followed by periods of relapse and depression. Depression may go unrecognized because the client and his/her family are often deeply troubled by the return to drinking or drugging. Families adapt to depression in similar ways, as they do to chemical dependence, and may not make any useful distinction between the two. The family's judgmental attitudes and moralistic beliefs ("if he only tried harder," etc.) may even interfere with accurately assessing the situation.

4. Sexuality is a particular concern for many clients and is commonly involved in the use–abstinence cycle. An educational approach to sexuality is often initially helpful, providing basic information, which many persons growing up in a chemical-dependent family of origin may never have received, and encouraging direct therapeutic discussions about sexual issues. Because chemical dependence and initial abstinence tend to profoundly impact sexual functioning, it is also important to educate and to encourage realistic expectations regarding sexuality. Sexual issues, and particularly sexual abuse, are highly charged subjects, and intense loyalty conflicts frequently appear. In Susan and Richard's case, the therapist's clarity and directness regarding sexual matters allowed the couple to openly discuss the role of alcohol in their intimate life.

Individual Diagnosis and Treatment
of Multigenerational Chemical Dependence

Our third principle is that *attention to multigenerational chemical-dependence patterns assures accurate individual diagnosis and appropriate treatment.* Absent a multigenerational family assessment, diagnoses of chemical dependence or codependence can be missed altogether, or such diagnoses can mislead, underemphasizing the central role of family chemical-dependence dynamics. Because alcohol and drug problems are usually not the presenting problem, routine screening for chemical dependence is essential: Substance abuse is not only the most common mental health disorder (26.6% of the adult U.S. population reports a current or past history of abuse or dependence) (Kessler et al., 1994), but also, up to 60% of couples seeking treatment for marital–family–relationship difficulties have a substance abuse problem (O'Farrell & Cowles, 1989).

A codependent spouse or lover may present for treatment with complaints of couple dissatisfaction, or with anxiety or depression; unless the alert clinician asks about chemical use within the family, however, the underlying and essential systemic chemical dependence problem may never be addressed. If anxiety or depression is treated in a codependent without also treating the systemic chemical dependence, positive results are often short-lived and may result in the codependent eventually feeling sicker, more despondent, and increasingly self-blaming. This problem is also common in female chemical dependents, who may come to treatment due to self-esteem problems or difficulties from "always choosing the wrong man," and often fail to reveal the role of chemicals in their difficulties.

A thorough family assessment also allows the family and social network to have input in determining the initial level of care necessary for the chemical dependent to establish abstinence. Table 17.1 illustrates the various options and tasks facing the therapist and family in achieving this goal. The time spent discussing family concerns, questions, opposition, and fears in the level of care determination process sets the groundwork for successful treatment. A typical network or family discussion regarding the level of addiction care required will bring up issues with profound systemic implications:

- Discussions of inpatient versus outpatient care will lead to questions about who is sick and who is to be treated (Washton, 1987);
- Discussions of whether living arrangements are supportive of recovery will lead to how others in the family and social system use alcohol and drugs;
- Discussions of motivation for recovery will lead directly to family loyalty concerns; and

TABLE 17.1. Options and Tasks Necessary to Achieving Abstinence

Level of formal chemical-dependence care	Indicators for this level of chemical-dependence care	Marriage and family therapist's tasks regarding addicted person	Marriage and family therapist's tasks with partner, family, and social network
Acute care inpatient detox (hospital care in a chemical-dependence-specific detoxification unit)	Physical withdrawal symptoms, risk of seizures or other physical problems, unstable living environment	• Arrange for evaluation of physical danger of withdrawal • Arrange for hospital admission	• Identify fear, anger, frustration or skepticism regarding hospitalization and short-term nature of detoxification • Get commitment to make the home alcohol- and drug-free for 6 months • Coordinate logistics for hospital admission • Educate regarding the necessity for detoxification • Obtain commitment for support of initial abstinence • Plan next meeting of family and support group either on the detoxification unit or the day the client is discharged from hospital
Ambulatory detox (outpatient-based care, utilizing medically supervised psychopharmaceutical and/or acupuncture detoxification [Smith & Khan, 1988; Bullock, Culliton, & Orlander, 1989])	High motivation to stop using, strong support network, stable living environment, medical clearance	• Arrange evaluation for appropriateness for ambulatory detox • Understand the protocol for ambulatory detox • Assure adequate resources for ambulatory detox	• Determine depth of support for ambulatory detox • Obtain support for the procedure (if unable to gain such support, advise inpatient detox) • Educate about the process and dangers, and the roles of the partner, family and network in this procedure • Develop emergency steps if client continues to use • Develop a plan so the client is not alone for any significant period of time during the detox procedure • Educate about the importance of establishing initial abstinence and the role of support during this time • Develop plan to take client to self-help meetings *(cont.)*

323

TABLE 17.1. *Cont.*

Level of formal chemical-dependence care	Indicators for this level of chemical-dependence care	Marriage and family therapist's tasks regarding addicted person	Marriage and family therapist's tasks with partner, family, and social network
Residential rehab (typically a 14- to 28-day inpatient treatment program, following detox)	Needs time away from current environment in order to stabilize, continuous relapses while in outpatient treatment, despite family work, psychiatric assessment, and treatment	• Utilize the referral within a strategic frame, to avoid undue focus on the chemical-dependent person	• Educate partner, family, and network about the limited role of residential treatment • Get commitment from partner, family, and extended family to engage in psychoeducational treatment • Evaluate use–abstinence cycle with the couple and integrate it into treatment planning • Inventory the pattern of systemic behaviors and beliefs that have led to residential treatment
Outpatient rehab (usually 4 to 5 full days or evenings for a minimum of 4 weeks)	Able to abstain from use only when seen on a daily basis	• Make referral to chemical-dependence treatment facility which has this level of care • Coordinate with addiction care clinicians to assure clinical consistency	• Refer family and/or partner to family education component of addiction treatment (most outpatient rehab programs have a distinct family program) • Educate family that change occurs more quickly with the chemical-dependent person than with the partner, and this can lead to spousal resentment and premature termination of treatment • Build couple therapy into the treatment plan, taking into account the anger, loss of trust, and fears that are normal at the early stage of recovery • Encourage family and support group to participate in those portions of treatment that include psychoeducational material about chemical dependence • Discuss the importance of self-help

Level of care	Criteria		
Outpatient counseling (addiction-specific counseling two or fewer times per week)	Demonstrates ability to establish abstinence with minimal treatment or is the only option client will agree to at the initial stage of treatment	• Engage client with abstinence agreement and monitor ability to remain abstinent • Build in agreement that if stable abstinence is not achieved at this level of care, couple agree to enter more intensive treatment	• Get commitment from partner, family, and network to participate in counseling • Utilizing all involved, develop concrete and specific abstinence support plan, including self-help group attendance • Develop commitment from support group for client to enter a more intense level of treatment if abstinence is not maintained • Encourage family attendance at self-help meetings such as Al-Anon, Nar-Anon, Codependents Anonymous, etc.
Aftercare (supportive group counseling on a weekly, or less often, basis)	Maintains 6 + months of stable recovery	• Provide couple and family therapy in conjunction with aftercare	• Renegotiate treatment goals for the couple • Involve children in treatment, as appropriate • Educate couple regarding the phases of recovery and what they can expect, given their functioning in the use–abstinence cycle • Determine whether the goals of the support group have been accomplished • End meeting with them or renegotiate treatment goals for future meetings • Educate about the next 6 months of recovery, so some of the surprises can be eliminated
Self-help meetings	Recommended for use with all levels of care	• Familiarity with self-help meetings • Have self-help literature in office • Encourage attendance at meetings	• Weave self-help philosophy, slogans, and meeting topics into couples' treatment • Encourage each family member to attend self-help meeting through all phases of treatment

• discussions of how trust can be restored when previous treatment has been unsuccessful, will lead to the issue of *why now* the family is ready to make changes.

Practice Guidelines

1. Routine questioning about the role of alcohol and drugs in family and social functioning is essential to thorough diagnostic assessment. Explore when, where, and how much alcohol and drugs are used by nuclear and extended family, and friends: Understand the role of alcohol and drugs within a three- or four-generation framework. Families with a history of alcohol and drug problems often produce offspring who are alcohol- and drug-free but whose loyalty is expressed in an obsessive and unhealthy preoccupation with chemicals (i.e., parents with a clean and sober teen may still routinely search the adolescent's room and clothes for evidence of chemical use) and whose behavior can actually contribute to rebellious adolescent experimentation with chemicals.

2. Traditional chemical dependency terms such as *codependent* and *alcoholic personality,* derived from an individual approach to chemical dependence, should be applied only with an understanding of their systemic meaning. Codependent family members should be honored for their willingness to adapt to the chronic, invasive nature of chemical dependency. In the early stage of chemical dependence, classically codependent behavior, such as taking over functions once performed by the chemical dependent, may be extremely adaptive for continued family functioning. The codependent who feels honored and respected by the clinician will more easily see that his/her attempt to maintain the family's functioning supports continued chemical use instead and undermines healthy family behavior. Denial of personal problems by the codependent when he/she first presents for treatment is often entrenched: Such codependent behavior must be treated as an act of loyalty and will only change if treated from a position of respect. Similarly, the "alcoholic personality" is an artifact of the biopsychosocial nature of the illness and should never be an object of treatment in and of itself.

3. Once family and network concerns regarding the level of treatment have been verbalized, the next step for the therapist is to stretch the polarities that have been discussed. The goal is to develop a supportive consensus among the involved family and network members, even though many concerns may be unaddressed. The time spent with the family in this process honors their history and engages them for the longer-term process of systemic change. The therapist's observations of intergenerational transitional conflicts, loyalties, roles, problem-solving behavior, and intrusiveness of the substance use into family functioning facilitate systemically based treatment planning.

4. Treatment goals must include family and social systemic as well

as individual outcome expectations. Thus, routine treatment goals might include not only abstinence by the chemical dependent (verified, as needed, by urine screens) and focus on self by the codependent but also the following:

- Enhanced functioning by both the chemical dependent and significant others, as reflected, for example, in improved marital and family problem solving and increased affection.
- Development of new "clean and sober" family and social systemic coping mechanisms with sufficient adaptational value to effectively resist the pull toward returning to chemical use for its stabilization effects. This may involve superficially minor changes at key leverage points: new family coping mechanisms might include changes in family rituals; new social system coping mechanisms might include involvement with self-help or religious groups.
- Development of a healthy frame of reference regarding personal and family recovery.

Despite the complexities of treating the chemical-dependent couple and family, treatment should be brief and directive. It is essential for the clinician and family to agree clearly and specifically, in writing, what the treatment goals are and to stop clinical treatment when these goals are met.

Systemic Recovery and Family Life-Cycle Stages

Our fourth principle is that *systemic recovery occurs consistent with family life-cycle stages.* Treatment must take into account each life stage; systemic considerations determine the outcome of the interaction of chemical dependence with developmental dramas (Haley, 1977).

For each family, the therapist must take into account the life-cycle stage, the family's related tasks, and the likely impact of chemical dependence (while keeping in mind cultural, ethnic, economic, and sexual orientation differences). Often, recovering individuals will comment, "I never had a family role model when I was growing up," and look to the therapist for guidance on how to address developmental tasks. When both persons in a recovering couple come from alcoholic or drug-dependent families, the couple often reports a lack of direction in how to soberly resolve "normal" life-cycle problems. Therapeutic attention to life-cycle issues ensures that family identity is focused on real and current concerns, so that chemical dependence need no longer be the primary organizational factor in family life. This applies not only to the newly recovering couple but also to couples and families with many years of recovery, who remain fixated on a narrow vision of "working my program" (i.e., going to meetings every day and living a social life entirely built around 12-Step involvement) rather than living a full life today. Attention to life-cycle tasks promotes treatment focus and gives families hope by allowing them to solve problems in a way that supports living life fully.

Here are some typical life-cycle issues faced by family therapists:

1. For many couples, chemical dependence is involved in the relationship from the beginning. *In the first stage of family life, when romance and courting are emphasized and rules of intimacy are established, chemical dependence often invades connectedness: Intimacy may be primarily facilitated by chemical use.* For such couples, treatment needs to focus on developing sober intimacy skills as a core recovery process. Primary issues for attention will be helping the newly recovering couple to individuate from their families of origin. Sex education may be an essential component of treatment for such couples. Richard and Susan's difficulties (see case discussed earlier) reflect the basic intimacy issues involved in this stage of their marriage. They readily reported using alcohol to deal with each stage of the relationship: Romance and courtship were marked by one basic family of origin "rule"—drinking leads to love and emotional and physical intimacy. Their initial couple identity was flawed by this "rule," so they felt increasing emotional distance and "bareness," and both became more married to work than to each other.

Susan and Richard could not resolve this conflict on their own, as all their attempts led only to an endless repetition of their abstinence–use cycle. If this couple were not treated at this time, their intimacy would continue to be mediated by alcohol; only short-term and marginally effective solutions would probably be developed. The distortions in the couple relationship would grow deeper over time, and the couple would increasingly solidify an alcoholic identity (Steinglass et al., 1987).

2. Other couples describe the impact of chemical dependency in terms of the *early marriage issues of defining couple identity, developing rules for daily living, boundaries definitions, and conflict resolution skills.* Such couples often come to treatment presenting issues of infidelity, inability to resolve conflict, and overinvolvement with family of origin The therapist needs to help such couples focus on their couple identity and to develop rules for their relationship.

3. The early years with children will also tend to have their own characteristic tasks and common disease impacts. *Alcohol and drug dependence may interfere with the couple's need to define their priorities regarding child care, work, intimacy, and the degree to which they are child focused.* When chemical use invades these areas of functioning, the couple will commonly come in with problems of unduly rigid role definitions, inability to effectively discipline children, and, often, problems with children's bedtimes. Couples treatment needs to focus on helping such couples develop a balance among their family tasks, define how they will address their children's needs, and develop friendships with, and support from, peers in similar family life stages.

4. As the years with children progress, the impact of chemical dependence is expressed in the family's difficulty in addressing family identity issues related to children's school and homework behavior and the increasing need to address the individual needs of each family member. Family treatment must take into account the need to develop consistent, supportive family routines, encouraging individual interests while maintaining the parental hierarchy.

5. Finally, the older adult years and retirement years also have their own set of life tasks and specific areas of potential focus regarding the impact of chemical dependence. A life-cycle focus assures that the needs of a retired, African American couple in their sixties, who have three grown children, and seven grandchildren, are not, somehow, lumped into a narrow "disease concept" model of recovery based on the needs of a prototypical 45-year-old married, white male.

At every phase of life, chemical dependence interfaces with life-cycle issues. Therefore, life-cycle issues determine, to a considerable degree, the course of recovery.

Practice Guidelines

1. A focus on family life-cycle stages will guide the therapist to the appropriate recovery tasks. Clients appreciate clarity and specificity of tasks. A direct discussion of life-cycle stages and tasks invites open discussion of complicated issues and gives clients permission to bring up related and often unstated issues. For example, many families in recovery report severe financial difficulties, which they believe interfere with life-cycle-stage task completion. Arranging for practical assistance and guidance in such cases can help move clients along their developmental paths.

2. Life-cycle related homework is an essential part of both the educational and psychotherapeutic process. Homework assignments should always take into account the family life cycle and stage of recovery. Homework may include reading assignments, self-help group attendance, couple behavioral assignments, or family-specific suggestions regarding new rituals, traditions, or problem-solving methods. Homework is a routine intervention that can be useful in and of itself and also provides information about couple and family problem-solving styles. Homework is usually prescribed in a straightforward manner and checked at the next session. If it is not accomplished, it should be reworked in order to make it more effective, or a more indirect approach should be taken.

Recovery and Episodes of Brief Treatment

Our fifth principle is that *recovery may involve a number of episodes of brief treatment.* Many chemical dependents do not develop stable abstinence at the time of their first treatment episode. Usually, the sicker the chemical-dependent person and the more chemical-abuse patterns have invaded the family and social system, the more complex recovery is likely to be. As a result, repeated episodes of treatment are common: As individuals, couples, families, and the greater social system change over time, and as the chemical-dependence disease process progresses, new opportunities for recovery commonly appear. If the therapist has assumed a positive attitude toward family and friends in the chemical-dependent system, there will often be more than one opportunity for treatment, and each opportunity will offer a greater likelihood of success than did the previous one. This is due to evolution of the social system, the increasing knowledge and experience of the identified patient(s) and therapist(s), and the increasing comfort of the social system members, honored and respected by the treatment clinician, and so more willing to trust the treatment process (Vaillant, 1987, p. 216).

Many clients keep coming back to treatment until they can effectively involve their family. For most alcohol- and drug-dependent persons it is when family are willing to be involved that recovery can fully blossom.

Practice Guidelines

1. Relapse should be anticipated as a normal aspect of chemical dependence treatment. The therapist may find it helpful, at times, to predict relapse. Relapse typically reflects unresolved systemic dilemmas and offers an opportunity for a greater level of systemic integration of recovery.

2. The longer the problem has existed and the more entrenched it is in the family system, the more likely the family will require a number of treatment episodes before recovery is successfully established. It takes time for families to "digest" the treatment process and incorporate recovery principles into everyday living. If a family is moving quickly to make changes, it may be helpful to slow them down in order to allay possible anxiety about the changes. This anxiety may not be felt directly but will be expressed within the system in the form of "resistance, denial, and minimization" by key family and social system participants.

3. Each treatment episode offers the opportunity to reach out to additional relevant persons in the clients' social system. The involvement of Susan's aunt and Richard's siblings illustrates this point: If we had not encouraged family involvement, we would have inadvertently reinforced loyalty conflicts, undermining the couple's attempt to develop sobriety and increased intimacy and reducing the systemic momentum for recovery. Sibling and auntly support gave Susan and Richard the support and encouragement they needed during the difficult early months of recovery.

Development of a "Seamless Treatment Web"

Finally, our sixth principle is that *the therapist respects and works with the natural support system, as well as the artificial addiction treatment system, developing a "seamless treatment web."* Life for active chemical dependents is often a seamless web of illness, in which they are surrounded by alcohol/drug-abusing or codependent family and friends and often live in neighborhoods, or work in job settings, supportive of chemical abuse. The chemical dependent expects inconsistent messages regarding recovery and looks for inconsistent behaviors from both professional helpers and the recovering community: The recovering addict often will remember the 1 counselor out of 50 who tells him, "It's OK to drink as long as you don't do crack," or "It's all right to smoke pot, as long as you don't drink." Similarly, inconsistencies in messages regarding addressing family recovery issues, guilt and secrecy, or how "dirty" urines are dealt with will be cited as proof that the family is right, that "you can't trust counselors," and that systemic loyalty is the only true guide to happiness. Because the chemical dependent will usually find inconsistencies and confusion among helpers, it is essential that every effort be made to address this problem:

- The natural support system of family and friends must be consistently involved as the primary recovery support system, and must consistently perceive support coming from the treatment professionals.
- The artificial support system of therapists, social service workers, criminal justice personnel, and others must establish and maintain mutually agreed-on goals and promote routine, clear communication and problem resolution.

Practice Guidelines

1. Evaluate the support system. The support system consists of all those persons and institutions that support healthy individual, couple, and family functioning. The support system consists of the natural support system of family, friends, employer, colleagues, etc., and the artificial support system of clinicians, other professionals, employee assistance programs, treatment programs, criminal justice, child welfare, and other specialized, paid support persons. The natural support system is what most people base their lives on; the artificial support system only becomes relevant when natural supports are inadequate. It is an essential goal of systemic substance abuse treatment to enhance the functioning of the natural support system (J. Landau-Stanton, personal communication, September 7, 1990). Enhancement can be accomplished by increasing existing supports for recovery, addressing areas of stress, and adding to the support system. Family treatment can increase support and reduce stress; self-help groups and new friendships can add to the system. It is particularly important to address the support system needs of more troubled chemical-dependent families: Such families tend to have little natural support and a great deal of "official" support in the form of probation, child

welfare, and other governmental service providers. It is essential to know the significance to the recovering family of each person in the support system. Participants' attitudes toward treatment and recovery and their willingness to participate in the treatment process help determine the value of the network. Expanding the natural support system helps move these families in the direction of sober, healthy, independent functioning.

2. Bring together the entire support system as early in the treatment process as possible. Bringing the support group together as part of the treatment planning process allows the clinician to see both the forces supporting abstinence and the tugs that are likely to impede recovery. The support network will address concerns and problems that the client may be reluctant to address alone or is totally unaware of. An outpatient setting allows for the maximum number of support network members to attend sessions and assist clients in achieving family treatment goals. This results in a better long-term outcome (Speck & Attneave, 1974).

3. Encourage the use of community self-help groups, including traditional groups such as Alcoholics Anonymous (AA) (Alcoholics Anonymous, 1976), and newer, nonspiritual programs, such as Rational Recovery (RR^SM) and Women for Sobriety. It is important for the therapist to know about these groups, have lists of group meetings available, and encourage attendance, at least for clients to "try it out." Such groups are important not only for the chemical dependent but for other family members as well: Al-Anon, the traditional program for those who love the alcoholic, has been joined in recent years by groups specific for those involved with drug addicts, as well as special groups for codependents, adult and young children of alcoholics and drug addicts, incest survivors, and so on. Traditional 12-Step groups, such as AA, Narcotics Anonymous, and Al-Anon, also offer participants the opportunity to establish sponsor (mentorlike) relationships, home group membership, and active involvement in helping the meeting function. Although not every client will find self-help attractive, the ones who do can be enormously helped. Furthermore, as in all other aspects of this disease, as clients and families change, so do attitudes toward self-help; the client who refuses AA involvement at one point in treatment may be quite enthusiastic at another. Finally, self-help not only provides significant additional support for recovery but also reduces demand on the professional part of the support system.

4. Ensure that addiction education and treatment are available for both the entire family and support network members. Most people, and especially chemical-dependent family members, know surprisingly little about this illness. The belief that chemical dependence is a shameful, morally reprehensible problem inhibits families from seeking treatment and makes entry into chemical dependence recovery more difficult. The disease concept gives every participant a clear, nonjudgmental recovery model while encouraging individual responsibility for self-care (Alcoholics Anonymous, 1976). Education in this conceptual framework is available in most addiction treatment centers.

Often a period of treatment for the codependent, preferably in a family program in a chemical dependence clinic, is essential before couples work can successfully begin. During the period of early abstinence, when the chemical-dependent person is creating a new habit of sobriety, the codependent is recovering a sense of self as distinct from the chemical dependence. In group treatment, he/she will typically rediscover self-worth and begin better habits of self-care while also learning to talk more directly and effectively to others.

Many couples prefer to start treatment separately in order to move away from previous habits with one another and to gain perspective on resentments and anger that developed during the dependence phase of their chemical use. Frequently, a period of 3 to 6 months of abstinence is necessary before both members of the couple have enough confidence in sobriety and new behaviors to face one another. It is essential, however, that treatment for both the chemical-dependent person and the codependent share the same approach, values, and philosophy: Clients must feel respected as members of a healing system to consistently act as such.

5. The marriage and family therapist must establish a clear and consistent relationship with local chemical-dependence clinics. A strong chemical-dependence clinic will offer an aggressive treatment approach from the first contact (Stark, Campbell, & Brinkerhoff, 1990). A smooth referral process, rapid assessment, and immediate entry into treatment will ensure that chemical dependence therapy can be routinely provided on an outpatient basis, and with a continual focus on systemic recovery. Such a focus can allow the marriage and family practitioner to remain actively involved in the treatment process, or available for continuing treatment once initial abstinence goals have been achieved. A conscientiously operated clinic will ensure that the referring clinician receives regular progress reports, participates in problem resolution case conferences, and feels invited to assist in the recovery process.

A well-established, community-oriented clinic will usually offer a range of specialized services that may not be readily available elsewhere. Special recovery programs for codependents, women, gays and lesbians, adolescents, adults molested as children, and other groups are often provided in larger clinics. It is particularly important to encourage clients to participate in chemical-dependence couples recovery groups (Gallant, Rich, Bey, & Terranova, 1970; McCrady, Stout, Noel, Abrams, & Fisher-Nelson, 1991; Noel, McGrady, Stout, & Fisher-Nelson, 1987). Such groups support the development of a larger and stronger support network by reducing couple isolation and encouraging the development of friendships, which quite often extend outside the treatment center.

8. Therapist should learn about the clinics to which they refer. They should take the time to visit chemical-dependence clinics in the area. Clients will benefit from treatment at these facilities and the therapist will benefit from referrals of clients who are stable in recovery and want more mental health-oriented therapy.

CONCLUSION

We have reviewed the dynamics of systemic treatment of family chemical dependency. We have proposed a brief treatment model emphasizing six principles:

1. The family, broadly defined, is the unit of treatment, and loyalty and love are the key systemic motivators for recovery. Therefore, we seek strategically to mobilize the recovery process within the social system, including the multigenerational family, as well as friends and other involved professionals.
2. Systemic adaptation includes a use–abstinence cycle (a broad adaptation of Steinglass's wet–dry alcoholism cycle) which may last days, weeks, months or years, and is often part of a multigenerational pattern.
3. Attention to multigenerational chemical-dependence patterns ensures accurate and effective individual diagnosis and appropriate treatment.
4. Systemic recovery occurs consistent with family life-cycle stages.
5. Recovery may involve a number of episodes of short-term care.
6. The therapist respects and works with the natural support system, as well as the artificial addiction treatment system, developing a "seamless treatment web."

Each of these treatment assumptions leads to particular therapy procedures, all of which emphasize positive reframing of individual and family chemical-dependence problems and which place chemical dependence within the larger concerns of the family. Applying these principles and practice procedures for treatment will help the marriage and family therapist to successfully treat chemical dependence.

REFERENCES

Alcoholics Anonymous. (1976). *The story of how many thousands of men and women have recovered from alcoholism* (3rd ed.). New York: Alcoholics Anonymous World Services.

Bullock, M. L., Culliton, P. D., & Orlander, R. T. (1989). Controlled trial of acupuncture for severe recidivist alcoholism, *Lancet 1*(8652), 1435–1439.

Galanter, M. (1993). *Network therapy for alcohol and drug abuse.* New York: Basic Books.

Gallant, D. N., Rich, A., Bey, E., & Terranova, L. (1970). Group psychotherapy with married couples. *Journal of Lousiana State Medical Society, 122,* 41–44.

Haley, J. (1977). *Problem solving therapy.* San Francisco: Jossey-Bass.

Haley, J. (1990). *Strategies of psychotherapy.* Rockville, MD: Triangle Press.

Kaufman, E., & Kaufman, P. N. (Eds.). (1979). *Family therapy of drug and alcohol abuse.* New York: Gardner Press.

Kessler, R. C., McGonagle, C. A., Zhao, S., Nelson, C., Hughes, M., Eshleman, S., Wittchen, H., & Kendler, K. (1994). Lifetime and 12-month prevalence of DSM-III-R psychiatric disorders in the United States. *Archives of General Psychiatry, 51,* 8–19.

Landau-Stanton, J. (1988). Competence, impermanence, and transitional mapping: A model for system consultation. In L. C. Wynne, S. H. McDaniel, & T. T. Weber (Eds.), *Systems consultation: A new perspective for family therapy* (p. 253–269). New York: Guilford Press.

McCrady, B. S., Stout, R., Noel, N., Abrams, D., & Fisher-Nelson, H. (1991). Effectiveness of three types of spouse-involved behavioral alcoholism treatment. *British Journal of Addiction, 86,* 1415–1424.

McDowell, T., & York, C. D. (1992). Family alcohol use: A progression model. *Journal of Strategic and Systemic Therapies, 11*(4), 19–26.

McGoldrick, M. (1985). *Genograms in family assessment.* New York: W. W. Norton.

Minuchin, S., Montalvo, B., Guerney, B. G., Russman, B. L., & Schumer, F. (1967). *Families of the slums.* New York: Basic Books.

Moos, R. H., & Moos, B. S. (1984). The process of recovery from alcoholism, III: Comparing functioning in families of alcoholics and matched control families. *Journal of Studies on Alcohol, 45,* 111–118.

Noel, N. E., McCrady, B. S., Stout, R. L., & Fisher-Nelson, H. (1987). Predictors of attrition from an outpatient alcoholism treatment program for couples. *Journal of Studies on Alcohol, 48,* 229–235.

O'Farrell, T. J., & Cowles, K. S. (1989). Marital and family therapy. In R. K. Hester & W. R. Miller (Eds.), *Handbook of alcoholism treatment approaches* (pp. 183–205). New York: Pergamon Press.

Prochaska, J. O., & DiClemente, C. C. (1983). Stages and processes of self-change of smoking: Towards an integrative model of change. *Journal of Consulting and Clinical Psychology, 51,* 390–395.

Prochaska, J. O., & DiClemente, C. C. (1986). Toward a comprehensive model of change. In W. R. Miller & N. Hester (Eds.), *Treating addictive behavior: Process of change* (pp. 3–27). New York: Plenum Press.

Rothman, S. (1994). *Living in the shadow of death.* New York: Basic Books.

Smith, M. O., & Khan, I. (1988). An acupuncture programme for the treatment of drug-addicted persons. *Bulletin on Narcotics, 11,* 35–41.

Speck, R., & Attneave, C. (1974). *Family networks.* New York: Vintage Books.

Stanton, M. D. (1994). *The ancestry: Its role in normality, nonshared environments and dysfunction.* Unpublished manuscript, University of Rochester.

Stanton, M. D. (1992). The time line and the "why now" question: A technique and rationale for therapy, training, organizational consultation and research. *Journal of Marital and Family Therapy, 18,* 331–343.

Stanton, M. D., Todd, T. C., & Associates. (1982). *The family therapy of drug abuse and addiction.* New York: Guilford Press.

Stark, M. J., Campbell, B. K., & Brinkerhoff, C. V. (1990). "Hello, may we help you?" A study of attrition prevention at the time of the first phone contact with substance-abusing clients. *American Journal of Drug and Alcohol Abuse, 16,* 67–76.

Steinglass, P., Bennett, L. A., Wolin, S. J., & Reiss, D. (1987). *The alcoholic family.* New York: Basic Books.

Vaillant, G. E. (1981). Dangers of psychotherapy in the treatment of alcoholism. In M. H. Bean, & N. E. Zinberg (Eds.), *Dynamic approaches to the understanding and treatment of alcoholism* (pp. 187–210). New York: Free Press.

Vaillant, G. E. (1987). *The natural history of alcoholism, causes, patterns, and paths to recovery.* Cambridge, MA: Harvard University Press.

Washton, A. M. (1987). Outpatient treatment techniques. In A. M. Washton & M. S. Gold (Eds.), *Cocaine: A clinician's handbook* (pp. 106–117). New York: Guilford Press.

18

Group Psychotherapy
with Substance Abusers
and Family Members

MARSHA VANNICELLI

INTRODUCTION

Over the past four decades, group psychotherapy has been gaining increasing acceptance as a treatment modality for substance abusers and their family members. Descriptions of group techniques for substance abusers appear in the literature as early as 1946 (McCarthy, 1946), for family members as early as 1959 (Igersheimer, 1959), and for adult children of alcoholics as early as 1980 (Pietler, 1980)—with scores of articles and books since then. Noteworthy among the vast group therapy literature are contributions describing group work with substance abusers (see Blume, 1985; Brown & Yalom, 1977; Brunner-Orne, 1956; Cooper, 1987; Doroff, 1977; Elder, 1990; Fox, 1962; Khantzian, Halliday, & McAuliff, 1990; Perez, 1986; Steiner, 1977; Vannicelli, 1982, 1988, 1992; Vannicelli, Canning, & Griefen, 1984; Vannicelli, Dillavou, & Caplan, 1988; Yalom, 1954), collaterals of substance abusers (see Cadogan, 1973; Vannicelli, 1987, 1992; Honig & Spinner, 1986; Igersheimer, 1959; Sands & Hanson, 1971), and adult children of alocholics (ACOAs) (see Brown & Beletsis, 1986; Cermak & Brown, 1982; Seixas & Levitan, 1984; Vannicelli, 1989, 1990, 1991).

The increasing acceptance of group psychotherapy for these populations has corresponded not only to increasing acceptance of group psychotherapy in general in this country but also to the increasing popularity and acceptance of self-help groups (Alcoholics Anonymous, Narcotics Anonymous, Al-Anon, Nar-Anon). Although the goals of a therapy and a self-help group differ in many ways, which are discussed in this chapter, the self-help movement has demonstrated that groups of people coming together to work on a common problem can be helpful in terms of sharing and identifying with others who are going through similar problems, and also in terms of understanding the impact of alcohol and drugs on those who abuse these substances as well as on those who are closely connected to the substance abuser.

Advantages and Limitations of Group Therapy

Advantages

This kind of group therapy is particularly helpful for substance abusers and their family members because it reduces the sense of isolation by grouping together people who have identified themselves as having a problem in common (substance abusers or ACOAs or family members living with a chemically dependent relative); provides an opportunity for members to see others who are getting better, thus instilling hope; provides an opportunity to learn from watching others who are struggling with similar kinds of conflicts; alters distorted self-concepts by providing an opportunity to examine one's own behavior in relation to others (and to get group feedback); and offers the possibility of a reparative family experience by providing an immediate "family context" in which to (1) explore the past as it is recreated in the present and (2) relive early conflicts correctively, as old nonadaptive behavioral patterns are challenged and new behaviors are tested out.

For substance abusers, group psychotherapy offers an additional advantage. Even when the patient is not in immediate danger with regard to substance abuse, coming to a weekly substance abuse group keeps the issue alive. The opportunity to hear about other members' struggle with abstinence underscores the need for constant vigilance. This is different from what often happens in individual psychotherapy (particularly traditional therapy) where weeks or months may go by in which the issue of substance abuse never comes up. Although a patient in individual therapy who is actively involved in a self-help program might also be able to maintain a focus on substance abuse issues, often when patients begin to waiver in their commitment to abstinence, they also slip away from Alcoholics Anonymous (AA) and Narcotics Anonymous (NA). Because a self-help group does not require the same kind of accountability as a therapy group, early warning signs may not be noticed.

Limitations

Within each of the three subgroups to be discussed, a wide range of patients (in terms of accompanying psychopathology, levels of functioning, sociodemographic characteristics, and personality traits) can be effectively treated with group psychotherapy as long as other treatment adjuncts are also used as needed (e.g., psychopharmacological treatment and individual therapy), group members are appropriately matched in terms in level of functioning (i.e., chronic patients with severe Axis I diagnoses and poor levels of functioning are not mixed with high-functioning patients), and severely paranoid patients are screened out, as well as others whose behavioral symptoms might seriously impede the ability of the group to function.

In addition, it is important that family members requesting treatment either as ACOAs or as collaterals of substance abusers have a thorough assessment in terms of their own use of alcohol and drugs. Should substance abuse problems prove to be part of the clinical picture for these individuals, it is important that they be placed in groups that will provide treatment for the substance abuse rather than focusing on "the ACOAs issue" or the "family issue" (which can be used defensively to avoid looking at one's own substance abuse problem). Similarly, ACOAs who are currently living with an actively abusing significant other should be considered for placement in a family members' group, rather than an ACOA group where they may defensively retreat to the problems of the *past* as a way of avoiding the pressing issues in their *current* lives (see Vannicelli, 1992, for elaboration regarding treating the problem of "highest crisis potential" first).

Overview of Chapter

This chapter examines dilemmas that arise in group psychotherapy with substance abusers, adult children of alcoholics, and other family members.[1] These dilemmas, or roadblocks to recovery—frequently referred to in the psychotherapy literature as forms of resistance—are erected to avoid work that may be painful or difficult. We will examine these roadblocks as they emerge within the individual group member, the group as a whole, and the therapist.

It should be noted that the line differentiating group, member, and leader roadblocks is not always clear because they often interact. Sometimes what appears to be a member roadblock may actually be a roadblock for the group as a whole, in which the group allows a single member to represent or "contain" some piece of resistance that is shared by other group members. Thus, for example, a member's resumption of drinking may begin as a resistance in that individual member. Yet, if the drinking continues, and the group as a whole fails to attend to it adequately, it is very likely that this individual is enacting something for the entire group (otherwise, the group would more effectively intervene). With this caveat about the potential overlap between the three categories of roadblocks, I begin with those roadblocks that are most clearly localized in the individual group member.

INDIVIDUAL MEMBER ROADBLOCKS

Misunderstanding the Contract

Many substance abusers and family members begin their group therapy experiences with prior (or simultaneous) experiences in 12-Step self-help groups (AA/NA, Al-Anon/Nar-Anon, etc.)—experiences that are likely to have a strong influence on their expectations about group therapy (and may give rise to some of the program-related roadblocks discussed in the section that follows). Although work in a self-help group and a psychotherapy group can be mutually complementary, it is important to clearly differentiate these two kinds of experiences because their goals and ground rules differ. Thus, after ascertaining that a patient is familiar with one of the 12-Step programs, I might support his/her continued use of the program while underscoring the ways in which the ground rules differ from those of a therapy group. Thus, I might ask, "Have you been using AA?" If the patient responds affirmatively, I might say, "Good, that can be very helpful. However, it may also be useful for us to review some of the ways that participation in a therapy group differs from participation in AA." Then, as I review the ground rules with the patient, I might highlight the ways in which they differ from membership in AA—namely, that membership in a therapy group carries with it the expectation that patients will be at the group every week and on time, will call in if for some reason they are unable to come, and will give advance notice to the group should they consider discontinuing membership. It may be helpful to say to the new member, "In a therapy group you are expected to attend every week and on time; it makes a difference to people whether or not you are at a particular session. And, unlike AA, where if one needed to leave early one could, in the group it would matter a great deal to other members if somebody had to depart from the group prior to the end of the session." The boundaries are much tighter in a therapy group than in AA, there is more accountability, and people's comings and goings from the group are attended to more carefully.

Although these ground rules are not unique to therapy groups for substance abusers and their family members, and would be stated as part of the initial treatment contract for any therapy group, it is particularly important that they be underscored at the pregroup interviews with these populations because they do differ substantially from the ground rules of AA and Al-Anon.[2] Other ways in which the therapy group may differ from AA and Al-Anon should also be clarified. These include the expectation that members will pay, that outside-of-group contact has to be brought back into the group, and that what goes on in the group itself will be talked about (i.e., exploration of the group process itself). It may be especially important to attend to the latter because most of the exchanges in large open AA groups occur between the "leader" (i.e., the speaker) and various members. Although this may be modified somewhat in smaller meetings or special step meetings, for many patients their experiences in 12-Step programs will have exposed them to serial dyadic communication rather than group interaction among many members.

Finally, it is important to underscore that the group will focus on feelings and learning to communicate them more clearly and will explore the past as well as the present with the goal of better integrating and understanding one's life experiences and feelings. Although patients sometimes feel that there is conflict between their AA or Al-Anon experience and group therapy because the formats are so different, the therapist should be clear in his own mind that the two are not in any way mutually exclusive but, rather, serve different functions and provide support in distinct but complementary ways.

Program-Related Roadblocks

Proselytizing for Alcoholics Anonymous or Al-Anon

A group member who has had tremendous success with one of the 12-Step self-help programs (AA/NA, Al-Anon/Nar-Anon) may be disquieted about the presence of others in the group who are not solidly hooked into the program. This member may spend a considerable amount of his/her time and energy proselytizing about "the necessity of being a regular AA or Al-Anon attender and the impossibility of recovering without it" and registering concerns about participation in a group in which other members are not sufficiently attached to "the program." For such individuals, the precariousness of their own recovery creates tremendous anxiety about the possibility of anyone *else* deviating from a program that they themselves have embraced. With such individuals, it may be useful to underscore that they have learned a lot in AA or Al-Anon that has been terribly helpful in supporting their recovery, and clearly for *them* this has been a critical support. Although it is important for the group leader to make it clear that he thinks that 12-Step programs are very useful, the message should also be given that there are other supports that may be useful to other group members.

It is also important to consider the possibility that the patient who struggles too ardently on this issue may be setting up a struggle with the group to avoid intimacy. As the group becomes polarized, group process becomes stalemated and group development is halted.

Taking the Program Too Literally

For other group members, initial resistance to full engagement in the therapeutic work may take the form of a very literal acceptance of the 12-Step dictum about "living in the present" and not "rehashing the past" or "projecting into the future." It is thus important that the leaders underscore in the pregroup interview, and whenever indicated through the life of the group, that the group provides an opportunity to understand how patterns from the past get repeated in the present. In early sessions, "slogan resistance" may first be apparent when leaders ask how something might connect to what was happening in the previous session, and a member responds, "I just think about what is happening for today. I don't think about the past, and I don't project into the future." This patient is, in a sense, a good student who has learned his lessons well—even if they have been taken a bit literally. To such a patient the leader might respond, "It's clear that you've learned a lot in the program that's been very helpful to you; and you've learned a lot about how 12-Step groups work. Some of the ground rules in here are a little bit different, though I think you will find that they operate in a complementary fashion."

Obfuscating through Program Lingo

"Program lingo" (i.e., idioms and slogans from AA, NA, Al-Anon, etc.) can also be used defensively in other ways. Thus, a family member in a group may say, "Well, clearly I just have 'to let go.' " Sometimes, the therapist feels as if he/she should know what the patient means—as if it is a requirement of the therapist working in the substance abuse field to know and to understand all the idioms and to accept them as complete communications when they come up. Instead, it is useful for the therapist to question further when idioms are used, asking, "How do you mean?" or "Can you say a little bit more about that?" If the patient responds with a tart, "Don't you know what 'letting go' means?" The therapist might respond, "I'm familiar with that expression, but I'm interested in knowing more about what it means in your particular situation." Or, "Letting go means something a bit different to each person." Basically, therapists need to take the same position in terms of making sure that they understand what their patients are talking about when program lingo and idioms are used as they would if a patient were a member of a rare religious sect whose terms were not altogether clear.

Creating a Sense of "Sameness" through Program Labels

Program labels can also be used to create an illusion of "sameness" that can be used defensively to avoid differences and conflict. Thus, members, at times of stress in the group, may attempt to abort further exploration with comments such as "That's typical alcoholic behavior" or "This is a typical ACOA issue." Such assumptions about sameness and shared understanding may create a "you know how it is" mentality in the group, leading to tunnel vision and a reluctance to explore "the obvious." It is thus important that leaders challenge this assumption when it emerges. A program label should not be accepted as an adequate summary or explanation of what is going on but, rather, should be understood as the patient's attempt temporarily to close the door on painful issues. Thus, when group members summarize what is going on as "That was a typical ACOA reaction" or "That's typical alcoholic thinking," the leader should ask, "How so?" and should inquire further about what *specifically* was going on. In addition, in order to further differentiation instead of supporting the defense of sameness, the leader should ask what different kinds of feelings or reactions others in the group might be having.

Member Roadblocks Specific to the Substance Abuser

In addition to articulating aspects of the contract that differentiate a therapy group from AA (as discussed above), for the substance abuser it is also essential that a commitment to abstinence is made explicit as part of the initial group contract. The contract should also indicate that any difficulties encountered in working toward this goal (in the form of either fears about substance use or actual use) will be discussed with the group. Although group membership is not specifically contingent upon abstinence, it does hinge on the patient's willingness to struggle honestly with the wish to use alcohol or drugs with a commitment to abstinence as a goal. Thus, when a slip does occur, the group and the "wavering" member should be engaged in a process of contracting that specifies a clear time frame for resuming abstinence and additional support that will be used toward this end (e.g., the patient must get a sponsor and must start attending additional AA/NA meetings). Because for many substance abusers the course of recovery is punctuated with periodic setbacks, lapses from abstinence will certainly occur. However, a slip should not suggest to either the patient or the therapist that all that was gained has now been lost. In fact, a "slip" handled appropriately by the patient (i.e., the patient solicits help or stops using alcohol or drugs soon after the onset of the episode and discusses it openly with the group) can be a useful learning experience for the patient as well as for other group members, underscoring the need for constant vigilance and adequate support for maintaining abstinence.

However, there is a lot of ground between an appropriately handled slip and other forms of drinking and drug use that occur within the context of group therapy. Two of the most common drinking/drugging hurdles are reluctance to discontinue use of alcohol and drugs and reluctance to discuss this reluctance (i.e., to discussing the continued use of substances).

Reluctance to Discontinue Use of Alcohol and Drugs

The patient who comes to the group intoxicated presents the most blatant version of resistance to giving up alcohol and drugs. This member, if allowed to remain, may also make it impossible for the group to proceed. If intoxication is immediately apparent to the group leaders, the member should be asked to leave and to return in a condition appropriate for participation the next week. (Provision must also be made for assuring patients' safety if they are not in condition to get themselves safely home.)

More difficult is the patient whose intoxication is not immediately apparent but who becomes disruptive during the course of the meeting. This patient should be told that his/her specific alcohol- or drug-related behaviors (e.g., talking while others are talking and inability to keep up with what is going on in the group) indicate that he/she is not able to participate appropriately in the group that evening. Whether or not the patient returns that evening, other group members should be encouraged to share their feelings and observations about both the patient's behavior and the therapist's request that the patient leave. When the patient returns the next week, group members should be asked to share their feelings about what happened the previous week, and the patient and the group should be asked to contract for added supports.

"Using" but Refusing to Acknowledge It (Reluctance to Discuss the Reluctance)

Often, a group member's use of alcohol or drugs is less obviously available to the group, but the leaders learn from sources outside the group (other staff, patients, a concerned spouse) that a patient has relapsed who is not talking about it in the group. Ideally, therapists will use such information to help patients disclose this substance use "on their own." This disclosure can be facilitated by starting out with a general comment such as "I understand, Bill, that you've been having rather a tough time for the past several weeks." If the patient acknowledges this, he is then asked to share as much about it as he can with the group. If Bill does not mention his use of alcohol or drugs, or if he denies that there have been any problems, the therapist should share the incoming information in a factual way. (It should be clear from the initial treatment contract that there will be no secrets and that any information the therapist receives *will* be shared with the patient.) Thus the therapist might say, "Your wife called in this evening and was concerned that you might be drinking." If denial persists, the patient should be asked what sense he makes of the discrepancy between the outside information and his own report.

If a patient is not able to trust the group enough to talk about the substance use, this dilemma should be stated by saying, for example, "It must be hard for you, Bill, to find yourself in a group in which you don't feel safe enough to talk about your drinking." (It may also be helpful at this point for the group as a whole to explore feelings of safety in the group and each member's sense of what he/she feels can and cannot be shared.) Ultimately, the patient must be reminded of the group contract committing members to talk about slips if they do occur. If the substance abuse continues and still is not discussed, the therapist must let the patient know (preferably in the group) that, at this point, the member and the group have an unworkable relationship, and he/she should be asked to leave.

Another difficult situation arises when a patient comes in showing signs of intoxication (disheveled appearance, slightly slurred speech, smelling faintly of alcohol) who denies use of any substances. To this individual it might be appropriate to say, "John, you seem somewhat less tidy about your appearance this week than usual, and I smell alcohol in the room. I'm concerned that you are drinking." Even if John denies that he has been drinking, the leader might further comment, "My hunch is that it's been difficult for you to acknowledge that you've been having a hard time with alcohol because you're afraid of disappointing people in here that you care about." This is an empathic response that indicates to the patient that his difficulty leveling with the group is understandable. If he gives a positive response to this empathic statement, the group should be asked what they think needs to happen in order to help him get "squared away" again—the time frame for the resumption of abstinence, additional supports that need to be added, and, possibly, some way of establishing a safer forum in the group so that John will be able to talk about the drinking if it does happen again.

Urine or saliva screens may also be helpful in these situations (particularly if the patient continues to deny alcohol or drug use).

Over a 3-month period, a group member intermittently arrived with bloodshot eyes and appearing emotionally labile. One co-leader or the other frequently believed that he was under the influence of Valium, but they rarely agreed about this on any given night. When one or the other would inquire as to how he was doing with his abstinence or would wonder whether his current problems were related to drug use, they always received responses that denied any drug use. Eventually the leaders decided that the uncertainty about the patient's status (as well as their intermittent concerns that he might not be leveling with the group) was jeopardizing his therapy.

The next week they addressed the issue, saying, "Mr. Smith, for several months now we have wondered off and on whether you might be back on Valium. Last week we had that concern again. We think it's bad for our relationship with you to be worried about this as much as we are—and also, that it must be troublesome to you to have us wondering and doubting. One way to resolve this is that the next time you come to group in a condition that leaves any doubt about your sobriety, you go downstairs to the Inpatient Unit after the group and give a urine sample."

The patient agreed. Though no urines were ever given, the impact of this clear intervention was that the next week the patient checked himself into an inpatient program. When he returned to the group he thanked them for confronting the issue and acknowledged that they had been right all along.

Whether or not urine or saliva screens are an option, it is essential that the group leaders tackle the problem and help define the impasse that exists. The steps involved in dealing with a patient who is actively using and coming to the group intoxicated involve (1) empathic enjoinment—letting the patient know that the therapist understands why it is hard to acknowledge the substance use to the group, (2) describing the impasse—namely, that it is important that the therapist and patient both feel that they are in a credible relationship (difficult when, week after week, there are substantial doubts), and (3) problem solving with the group to get past the impasse. In the second and third steps, the patient and the group are presented with the fact that it is not useful for these doubts to persist. The impasse is put out to the group as a whole, and members are challenged to think about what can be done to resolve it.

Roadblocks Specific to Family Members

Collaterals of substance abusers (spouses, grown children, and other relatives and significant others) can be treated either in conjunction with the substance abuser in a couples groups (Vannicelli, 1987) or separately in groups that are often referred to as relatives groups, significant others groups, or codependency groups. These groups for relatives are to be differentiated from ACOA groups (which are, of course, also for family members) based on proximity to the substance abuse conflict. Relatives groups are intended for those who are currently living with substance abusers or those in recent recovery—the partners and parents, and some times the grown children if they are still actively involved in the day-to-day life of the active (or recently recovering) substance abuser. This is differentiated from the ACOA group in which there is less immediacy to the present substance abuse issues of the parents. Certain forms of resistance are relatively common in all three groups for family members (couples groups, groups for relatives, and ACOA groups).

Resistance to Examining One's Own Substance Abuse

It is not uncommon for ACOAs and other collaterals to enter treatment to deal with the pain of living with a substance-abusing other (either in the past, if they are ACOAs, or currently, if they are spouses or other close associates) while ignoring their own very real abuse of substances. It is thus important that family members requesting group treatment either as ACOAs or as collaterals of substance abusers have a thorough assessment in terms of their own use of alcohol and drugs. Should substance abuse problems prove to be part of the clinical picture for these individuals, it is important that they be placed in groups that will provide treatment for the substance abuse rather than focusing on "the ACOA issue" or the "family issue" (which can be used defensively to avoid looking at one's own substance abuse problem—"hiding out" in a family or ACOA focus). Similarly, an ACOA who is currently living with an actively abusing significant other should be considered for placement in a family members group rather than an ACOA group where the client may defensively retreat to the problems of the *past* as a way of avoiding the pressing issues in his/her *current* life (see Vannicelli, 1992, for elaboration regarding treating the problem of "highest crisis potential" first).

Externalized Focus

ACOAs. A frequent theme in all groups involving family members is that "the substance abuser is the problem." For ACOA group members, this externalized focus is often a preferable alternative to the self-blame they have carried for years. For some, it appears that there is now an understandable "cause" for their problems. Thus, particularly in the early phases of group life, considerable group energy may be spent blaming the parents (both the parents of childhood and the parents of the present, who continue to perpetuate the crimes of the past). ACOA group members may also spend time focusing on ways to change members of their families of origin rather than focusing on themselves. When this happens, it may be useful for group leaders to refocus the group with comments such as, "My hunch is that the troublesome family members that we are hearing so much about have always gotten more than their fair share of the attention. What would it be like for the family members who *are* here to have more of the focus on you?"

Other Relatives. For spouses and other family members, too, the flamboyance of the substance abuser's craziness may make it easy for all family members to blame the substance abuser for their pain, despite the fact that the other family members may also feel and act crazy at times. Family and friends often contribute to the perpetuation of this myth, looking for some simple mechanism for understanding the family's distress or for assigning blame.

This externalized view of the problem held by many spouses or other relatives may involve them initially in a stance that seems antithetical to productive use of psychotherapy. Such individuals may even be reluctant, initially, to call themselves patients or to engage in any activity that is referred to as therapy. Yet they are clearly in pain, and the therapist's job is to align with them around this pain so that relief may ultimately be possible.

In groups for relatives, in particular, the forces of resistance often seem to overpower the forces for change. Whereas ACOAs come with an agenda to work on their family-of-origin issues and move quickly to a level of engagement with the past in an effort to understand its application in the present, and substance abusers have an immediate goal of making at least those changes necessary to maintain abstinence, family members are often more confused about their own personal goals as well as the group's task. Are they there to learn how to better tolerate an intolerable situation? (A somewhat entrenched position.) Are they there to make changes? If so, in whom? Some family members join with the hidden agenda of making changes in *somebody else*—to "get *him* to change."

The therapist can use the patient's confusion as a springboard to clarifying the group's task, by asking, "If group members mostly talk about their substance-abusing husbands and wives, how much do you think you will learn about yourselves?" and, "What other things do you think might be useful for the group to talk about?" The therapist's questions are a way of helping patients to formulate a clearer sense of the group's purpose—namely, to help patients better understand their own emotional lives and the pushes and pulls that motivate them, as well as the roles they play in maintaining their own untenable life situations. By examining the interactions of members as they connect—or fail to connect—to one another in the group, members learn more about the complexity of human relations and the ways in which members may sabotage the kind of connections they most want. These tasks will be only minimally addressed if the group stays focused on outside-of-group material and are furthered when outside-of-group material is tied to here-and-now interactions with the group.

GROUP ROADBLOCKS

Focusing on the Group Theme as a Defense against Group Work

In the early stages of group therapy for special populations, the population themes that bring members together tend to predominate. In groups for substance abusers, reminiscences about the "good old days" when "using" was still fun, "war stories" about how bad things finally got, and concerns about current wishes to use (or actual use) pervade the group discussion. Group members establish a sense of cohesiveness by focusing on the one thing—substance abuse—known to be held in common. In addition, though group members have picked a relatively safe way of beginning their involvement in the group, the discussion is relevant to one of the stated goals of the group: abstinence. Groups for collaterals or ACOAs often do the same kind of joining around their respective theme, as members attempt to safely connect with one another.

At times, however, a group may persist in talking about substance use (or the substance abuser, in the case of collaterals and ACOAs) to the exclusion of all else, or may periodically relapse to this limited form of interaction. When this happens, leaders are often bewildered—the group feels stuck and is usually dull, yet it appears to be doing what it is supposed to be doing. (After all, what could be more legitimate than discussions about drinking and drug use in a treatment group for substance abusers, or talking about the trials of living with a substance abuser in an ACOA or collateral group?) Another common example of defensive use of the group theme is the following: In the middle of an intense, affectively loaded discussion, a patient interrupts to ask, "What does all this have to do with alcohol or drugs (or with our ACOA issues)?" The question is heralded by a chorus of support by other group members. This protest is a defense against the painful feelings that are being stirred up in the group and expresses a wish to get back onto safer territory. It is, of course, the apparent legitimacy of the theme-focused talk that makes it such a beguiling group defense against exploring deeper issues.

Defensive retreat to the group "focus" is present when any of the following occur: (1) the group seems to talk about little else; (2) the group uses alcohol and drug-related talk (or talk about the relatives who abuse the substances) as a distraction, as in the above example; (3) a group member presents an account of a recent "disaster story" (his own recent use, or a family event involving the substance abuser) that is devoid of feelings associated with the event; and (4) group members, in turn, give advice or get distracted with their own "war memories."

In contrast, appropriate discussion of drinking and drugging or family problems (1) is but one of many topics discussed; (2) is characterized by expression and exploration of feelings; (3) is related to here-and-now interactions in the group, as family themes replay themselves in the present; and (4) for substance abusers, encourages an exploration of the circumstances (psychological as well as external) that led the troubled group member to feel that he/she could not cope without alcohol or drugs and, if a slip actually occurred, what went wrong with the relapse prevention plan.

Finally, although focusing on the group theme may be a way for some patients to avoid involvement and intensity, for the patient who feels particularly unworthy it may serve the opposite end. For this patient, talking about the group's "official theme" may seem like the only "legitimate" way to get a share of the group's time. It is thus essential that the group leader be aware of the many functions of theme-focused talk in terms of both individual and group dynamics.

Rigidly Embraced Roles

In ACOA groups, members may find themselves solidly entrenched in specific, relatively limited roles, with the collusion and support of the group. Although, to some extent, this dynamic is possible in all psychodynamically oriented therapy groups, it may be exaggerated in ACOA groups because dysfunctional families may be particularly likely to develop stereotyped and rigid roles that keep the family system in balance (Davis, Berenson, Steinglass, & Davis, 1974; Steinglass, 1979; Steinglass, Davis, & Berenson, 1977). This dynamic is probably due, in part, to a need to increase predictability in an arena in which predictability is frequently lacking. The quest for predictability, and with it constriction of roles, is often particularly noticeable in the group's assignment of an "identified patient" (the family problem) and "rescuer."

Searching for the Identified Patient

ACOA groups often eagerly engage in targeting "an identified patient" (IP), whom they first "try to cure," ultimately decide is "too sick," and finally attempt to extrude. As in most instances of scapegoating, the chosen IP complies in some way, as he/she shares the group fantasy and lends him/herself to its enactment. The collective myth is that the family will finally be restored to happiness when the "problem" is removed; that is, when the troubled (alcoholic) member is gone. In fact, the group may move from one member to another, attempting to discover "who is the sickest," in order to target the IP so that the group can either cure or extrude this member and thereby restore the health of the family.

Searching for a Rescuer

The group's search for the "problem" patient is paralleled by the search for a powerful figure who will "come to the rescue." Although this wish may initially be projected onto the group leaders, as the group moves on (and particularly as the group leaders come to be viewed more ambivalently), the members may look for a "rescuer" among themselves. Like the IP, the patient who is assigned the rescuer role (and who, often, all too willingly complies) may soon find the role difficult to shed.

With both the scapegoated IP and the assigned "hero," it falls to the group leader to help the group understand its need to have these roles filled and to suggest that the targeted individual might in some way be serving a function for the group. Thus the leader might comment, "It seems as if the group has a powerful wish to see Jane as the 'rescuer' in here. I wonder if her portrayal of herself as so much healthier than other members, and the group's readiness to buy this, might be a 'solution' that could be understood from the past." Although the entire group's involvement in the enactment will be important, the particular individual's willingness to play a particular role should also be explored.

LEADER ROADBLOCKS

Countertransference Related to "Having Been There"

An unusual characteristic of the treaters of substance abusers and their family members is that many, themselves, have histories of personal or familial substance abuse. The extent to which a group leader personally resonates with the clinical material may be his/her greatest treasure in working with these populations or may get the leader into trouble if not adequately examined and understood. Familiarity with the issues is helpful as long as distance and perspective are not lost.

Wood (1987) describes some of the specific dilemmas of the ACOA therapist. She points to the ACOA therapist's propensity, at times, to block or dampen patients' expressions of painful feelings because in the therapist's own family of origin, "emotionality and conflict never came to a good end" (p. 146). Through Wood's discussion, we come to understand how the ACOA therapist may hinder the work of his/her patients by employing the same blocking maneuvers that were once used to "restore the false harmony" of his/her own alcoholic family (p. 154). However, because the goal of therapy is not to eliminate painful feelings but to help the patient experience them in a safe context in which they can become reintegrated, ACOA therapists need to stay on top of their own reactions as strong feelings emerge. A particularly clear instance of leader resonation with a group theme (and this kind of blocking maneuver) was evident in the following case example:

This ACOA group, during the first few weeks of its formation, struggled to identify the "most problematic patient." The leader found herself, by the end of the first session, colluding with the group—feeling, with them, that a particular "problem patient" did not "fit" in the group and allowing the group to persuade this member that he did not belong. When the patient did not return the following week, the leader expressed relief, stating in supervision "that the group would be better off without this patient, who was too sick." The leader's own wish to "save the family" by "ridding it of its troubled member"—a dynamic that she was all too familiar with from her own family of origin—blinded her to the realization of what the group (and she) was reenacting. Instead, she colluded with them and helped this "unfit" patient leave the group, thus recapitulating the family fantasy that everything would be fine if only the problem member were removed. A few weeks later the group took up the same cause again, searching anew for a problem patient to eliminate. At this point, the leader, understanding her own earlier collusion, was able to intervene more effectively and this time helped the group retain and work with the new problem patient that it had identified.

12-Step-Related Roadblocks

Another potential hazard for group therapists who are, themselves, recovering substance abusers, ACOAs, or other family members is that they may find themselves pulled toward the "self-help" model with concomitant pressures to self-disclose and share personal experiences (as one might do in the role of an AA or Al-Anon sponsor). For therapists who are in 12-Step programs, it may, at times, be confusing as to how the role of therapist differs from or converges with that of the sponsor. It is essential to recognize that the two roles are quite different. A sponsor continues to help him/herself while also helping the other. Although we, as therapists, also continue to grow in the course of our work, our growth is never the focus of the therapeutic relationship. Unlike the "therapeutic" reciprocity in the sponsor–pigeon relationship, therapeutic interventions by necessity are geared to meeting the patient's needs rather than those of the therapist. Although there is always the possibility that the therapist can grow along with his/her patients, or with the group, it is the therapist's responsibility to take care of his/her own mental health in another arena (i.e., in the therapist's own psychotherapy). In this regard, being an effective group therapist is clearly differentiated from effective functioning as a 12-Step sponsor.

Group Leader's Reluctance to Deal with Uncertainty

In our earlier discussion of patient resistance, we talked about the situation in which a patient arrived at the group intoxicated. A special variation of this problem emerges when there is a distinct odor of alcohol in the room (*someone* in the group has been drinking) but the leader is uncertain from whom the odor is coming. In this instance, the patient's resistance is often matched by a roadblock in the therapist—who is reluctant to process the data given his/her uncertainty about the source. It is essential, however, that the leader actively attend to this important piece of data (the smell of alcohol). For example, the therapist might inquire, "I wonder if what is going on in here right now might relate in some way to the faint odor of alcohol in the room?" (Thus, the presence of the odor is presented as a *fact*.) Or, the leader might simply state, "There is a faint smell in here that seems like it could be alcohol"—inquiring then about members' thoughts and feelings about this. Even if it is not immediately apparent who in the room may be drinking, the issue has not been ignored, and with time, clarity is likely to emerge.

The Overly Zealous Therapist

Sometimes group leaders dealing with a member whose abstinence is wavering may become so concerned about limit setting that they respond by hastily and unilaterally imposing stiff treatment contracts without attending to the state of the treatment alliance (thus dealing perhaps with the therapist's anxiety more effectively than with the patient's treatment). For example, a recently abstinent patient might be told during the pre-group interview that if a drinking slip occurred, she would have to begin taking Antabuse [disulfiram] and attend seven AA meetings per week. Although she may agree to this without much reflection, should a slip actually occur, it is not likely that she would follow through on such stiff terms. It would be more likely that she would drop treatment instead.

It is important whenever a new contract has to be initiated, or the old one updated, to have the patient actively and *realistically* engaged in the contracting process. Tough, unilateral contracts "imposed" by the therapist are clinically effective only in relatively rare, medically dangerous situations in which any time lost between alcohol or drug use and getting the patient into a detoxification or inpatient facility would seriously jeopardize the patient's health. Except for these extreme cases, tough, unilateral contracts will generally be effective only in keeping less motivated patients *out* of treatment.

A carefully negotiated contract is sensitive to the current status of the patient's alliance and offers gradations of increasing support that the patient is actively involved in selecting and can readily endorse. This means that the therapist and patient together must decide what would be an effective and workable plan. "Packaged" proposals by the patient (e.g., "90 meetings in 90 days") should be carefully challenged with questions such as, "Given all that you've got going right now, will you be able to do that?" A more modest plan that the patient can reliably carry out is more likely to succeed than one that is too ambitious.

COST CONSIDERATIONS AND EFFECTIVENESS

Monumental changes are currently under way in the delivery of health care services. Third-party payers are increasingly reluctant to support lengthy hospital stays for psychiatric treatment and are escalating the criteria necessary to enter an inpatient facility, even for relatively brief periods. Patients with substance abuse problems have been among the hardest hit, with insurance companies even more reluctant to allow inpatient hospitalization for these individuals than for other patient populations. These changes challenge substance abuse providers to increase the availability of effective, *affordable* outpatient services. In terms of cost-effectiveness, group therapy has much to recommend it. The charge for 90 minutes of group psychotherapy is generally one half to one third the charge for individual therapy—an especially important consideration given treatment outcome data for substance abusers that generally point to results that are at least as favorable for group psychotherapy as for individual psychotherapy (Brandsma & Pattison, 1985; Solomon, 1983; Emrick, 1975; Kanas, 1982).

It is important to emphasize, however, that delivery of effective group psychotherapy services for these populations requires a group leader who is adequately trained in terms of both group psychotherapy skills more generally and specific training regarding pertinent issues for substance abusers and their family members. This is perhaps particularly important to underscore in an arena in which so much of what is seen as helpful has been the self-help movement. However, to be an effective group psychotherapist, having shared similar experiences in terms of one's own or one's family's history of substance abuse is neither a necessary nor a sufficient qualification. Although often serving as an incentive to do the work, and sometimes helpful in terms of resonating with the issues of group members, one's own personal or familial substance abuse history can also at times produce tunnel vision or resonating countertransference reactions that need to be adequately attended to (see Vannicelli, 1989, 1990, 1991, 1992). Adequate training and preparation, along with a desire to help and sensitivity to the issues, are essential.

NOTES

1. Much of the material for this chapter is adapted from *Removing the Roadblocks: Group Psychotherapy with Substance Abusers and Family Members* (Vannicelli, 1992).

2. I refer here to AA and Al-Anon for the sake of brevity but include also NA and Nar-Anon.

REFERENCES

Blume, S. B. (1985). Group psychotherapy in the treatment of alcoholism. In S. Zimberg, J. Wallace, & S. Blume (Eds.), *Practical approaches to alcoholism psychotherapy* (2nd ed., pp. 73–86). New York: Plenum Press.

Brandsma, J. M., & Pattison, E. M. (1985). The outcome of group psychotherapy alcoholics: An empirical review. *American Journal of Drug and Alcohol Abuse, 11*(1, 2), 151–160.

Brown, S., & Beletsis, S. (1986). The development of family transference in groups for the adult children of alcoholics. *International Journal of Group Psychotherapy, 36*(1), 97–114.

Brown, S., & Yalom, I. D. (1977). Interactional group therapy with alcoholics. *Journal of Studies on Alcohol, 38*(3), 426–456.

Brunner-Orne, M. (1956). The utilization of group psychotherapy in enforced treatment programs for alcoholics and addicts. *International Journal of Group Psychotherapy, 6,* 272–279.

Cadogan, D. A. (1973). Marital group therapy in the treatment of alcoholism. *Quarterly Journal of Studies on Alcohol, 34*(4), 1187–1194.

Cermak, T. L., & Brown, S. (1982). Interactional group therapy with the adult children of alcoholics. *International Journal of Group Psychotherapy, 32*(3), 375–389.

Cooper, D. E. (1987). The role of group psychotherapy in the treatment of substance abusers. *American Journal of Psychotherapy, 41*(1), 55–67.

Davis, D. I., Berenson, D., Steinglass, P., & Davis, S. (1974). The adaptive consequences of drinking. *Psychiatry, 37,* 209–215.

Doroff, D. R. (1977). Group psychotherapy and alcoholism. In B. Kissin & H. Begleiter (Eds.), *The biology of alcoholism: Vol. 5. Treatment and rehabilitation of the chronic alcoholic* (pp. 235–258). New York: Plenum Press.

Elder, I. R. (1990). *Conducting group therapy with addicts: A guidebook for professionals.* Blue Ridge Summit, PA: TAB Books.

Emrick, C. (1975). A review of psychologically oriented treatment of alcoholism II: The relative effectiveness of different treatment approaches and the effectiveness of treatment versus no treatment. *Journal of Studies on Alcohol, 36*(1), 88–108.

Fox, R. (1962). Group psychotherapy with alcoholics. *International Journal of Group Psychotherapy, 12*(1), 56–63.

Honig, F., & Spinner, A. (1986). A group therapy approach in the treatment of spouses of alcoholics. *Alcoholism Treatment Quarterly, 3*(3), 91–105.

Igersheimer, W. (1959). Group psychotherapy for the non-alcoholic wives of alcoholics. *Quarterly Journal of Studies on Alcohol, 20,* 77–85.

Kanas, N. (1982). Alcoholism and group psychotherapy. In E. M. Pattison & E. Kaufman (Eds.), *Encyclopedic handbook of alcoholism* (pp. 1011–1021). New York: Gardner Press.

Khantzian, E. J., Halliday, K. S., & McAuliffe, W. E. (1990). *Addiction and the vulnerable self: Modified dynamic group therapy for substance abusers.* New York: Guilford Press.

McCarthy, R. G. (1946). Group therapy in an outpatient clinic for the treatment of alcoholism. *Quarterly Journal of Studies on Alcohol, 7,* 98–109.

Perez, J. F. (1986). *Counseling the alcoholic group.* New York: Gardner Press.

Pietler, E. J. (1980). A comparison of the effectiveness of group counseling and Alateen on the psychological adjustment of two groups of adolescent sons of alcoholic fathers (Doctoral dissertation, St. John's University, 1980). *Dissertation Abstracts International, 41*(4), 1520B.

Sands, P. M., & Hanson, P. G. (1971). Psychotherapeutic groups for alcoholics and relatives in an outpatient setting. *International Journal of Group Psychotherapy, 21*(1), 23–33.

Seixas, J. S., & Levitan, M. L. (1984). A supportive counseling group for adult children of alcoholics. *Alcoholism Treatment Quarterly, 1*(4), 123–132.

Solomon, S. D. (1983). Individual versus group therapy: Current status in the treatment of alcoholism. *Advances in Alcohol and Substance Abuse, 2*(1), 69–86.

Steiner, C. M. (1977). *Games alcoholics play.* New York: Grove Press.

Steinglass, P. (1979). The alcoholic family in the interaction laboratory. *Journal of Nervous and Mental Disease, 167*(7), 428–436.

Steinglass, P., Davis, D. I., & Berenson, D. (1977). Observations of conjointly hospitalized "alcoholic couples" during sobriety and intoxication: Implications for theory and therapy. *Family Process, 16,* 1–16.

Vannicelli, M. (1982). Group psychotherapy with alcoholics: Special techniques. *Journal of Studies on Alcohol, 43*(1), 17–37.

Vannicelli, M. (1987). Treatment of alcoholic couples in outpatient group therapy. *Group, 11*(4), 247–257.

Vannicelli, M. (1988). Group therapy aftercare for alcoholic patients. *International Journal of Group Psychotherapy, 38*(3), 337–353.

Vannicelli, M. (1989). *Group psychotherapy with adult children of alcoholics: Treatment techniques and countertransference considerations.* New York: Guilford Press.

Vannicelli, M. (1990). Group psychotherapy with adult children of alcoholics. In M. Seligman & L. A. Marshall (Eds.), *Group psychotherapy: A practitioner's guide to interventions with special populations* (pp. 195–217). Boston: Allyn & Bacon.

Vannicelli, M. (1991). Dilemmas and countertransference considerations in group psychotherapy with adult children of alcoholics. *International Journal of Group Psychotherapy, 41*(3), 295–312.

Vannicelli, M. (1992). *Removing the roadblocks: Group psychotherapy with substance abusers and family members.* New York: Guilford Press.

Vannicelli, M., Canning, D., & Griefen, M. (1984). Group therapy with alcoholics: A group case study. *International Journal of Group Psychotherapy, 34*(1), 127–147.

Vannicelli, M., Dillavou, D., & Caplan, C. (1988). Psychodynamically oriented group therapy with alcoholics: Making it work despite the prevailing bias. *Group, 13*(2), 95–100.

Wood, B. L. (1987). *Children of alcoholism: The struggle for self and intimacy in adult life.* New York: New York University Press.

Yalom, I. D. (1975). Group therapy and alcoholism. *Annals of the New York Academy of Sciences, 233,* 85–103.

19

Network Therapy

MARC GALANTER

INTRODUCTION

Substance abuse is the most common mental illness, but despite this, there is no format in general use for treating addicted people in an office practice. This stark fact stands in contrast to the management of other psychological problems. Many therapists address character disorder by means of psychodynamic treatment, phobic and eating disorders by means of behavioral therapy, and psychotic disorders with medication and hospitalization.

This chapter describes how family and friends can be engaged concomitant with individual therapy and 12-Step involvement to treat addiction in a focused therapeutic approach. A group of people close to the patient can provide effective support for rehabilitation of addictive illness in "network therapy" (Galanter, 1993), an innovative and pragmatic format for treatment. By means of the network approach to social support, we can take concrete steps to overcome the destructive forces that are so compromising to the continuity of care for the substance abuser.

It is helpful here to give an operational definition of network therapy. It is an approach to rehabilitation in which specific family members and friends are enlisted to provide ongoing support and to promote attitude change. Network members are part of the therapist's working "team" and not subjects of treatment themselves. The goal of this approach is the prompt achievement of abstinence with relapse prevention and the development of a drug-free adaptation.

Network therapy confronts the confounding problem that therapists have only a marginal ability to influence patients' behavior outside the office. If patients "slip" into drug abuse, their therapists may not be apprised, and if their therapists know, they can bring little influence to bear. Therapists on their own are limited in the degree to which they can make demands on the patient's life, and the patient is free to walk away from the therapeutic situation if it is uncomfortable for him/her, that is, if the situation challenges a potential relapse to addiction. All these factors make the engagement and orchestration of family and friends into the therapy with a substance-abusing patient invaluable resources, which offer remarkable opportunity for the modification of traditional psychotherapeutic techniques to treat the substance abuser.

NETWORK THERAPY EXAMPLE

We can begin to understand the nature of this option with the example of one particular patient. I was contacted by Paul, a physician practicing at a local hospital, who was concerned that the woman he hoped to marry was alcoholic. As he explained, when they were getting to know each other, there were periods when Nancy, seemingly well adapted, was unavailable in person or by telephone. But it was only after they moved in together that he realized the reason for these absences, as he soon became aware that Nancy would regularly go on drinking binges and that she sometimes did not show up the next day at the law office where she worked. She once threatened to kill herself when she was drunk.

Paul turned to her parents, but they preferred to minimize the issue, apparently not wanting to tarnish their daughter's image. He pleaded with Nancy to go to Alcoholics Anonymous (AA); she said she would think about it.

Nancy had been in treatment for a few years with a reputable psychiatrist, whom I later found out had tried to convince her to stop drinking. The problem this insight-oriented therapist encountered was so typical of those confronted with addicted patients.

A few weeks after Paul and I met, Nancy herself came to see me at Paul's behest, and I tried to get her to look at her problem. She, however, said that she was quite comfortable in her analysis and that it was offering her valuable insights. Furthermore, she did not think it useful for me to speak directly with her doctor. When I pointed out that her continued drinking argued for additional intervention, or at least some visits to AA, she fell back on the contention that her relationship in therapy should be enough to deal with her problems.

My later experience with Nancy will help to introduce the concept of network treatment. Nancy's resistance to seeking help for her alcoholism was typical of the way denial shows itself over the course of the disease. A few months after I initially saw her, she became annoyed at her psychiatrist for "pestering her" about going to AA and dropped out of treatment. The drinking continued unabated, and later that year she lost her job at the law office because of her unreliability. Paul was ready to walk out as well but said he would give her one more chance if she saw me, "the doctor who said she had to stop drinking." Nancy came in saying that her problem was that she needed "to get a handle on the depression" she had felt since losing her job.

Clearly, it was not a time to let her ventilate her feelings in isolation and fall into the same trap as her first therapist. I told her that because drinking played a role in her problem, it was important that we get some support for her, to help her look at her situation. I asked her to bring Paul and a friend of hers to our next session to discuss the issue. This was the beginning of her network therapy.

The two network members were certainly more revealing about the extent of Nancy's alcoholism than Nancy had been. They described how alcohol now often left Nancy in awkward social situations and incapacitated as well in facing the day that would follow her heavy drinking. I encouraged Paul and the friend to voice their feelings and concerns, to soften Nancy's inclination to avoid the problem. The impact of this network session moved Nancy to acknowledge that she had a problem with alcohol. The network members helped me to prevail on her to accept the idea of abstinence.

Together, the four of us developed a regimen to support Nancy's recovery, one that included individual sessions as well as meetings with this network. To this we added AA meetings, and the network members supported her in attending the meetings during later sessions, when she expressed misgivings about them. Importantly, Nancy and I *continued* to meet with her network while she focused on ways to protect her continued abstinence and on the psychological issues that would allow her to achieve a full recovery.

Nancy had a few slips back into drinking while in treatment and was once prepared to give it all up. Her network was behind her continued abstinence, though. We all consulted together at these times of crisis. With each slip we would work together to understand what certain drinking cues—situations and emotional states—led to the relapses. We would then plan together how Nancy could handle these cues when they came up again.

As time went on and Nancy's abstinence was secured, our network sessions were held less frequently but were not called off, and Nancy's individual therapy continued. In network sessions, the three of us would act as a sounding board for Nancy's recovery. We also provided the assurance that if Nancy slipped again, even after treatment was over, there would be a resource to draw on to secure her return to sobriety.

The nature of network support is further evident in the way we drew on one particularly meaningful relationship to bolster Nancy's abstinence. We often spoke with her sister on my speaker-phone during our network sessions. Although her sister lived in a remote city, Nancy had a particularly trusting relationship with her, and the sister had been very distressed for years over her drinking problem. This relationship was one that added strength to the bonds of affiliation that supported Nancy's recovery.

How does network therapy fit into our evolving understanding of addiction? Addicted persons generate great conflict and resentment among their family and friends. On the one hand, persons close to the addict have long been angered by his lack of responsiveness and by a history of many disappointments that he has conferred on them. On the other, they are remorseful over his unhappiness and the losses that he has suffered. The tension between anger and guilt makes it all but impossible for those close to the addicted people to approach them in an objective way. They are likely to overreact at one time and castigate them, and at another time they may shrink from asserting their concerns and be overly permissive, even enabling their addictive behavior.

In recent years, professionals have begun to consider the orchestration of family dynamics to move the addicted person toward recovery. A very important contribution has been the technique of the "intervention" for the reluctant substance abuser, which brings his family together to plan a confrontation designed to impress him with the immediate need for hospitalization. With aid from a professional, family members can thereby work together to have a meaningful impact, spurring the patient onto action. Multiple family therapy groups for substance abusers have also come into use so as to create a setting where a diversity of issues are melded together to neutralize individual resentments. The sense of community engendered in such groups can be supportive, and at the same time aid in achieving compliance with an expected norm of abstinence. These trends have been invaluable in developing our thinking about bringing the family into addiction treatment.

A LEARNING THEORY APPROACH

An important explanatory model of drug dependence was elaborated by Wikler (1973), based on his clinical investigations. The model, drawn from learning theory, helps to explain how the therapist employs cues to substance use in a network context.

In an attempt to understand the spontaneous appearance of drug craving in the absence of physiological withdrawal, Wikler looked to certain stimuli which may have been conditioned to evoke withdrawal phenomena. He pointed out that addictive drugs produce counteradaptive responses in the central nervous system at the same time that their direct pharmacological effects are felt, and that these are reflected in certain physiological events. With alcohol, for example, under certain circumstances, electroencephelogram-evoked response changes characteristic of withdrawal may be observed in the initial phases of intoxication (Begleiter & Porjesz, 1979). With opiates, administration of a narcotic antagonist to an addict who is "high" will precipitate a withdrawal reaction, which may be said to be present in a latent form. Such responses are overridden by the direct effect of the drug and are generally only observed after the cessation of a prolonged period of administration, when they are perceived as physiological withdrawal feelings or craving.

Thus, the drug euphoria is inevitably followed by the counteradaptive responses that occur on a physiological level, shortly after the initial drug administration. The pairing of this administration with stimuli from the environment or with internal subjective stimuli in a consistent manner will cause these stimuli to elicit the central counteradaptive response in the absence of prior drug administration. In the case of central nervous system depressant drugs such as the opiates and alcohol, the central response is subjectively experienced as an excitatory state, which is perceived by the addict as an abstinence or craving state. This state and its behavioral correlate of drug seeking are ultimately precipitated by the conditioned stimulus, namely, the sight of the drug, the associated context, or an initial dose of the drug itself.

Feelings such as anxiety and depression may regularly lead to the administration by the substance abuser of his/her drug of abuse. Such feelings may therefore also become conditioned stimuli for the excitatory conditioned response experienced as craving. They may therefore precipitate drug taking without conscious decision on the part of the addict. The same is true for a particular context in which alcohol or drugs were repeatedly taken; it may become a conditioned stimulus for drug-seeking behavior or subsequent occasions. For this reason, the recovering alcoholic is wise to avoid bars, as they have become for him/her conditioned stimuli for conditioned abstinence feelings, leaving the recovering alcoholics more vulnerable to "need" a drink.

Wikler (1973) primarily discussed conditioning or a psychophysiological response. With regard to the issues presented here, however, it should be pointed out that the conditioned stimulus of the drug or the affective state may lead directly to the behavioral response before the addict consciously experiences withdrawal feelings. The addict may therefore automatically act to seek out drugs by virtue of this conditioning upon entry into his/her old neighborhood, or upon experiencing anxiety or depression, all of which may have become conditioned stimuli. O'Brien, Testa, and O'Brien (1977) demonstrated the conditioning of addicts of opiate withdrawal responses to neutral stimuli such as sound and odor. This conditioning, produced in a laboratory setting, provided experimental corroboration of Wikler's hypothesis. Ludwig, Wikler, and Stark (1974) demonstrated the direct behavioral correlates of such conditioned stimuli in relation to alcohol administration. They found that for the alcoholic, the alcohol dose itself might serve as a conditioned stimulus for enhancing craving, as could the appropriate drinking context.

The following example illustrates the precipitation of drug seeking by a stimulus previously conditioned through its association with drug-taking behavior. Two conditioned stimuli, a subjective anxiety state and the visual cue of the bottle, both combined to precipitate a relapse into drug-seeking behavior without intermediate steps of deliberation, and without the intervening sensation of craving.

> A 41-year-old recovered alcoholic had been abstinent for 6 years. She was a regular if infrequent attender at AA meetings and had no interest in resuming drinking. One day, her 10-year-old daughter had not returned home from school. The daughter was sufficiently late so that the mother called the homes of her daughter's friends and then the police to find out whether there had been any reports of her whereabouts. The mother was sitting in her living room near the telephone awaiting a possible call and was quite anxious. At one point, she glanced over at a liquor cabinet and her attention was caught by a bottle of gin, which had been her preferred alcoholic beverage before achieving sobriety. The liquor cabinet was placed in the open because of her confidence and that of her family in the reliability of her maintaining abstinence. Without thinking, she went over to the bottle and poured a drink. This information was obtained from her in an interview on a detoxification service, some 6 months later; her drinking had increased to the point that she required hospital admission. The particular incident had been forgotten and was only elicited after a lengthy guided interview.

It should be noted that the initial dose of alcohol described here itself served as a conditioned stimulus for further alcohol seeking. As noted above, the enhancement of craving by an initial alcohol dose has been demonstrated in an experimental context. It is by this mechanism that a small amount of the addictive agent has been observed to precipitate "loss of control," that is, unmoderated alcohol or drug use.

Cognitive Labeling

The question may then be raised as to what would serve as a minimally noxious aversive stimulus that would be both specific for the conditioned stimulus and unlikely to be generalized, thereby yielding a maximal positive learning experience. To answer, let us look at Wikler's (1981) initial conception of the implications of this conditioning theory. He pointed out the following:

The user would become entangled in an interlocking web of self-perpetuating reinforcers, which perhaps explain the persistence of drug abuse, despite disastrous consequences for the user, and his imperviousness to psychotherapy which does not take such conditioning factors into account, because neither the subject nor the therapist is aware of their existence.

In addition, Ludwig et al. (1974) point out that the conditioned stimuli can be cognitively labeled so as to manipulate their role in precipitating craving and drug-seeking behavior. That is, by tagging the stimulus with some perceived label, the effect of the stimulus itself can be manipulated.

Because of the unconscious nature of the conditioned response of drug seeking, the patient's attempt to alter the course of the stimulus–response sequence is generally not viable, even with the aid of a therapist. Neither party is aware that a conditioned sequence is taking place. Sufficient exploration, however, may reveal the relevant stimuli and their ultimate effect through conditioned sequences of drug-seeking behavior. By means of guided recall in a psychotherapeutic context, alcoholics or addicts themselves can become aware of the sequence of action of conditioned stimuli. They can then label those stimuli themselves. The therapeutic maneuver consists of applying an aversive stimulus to the conditioned responses that are to be extinguished.

At this point, the patient's own distress at the course of the addictive process, generated by the patient's own motivation for escaping the addictive pattern, may be mobilized. This motivational distress then serves as the aversive stimulus. The implicit assumption behind this therapeutic approach is that the patient in question is desirous of altering his/her pattern of drug use and that the recognition of a particular stimulus as a conditioned component of addiction will allow the patient, in effect, to initiate the extinction process. If a patient is committed to achieving abstinence from an addictive drug such as alcohol or cocaine but is in jeopardy of occasional slips, cognitive labeling can facilitate consolidation of an abstinent adaptation. Such an approach is less valuable in the context of inadequate motivation for abstinence, fragile social supports, or compulsive substance abuse unmanageable by the patient in his/her usual social settings. Hospitalization or replacement therapy (e.g., methadone) may be necessary here, because ambulatory stabilization through psychotherapeutic support is often not feasible. Under any circumstances, cognitive labeling is an adjunct to psychotherapy and not a replacement for group supports such as AA, family counseling, or ambulatory therapeutic community programs where applicable.

The following clinical example may be helpful in illustrating this approach.

A 40-year-old writer–publicist had been drinking heavily since his late teens, at least a pint daily for the past 10 years. He was referred to consultation by his child's therapist. This and a recent work-related crisis led him to appreciate the extensive damage caused by his drinking. He agreed to undertake abstinence and take disulfiram but refused to attend AA. Although drinking only presented a problem during one subsequent episode, conditioned drinking cues emerged as an issue in therapy. These were illustrated by three contexts previously associated with drinking in which the patient experienced malaise and restlessness. All three were examined in depth in terms of the drinking antecedents as well as his contemporaneous feelings. This allowed the patient to understand his malaise and consciously mobilize himself to deal with craving he felt in these situations. The first setting was when he stayed up late at night, as was his wont, to do his writing; he regularly drank heavily at these times to allay anxiety aroused by his conflicts over his creative work. Second, he suffered from a mild phobia of airplane flights and would drink heavily before flying. Third, before major speeches out of town, he would spend the evening in a bar, sometimes to the point of affecting his ability to present his material the next day. Addressing the symptoms experienced at these times was as a basis for understanding the patient's conflicts, as well as helping to bolster his commitment to abstinence. They were discussed in the context of network sessions as well, a technique described below.

This case example therefore illustrates enhanced means for approaching psychotherapy with the alcohol and drug abuser in the context of network supports. It provides the therapist with another tool to assist the patient at a time when more traditional therapeutic maneuvers may be less successful.

THE TECHNIQUE OF NETWORK THERAPY

Patient Selection for Network Therapy

A broad range of addicted patients characterized by the following clinical hallmarks of addictive illness can be treated. They are substance-dependent patients who, upon initiating consumption of their addictive agent, be it alcohol, cocaine, opiates, or depressant drugs, frequently cannot limit that consumption to a reasonable and predictable level. This phenomenon has been termed *loss of control* by clinicians who treat alcohol- or drug-dependent persons (Ludwig, Bendfeldt, Wikler, & Cain, 1978; Galanter, 1983). Also included are patients who consistently demonstrate relapse to the agent of abuse; that is, they have attempted to stop using the drug for varying periods but return to it, despite a specific intent to avoid it.

This treatment approach is not necessary for those abusers who can, in fact, learn to set limits on their alcohol; their abuse may be treated as a behavioral symptom in a more traditional psychotherapeutic fashion. Nor is it directed at those patients for whom the addictive pattern is most unmanageable, such as alcoholics with unusual destabilizing circumstances such as homelessness, severe character pathology, or psychosis. These patients may need special supportive care such as inpatient detoxification or long-term residential treatment. What therefore differentiates patients regarding their suitability for treatment? Factors that are relevant are intensity of addiction, the drug abused, and the severity of the patient's social disability.

As in all office practice, patients tend to self-select relative to the therapist and the modalities offered. Although the therapist may encounter a variety of patients, those encountered typically appear voluntarily for assistance with alcohol or drug dependence. These patients tend to be less compromised than inpatients, whose abuse has been so severe that they required hospitalization. Nonetheless, after a period of hospitalization, the latter group may be quite suitable for network treatment. Furthermore, patients engaged in self-help treatment, such as AA or a therapeutic community, can be seen concomitantly with a network approach. However, care must be taken to ensure that the variety of modalities combined act in a complementary way.

How to Begin Network Therapy

Let us consider how one embarks on the use of a network in treatment. At the outset, the patient should be asked to bring a spouse or a close friend to the first session. Substance abusers often balk at a confrontation with the therapist upon first coming for treatment and may deny or rationalize even if they have voluntarily sought help. Because of their denial of the problem, a significant other is essential both to history taking and to implementing a viable treatment plan. A close relation can often cut through the denial in the way that an unfamiliar therapist cannot and can therefore be invaluable in setting a standard of realism in dealing with the addiction.

Some patients make clear that they wish to come to the initial session on their own. This is often associated with their desire to preserve the option of continued alcohol abuse and is born out of the fear that an alliance will be established independent of them to prevent this. Although a delay may be tolerated for a session or two, there should be no ambiguity at the outset that effective treatment can only be undertaken on the basis of a therapeutic alliance built around the alcohol issue that includes the support of significant others, and that it is expected that a network of close friends and/or relations will be brought in within a session or two at the most.

The therapist should be available for consultation on the telephone and should indicate to the patient that he/she wants to be called if problems arise. This makes the therapist's commitment clear and sets the tone for a "team effort." It begins to undercut one reason for relapse, the patient's sense that perceived mobility to manage the situation. The astute therapist, though, will be able to avoid spending excessive time on the telephone or in emergency sessions. The therapist can develop a support network that can handle the majority of problems involved in day-to-day assistance to the patient. This will generally leave the therapist only to respond to occasional questions of interpreting the terms of the understanding between him/herself, the patient, and support network members. If there is question about the ability of the patient and network to manage the period between the initial sessions, the first few scheduled sessions may be arranged at intervals of only 1 to 3 days.

What is most essential, though, is that the network be forged into a working group to provide necessary support for the patient between the initial sessions. Contacts between network members at this stage typically include telephone calls at the therapist's or patient's initiative, dinner arrangements, and social encounters and should be preplanned to a fair extent during the joint session. These encounters are most often undertaken when alcohol or drug use is likely to occur. In planning together, however, it should be made clear to network members that relatively little unusual effort will be required for the long term, that after the patient is stabilized, their participation will come to little more than attendance at infrequent meetings with the patient and therapist. This is reassuring to those network members who are unable to make a major time commitment to the patient, as well as to those patients who do not want to be placed in a dependent position.

The Network's Role

The network is established to implement a straightforward task: aiding the therapist to sustain the patient's abstinence. It must be directed with the same clarity of purpose that a task force is directed in any effective organization. Competing and alternative goals must be suppressed, or at least prevented from interfering with the primary task. Unlike family members involved in traditional family therapy, network members are not led to expect symptom relief or self-realization for themselves. This prevents the development of competing goals for the network's meetings. It also assures the members that they will be protected from having their own motives scrutinized, and thereby supports their continuing involvement without the threat of an assault on their psychological defenses. Because network members have volunteered to participate, their motives must not be impugned. Their constructive behavior should be commended. It is useful to acknowledge appreciation for the contribution they are making to the therapy. There is always a counterproductive tendency on their part to minimize the value of their contribution.

At the outset of therapy, it is important to see the patient with the group on a weekly basis, at least for the first month. Unstable circumstances demand more frequent contacts with the network. Sessions can be tapered off biweekly and then at monthly intervals after a time.

In order to sustain the continuing commitment of the group, particularly between the therapist and the network members, network sessions should be held every 3 months or so for the duration of the individual therapy. Once the patient has stabilized, the meetings tend less to address day-to-day issues. They may begin with the patient's recounting of the drug situation. Reflections on the patient's progress and goals, or sometimes on relations between the network members, may then be discussed. In any case, it is essential that network members contact the therapist if they are concerned about the patient's possible use of alcohol or drugs, and that the therapist him/herself contact the network members if the therapist becomes concerned about a potential relapse.

Alcoholics Anonymous Is Network Therapy

Use of self-help modalities is desirable whenever possible. For the alcoholic certainly, participation in AA is strongly encouraged. (Groups such as Narcotics Anonymous, Pills Anonymous, and Cocaine Anonymous are modeled after AA and play a similarly useful role for drug abusers.) One approach is to tell the patient that he/she is expected to attend at least two AA meetings a week for at least 1 month so as to familiarize him/herself with the program. If after 1 month the patient is quite reluctant to continue, and other aspects of the treatment are going well, the patient's nonparticipation may have to be accepted.

Some patients are more easily convinced to attend AA meetings. Others may be less compliant. The therapist should mobilize the support network as appropriate, in order to continue pressure for the patient's involvement with AA for a reasonable trial. It may take a considerable amount of time, but ultimately a patient may experience something of a conversion wherein he/she adopts the group ethos and expresses a deep commitment to abstinence, a measure of commitment rarely observed in patients who experience psychotherapy alone. When this commitment occurs, the therapist may assume a more passive role in monitoring the patient's abstinence and keep an eye on the patient's ongoing involvement in AA.

Using Disulfiram

Disulfiram can be a useful tool when taken daily to avert relapse, as it blocks the intermediary metabolism of alcohol, producing high blood levels of acetaldehyde, a metabolite of alcohol (Fuller et al., 1986). Patients taking disulfiram will therefore experience considerable distress if they drink, because acetaldehyde in high concentrations causes nausea, headache, and facial flushing. If this alcohol–acetaldehyde reaction is explained to the alcoholic upon the initiation of disulfiram treatment, the anticipation of this highly unpleasant experience serves as a deterrent for alcohol use. For this reason, if the patient takes disulfiram each morning, he/she will be cognizant of the vulnerability to drinking and will avoid drinking at least for that day.

In order for the regimen to be effective, however, the patient must continue taking disulfiram every day. If the patient knows he/she will be observed taking disulfiram each morning, the patient will avoid inadvertently "forgetting" the medication for a day or two, which would allow for the possibility of losing the intended effect of this medication. An observation regimen can be established with a person in the network close to the patient, generally the spouse, as this is easily adapted to a couple's morning routine. Thus, although, disulfiram may be of marginal use in a traditional counseling context (Fuller et al., 1986), it therefore becomes much more valuable when carefully integrated into work with the patient and network.

It is a good idea to use the initial telephone contact to obtain the patient's agreement to be abstinent from alcohol for the day immediately prior to the first session. The therapist then has the option of prescribing or administering disulfiram at that time. For a patient who is in earnest about seeking assistance for alcoholism, this is often not difficult if some time is spent on the telephone making plans to avoid a drinking context during that period. If it is not feasible to undertake this on the telephone, it may be addressed in the first session. Such planning with the patient almost always involves organizing time with significant others and therefore is a basis for developing the patient's support network.

The administration of disulfiram under observation is a treatment option that is easily adapted to work with social networks. A patient who takes disulfiram cannot drink; a patient who agrees to be observed by a responsible party while taking disulfiram will not miss his/his dose without the observer's knowledge. This may take a measure of persuasion and, above all, the therapist's commitment that such an approach can be reasonable and helpful.

As noted previously, individual therapists have traditionally seen the abuser as a patient with poor prognosis. This is largely because in the context of traditional psychotherapy, there are no behavioral controls to prevent the recurrence of drug use, and resources are not available for behavioral intervention if a recurrence takes place—which it usually does. A system of impediments to the emergence of relapse, resting heavily on the actual or symbolic role of the network, must therefore be established. The therapist must have assistance in addressing any minor episode of drinking so that this ever-present problem does not lead to an unmanageable relapse or an unsuccessful termination of therapy.

Concomitant Individual Therapy

As noted above, network sessions are scheduled on a weekly basis at the outset of treatment. This is likely to compromise the number of individual contacts. Indeed, if sessions are held once a week, the patient may not be seen individually for a certain period. This may be perceived as a deprivation by the patient unless the individual therapy is presented as an opportunity for further growth *predicated* on achieving stable abstinence assured through work with the network.

When the individual therapy does begin, the traditional objectives of therapy must be ordered so as to accommodate the goals of the substance abuse treatment. For insight-oriented therapy, clarification of unconscious motivations is a primary objective; for supportive therapy, the bolstering of established constructive defenses is primary. In the therapeutic context we are describing, however, the following objectives are given precedence: Network therapy sessions are conducted on a weekly basis for the first month of treatment, and thereafter tapered to a biweekly format for the ensuing month, and then less frequently, such as monthly or bimonthly after 1 year. This schedule is introduced within an overall format of once- or twice-weekly sessions. Network therapy typically continues for at least 1 year, after which these sessions may be terminated with the understanding that they can be reconvened if the need arises. Individual therapy may come to an end at that time as well, or it may continue as appropriate.

Of primary importance is the need to address exposure to substances of abuse, or exposure to cues that might precipitate alcohol or drug use. Both patient and therapist should be sensitive to this matter and explore these situations as they arise. Second, a stable social context in an appropriate social environment—one conducive to abstinence with minimal disruption of life circumstances—should be supported. Considerations of minor disruptions in place of residence, friends, or job need not be a primary issue for the patient with character disorder or neurosis, but they cannot go untended here. For a considerable period, the substance abuser is highly vulnerable to exacerbations of the addictive illness and must be viewed with the considerable caution, in some respects, as one treats the recently compensated psychotic.

A formal understanding is established with the patient and members of the network regarding confidentiality of communication. All information directly related to the consumption of alcohol and drugs should be shared by the patient, the network members, and the therapist. Thus, information regarding drug use, conveyed by a member of the network, would be conveyed to both the patient and other members of the network. Similarly, the patient is obliged to reveal episodes of substance use to the group. On the other hand, issues discussed in individual therapy are not subject to exposure by the therapist, nor is the patient under any obligation to reveal personal matters to members of the network. Furthermore, it is understood that members of the network will not reveal to outside parties anything discussed with the patient in the network sessions.

Finally, after attending to these priorities, psychological conflicts which the patient must resolve, relative to his own growth, are considered. As the therapy continues, these conflicts assume a more prominent role. In the earlier phases, they are likely to directly reflect issues associated with previous drug use. Later, however, as the issue of addiction becomes less compelling from day to day, the context of the treatment will come increasingly to resemble the traditional psychotherapeutic context. Given the optimism generated by initial success over the addictive process, the patient will be in an excellent position to move forward in therapy with a positive view of his future.

NETWORK GUIDELINES

At the outset of therapy, it is important to see the patient with the group on a weekly basis at least for the first month. Unstable circumstances demand more frequent contacts with the network. Sessions can be tapered off biweekly and then at monthly intervals after a time.

In order to sustain the continuing commitment of the group, particularly between the therapist and the network members, network sessions should be held every 3 months or so for the duration of the individual therapy. Once the patient has stabilized, the meetings tend less to address day-to-day issues. They may begin with the patient's recounting of the drug situation. Reflections on the patient's progress and goals, or sometimes on relations between the network members, may then be discussed. In any case, it is essential that network members contact the therapist if they are concerned about the patient's possible use of alcohol or drugs, and that the therapist him/herself contact the network members if the therapist becomes concerned about a potential relapse.

The following guidelines should be made clear from the first so that network members can collaborate in implementing their respective work with the patient. Above all, they should be conveyed by example. The correction of misapprehensions about these norms should be given a high priority; similarly, violations of these guidelines are discussed as soon as detected, and in a supportive manner.

1. The purpose of the network is to help patients maintain their abstinence; unrelated benefits for other members are not pursued

in network sessions by the patient, network members, or the therapist.

2. Information relevant to the patient's abstinence or slips into drug use will be promptly reported to the therapist and to other network members.

3. Supportiveness for the patient is primary. Members should help the patient to deal with problems he/she confronts regarding abstinence but not be critical of his/her difficulties in achieving a recovery.

4. If a slip is detected by a network member, the network member will offer the patient assistance but will not impose a course of action without consulting with the therapist.

5. The nature of confidentiality is important. The patient's own exchanges with the therapist that are unrelated to drug problems are kept in confidence. Information revealed by network members to the therapist, however, will be brought up in the group if relevant.

REFERENCES

Begleiter, H., & Porjesz, B. (1979). Persistence of a subacute withdrawal syndrome following chronic ethanol intake. *Drug and Alcohol Dependence, 4,* 353–357.

Fuller, R., Branchey, L., Brightwell, D. R., Derman, R. M., Emrick, C. D., Iber, F. L., James K. E., LaCousiere, R. B., Leek, K., Lowenstein, I., Maany, I., Niederheiser, D., Nocks, J. J., & Shaw, S. (1986). Disulfiram treatment of alcoholism. A Veterans Administration cooperative study. *Journal of the American Medical Association, 256,* 1449–1455.

Galanter, M. (1983). Psychotherapy for alcohol and drug abuse: An approach based on learning theory. *Journal of Psychiatric Treatment and Evaluation, 5,* 551–556.

Galanter, M. (1993). *Network therapy for alcoholism and drug abuse: A new approach in practice.* New York: Basic Books.

Ludwig, A. M., Bendfeldt, F., Wikler, A., & Cain, R. B. (1978). "Loss of control" in alcoholics. *Archives of General Psychiatry, 35,* 370–373.

Ludwig, A. M., Wikler, A., & Stark, L. M. (1974). The first drink. *Archives of General Psychiatry, 30,* 539–547.

O'Brien, C. P., Testa, T., & O'Brien, T. J. (1977). Conditioned narcotic withdrawal in humans. *Science, 195,* 1000–1002.

Wikler, A. (1971). Some implications of conditioning theory for problems of drug abuse. *Behavioral Science, 16,* 92–97.

Wikler, A. (1973). Dynamics of drug dependence. *Archives of General Psychiatry, 28,* 611–616.

III

SPECIAL POPULATIONS
AND CONSIDERATIONS

20

Dual Diagnosis: Outpatient Treatment of Substance Abusers with Coexisting Psychiatric Disorders

LISA DIRECTOR

INTRODUCTION

The incidence of psychiatric disturbance is high among those who suffer from chemical dependency. Estimates vary of the number of substance abusers who are thought to carry a so-called dual diagnosis, based on the category of psychiatric disorder that is used as an index and the group of substance abusers that is selected for study. However, it is safe to conclude, as Wallen and Weiner (1989) do, that "a significant minority" of all chemically dependent persons are dually diagnosed. These authors estimate—conservatively, alongside others—that 5% to 10% of drug-dependent individuals are likely to suffer from a major psychiatric disorder, such as affective illness, anxiety disorder, schizophrenia, or schizoaffective disorder, whereas an even larger number, 25% to 35%, are likely to suffer from an underlying personality disorder.

Although psychiatric illness of one form or another has always existed among a subgroup of substance abusers, the problem has drawn particular attention in recent years. The increased interest and attention may be due to converging public and professional events.

Publicly, the effects of deinstitutionalization, homelessness, and the availability of cheap drugs have combined to lend urgency to the discussion of dual diagnosis and to give the problem a human face. Residents of every urban neighborhood have grown used to the familiar sight of the homeless, including a certain number who are psychiatrically disturbed (most of whom are hardly threatening, due to their impairment). However, the recent influx of street drugs—crack, in particular—has transformed some of this number into public nuisances or, worse, dangerous individuals whose psychiatric symptoms have been exacerbated to tragic end. In a few publicized cases—where such individuals have succeeded in overturning care, terrorizing neighborhoods, even committing violent crimes—the potentially explosive interaction of mental illness and drug abuse has gained widespread recognition, as has the need for a response (Treaster & Tabor, 1993).

More quietly, an important development has been taking place in the fields of addiction treatment and mental health. A historic gulf between these two fields—based on differing views of problem behavior and differing approaches to treatment—has been gradually eroding (Wallen & Weiner, 1989; Zweben, 1992). This has permitted the evolution of a new breed of clinician, trained in both disciplines, with the skills and flexibility to respond to the needs of patients whose dual diagnoses require application of more than one theory and technique. In hospitals, mental health facilities, and drug treatment clinics, "integrated" approaches to treating the dually diagnosed have been evolving, reflecting the growing awareness that these patients make up a unique clinical population requiring a unique treatment methodology and response (Minkoff, 1989; Wallen & Weiner, 1989; Zweben, 1992).

In this chapter, one such model for treating dually diagnosed patients in an outpatient addiction facility is presented. The model is integrated in that elements of varied and distinct treatment approaches—addiction treatment, supportive psychotherapy, education, and psychopharmacology—are brought together to meet the special needs of these patients. First, however, before considering treatment, basic information particular to this group of patients needs to be addressed.

TERMINOLOGY AND MEANING

Dual diagnosis is itself a vague term, contributing to our inability to get a clearer picture of these patients (Sciacca, 1991). Theoretically, the term could apply to any combination of disorders taken from the *Diagnostic and Statistical Manual of Mental Disorders* (DSM-III-R), which is published by the American Psychiatric Association (APA, 1987) to serve as a classification system and diagnostic guide. Practically speaking, however, the term *dual diagnosis* has come to connote any individual with a diagnosis of substance abuse or dependence who also exhibits a distinct, coexisting psychiatric disorder. Note that this is not the same as an individual who is considered "dually addicted"—that is, addicted to more than one substance or behavior, as in the case of an alcoholic who compulsively gambles or a cocaine addict who engages in compulsive sexual activity when he/she is high. The additional diagnosis that an "addicted" person must carry to warrant designation as "dually diagnosed" must be of a separate and different psychiatric disorder. This still leaves a wide domain. It should also be noted that many believe that all chemically dependent persons suffer from a certain amount of mood dysfunction and personality deficit (Khantzian, Halliday, & McAuliffe, 1990). However, the term *dual diagnosis* is usually reserved for those who suffer from a more pronounced disturbance, worthy of additional diagnosis and separate psychiatric attention. Granted, these distinctions can be hard to make.

The psychiatric disorders that may affect substance abusers fall under two main headings. First, there are the major clinical syndromes classified under Axis I of the DSM-III-R diagnostic code, which break down into further categories. Of particular relevance to substance abusers are mood disorders, including depression and bipolar disorder; anxiety disorders, including panic disorder, generalized anxiety disorder, and obsessive–compulsive disorder; and psychotic disorders, including schizophrenia and schizoaffective disorder. (Of course, the condition of substance abuse or dependence is itself an Axis I diagnosis.)

Grouped under Axis II of the DSM-III-R diagnostic code are the so-called personality disorders, believed to reflect maladaptive traits that take shape early in a person's life, persist throughout development, and result in marked impairment or distress (APA, 1987). Among this class of disorders, borderline, narcissistic, and antisocial personality disorders are especially common among the chemically dependent.

If we add to this the menu of possible drugs of abuse—stimulants such as cocaine, depressants like alcohol and opiates, sedative and analgesic drugs such as benzodiazepines and barbiturates—one can see that the dual-diagnosis designation applies to a broad group. For example, a homeless schizophrenic who is addicted to crack can be seen as dually diagnosed, as can be a depressed but functional teacher who quietly abuses alcohol at night. Clearly, the dually diagnosed are not a uniform clinical entity but a heterogeneous group who differ in psychiatric disorder, level of functioning, social support, and capacity for independent living. Thus, there is no one treatment methodology that could singly serve the needs of the dually diagnosed. Rather, various approaches need to be developed that are carefully tailored to selected segments of this population. In fact, it is questionable whether all dually diagnosed individuals require special treatment at all: substance abusers who are rather high functioning, and only mildly impaired by coexisting disorders, may successfully be treated in mainstream chemical dependency settings.

One further distinction needs to be made. The term *mentally ill chemical abuser* (MICA) has also gained currency in the discussion of these patients. The term MICA has sometimes loosely been used to suggest any individual, or group of patients, who is dually diagnosed. (In common usage, when used more as a label, MICA has become associated with a suggestion of difficulty, reflecting the popular, even professional belief that these are "problem patients," given their multiple diagnoses and needs. Other labels that have emerged for these patients capture this same perception: According to a list of names cited by Ries & Ellingson, 1990, the dual-diagnosis patient has been called the new, chronic patient and even the 3-D patient—for "drinking, drugging, and disturbed.") MICA more accurately refers to a specific subgroup of the dually diagnosed: those who suffer from severe mental illness. Severe mental illness is defined by most practitioners as consisting of an Axis I psychotic disorder—principally schizophrenia, but also schizoaffective disorder or major affective disorder with psychotic features (Minkoff, 1989; Sciacca, 1991). Because patients so diagnosed often suffer from the ongoing effects of their disorders and limitations in their functioning that require that they be treated in partial hospitalization, services that are suited to their needs differ markedly from those that could be designed for patients who do not suffer from psychotic symptomatology or sequelae (Sciacca, 1991).

It is useful, then, to distinguish between two groups of the dually diagnosed: those who, in addition to chemical dependency, suffer from psychotic mental disorders (MICA) versus those who suffer from non-psychotic mental disorders, including depression, bipolar disorder, anxiety disorders, or serious personality disorder. Because such disorders are less likely to seriously curtail functioning or prevent employment, such patients can be effectively treated in an outpatient treatment program. The program presented later in this chapter was developed for the latter group; treatment considerations for MICA patients are not addressed in this chapter.

CONSIDERATIONS IN ASSESSMENT

The basic criterion for a dual diagnosis in a chemically dependent person is the presence of an independent psychiatric disorder. Determining this becomes tricky simply because drug effects mask underlying mental functioning and sometimes mimic actual psychiatric syndromes. There are many examples of this problem. In the stage of acute intoxication, stimulants such as cocaine can induce a paranoid psychotic state that resembles schizophrenia (Kosten & Kleber, 1988). And addiction to many different drugs, including stimulants, opiates, and alcohol, can leave users in a state of protracted withdrawal that looks and feels like depression, featuring problems such as sleep and appetite disturbance, fatigue, anxiety, and irritability (Group for the Advancement of Psychiatry, 1991). Given the confounding effects of drugs, how can one accurately assess?

Clinicians have arrived at a set of working guidelines to assist them in establishing whether disturbance in an active or newly sober patient exists independently of the drug use itself. First, the patient's history serves as a guide. If the patient reports a history of psychiatric disturbance well before he/she became involved in drugs, this clearly establishes an independent origin and the likely presence of a dual diagnosis. However, because patients often fail to serve as reliable historians, and family members are not always available for the assessment process, history alone is not an adequate guide.

Most clinicians rely on their own observations of a patient, within the first few weeks of treatment, to see whether the patient's psychiatric symptoms resolve with the onset of abstinence. There is a range of opinion as to how much sober time to allow in order to unmask true, drug-free mental status: By conservative estimate, it could take 6 months of abstinence before a picture of a patient's baseline functioning emerges, but most clinicians use a timetable of 4 to 6 weeks to allow for full detoxification from drug use and for sufficient sobriety to be in place to assume that a patient's functioning and feelings are relatively free of the influence of drugs (Evans & Sullivan, 1990). If a patient's psychiatric complaints persist beyond this point they are more likely to stem from actual psychopathology—indicative of dual diagnosis—than they are from drug toxicity and effect (Zweben, 1992). Conversely, if by this point a patient's symptoms subside, they are likely to have been by-products of drug use and not evidence of mental disorder. In the latter case, where symptoms arise secondary to drug use, dual diagnosis does not exist. Such patients are helped to tolerate the discomfort of drug withdrawal and loss, which is itself a critical task as all drug users suffer from deficits in their capacity to regulate affect; however, no other specialized treatment is offered. These patients, misleading in their resemblance to the dually diagnosed in early stages of sobriety, have earned their own acronym: CAMI ("chemical abusing mentally ill")—the positioning of the letters in their name reflecting the derivative nature of their "mental illness" (Sciacca, 1991).

The need to allow for time and repeated observation in diagnosing newly sober patients has led experts to agree that a "longitudinal" approach to assessment is in order with individuals considered likely to be dually diagnosed (Zweben, 1992). The experience, in work with all recovering patients, of witnessing metamorphosis, especially occurs with the dually diagnosed: The nature of the work, and of the patients themselves, constantly changes throughout the first year. One first meets these

patients in the throes of active drug use, observes the emergence of their
"real" personalities and disorders as sobriety settles in, works to introduce
patients to certain aspects of their selves as they become available to view,
then helps patients cope with impingements to their psyches, as these
impingements are experienced without relief of drugs.

Whereas history and time are the objective criteria used in assessment, many clinicians rely on a subjective guide to determine whether
patients are dually diagnosed: their different "feel" from other substance
abusers, even early in sobriety. It is easiest to get at the way these patients offer an exception by first commenting on the "rule": Substance
abusers who lack significant psychiatric disorders are remarkable for the
simple fact that they can look and sound "normal." Even the most out-
of-control drug user, whose spiraling addiction has brought him to his
knees—through daily bingeing, depletion of funds, ultimatums from his
spouse, termination from his job—can arrive at treatment, articulately
tell his story, relate to a group of strangers, and display appropriate affect in the process. Although this superficial appearance of normalcy is
itself problematic, serving as it can to defensively veil underlying deficit,
most substance abusers have the disarming ability to speak, function, and
interact in an appropriate way.

Those who are dually diagnosed do *not*—not because of their chemical dependency but because of their psychiatric impairment. Something
is markedly "off" in their presentation, with disorder appearing in one
or another domain of mental status. Mood might be grim and leaden or
anger unusually intense and uncontained. Thinking might be idiosyncratic
or speech rambling and circumstantial. Of particular diagnostic value are
any impairments in relatedness, a problem often on display in a patient's
response to the evaluating clinician. Keeping in mind that absent mental
illness, those who are chemically dependent are often adept, even facile,
in their management of social roles and exchanges, gross deficits in relatedness or inappropriate behavior are often telling. For example, if a patient fails to make normal eye contact or expresses marked paranoia
toward the interviewer, or, conversely, is excessively ingratiating in his
efforts to charm, such aberrant responses often tip the presence of additional disorder.

In sum, whereas psychiatric assessment of the chemically dependent
is a challenge, using clinical judgment and allowing for a longitudinal approach can make for accurate detection of dual diagnosis.

PRINCIPLES OF TREATMENT:
AN INTEGRATED APPROACH

The model described here, the dual-focus program, was developed at the
Washton Institute, an outpatient treatment facility in New York. The institute specializes in providing structured, intensive treatment to alcohol-

and substance-abusing individuals. Because of the effectiveness of its approach, described in an earlier chapter, and because outpatient treatment can be undertaken without causing disruption to a patient's home or work life, the institute attracts a client base who are largely employed.

In recent years, within the same client base at the institute, we began seeing a certain number of patients who appeared more disturbed than their "mainstream" chemically dependent cohorts. Frequently, one of the ways in which their disorder was apparent was that they were unable to work, because they had been either placed on medical leave following psychiatric hospitalization or fired for inappropriate behavior. As it became clear that a stable and significant minority of our patients were, in fact, dually diagnosed and in need of special services, we developed the dual-focus program, with its own assessment and treatment protocol. Although these patients were more impaired than those in our mainstream program, because they tended to come from the same referral sources and were potential members of the work force, they were not seriously dysfunctional. Thus, the dual-diagnosis program that we developed was not created to meet the needs of the more severely impaired MICA population. Rather, the kinds of psychiatric disorders that we expected to attract, and did in fact treat, alongside drug dependence, included major depression, bipolar disorder, panic disorder, obsessive–compulsive disorder, and antisocial, borderline, and mixed personality disorders. Although patients who suffered from a primary psychotic mental disorder were, as a rule, excluded from our program, some of our patients had experienced discrete psychotic episodes in the past.

The clinical and theoretical thrust of the dual-focus program is eclectic. The one guiding philosophy is the belief that dually diagnosed patients suffer from interacting but disparate disorders whose differences require varied treatment and response. In this regard, we take a different approach from other experts in the field who believe that in working with the dually diagnosed, "parallels" between their two disorders should be emphasized, as should the need for a like response (Minkoff, 1989; Sciacca, 1991). For example, in this view, patients are taught that chemical dependency and psychiatric disorder are both forms of "illness" that share a biological base and chronic course, with periods of "active" symptoms that can be brought under control; likewise, the goal in both disorders is to prevent relapse rather than to arrive at a permanent "cure" (Minkoff, 1989; Sciacca, 1991). While such a view of parallel phenomena might be applicable with a chemically dependent patient who also suffers from schizophrenia—where concepts of disease, active symptoms, and relapse apply—it is less useful with a patient who has a personality disorder or dysthymia. In these disorders, etiology is complex and distress ongoing, with symptoms hardly obeying an episodic course of clear onset and remission. In further contrast to chemical dependency, where disorder appears in the form of behavior, in most psychiatric syndromes disorder is internal, evidenced in abnormal mood, distortions in sense of self, etc., and therefore cannot be undone in quite the same way as addiction.

Thus, our treatment model embodies diversity: differing theories are drawn on to explain and treat and differing interventions are woven together. Elements of addiction treatment, supportive psychotherapy, psychoeducation, and pharmacotherapy are integrated with the result that treatment operates on several planes at once, moving freely among schools of thought, techniques, and target behaviors. Let me illustrate this with the hypothetical example of an alcoholic patient who also suffers from bipolar and mixed personality disorders. The approach of addiction treatment would be used to challenge such a patient to address a relapse by making specific behavior changes, such as attending self-help daily, enlisting a sponsor, and planning free time; the principles of dynamically oriented psychotherapy would be applied to help the patient see how he responds to group inquiry with hurt and anger that quickly escalate into conflict, resembling problems he has elsewhere in his life; the occasion of his relapse might also be used to educate the patient about the concept of mood variation and to ask him to identify the signs of his own cycle and how they can be used to alert him to impending relapse; and the question of medication would be raised, with the patient urged to consider lithium.

Although this eschews simplicity, and calls on patients as well as therapists to constantly shift hats, nonetheless such an integrated approach addresses these patients' true diagnostic complexity, and trains them to become versatile in their own management of their disorders.

In the dual-focus program, treatment is viewed as taking place in stages, the specifics of which are described here.

Stage 1: Initial Assessment and Engagement

A chemically dependent patient, new to the institute, who shows signs of possible dual diagnosis—through report of psychiatric hospitalization, use of psychotropic medication, or the patient's own account—is assigned to undergo a special assessment.

In an initial interview, the standard drug and alcohol history is taken and a full psychological evaluation conducted, complete with mental status examination and psychiatric and treatment history. Although a diagnostic impression is formed, most of our dually diagnosed patients are not assigned to enter group therapy immediately. In contrast to our "regular" substance-abusing patients, we continue to work with dually diagnosed patients in an extended assessment format, involving individual sessions alone for a period of up to 4 weeks. There are many reasons for extending this procedure.

First, the additional time allows for the unfolding of the assessment process as is ideally called for, and previously described, with dually diagnosed patients who are newly sober. This period also allows the clinician to refer the patient for a psychiatric consultation if evaluation for medication appears to be in order. As psychiatrists often want a patient drug-free for at least 2 weeks before starting medication, an initial start-up period in the treatment, during which sobriety can be closely monitored, plays a useful role.

Most important, the extended procedure lends itself to the critical task of engagement and to the development of a therapeutic alliance between patient and clinician. Whereas engagement is the essential first step in any treatment, it is especially important with the dually diagnosed. Because of their psychiatric impairments, these patients have often failed to develop the social and vocational supports that surround other substance abusers and whose preservation provides motivation for treatment (Kofoed, Kania, Walsh, & Atkinson, 1986). Specifically, dually diagnosed patients are often unmarried or estranged from families and living alone; they are often unemployed or working in marginal, per diem jobs. They therefore lack the personal and professional "assets" that serve as incentives to other substance abusers to consider sobriety and change.

Although this makes dually diagnosed patients less inclined to undertake treatment—and the task of engagement more difficult—they also stand to gain more than others by entering treatment: the value of the therapeutic relationship itself. More than with other patients, the treatment professional assumes special importance in these patients' lives, serving not only as therapist and related transference object but also as adviser, teacher, respected "friend" of the family, and social liaison. A therapist's place in his/her patient's object world is always laden with meaning; however the therapist who works with the dually diagnosed actually fills several of these real-world roles. He or she exerts far greater influence by sheer dint of the psychosocial limits in these patients' lives.

Therefore, in our treatment model for the dually diagnosed, we emphasize the contribution of the therapeutic alliance. We not only set aside time at the outset for patient and therapist to cultivate this tie but also reserve a role for individual therapy throughout the course of treatment, alongside other modalities. Note that this is a departure from the standard approach of addiction treatment and from the methodology of Alcoholics Anonymous (AA); in both, it is the *group* that is accorded special status as the primary agent of change and not the individual therapist. Indeed, in prototypical form, as pioneered by AA, the model of change for alcoholics and addicts does not hinge on individual alliances but rather on the collective alliance, ego, and power of a "fellowship" (Mack, 1981).

Stage 2: Primary Care

At the conclusion of assessment, patients enter the dual-focus group, and at this point, the focus of treatment shifts to the group modality. This stage of treatment runs approximately 16 weeks, with each patient's length of stay determined by his/her particular progress and needs. The group itself meets for three sessions a week, 90 minutes a session. The group has an enrollment of 7 to 10 members, and although admission remains open, allowing patients to complete the program and others to take their place, membership remains by and large stable. Patients entering the group can expect to undergo treatment with roughly the same cohort of patients. Regarding issues of size and boundary, care is taken to limit the number of members to a lower threshold than is generally maintained in other chemical dependency groups and to closely monitor the timing of new arrivals. This is done in the belief that dually diagnosed patients are less resilient to change and in greater need of a holding environment than are other chemically dependent patients.

The task in the primary-care stage is stabilization of both areas of dysfunction in patients' lives. The agenda includes the goals of helping patients achieve abstinence and reducing their target psychiatric symptoms. Clearly leading the agenda is the task of breaking the cycle of addiction in patients' lives and helping them achieve abstinence (Tatarsky & Washton, 1992). The reason this task assumes priority is that sobriety *is* the first step in reversing psychiatric decline and helping patients learn how to regulate mood and functioning in a healthy fashion. But also, sobriety takes precedence in the treatment agenda because the steps involved in maintaining sobriety give shape and definition to the other work that dually diagnosed patients need to do on themselves.

Our approach to helping patients establish sobriety is taken directly from standard outpatient addiction treatment. Because this is described at length elsewhere in this book, I will only summarize it here. Principally, we rely heavily on direct behavioral guidelines to help patients stay sober early in treatment. We advise them to clean out drug paraphernalia from their homes, avoid companions and places that are associated with drugs, limit their access to cash, and structure their free time (Tatarsky & Washton, 1992; Washton, 1989). We strategize with patients about "high-risk" situations (holidays, conferences away from home, etc.) and how to cope with potential pitfalls. In addition to such behavioral tips, we also focus on cognition. We point out how patients resort to such defensive strategies as rationalization ("I had to have a drink because of the day I had at work") and minimization ("I only had one joint") to allow them to turn to drugs. We work to make this thinking conscious, to extend decision-making moments in time, and to help patients identify the counterbalancing thoughts ("How will I feel when my wife finds out that I got high?") that enable them to control their behavior. Although the task of first achieving sobriety favors cognitive and behavioral techniques, we also help patients see how their use of drugs is often a response to their own uncomfortable feelings or unsatisfied longings and needs (Tatarsky & Washton, 1992). In sum, treatment in early sobriety seeks to make patients knowledgeable about their own patterns of use and particular external and internal triggers, and to provide them, in response, with effective coping strategies.

How, then, do we adapt this approach to incorporate the two fold treatment agenda of patients who are dually diagnosed? Broadly speaking, we try to capitalize on the clear, empowering elements of addiction treatment and to graft patients' psychiatric needs onto the same set of strategies. We do this out of a belief that dually diagnosed patients feel overwhelmed, even immobilized, by their psychiatric disorders, in contrast to their substance abuse problems. How *does* one "cure" depression or mood disorder? How *does* one bring about an end to problems with "anger"? The elusive etiology and course of such problems leave these patients feeling helpless; they lack a strategic handle on their psychiatric problems that compares with the role sobriety plays in affording them control over addiction. Compounding this effect is the sense of shame patients feel about their so-called mental problems. Although these patients suffer from two, coexisting disorders, they do not view their dual disorders as equal: It is far more threatening and scary for them to consider being "crazy," and therefore much harder to face, than it is to be chemically dependent.

Therefore, we seek to ground our patients' preliminary psychiatric care in the organizing principles of addiction treatment. The specific tenets of addiction treatment that lend themselves to such broader application are a greater emphasis on behavior, rather than on meaning or conflict, early in treatment; a belief that patients need to take a proactive stance toward their problems; a view of disorder as biopsychosocial, requiring patients to make efforts in all areas of their lives; and a view of change as an incremental process, taking place "one step at a time."

Let me offer a few examples of the way these themes might translate into practice in our program. A patient who complains of worsening depression, including symptoms of fatigue and excessive sleep, would be advised to consider antidepressants but might also be asked to make the effort to join another member of the group at morning AA meetings. An anxiety-ridden patient may be urged to consider an exercise regimen that would supplement his medication and might assist in regulating his sleep. For a patient who suffers from mixed personality disorders and is prone to outbursts of anger whenever slighted, we may reframe his angry impulses as "urges" that need to be managed in much the same way as drug urges; the patient might be asked to avoid "high-risk" situations that set him off, or if he finds himself in a situation where his temper is rising, to be prepared to call his sponsor or available list of group members.

In borrowing the biases of addiction treatment to assist patients in their work on other issues, we are only borrowing a set of tools. We are not attempting to equate all disorder with addiction. What we are trying to make available to our patients, for the initial work on their psychiatric problems, is a pragmatic, "how-to" approach that can instill a sense of hope and organization into their efforts. Addiction treatment *is* successful at drawing on patients' agency and responsibility for their substance use or sobriety. The ego-strengthening value of such a focus is the most celebrated feature of addiction treatment and is the ingredient that transforms an experience of mere sobriety into the uplifting phenomenon of "recovery." It is this ego-enhancing benefit that we seek to extend to patients' work on their other problems.

Education is another device we use to strengthen ego functioning and combat patients' sense of shame. With dually diagnosed patients, special attention needs to be paid to the myths and concerns that arise in treatment. Patients often ask questions about diagnostic terminology ("dual diagnosis," "bipolar disorder"), or about other loosely used labels ("crazy"). Medication typically arouses so much anxiety that it is practically an educational topic unto itself: Any therapist working with the dually diagnosed should be prepared to respond to questions about the workings of the different classes of psychotropic drugs and to address patients' common fears about their use ("Will I get 'hooked'?" "Do I have to take them forever?"). Education can be supplied in the form of organized didactic units that address specific topics or in brief, spontaneous digression from other group discussion. Either way, giving patients information about their disorders serves to clarify misconceptions. With the dually diagnosed in particular, knowledge gives a sense of mastery and boosts self-esteem.

Group psychotherapy with dually diagnosed patients is not solely devoted to behavior change and education. There is a place and a need for insight-oriented work as well, to address the characterological problems and difficulty with feelings that patients typically display during treatment and that form the root causes of their use of drugs. If, according to Khantzian et al. (1990), addiction can be viewed as the "self-medication of psychological suffering" (p. 4), then nowhere is the weave tighter between disturbance and use of drugs than with the dually diagnosed. Patients with mood and anxiety disorders are beset by painful affects; those with personality disorders by disturbances in self-esteem, reinforced by their impaired efforts to relate to others (Khantzian, 1985). As these problems are set in motion by the therapeutic process itself, the group therapist is ideally positioned to point out to patients moments when their maladaptive defenses and inadequate regulation of feeling are called into play. The therapist can make connections between such moments and the dynamics that surround them and the patients' past use of drugs as a remedial solution (Khantzian, 1985). Thus, group becomes a learning laboratory: Patients' core difficulties inevitably emerge, but through the therapist's selective use of observation and interpretation, patients can be given some insight into their characters as well as an opportunity to try alternative ways of being within the treatment experience itself (Khantzian et al., 1990).

Finally, although group is the principal treatment modality during the phase of primary care, individual therapy takes place as well. Individual therapy always serves a useful function in addiction treatment as a way of helping patients who struggle in recovery through the medium of group alone, and who require closer attention to personal conflicts in order to maintain sobriety. This need for close attention is always the case with the dually diagnosed, whose psychiatric problems simply cannot be shelved. As a result, in our model, patients are seen individually twice a month, or more frequently if needed, to address their underlying issues and problems. In addition, from a larger perspective, we create an ongoing place for individual therapy because, in our view of the dually diagnosed, the therapeutic alliance provides needed ballast for their treatment overall. Individual sessions are scheduled at regular intervals throughout the program—at times to augment and at other times to correct the treatment experience that is taking place in group, and at all times to sustain these patients, whose fragile characters and tenuous holds on sobriety require support.

Stage 3: Continuing Care

Continuing care is open-ended in duration, running at least until the end of the first year that the patient is in treatment and usually longer. The primary tasks are to broaden the base of sobriety and to strengthen symptom control and management of psychiatric condition. Treatment can take place in combined group and individual modalities or in individual therapy alone. In our program, once sobriety and psychiatric functioning are stabilized, patients are prepared to advance from primary care by gradually phasing out of the dual-focus group. They spend the final month decreasing attendance from three to two times a week and at the same time mark their imminent "graduation" by addressing the group, reviewing their progress, and outlining the work that still awaits them. Patients then join a separate, once-a-week aftercare group and/or undertake extended, individual psychotherapy, with a recovery focus.

Individual therapy is the preferred modality in later stages of recovery because once sobriety is established, character structure, and in this case disorder, is more sharply exposed (Khantzian et al., 1990). Treatment naturally shifts inward. This is a precarious time with the dually diagnosed because their disorders are finally fully on view, and more keenly felt, without the limiting effects of drugs: Anxiety may go unchecked, extremes of mood may appear, and disturbances in object relations become apparent. The therapist provides critical support during this process of unveiling and helps patients gain awareness of their core difficulties and the way their drug of choice served as a compromise solution. Such core difficulties may include narcissistic disturbance and its sequelae, phobic ideation and anxiety, pervasive depression and anergia, and primitive aggression and sadomasochistic impulses (Khantzian, 1985; Wurmser, 1980). Sobriety, then, literally creates the potential for a deeper, uncovering psychotherapy in later stages of recovery.

For most of the dually diagnosed, however, such deeper work may have to await further progress in stabilization or get carefully integrated into a treatment agenda that remains primarily focused on normalization of functioning. The main thrust of continuing care is to restore patients to the day-to-day routines and responsibilities of their lives. Vocational planning in particular is emphasized during this stage. Patients are helped to return to work following periods of disability, to reorganize their job responsibilities and schedules so as to reduce stress, to rethink vocational choices altogether when particular jobs have served to promote disturbance, and to undertake training for new vocational options wherever appropriate. There is a similar attention to social rehabilitation. Once sober, patients are strengthened to disengage from destructive relationships, and with the help of couple and family therapy, if needed, to address dysfunctional ties. Care is also taken, in this stage, to make sure that patients are working to develop independent support networks outside treatment, through AA and other fellowships.

All in all, treatment of the dually diagnosed obeys a longer timetable, with change expected at a more gradual pace than with other chemically dependent persons. Sobriety simply does not occasion the dramatic turnarounds in these patients that are sufficiently common in other substance abusers to have won recognition as the phenomenon of "recovery." Because of their psychiatric disturbance, dually diagnosed patients enter treatment at a point of greater characterological collapse, and with their lives in further disarray, than do other substance abusers. They are likely to have undergone suicide attempts or psychotic episodes or to have achieved extremes of vegetative depression. Because of the scope of damage they have suffered, it is more realistic to view dually diagnosed patients as undergoing a period of "convalescence" (Minkoff, 1989, p. 1034) in the first year rather than actual "recovery." Expectations for their progress need accordingly to be revised. They should be seen as working to retrieve levels of baseline functioning and as laying the groundwork for future progress rather than as bearing signs of immediate change (Minkoff, 1989).

SPECIAL CLINICAL ISSUES

There are many factors, both objective and subjective, that make treatment of the dually diagnosed distinct from work with other substance abusers.

First, one has to recognize the need to individualize treatment when working with these patients. The diagnostic variation brought together under the heading of dual diagnosis makes it impossible for one treatment approach to successfully meet all these patients' needs. Although the idea of individualizing treatment makes for sound clinical practice in general, it challenges the programmatic bias of traditional addiction treatment, which originated in AA. AA offers *one* philosophy and method to any person seeking help with any drug or alcohol problem. The AA program is based on acceptance of central tenets known as the 12 steps, discussed and given meaning at daily meetings—and it is invariant. The idea that one approach is all that is needed to guide people to sobriety and the view of alcohol as a great leveler, removing differences among people as it democratically ruins lives, are powerful beliefs that pervade the field of chemical dependency.

With the dually diagnosed, however, it is impossible to mandate a single program. In fact, it is the very belief in the superiority of a "program" that itself must be set aside. With these patients, individual differences and needs take priority, and any treatment approach that is fashioned for them must be flexible. Treatment agendas must take into account their fragile characters and inconsistencies in performance. This can be illustrated with the subject of AA itself. Almost every treatment program for the newly sober recommends that patients regularly attend AA. However, there are dually diagnosed patients for whom going to meetings with unfamiliar people stirs so much anxiety that it can only be undertaken on an irregular basis, when companions have been found and facilitating arrangements made. Likewise, there are character-disordered patients whose identities are so unformed that they fear the power and influence of the fellowship and see in it a threat of mind control. The point is, based on their psychopathology, these patients' objections to elements of the treatment plan may be well founded and not merely defensive in nature. Clinicians need to know the difference and be able to act on their judgment by challenging the patient or, at other times, setting aside the treatment plan. In this and other respects, with the dually diagnosed, the treatment program needs to be adapted to patients' needs, not the other way around.

Another characteristic of work with the dually diagnosed is that their progress is unpredictable. Because of their two disorders, sobriety alone does not do the job of delivering them to health. In fact, without the self-medicating effects of drugs, patients' symptoms may emerge full-blown and cause them more suffering. Viewed another way, from the standpoint of those who believe that chronic users turn to drugs in an effort to replace a missing piece of their psychic structure (Kohut, 1977), it stands to reason that giving up the drug would lay bare their character deficits and actually serve to weaken them. Indeed, one comes to appreciate the structural function of drug use when one sees a certain number of these patients suffer episodes of decompensation once they have stopped using drugs. Psychotropic medication is prescribed to alleviate patients' distress, but realistically, it can take time and experimentation to arrive at a suitable medication regimen; this process in itself creates discomfort. Thus, sobriety may well occasion a heightened degree of distress in these patients.

Moreover, because their disorders are related but independent, these patients can undergo psychiatric decline at any point during sobriety. Hospitalization itself needs to be "decatastrophized," as it is a more routine step and occurrence with these patients than with other substance abusers. Thus, to work with this population, the therapist must be comfortable working with patients whose status is uncertain and whose course of treatment is inconsistent at best.

Having said this, the question of countertransference arises. Work with the dually diagnosed is more difficult than work with other chemically dependent people. As already discussed, many more variables enter into their treatment and confound their prognosis, including fragile motivation, inadequate social support, and the uncertain interplay of their two disorders. They are more prone to crisis and acute distress and therefore needier of close attention. Therapists who work with these patients can feel as if they are always working to fend off the twin "sirens" of relapse and regression without ever knowing whether the patient is finally in the clear. In addition, work with the dually diagnosed can fail to deliver the "uplifting" experience that most clinicians come to expect in their work with other recovering patients, where they can count on the curative power of sobriety to bring about dramatic transformation on its own.

Balancing these problems are the differing rewards of working with this population. The dually diagnosed are a clinically challenging group of patients. To be effective with them, the therapist must bring to bear a varied and complete repertoire of clinical skills, not only skills related to drug use and sobriety. The therapist must exercise expertise in such areas as assessment, developing a therapeutic alliance, overcoming resistance, and treatment of character disorder. It is as if the therapist gets to be more of a therapist with the dually diagnosed. And, indeed, the contribution of the therapist is valued as more central to the treatment of dually diagnosed patients as compared with other substance abusers. Whereas sobriety alone can bring about the change that is needed in the lives of other substance abusers, it is not a sufficient antidote for the multiple problems of those who have serious psychiatric disturbance. Here, other skills are needed, and they are the therapist's to give.

However, to meet these patients' needs, the therapist must be properly trained in the varied disciplines and approaches of chemical dependency and mental health. On the substance abuse side of the skills that must be acquired, the therapist must be trained in recognizing signs of abuse and addiction, understanding the disease concept, the workings of the 12-Step programs, and strategies for relapse prevention. On the mental health side, the therapist needs training in assessment, the fundamentals of providing group and individual psychotherapy, strategies for handling psychiatric emergencies, and the basics of psychopharmacology (Wallen & Weiner, 1989). It is this very need to be proficient in the perspectives of both fields that has led to the use of a new term—"cross-training" (Zweben, 1992)—to signify the extent, and perhaps rigor, of the preparation needed to work with dually diagnosed patients. Moreover, in the model of treatment that has been presented in this chapter, clinicians must also be versatile in their familiarity with technique. At times, in our model, the therapist is called on to take a direct, counseling approach to patients, providing behavioral interventions and other specific strategies designed to maintain sobriety; at other times, the therapist adopts a didactic role, furnishing facts and information; still at other times in the treatment cycle, a psychotherapeutic stance is in order, with the therapist encouraging exploration and pacing it with his/her own inquiry and observation. All in all, depth of training and comfort with many styles are required.

The effort to expand and integrate skills in the service of the dually diagnosed, cannot take place only at the level of the individual therapist; it must also take place at higher clinical and administrative levels to effectively address these patients' problems (Wallen & Weiner, 1989). Although "hybrid" treatment programs, such as the one described in this chapter, are clearly gaining ground, many more such services need to be developed. Badly needed, in particular, are specialized inpatient units and longer-term residential facilities that can cater to these patients (Wallen & Weiner, 1989; Zweben, 1992). Government agencies have also been slow to respond to the dually diagnosed. In most states, the departments that regulate mental health and drug treatment services are separate; the collaboration and awareness that are needed to respond to the crossover problems of the dually diagnosed do not yet have a formal home within the structure of most state agencies (Wallen & Weiner, 1989).

Finally, insurance companies, too, have failed to recognize dually diagnosed patients as a distinct group that warrants its own consideration in determining need for treatment and reimbursement guidelines. Benefits plans are currently designed to cover psychiatric complaints or chemical dependency but do not yet exist in a way as to address the phenomenon of their co-occurrence. Insurance plans thus perpetuate the wrongheaded, either–or view of these patients who nonetheless do not fit into either diagnostic camp and who remain ill-served by single-minded treatment planning. The clinician ends up having to justify the need for additional services for a dually diagnosed patient merely because the course of treatment represents a departure from standard care. If, however, benefits were conceived—as treatment itself must be—with the unique needs of the dually diagnosed in mind, such maneuvering could be eliminated at the point of reimbursement.

CONCLUSION

Within the field of chemical dependency, the phenomenon of dual diagnosis is claiming new attention. Although it may be true that the problem itself is growing, or at the very least appearing in more flagrant form through the increasing availability of cheap drugs, it is certainly true that these patients have been underserved in the past. Often viewed as wayward or impossible to treat, the dually diagnosed have only recently been gaining recognition as a distinct group deserving of a set of treatment strategies tailored to their needs.

A model of treatment was presented in this chapter that was developed in the setting of an outpatient addiction treatment facility intended for patients with nonpsychotic disorders. Ours is a composite model, drawing on several genres of treatment—including addiction treatment, supportive psychotherapy, psychoeducation, and pharmacotherapy—to address the differing problems of the dually diagnosed. We also use diverse techniques in our approach to treating these patients. Early in treatment, our model borrows heavily from standard addiction treatment to emphasize behavioral initiatives; as patients stabilize, we broaden our focus, to permit insight-oriented work as well. Above all, we do not take a doctrinaire approach, as we believe that dually diagnosed patients require treatment that is flexible, and can adapt to their changing needs.

Although this model may not be suited to the needs of all the dually diagnosed, we believe that an integrative approach to treatment best captures the complex makeup of these patients and holds the greatest promise of success. It is also important that the interest and consideration that these patients are stirring be matched at higher institutional levels for there to be a broader-based possibility of success with this challenging group.

REFERENCES

American Psychiatric Association. (1987). *Diagnostic and statistical manual of mental disorders* (3rd ed., rev.). Washington, DC: Author.

Evans, K., & Sullivan, J. M. (1990). *Dual diagnosis: Counseling the mentally ill substance abuser.* New York: Guilford Press.

Group for the Advancement of Psychiatry, Committee on Alcoholism and the Addictions. (1991). Substance abuse disorders: A psychiatric priority. *American Journal of Psychiatry, 148,* 1291–1300.

Khantzian, E. J. (1985). The self-medication hypothesis of addictive disorders: Focus on heroin and cocaine dependence. *American Journal of Psychiatry, 142,* 1259–1264.

Khantzian, E. J., Halliday, K. S., & McAuliffe, W. E. (1990). *Addiction and the vulnerable self: Modified dynamic group therapy for substance abusers.* New York: Guilford Press.

Kofoed, L., Kania, J., Walsh, T., & Atkinson, R. M. (1986). Outpatient treatment of patients with substance abuse and coexisting psychiatric disorders. *American Journal of Psychiatry, 143,* 867–872.

Kohut, H. (1977). Preface. In J. D. Blaine & D. A. Julius (Eds.), *Psychodynamics of drug dependence* (Research Monograph Series No. 12, pp. vii–ix). Rockville, MD: National Institute on Drug Abuse.

Kosten, T. R., & Kleber, H. D. (1988). Differential diagnosis of psychiatric comorbidity in substance abusers. *Journal of Substance Abuse Treatment, 5,* 201–206.

Mack, J. E. (1981). Alcoholism, A.A., and the governance of the self. In M. H. Bean & N. E. Zinberg (Eds.), *Dynamic approaches to the understanding and treatment of alcoholism* (pp. 128–162). New York: Macmillan.

Minkoff, K. (1989). An integrated treatment model for dual diagnosis of psychosis and addiction. *Hospital and Community Psychiatry, 40,* 1031–1036.

Ries, R. K., & Ellingson, T. (1990). A pilot assessment at one month of 17 dual diagnosis patients. *Hospital and Community Psychiatry, 41,* 1230–1233.

Sciacca, K. (1991). An integrated treatment approach for severely mentally ill individuals with substance disorders. In K. Minkoff & R. E. Drake (Eds.), *Dual diagnosis of major mental illness and substance disorder* (pp. 69–84). San Francisco: Jossey-Bass.

Tatarsky, A., & Washton, A. (1992). Intensive outpatient treatment: A psychological perspective. In B. C. Wallace (Ed.), *The chemically dependent: Phases of treatment and recovery* (pp. 28–37). New York: Brunner/Mazel.

Treaster, J. B., & Tabor, M. B. W. (1993, February 8). Little help for mentally ill addicts: Two treatment bureaucracies compete to avoid them. *The New York Times,* pp. B1, B4.

Wallen, M. C., & Weiner, H. D. (1989). Impediments to the effective treatment of the dually diagnosed patient. *Journal of Psychoactive Drugs, 21*(2), 161–168.

Washton, A. (1989). *Cocaine addiction: Treatment, recovery, and relapse prevention.* New York: Norton.

Wurmser, L. (1980). Phobic core in the addictions and the paranoid process. *International Journal of Psychoanalytic Psychotherapy, 8,* 311–335.

Zweben, J. E. (1992). Issues in the treatment of the dual-diagnosis patient. In B. C. Wallace (Ed.), *The chemically dependent: Phases of treatment and recovery* (pp. 298–309). New York: Brunner Mazel.

21

Adolescent Chemical Dependence: Assessment, Treatment, and Management

ROBERT MARGOLIS

INTRODUCTION

Successful treatment of chemically dependent adolescents requires a multipronged approach. The therapist provides a structure of hope and support, sets appropriate limits with the help of the family, teaches specific coping skills, addresses deficits and delays that result from drug use, and encourages the entire family to begin their own process of recovery. In so doing, the therapist is a vital link in the recovery process.

For purposes of this chapter, chemical dependency is viewed as a primary progressive disorder with biopsychosocial antecedents and a discrete set of symptoms. For both adults and adolescents, symptoms include denial, genetic and environmental antecedents, craving, shame, family dysfunction, and continued use despite negative consequences.

Denial

Most chemically dependent individuals experience denial. Typically, they are the last to recognize the disorder and may be resistant to treatment in the early stages. They try to maintain both the appearance and the inner conviction of their normality while in fact their life becomes increasingly unmanageable and out of control. The therapist may need to be more directive with these clients to highlight the discrepancy between their perception and the reality.

Genetics and Environment

Research data show that alcoholism and other drug dependencies have genetic and environmental antecedents. Data from studies of neurochemistry, animals, twins, adoptions, and sons of alcoholic fathers strongly suggest the genetic connection. In addition, some individuals without the genetic factor have psychodynamic issues that predispose them to chemical abuse (Brehm & Khantzian, 1992).

Craving

Regardless of the precipitating factors, individuals who abuse drugs often develop intense craving. They desire to use drugs to satisfy this craving and to block out negative affect states. As a result, the use of chemicals becomes an increasingly potent force in the person's life; more and more activities revolve around the use of chemicals.

Shame

Most chemically dependent individuals have to come to terms with a sense of shame. The shame stems from negative feedback from family, society, and their own value systems. These individuals neither lack a sense of right and wrong nor suffer from a character disorder. They know that they are doing wrong, but they are unable to stop. They are driven by physical and emotional craving, which is a more primitive drive in the hierarchy of needs.

The sense of shame begins to emerge as the individual becomes sober. Uncovering affect too quickly may result in the patient's being overwhelmed with a sense of shame and thus trigger a relapse.

Family Dysfunction

Family dysfunction plays a crucial role in chemical dependence especially with adolescents. Frequently there is more than one substance abuser in the family. In addition, family members become locked into dysfunctional roles. The therapist must include the family in didactic and psychotherapeutic experiences to increase sensitivity to the dynamics of addiction and to improve communication.

Continued Use Despite Negative Consequences

Chemically dependent individuals continue to use drugs or alcohol despite the consequences. People who abuse drugs but have not moved into full dependency may experience some negative consequences and they alter their behavior. Chemically dependent individuals continue to use despite negative consequences. For example, the adolescent who is expelled from school for doing drugs is often out smoking marijuana that very same night.

KEY CHARACTERISTICS
OF ADOLESCENT DRUG USE

In working with adolescents there is a group of special characteristics. First, adolescent drug abuse manifests itself through problem behaviors rather than overt signs of drug abuse. Typically, family members come for consultation about school or home problems instead of drug use. Second, the disorder progresses more rapidly in adolescents than it does in adults. Adults may take 2 to 7 years to progress from first use to full chemical dependency. Adolescents often make this progression in 6 to 18 months. Third, adolescents abuse more than one drug; they may have a "drug of choice," but they almost always use several drugs. Fourth, adolescents experience stronger denial because they have not experienced the years of negative consequences that an adult has experienced. They have difficulty connecting their school and family problems to their drug use. Fifth, the enabling system surrounding adolescents is stronger than is usually found with adults. Usually drug use is universally accepted in their peer group. "But everyone does it" is a typical statement.

Sixth, adolescents experience developmental delays directly caused by drug use. When drug abuse begins, the normal maturation and growth process slows down or ceases. These adolescents fall behind their age group in academics, social skills development, impulse control, and tolerance of delayed gratification. The diagnosis and treatment of these adolescents must take these delays into account because addressing these delays is the single greatest factor in the success of treatment. Treatment must be longer and more intense for adolescents than for adults.

The Comprehensive Assessment and Treatment Model (Figure 21.1) is helpful in assessing the degree of impairment in functioning. The model is based on the assumption that as the chemical dependence increases, functioning in all areas of life decreases. This model can be used in the assessment, treatment, and aftercare phases of recovery. In addition, outcome studies and follow-up questionnaires can be keyed to the domains of functioning contained in the model.

FIGURE 21.1. Comprehensive Assessment and Treatment Model for Adolescent Substance Abuse and Chemical Dependence. This figure depicts the scope of diagnostic and treatment domains associated with adolescent substance abuse and chemical dependence. The model facilitates a viable fit between the assessment, treatment, and aftercare services offered by the programs.

ASSESSMENT

Assessment of the adolescent for chemical dependency requires an evaluation of each of the areas on the comprehensive model. It is necessary to determine whether the presenting problem is due to drug or alcohol use and where along the progression from first use to full dependency a particular adolescent falls. The main tools are psychological testing, structured questionnaires, urine drug screens, and the diagnostic interview.

Psychological Testing and Structured Questionnaires

Psychological testing is primarily useful in developing treatment plans. The tests will not reveal chemical dependence per se, but they do highlight psychological and interpersonal problems that need to be addressed in treatment.

Structured questionnaires regarding drug and alcohol use can be helpful if they are designed for adolescents. Questionnaires such as the Michigan Alcoholism Screening Test (MAST), which is designed for adults, are not appropriate for adolescents and are not effective for them. The Personal Experience Inventory (PEI) (Winters & Henley, 1989) is designed for adolescents and asks information about patterns of drug use as well as behaviors associated with drug use.

The PEI provides two sets of norms: one that compares an individual to a group of normal adolescents; a second that compares an individual to a subgroup of adolescents who appear in treatment centers. The results of this test can break down denial effectively when an adolescent's score is similar to the second norm.

Urine Drug Screens

An initial urine drug screen and subsequent random drug screens are an essential part of the assessment process. The individual screens must occur on a truly random as well as regular basis. Because the quality of drug screens is variable, some specific points need to be emphasized. First, as most adolescents are polydrug users, the test should screen for a panel of drugs and not just one or two drugs. Second, certain drugs leave the system almost immediately while others remain for extended periods of time. Cocaine is often undetectable after 24 to 48 hours. Marijuana, on the other hand, is detectable for at least 4 or 5 days and may remain in the system for 2 weeks.

Marijuana screens are variable in their accuracy. Many laboratories have increased the cutoff point from 20 ng/ml to 50 ng/ml or higher in order to avoid legal liability. Screens at the 50-ng-or-higher level often miss all but the most chronic heavy marijuana users. It is important to find a laboratory that uses the cutoff of 20 ng/ml.

LSD is almost undetectable in a drug screen. It is not included in the regular panel of drugs on most drug screens. There is a separate screen for LSD, but it is expensive and unreliable due to the small quantity of LSD consumed. Alcohol is also not a part of the regular panel of drugs because it leaves the system in 12 to 24 hours. Other devices such as a breathalyzer or chemstrips, which change color when they are placed on a subject's tongue, are better screens for alcohol use. Finally, the collection of urine drug screens must be observed or monitored in some manner in order to assure the validity of the sample.

Diagnostic Interview

The diagnostic interview is the most significant and crucial part of the assessment phase. It enables the clinician to target questions to the areas contained in the Comprehensive Assessment and Treatment Model. Certain areas of discussion are best addressed with the parents and adolescent together. Other areas are best addressed with the adolescent alone.

In the joint interview, the clinician can investigate the history of the presenting problem, family history of chemical use, and developmental problems of the child. In many instances parents do not identify alcohol and drug use as the presenting problem. The parents usually speak of the problem as related to school difficulties, family conflicts, or behavioral problems. The clinician must get a complete history of these problems and especially look for shifts in behavior, mood, interpersonal style, or peer group.

Family history of alcohol and drug problems and psychiatric problems is particularly significant. It also can be difficult to obtain. It requires asking questions in such a way that the family thinks of the issues in a new light. Frequently, addiction and psychiatric problems are "in the closet" and emerge only after thorough questioning. It can be helpful to ask specifically about extended family members and people who were not identified or treated as chemically dependent. The family history often establishes a genetic susceptibility to the disorder. If there is abuse in the immediate family it points to a negative environmental influence in that the parents are modeling chemically dependent behavior for the child.

Inquiries should be made about the overall health and developmental history of the adolescent. Once again, the clinician is looking for marked shifts that may have followed the onset of chemical use. Learning disorders and attention deficit disorder appear to correlate with later chemical use.

In an interview with the adolescent alone, the clinician should get a chemical use profile, the history and progression of that use, and a mental status examination. The profile can be done either through questionnaires or through dialogue with the adolescent. In dialogue, simply asking the adolescent what drugs he/she has done is not sufficient. Although the clinician may begin in this manner, he/she needs to ask about specific drugs that the adolescent may consider unimportant. For example, adolescents frequently consider alcohol use to be trivial and unproblematic. Inhalants and stimulants such as diet pills are frequently not mentioned in their initial response.

The history of chemical use involves a variety of specific questions about the progression. How old was the adolescent when he/she first began to use drugs? Whom did he/she use with? What is the progression of use from the first time until the present? Have there been significant periods of sobriety? Has the adolescent ever found the need to cut down use on his/her own? If so, why? Has the person ever behaved in a way that is inconsistent with his/her own value system, such as sexual acting out, violence, or illegal acts while under the influence of chemicals? Has the person ever said or thought, "There are certain things I would never do like using IV drugs, mixing different types of drugs, using 'hard' drugs?" Questions such as these help the clinician to assess the degree of unmanageability and severity of the adolescent's drug use and they help adolescents to think about the consequences of their drug use and how far the chemical use has progressed.

A final element of the diagnostic interview with the adolescent is the mental status examination. The clinician should pay attention to sudden, unexplained mood swings as well as unexplained difficulties with judgment and insight. The adolescent's affective state and motivation for treatment are important elements of the mental status examination.

In doing the diagnostic interview, there are a number of troublesome signs that the clinician should watch. An adolescent who begins to use drugs will usually shift to a peer group composed solely of other drug-using adolescents. Parents often register this shift in peer group as a major concern and source of friction in the family. The adolescent frequently complains, "You don't like any of my friends."

Problems with compliance with family and school structure also may be a telling sign of chemical use. As chemical use increases, the individual's life becomes more and more unmanageable. Initially, the person can hide and cover the use of drugs or alcohol, but as the dependence progresses the ability to hide and cover up decreases. If there are signs of marked deterioration in conduct, family functioning, and academic performance, the adolescent's chemical use may have progressed so that covering up is no longer possible. Sometimes the adolescent tries to avoid the parents as much as possible to prevent detection. Parents in these cases may complain that their child is increasingly secretive, spends large amounts of time alone in the bedroom, and never wants to be with the family.

Indicators that drug use is rapidly progressing out of control include running away; legal difficulties, especially if related to possession, sale, or distribution of drugs; and the total inability to function at school or employment. In these cases, immediate intervention is necessary to reverse a rapidly deteriorating process.

In the feedback portion of the diagnostic interview the parents, adolescent, and clinician meet together again to discuss the findings. The clinician can review the findings stressing the salient points. For example, there is a positive family history of addiction, Johnny's drug use has progressed to a point where he began using on the weekends, and he is now smoking marijuana before school. His grades have deteriorated. He has been sneaking out at night. His peer group has changed and many of his peers have either dropped out of school or are having significant difficulties. Although Johnny has tried to cut back on several occasions and has even been successful for a period of several months, his use has progressed and increased over the last several years.

Confidentiality

It is, of course, essential to obtain the adolescent's permission to share this information with the parents. If the adolescent is reluctant to share specifics, perhaps he/she will give permission to generally share concerns about the progression of drug use so that the parents can have some understanding of the problem.

The issue of confidentiality is a difficult judgment call, especially when adolescents are engaged in high-risk or life-threatening behavior. If the therapist intends to violate the adolescent's confidentiality to ensure the adolescent's safety, it is important to inform the adolescent of what the therapist is about to do and his/her reasons for this breach of the confidential relationship. The issue must be handled delicately in order to preserve the therapeutic relationship with the adolescent and also to help the parents understand the need and the specific recommendations for treatment.

Drawing Conclusions

When the psychological testing, structured questionnaires, urine drugs screens, and the diagnostic interview are completed, the therapist faces three possible conclusions. First, the adolescent is clearly chemically dependent and requires some type of structured treatment. Second, the adolescent is not chemically dependent and the presenting problem is not drug related. Third, the role of drugs in the presenting problem is possible or probable but not yet clearly determinable. Unfortunately, this last conclusion is the most common. It calls for an extended assessment process in order to more fully define the role chemical use plays in the adolescent's life.

The extended assessment is based on the fact that the disorder progresses to greater unmanageability. Adolescents who are moving from first use to full dependency will continue to use despite therapy, behavioral contracts, and urine drug screens. The only way to separate the adolescent who is experimenting from the adolescent who is dependent is to ask the adolescent to stop. Those who can stop will if the consequences are severe enough. Those who cannot stop will continue to use despite the negative consequences. The family and the therapist draw up a behavioral contract with specific limits and consequences. The parents are asked to assist in monitoring the adolescent's drug use. The adolescent is given a clear unequivocal message that any type of drug or alcohol use is unacceptable at this point. The therapist may state that he/she does not work with adolescents who use alcohol or drugs because it undermines the therapeutic process.

This conversation sometimes engenders resistance and anger from the adolescent, but the anger or alienation is usually shortlived. Adolescents who are never forced to come face to face with the consequences of their chemical abuse lose respect for the therapist and adults involved. They also lose respect if the therapist is easily manipulated. The therapist may become a "professional enabler" if he/she gives the impression that something is being accomplished (i.e., psychotherapy) when in fact the adolescent is continuing to use drugs at greater and greater levels. As the disorder progresses, the parents become even more reluctant to confront the child because they feel secure that the therapist is addressing the problem.

In addition to a behavioral contract, group therapy is of tremendous value in the extended assessment period. It is particularly valuable if the group has recovering adolescents who are chemically free and engaged in an ongoing recovery process. The recovering adolescents are particularly adept at eliciting information from other adolescents who are in denial or trying to hide their chemical use. Often simply by sharing their personal experiences they normalize the process of talking about drug use in an open, nonjudgmental manner. They will often do much of the therapist's work by confronting the adolescent and encouraging him/her to share more information.

These adolescents can also introduce the adolescent to a recovering life-style. They can encourage the adolescent to attend community support groups with them. Often, the adolescent who is in denial begins to see the positive effects of recovery and the obvious difference between the drug life-style and the recovering life-style.

Finally, the adolescent will continue to be monitored by random urine drug screens during the extended assessment period. The drug screens should not be on the same day as the day of group therapy. It becomes too easy for the adolescents to time their drug use to be drug-free for the group therapy. All adolescents in the group need to be tested. For the protection and integrity of the group, regular drug screening is essential.

The extended assessment period may continue for a period of weeks or months. During this time, the therapist should continue to focus on the role chemical dependence plays in the adolescent's life. Often ongoing therapeutic efforts can be undermined by chronic drug use that is undiagnosed and undetected. The therapist should have a healthy skepticism and continually listen for signs of drug use. Ironically, attempts to develop a bond with the patient can work contrary to the interest of the patient by making the therapist less likely to see the signs of drug use. It is only by maintaining some reserve in judgment and an attitude of healthy skepticism that therapists can avoid the denial process and serve the patients well.

THERAPEUTIC INTERVENTIONS

In designing a treatment plan for chemically dependent adolescents, we return to the Comprehensive Assessment and Treatment Model, which emphasizes the impact of substance abuse on functioning and development.

Therapeutic interventions are structured to address the different spheres that have been impaired and to assist the adolescent to move to a higher level of functioning in each of these spheres. Unless these specific deficits are addressed, long-term sobriety is likely to be compromised.

Unlike adults, who often arrive at the chemically dependent stage with a range of coping strategies and social skills, adolescent substance abuse is such that the development of these coping strategies is curtailed at the stage in which they began abusing chemicals. For this reason, treatment of adolescent chemical dependence is sometimes referred to as habilitation (Morrison, Knauf, & Hayes, 1989) as opposed to the traditional view of treatment as rehabilitation. It is this need for primary habilitation as opposed to rehabilitation that accounts for the fact that treatment of the chemically impaired adolescent is more long term and intensive than adult rehabilitation.

Continuum of Care

As a result of the intensity and complexity of adolescent treatment, Morrison et al. (1989) stress the need for a continuum of care (Figure 21.2) when treating adolescent substance abusers. In the past, most chemically dependent adolescents were treated in inpatient settings. Within the past several years, more adolescents have been treated in other settings including partial hospitalization programs, day programs, recovery residences, and even traditional psychotherapy in an outpatient practice. If outpatient treatment is the foundation for the treatment plan, it is important to emphasize the possibility of continued use of chemicals and the accompanying risks. This possibility needs to be weighed and routine urine drug screening is essential.

Zweben (1993) has addressed the issue of urinalysis by stating, "Drug and alcohol testing should be presented as something taken for granted given the nature of addictive disorders, not a personal issue for mistrust in the individual case" (p. 264). This is an important point because many therapists are reluctant to utilize urine drug screens, fearing loss of trust or a destruction of the therapist–patient bond. In my experience, it is

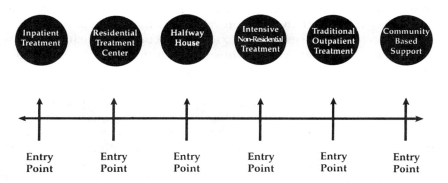

FIGURE 21.2. Continuum of treatment services.

the therapist's attitude and degree of comfort with urinalysis that most determines whether the therapist–patient bond is negatively impacted.

The continuum of care should be in place before the therapist begins to work with adolescent substance abusers. The therapist should have a relationship with a treatment center that provides this continuum for those adolescents who are unable to maintain sobriety through traditional outpatient treatment.

Sometimes nonmedical psychotherapists have a degree of discomfort in functioning as a member of a multidisciplinary team. The therapist should seek out a treatment center that provides high-quality care and is sensitive to the needs of nonmedically trained therapists to direct the clinical–behavioral aspects of the patient's treatment.

CONFLICTS BETWEEN PSYCHODYNAMICS AND THE DISEASE MODEL

Within the addiction field, there is a controversy between traditionally trained, psychodynamic psychotherapists and addiction-oriented therapists working from a disease model. Zweben (1993) elaborates this controversy: "While conventional psychotherapy has usually erred in the direction of promoting exploration without stating clear expectations about action toward abstinence, addiction treatment personnel often become quickly frustrated by this ambivalence and may justify early termination on the grounds of avoiding collusion and drug using behavior" (p. 261).

By examining the contributions of each point of view, it is possible to integrate the best characteristics of each approach.

MINNESOTA 12-STEP MODEL

The Minnesota model of therapy offers a specific set of coping mechanisms, which the recovering individual can immediately access for relief of the anxiety and pain that is so prevalent in early-stage recovery. These coping mechanisms strongly emphasize connection with an outside support group. The recovering individual can substitute the strength of the group for the personal powerlessness that is an essential part of the recovering person's experience. The group offers the individual a sober network of peers who have worked through the pain, depression, and anxiety of early-stage recovery. Thus, the recovering person begins to see a sense of possibility for remaining sober. This connection to a nonusing peer group is especially important in working with adolescents. At our center, we have collected follow-up data that underscore this point. In July 1988, an outcome study was conducted with 160 patients and their parents. The response rate was 59%. The patients were divided into three groups: continuously sober (55%), relapsed but sober at the time of treatment (25%), and relapsed at the time of treatment (19%). All (100%) of the adolescents in the continuously sober group associated with drug-free peers. In the relapsed but currently sober and the relapsed group the percentage of adolescents with a drug-free peer group were 50% and 10%, respectively.

Focus on Problem

The Minnesota model approach also helps the recovering person to stay focused on the problem. The skilled recovery-oriented therapist is constantly refocusing the patient on the task at hand, which is the achievement of abstinence from psychoactive chemicals and a sober frame of mind, with self-satisfaction and serenity. The therapist is reframing the patient's experience as part of a normal continuum of recovery with its inherent ups and downs. Adolescents in particular are prone to view situations as either black or white. When the recovering adolescent is depressed, it often seems as if this is a permanent condition. By framing the recovering patient's depression as normal and offering specific nonchemical coping techniques to deal with depression, the recovery-based therapist provides an essential ingredient which moves the patient further along the continuum toward abstinence and sobriety.

Appropriate Confrontation

Finally, the Minnesota model of therapy is more confrontational than traditional psychodynamic psychotherapy. In the treatment of chemical dependence, there is unquestionably an appropriate role for confrontation. Unfortunately, many psychodynamic psychotherapists are uncomfortable with appropriate confrontation. Johnson (1980) has provided an excellent set of guidelines for appropriate use of confrontation which is neither shaming nor likely to elicit defensiveness from the patient. These guidelines include the following points:

1. Give realistic feedback about behavior, not character assassination;
2. Speak with empathy in a respectful tone of voice;
3. Describe what you have observed, excluding guesses, interpretations, and criticisms; and
4. Include a statement of your concerns and when possible give an example of self defeating behavior from your past.

PSYCHODYNAMICS

Psychodynamic therapists bring their own set of strengths to the treatment process. Psychodynamic therapists recognize that heavily confrontational techniques can often drive the adolescent and the family away from treatment prematurely. Statements from untrained recovering therapists such as, "Clearly, you are not ready for recovery," do not take into the account the struggle that the adolescent has with even conceiving the notion of sobriety. Miller and Rollnick (1991), in their book on motivational interviewing, apply five psychodynamic principles to the area of chemical dependence. These principles are designed to enhance motivation for treatment.

Express Empathy

The first principle involves expressing empathy. Miller and Rollnick (1991) point out the paradox that through the use of accurate empathy techniques, the patient develops a sense of acceptance which "seems to free them to change whereas inconsistent non-acceptance . . . can have the effect of keeping people as they are" (p. 56). The patient's ambivalence about maintaining sobriety is framed as a normal part of human experience rather than a lack of motivation for change or a lack of seriousness about the therapeutic process.

Develop Discrepancy

The second technique is to develop discrepancy. Stated succinctly, this includes "a discrepancy between where one is and where one wants to be" (Miller & Rollnick, 1991, p. 57). This is a particularly important technique in helping the adolescent to realize how substance abuse has affected their lives. Specific statements focusing on the personal cost of one's substance abuse are effective. The therapist should be sensitive to those statements by patients that reflect their own awareness of a discrepancy between their achievements and their goals. As Miller and Rollnick (1991) point out, "a goal of motivational interviewing is to develop discrepancy—to make use of it, increase it, and amplify it until it overrides attachment to the present behavior" (p. 57). When this technique is used properly, it is often the patient him/herself who is able to give voice to this concern.

Avoid Arguments

The third technique is to avoid argumentation. Miller and Rollnick (1991) stress the importance of shifting strategies when resistance is encountered. Arguments over whether one is or is not an addict/alcoholic are completely fruitless. Fighting against patients always detracts from the goal of motivating them for change. In working with adolescents, this general principle is helpful, but a certain degree of limit setting is imperative. Resistance, in the form of continued acting-out behavior, needs to be addressed directly. Failure to do so will lose support of the family and undermine the therapist's credibility with the adolescent who begins to see the therapist as easily manipulated. Although there is a dilemma here between avoiding argumentation and appropriate limit setting, the therapist is encouraged to tread a fine line. Often the dilemma can be resolved by clearly delineating the contract between the patient and therapist at the start of therapy in regard to expectations for a successful therapeutic outcome. Specific consequences such as moving to a more intensive level of care should also be delineated and defined not as punishments but as support for the adolescent who is trying to achieve sobriety.

Accept Resistance

A fourth technique in motivational interviewing involves rolling with resistance. "An attack is not met with direct opposition, but rather the attacker's own momentum is used to good advantage" (Miller & Rollnick, 1991, p. 59). When the therapist encounters defensiveness, rather than attacking it directly, he/she is encouraged to retreat briefly and come at the problem from a slightly different direction. The client is invited to consider new information or to look at the problem from a different perspective. Commonly turning questions back to clients and allowing them to struggle with their own answers is particularly important in this regard. As the therapist watches the client struggle, he/she becomes a participant with the client to support but never directly oppose his/her views of a situation. It is assumed in this regard that the client is capable of developing insight and moving in a healthy direction.

Support Self-Efficacy

A fifth concept is to support self-efficacy, which refers to the therapist's confidence in the patient's ability to "cope with a specific task or challenge" (Miller & Rollnick, 1991, p. 61). Adolescents who see the possibility of sobriety will view it as a positive step in their lives. Exposing adolescent patients to other recovering adolescents is an important step in developing self-efficacy. Attendance at 12-Step meetings can be particularly important for adolescents.

Zweben (1993) underscores the desirability of the Therapist's being familiar with 12-Step programs. "It is difficult, if not impossible for the clinician to make successful referrals and deal effectively with resistance if he or she has no direct experience of meetings. To this end, the author suggests attending a variety of meetings. At least six is recommended'' (p. 266). By learning the language of Alcoholics Anonymous (AA) and its specific techniques, therapists can bond with their client by joining them in their recovery process. Both the therapist and the client are aware of the efforts toward self-efficacy and the therapist can support these efforts knowledgeably. Therapists who are not familiar with the strategies and techniques of self-help support groups often unwittingly make suggestions that run contrary to the suggestions of the support group. They eventually lose the respect of their patients.

KEY ELEMENTS OF RECOVERY

Whether one is trained in the Minnesota model or in traditional psychodynamic psychotherapy, the therapist needs to be constantly aware of the struggle the recovering patient experiences on a daily basis in the early stages. Earlier, Margolis (1993) compared the addict's struggle to maintain sobriety with a child who is first learning to ride a two-wheel bicycle. When a child first views a two-wheeler lying on its side, the concept that this will stay upright seems beyond belief. It is only through the parent's gentle coaching and support that the child takes a leap of faith and has the courage to get on the bike and begin pedaling. The paradox is that the faster the child pedals, the more stable the child becomes. In much the same light, early recovery for adolescents seems unattainable. It is only through immersing oneself in a recovery-oriented life-style based on nonchemical coping skills that the adolescent is able to achieve any stability in his/her life. Early-stage treatment with the adolescent must incorporate many nurturing parent skills such as gentle coaching and specific techniques for achieving sobriety.

At the same time, however, early-stage therapy must be more directive. The therapist must offer specific strategies to the adolescent, such as "Let me help you find a support group," "Avoid old using grounds and other potential trigger experiences," etc. Traditional limit setting is also an important aspect of early-stage therapy; the therapist must be prepared to intervene when the adolescent is careening out of control. Some therapists have difficulty identifying the need for clear limits and appropriate intervention. The therapist learns to recognize when limits are necessary by referring back to the functional impairment model of addiction.

Psychotherapy with chemically dependent adolescents requires the ability to switch between a nurturing, self-exploration-based therapy to a limit-setting, directive, or even confrontational stance as appropriate. The appropriate technique is dictated by the adolescent's ability to comply with clear therapeutic goals. For those adolescents whose behavior indicates that they cannot achieve therapeutic goals, a more confrontational approach is indicated with appropriate recommendations for more intensive levels of care.

In employing the techniques of motivational interviewing and Zweben's (1993) developmental model of recovery, individual and group psychotherapy are important. Through individual therapy the adolescent derives the courage and support to take the first steps toward abstinence and bonding with a community support group. Through group therapy, the adolescent benefits from the "mirror image" that the experiences of others provide and derives a sense of support and an awareness of the healing process of recovery. Adolescents can place themselves along a continuum of recovery and realize that recovery progresses in stages, each with its own set of rewards and complications.

Family Therapy

Family therapy is essential. Adults are free to leave dysfunctional families, but most adolescents must deal with the individual family members and the dynamics that exist within their home structure. Drug or alcohol abuse by parents or other family members is of the utmost concern and must be assessed thoroughly. Returning an adolescent to a home in which there is active chemical abuse is a recipe for failure.

Limit Setting

Early family therapy sessions usually center around limit setting and appropriate rules and consequences. As mentioned in the extended assessment section, a behavior contract is drawn up with specific limits and consequences. The rules are geared as closely as possible to normal adolescent rules, taking into account the parents' ability to set limits appropriately. The therapist can meet separately with the parents if they are at odds with each other or have difficulty with setting rules. In the early part of treatment, the family needs to learn about the dynamics of addictive disorder. Didactic lectures on the nature and stages of chemical dependence can be very helpful. The educational approach sensitizes the parents to the child's experience and helps them to avoid shaming responses.

Family Dynamics

As therapy progresses, discussion usually evolves from limit setting to family dynamics. Frequently the roles of the parents have become polarized, with one parent assuming an enabler role and the other parent assuming the role of enforcer. Much conflict and distress between the parents result. The therapist can help the parents to see how they got into this position and help them to move toward a middle ground. Real change for the parents occurs as they struggle individually with their own personality styles and childhood situations. As they come to greater understanding, they view the change not as a defeat or surrender but as a movement toward health and centering. They come to accept that parenting a chemically dependent adolescent is virtually impossible and to release their own guilt and shame.

Parents are encouraged to develop their own support network through Al-Anon or Nar-Anon. These meetings provide the parents with a recovery model similar to the one that the adolescent is learning. They help the parents to understand the unmanageability of chemical dependence and the need to "detach with love." Adolescents receive a powerful message of trust and support as they watch their parents recover.

Developmental Delays

As stated earlier, adolescents who abuse chemicals experience specific developmental delays. This is the primary reason why the therapist must consider utilizing more intensive interventions along the continuum of care, because comprehensive treatment programs can usually address the full complement of developmental delays adolescents experience.

Educational Delays

Many adolescents experience educational delays as a result of their chemical abuse. To place these adolescents back into normal public school, even schools with resources classes, can set them up for failure. Comprehensive treatment programs can offer individualized educational programs designed to address the educational deficits. The delay in achievement scores as well as the lack of appropriate study skills, inability to set and achieve long-term goals, and a lack of awareness about appropriate classroom behavior causes problems for these adolescents. Comprehensive treatment centers are aware of these problems and provide specific academic and behavioral goals for the adolescents to meet. Often, level systems are effective in structuring an adolescent's behavior in a more positive direction.

Social Skills Deficits

In addition to educational delays, many adolescents have glaring deficits in social skills. Comprehensive treatment programs provide social skills groups that are an essential part of reintegrating into a larger world. For many adolescents, the concept of socializing without chemicals to relieve anxiety is a foreign experience. The self-consciousness and lack of self-confidence that these adolescents experience is often masked by a gruff or *macho* facade. Many adolescents who do not develop appropriate social skills are likely to slip back into the drug culture, where acceptance is based on one criterion, the use of chemicals. The issue of sexual relationships is a major factor in adolescent recovery. Many early-stage recovering individuals, especially adolescents, begin to use sexual behavior as self-medication in order to alleviate psychological–emotional pain. Through milieu-based, group psychotherapy, these adolescents can look at the dysfunctional nature of these relationships. The therapist can point out how these relationships can easily lead back to chemical abuse because they are keeping the adolescent from developing appropriate coping skills and they serve the same function as chemicals for the adolescent.

A final set of coping skills which must be addressed in treatment includes the inability of early-stage recovering people to deal with their own feelings. This is an area in which more traditional psychodynamic group psychotherapy can be beneficial. In an atmosphere of acceptance and caring, the adolescent is encouraged to explore his/her feelings in a nonjudgmental way. These feelings, which have often been medicated for years by the adolescent, are scary and potentially overwhelming. The rate at which affective material is exposed needs to be monitored by the therapist. Patients are encouraged to move at their own rate of uncovering. Techniques such as allowing adolescents who are threatened by their feelings to physically relocate themselves within the group room, either closer or further away from the group as needed, give adolescents a sense of control and a feeling that they can uncover affective material without being overwhelmed.

Although not every adolescent must go through a formal treatment program, these are modalities that should not be overlooked given the massive developmental delays many adolescents experience. The therapist who chooses to work in a less structured setting must design a treatment plan that addresses these developmental delays. For example, working closely with the schools to develop appropriate resource classes might be an option. In addition, providing structured outpatient group experiences for the adolescent to work through social skills and to develop feeling-oriented coping skills is also crucial. A therapist who chooses not to affiliate with a treatment program, however, must develop appropriate guidelines for when to refer. In many cases, this therapist should confine his/her practice to assessment and early-stage intervention rather than full treatment and management of this disorder.

In conclusion, the goals of therapeutic intervention with chemically dependent adolescents are first abstinence and second a sober state of mind with nonchemical coping skills. Achievement of these goals requires a continuum of care from inpatient structured treatment centers to outpatient private practice. The therapist should be willing and able to use the appropriate level of care as indicated by the adolescent's behavior. The therapist should also use individual and group psychotherapy, urine drug screens, and family therapy to achieve the goals.

Finally, an attitude of humility on the part of the therapist is essential. Brown (1985) states:

> Therapists must recognize loss of control for the alcoholic and must accept their own loss of control in being able to make the patient change. Therapists who recognize their own limits can then begin to help the alcoholic accept the diagnosis of alcoholism, the lack of control that goes with it, and the abstinence required. Therapists can then help the patient learn how to stay abstinent. (p. 15)

Ultimately the therapist is not in control of whether the patient uses or remains sober. In this process, the therapist participates as the lives of the adolescents and their families move from failure to success, chaos to order, and despair to hope.

REFERENCES

Brehm, N. M., & Khantzian, E. J. (1992). A psychodynamic perspective. In J. H. Lowinson, P. Ruiz, & R. B. Millman (Eds.), *Substance abuse: A comprehensive textbook* (pp. 106–117). Baltimore: Williams & Wilkins.

Brown, S. (1985). *Treating the alcoholic: A developmental model of recovery.* New York: Wiley.

Johnson, V. E. (1980). *I'll quit tomorrow: A practical guide to alcoholism treatment.* San Francisco: Harper & Row.

Margolis, R. (1993). Recovery: Leaps of faith for addicts and psychologists. *Psychotherapy, 30*(2), 187–193.

Miller, W. R., & Rollnick, S. (1991). *Motivational interviewing: Preparing people to change addictive behavior.* New York: Guilford Press.

Morrison, M. A., Knauf, K. J., & Hayes, H. R. (1989, November). A comprehensive treatment model. *Alcoholism and Addiction,* pp. 12–17.

Winters, K. C., & Henley, G. A. (1989). *Personal Experience Inventory manual.* Los Angeles: Western Psychological Services.

Zweben, J. E. (1993). Recovery oriented psychotherapy: A model for addiction treatment. *Psychotherapy, 30*(2), 359–268.

22

The Elderly

SHELDON ZIMBERG

INTRODUCTION

In recent years there has been an increasing awareness that alcohol abuse and alcoholism and prescription drug abuse are significant problems among the aged. This awareness has been supported by studies that looked at this problem from a variety of viewpoints including community-based prevalence studies, hospital admissions, arrests for public intoxication, outpatient treatment programs, and interviews with the staff of health, social service, and information and referral agencies.

In the Washington Heights area of Manhattan, a household-prevalence study survey was conducted which involved questions related to alcoholism (Bailey, Haberman, & Alksne, 1965). This study noted that for individuals age 20 and over, a peak prevalence of 23 per 1,000 population occurred in the 45–54 age group. The prevalence decreased to 17 per 1,000 for the age group 55–65 and then increased to a prevalence of 22 per 1,000 at the 65–74 age group. This study noted that elderly widowers had a rate of 105 per 1,000 in contrast to the overall rate of 19 per 1,000. In addition to this study, a sample of United Automobile Workers Union members age 21 and over was conducted in the Baltimore metropolitan area (Siassi, Crocetti, & Spiro, 1973). This study found that 10% of the men and 20% of the women age 60 and over were heavy escape drinkers and considered to be alcoholics.

A study conducted on 534 patients over age 60 admitted to a psychiatric observation ward in San Francisco General Hospital noted that

23% were alcoholic (Simon, Epstein, & Reynolds, 1968). Another study conducted at a county psychiatric screening ward in Houston, Texas, noted that 44% of 100 consecutive admissions age 60 and over were alcoholic (Gaitz & Baer, 1971). A prevalence study on alcoholism conducted at Harlem Hospital Center in New York City noted that 60% of the male admissions to the medical service and 43% of the female admissions were alcoholic (McCusker, Cherubin, & Zimberg, 1971); five of the male patients (56%) in the age 70 and over group were alcoholic but none of the women were. A survey of patients were 65 and over admitted to the acute medical ward of a California Veterans Administration Hospital noted that 18% of these patients were alcoholic (Schuckit & Miller, 1975).

In San Francisco, in a study of 722 individuals age 60 and over arrested for minor crimes, it was noted that 82.3% were charged with drunkenness (Epstein, Mills, & Simon, 1970). This proportion of drunkenness arrests was much higher than for any other age group.

In an outpatient geriatric psychiatry program conducted at Harlem Hospital, 12% of the elderly patients were noted to have a drinking problem (Zimberg, 1969). In a medical home-care program, 13% of the elderly patients requiring psychiatric consultation were diagnosed as alcoholic (Zimberg, 1971). The author noted that 17% of patients age 65 and over admitted to a suburban New York community mental health center had alcohol abuse as a problem on admission.

More recent studies of hospital admissions under Medicare (Adams, Zhung, Barboriak, & Rimm, 1993) showed that elderly patients with alcoholism or alcohol-related medical conditions were admitted at a rate of 48 per 10,000 population, similar to the rates of admission for myocardial infarction for this age group. The prevalence of alcoholism among the elderly seen in an emergency room was 24% lifetime and 14% current (Adams, Magruder-Habib, Trued, & Broome, 1992).

Other substance abuse problems occur in the elderly although opiate and cocaine abuse is rare. The most common drugs abused by the elderly currently are benzodiazepines (Schuckit, 1979). These are drugs widely prescribed by physicians for the treatment of anxiety and insomnia. Patients can become dependent and seek other prescriptions from various doctors. The issues regarding identification and treatment of benzodiazepine dependence in the elderly are similar to alcoholism, so this chapter will deal largely with alcoholism. It should be noted that benzodiazepine abuse is often found coexisting with alcohol abuse in the elderly.

The prevalence of alcohol problems in the elderly is in the range of 10% to 15%. Higher prevalences occur in hospitalized elderly and in other health and mental health settings. The problem is that few are diagnosed and referred for treatment. The paradoxical state exists where there is a relatively *high prevalence* with a *low index of suspicion* among health care practitioners. Few programs for elderly alcoholics exist in either the alcoholism treatment system or the aging services network. This is in sharp contrast to the well-developed system of care for younger alcoholics. Reasons for this lack of services for elderly alcoholics are discussed below.

RESISTANCE TO IDENTIFICATION
AND TREATMENT OF ELDERLY ALCOHOLICS

The reasons for this resistance in spite of a high prevalence of alcoholism in the elderly are the difficulty in establishing a diagnosis, prejudicial attitudes, and severe countertransference reactions to working with the elderly. Also, there is a lack of acceptance of a modified elder-specific treatment model that differs from the accepted 12-Step disease model of alcoholism. There have been great difficulties in utilizing existing screening tests and diagnostic interviews to identify elderly alcoholics. The problems involve significant difference in the level of alcohol consumption of elderly alcoholics, much greater denial, often less severe health consequences of alcoholism, and confusion with the manifestations of health problems common in the elderly. There is less social, legal, occupational, and interpersonal consequences of alcoholism because the elderly are often not working, live alone, and have less evidence of alcohol dependence and withdrawal, which, if present, can be confused with other physical conditions (Graham, 1986). Graham (1986) says that more appropriate indicators of an alcohol problem might be housing problems, falls or accidents, lack of physical exercise, poor nutrition, inadequate self-care, and social isolation.

In recent years, there has been improvement in the use of screening instruments for the elderly alcoholic The CAGE questionnaire has been used on the elderly with some success (Buchsbaum, Buchanan, & Lawton, 1991). The four CAGE questions are as follows:

Have you ever felt you should *C*ut down on your drinking?
Have people *A*nnoyed you by criticizing your drinking?
Have you ever felt bad or *G*uilty about your drinking?
Have you ever had a drink first thing in the morning to steady your nerves or to get rid of a hangover (*E*ye opener)?

Any yes response is suspicious; two yes responses are a strong indicator that an alcohol problem exists. I have used the CAGE on the elderly and found the first and third questions most likely to be answered yes by an elderly alcoholic.

A recent development of a geriatric version of the MAST (Michigan Alcoholism Screening Test) has been developed and tested (Blow et al., 1992) This test is reported to have very good sensitivity and specificity for alcoholism in the elderly.

Blood testing for liver function abnormalities and indices of red blood cell size are frequently abnormal in younger alcoholics but not frequently enough to be diagnostic. However, in elderly alcoholics a Mayo Clinic study found that abnormalities in the mean corpuscular volume (MCV) and mean corpuscular hemoglobin (MCH) red blood cell tests of the complete blood count were abnormal in a majority (70%) of more than 200 elderly alcoholics admitted to the Mayo Clinic for treatment (Hunt, Finlayson, Morse, & Davis, 1988).

Using the CAGE and the geriatric MAST in combination with abnormal MCV and MCH can be a useful way to identify elderly alcoholics in a health care setting. In addition, using the parameters suggested by Graham (1986) can further help in the identification process. I have developed a series of questions that can be helpful in establishing an alcoholism problem in an elderly person. These questions are illustrated in Table 22.1.

Another major area of difficulty is the attitude many health care workers have toward the elderly. They tend to infantilize elderly patients, ignore their complaints, and label all medical and social problems as manifestations of senility. This attitude has been termed *ageism*. There is also a predominant patronizing attitude toward elderly people with alcohol problems that suggest, "Why take away the alcohol, that's all they have left." This is a destructive attitude that ignores the reality that working with the elderly can be very rewarding because they are responsive, and helping an elderly person regain a feeling of self-worth can contribute to giving up the use of alcohol.

The third problem involves lack of specific knowledge about alcoholism in the elderly and the belief that the standard treatment of alco-

---

TABLE 22.1. Key Questions for the Suspected Elderly Alcoholic

1. Has there been any recent marked change in behavior or personality?
2. Are there recurring episodes of memory loss and confusion?
3. Has the person tended to become more socially isolated and stay at home most of the time?
4. Has the person become more argumentative and resistant to offers of help?
5. Has the person tended to neglect personal hygiene, not been eating regularly, not been keeping appointments, especially doctor's appointments?
6. Has the individual been neglecting his/her medical treatment regimen?
7. Has the individual been unable to manage his/her income effectively?
8. Has the individual been in trouble with the law?
9. Has the individual caused problems with neighbors?
10. Has the individual been subject to excessive falls or accidents?
11. Does the individual frequently use benzodiazepines (Valium, Librium, Xanax, etc.)?
12. Has drinking been associated with any of the above situations?

holism based on the disease model is the *only* effective approach for *all* alcoholics. The health care and social service care workers in the aging field are lacking in any significant knowledge about alcoholism in general or the elderly in particular. There have been sporadic attempts in the alcoholism field to develop special programs for the elderly or to mainstream them within existing outpatient or rehabilitation programs. The problem has been the application to the elderly of the alcohol-specific approach when alcoholism is the only or the major problem as the focus of treatment. This approach is only successful with a minority of elderly alcoholics. A modified approach directed at the stresses of aging, which can include a problem with alcohol as a reactive condition, is a more effective approach (Rosin & Glatt, 1971; Zimberg, 1990). What works well with younger alcoholics is generally not effective with elderly alcoholics for reasons discussed later. Today, many alcoholism therapists are caught in the dilemma that their alcohol-specific approach does not work with the elderly and they are unwilling or unable to modify the approach. This is exactly the situation that faced psychoanalysts in the 1940s and 1950s when they found that psychoanalysis was not effective in the treatment of alcoholism, leading to the abandonment of these patients by psychiatry. It was not until the work of psychiatrists Harry Tiebout and Ruth Fox, who developed a modified psychotherapeutic approach that first dealt with the drinking and later with psychological conflicts, that psychiatrists began to work more effectively with alcoholics. A modified approach is necessary for the successful treatment of most elderly alcoholics.

CLASSIFICATION OF ELDERLY ALCOHOLICS

A number of authors have noted that elderly alcoholics can be differentiated into several diagnostic groupings. Simon et al. (1968) and Gaitz and Baer (1971) made distinctions between elderly alcoholics with and without an organic mental syndrome. Such a distinction would imply differing prognoses and treatment approaches. Simon et al. (1968) indicated that alcoholics with an organic mental syndrome had a poor prognosis with respect to dying at an earlier age than did elderly alcoholics without an organic mental syndrome. Simon et al. (1968) also noted that of the 23% elderly alcoholic admissions, 7% became alcoholic after age 60 and 16% became alcoholic before age 60 and had long histories of alcohol abuse, thus indicating that about one third of these patients developed a drinking problem in later life and two thirds were long-standing alcoholics.

In developing a classification of elderly alcoholics, it would appear that a distinction between *late-onset* problem drinking and *early-onset* problem drinking would be a more useful approach than one based on a distinction of psychiatric diagnosis, particularly the presence or absence of an organic mental syndrome. The late- and early-onset problem-drinking classification can permit observations regarding the effects of the stresses of aging that contribute to the onset of other mental health problems in the aged in contrast to factors that existed in alcoholics long before they became elderly and may be unrelated to the developmental problems associated with aging.

Rosin and Glatt (1971) reviewed 103 cases of patients age 65 and over who were seen in psychiatric home consultations or admitted to a regional alcoholism unit or to a hospital's geriatric unit. They also found two distinct groups of alcoholics and noted that two thirds of the patients were long-standing alcoholics, with their alcoholism persisting as they grew older, while the other one third developed their alcoholism in later life. The long-standing alcoholics had personality characteristics similar to those found among younger alcoholics, but the late-onset alcoholics seemed to have developed their drinking problems associated with depression, bereavement, retirement, loneliness, marital stress, and physical illness. Alcoholism in the late-onset alcoholics seemed related to the stresses of aging.

Based on their data from social service and information and referral agencies, Carruth, Williams, Mysak, and Boudreaux (1975) reported three distinct types of alcoholics. One type consisted of individuals who had no history of a drinking problem prior to old age and who developed the problem during old age (late onset); a second group consisted of individuals who intermittently experienced problems with alcohol but in old age developed a more severe and persistent problem of alcohol abuse (late-onset exacerbation); the third group consisted of individuals who had a long history of alcoholism and continued their problem drinking into old age (early onset). The authors did not indicate the relative percentage in the three groups described. It seems possible to conclude, however, that the two latter groups could be considered alcoholics of long standing with different drinking patterns in their younger years. The terms *late onset, late-onset exacerbation,* and *early onset* are my designations.

The concept of early-onset alcoholism (two thirds) and late-onset alcoholism (one third) among the elderly appears to be a more useful classification. First, it is possible to determine, through the history of the use of alcohol in relation to problems, in which group an elderly alcoholic might be classified. Second, the long-standing alcoholics are more likely to be experiencing medical complications of alcoholism and therefore to require medical care. Third, recognizing factors contributing to the development of the problem may make interventions more effective.

Important questions arise, however, if we accept this classification of early and late onset of alcoholism among the elderly. These questions deal with possibly different treatment approaches for these two groups based on the differing psychological and social characteristics that may be found among these patients.

PSYCHOSOCIAL STRESSES OF AGING

As people age and reach the age of 60 and above, a variety of stresses are more likely to occur as part of this developmental stage of the life cycle. These stresses include retirement from work, loss of loved ones, deteriorating physical health, less cognitive abilities, housing problems, financial problems, loneliness, lack of interesting activities, and social withdrawal. These stresses can often lead to the development of clinical depression, which is often unrecognized as a treatable condition but is viewed rather as a result of getting old. This depression can become another source of dysfunction and stress. People adjust to these stresses in varying ways. Increasingly older people will turn to alcohol to feel better or escape these problems. This clearly describes the late on-set alcoholic as a reactive alcoholic.

What about the early-onset alcoholic who was drinking for many years and just continued to drink alcohol excessively in late life? Most clinical descriptions of these patients, including mine, suggest that they have a family history of alcoholism and personality, behavioral, and treatment histories similar to those of younger alcoholics. There is evidence that many younger alcoholics as they grow older tend to have their condition burn out in spontaneous remissions (Drew, 1968), and that people in general tend to drink less as they age (Cahalan, Cisin, & Crossley, 1974). Could the early-onset alcoholics prolong their abusive drinking because they are also reacting to the stresses of aging rather than giving up drinking as expected?

Some evidence of this possibility was developed by Schonfeld and Dupree (1991). They studied early- and late-onset elderly alcoholics of both sexes admitted for treatment. They found that "depression, loneliness and lack of social support were the most likely antecedents to preadmission drinking behavior for both groups" (p. 587).

Therefore, we have some research evidence to support clinical findings of several clinicians in different clinical settings (Rosin & Glatt, 1971; Droller, 1964; Zimberg, 1969) to suggest that the stresses of aging may prolong abusive drinking in early-onset alcoholics and contribute to the development of alcoholic problems in late-onset elderly alcoholics.

PSYCHOSOCIAL TREATMENT TECHNIQUES

Although awareness of alcoholism among the elderly has developed only recently, there have been reports of successful interventions in relation to elderly alcoholics. Droller (1964) reported on seven cases of elderly alcoholics he visited at home. He found that in addition to medical and supportive treatment, therapy that was primarily social was the most beneficial to these patients. Rosin and Glatt (1971), in their treatment of 103 elderly alcoholics, noted that environmental manipulation and medical services along with day hospital and home visiting by staff or good neighbors were the services that were most beneficial. More recently, Kofoed, Tolson, Atkinson, Toth, and Turner (1987) found that elder-specific treatment was more effective than mainstreaming elderly alcoholic patients in standard alcoholism treatment in an outpatient setting. Another article comparing outcomes of elder-specific inpatient alcoholism treatment compared to traditional alcoholism-specific treatment produced 2.1 times more abstinence and was slightly less costly (Kashner, Rudell, Ogden, Guggenheim, & Karson, 1992).

In my experience in an outpatient geriatric psychiatry program (Zimberg, 1969), as a psychiatric consultant to a medical home-care program (Zimberg, 1971), and as a psychiatric consultant to a nursing home, I noted similar responses to aging-specific social interventions. The use of group socialization and at times antidepressant medication in depressed patients was effective in eliminating alcohol abuse as a problem among the patients in these programs. The use of disulfiram, Alcoholics Anonymous (AA), or referral to alcoholism treatment programs required by younger alcoholics was not necessary for these patients. It is of even further interest to note that both early-onset and late-onset alcoholics responded equally well to these psychosocial interventions, suggesting common etiological factors for these two groups of elderly alcoholics, namely, the stresses of aging.

The hypothesis that psychosocial factors are the major contributors to alcoholism among the aged has been supported by the successful use of treatment interventions based on a psychosocial model. In young-adult and middle-aged alcoholics, the treatment approaches are directed at the drinking behavior itself first. In contrast, the elderly alcoholic is responding to severe social and psychological stresses associated with aging and is drinking in response to these stresses. If these stresses can be eliminated or attenuated, the secondary use of alcohol is diminished, thus leading to sobriety.

The treatment techniques utilized with such patients are based on my experience in a geriatric psychiatry outpatient program and involve the use of group therapy. Prior to admission to the group, every patient should have a complete physical and psychiatric evaluation so that physical or psychiatric disorders can be diagnosed and appropriate treatments instituted.

The group therapy can involve up to 10 to 15 patients and should not be insight oriented or directive as far as alcoholism is concerned. The patients should be elderly persons with a variety of social, psychological, organic mental, and physical disorders, not just alcoholism. The patients with alcoholism should be told that they have a drinking problem and that is probably related to the difficulties they are having in adjusting to their current life situation.

The group should meet at least once a week and last for 1½ to 2 hours. Cookies, coffee, and tea should be made available. If meals can be provided, eating together as a group would be helpful. The approach utilized by the group leaders should be supportive and oriented toward problem solving. Drinking problems should be one of the problem areas discussed but not the only one. Members of the group should be encouraged to discuss other members' problems as well as their own and to give advice and suggestions to other group members.

The group sessions could be divided into an informal social and/or eating period during the beginning of sessions, then a discussion and problem-solving period, followed by a socializing period at the end. The socializing period could be expanded through the use of activities therapy involving occupational therapy and/or planning for trips and outings, development of a patient government, and establishment of a patient kitty or dues. Patients requiring medication or medical follow-up can be seen by the physician individually after the group activities are completed.

The staffing of group programs should ideally consist of a psychiatrist knowledgeable about the problems of aging and alcoholism, a nurse or social worker, and one or two paraprofessional workers. These paraprofessional workers can provide a great many services for the patients, who will have many areas of difficulty. Such services should include visiting the homes of patients who miss clinic appointments; accompanying patients to other clinics and community agencies to act as liaison and patient advocates; observing and reporting patient behavior to the professional staff; contacting the Department of Social Services to help with patients' economic and housing needs; interviewing patients' friends, relatives, and neighbors to help support the patients living at home; and participating in the group sessions. If paraprofessional staff are not available, home attendants of the patients can attend the group with some preliminary education and supervision. Most home attendants can serve as therapeutic agents and carry out many of the activities of a paraprofessional staff.

Many of the patients treated in such groups will be noted to be clinically depressed. The judicious use of antidepressant medication can be helpful for such patients.

Although the most important goal of the elder-specific treatment of alcoholism is not necessarily producing abstinence from alcohol use and the efforts are directed mainly at the psychosocial stresses of aging, abstinence is often a quick response to this treatment. In addition, abstinence is more easily maintained with few if any relapses to drinking. Relapse prevention strategies with the elderly take the form of dealing with maladaptations to the stresses of aging, treatment of coexisting depression, mutual support and caring among group members, and the development of meaningful life activities that give reasons to continue to live.

With increasing interest in the treatment of elderly alcoholics, some new clinical observations have been made by myself and others interested in this area. Elderly alcoholics who are well off financially and retired from previously prominent positions seem to experience fewer of the social and economic stresses of aging and respond to more alcoholism-specific approaches. They need counseling and support to help them deal with a changed way of life, but the treatment of alcoholism must take priority. Another observation has been that elderly alcoholics who do find their way to alcoholism programs can also be treated in an alcoholism-specific way with the addition of psychosocial group interventions for the stresses of aging. Most elderly alcoholics, however, still resist referral to alcoholism programs and are more comfortable in senior-oriented programs.

CASE HISTORIES

Late-Onset Alcoholism

One of the patients with a drinking problem treated in such a group illustrates the value of this psychosocial approach. This case presents a patient with late-onset alcoholism. The patient was a 64-year-old widower who was a retired railroad mechanic. He was living with his son. He had become quite depressed since his wife's death and had greatly increased his alcohol intake so that it became a serious problem. He was behaving strangely and was often observed giving money away to strangers. He was referred to the program by a local block association. He had retired from work; his wife's death was a severe blow. Shortly after his referral he became involved in the group and was started on antidepressant medication. He responded quickly to the medication and experienced a significant reduction in depression. He became an enthusiastic participant in the group and soon stopped drinking alcohol. He was visited at home on several occasions by one of the paraprofessional workers, who was able to improve the strained relationship the patient had with his son as a result of his symptoms.

Early-Onset Alcoholism

Another patient treated by this group approach was a 70-year-old retired longshoreman who was living alone. He had been divorced from his wife for many years and had no children. He had at least a 40-year history of excessive drinking and had continued to drink heavily since his retirement from work 2 years prior to his referral to the group geriatric psychiatry program. He was referred by the psychiatric emergency room staff of the hospital because he had developed hallucinations and confusion. When seen initially, he was in a physically debilitated state and was suffering from urinary incontinence in addition to psychotic symptoms. He was attempting to get work on the docks and was unable to accept the fact that he was physically unable to do such work. He had several general hospital admissions and was followed in the medical and urology clinics. He was visited by paraprofessional staff members while in the hospital and had his clinic follow-up arranged by them. He was treated with a phenothiazine drug at bedtime and antidepressants during the day. Between admissions to the hospital, he attended many group sessions. Gradually his health improved, his confusion cleared, and he gave up drinking. He made several friends in the group and accepted his retirement.

Alcoholism-Specific Therapy in an Elderly Alcoholic

The patient, who was treated in a private practice setting, was a 65-year-old woman who was married for 33 years. She was from Texas and was a very attractive woman. She married a wealthy man in New York City who was of a different religion. She found the adjustment to New York City difficult and began to drink more. After the birth of her daughter 32 years ago, her husband became devoted to the child and tended to neglect her. Her drinking increased and reached a level of alcohol addiction about 10 years ago. She drank primarily beer.

She developed serious liver problems due to the drinking and the liver damage reached the stage of early cirrhosis. She had tried numerous attempts at treatment including several hospital detoxifications, AA, and inpatient treatment at several different facilities. She stopped drinking for short periods but always resumed the alcoholic drinking in a matter of weeks.

She became increasingly estranged from her husband and her daughter. Her husband was verbally and at times physically abusive to her when she was intoxicated. She had several falls and sustained fractures while intoxicated.

Her internist sent her to me for alcoholism treatment as a last resort. When I first saw her, she had been drinking heavily and was in need of detoxification. Detoxification was carried out on an outpatient basis using diazepam. She was quite agitated and tremulous during the first week of detoxification. She completed the detoxification and did not resume drinking. Medical clearance was obtained and she was started on disulfiram 250 mg a day.

The patient appeared quite physically debilitated and unstable on her feet during the first 2 weeks of treatment. After 4 weeks of treatment her physical status was somewhat better but she appeared severely depressed. She had a history of depression. She had no appetite and showed psychomotor retardation. She was started on desipramine which was gradually increased to 300 mg a day. After 2 months of treatment she felt much better physically and was less depressed.

The patient began attending AA meetings four to six times a week and her husband went to a few Al-Anon meetings. After she became sober, the relationship between herself and her husband gradually improved.

The desipramine was gradually reduced and then discontinued, but she was maintained on disulfiram. Her liver began to heal and she felt increasingly better. She renewed her activities at her church and became committed to long-term sobriety which so far has been more than 2 years.

This elderly patient with long-standing alcoholism had not responded to many previous attempts at alcoholism treatment. Her "last chance" referral for alcoholism treatment was successful because the patient had "hit bottom" and because her seriously deteriorating physical condition and the severe coexisting depression were recognized and effectively treated.

LOCATION OF TREATMENT PROGRAMS AND COST EFFECTIVENESS

The question arises as to where these treatments should be provided in order to reach the greatest number of elderly alcoholics. In addition, there is the common question of how one deals with the significant number of elderly unwilling or unable to leave their homes. It has been found that elderly alcoholics perceive their alcoholism in ways different from younger alcoholics. First, older alcoholics generally consume smaller quantities of alcohol because of a lower tolerance and therefore have fewer *acute* medical problems associated with their alcohol consumption. For most elderly alcoholics the alcohol that is consumed produces social problems but less often acute physical problems. Chronic medical problems such as cirrhosis of the liver or peptic ulcer may be present, but the need to detoxify from alcohol and treat alcohol withdrawal manifestations is much less. Therefore, the physical stress associated with alcoholism is seen less in elderly alcoholics which leads to a greater reluctance of the elderly to utilize specialized alcoholism treatment programs.

Denial exists in elderly alcoholics as it does in younger alcoholics, but the confrontation required to reach younger alcoholics to get them to recognize that they are alcoholic has not been found to be necessary in most cases. In view of these clinical observations, as well as the responses of elderly alcoholics to sociopsychological approaches related to the stresses of aging and their multiplicity of complex problems (only one of which is problem drinking), it would seem inappropriate to refer such patients to alcoholism treatment programs except when they may have serious medical problems associated with their drinking or because they are more insulated from the stresses of aging due to other circumstances. Treatment interventions will, in general, be much more effective when delivered through facilities serving the aged, such as senior citizen programs, outpatient geriatric medical or psychiatric programs, nursing homes, or home-care programs.

The development of specialized AA programs for elderly alcoholics might be an exception to this suggestion. Such AA programs should utilize elderly alcoholics as speakers to help the participants identify with similar problems. In addition, the group nature of an AA meeting could be enhanced by providing socialization and recreational activities after the formal AA meeting. Conducting such meetings in a senior citizen center would be ideal in regard to location and in regard to the availability of recreational activities.

The problems associated with delivering services to the elderly in general also apply to elderly alcoholics. Many people are unwilling or unable to leave their homes to go to outpatient programs or to participate in groups once they get there. Therefore, the delivery of comprehensive services to the elderly must include outreach and case-finding services as well as an effective home-care program. Elderly individuals unwilling to participate in group activities as part of their lifelong style and personality have to be dealt with individually in an effort to learn what particular interests and competence they have that might be utilized to catalyze involvement in some aspect of a program. These considerations apply to elderly alcoholics as well.

The emergency room study (Adams et al., 1992) and the alcohol-related hospitalization study (Adams et al., 1993) suggest high medical utilization by elderly alcoholics. Effective treatment has been shown to improve functioning, eliminate alcohol abuse, and reduce depression thus reducing the need for hospital and emergency room treatment (Kofoed et al., 1987; Kashner et al., 1992). This is certainly a major cost benefit to an already over burdened health care system.

GUIDELINES FOR ELDERLY ALCOHOLISM TREATMENT

Several major principles must be applied in order to successfully identify elderly alcohol abusers, engage them in treatment, and produce a good outcome, namely, abstinence from alcohol and reduced or eliminated adverse effects of the stresses of aging. These principles include the awareness that alcoholism can occur in the elderly but its manifestation will be different from that in younger individuals. The impact of alcohol use on functioning should be sought and differentiated from medical abnormalities and organic mental problems. There should be a careful evaluation for depression, which is so common in the elderly. A review of the elderly person's medical, psychological, social, financial, housing, environmental, and family relationships should be done. The confrontation of the elderly person's alcohol problem should be done as part of a series of difficulties the person is experiencing rather than as *the* problem. Such a confrontation should indicate that the person may have a problem with alcohol along with depression, social isolation, and medical problems, not that the person is an "alcoholic." The re-

TABLE 22.2. Principles of Elderly Alcoholism Treatment

1. There should be a high index of suspicion of alcoholism in the elderly.

2. Diagnosis should be made by impact of alcohol consumption on functioning rather than by quantity or medical consequences.

3. Look for depression, which is common in the elderly alcoholic.

4. An alcohol problem should be presented to the elderly person in the context of problems of adjustment to aging.

5. Treatment should be directed at the stresses of aging with a problem-solving orientation in a group setting.

6. Clinical depression should be actively treated.

7. Outreach and follow-up should be provided to help with the obtaining of services and when patients do not keep appointments.

ferral for treatment should emphasize this need to help with all the problems in a group for "senior citizens" rather than an alcoholism program. The group should be oriented to self- and mutual help rather than engaging in psychoanalytical uncovering or alcoholism-specific treatment. The patients should take a leadership role in the group's organization and development. The many social, economic, housing. and family problems should be addressed. Clinical depression should be actively treated with antidepressant medication. Outreach, including home visiting and assistance in obtaining services, should be part of the treatment.

If these principles are carried out, most elderly patients will respond quickly and remain in treatment, eliminating the alcohol problem and experiencing an improved quality of life. These principles are summarized in Table 22.2.

REFERENCES

Adams, W. L., Magruder-Habib, K., Trued, S., & Broome, H. L. (1992). Alcohol abuse in elderly emergency department patients. *Journal of the American Geriatrics Society, 40,* 1236–1240.

Adams, W. L., Zhong, Y., Barboriak, J. J., & Rimm, A. A. (1993). Alcohol related hospitalizations of elderly people. *Journal of the American Medical Association, 270,* 1222–1225.

Bailey, M. B., Haberman, P. W., & Alksne, H. (1965). The epidemiology of alcoholism in an urban residential area. *Quarterly Journal of Studies on Alcohol 26,* 19–40.

Blow, F. C., Brower, K. J., Schulenberg, J. E., Demo-Daranber, L. M., Young, M. S., & Beresford, T. P. (1992). The Michigan Alcoholism Screening Test: A new elderly specific screening instrument. *Alcoholism: Clinical and Experimental Research, 16,* 372–377.

Buchsbaum, D. L., Buchanan, R. G., & Lawton, M. J. (1991). Alcohol consumption patterns in a primary care population. *Alcohol and Alcoholism, 26,* 215–220.

Cahalan, D., Cisin, I. H., & Crossley, H. M. (1974). *American drinking practices: A national survey of drinking behavior and attitudes.* New Brunswick, NJ: Rutgers Center of Alcohol Studies.

Carruth, B., Williams, E. P., Mysak, P., & Boudreaux, L. (1975, July). Community care providers and the older problem drinker. *Grassroots,* pp. 1–5.

Drew, L. R. H. (1968). Alcohol as a self-limiting disease. *Quarterly Journal of Studies on Alcohol, 29,* 956–967.

Droller, H. (1964). Some aspects of alcoholism in the elderly. *Lancet, 2,* 137–139.

Epstein, L. J., Mills, C., & Simon, A. (1970). Antisocial behavior of the elderly. *Comprehensive Psychiatry, 11,* 36–42.

Gaitz, C. M., & Baer, P. E. (1971). Characteristics of elderly patients with alcoholism. *Archives of General Psychiatry, 24,* 327–378.

Graham, K. (1986). Identifying and measuring alcohol abuse among the elderly: Serious problems with existing instrumentation. *Journal of Studies on Alcohol, 47,* 322–326.

Hunt, R. D., Finlayson, R. E., Morse, R. M., & Davis, L. J. (1988). Alcoholism in elderly persons: Medical aspects and prognosis of 216 inpatients. *Mayo Clinic Proceedings, 63,* 753–760.

Kashner, M. T., Rudell, D. E., Ogden, S. R., Guggenheim, F. E., & Karson, C. N. (1992). Outcomes and cost of two VA inpatient treatment programs for older alcoholic patients. *Hospital and Community Psychiatry, 43,* 985–989.

Kofoed, L. L., Tolson, R. L., Atkinson, R. M., Toth, R. F., & Turner, J. A. (1987). Treatment compliance of older alcoholics: An elder specific approach is superior to "mainstreaming." *Journal of Studies on Alcohol, 48,* 47–51.

McCusker, J., Cherubin, C. F., & Zimberg, S. (1971). Prevalence of alcoholism in general municipal hospital population. *New York State Journal of Medicine, 71,* 751–754.

Rosin, A. J., & Glatt, M. M. (1971). Alcohol excess in the elderly. *Quarterly Journal of Studies on Alcohol, 32,* 53–59.

Schonfeld, L., & Dupree, L. W. (1991). Antecedents of drinking for early and late-onset elderly alcohol abusers. *Journal of Studies on Alcohol, 52,* 587–592.

Schuckit, M. (1979). Geriatric alcoholism and drug abuse. *The Gerontologist, 17,* 168–174.

Schuckit, M. A., & Miller, P. L. (1975). Alcoholism in eldery men: A survey of a general medical ward. *Annals of the New York Academy of Science, 273,* 558–571.

Siassi, I., Crocetti, G., & Spiro, H. R. (1973). Drinking patterns and alcoholism in a blue collar population. *Quarterly Journal on Studies of Alcohol, 34,* 197–926.

Simon, A., Epstein, L. J., & Reynolds, L. (1968). Alcoholism in the geriatric mentally ill. *Geriatrics, 23,* 125–131.

Zimberg, S., (1969). Outpatient geriatric psychiatry in urban ghetto with nonprofessional workers. *American Journal of Psychiatry, 125,* 1697–1702.

Zimberg, S. (1971). The psychiatrist and medical home care: Geriatric psychiatry in the Harlem community. *American Journal of Psychiatry, 127,* 1062–1066.

Zimberg, S. (1990). Management of alcoholism in the elderly. *Addictions Nursing Network, 2,* 4–6.

23

HIV and AIDS

MARK G. WINIARSKI

INTRODUCTION

In the second decade of the AIDS epidemic, human immunodeficiency virus (HIV) infection and the condition it causes, acquired immune deficiency syndrome (AIDS), no longer threaten someone else's community and someone else's clients. HIV threatens all our communities and all our clients. All mental health providers, and especially those with clients with substance abuse issues, must now include HIV-related content in their counseling and psychotherapy.

Originally construed as a biomedical condition with almost exclusively medical interventions, HIV infection and HIV-related illness are now better understood as biopsychosocial–spiritual conditions with large prevention and treatment roles for the psychotherapist.

In fact, the roles a psychotherapist can play in the HIV epidemic are important and many. At the least, psychotherapy must include fact-based prevention messages and, even better, risk-prevention skills building. And, with the Centers for Disease Control and Prevention (CDC) estimate that one in 250 persons in the United States is HIV infected, mental health professionals will require significant additional knowledge and skills to work with persons with a chronic, life-threatening condition. This work may include assisting an HIV-infected person or a family member to come to terms with death, accompanying clients to the threshold of death, ensuring that this generation's HIV-affected children will be cared for, and advocating for "upstream" socioeconomic systemic solutions rather than waiting downstream for the bodies to float by.

Special chapters and books on HIV-related psychotherapy (e.g., Winiarski, 1991; Dilley, Pies, & Helquist, 1989; Kain, 1989) are written because work with HIV-related issues is different. When HIV is discussed, disconcerting issues and feelings may also surface, including:

- Moral judgments regarding sex and substance use;
- Psychological discomfort regarding alternative sexual practices and substance use, including but not limited to injection drug use;
- Judgments regarding women, their sexual activity, and childbearing responsibilities;
- Racism and classism that includes anger at disadvantaged urban minority-culture members;
- Feelings of helplessness; and
- Seeming inevitable loss.

HIV-infected individuals, as is true with substance users, have been ill served by society's tendency to blame, stigmatize, and ostracize rather than to understand, respond therapeutically, and console. We find fault in individuals for "internal defects" rather than see many behaviors, such as substance abuse, as symptoms of societal conditions such as lack of employment opportunities and treatment resources (see Humphreys & Rappaport, 1993, for an extended discussion). Readers of this volume are urged to note the many significant parallels between societal attitudes, understandings, and treatment of both substance users and HIV-affected individuals. Those parallels include the following:

- Those with HIV infection, as those with addictions, are often viewed with derision and disgust or are, at best, ignored.
- HIV-infected people and those with addictions are stereotyped as irresponsible, "lowlifes," sociopaths, and human garbage.
- HIV-positive people, as well as substance users, may have internalized or "introjected" many of the societal messages, resulting in self-hate.
- Reflecting society's judgments, services to substance users and HIV-positive people are inadequate in many communities.
- Despite the complexities and difficulties of their work, psychotherapists—including psychiatrists, psychologists, social workers, and counselors—who treat substance users and/or HIV-affected people are viewed as less adequate than other practitioners. Societal attitudes seem to affect everyone.

It would be tragic if psychotherapists—who should be, after all, healers—consciously or not recapitulate the stigmatization and rejection, described in this volume and chapter, that society offers clients. This can occur by discriminatorily declining to provide services or, worse, by providing mental health services that lack compassion and competence.

The following sections contain information to enable practitioners to provide compassionate and competent care to people affected by HIV:

1. Transmission and epidemiological trends;
2. The controversy and clinical implications regarding links between substance abuse and behavior that is high risk for HIV infection, including implications for prevention;
3. A biopsychosocial–spiritual model for understanding and treating HIV infection;
4. Exercises regarding attitudes that may interfere with compassionate practice;
5. Information regarding competent psychotherapy and counseling with HIV-positive people; and
6. Practical suggestions for building and maintaining HIV-related competence.

STATISTICS AND STEREOTYPES

Unfortunately, in regard to both substance abuse and HIV, too many psychotherapists maintain an "HIV is not my problem" stance through a stereotypical view of vulnerable persons, a simplistic use of statistics, a poor understanding of risk, and cultural stereotypes.

The original view of HIV-infected persons as either gay or intravenous drug users is antiquated and dangerous in that it minimizes the risks to everyone. By now, most people understand that the virus does not know whether people are of a certain race, sexual preference, or economic group. The virus goes where it is transported by bodily fluids. The transportation occurs through fluid exchange from an infected person in the following ways:

- During sex;
- Through injection drug use. Risk occurs when an HIV-infected person uses a syringe to shoot up and leaves some infected blood in it; then another person uses the same syringe, thereby injecting infected blood along with the drug or drugs;
- From the infected mother to the fetus in the womb: because of the presence of the mother's HIV antibodies, all babies born of HIV-infected mothers test HIV positive immediately after birth; the mother's antibodies disappear and about 30% of the babies subsequently develop their own antibodies and become HIV positive themselves;

- Through breast-feeding from the infected mother to the baby; and
- By way of transfusions and blood products that have not been correctly tested for the presence of HIV. Routine testing in the United States has decreased the risk to negligible size. To avoid even that negligible risk, U.S. surgeons who plan procedures suggest that patients stock their own blood for transfusion, a procedure known as autologous transfusion. There have been reports from other countries, however, that companies have failed to test blood products, thus endangering recipients.

In the United States, hemophiliacs who received blood products before testing commenced in the mid-1980s, gay men, and injection drug users (IDUs) were most affected in the early epidemic because those groups were entry points for the virus here. The communities of gay men and IDUs then became large pools of infected persons. In developing countries, the pool of infected individuals is heterosexual. The epidemic in the inner city of the United States—largely scorned and tragically ignored—portends the future for the epidemic in the United States: Individuals infected through injection drug use are having unprotected sex, leading to a startling increase in numbers of infected women and, subsequently, their children. In one epicenter of the epidemic, the Bronx, New York, a state seroprevalence study indicated that 1.58% to 1.8% of all women giving live birth in the last few years are HIV infected. The most recent statistics available, for 1992, show an infection rate of 1.58% in all Bronx women who gave live birth. However, black women in the Bronx who gave live birth in 1992 have an infection rate of 2.32% (W. Pulver, personal communication, November 1993; see also Novick et al., 1991, for methodology).

In late 1993, the CDC was estimating about 1 million infected people in the United States—1 in 250. National data from Job Corps applicants, people primarily from disadvantaged areas, indicate that about 3 in 1,000 of these youth, ages 16–21, are infected (Conway et al., 1993). Seroprevalence in young men in that sample ranged from 3.6 per 1,000 in 1988 to 2.2 per 1,000 in 1992. For young women in the study, the seroprevalence increased from 2.1 per 1,000 in 1988 to 4.2 per 1,000 in 1990 and through 1992. However, Conway et al. (1993) note that Job Corps applicants are not representative of disadvantaged youths generally, failing to include IDUs, people incarcerated, and those prostituting or involved in other illegal activities.

Do not succumb to the temptation to use these data to support a view that HIV remains isolated and does not touch your community. College campus data spanning 1987–1990, presumably from people in a different socioeconomic stratum than Job Corps applicants, indicate that overall 2 in 1,000 are infected, with the rate for men 5 in 1,000 (Gayle et al., 1990; see also Anonymous, American College Health Association, personal communication, November 17, 1993). In low-incidence communities, people are nevertheless touched by HIV and require related counseling services: A neighbor's son returns home to die, condoms are in plain view in every drugstore, adults and teenagers continue to have unprotected sex, and rumors of infection rise and disappear. Indeed, a myopic view of statistics combined with the antiquated view of stereotypical "risk groups" may lead a college student or a sports bar goer to decide risk of infection is minuscule in his/her town. However, if the sexual partner is infected, HIV transmission during a single act of unprotected intercourse is possible (although the real risk is difficult to estimate). In gay men, Kingsley et al. (1987) found that relatively low rates of unprotected anal intercourse predict greatly elevated risk for HIV seroconversion. The fact is, everyone who may receive someone else's bodily fluids can be infected if HIV is present in those fluids.

SUBSTANCE ABUSE AND HIV

Although it is indisputable that substance abuse that includes exchange of blood is a high-risk behavior for HIV infection, the belief that the use of substances such as alcohol or crack cocaine is a *direct* cause of high-risk sex is still controversial. That controversy has clinical implications.

In their exhaustive review of research regarding this link, Leigh and Stall (1993) concluded: "It is clear that there is a positive relationship between substance use and high risk sex; what is less clear is the level at which this link exists. People who drink more, use more drugs, or do either in conjunction with sex are more likely to engage in high-risk activities" (p. 1038). Yet, the authors suggest that the picture is very complex and caution against attributing those activities to the substance abuse alone. For example, people who use substances and have high-risk sex may be thrill seekers or have impulse control problems. Hypothesized links, with clinical implications, between substance abuse and high-risk sex include the following:

- Use of the substance, such as alcohol, to excuse bad behavior;
- Disinhibition, or loss of judgment that would prevent a high-risk behavior;
- Hypersexuality, the physiological stoking of sexual desire, most notably seen in crack cocaine users;
- Sex work for drugs, which may include higher-paying high-risk sex, as an economic imperative driven by addiction; and
- Diminishment of capacity for safer sex, for example, diminished ability to say no to unsafe sex, or diminished ability to put on or remove a condom to avoid leakage.

Prevention Implications

Mental health providers have resisted discussing HIV with their clients for too long in the face of disturbing data regarding the epidemic's spread. Or, if the discussion occurred, it likely was without adequate depth. This is curious because doubtless most therapists would discuss reproductive implications with a sexually active client. A religious counselor may suggest abstinence, whereas others would discuss birth control. Why not discuss HIV prevention?

When working with substance-using clients, the clinician should be concerned with two aspects of prevention: The first I call the mechanics of prevention, which are necessary but insufficient, and the second I call the motivational aspects, also necessary but insufficient without mechanical "know-how."

The therapist has, in the context of a relationship, the ability to teach the client that HIV transmission can be prevented by:

- Abstinence;
- Beginning and remaining in a relationship with an HIV-negative individual, as determined by a test no less than 6 months after the last encounter with another person;
- Safer sex practices, including correct condom use to avoid contact with bodily fluids, avoidance of anal sex which is high risk, masturbation, and mutual masturbation;
- Termination of needle sharing by ending injection drug use or, if that is not possible, using only new syringes; and
- Avoidance of substance use, which may lead to unsafe sex, directly or indirectly.

The clinician should be warned, however, that even discussion of the mechanics should be based on an assessment of the person's ability to understand the directions, motivation to employ the information, and sexual functioning and attitudes. Chabon (1993) surveyed condom use and attitudes and sexual dysfunction in methadone clinic clients. She found that 92% of both men and women surveyed showed impaired sexual functioning—indicating that we need to understand these issues' impact on reluctance to use condoms. And, some persons still hold views or have feelings that prevent them from purchasing condoms.

These statistics suggest that the mental health provider must consider motivational aspects of both the substance use and high-risk sexual behaviors. Regarding the link, the clinician must not accept the simplistic premise, which may be the client's and society's, that demon rum (or cocaine, or whatever drug) forced an individual into the high-risk behavior. The client may have used substances to aid, abet, excuse, defer responsibility for, or justify the risk. Or, an unconscious psychodynamic link may exist between the high-risk sex and the drug use. Furthermore, the client may have engaged in unsafe sex, with or without a link to substance use, for a variety of reasons, including a need for closeness and nurturance or as a result of coercion. The complexities underpinning both the sexual behavior and the substance abuse behavior must be understood and addressed in the treatment. Clinicians should be warned, however, that understanding the behavior–risk link may not result in behavioral change. For example, I had a woman client who knew her partner was HIV positive and knew about safer sex practices but for complex reasons was careless and subsequently seroconverted.

A MODEL FOR UNDERSTANDING HIV INFECTION

As occurs also with substance abuse, HIV infection and AIDS are usually incompletely viewed as biomedical conditions. The result is incomplete treatment that denies the many facets of the condition and the person. In actuality, HIV infection and related illnesses—and substance abuse—are better addressed when understood as a biomedical, psychological, social, and spiritual condition:

- Biomedical in that as either cause or effect or both, biological factors are present. With HIV, for example, a virus is implicated in the collapse of immune functioning as well as having a direct effect on the body.
- Psychological in that the well-being of the inner person, or psyche, leads to or is affected by substance abuse or HIV infection.
- Social in that families, neighborhoods, affinity groups such as churches, and communities, affect both our vulnerability to and response to stresses, including HIV infection.
- Spiritual, by which we mean not an attachment to ecclesiastical institutions, although that may be present, but a sense of an "other," which may be a presence or meaning that surpasses current reality. Fortunato (1993) discusses our responding "to a client's need for eschatological hope. The word *eschatological* derives from the Greek word *eschaton,* meaning end times. It alludes to what happens to us after death" (p. 1). Fortunato (1993) suggests that counselors should form no opinion about clients' belief systems. Atheistic caregivers, he says, can be helpful to clients who believe in life after death. "Perceiving a client's eschatological beliefs as illusory is fine, as long as the caregiver understands that they are useful, functional illusions (and as long as the caregiver can respect the client's perception of atheism as equally illusory)" (p. 3).

The biopsychosocial/spiritual model has several uses. It allows us to think through what we know intuitively: No aspect of HIV falls into just one of these categories. Each aspect affects and is affected by others. Second, this consciousness allows a sophisticated response to a client who learns that he/she is HIV positive. Typically, the person is then sucked into a medical whirlwind of laboratory tests and numerical results, advice on prophylactic treatment, and subsequent medical appointments. But the person's psychological status, which is likely to include high levels of fear and anxiety and concerns about support, and that person's partners and family members are frequently ignored in the medical tornado. In contrast, the sophisticated practitioner will view HIV as not only a biomedical condition to be treated with prescription medication, but a condition of the psyche, family and community, and soul. As preparation for doing HIV-related psychotherapy, clinicians should consider how they would conceptualize these cases and respond in terms of the biopsychosocial/spiritual model:

Situation One

A senior-year woman at a state college has heard 4 years of HIV prevention messages, especially those regarding condoms. She has taken assertiveness training in negotiating condom use with men, and she carries a condom in her purse. One night she meets an attractive man at a party and has sex with him. However, she drank too much that night and failed to use her skills at negotiating condom use. A few days later she is frantic and comes to you for counseling.

Situation Two

A 12-year-old boy in a small town gradually weakens during his year in the sixth grade and loses weight. He develops thrush, a white coating, in his mouth. His physician orders an HIV test at a local laboratory, and word spreads that the boy is HIV positive. School officials, at the urging of a small group of parents, ask to meet with the mother (the father has died) with the intention of dismissing him "so other children won't be infected." You are the school's mental health consultant and have been ordered to be at that meeting.

The model provides theoretical and practical underpinnings to the type of psychotherapy with HIV-affected people that we describe later in this chapter—a relationship that responds flexibly to the person's biomedical, psychological, social, and spiritual needs.

This model can help therapists organize the conduct of their psychotherapy and detect areas of avoidance. For example, if a client focuses only on the biomedical, the practitioner may inquire regarding several issues, including: Why is the client unable to request necessary information from a medical provider? If the information has been communicated, why does the client request repetition? Is the focus on the biomedical, especially with a therapist, a means to escape discussing emotions or relationships? Similarly, a focus on emotional, or psychological, content should not obscure neglect of the physical.

In multidisciplinary settings, such as hospitals, this way of viewing HIV can serve as a metamodel facilitating multidisciplinary treatment by persons of different disciplinary cultures. Often, although all these practitioners speak English, they misunderstand or devalue each other because different disciplines each have different professional cultures, with different presuppositions about etiologies, primary problems, and treatments. The metamodel enables professionals with different cultures to work together without invalidating disciplinary premises and gifts. They all fit under this umbrella.

COMPASSION IN WORK
WITH THE HIV-POSITIVE CLIENT

Work with the HIV-positive client involves two simple-sounding but complex elements: compassion and competence. Compassion involves the therapist's attitudes, what some would term *countertransference*. Competence involves one's body of related knowledge and its skillful applications.

In HIV-related psychotherapy, a great deal of attention is paid to provider attitudes because these so often interfere with skillful practice: Providers may know what to say or do but for countertransferential reasons act unskillfully. Similarly, when I teach, I address the attitudes first. If attitudes are negative, little useful information sticks. Compassionate work can be blocked in two ways: first, by stereotypical attitudes regarding the clients, and second, by processes within the therapy that touch the provider.

Many of the stereotypical attitudes are unfounded beliefs. For example, Miller and Rollnick (1991) ask how professionals "become so convinced that alcoholics and other drug abusers are characterologically denying, lying, rationalizing, evasive, defensive, and resistant people and need to be treated as such?" (p. 10). They suggest processes of selective (mis)perception, misinterpretation of normal behaviors, and creation of reactions through certain styles of addictions counseling. Other issues believed to be substance abuse-related are in fact not related primarily or singularly to the substances but to the fact of being disadvantaged. The same is true for HIV-positive people. How have they come to be categorized as abnormal and "not us," as people who chose to become infected, as worthy of scorn? And how often are our therapies affected by these types of judgments? We are, despite our denials, not that different from society and our communities.

In HIV-related therapy, our deepest fears and emotions are touched. Some providers attempt to protect themselves by removing themselves emotionally from the client. But that countertransferential stance not only communicates to the client another message of ostracism but halts the provider's emotional growth. Indeed, oftentimes we can be painfully flooded with emotion: In my private practice, a client suddenly began pounding me with angry statements such as, "What good is it? What's the point of this so-called therapy?" I became severely anxious, questioning my competence and doubting the therapy. I had been caught up in a parallel anxiety, and my mind lost the words: "We are here to come to terms." I had in fact experienced a gift of parallel process. I had experienced, rather than cognitively learned, what the client was feeling. Those who conduct therapy at an emotional distance will never experience the client and will never understand and, consequently, do therapeutic work.

It is better that a therapist confront the possibilities of being uncomfortable or reluctant to discuss sex, death, loss, and illness than to enter a relationship and be unable to be therapeutic because of discomfort. This confrontation can lead to exploration and growth for the therapist.

Following are some questions, by no means all, that should be considered before working with HIV-affected people. The first set of questions is adapted from an exercise (Winiarski, 1991) that involves several steps: Practitioners should read each question while imagining that the HIV-positive client is sitting with them and asking the question. Then, first, they should answer the question immediately, as quickly as they would need to respond to the client. They should write down that answer as well as their emotional reaction to being placed on the spot. Then, they should take time to consider their more authentic response and jot that down. Practitioners should attempt to understand why the first and second responses differ and to understand the emotional component.

Question 1: Client to therapist: Will you stay with me until the end?
Question 2: Would you kill yourself if you were me?
Question 3: I know I am dying. Will you hold me?

When this exercise is completed, practitioners should ask themselves whether they used technique to distance themselves from anxiety. What was the comfort level with these profound questions? What will they say and do when asked these questions in reality?

To further explore attitudes regarding HIV-positive persons, consider the following:

Question 4: True or false: Dysfunctional or pathological persons are most vulnerable to HIV infection.

Some psychotherapists are able to admit that they believe their clients are abnormal and that pathology led to the HIV infection. That defensive posture may allow someone to feel superior and to feel invulnerable ("If I'm not abnormal I won't contract HIV"). At a deeper level, there may be issues regarding sexuality, status, and blame. Most either do not acknowledge this bias or believe they can cover it up. Yet, we all know that our attitudes are conveyed to the client in our facial expressions, body language, or plainly unskillful attempts at psychotherapy. For example, a 23-year-old HIV-positive African American woman complained to me about another provider: "I told her that I had been arrested with crack. She then asked me, 'How long have you been using drugs?' I told her I hadn't been using. But how dare she make that assumption?"

Question 5: Am I willing to give up the perception of control?

In a training exercise, one person plays the therapist and another the client who describes a risk behavior and seeks help for it. The therapist can say only one thing, "Is there anything I can say or do to make you change your risk behavior?" Ultimately the realization dawns that there is nothing the therapist can say or do except support; the determination to change resides in the client. This is, of course, true for all therapies, no matter what we believe. Unfortunately, with HIV, our anxiety propels us to believe that we should be able to do something about the client's risk behaviors or his/her final illness. A chronic, life-threatening condition such as HIV challenges our perceptions of control.

Question 6: To what extent are my presuppositions about substance users and HIV-positive persons based on stereotypes about race, ethnicity, and disadvantaged status? Am I willing to allow the client to teach me about other cultures?

Often the view of a client is confounded by race, ethnicity, and other factors. For example, a white Irish alcoholic may be seen as a more tractable and desirable client than an African American. Why? Gay men are viewed by many as more desirable clients than those infected through substance use. But gay men also abuse substances.

Question 7: Will I treat an HIV-positive person who is not in recovery?

Controversy exists regarding whether the primary goal of treatment should be abstinence first or dealing with HIV. Those counselors whose training is in substance abuse generally take the former stance, arguing that a client who is not sober is not available for counseling. Those who have health-related or hospital-based practices are reluctant to reject a client and often will use HIV issues, over the course of the treatment, to underline the need for abstinence from substances.

> Question 8: What judgments do I make, consciously or unconsciously, about physicians, psychiatrists, social workers, psychologists, counselors, and others who work with substance abusers or HIV-positive people?

Many HIV-positive clients who have histories of substance use have been marginalized and devalued. It is notable that practitioners who work with substance-using or HIV-positive clients are often also devalued. As overheard in a Cape Cod restaurant: "He's working with substance abusers? How can he stand that work?" The reply: "He's doing research." Perhaps one avoids substance abuse- and HIV-related work because the devaluation of the client has led to a devaluation of their providers.

These questions and the responses comprise a brief self-assessment that may suggest whether a practitioner is willing to enter into a therapeutic relationship with someone affected by HIV.

HIV-RELATED PSYCHOTHERAPY

A compassionate psychotherapy also requires competence, by which I mean HIV-specific knowledge and psychotherapeutic skills. HIV-related psychotherapy should be responsive to the needs of people who face a chronic, life-threatening condition that can change suddenly and often over many years. How have psychotherapists who work with HIV-positive people responded?

When mental health specialists in HIV issues gather, they often close the door and talk among themselves about how the work involves many roles that were neither taught in graduate or postdoctoral psychotherapy programs nor included in traditional "frames" of psychotherapy. These are just a few of the many stories told at these meetings:

- The psychoanalytic candidate who washed and bathed his very ill analysand.
- The New York analyst who visited his client in a hospital and told me later, "I don't know if he even knew I was there."
- The Bronx psychologist who took a grieving mother to her son's grave, so she could speak to his spirit.

These acts of compassion do not conflict with but, rather, illustrate competent HIV-related service delivery. These are therapists who, secure in their training, are confident enough to go beyond that training to provide, in the context of a relationship, what is needed. Therapists who work with HIV-positive clients, regardless of race or socioeconomic class, quickly learn that they should have the following:

> Flexibility to move to different points on the paradigmatic continuum, depending on the client's changing circumstances. . . . It may be that, early on, self-exploration is useful, especially as it helps a client approach his or her anxieties and yearnings. It may be that as the disease progresses, the therapist may make hospital visits, conduct support sessions by telephone, or take a greater role in case management. (Winiarski, 1991, pp. 3–4)

The advice to "bend the frame" does not challenge paradigms of therapies, each of which works well with specific subgroups of clients. My advice suggests that HIV-affected persons comprise yet another subgroup that requires special care.

This special care requires attention to complicated issues that only rarely exist in therapies with noninfected individuals. As noted in the section on compassion, practitioners first must assess their ability and willingness to work with HIV-affected people. Then, they must assess the client's needs. The contract, preferably spoken, with a client must be based on these two assessments plus anticipation of the client's needs as the relationship and illness progresses. Successful "anticipatory management" (Winiarski, 1991) is informed by knowledge of HIV disease. Because medical information regarding HIV changes so rapidly, rather than provide perishable information this chapter concludes with suggestions for obtaining current medical information.

Client Assessment

A more comprehensive and compassionate view of the HIV-positive client is required before entering into the therapeutic relationship. This includes considerations of the following:

- Multiple traumas, including sexual, physical, and psychological, with an eye to how HIV infection recapitulates the trauma;
- Shame and guilt related to HIV, substance use, or sexual practice and how those feelings will be expressed in the therapy;
- Experiences of stigmatization in the family, cultural group, and community and how the therapist too may stigmatize that person;
- Experiences of inadequate or culturally inappropriate treatment and the therapist's cultural sensitivity and competence; and
- Functionality of the client's support system in face of HIV. Are others in the client's system also infected and with what impact?

It is also helpful to understand that for many HIV-affected clients, the issues around the medical condition are not a top priority. This is seen among clients of all socioeconomic classes who, when exhorted by a medical provider to go to the emergency room, will respond, "But I have an important meeting this afternoon" or "I have to go home and feed the cats." For many, HIV is just another on a long list of physical and emotional insults and is experienced as only an inconvenience, regardless of the anxiety of medical staff. In the practitioner's work as well, HIV may seem to be the foremost issue, while the client may seem to ignore it for reasons the practitioner needs to understand.

To obtain a well-rounded view of the client, based on the biopsychosocial/spiritual model outlined earlier in this chapter, the following information should be obtained.

Medical Condition

In order to understand the client, the therapist must understand the medical situation. Queries here should strive both for objective information and the meaning the information has for the client, and would include these topic areas:

- Current HIV medical status. Occurrence of HIV-related symptoms and conditions, and any lasting effects.
- Other medical conditions (e.g., diabetes, sickle cell anemia, and hypertension).
- Medications being taken, and those that have been recommended but declined. Ask about side effects, but they may have to be researched. Include here prescription and drugs obtained on the street or through buyers' networks, as well as herbal and other complementary remedies.
- Other treatments, including chiropractic care, acupuncture, and self-treatment.
- Names of all medical (and nonmedical) caregivers, including dentist, ophthalmologist, occupational therapist, physical therapist, visiting nurse, nutritionist, Christian Scientist practitioner, chaplain, and others. Understand their roles and the client's choices. Are these persons with HIV experience and expertise?
- Response to treatment, generally.

Neurological Condition

Because HIV has a neurotoxic effect, as do certain medications, and these affect the client's quality of life, consider the following:

- Client's baseline cognitive functioning.
- Symptoms of central nervous system involvement, such as cognitive slowing and memory loss.

- Client use of compensatory strategies, such as note taking, a reminder system.
- Peripheral nervous system involvement, indicated by pain, numbness, or other symptoms in arms, hands, legs, or feet.

Client Knowledge, Attitudes, and Emotional Response to HIV

It is important to assess whether the client is knowledgeable and realistic about his/her condition.

- Does the client have a good understanding of HIV-related conditions and his/her own condition specifically?
- Degree of denial and realism, the nature of the client's fighting spirit.

Psychological and Psychiatric Issues

The therapist should conduct a standard inquiry into baseline psychological functioninng and preexisting and current conditions, while adding questions in the following areas:

- Axis I symptoms that the client attributes to HIV status (e.g., anxiety, unhappiness, depression, and despair).
- History of, and attitudes regarding, current or past mental health professionals, who may include substance abuse program counselors and past or current participation in 12-Step programs, such as Narcotics Anonymous and Positives Anonymous.
- Use of psychiatric medications, either prescribed or obtained from street dealers. Clinicians must not overlook the abuse of prescriptions and the possibilities of substance abuse in people who do not meet their stereotype of someone abusing drugs. The very respectable looking actor River Phoenix died in November 1993 with cocaine, heroin, diazepam, marijuana, and an over-the-counter cold remedy in his bloodstream. When inquiring of substance use, use both street names and brand names. I usually ask, "Have you ever taken Librium [chlordiazepoxide], Valium [diazepam], etc.? Have you ever done speedball, etc.?"

Psychosocial Background

Through questioning about psychosocial background, the therapist begins to understand the client's social context. Information obtained in these areas will also help determine if case management services will be required:

- The client's cultural affiliations, which may be multiple. How does the client identify him/herself culturally? Practitioners should ask the client to teach them about the culture and, especially, how that culture regards the HIV-positive person.
- Names and positions of caregivers. Does the client have two families—one of blood relatives and another of affiliation, such as gay friends and a partner.
- Response of "relatives," and an understanding of longtime family patterns of care and current support. Are any apt to flee during a crisis?
- Are others in the support system HIV positive?
- Whom does the client designate to make treatment decisions if incapacitation occurs? Are the proper documents signed and filed with physicians and others?
- Are children involved? What is their biopsychosocial status?
- If there is social isolation, what is the cause?
- Whom should the therapist contact in an emergency, who can be counted on?
- What should the therapist do if the client misses an appointment and the therapist cannot reach him/her?

Sexual Functioning

Individuals often respond to their HIV infection with extreme changes in their sexual behaviors, provoked by extreme feelings. The following should be asked:

- Assess history and current sexual functioning.
- Does the client practice safer sex?
- Type of sex preferred? Anal, oral, receptive?
- What has changed since diagnosis or symptoms?
- Unwanted sexual occurrences?
- If gay or lesbian, the client's comfort with his/her sexual preference.

Spiritual Issues

Unfortunately, too many of us have been trained to avoid spiritual issues. Yet, many clients are yearning to discuss these concerns. A fuller understanding of our clients will come if we ask the following:

- Does the client have any spiritual beliefs or practices, such as belief in an afterlife?
- Are these beliefs comforting or a source of discomfort?

- With whom does the client discuss spirituality?
- What are the client's spiritual concerns?

This is by no means a comprehensive list of information that should be obtained (see Winiarski, 1991, for a broader list). Information gathered should be additionally expanded to encompass the client's specific circumstances. Based on the information obtained through this process and the clinician's knowledge of HIV illness, clinician and client can enter into a realistic therapeutic contract that anticipates, as well as reacts to, biopsychosocial and spiritual issues.

Goals and Themes

No consensus exists on the goals of psychotherapy, let alone HIV-related psychotherapy. Some argue that insight is the goal, whereas others require behavioral change. Some therapists claim as a goal the lifting of the client's spirits. In the practice of the federally funded AIDS Mental Health and Primary Care Integration Project, which I have directed at Montefiore Medical Center, the overarching goal is to have a relationship with clients, many of whom have not had helpful relationships. Many have histories of psychological deprivation and have come to learn that their feelings and needs were not important. We do not submit these people to additional deprivation to create a transference neurosis from which insight theoretically springs. Rather, we work to establish a relationship. Then, we find, oftentimes behavioral change and insight occur in the safe relationship. For example, project staff member Noel Elia (personal communication, October 1993) tells how one woman, who had been using drugs since age 12, suddenly connected her drug use to the painful experience of childhood sexual abuse.

Rather than impose our own specific goals beyond relationship, it is suggested that we listen more carefully to what the client wants the goal to be. Their goals may include coming to terms with death, not dying a substance abuser, connection and reconnection, planning for the future, learning more about the condition and coping strategies, avoiding relapse, and dying a righteous death, however that is defined by the individual.

The psychotherapist or counselor working with HIV-positive individuals may hear the following psychotherapeutic themes:

- Exploration of group membership, that is, what it has been like in the family and community. What groups does the client identify with? What roles did the client play in those groups? (Fred Millan, also of our project, conducts a group in the Bronx that is based on identification as a member of an oppressed minority group.)

- Reflections on the relationships between substance abuse and other aspects of life, including HIV infection.
- Current and historical relationships and the effects of HIV infection.
- Issues of abandonment, ostracism, and betrayal.
- Why me? Why me after I have been sober and clean and "gotten my act together"? Existential issues regarding fairness and randomness.
- It's not me!: denial, with the possibility that necessary work isn't getting accomplished.
- Shame and guilt, two all-pervasive themes in many psychotherapies.
- Dependency, loss of control.
- Fear of dying alone, in pain, or in a shameful way.
- Fear of living with HIV infection.
- Relationships with majority culture providers.

Obviously these are just a sample of the themes that can emerge. Each client brings a multitude of themes.

Other "Bending the Frame" Roles for the Therapist

As noted, the biopsychosocial/spiritual complexities of HIV-related conditions require psychotherapists to consider other roles as they bend the frame of therapy. Other functions are briefly described.

Case Management

Depending on one's training, case management may have been emphasized or overlooked. Even some social workers, trained in case management, may consider it "scut work" and avoid it. Others avoid it simply because they know little about it or view it as too time-consuming. But providers who have embraced a larger role have found that case management is often crucial to the client and embraces issues that come before insight in the hierarchy of needs. Case management can connect the client to entitlements that mean food and medical care and can reduce stress. Skillful case management, in fact, may not manage the client but rather the systems that service the client. Case management can include many functions:

- Creating linkages between all the professional and nonprofessional providers identified during the assessment. To avoid complicated and duplicated communications, some case managers ask families to designate one spokesperson who addresses the professionals.

- Responding to substance abuse relapses by reconnecting the client to treatment, including 12-Step programs.
- Monitoring and care for family members. Many loving partners and others neglect their own needs and, as a result, are unable to care for the HIV-positive person. The case manager may address care and sustenance of others in the system.
- Preventing overmedicalization of the client. The case manager will remind all involved that the client and the systems also have nonmedical components and needs.
- Ensuring entitlements and services. The client will be connected to governmental benefits and other services available.
- Shoring up the care systems during crisis.
- Advocating for new models of care that provide "upstream" solutions, that is, solutions that are proactive and creative rather than reactive.

Many psychotherapists ask why they should provide case management. Often the therapist has the longest and deepest relationship with the client and, in the absence of an active family member or other caregiver, best knows the client's needs and desires and is best able to maintain objectivity. Of course, others in a client's family or community may better serve this function, but the therapist should communicate with that person, especially at the end of the illness.

Monitoring

HIV-related psychotherapy must attend to acute symptoms. With HIV, the therapist must not only ask the client how he/she feels about a new symptom but assess it and, if serious, recommend immediate action or provide it. The therapist must give serious attention to the following acute, or new-onset, symptoms:

- Difficulties in communication, including the inability to speak or difficulty speaking;
- Hallucinations, either visual, auditory or olfactory;
- Other acute cognitive impairment;
- Delirium, the symptoms of which develop over a short period of time and fluctuate during the day. Symptoms may include impaired ability to focus, sustain or shift attention; easy distractability; changes in cognition that may include problems with recent memory and disorientation to time and place; changes in speech patterns, and perceptual disturbances. Consult the fourth edition of the *Diagnostic and Statistical Manual of Mental Disorders* (American Psychiatric Association, 1994, pp. 124–133) for additional information:

- Significant shortness of breath or chest pain;
- Fever, especially increases in fever over baseline, or new onset fever;
- Headaches, especially without a previous history of tension or migraine headaches;
- Seizure activity; and
- Incontinence.

If any of these symptoms occur, the therapist should immediately discuss with the client the need for medical attention.

Monitoring in the psychosocial/spiritual spheres should include attention to new agitation, frustration, violence, substance abuse relapse, hopelessness, despair, new negative attitudes toward medical care, and suicidal intent. Therapists should also watch for changes in social, vocational, or parental functioning and changes in social systems such as supporters' and children's crises and monitor entitlement problems, workplace concerns, termination of substance use treatment, or 12-Step attendance.

Practitioners should not be reticent about voicing their concerns and discussing the client's reluctance to take action. Many therapists seem afraid to be intrusive; I believe our clients appreciate our expressions of concern. If the client appears delirious, incoherent, or in other ways unable to take care of him/herself, the provider should immediately call for emergency medical assistance while also contacting a caregiver.

Supervision

HIV-related psychotherapy is obviously as complicated and emotionally taxing as it is rewarding. So it would seem that those who do the work would seek expert advice. As I travel and teach, I ask how many attendees working with HIV-positive clients are in regular (weekly or, at least, semiweekly) supervision. It is shocking that in each audience the number of professionals in supervision is extremely low.

Several aspects of practice need consideration and supervisory advice that we cannot give ourselves.

Rescue Fantasies

Two rescue fantasies that intrude into skillful HIV-related practice are (1) a biomedical solution will soon be found or that the psychotherapy will somehow lead to physical cure, and (2) the therapy may create significant lasting personality changes that will contribute to an emotionally healthier dying. For example, a therapist may believe that a person with significant narcissistic traits may somehow die as a healthier person. While we may wish it to be so, it is perhaps healthier on our part to be realistic. The quickest route to feelings of helplessness and hopelessness is creation of a goal that is unreachable.

Belief in the Efficacy of Concrete Plans

Tunnell (1987) suggested that psychotherapists who pursue concrete problem solving may be attempting to avoid their own feelings of helplessness and anger: "As long as the *patient* has a plan to avoid the adversity and negativity of life, he won't have to deal with feeling helpless. As long as the *therapist* has a plan to avoid dealing with the patient's adverse situation and negative feelings, he or she won't have to deal with feeling helpless in the therapy hour" (p. 4).

Reluctance to Act in the Face of Clear Evidence of a Serious Situation

For example, providers seem notoriously reluctant to confront clients regarding unsafe practices, whether they be unsafe sex or dangerous parenting. Supervision will help the therapist understand wheter an unsafe situation actually exists and whether it needs immediate action, such as notification of the child welfare authorities.

Feelings of Despair and Demoralization

These feelings may be part of a parallel process splashed on a therapist by a despairing client, or they may result from the therapist's own psychological state. In either case, they require attention.

BUILDING AND MAINTAINING HIV COMPETENCE

Several concrete suggestions will help in developing more HIV-related knowledge and skills. Those interested can familiarize themselves with HIV counseling and psychotherapy issues by reading some of the following books and articles: *AIDS-Related Psychotherapy* (Winiarski, 1991); *Face to Face: A Guide to AIDS Counseling* (Dilley, Pies, & Helquist, 1989); *AIDS: A Complete Guide to Psychosocial Intervention* (Land, 1992); *No Longer Immune: A Counselor's Guide to AIDS* (Kain, 1989); and a review in the *Journal of Counseling and Development* (Dworkin & Pincu, 1993). New books are appearing every year.

Moreover, clinicians should regularly read newsletters about HIV-related work. *FOCUS: A Guide to AIDS Research and Counseling* is available from the AIDS Health Project, University of California at San Francisco (Box 0884, San Francisco, CA 94143-0884), for about $45 annually. *HIV Frontline* is available free from NCM Publishers (200 Varick Street,

New York, NY 10014). Those who do regular HIV-related work read the somewhat pricy medical newsletter, *AIDS Clinical Care* (it can be found in most medical libraries and subscriptions are available from P.O. Box 9085, Waltham, MA 02254).

Volunteering at a local or regional HIV-related service center will help clinicians enter a network of providers who share information and support and may provide referrals to their practice.

It may be helpful for the provider to query his/her national professional organization regarding training. For example, both the American Psychological Association and the American Psychiatric Association have national training programs in HIV-related issues, with trainers locally teaching a general curriculum and specialized tracks such as substance abuse. The federal government also has funded regional education and training centers that provide training to medical and mental health professionals.

Clinicians can obtain access to an academic library and occasionally check databases for articles they have missed in the general press. Many AIDS-related databases are now available on CD-ROM.

It can be useful to start an HIV supervision group with colleagues or locate and contact a local or regional HIV psychotherapy expert in HIV issues for case supervision, even if only by telephone.

In 1991, I wrote that HIV-related work is a "psychotherapeutic relationship that is unlike any other; a relationship that can encourage and reveal the human spirit, but always against the stark contrast of anxieties about life, the difficulties inherent in a life-threatening chronic illness, and loss" (Winiarski, 1991, p. 3). The work is difficult, but the dangers of HIV are no longer theoretical, not in any community.

ACKNOWLEDGMENTS

The writing of this chapter was supported in part by Contract BRH 970025-03-0 from the Health Resources and Services Administration, with funding from the Ryan White Comprehensive AIDS Resources Emergency Act, Title II, Special Projects of National Significance.

REFERENCES

American Psychiatric Association. (1994). *Diagnostic and statistical manual of mental disorders* (4th ed.). Washington, DC: Author.

Chabon, B. (1993, August). *Sexual dysfunction, condom attitude and use in a sample of methadone patients.* Paper presented at the 101st Annual Meeting of the American Psychological Association, Toronto, Ontario.

Conway, G. A., Epstein, M. R., Hayman, C. R., Miller, C. A., Wendell, D. A., Gwinn, M., Karon, J. M., & Peterson, L. R. (1993). Trends in HIV prevalence among disadvantaged youth. *Journal of the American Medical Association, 269,* 2887–2891.

Dilley, J. W., Pies, S., & Helquist, M. (Eds.). (1989). *Face to face: A guide to AIDS counseling.* Berkeley, CA: Celestial Arts.

Dworkin, S. H., & Pincu, L. (1993). Counseling in the era of AIDS. *Journal of Counseling and Development, 71,* 275–281.

Fortunato, J. E. (1993, June). A framework for hope. *Focus: A guide to AIDS Research and Counseling, 8*(2), 1–4.

Gayle, H. D., Keeling, R. P., Garcia-Tunon, M., Kilbourne, B. W., Narkunas, J. P., Ingram, F. R., Rogers, M. F., & Curran, J. W. (1990). Prevalence of the human immunodeficiency virus among university students. *New England Journal of Medicine, 323,* 1538–1541.

Humphreys, K., & Rappaport, J. (1993). From the community mental health movement to the war on drugs: A study in the definition of social problems. *American Psychologist, 48,* 892–901.

Kain, C. (1989). *No longer immune: A counselor's guide to AIDS.* Alexandria, VA: American Counseling Association.

Kingsley, L. A., Detels, R., Kaslow, R., Polk, B. F., Rinaldo, C. R., Chmiel, D. K., Kelsey, S. F., Odaka, K., Ostrow, D. G., Van Raden, M., & Visscher, B. (1987). Risk factors for seroconversion to human immunodeficiency virus among male homosexuals. *Lancet, 1,* 345–349.

Land, H. (Ed.). (1992). *AIDS: A complete guide to psychosocial intervention.* Milwaukee, WI: Family Service America.

Leigh, B. C., & Stall, R. (1993). Substance use and risky sexual behavior for exposure to HIV. *American Psychologist, 48,* 1035–1045.

Miller, W. R., & Rollnick, S. (1991). *Motivational interviewing: Preparing people to change addictive behavior.* New York: Guilford Press.

Novick, L. F., Glebatis, D. M., Stricof, R. L., MacCubbin, P. A., Lessner, L., & Berns, D. S. (1991). II. Newborn seroprevalence study: Methods and results. *American Journal of Public Health, 81*(May Suppl.), 15–21.

Tunnell, G. (1987, December). *Counseling AIDS patients and their families.* Paper presented at Queens College, Flushing, NY.

Winiarski, M. G. (1991). *AIDS-related psychotherapy.* Elmsford, NY: Pergamon Press (now distributed by Allyn & Bacon).

24

The Role of Incest Issues in Relapse and Recovery

ENID B. YOUNG

INTRODUCTION

One of the greatest unacknowledged contributors to recidivism in alcoholism and other addictions may be the failure to identify and treat underlying childhood sexual abuse issues. The occurrence of relapse—a breakdown or setback in a person's attempt to change a target behavior—has been recognized as the most common outcome of treatment in recovery programs. Traditionally, relapse has been addressed both in 12-Step recovery programs and in the addiction field and, even more recently, in the area of relapse prevention. However, the possible existence of childhood sexual abuse issues as a predisposing factor of relapse has not been comprehensively explored.[1]

HISTORICAL OVERVIEW OF RELAPSE THEORY

Relapse has been studied primarily in the field of alcoholism and drug addiction. Classic theories of addiction (Jellinek, 1952; Jelinek & Williams, 1987) maintain that relapse is motivated and reinforced by relief from withdrawal; that is, traditional theory has focused on the role of physical withdrawal or the craving for a substance to alleviate the unpleasant symptoms associated with withdrawal distress. Others (Ludwig, Wikler, & Syark, 1974) have defined craving in terms of the environmental cues or conditioned stimuli previously associated with the substance as initiating factors of craving.

Current theories (Marlatt & Gordon, 1985; Litman, Eiser, & Rawsom, 1977; Chaney, O'Leary, & Marlatt, 1978) recognize the role played by social, psychological, cultural, and situational factors in the relapse process. Such models reject theories that regard craving as the principal determinant of relapse, focusing instead on environmental, intrapersonal, and interpersonal determinants of relapse.

Relapse prevention theory (Marlatt & Gordon, 1985) holds that it is the effect of high-risk situations and the individual's response to them that is most closely associated with relapse. For example, an alcoholic choosing to enter a bar and a cocaineuser going to a party where cocaine will be used may be placing themselves in high-risk situations for relapse. Relapse prevention draws on social learning theory and the acquisition of new cognitive-behavioral techniques that can help the individual to define high-risk situations and covert antecedents of a relapse situation (triggers) as well as to develop "coping" strategies for maintaining abstinent behavior (life-style change). Intervention strategies are designed to deal with relapse when it does occur in order to ensure an immediate return to abstinence.

Common agreement among all theories has been that relapse is a highly probable, complex, multifaceted phenomenon. In fact, relapse is so common that it warrants the defining of addiction as "a relapsing condition."

THE ROLE OF CHILDHOOD SEXUAL ABUSE ISSUES IN RELAPSE

Classical theories of dependence and current theories of relapse prevention have not addressed the potential high risk for relapse associated with internally generated phenomena such as the effects of early childhood sexual abuse. The association between addictive behaviors, such as alcoholism, other drug abuse and eating disorders, and the incidence of childhood sexual abuse has been increasingly documented (Brown & Finkelhor, 1986; Courteois & Sprei, 1988). However, because denial is a principal defense mechanism in handling the effects of childhood sexual abuse, these experiences and the resultant symptoms are frequently masked. They remain untreated and become a high potential risk for relapse in recovery from addiction. Therefore, relapse prevention must explore the possible existence of childhood sexual abuse as a precipitating factor of relapse.

Many of the relapses that appear to be stimulus contingent, as current theory proposes, may in fact turn out to be internally generated. This would help to explain the persistent, repetitive occurrence of relapse when attempting to abstain from addictive behavior. Relapse should be viewed not only as a regression in terms of a defined goal of abstinence but, more important, as an indication of the existence of underlying material and the resultant inner psychic impairment that has contributed to the etiology of the addiction. When viewed in this way, relapse becomes an opportunity to strengthen the process of abstinence through the resolution of precipitating factors in the development of the addictive behavior.

CESSATION OF ADDICTIVE ACTIVITY INVOLVES MORE THAN ABSTINENCE

Alcoholics Anonymous (AA) and other 12-Step programs for addictive behaviors all emphasize that although abstinence is essential to relapse prevention, it is not the only issue. Recovery can be achieved only when the attitudes and behaviors that led to and/or were associated with the addictive behavior are changed. In other words, although relapse has usually been defined in terms of abstinence, or the total cessation of the addictive behavior (Marlatt & Gordon, 1985; Washton, 1988; Litman et al., 1977), it is important to understand that cessation of an addictive activity involves more than abstinence. As Washton (1988, p. 36) asserted:

> Abstinence is merely a prerequisite to recovery, because only during sustained abstinence can a chemically dependent person make the psychological, behavioral and attitudinal changes that are necessary to initiate and continue recovery from the addictive illness. If patients manage to stay abstinent for a while by sheer willpower and dogged determinism . . . but do not make fundamental changes in their way of living and behaving, they often continue to act in the same self-defeating and maladaptive manner as when they were actively using drugs. Moreover, their relapse potential remains extraordinarily high. In alcoholism treatment, this phenomenon is known as the "dry drunk."

When indicating the presence of unresolved traumatic experiences, relapse may be viewed not as a failure but rather as an opportunity to understand and thereby resolve psychological, behavioral, attitudinal, and spiritual material that has contributed to the addictive behavior. The resolution of this previously unresolved material strengthens the recovery process by initiating a process of inner psychic integration and is a critical factor in the prevention of further relapse.

THE PHENOMENON OF MULTIADDICTIONS

Another result of the underlying impairment that may contribute to the persistence of relapse is the phenomenon of multiaddictions. The prevalence of multiple addictions as an unacknowledged contributing factor to relapse is explored later. In particular, an increasingly recognized addiction, sex and love addiction, will be discussed.

WHAT IS CHILDHOOD SEXUAL ABUSE?

Childhood sexual abuse may be defined as "contacts or interactions between a child and an adult when the child is being used as an object of gratification for adult sexual needs or desires" (De Vine, 1988). When this contact happens within the family system (e.g., father, mother, cousin, brother, sister, or stepfather) it is defined as incest. Childhood sexual abuse occurs on a continuum, from covert to overt. Overt sexual abuse involves actual sexual contact, whereas covert sexual abuse includes more subtle sexual behaviors such as exhibitionism, sexualized language, a lack of appropriate privacy, and a misappropriarion of roles in the family system. It is a traumatic experience that interferes with a child's normal, healthy development. Although the focus of this article is childhood sexual abuse within the family system (i.e., incest), the theorizing is not limited to abuse within the family alone. Childhood sexual abuse often happens outside the family with similar dynamics, such as denial, repetitiveness, and trauma. Therefore, I use the terms *incest* and *childhood sexual abuse* interchangeably.

Historically, sexual abuse in childhood has been characterized by one of the most common reactions to the abuse experience itself: denial. During the past decade, however, the prevalence of all forms of child sexual abuse, including incest, has been discovered and has received unprecedented societal recognition (Brown & Finkelhor, 1985, 1986; Butler, 1985; Courtois, 1988; Covington & Beckett, 1988; Crewdson, 1988; Russell, 1983). It is now accepted that a substantial percentage of women have experienced childhood sexual abuse (Wyatt, 1985). Although the statistics on sexual abuse among men have been more difficult to document, in part because the taboo against men reporting such abuse is even greater than for women, it has been increasingly reported as significant.

CHILDHOOD SEXUAL ABUSE PREDISPOSES VICTIMS TO THE DEVELOPMENT OF ADDICTIVE BEHAVIORS

High Correlation between History of Sexual Abuse and Subsequent Manifestation of Addiction

Does the experience of childhood sexual abuse predispose an individual to the development of addictive behaviors? The etiology of addiction has been and continues to be studied extensively. It is clear that addiction is multidetermined; biological, social, and psychological factors all contribute to the development of addictions.

Increasing evidence reveals a high correlation between a history of sexual abuse and the subsequent manifestation of addictive behavior. Studies indicate that early sexual trauma may lead to alcohol problems in women (Kouach, 1983; Nielsen, 1984). When asked about experiences with incest or rape, a majority of alcoholic women state that they experienced incest and other childhood sexual abuse (Covington, 1986).

In a survey of 78 eating-disordered patients, Oppenheimer, Howells, Palmer, and Chaloner (1985) reported that 66% revealed a history of adverse sexual experience, 80% of which occurred in childhood. Kearney-Cooke (in press) reported a 90% reduction in binge–purge frequency in bulimic women whose treatment included a focus on the aftereffects of child sexual abuse. Kearney-Cooke (in press) also asserted that "abusive sexual experiences, as well as the feelings of powerlessness which result from them, can be important contributing factors in the development of an eating disorder and require specific treatment."

Odyssey House, a well-established, residential drug treatment program, reported that 44% of its female drug addicts were sexually abused as children. John Siverson, a Minneapolis therapist specializing in treating teenage drug addicts, estimates that figure to be closer to 70% (Forward & Buck, 1978). Bass and Davis (1988), experts in the field of incest recovery, state that addictions are common ways of coping with the pain of sexual abuse. They suggest that eating disorders, as well as alcohol and other drugs, are often used to numb feelings, suppress memories, and escape from the pain of sexual abuse.

Victimized Children at High Risk for Development of Negative Aftereffects

It has been increasingly documented that children victimized by sexual abuse are at high risk for the development of negative aftereffects both immediately and in adulthood (Courtois, 1988; Browne & Finkelhor, 1985, 1986; Russell, 1983; Butler, 1985; Gelinas, 1983). The range of problems most commonly includes such difficulties as low self-esteem, "low" functioning or "driven" functioning, depression, anxiety, alienation and the inability to sustain relationships, the repetition of abusive relationships, sexual dysfunctions, and dependence on alcohol and drugs, as well as other addictions.

Trauma and Childhood Sexual Abuse

Why does childhood sexual abuse predispose one to the development of addictive behaviors? Current models conceptualize the impact of childhood sexual abuse in terms of the relation of "trauma" to the development of mental health problems (Figley, 1985; Green, 1983; Herman, 1981). At the time of the abuse, victims develop symptomatology associated with acute posttraumatic stress disorder (Courtois, 1988; Briere & Runtz, 1987; Conte & Schuerman, 1987). Because the original effects of the trauma generally remain untreated, they become chronic and appear in delayed fashion, disguised in such secondary symptoms as depression, anxiety disorders, substance abuse, sexual difficulties, sleep disturbance, revictimization, and dissociative disorders.

The direct result of the trauma is an assault to the self. The secondary symptoms, including various addictive behaviors, are manifestations of the underlying self-impairment. Therefore, the occurrence of sexual abuse and the resultant damage to the self are often hidden behind the secondary symptoms. It is not until the secondary symptoms are treated that the recognition and repair of the original trauma becomes possible. In the recovery process, abstinence may lead to the emergence of sexual abuse memories previously masked by the addiction. The emergence of these childhood memories may become a high-risk, precipitating factor for relapse. As previously stated, addressing this possibility is essential for effective relapse prevention. It may initiate a process of the restoration of the self that has been impaired by the abuse. The specific ways in which addressing these childhood memories will assist the prevention of relapse and the reparation of the self are discussed here.

Traumatic Effects of Childhood
Sexual Abuse on Developing
Child's Sense of Self

In *The Phenomenology of the Self,* Meissner (1986) addressed the issue of the self as an integrating and organizing principle in a child's development. Self-organization is expressed in the capacity for trust, autonomy, and initiative, as well as in the ability to set meaningful goals and undertake to achieve them (Erikson, 1980; Kohut, 1977). An individual's sense of self (perception of self) and functioning self (expression of self) will determine his/her ability to live a productive and creative life and to form fulfilling relationships with others.

The child victim of sexual abuse is deprived of an environment that facilitates the development of a sense of self as valuable in its own right. The ability to define one's own feelings, needs, and perceptions and one's growing capacities to interact with the environment—an ability that is dependent on the caretaking adult's capacity to provide such an environment (Winnicott, 1965)—is superseded by the necessity to conform to the adult's needs and requirements. Therefore, maturational development is halted and the child is forced to conform to another's reality (needs, expectations, perceptions) rather than to engage in the developmental process of defining his/her own reality (sense of self). The sexually abused child learns *fusion,* which entails a confusion of self and others, rather than *individuation,* which means a differentiation between self and others. The laws of fusion that the child develops are discussed later in greater detail.

The child victim is abused twice: the cessation of the development of the self is a result of (1) the actual event of the abuse (both singular and repeated) and (2) the conditions of secrecy and denial within which the abuse occurs. The sacrifice of self and the enforced denial of the abuse and its effects evoke overwhelming terror, rage, and despair in the child. The terror, rage, and despair, which are intolerable to a child, force the child to form maladaptive defense mechanisms to survive.[2] These defenses deny both the powerlessness of the child to stop the abuse and the terror, rage, and despair associated with that powerlessness. They allow the self, impaired by the trauma of the abuse, to survive.

When the effects and defenses associated with the trauma of childhood sexual abuse are left untreated, secondary symptoms develop that mask them. Addictive behaviors may serve such a function. They keep the self impaired by covering over the trauma and maintaining the lies and denial that have surrounded the abuse. At the same time, they allow the impaired self to function more or less with its restrictions for a certain period. (The impaired self, for example, has been cut off from learning how to care for itself. A person in psychological pain, therefore, may take a drink or overeat to soothe the pain. A healthy person would be capable of addressing the pain directly.) Eventually, through the progressive and pathological effects of the addictive behavior, the impairment of the self increases.

Addictive behaviors develop and become serious problems in themselves. Indeed, in their manifestations, they recreate many elements of the repressed trauma such as denial, secrecy, numbness, shame, powerlessness, and pain. They become one possible "disguised presentation" of childhood sexual abuse that keeps the individual and others in denial about the abuse. When the addictions themselves are treated, the hidden trauma is often revealed.

TREATMENT

Withdrawal

The incest survivor who enters treatment for addictive behaviors will in most cases be unaware of the childhood trauma underlying his/her behavior. The addictive behavior is at this time the primary pathology. A disease in itself, it must be addressed as such. Following a progressive course of destruction to the physical, emotional, social, and spiritual well-being of the individual, the addictive disease has become the preoccupying focus of the addict's life. The addict's ability to function has increasingly deteriorated and, if left untreated, the addiction will lead to death. In abstinence, the working of the 12 steps provides a foundation for integration.

AA and the many addiction treatment programs that follow the 12-Step program model emphasize that total abstinence from the addictive behavior is a prerequisite for recovery from the addictive disease (Alcoholics Anonymous World Services, 1976; Johnson, 1973; Maxwell, 1984; Washton, 1988). Abstinence is the condition that allows the tasks of recovery to take place, including the development of a new way of life and the reparation of the impaired self. In each stage of abstinence—early, middle, and long-term—there is a potential for relapse to addictive behavior. Relapse is viewed as a "return to the former coping style in a context of recovery" (Rankin, 1989, p. 90). As stated previously, relapse may be a tool in strengthening abstinence when the underlying state of the addictive behavior is revealed and a program of recovery is initiated (Brown, 1989, p. 90).

Abstinence, the first task in the treatment process, begins a period of "withdrawal" from the addictive behavior, which initially involves "cleaning out" the effects of the addictive behavior as well as a strong pull back toward the addictive behavior. In later stages of abstinence, withdrawal will involve the emergence of underlying material and will reveal deeper characteristics of the addictive behavior. At each stage, withdrawal presents a risk for relapse as new material emerges, new addictive behaviors are revealed, and a new life-style is developed. Withdrawal is viewed here as the movement from a life-style dependent on addictive behaviors (impaired self) to a life-style based on healthy, self-determined, and creative choices (restored self).

The incest survivor in addiction recovery will be at risk for relapse in four major areas: (1) memories are unknown but begin to surface; (2) affects associated with the incest as well as feelings in general begin to emerge; (3) life experiences are met without the aid of addictive behaviors; (4) addictive behaviors surface other than the identified addiction. These risk factors do not occur sequentially but are all present throughout recovery. How can this issue of relapse best be addressed as recovery proceeds?

Memories Are Unknown but Begin to Surface

Relapse may occur at any time in the withdrawal process without any awareness of the traumatic events. In this case, relapse may be used as a signal to investigate the possibility of childhood sexual abuse. This investigation may lead to uncovering sexual trauma, or childhood sexual abuse memories may surface at once in the abstinence process. Abstinence from the addictive behavior will initiate withdrawal from the effects of the addiction, one of which has been to effectively block sexual abuse memories. As one incest survivor stated:

> At the point I decided to put down drinking, I had to start feeling. The connection to the abuse was almost immediate. And I watched other people come to AA and do the same thing. They have just enough time to get through the initial shakes and you watch them start going through the memories. And you know what's coming. But they don't. (Brown, 1985, p. 184)

Thus, memories may surface immediately or at any point along the recovery continuum. An attempt to once again block these painful, often overwhelming memories may lead to relapse.

From the point at which childhood sexual abuse issues have been identified as a precipitant of relapse, the recovery process must continually proceed along two axes. First, the recovery program will need to support the individual in returning to abstinence. This will mean increased use of the tools of the program, including additional meetings, telephone calls, and 12-Step work. Participation in a self-help group such as Incest Survivors Anonymous may be helpful. Second, the uncovering of the sexual abuse material underlying the addictive behavior will need to be specifically addressed. If not already in process, individual therapy is indicated, in order to address and repair the unintegrated self. A parallel process of individual therapeutic work and 12-Step program recovery work is emphasized.

It is important to understand that the treatment program for the originally identified addictive behavior is a crucial, ongoing support for recovery related to the childhood trauma. Abstinence is supported by this treatment. The original treatment setting provides a consistent, reliable base as the exploration and working through of the trauma proceed. The new attitudes and behaviors learned in the treatment group will become even more important in establishing a new orientation as the old coping mechanisms instituted to deal with the trauma are lifted. Defining the incest experience and forming connections with others who have had similar experiences can be an enormous relief to the survivor. Understanding that one is not "crazy"—his/her difficulties have a source in reality—or "alone"—others have suffered in the same way and with similar effects—breaks the forced isolation, secrecy, and shame of the original abuse conditions. Specific details of treatment involving the parallel process of individual therapy and 12-Step programs are elucidated here.

Affects Associated with the Incest and Other Feelings Begin to Emerge

The second risk for relapse facing the incest survivor is the emergence of feelings. Addictive behaviors mask the effects of the original trauma. Feelings have either been repressed or never experienced at all. Therefore, at all stages of abstinence, withdrawal will involve the surfacing of feelings. The emergence of feelings will bring discomfort to the incest survivor whose survival has depended on not feeling. He/she will experience both the painful feelings associated with the trauma and newly experienced feelings of joy and excitement as life begins to be "well lived." Relapse will be a possible defense in relation to the emergence of these feelings.

All feelings are associated with the intolerable affects of trauma. The recovering survivor will need to learn that feelings are not dangerous or destructive (Gil, 1988). The addiction treatment group provides a context for the relearning of the meaning of feelings. The spiritual orientation of the group, the belief in a power greater than oneself that offers unconditional acceptance and love, and the unconditional acceptance offered by group members provide a safety net for the incest survivor who risks experiencing both painful and joyful feelings.

Rather than fearing and avoiding feelings, the incest survivor learns to identify, experience, and trust his/her own feelings and learns to use feelings as guides for defining needs, desires, and perceptions. As feelings become familiar and helpful, the necessity to mask them is reduced. Self-determination is strengthened by experiencing feelings as a resource rather than a liability. Feelings become a tool for defining oneself as distinct from others. The likelihood of relapse is gradually reduced.

Life Experiences Are Met without the Aid of Addictive Behaviors

The third possible risk for relapse facing the recovering incest survivor is that ordinary life experiences and life challenges are likely to trigger the underlying negative effects of the incest. Because the self is impaired, the incest survivor is unequipped to deal with life processes without the mediating effects of the addictive behavior.

> Many of the survivors I interviewed . . . told me that they felt the incest irreparably changed them and that they did not develop as they might have been. . . . Survivors described themselves as feeling as though they have holes in themselves and in their development, as

though they don't know where other people leave off and where they begin, and as so burdened with the demands of others that their own needs remain undefined. (Courtois, 1988)

As the survivor attempts to meet life experiences that he/she is developmentally unprepared to handle, there may be a reversion to the addictive behavior that has substituted for adequate development. As the incest survivor "withdraws" from the use of addictive behaviors that mask the impaired self, he/she builds a healthy self through the acquisition of new thinking, feeling, and behavioral processes. This involves attempts to assert needs and desires and to actualize creative endeavors. Each step may "trigger" the fear of repraisal for self-assertion that characterized the survivor's childhood experience. Relapse may be a response to this fear.

To deal with the issue of developmental triggers, relapse prevention must involve a maturational process. As treatment provides an opportunity to move through maturational levels and develop at one's own pace, acknowledgement of the "child within" emerges. The addiction recovery group provides functions that were absent or distorted in the original family that are necessary for healthy development (Rist, 1979). The recovery group supports individuation rather than fusion. The concept of boundaries is introduced through the sharing of one's own experience without "cross-talk"—judgments or advice giving from others. The 12-Steps articulate a new set of attitudes and behaviors that provide a framework for relating to oneself and others. Modeling is provided by members of the group who are in sustained recovery. Breaking silence by sharing experiences (identification) allows acceptance of the individual's unique self as it is revealed to the group (mirroring) and affirms the individual's steps in the recovery process (validating). The group provides the tools that were unavailable in the original family system. Maladaptive mechanisms are replaced with healthier and more appropriate ones, and a positive feeling toward oneself replaces defeatist, destructive attitudes (Coles, 1985).

The individual therapeutic relationship and the 12-Step program recovery group provide the context within which this difficult work can take place. The goal of treatment is to ameliorate the developmental deficits and arrest that have resulted from sexual abuse. Specifically, how does recovery proceed in the individual therapeutic setting?

The Effects of Childhood Sexual Abuse Experiences and Their Manifestation in the Therapeutic Setting

Patients will often set up the therapeutic relationship as if it is governed by the "laws of fusion," the laws that govern how people operate when they do not have a developed sense of self. They will draw the therapist in to cooperate with these laws.

Without an integrated self, boundaries cannot be differentiated. Therefore, everyone and everything becomes part of the patient's internal world in an attempt to resolve unsatisfactory early relations and deficits. Current relationships are based on the acting out of these early traumatic conflicts. It is therefore inevitable and necessary that these dramas get acted out with the therapist in the therapeutic setting. The laws of fusion are characterized by the following behaviors:

1. *Shifting boundaries and sudden reversals:*
   a. There is a constantly shifting view of self and others (a person may be experienced as an ally at one moment, an enemy in the next moment).
   b. Self and others are alternately idealized or devalued. The therapist is alternately omnipotent or useless and denigrated.
   c. There is a denial of the significance of the therapeutic relationship, alternating with attempts to create extreme dependency (telephone calls, etc.).
   d. Others are experienced as past significant figures (become a part of internal, unresolved issues). Viewed subjectively rather than objectively, others are perceived to rapidly change characterizations and therefore are perceived as entirely different people.
   e. The therapist is experienced as actual past significant figures, and therefore as variable rather than as the therapist, on whom characteristics of past significant figures are attributed (displacement). For example, the therapist becomes "father" rather than like the father.
2. *Indirect and masked communication:*
   a. Saying the opposite of what what one means is used as a defensive maneuver.
   b. Communication is based on the use of "projective identification." Projective identification is a means of communication whereby communication in personal relationships is based on a need to make others *feel* what one is trying to avoid or reject in oneself and to coerce people into specific behaviors. Communication in therapy is not direct: Rather than explaining feelings and experiences from the past (significant relationships and their effects), emotions are "put into" the therapist so that the therapist "must experience" as his/her own the projector's past experience.
   c. Anger is either avoided through defenses of denial, splitting, or projection or used to mask unsafe, vulnerable feelings (expressing anger, for example, rather than hurt).

3. *Power dynamics.* All relations are based on struggles over power and are characterized by the following: dominance–submission; victim–perpetrator (blame); focus on who is controlling whom; compliance versus rebellion.
4. *Fear.* Fear defines behavior and responses. Survival is always at stake.
5. *Keeping secrets:*
   a. Lying and misrepresenting are used as a means of denying reality to oneself and to others.
   b. Misrepresentation and concealment are used in the therapeutic setting.
6. *Covert operations:*
   a. Control of others operates through taking responsibility for other people as well as asking other people to take responsibility for oneself.
   b. Behavior is designed to conceal motivations both from oneself and from others. Honesty is considered dangerous to self-preservation and is therefore avoided.
   c. "Niceness" replaces caring because self-preservation is the fundamental concern.
   d. Triangulation (talking to other people about other people) is dominant.
   e. Relating is based on "bargaining" ("If you take care of me, I'll take care of you").
7. *Sexualization of all relationships.* Underlying motivations of seduction and intrigue are predominant, as well as the suspicion of these underlying motivations in others.
8. *Paranoia:*
   a. Interactions with others are taken personally; that is, as a statement toward oneself (rejection, seduction, hostility, etc.). An accusatory attitude prevails.
   b. Insecurity is pervasive.
   c. The world is considered dangerous (war zone).
9. *Persecutory attitude:*
   a. An attacking attitude toward one's self and others is reflected in critical and judgmental thinking.
   b. Others are blamed for one's feelings and actions, rather than questioning, exploring, and understanding one's own motivations.
   c. The underlying belief "I am bad" is always being proven and/or defended against.
10. *A lack of an inner regulatory mechanism:* Behavior is characterized by extremes such as perfectionism versus carelessness, workaholism versus procrastination, overeating versus starvation, compulsive sexuality versus sexual celibacy, minimizing

versus creating catastrophes, clinging versus isolation, and hysteria versus stoicism.

11. *Intimacy is felt as a threat to self-preservation:*
    a. Intimacy is perceived as intrusiveness or possible abandonment and is therefore avoided. Rather, chaotic, dependent relationships substitute for intimacy by creating an illusion of relatedness.
    b. Interactions are based on fantasy rather than reality.
    c. A chronic feeling of inadequacy and emptiness prevails.
    d. Relationships are based on the need to make up for deficits in the self.

How Unintegration Presents Itself in the Therapeutic Setting

The therapeutic relationship is the vehicle for the intrapsychic transformation of the patient's unintegrated internal world. A unique relationship, it is the staging ground for the emergence of internal and external relational pathology. The therapist provides a "holding environment" (Winnicott, 1965) within which the patient can reinstate the development of the self that was thwarted by a traumatic early environment. It is essential that the therapist enter the relationship with the knowledge that the interaction will reflect the chaotic, unintegrated inner world described by the laws of fusion. Through projective identification, the patient reveals the early fragmented intrapsychic structures of the unintegrated self that reflect early pathological relationships and need to be identified and reworked. Without reacting to the chaos, but rather observing and defining the projections, the therapist offers a neutral field within which the internal psychic dramas can unfold and be transformed. The therapist must strive to maintain an attitude of calm, optimistic interest toward all that arises in the therapeutic setting. The therapist strives for an "evenly suspended attention" (Freud, 1962) within which all that arises between and within patient and therapist can be observed and examined. The therapist's neutrality provides the atmosphere within which all patient and therapist reactions and responses can be recognized and examined. It is an attitude of neutral interest that is essential for the transformational process of the patient's inner world and outer relationships to take place.

The Importance of the Frame of the Therapy

Because the patient's inner and outer worlds have been characterized by chaos, the importance of maintaining a clear and consistent frame in the therapeutic setting cannot be overly stated. Establishment of a secure and stable frame and an atmosphere of empathic neutrality are essential in order to transform the chaos and to develop the trust that is essential for the formation of a therapeutic alliance. Fees, payment for missed hours, time of meetings, policies with regard to vacations, the use of surnames, and the exclusion of physical contact are necessary parameters in creating a clear, consistent and firm boundary within which the laws of fusion can be enacted, identified, and transformed. A clear frame provides a firm grounding for both the therapist and patient as the therapist is pulled into chaotic dramas. Pushing against a frame that is consistent will be a vehicle for the patient and a test for the therapist that will yield important therapeutic material. A new model of behavior will also be taught. Without the consistency of a clear and firm frame, the therapeutic process cannot take place.

Multiaddictions

The fourth factor creating a high risk for relapse throughout abstinence and withdrawal is when addictions surface other than the identified addiction: Individuals may relapse "into" an unidentified addiction.

Clinical observation has shown that abstinence from one addictive behavior often leads to the substitution of a different addictive behavior. For example, the alcoholic who stops drinking may start eating compulsively. How are we to understand the surfacing of multiaddictions? Our view is that the factors predisposing an individual to addictive behavior, such as childhood sexual abuse, result in an impairment of the self that predisposes an individual to addictive behaviors in many arenas. Relapse in the context of an abstinence program of recovery from an identified addictive behavior may in fact stem from an underlying addiction that has not yet been identified.

A recovering alcoholic successfully withdrawing from the effects of alcoholism, for example, may discover codependency issues (the compulsion to control people, places, and things). Or, after the effects of an eating disorder have been treated, a compulsive eater may discover a craving for other substances such as alcohol. As with the primary addiction, these "hidden" addictions arise out of the self-impairment caused by the incest trauma. The awareness of the interconnectedness of addictions is crucial to relapse prevention.

Sex and Love Addiction

There is one hidden addiction, often underlying other addictions, that the incest survivor is likely to display: sex and love addiction—the compulsive fusion with others, or, as one sex and love addict put it, "involuntary enmeshment." Sex and love addiction may manifest in a compulsive engagement in sexual relationships, compulsive sexual fantasies, and/or compulsive solitary sexual activity (Carnes, 1983). On the other hand, the addiction may take the form of a compulsive avoidance of sexuality and relationships because of a fear of suffocation or annihilation (Schaef, 1989). What characterizes sex and love addiction is fusion—defining oneself through others rather than through oneself. Sex and love addiction has its roots in incestuous abuse. It is a generationally transmitted addiction, usually hidden and unidentified. The perpetrator of childhood sexual abuse is a sex and love addict who uses the child for his/her own sexual and emotional needs. For the child, early relationships are sexualized. The child learns that sex and affection are synonymous and that sexuality is involved in all close interpersonal interactions. The child who is used in this manner learns fusion as a survival coping mechanism. One way this manifests is in "fusion with the perpetrator." In order to accommodate the adult abuser and to maintain a relationship with the abuser on whom the child is dependent, the child incorporates the perpetrator's world view as part of his/her identity. Separation from the "abuser within" is a major aspect of recovery for the incest survivor.

When unrecognized and untreated, the patterns that are learned in the incestuous abuse experience, will repeat themselves in adult relationships. Thus the survivor acts out these patterns in sex and love addiction in adulthood. Furthermore, sex and love addiction may be viewed as one aspect of posttraumatic stress. On the one hand, compulsive inappropriate sexual relationships are engaged in, repeating the dynamics of fusion (e.g., using and being used by another person) in the original sexual abuse. This is done in an attempt to master the original situation as well as in the hope that the outcome might, this time, be different (Norwood, 1985). On the other hand, relationships are compulsively avoided in an effort to ward off triggers of affects related to the original abuse.

Sex and love addiction is often hidden by other addictions and is not revealed until abstinence from the identified addiction is initiated. One recovering alcoholic commented: "I see now that my alcoholism developed to support my sex and love addiction." This is becoming clear in the area of cocaine addiction, where it is observed clinically that cocaine is very often used to support sexual compulsivity. In this case, it is only when one abstains from the originally defined addiction that the manifestations of the sex and love addiction, which it is has been supporting, appear. (This may also be true for codependency, where codependent patterns of behavior support sex and love addiction.)

If left unrecognized and untreated, sex and love addiction remains a high-risk factor of relapse during recovery, and it is an area that must be addressed in relapse prevention.

CONCLUSION

As memories appear, as the feelings associated with the original trauma resurface, as feelings in general are experienced, and as the challenge is faced of living a life-style free of addictive behaviors that have both maintained and further destroyed the impaired self, relapse will be both a risk—diminishing over time as the self is strengthened—and a tool. Relapse may be a bridge between repressed childhood sexual abuse issues and disclosing and working through material necessary for a successful recovery. In this respect, a successful recovery is defined as the restoration and healing of the impaired self. Indeed, it is the restored self that is the ultimate prevention of relapse from addictive behaviors.

NOTES

1. This chapter is an adaptation of an article entitled "The Role of Incest Issues in Relapse" (Young, 1990) and a presentation given at the 1991 conference of the California Association of Marriage and Family Therapists.

2. Among the defenses most commonly documented as responses to the trauma of sexual abuse are the following: the assumption of responsibility for the abuse in order to protect the depended on adult and the child's feelings toward that adult; the numbing of affect in relation to the abuse as well as general affect; the turning of the rage at the abuser toward the self instead; preoccupation with the abuser in the repeated attempt to ward off further abuse; a compulsion to repeat the trauma, as well as to avoid the return of the traumatic state; dissociation during the experience of abuse; repressing the memory of the abuse; and adaptation through the assumption of various roles in relation to others based on fusion.

REFERENCES

Alcoholics Anonymous World Services. (1976). *Alcoholics Anonymous.* New York: Author.

Anonymous. (1989). *Growing through the pain.* Park Ridge, IL: Parkside.

Bass, E., & Davis, L. (1988). *The courage to heal.* New York: Harper & Row.

Briere, J., & Runtz, M. (1987). Post sexual abuse trauma, data and impliciitons for clinical practice. *Journal of Interpersonal Violence, 2,* 367–379.

Brown, R. (1989). Relapses from a gambling perspective. In M. Gossop (Ed.), *Relapse and addictive behavior.* London: Routledge.

Brown, S. (1985). *Treating the alcoholic: A developmental model of recovery.* New York: Wiley.

Browne, A., & Finkelhor, D. (1986). Impact of sexual abuse: A review of the literature. *Psychological Bulletin, 99,* 66–77.

Butler, S. (1985). *Conspiracy of silence: The trauma of incest.* San Francisco: Volcano Press.

Carnes, P. (1983). *Out of the shadows: Understanding sexual addiction.* Minneapolis: CompCare Publications.

Chaney, E. F., O'Leary, M. R., & Marlatt, G. A. (1978). Skill training with alcoholics. *Journal of Consulting and Clinical Psychology, 46,* 1092–1104.

Cole, C. (1985). A group design for adult female survivors of childhood incest. *Women and Therapy, 4*(3), 71–82.

Conte, J. R., & Schuerman, J. R. (1987). The effects of sexual abuse on children, a multi-dimensional view. *Journal of Interpersonal Violence, 2,* 381–390.

Courtois, C. (1988). *Healing the incest wound: Adult survivors in therapy.* New York: Norton.

Courtois, C., & Sprei, J. E. (1988). Restrospective incest therapy for women. In L. E. Walker (Ed.), *Handbook on sexual abuse of children.* New York: Springer.

Covington, S. S. (1986). Facing the clinical challenges of women alcoholics: Physical, emotional and sexual abuse. *Focus on Family, 3,* 10–11; *9*(37), 42–44.

Covington, S., & Beckett, L. (1988). *Leaving the enchanted forest.* San Francisco: Harper & Row.

Crewdson, J. (1988). *By silence betrayed.* Boston: Little & Brown.

De Vine, R. (1988). Sexual abuse of children: An overview of the problem. In K. MacFarlane & B. McComb Jones (Eds.), *Sexual abuse of children: Selected readings.* Newark, NJ: National Center on Child Abuse and Neglect.

Erikson, E. H. (1980). *Identity and the life cycle.* New York: Norton.

Figley, C. R. (Ed.). (1985). *Trauma and its wake: The study and treatment of post-traumatic stress disorder.* New York: Brunner/Mazel.

Finkelhor, D., & Browne, A. (1985). The traumatic impact of child abuse: A conceptualization. *American Journal of Orthopsychiatry, 55,* 530–541.

Finkelhor, D., & Browne, A. (1986). The impact of child sexual abuse: A review of the literature. *Psychological Bulletin, 99,* 66–77.

Forward, S., & Buck, C. (1978). *Betrayal of innocence: Incest and its devastation.* Los Angeles: J. P. Tarcher.

Freud, S. (1962). *General introduction to psychoanalysis.* New York: Washington Square Press.

Gelinas, D. J. (1983). The persisting negative effects of incest. *Psychiatry, 46,* 313–332.

Gil, E. (1988). *Treatment of adult survivors of childhood abuse.* Walnut Creek, CA: Launch Press.

Green, A. (1983). Dimensions of psychological trauma in abused children. *Journal of the American Academy of Child Psychiatry, 22,* 231–237.

Herman, J. (1981). *Father–daughter incest.* Cambridge, MA: Harvard University Press.

Jelinek, J. M., & Williams, T. (1987). Post-traumatic stress disorder and substance abuse: Treatment problems, strategies and recommendation. In T. Williams (Ed.), *Post-traumatic stress disorders: A handbook for clinicians.* Cincinnati: Disabled American Veterans.

Jellinek, E. M. (1952). The phases of alcohol addiction. *Quarterly Journal of Studies on Alcohol, 13,* 673–684.

Johnson, V. (1973). *I'll quit tomorrow.* New York: Harper & Row.

Kearney-Cooke, A. (in press). Group treatment of sexual abuse among women with eating disorders. *Women and Therapy.*

Kohut, H. (1977). *The restoration of the self.* New York: International Universities Press.

Kovach, J. A. (1983). The relationship between treatment failures of alcoholic women and incestuous histories with possible implications for post-traumatic stress disorder symptomatology. *Dissertation Abstracts International, 44*(3A), 710–712.

Litman, G. K., Eiser, J. R., & Rawsom, N. (1977). Towards a typology of relapse: A preliminary report. *Drug and Alcohol Dependence, 2,* 157–162.

Ludwig, A. M., Wikler, A., & Syark, L. H. (1974). The first drink: Psychobiological aspects of craving. *Archives of General Psychiatry, 30,* 539–547.

MacFarlane, K., & McComb Jones, B. (Eds.). (1980). *Sexual abuse of children: Selected readings.* Newark, NJ: National Center on Child Abuse and Neglect.

Marlatt, G. A., & Gordon, J. R. (1985). *Relapse prevention: Maintenance strategies in the treatment of addictive behaviors.* New York: Guilford Press.

Maxwell, M. (1984). *The AA experience.* New York: McGraw-Hill.

Meissner, W. W. (1986). The earliest internationalizations. In R. F. Lax, S. Bach, & J. A. Burland (Eds.), *Self and object constancy: Clinical and theoretical perspectives* (pp. 29–72). New York: Guilford Press.

Nielsen, L. A. (1984). Sexual abuse and chemical dependency: Assessing the risk for women alcoholics and adult children. *Focus on Family and Chemical Dependency, 7*(6), 10–11.

Norwood, R. (1985). *Women who love too much.* Los Angeles: J. P. Tarcher.

Oppenheimer, R., Howells, K., Palmer, R. L., & Chaloner, D. A. (1985). Adverse sexual experience in childhood and chinical eating disorders: A preliminary description. *Journal of Psychiatric Research, 19,* 357–361.

Rankin, H. (1989). Relapse and eating disorders: The recurring illusion. In M. Gossop (Ed.), *Relapse and addictive behavior.* London: Routledge.

Rist, K. (1979). Incest: Theoretical and clinical views. *American Journal of Orthopsychiatry, 49,* 680–691.

Russell, D. E. H. (1983). The incidence and prevalence of intrafamilial and extrafamilial sexual abuse of female children. *Child Abuse and Neglect, 7,* 133–146.

Schaef, A. W. (1989). *Escape from intimacy.* New York: Harper & Row.

Washton, A. M. (1988). Preventing relapse to cocaine. *Journal of Clinical Psychiatry, 49,* 34–38.

Winnicott, W. W. (1965). *The maturational processes and the facilitating environment.* New York: International Universities Press.

Young, E. B. (1990). The role of incest issues in relapse. *Journal of Psychoactive Drugs, 22,* 249–258.

Young, E. B. (1991, May). *Incest: A root of addiction.* Paper presented at the conference of the California Association of Marriage and Family Therapists, Oakland, CA.

25

Women and Minorities
in Treatment

BARBARA C. WALLACE

INTRODUCTION

A current trend in the field of substance abuse treatment involves the identification of subsets of the population of potential clients as belonging
to a special population. The term *special population* in this context con-
notes that aside from invoking the biopsychosocial paradigm, a comprehensive approach to individualized assessment, matching of clients based
on assessment findings to appropriate interventions, and "timing" interventions across phases of recovery (Donovan & Marlatt, 1988; Wallace,
1991a, 1992a), we aspire to consider yet something more. This something more or "something special" which practitioners need to consider
throughout the assessment and treatment process involves the characteristics and characteristic experiences of women and minorities and the
resulting special challenges that attend the task of treating a female or
minority substance abuser.

As an African American female clinician, I have worked within an
inpatient detoxification unit as a staff psychologist, within a residential
therapeutic community as a consultant, and in outpatient settings. As an
introduction to this something more or something special, let us first briefly consider selected observations of women in treatment in these various settings and the case of a male minority consumer of substance abuse

470

services. I begin with observations that raise disturbing questions regarding the treatment experiences of the special populations of women and minorities.

Observations of Women in Treatment

While observing women in treatment in the middle to late 1980s, I noted many symbols of women having less power than men in treatment facilities. For example, on the co-ed inpatient detoxification unit where I worked, women were in the minority by virtue of the number of beds assigned to men versus women on the unit (Wallace, 1991a, 1992b). Although perhaps quite trivial, this suggests nonetheless the reality that women in 1986–1988, at the height of the crack cocaine epidemic, entered a treatment system oriented to the expectation that they were a minority of the treatment population. Fortunately, the inpatient detoxification unit on which I worked did accept pregnant women for detoxification, adjusting the protocol accordingly (Wallace, 1991a, 1991b). On the other hand, Chavkin (1990) offers disturbing observations and data on the way in which a female crack cocaine-abusing pregnant woman would likely find rejection in her attempt to seek treatment in the New York metropolitan area, with the problem being compounded if that woman was also utilizing Medicaid to pay for treatment services. As women in the 1980s presented serious substance abuse problems complicated by the realities of being in their childbearing years, these women entered a treatment system ill-prepared and often downright unwilling to adjust treatment protocols. Moreover, these protocols were admittedly designed for men and with the characteristics and needs of men in mind. Indeed, to be a woman and to be a pregnant woman in the 1980s meant encountering potential barriers to obtaining treatment. These barriers took the form of fewer or no treatment slots. Moreover, the 1980s and 1990s saw more negative attitudes toward and greater stigma for women substance abusers, and in particular for pregnant women who were engaged in substance abuse (Harrison, 1991; Wallace, 1991b).

Having worked as a consultant to a residential therapeutic community in the early 1990s within the New York metropolitan area (Wallace, 1992c), I made other observations. Men had access to an equipped exercise room, while women did not; men had a basketball team with league participation, while women were never organized into a basketball or softball team despite some discussion. Men held the high-prestige job of van driver, while women did not. And consistent with the reality of female substance abusers being in their childbearing years, among women routinely admitted without a pregnancy test, several per year faced the crisis of forming a 2-month attachment to a new stable treatment environment while facing the decision to have an abortion or leave because the residence could not accommodate pregnant women.

Although discussion around these issues within the residence led to some policy changes, symbols of the relative power and status of women versus men in the residence may justify our asking the following question: Are there subtle ways in which women, and perhaps members of ethnic and racial minority groups, receive differential treatment within our various inpatient, residential, and outpatient treatment settings, negatively impacting the treatment and recovery experiences of women and minorities? The following case of a minority male during inpatient treatment further suggests the appropriateness of asking this question, as we aspire to prepare practitioners to work effectively with the special populations of women and minority substance abusers.

The Case of Mr. D.

A middle-class, well-educated African American male, Mr. D., an outpatient, described his experiences as the only African American male patient in a well-respected urban addiction treatment center during a month-long inpatient treatment cycle, which cost his insurance company nearly $30,000. According to this articulate consumer, he felt his inpatient treatment had been "compromised" because he was an African American. As an example, Mr. D. focused on his group therapy experiences and how he had been asked to take a white female group member to a local Narcotics Anonymous (NA) meeting on an evening pass in the urban area near the treatment center. When, within group on the rehabilitation unit, this female asked the therapist why she should go along to these NA meetings when her real problem was compulsive overeating, the therapist responded that she might learn some social skills via the outings and NA meetings: She would then take these social skills back with her when she returned to her own environment. The African American male felt as though both he and his minority contemporaries at the urban NA meeting were merely "being used" to benefit the white female, who would return to her suburban environs enriched by the experience. He also shared a few other incidents and experiences conveying the same theme of his feeling slighted and uncomfortable.

Mr. D.'s exposure to relapse prevention seemed to be quite heavily laden with negative expectations that relapse was nearly inevitable. Moreover, I was quite disappointed that his exposure to this brief relapse prevention education was not balanced with the facility's provision of training regarding what to do in specific high-risk situations. This raised yet other questions: Could the relapse prevention component of this treatment center really be so inferior, based on Mr. D.'s description of relapse prevention he personally received, betraying the reputation of the center? Does the attribute of one's ethnic or racial difference contribute to a more negative prognosis, and the conveying of more negative expectations regarding relapse? And finally, can we train clinicians so that clients do not emerge feeling that their treatment was somehow compromised to their detriment because of their gender, race, or ethnicity?

Toward a Training Model for Gender and Cultural Sensitivity

In searching for answers to these questions, this chapter aspires to provide the practitioner with knowledge of that something more or something special that confronts the practitioner and creates a special assessment and treatment challenge in work with women and minorities. Even as we remain cognizant of the need to avoid perpetuating new stereotypes, the goal of this chapter is to expose practitioners to a training model for gender and cultural sensitivity. In order to prepare the practitioner for clinical work with the special populations of women and minority substance abusers, this chapter (1) describes key characteristics and characteristic experiences of women and minorities who enter substance abuse treatment settings, (2) discusses the implications of these characteristics and experiences for substance abuse treatment and the training of practitioners, and (3) briefly describes a multifaceted clinical technique developed in clinical work with women and minority substance abusers. Case examples are utilized throughout the chapter to further elucidate material, drawing on cases from my past work in either inpatient, residential therapeutic community, or outpatient treatment settings.

KEY CHARACTERISTICS AND CHARACTERISTIC EXPERIENCES OF WOMEN AND MEMBERS OF ETHNIC AND RACIAL MINORITY GROUPS

Women and members of racial and ethnic minority groups possess certain characteristics and have certain characteristic experiences. In discussing the implications of these characteristics and experiences for treatment and the training of practitioners, the characteristics and experiences of women and then minorities are considered in turn.

Characteristics of Women and Characteristic Experiences

The 1980s phenomenon of a cocaine and crack cocaine epidemic permitted women to gain access to this equal opportunity drug. The affordable price of ready-to-smoke crack cocaine also meant that women of diverse socioeconomic status could purchase a highly addictive substance, ensuring a different kind of equal access to what had been the chic and expensive cocaine product of the rich and famous in the 1970s. Because the cohort of women who became abusers of cocaine, crack cocaine, and other substances in the 1980s and 1990s are generally in their childbearing years, this poses the risk of intrauterine drug exposure to the fetus. It also poses the potential risk of future developmental delays in children, which could lead to special education placements and a more difficult and challenging parenting experience for the recovering substance abuser.

Evidence of developmental delays or anomalies across each developmental era in women's children, after a history of intrauterine drug exposure, also results in the maternal experience of resurgent feelings of guilt across the life-span. Feelings of guilt and shame may contribute to slips and relapse episodes in recovering women far beyond the birth of the infant. Unresolved feelings of guilt and shame may also lead women to engage in other compulsive behaviors (e.g., compulsive sex, overeating, gambling, and workaholism), as the ego utilizes compulsive behavior as an elaborate behavioral defense against the painful feelings of shame and guilt that threaten to emerge. Both periods of substitution with other compulsive behaviors and periods of relapse to substance abuse readily occur in recovering women who harbor unresolved maternal guilt and shame, as well as a range of affects.

We might alternatively observe instead of compulsive behaviors, periods in which there is a characteristic ego rigidity. This ego rigidity, resulting lack of flexibility, and perception of limited possibilities occur because the ego is engaging in the overuse of ego defenses against the feelings of shame and guilt that threaten to emerge. Following a history of intrauterine drug exposure, women may harbor unresolved maternal guilt and shame. A syndrome of unresolved maternal guilt and shame suggests a common characteristic and invokes a common set of characteristic experiences among female substance abusers, as the following case highlights.

The Case of Ms. U.

The case of Ms. U., a 48 year old Caucasian female outpatient in individual psychotherapy who is in the first decade of her recovery, suggests the kind of maternal feelings of guilt and shame that can plague a woman's recovery. Once Ms. U. was sober, what characterized her first years of recovery from alcohol, heroin, and cocaine addiction was an attempt to be the very best nurturer for her school-age son. What her son needed and found in her was also an advocate who fought for his special education and treatment needs. As a sober parent, Ms. U. persevered as an actively engaged parent throughout the elementary school years replete with special education placements and the extensive testing associated with her son's learning disability. She often faced the judgmental attitudes of professionals who exacerbated her personal feelings of guilt for intrauterine drug exposure and a 2-year period of loss of custody of her son to foster care when he was a very young child. Beyond latency, her son's early adolescent years posed the challenge of managing his increasing aggression, juvenile mischief with peers, drug use, and truancy. Late adolescence brought more pain, as it became clear that this young man faced limited employment opportunities. Feelings of acceptance gradually came to replace intense feelings of maternal guilt and shame—which had posed a central treatment challenge in our outpatient work.

African American Women Face a Greater Risk of Loss of Infants

Whereas the case of Ms. U. presents the characteristic experiences of female heroin abusers and methadone-maintained pregnant women in the late 1960s and 1970s, the 1980s crack cocaine epidemic came to include much more rigorous detection of intra uterine drug exposure. Researchers found that pregnant African American women were 10 times more likely to be reported by physicians for a positive illicit drug toxicology than were their white counterparts (Chasnoff, Laundress, & Barrett, 1990). The possible existence of more aggressive reporting of positive drug toxicologies for African American women by physicians in some areas of the country may lead to characteristic traumatic experiences among minority women. Characteristic traumatic experiences for many women involve the loss of custody of an infant at birth and often the loss of custody of other older children as well. Extended family networks and grandmothers in particular have played a critical role in keeping infants and children taken away from substance-abusing mothers. The outcome of some women who lose custody of infants who show a positive drug toxicology at birth means that issues of separation and depression may compound maternal feelings of guilt and shame. A maternal syndrome involving separation anxiety, depression, guilt, and shame arises from such trauma as women have lost custody of infants and other older children to foster care or extended family placements.

Raskin (1992) emphasized the importance of recognizing a long-standing underlying depression or the maternal bereavement that characterizes a cohort of women who have lost even multiple births to the foster care system or death. According to Raskin (1992), because of unresolved feelings of loss surrounding an infant, the mother may find that several years later, a subsequent pregnancy or opportunity to parent triggers feelings of inadequacy and being unworthy of the parenting role.

Patterns of possible overreporting of pregnant African American and Latina women for positive drug toxicologies may mean greater presence of an underlying unresolved maternal bereavement in this population. To be both female and minority, then, means the possibility of facing greater trauma and stigma when hitting "rock bottom." This trauma and stigma include possible criminal sanctions and loss of infant custody. Following Raskin's (1992) observations, we may also anticipate in recovering women some rejection of the parenting role, inadvertent rejection of surviving children, and expressions of parental inadequacy, as the following case illustrates.

The Case of Ms. B.

Ms. B. is a 29-year-old Puerto Rican female who was being treated for heroin dependence in a residential therapeutic community. When Ms. B. was just 2 months in recovery, she had to negotiate in a sober state— the first time in many years—the anniversary of the birthday of her first child who had died in infancy after struggling with multiple illnesses. With this first problematic pregnancy, any relationship to illicit chemical use would have been traced to her husband's heroin addiction. After the traumatic death of her first child, Ms. B. began to self-medicate with the heroin her husband had in the home. Several years later, this heroin abuse led to the delivery of an intrauterine drug-exposed infant who died shortly after birth. Unresolved feelings of maternal bereavement led to a tendency to reject and avoid her third child. Ms. B. was startled by her latency-age daughter's spontaneous expressions of love and affection toward her while visiting her daughter on a pass from the residential therapeutic community. Ms. B. felt unworthy of these expressions of love and struggled with a deep and basic sense of being unworthy as a mother, as well as with deep feelings of guilt, shame, and depression. At the height of her depression, Ms. B.'s suicidal ideation focused on how she would kill herself and this surviving child. In women's group, we assisted Ms. B. in working through and integrating her traumatic memories of her first infant's death in her arms at the hospital. This work also eventually focused on her traumatic memories of the sight of the dead body of her second infant shortly after birth—memories she tearfully articulated in group. In later sessions, the treatment challenge involved working with Ms. B. to prevent her from unconsciously sabotaging any movement toward more closeness with her surviving daughter. Ms. B. struggled with internal self-statements and cognitions of worthlessness as a mother.

Other Characteristic Trauma of Women

As the case of Ms. B. illustrates, substance abuse can be quite traumatic for women in their childbearing years. Narcissistic injuries (Wallace, 1991a) from the trauma of hitting rock bottom and experiencing multiple losses often follow for women. These narcissistic injuries constitute core injuries to the inner self and suggest a moment of trauma or overstimulation, as with the experience of overwhelming feelings of shame and guilt when infant or child custody is lost or an infant dies. Such injuries typically lead to the use of narcissitic defenses of grandiosity, inflation, arrogance, and aloofness, which leads to yet another characteristic frequently observed—a predominance of narcissistic traits (Wallace, 1991a; Levin, 1987).

Fullilove (1993) offers the term *injury event* to characterize the moment of some significant trauma in the lives of the crack cocaine-dependent women she and her colleagues studied. This work documented the multiple traumas of women across their lives. A body of literature has documented the way in which traumas across the life-span include childhood sexual abuse, exposure to dysfunctional family dynamics of one kind or another, exposure to parental alcoholism and substance abuse, and, all too frequently, exposure to attendant experiences of domestic violence, physical abuse, and verbal abuse when growing up within dysfunctional families (Young, 1990; Bollerud, 1990; Wallace, 1991a, 1993).

Many cocaine abusers have also discovered the aphrodisiac effects of cocaine and an increased level and range of sexual activity. They may encounter the presence of a compulsive sexuality together with compulsive cocaine use (Washton, 1989). Some cases suggest that users rent hotel rooms for the weekend and engage in compulsive cocaine use and compulsive sexual activity with paid prostitutes (Washton, 1989), whereas others document via ethnographic work, across the nation, the phenomenon of sex-for-crack exchanges (Ratner, 1993).

The Nexus of Compulsive Substance Abuse, Sexuality, and HIV/AIDS

The reality of the overlap of compulsive sexuality and compulsive cocaine and crack use introduces the risk of HIV/AIDS (human immunodeficiency virus-acquired immunodeficiency syndrome) transmission during high-risk sexual behavior, raising another possible characteristic of contemporary women in treatment—being HIV positive or having AIDS. Other women may be injection drug users or polysubstance abusers who have sex with men who are also injection drug users. This suggests multiple routes for exposure to HIV/AIDS for women. Inciardi, Lockwood, and Pottieger (1993) provide graphic description of the kind of experiences women have had in the world of sex-for-crack exchanges, clearly highlighting the risk of HIV/AIDS.

Other women have experienced the trauma of being raped by ''Johns'' in the drug culture or by virtue of being women in unsafe situations related to the purchase and communal use of drugs at all hours of the day and night. Trauma in the drug culture from such experiences of rape and sexual abuse suggests how trauma characterizing recovering women in treatment includes even the current adult developmental era.

Whether lower, upper, or middle income, and regardless of race or ethnicity, recovering women often possess histories of some degree of sexual activity about which they feel shame, and for which they may subsequently present an HIV-positive or AIDS status as they enter treatment. Among those not yet tested, a ''nagging question'' remains as to the possibility that some degree of high-risk behavior—ranging from disinhibited sexual activity without a condom to compulsive sexuality to sex-for-crack exchanges to a rape experience—has left them in danger of being HIV positive. Denial may extend to this high-risk behavior, whatever its degree, or to rape trauma. Clinicians therefore need to understand the nexus of compulsive substance abuse, sexuality, and the risk of HIV/AIDS transmission. The clinical task therefore includes not only providing HIV/AIDS education but also clinically managing denial and the range of feelings women may harbor about their sexual experiences. These feelings may run the gamut from feelings of power over men and pride in making money for sex exchanges to well-hidden feelings of shame and guilt. Initially, they may present bravado and pride, while with time, empathy, and support they may share feelings of shame and guilt, or a rape trauma can be therapeutically processed.

HIV/AIDS: Issues of Bereavement, Death, Dying, and Orphans

As a result of their own HIV/AIDS status, many women have had intimate and loving relationships with individuals who have already died of AIDS. Such women may enter treatment with unresolved feelings of bereavement due to the death of a partner. A community of recovering substance abusers finds itself increasingly devastated by the deaths of community members, including relatives, spouses, and parents of children. Women may find that as they enter recovery, the need for HIV testing and for coming to terms with the death of a past lover from AIDS complicates the tasks and process of recovery.

The reality of histories of high-risk sexual behavior means that psychoeducation on HIV/AIDS and discussion of testing issues are necessary in treatment in this era of HIV/AIDS (Schleifer, DeLaney, Tross, & Keller, 1991; Wallace, 1992e). The timing of testing for HIV becomes an issue when some women are admittedly so vulnerable in early stages of recovery that they anticipate coping with news of a positive test result with immediate relapse and self-medication of their pain.

Aside from debating the best time to test for HIV/AIDS and the pros and cons of risking a catastrophic reaction and immediate relapse to substance abuse when testing occurs relatively early in recovery (first 3 months), practioners in the field of substance abuse treatment must consider the special issues facing women who are also mothers. Not only may women have unresolved bereavement for a spouse or partner who died of AIDS, they may also need assistance from practitioners with issues of death and dying as the women themselves advance to AIDS. Moreover, women who are mothers experience the pain of anticipating what will follow in the lives of those children they leave behind if they advance to full-blown AIDS and eventually die. A special sensitivity is required in work with women who bring multiple needs for bereavement counseling, death and dying counseling, and assistance in preparing for the care of their surviving children. Several cases illustrate this complex treatment challenge.

The Case of Ms. R.

Ms. R. is an African American crack cocaine-dependent patient, 34-year-old mother of three school-age children, and the wife of a drug-free spouse. Within a women's group setting in an urban residential therapeutic community, Ms. R. shared her feelings over the course of several weeks regarding her HIV-positive status. Ms. R. sat in group with tears pouring down her cheeks as she described the manner in which her mother-in-law told her that she could not utilize utensils, cups, or plates whenever she came to visit. She also lamented over the negative and rejecting reactions of her husband to her HIV-positive status. As Ms. R. spoke of her experiences, she challenged other women in the group to break through their denial surrounding sexual activity during their period of active substance abuse.

The Case of Ms. G.

Ms. G., member of the same women's group, surrendered her denial and responded as though she had found a peer role model for coping with the reality of her own past high-risk sexual activity while abusing drugs. As a 23-year-old African American crack cocaine abuser with two young children, Ms. G. had already suffered the rage and physical violence of her husband who suspected sexual activity while she was out of the home abusing crack. Aside from fear of spousal violence, Ms. G. felt totally unprepared to contemplate the possibility of being HIV positive. But, she studied the coping strategies of Ms. R. while in the group with her. Ms. G. thought that if she took an HIV/AIDS test and the results were positive she would immediately relapse to crack cocaine. She also recognized that she would eventually need to be tested. In this manner, even with 5 months in treatment, Ms. G. may have accurately assessed her own coping abilities, declining to be tested for HIV until she could anticipate a better ability to cope.

The Case of Ms. N.

Ms. N. responded with tremendous empathy to the pain Ms. R. shared in group surrounding rejection by her family for being HIV positive. As a 38-year-old Caucasian polysubstance-abusing woman with grown children of her own, Ms. N. went on to share her fears of being HIV positive and dying of AIDS the way her lover had died just 5 months previously. Ms. N. had met this sober man while she was in recovery. The ultimate course of events led to his death from AIDS and Ms. N.'s immediate relapse to drug use. In pursuit of recovery and abstinence yet again, Ms. N. decided on her own that she was ready with just 2 months of sobriety to take an HIV test. While the results of this test were negative, Ms. N. understood all too well the possibility of seroconversion to an HIV-positive status and the possibility that her children might surround her deathbed, just as she stood at her lover's deathbed. Her unresolved feelings of bereavement for this lover found an outlet for expression in women's group.

Implications of Women's Characteristics and Experiences

The case vignettes underscore the nature of the difficult work that confronts the practitioner in individual or group work in inpatient, residential therapeutic community, and outpatient settings in the era of overlapping drug and HIV/AIDS epidemics. Clearly, our training must extend to being able to facilitate and support the process of grieving for a loved one's loss to HIV/AIDS. However, not to be forgotten is the culture of violence as the setting for service delivery (Wallace, 1993). The reality of our culture of violence also implicates unresolved bereavement for violent deaths of loved ones among our population; several alternative cases could have been presented highlighting the impact on a young mother from the death of her husband to a gunshot wound and her eventual self-medication with chemicals. Or, this bereavement work may also extend to infants and children lost by women, especially in light of practices wherein minority women may face more aggressive detection for and reporting of drug use during pregnancy—frequently resulting in loss of infant and child custody as well as criminal sanctions (Wallace, 1991b; Harrison, 1991). Practitioners may even prepare clients to negotiate death and dying—with all the implications for women's surviving children. Arrangements for these women's children, which may even involve legal preparations and selection of future guardians for children, become important therapeutic issues with which the practitioner may need to become involved.

It becomes apparent that practitioners may need to gain skill and competence in managing narcissistic traits in the newly abstinent, as discussed elsewhere (Wallace, 1991a). In essence, narcissim, grandiosity, and inflation represent attempts to defend against the painful shame and guilt overwhelming the inner self. Interpretation of the use of defenses to the client and the expression of empathy for the client's inner self struggling with painful affects are both recommended.

Practitioners may also need to gain skill and competence in addressing compulsive behaviors other than substance abuse. Compulsive and destructive behaviors may represent elaborate defensive strategies relied on by women to block painful affects and memories. The potential, spontaneous emergence of affects, impulses, and images represents a legacy of past trauma. A biopsychosocial approach, individualized assessment, and matching of clients to specific interventions permit those with compulsive sexuality, compulsive overeating, bulimia, or anorexia, for example, to receive services tailored to women's needs.

A women's group permits therapeutically addressing issues about which women feel the greatest levels of shame and guilt. A women's group also permits discussion of sensitive issues ranging from HIV/AIDS to past sexual behavior to bereavement and death and dying issues, as the cases presented here revealed. This suggests that a women's group (Wallace, 1992c) may constitute an ideal setting for the delivery of interventions tailored to women's needs, and it may also be combined with individual sessions or other interventions in order to meet the unique needs of any particular woman.

Typically, women's needs include exposure to a therapeutic approach that will address or resolve their past trauma (Bollerud, 1990). Aside from the trauma of multiple losses and hitting rock bottom, women also face the legacy of childhood, adolescent, adult, and drug culture trauma. In light of these experiences of trauma across developmental eras, our task as practitioners frequently includes trauma resolution. Critical therapeutic tasks closely tied to the resolution of trauma can be operationalized as involving the remediation of underlying psychopathology or improving problems in self-regulation (Wallace, 1992c; Khantzian, Halliday, & McAuliffe, 1990). Following Khantzian (1985; Dodes & Khantzian, 1991), we can understand poor self-regulation as it involves the realms of affect, impulse, self-esteem, and interpersonal behavior. To remediate underlying psychopathology or improve self-regulation may also reduce the risk of relapse, symptom substitution, and engagement in other compulsive behaviors. Substance abuse and compulsive behavior may be viewed as elaborate defense against poorly regulated affects (shame, guilt) that might be threatening to spontaneously emerge with traumatic memories.

Considerations of the therapeutic "timing" of the articulation and integration of trauma in treatment of the substance abuser are important. Some practitioners acknowledge the need for attention to sexual abuse trauma in early months of recovery, permitting women to avoid relapse from the spontaneous emergence of memories of traumatic sexual abuse during early sobriety (Young, 1990). Other practitioners caution modification of psychoanalytic techniques so that dynamic work addressing depth issues can be delayed until many months of sobriety have been established (Yalisove, 1992). Conducting a thorough, individualized assessment determines individual patient needs.

Initial emphasis in treatment on asking assessment questions, providing psychoeducation, and engaging in cognitive restructuring via psychoeducation results in increased capacity for clients to participate in good ego observation of their inner self experience. In early phases of recovery, psychoeducation and cognitive restructuring actually prepare the patient for the eventual possession of an ego grown sufficiently strengthened with enhanced ability to self-observe. A 1-to-3-month period of therapy with emphasis on psychoeducation may accomplish this goal. This strengthened ego may, in later phases of psychotherapy, with use of psychoanalytic techniques, undergo a guided therapeutic regression in the service of the observing ego to actual moments and memories of trauma; this work may occur as early as the third month in treatment and is well suited for the period between 6 and 9 months in a women's group, following a suggested model (Wallace, 1992c) with variability in light of individualized assessment findings.

Having considered the special population of women and the implications of their characteristics and experiences for treatment and the training of practitioners, we can now consider minorities as a special population of substance abusers.

Characteristics of Minorities and Characteristic Experiences

One approach to the characteristics and characteristic experiences of minorities is to discuss a variety of distinct ethnic and racial groups and to convey those cultural values, practices, and behaviors that might be relevant to the task of working cross-culturally. The result of codifying these cultural values and practices might be a set of anthropological guidelines. We would likely qualify the resulting anthopological guidelines for social interaction with Puerto Ricans, Dominicans, Cubans, Mexicans, African Americans, Jamaicans, Haitians, Chinese, Japanese, Koreans, Vietnamese, or a host of others. We might feel compelled to further qualify anthropological guidelines by drawing distinctions based on urban versus rural, rich versus poor, and educated versus uneducated characteristics of individual members of these cultural groups. In light of immigration and migration to and within the United States, we might feel compelled to further qualify anthropological guidelines in view of length of time in this country and degree of assimilation or acculturation to the ways, practices, and traditions of mainstream Americans. In the process, we are likely to offend many who view their particular ethnic, racial, or cultural group as having been reduced to an offensive stereotype in anthropological guidelines, as well as a host of others who find that their particular cultural group has been left out.

Moreover, we would continually have to expand the list of groups for whom we must learn a new set of anthropological guidelines for social interaction. But, suggesting the importance of this approach, another dimension to anthropological guidelines involves understanding some of the historical and regional experiences of immigrants in their homeland and in immigration and migration. The regional history of a cultural group may bear an important relationship to understanding patterns of addiction as they are transferred to and emerge in immigrant communities within the United States. However, there are limits to such an approach as well.

Rate, degree, and extent of acculturation introduce important qualifying variables that modify anthropological guidelines. We arrive at a familiar recommendation for performance of a thorough individualized assessment (Donovan & Marlatt, 1988; Wallace, 1991a). An alternative approach involving an individualized and ongoing assessment of any minority substance-abusing client also permits determining the extent of acculturation clients bring with them into the treatment setting and their unique experiences. An individualized assessment, for example, might reveal that a Puerto Rican family actually felt insulted when a clinician automatically spoke to them in Spanish, failing to appreciate that the extent of this particular family's acculturation extends to a preference to speak in English (Curtis, 1990). Or, consider the way assessment might indicate markedly different rates of acculturation within a Chinese family—with grandparents at home, adults in the work force, and adolescents who have been educated in the public school system (M. Lee, personal communication, January, 1992).

The resulting psychological approach to treatment should not, as Harris-Offut (1992) challenges, resort to habitually applying a Eurocentric view in work with new and different cultural groups. Instead, we may need to consider an Afrocentric world view and resulting psychology. Extending this thinking, we may also need to consider and enter—via a therapeutic alliance and continuing assessment of clients—the world views of Asians or Latinos. Similarly, we may need to consider as clinicians working with diverse members of various cultural groups the world view of each client with whom we work, entering that world to the extent that we engage in an assessment and interact with clients in a therapeutic context. We are likely to discover the extent to which each client's world view is shaped by multiple factors: the family's ethnic, racial, or cultural experiences; the degree, extent, and rate of acculturation to U.S. culture; and education, socioeconomic status, and employment experiences.

Characteristic Experiences of Immigrants: Xenophobia and Nativism

Common characteristics and characteristic experiences of immigrants and minority group members undergoing a process of acculturation and assimilation, or attempting in the 1990s to be a part of an emerging pluralistic society, can be considered in an attempt to prepare clinicians for effective cross-cultural work with minority substance abusers. This approach represents an alternative to considering a plethora of anthropological guidelines for different cultural groups.

Historically, characteristic experiences of immigrants involve ex-

posure to xenophobia where citizens react with fear to the new or different immigrant arrival seen working at the factory or living nearby. Nativism leads those who have been citizens longer, or already feel that they
are U.S. citizens, to assume an attitude of superiority over the new and
different immigrant arrival. It is not a long road to interethnic or inter-
racial prejudice, discrimination, mob attacks, church burnings, and riots
(Takaki, 1987, 1990). A question arises as to what extent these historical
experiences of immigrants in the United States continue to the present
day.

Possession of Salient Stimuli of Membership in Cultural Groups

A key characteristic of minority group members, or members of various
immigrant groups, is possession of traits, mannerisms, customs, or beliefs that distinguish the minority group member to the point that he/she
might be said to possess salient stimuli that indicate membership in a certain racial or ethnic group. Once in possession of certain salient stimuli
indicating membership in a particular cultural group, that individual may
also automatically be thought to possess certain negative attributes associated with that ethnic or racial group. The U.S. citizen has knowledge
of these negative attributes and stimuli indicative of group membership
because of a process of social conditioning. Socialization permits acquisition of conditioned cognitions, the content of which includes stereotypes and negative expectations regarding the "different other" (Wallace,
1993). The perception of salient stimuli may trigger our conditioned cognitions, as we attach stereotypes and negative expectations to the "different other." Or, we may consciously respond to perception of salient
stimuli with ego inhibition of conditioned responses, perhaps permitting
opportunities for new learning regarding the "different other."

Unconscious, Covert, and Invisible Processes: Projection

Having been cognitively conditioned as U.S. citizens, we typically utilize our knowledge of the content of stereotypes and negative expectations as something we attach to, or project on the "different other" during
an interpersonal process. This interpersonal process can be said to be unconscious, covert, and invisible. Others (Fanon, 1968) may prefer to emphasize the kind of social conditioning process that results in common
knowledge of salient stimuli (skin color, hair texture, physical appearance, distinct clothing) and negative expectations and stereotypes.

　　Fanon (1968) long ago described the way in which the African American was a cause of fear, phobia, and anxiety in the white colonialist. One
might view contemporary responses to the stimulus of a contemporary

African American as including cognitions or negative expectations that an African American, and male in particular, is a criminal. The African American is therefore considered likely to engage in criminal or anti-social behavior, appears sociopathic, and has a poor prognosis. Dark skin color alone may be a necessary and sufficient stimulus to evoke the conditioned cognitions associated with the phobic object of the African American. In this way, Jamaicans, Dominicans, Puerto Ricans, and Haitians with dark skin color may find that their dark skin color alone represents a salient stimulus that triggers responses of fear and defensive aggression in white Americans. Similarly, negative cognitions toward Japanese, conditioned because of Pearl Harbor and World War II, may inform some contemporary responses of fear and suspicion toward a range of Asian immigrants in contemporary U.S. society who possess yellow skin color or other distinct physical characteristics.

Possession of salient stimuli, such as skin color or physical characteristics, suggesting membership in a cultural group creates characteristic experiences among minorities. These characteristic experiences include exposure to prejudice, discrimination, or invisible interpersonal processes involving projection of negative or stereotypical expectations. Hence, a characteristic experience of individuals with black, brown, yellow, or red skin color is to be the recipient of the projection of negative expectations and stereotypical assumptions. These unconscious, invisible, and covert processes of projection are important to acknowledge because in work with the minority client, we discover the kind of low ethnic self-esteem (Harris-Offut, 1992), the kind of narcissistic injuries (Wallace, 1991a), and pain, anger, and ambivalence that can result from the experience of prejudice, discrimination, and tense interpersonal interactions. On one level, we may observe what appears to be a relatively benign interaction occuring cross culturally between client and practitioner; yet, on a another level, we might come to recognize the damage and injury sustained by clients from invisible and covert processes of projection.

To project negative expectations means that I, as a practitioner, may err in overemphasizing the possibilities of relapse, conveying a negative prophecy, or being a doomsday prophet who holds a negative prognosis. Myths and misinformation, relating to the content of socially conditioned cognitions, stereotypes, and negative expectations, may threaten to affect our interpersonal interactions with minority substance abusers, so we hold a greater expectation of relapse. Or, at the other extreme, we may assume no problem exists; as in the case of Asians, one must not stereotypically assume that a flushing reaction suggests such a low prevalence of alcoholism among Asians that false stereotypes of "flushing Asians" flourish and bar adequate assessment of a Chinese or other Asian patient for the presence of alcoholism (M. Lee, personal communication, January, 1992).

Implications of Minorities' Characteristics and Experiences

Somehow, training must enable practitioners to avoid the unconscious, invisible, and covert projection of socially conditioned cognitions, stereotypes, and negative expectations that may serve as a barrier to adequate assessment and matching of clients to appropriate treatment interventions. Moreover, in a field in which motivating clients becomes a critical task (Miller & Rollnick, 1991), training must ensure that practitioners do not differentially motivate clients because of covert, invisible processes of projection or possession of negative stereotypical expectations. Thus, one implication of our discussion of the characteristics and characteristic experiences of substance abusers who are members of diverse ethnic, racial, and cultural groups addresses the need to train practitioners in an effective cross-cultural counseling technique.

Within training for cross-cultural counseling, it has been recommended that a culturally sensitive empathy be deployed as a clinical technique for use with minority substance abusers (Wallace, 1993). Within the deployment of a culturally sensitive empathy, practitioners may recognize that they themselves never had the experience of personally negotiating childhood, adolescence, or adulthood as an immigrant or a member of a particular ethnic or racial group. However, practitioners can sit with a client from any cultural group and attempt to utilize their own inner self as an instrument that attempts to attune to the inner self experience of the "culturally different" client. In this way, practitioners can attempt to achieve empathy via the process of empathic attunement with the inner self experience of the client—while listening to the content and interpreting the meaning of a client's verbalized distress. A next step involves gently holding up a mirror to this client and reflecting back to the client what the clinician feels may be the client's inner self experience and own internal experience of affect. This involves a kind of empathic mirroring (Wallace, 1991a) wherein the practitioner validates the inner self experience of the client.

As preparation for the deployment of this clinical technique of culturally sensitive empathy, practitioners may contemplate their own family's immigrant experience in prior generations and should attempt to achieve empathy with their own relatives' experiences of the pain and violence that followed from xenophobia and nativism. Perhaps, for example, this past violence ensued because of an ethnic or religious difference involving being Irish, Italian, Polish, Jewish, or Catholic. In this reflective process, we may recognize that some immigrants, perhaps in our own families, changed their last names or avoided salient stimuli suggestive of their membership in a particular cultural or religious group. We may also reflect on how skin color remains a highly salient stimulus to the present day which is not changed as readily as a last name.

Practitioners must also debunk a host of myths that are potential obstacles to effective cross-cultural work (Wallace, 1991a). Practitioners can restructure their own cognitions, freeing themselves from performance of socially conditioned cognitive responses and adherence to myths. As we also engage in good ego observation of our own internal cognitions, practitioners can practice consciously retracting projections during moments when they find themselves having regressed to automatic conditioned cognitions. Individual practitioners may choose personal reading, participation in cross-cultural training workshops, and personal supervision to ensure that reflexive and unconscious assumptions do not serve as a barrier to effective cross-cultural work.

A MULTIFACETED CLINICAL TECHNIQUE AND MULTIDIMENSIONAL APPROACH TO RELAPSE PREVENTION

In other contexts, a multifaceted clinical technique has been recommended that combines cognitive, behavioral, psychodynamic, psychoeducational, and metaphorical interventions (Wallace, 1991a). Although a technique originally developed in clinical work with largely African American and Latino clients, as well as with women, it has been recommended for application with a range of diverse substance abusers. Perhaps by virtue of its design largely with two special populations, women and minorities, such an intervention approximates or begins to suggest a culturally sensitive and gender-sensitive clinical technique.

Psychoeducation as an Important Cognitive Intervention

The recommended multifaceted clinical technique recognizes a key role for cognitive or psychoeducational techniques that focus on actively restructuring cognitions, strengthening the ego, and improving ego observation of inner self experience. Cognitive interventions thereby prepare clients' egos for later phases of therapeutic work. Later phases of therapeutic work may involve the use of psychoanalytic techniques for improving self-regulation (of affects, impulses, self-esteem, and interpersonal behavior) and for trauma resolution. These psychoanalytic techniques may include a guided therapeutic regression of clients to memories of trauma for purposes of integration and working through these traumatic memories (Wallace, 1992c). This process, following a behavioral approach, also recognizes the importance of teaching clients alternative behaviors for performance in high-risk situations. Practitioners therefore actively shape and reinforce new, more adaptive behavior in clients.

Metaphorical Forms of Communication

Metaphorical forms of communication bypass clients' defenses and may even bypass subtle cognitive deficits from either the effects of substance abuse or an HIV/AIDS dementia (Kovner et al., 1992; Gillen, Kranzler, Kadden, & Weidenman, 1991). Metaphors powerfully convey the content of psychoeducation. Metaphorical forms of communication and storytelling may also draw on an African oral tradition and further enhance retention of vital psychoeducation conveying information on avoiding relapse or HIV/AIDS transmission. Also, by combining theories and corresponding techniques into an integrated theory and mulitifaceted clinical technique, and by empahsizing the use of cost-effective group modalities, we may facilitate fairly expeditious or rapid recovery. An informed eclecticism (Hester & Miller, 1989) or multifaceted clinical technique (Wallace, 1991a) may result in a clinical technique that permits a more rapid recovery from substance abuse and resolution of trauma than if we relied on any one school of thought or clinical technique alone.

A Multidimensional Approach to Relapse Prevention

The multifaceted clinical technique also addresses multideterminants of relapse brought to light in research with African American and Latino substance abusers (Wallace, 1991a). This research highlighted internal and external determinants of relapse, offered a typology of relapse determinants that involve a psychological–personality domain and an environmental–interpersonal domain, and underscored the role of multiple determinants in the relapse process. The resulting model of relapse prevention actively strives to prepare clients for those classic high-risk situations in which their peers previously relapsed. Whereas some contemporary notions of substance abuse suggest that it is a chronic relapsing condition, the model of relapse prevention I advanced ensures that a prophecy of inevitable relapse is not conveyed. Instead, specific high-risk situations and the performance of alternative behaviors, instead of conditioned responses of substance abuse, are emphasized for active performance in high-risk situations for relapse. Clients learn to perceive triggers or conditioned stimuli for substance abuse which may abound in the environment and to perform alternative behaviors to past conditioned responses.

The resulting multidimensional approach to relapse prevention (Wallace, 1992d) also recognizes the use of pharmacological adjuncts, especially during a withdrawal phase or in later phases of recovery for underlying psychiatric conditions. Whether teaching alternative behaviors for performance in high-risk situations for relapse or remediating underlying psychopathology and problems in self-regulation, this multidimensional approach to relapse prevention is comprehensive insofar as it recognizes multiple etiological factors underlying addiction and strives to address these factors proactively as they may possibly contribute to a risk of relapse.

Overall, the recommended multifaceted clinical technique and multidimensional approach to relapse prevention were developed in clinical work with female and minority substance abusers and reflect the perspective of an African American female clinician. The approach also attempts to foster in other practitioners gender and cultural sensitivity in work with the two special populations of women and minority substance abusers. As clinicians, we must strive to learn, deploy, and refine a clinical technique that is gender and culture sensitive in light of the critical treatment needs and special challenges we face in our work with women and minority clients.

CONCLUSION

This chapter described key characteristics and characteristic experiences of women and minorities within treatment settings. The implications of these characteristics and characteristic experiences for treatment and the training of practitioners were discussed. In addition, this chapter briefly described a culturally sensitive empathy and a multifaceted clinical technique developed in clinical work with the special populations of women and minority substance abusers. The chapter also briefly outlined what may be an effective clinical technique in work with these two special populations.

However, a limitation in our discussion is the lack of outcome evaluation data on the effectiveness of the multifaceted clinical technique, model of relapse prevention, and model of trauma resolution briefly described here. Grant-funded evaluation is necessary to determine to what extent my models can be replicated with success in other settings and with other patients; their potential value to other practitioners working with minority and female clients suggests the importance of evaluating these models.

This chapter also brought to light the special challenges posed in work with these two special populations in an era of overlapping drug and HIV/AIDS epidemics. In our discussion of women in particular, it became clear that the degree of access to substance abuse which contemporary women discover, the fact that most of these women are in their childbearing years, and the realities of disinhibited and compulsive high-risk sexual activity in the drug culture combine to create a daunting treatment challenge. As a result, training needs for practitioners include preparation for engaging women in bereavement, death and dying, and HIV/AIDS counseling. In our discussion of minorities, it similarly became clear that training in cross-cultural counseling, following the model and approach described here, means that practitioners are challenged to reflect on and restructure their own socially conditioned cognitions—as these cognitions may serve as a barrier to effective cross-cultural work.

In this way, we have considered that "something more" or "something special" that dictates the practitioner's taking some extra time to prepare for work with the special populations of women and minority substance abusers. Consideration of the characteristics of these special populations and of characteristic experiences of members of these groups was augmented by an attempt to steer clinicians away from certain pitfalls, such as avoiding the projection, ever so subtly, of negative expectations of a poor prognosis or a greater chance of relapse.

Unfortunately, until the training of practitioners in substance abuse and in cross-cultural counseling improves, a greater risk of relapse may indeed exist and result for women and minorities, even those who have access to the very best treatment facilities, utilizing the very best medical coverage. This disturbing possibility underscores the importance of this chapter's attempt to provide a handbook or guide for the practitioner pursuing this challenging but satisfying work with women and minorities.

REFERENCES

Bollerud, K. (1990). A model for the treatment of trauma-related syndromes among chemically dependent inpatient women. *Journal of Substance Abuse Treatment, 7,* 83–87.

Chasnoff, I. J., Landress, H. J., & Barrett, M. E. (1990). The prevalence of illicit-drug or alcohol use during pregnancy and discrepancies in mandatory reporting in Pinellas County, Florida. *New England Journal of Medicine, 322*(17), 1202–1206.

Chavkin, W. (1990). Drug addiction and pregnancy: Policy crossroads. *American Journal of Public Health, 80*(4), 483–487.

Curtis, P. A. (1990). The consequences of acculturation to service delivery and research with Hispanic families. *Child and Adolescent Social Work, 7*(2), 147–159.

Dodes, L. M., & Khantzian, E. J. (1991). Individual psychodynamic psychotherapy. In R. J. Frances & S. I. Miller (Eds.), *Clinical textbook of addictive disorders* (pp. 391–405). New York: Guilford Press.

Donovan, D. M., & Marlatt, G. A. (Eds.). (1988). *Assessment of addictive behaviors.* New York: Guilford Press.

Fanon, F. (1968). *Black skin, white masks.* New York: Grove Press.

Fullilove, M. (1993, October 13–16). *Trauma in the lives of crack cocaine dependent women.* Paper presented at the First Annual Conference on Psychopathology, Psychopharmacology, and Ethnicity, sponsored by the National Institute of Mental Health, the National Insitute of Drug Addiction, and Drew Medical School, Los Angeles.

Gillen, R. W., Kranzler, H. R., Kadden, R. M., & Weidenman, M. A. (1991). Utility of a brief cognitive screening instrument in substance abuse patients: Initial investigation. *Journal of Substance Abuse Treatment, 8,* 247–251.

Harris-Offutt, R. (1992). Cultural factors in the assessment and treatment of African-American addicts: Africentric considerations. In B. C. Wallace (Ed.), *The chemically dependent: Phases of treatment and recovery* (pp. 289–297). New York: Brunner/Mazel.

Harrison, M. (1991). Drug addiction in pregnancy: The interface of science, emotion, and social policy. *Journal of Substance Abuse Treatment, 8,* 261–268.

Hester, R. K., & Miller, W. R. (1989). (Eds). *Handbook of alcoholism treatment approaches: Effective alternatives.* New York: Pergamon Press.

Khantzian, E. J. (1985). On the psychological predisposition for opiate and stimulant dependence, *Psychiatry Letter,* p. 1.

Khantzian, E. J., Halliday, K. S., & McAuliffe, W. E. (1990). *Addiction and the vulnerable self: Modified dynamic group therapy for substance abusers.* New York: Guilford Press.

Kovner, R., Lazar, J. W., Lesser, M., Perecman, E., Kaplan, M. H., Hainline, B., & Napolitano, B. (1992). Use of the Dementia Rating Scale as a test for neuropsychological dysfunction in HIV-positive IV drug abusers. *Journal of Substance Abuse Treatment, 9,* 133–137.

Levin, J. D. (1987). *Treatment of alcoholism and other addictions: A self-psychology approach.* Northvale, NJ: Jason Aronson.

Miller, W. R., & Rollnick, S. (1991). *Motivational interviewing: Preparing people to change addictive behavior.* New York: Guilford Press.

Raskin, V. D. (1992). Maternal bereavement in the perinatal substance abuser. *Journal of Substance Abuse Treatment, 9,* 149–152.

Ratner, M. (1993). (Ed.). *Crack pipe as pimp: An ethnographic investigation of sex-for-crack exchanges.* New York: Lexington Books.

Schleifer, S. J., DeLaney, B. R., Tross, S., & Keller, S. E. (1991). AIDS and addictions. In R. J. Frances & S. I. Miller (Eds.), *Clinical textbook of addictive disorders* (pp. 299–319). New York: Guilford Press.

Takaki, R. (1987). (Ed.). *From different shores: Perspectives on race and ethnicity in America.* New York: Oxford University Press.

Takaki, R. (1990). *Iron cages: Race and culture in 19th century America.* New York: Oxford University Press.

Wallace, B. C. (1991a). *Crack cocaine: A practical treatment approach for the chemically dependent.* New York: Brunner/Mazel.

Wallace, B. C. (1991b). Chemical dependency treatment for the pregnant crack addict: Beyond the criminal sanctions perspective. *Psychology of Addictive Behavior, 5*(1), 23–35.

Wallace, B. C. (1992a). Treatment and recovery in an evolving field. In B. C. Wallace (Ed.), *The chemically dependent: Phases of treatment and recovery* (pp. 3–14). New York: Brunner/Mazel.

Wallace, B. C. (1992b). Inpatient treatment for the first phase of recovery. In B. C. Wallace (Ed.), *The chemically dependent: Phases of treatment and recovery* (pp. 15–27). New York: Brunner/Mazel.

Wallace, B. C. (1992c). The therapeutic community as a treatment modality and the role of the professional consultant: Spotlight on Damon House. In B. C.

Wallace (Ed.), *The chemically dependent: Phases of treatment and recovery* (pp. 39–59). New York: Brunner/Mazel.

Wallace, B. C. (1992d). Multidimensional relapse prevention from a biopsychosocial perspective across phases of recovery. In B. C. Wallace (Ed.), *The chemically dependent: Phases of treatment and recovery* (pp. 171–186). New York: Brunner/Mazel.

Wallace, B. C. (1992e). Treatment models for special groups: Criminal, pregnant, un-insured, adolescent, HIV positive, methadone-maintained, and homeless populations. In B. C. Wallace (Ed.), *The chemically dependent: Phases of treatment and recovery* (pp. 310–336). New York: Brunner/Mazel.

Wallace, B. C. (1993). Cross-cultural counseling with the chemically dependent: Preparing for service delivery within our culture of violence. *Journal of Psychoactive Drugs, 24*(3), 9–20.

Washton, A. M. (1989, December). Cocaine abuse and compulsive sexuality. *Medical Aspects of Human Sexuality,* pp. 32–39.

Yalisove, D. L. (1992). Survey of contemporary psychoanalytically oriented clinicians on the treatment of the addictions: A synthesis. In B. C. Wallace (Ed.), *The chemically dependent: Phases of treatment and recovery* (pp. 61–81). New York: Brunner/Mazel.

Young, E. B. (1990). The role of incest issues in relapse. *Journal of Psychoactive Drugs, 22*(2), 249–258.

Index